1849—1869

海上絲綢之路史料叢刊·中外關係卷

美國駐澳門領事館領事報告

(1849—1869)

DESPATCHES FROM UNITED STATES CONSULS IN MACAO

(1849-1869)

郝雨凡　林廣志　葉　農　整理

澳門大學
UNIVERSIDADE DE MACAU
UNIVERSITY OF MACAU

SPM
南方出版传媒
广东人民出版社
·廣州·

圖書在版編目（CIP）數據

海上絲綢之路史料叢刊・中外關係卷・美國駐澳門領事館領事報告（1849～1869）/ 郝雨凡，林廣志，葉農整理. —廣州：廣東人民出版社，2016.7

ISBN 978-7-218-10792-9

Ⅰ. ①海… Ⅱ. ①郝… ②林… ③葉… Ⅲ. ①海上運輸—絲綢之路—史料—中國—1849～1869 Ⅳ. ①K203

中國版本圖書館 CIP 數據核字（2016）第 062159 號

HAISHANG SICHOUZHILU SHILIAO CONGKAN ZHONGWAI GUANXI JUAN MEIGUO ZHU AOMEN LINGSHIGUAN LINGSHI BAOGAO（1849–1869）

海上絲綢之路史料叢刊・中外關係卷・美國駐澳門領事館領事報告（1849—1869）

郝雨凡　林廣志　葉農　　整理

出 版 人：曾　瑩

特約策劃：暨南大學港澳暨海外文獻出版傳媒中心
策劃編輯：肖風華
責任編輯：梁　茵　廖志芬
裝幀設計：陳　毅
責任技編：周　傑　黎碧霞

出版發行：廣東人民出版社
地　　址：廣州市大沙頭四馬路10號（郵政編碼：510102）
電　　話：（020）83798714（總編室）
傳　　真：（020）83780199
網　　址：http：//www.gdpph.com
印　　刷：廣州家聯印刷有限公司
開　　本：889毫米×1194毫米　1/16
印　　張：32　　**插　頁**：2　　**字　數**：520千
版　　次：2016年7月第1版　2016年7月第1次印刷
定　　價：380.00圓

如發現印裝質量問題，影響閱讀，請與出版社（020-83795749）聯繫調換。
售書熱綫：（020）83795240

ISBN 978-7-218-10792-9

Extract from the Chinese Proclamation.

粵東與外國人通商二百餘年矣。花旗官
商向來安分謹守不恃富强華民歡悅各
夷矜式 天朝實深為嘉尚。其餘各國亦
均公平交易毫無相欺。茍非暎夷無端召
釁兇燄迫人上干天怒下失人和十三行
洋樓何至一片瓦礫玉石俱焚。衆商人豈
至斷絕買賣數年之久不聞開艙故各國
之貨物阻滯資本損折實暎夷階之厲也。

原檔案樣張一

Macao. 22d Sept. 1857

I hereby certify that William A. Macy, a native of the State of New York, is known to me, and I regard him as a suitable person for, and competent to the discharge of the duties of the Consulate in this colony.

S. Wells Williams
Chargé d'affaires ad int.
U. S. A. in China

原檔案樣張二

Recd 18. Sept.

Consulate of the United States of America

Macao, July 2d 1858.

Sir,

I have the honor to inform you that in consequence of continued ill-health and physical infirmity I have availed myself of the power conferred by Section 36 chapter 4 of the Consular Regulations of 1856 to appoint as Deputy Consul for this place Mr Gideon Nye Jr a native of the State of Massachusetts, long a resident Merchant in China and Consul of the Republic of Chile in Canton from 1845 to his resignation of that office in 1855.

His temporary Testimonials will probably be obtained from Mr Consul Perry and Mr Acting Consul Roberts pending the return of the Legation of the United States to the South of China, when I expect to be favored with the approval of his appointment by His Excellency Mr Reed. According to Section 38 of the Regulations I await

The Honorable
Lewis Cass
Secretary of State of the United States
City of Washington

原檔案樣張三

Recd. Jan. 22.

No. 17.

United States Consulate,
Macao, October 28. 1865.

Sir:

Referring you to my No 16 for explanation of my rendering accounts at this time in the Quarter, I now have the honor to hand you my account for Consular Office Rent, from Oct. 1st to Oct 31st 1865. Please see Enclosure No. 1, being the said account for $12.50 and loss per exchange in the sale of my draft $4.12, together with vouchers Nos 1 & 2 in support of the same.

No. 1. Rent a/c for October 1865

Vouchers Nos 1 & 2

An examination of the vouchers accompanying my September accounts will show my landlord's acknowledgement for receipt of rent to Oct 31st — agreeing with my own voucher above. The vouchers for the past two years have all shown this anticipation of the one month's rent now claimed — and thus doubly vouched for by myself and the landlord.

I have the honor to be
Your Obedient Servant
W. T. Jones.
U. S. Consul.

The Hon
W. H. Seward,
Secretary of State for the United States
Washington. D.C.

原檔案樣張四

整理者簡介

郝雨凡，澳門大學社會科學學院院長、講座教授，1989年畢業於美國霍普金斯大學，獲博士學位。主要從事中國外交政策、中美關係、國際政治經濟學、澳門學等領域的研究工作，曾在《歷史研究》等學術刊物發表相關學術論文，出版過一批學術研究著作。

林廣志，澳門大學澳門研究中心訪問學者兼學術總監，暨南大學客座教授，歷史學博士。主要從事澳門學（澳門經濟史、澳門華商史）研究，發表相關學術論文數十篇，出版著作十餘部。

葉農，暨南大學港澳歷史文化研究中心主任、教授，歷史學博士。主要從事明清史（港澳史）、基督教傳華史、海外漢學的研究工作，發表相關學術論文數十篇，出版過相關的研究著作。

目錄

序　言

澳門從十六世紀至十九世紀中葉成爲中西文化交流的橋梁；同樣，澳門在中國與美國早期接觸中也扮演了重要角色。中美之間的第一個條約於1844年在澳門望廈村簽訂。隨後美國政府於1849年在澳門開設領事館，至十九世紀七十年代初纔關閉。在此期間，澳門在美國東亞擴張、中美關係中所扮演的角色，近年來日益受到國內外學術界的重視。

美國政府檔案——《美國駐澳門領事館領事報告（1849—1869）》原系美國國家檔案館檔案的組成部分，收錄了1849至1869年間美國駐中國澳門領事館的信件及其附件（包括當地英文與葡文報刊的剪報等），記錄了當時美國在中國澳門及其他地區、東南亞的許多重大活動及事件，對澳門史、中美關係史、美國東亞擴張史、現代東南亞國際政治關係之研究具有重要學術價值。

首先，透過駐澳門領事館的置撤，可了解美國在東亞地區的擴張歷程。1849年（道光二十九年），美國決定設置駐澳門領事，這無疑是十九世紀中葉美國與澳門關係中最爲重要的事件。在距離澳門咫尺的廣州、香港皆已設置了領事，而且駐廣州、香港領事以及駐華專員經常往來澳門的情況下，爲什麼美國政府還要獨立設置駐澳門領事？是出於商業利益的考量，還是另有他圖？是什麼原因促使美國做出這一決定？

通過對美國駐澳門領事館檔案等史料的分析，可以看到，基於澳門特殊的政治經濟環境以及商業利益的考慮，美國不僅利用澳門開展早期在華外交活動，而且希望將澳門變成太平洋西岸的一個理想港口與戰略據點，以此作爲向東亞地區前進的一個基地，鞏固其在東亞的勢力範圍，確保並拓展其在東亞的利益。美國在東亞擴張的這一走向，在澳門領事館的設置及其相關活動中已初露端倪。

其次，透過駐澳門領事的活動，可了解美國早期駐澳門領事的身份及其職責。美國駐澳門領事前後共有五任：首任領事斯爾弗（Robert P. de Silver, 1849–1856）是一名商人，生於費城（Philadelphia）；第二任領事薩繆爾·柏格·羅爾（Samuel Burge Rawle, 1856–1858），也是早期來華的商人，生於費城，在廣州、澳門、香港經商二十餘年，曾任副領事，1858年在澳門去世，葬於澳門基督教墳場。薩繆爾在臨終前任命麻西（Rev. William A. Macy，亦作"咩士"）牧師代理澳門領事。同年，麻西辭職，薩繆爾又任命其密友吉迪恩（Gideon Nye Jr.）爲代理領事；隨後，吉迪恩出任第三任領事，直到1863年；第四任領事是威廉·帕特森·瓊斯（William Patterson Jones, 1863–1865），並由美國海軍中尉巴頓（J. Q. Barton）任副領事；後瓊斯調任廈門領事，因巴頓退役而無人再任副領事，乃指定額必勒（Heinrich Ebell, 1865–1869）任執行副領事一職，執行領事的職責。

以上幾位駐澳門領事、一位代理領事和一位執行副領事，其身份各異，有商人、學者、牧師、外交人員，甚至還有非美國籍人士，但主要爲在華的美國商人，因當時美國經濟實力有限，允許領事人員從事商業活動以自養，美國駐澳門領事館的"商人領事"色彩一直沒有變化。這顯示出美國當時對華政策尚未上升到政治層面，主要由商人主導對華政策。領事人員變動相當頻繁，主要原因可能是薪酬待遇太低，無人願意擔任並長期服務。由於中美貿易帶來的商業利益，領事們仍然接受了這種安排。

雖然這些領事多爲商人，但作爲美國在澳門（中國）的利益代表，他們還是履行了領事的職責：向美國國務院提交美國船隻進出澳門港的季度、半年或年度報表；向美國國務院報告澳門、珠江三角洲以及中國內地的各種動態；救助有需要的美國人；簽發證書，處理與第三國的關係等；交涉一些涉及美國人利益的案件等等。

此外，透過駐澳門領事的活動，可爲十九世紀中葉美國與中國關係的研究提供重要線索。《中美望廈條約》簽訂後，中美關係進入了一個新時期。美國通過確立與澳門的新關係，使澳門成爲其東亞戰略前進基地。以此爲基地，美國積極展開對華外交活動。通過對美國駐澳門領事館檔案等史料的分析，可窺探此一時期美國對華外交從下列方面展開：1. 插足穗港澳三角關係圈，爲美國利益服務。穗港澳三角關係圈實際上代表着當時的中葡、中英、葡英關係。美國涉足其中，實際上也就是以澳門爲基地開展對華外交行動。2. 覬覦臺灣，展開入侵台灣的前期活動，包括爲佔領臺灣制造輿論、在臺灣地區展開調查活動等。3. 利用第二次鴉片戰爭時英法聯軍占領廣州、太平天國運動等重大事件，企圖從中國獲得新的權益。

顯然，這份重要檔案的價值還可從多個視角進行研究和解讀。廣西師範大學出版社早具卓識，於2012年出版了《美國駐中國澳門領事館領事報告（1849—1869）》（桂林：廣西師範大學出版社，三卷，1163頁，影印本），引起了學界的關注。近年來，我們在從事澳門學的研究，尤其是近代澳門與美國關係問題研究時，主要以此影印本爲基本材料。但是在使用過程中，我們發現，該影印本採用縮微膠卷形式，受技術水平的限制，許多文字難以辨認，甚至無法使用，導致該檔案目前沒有被學術界廣泛使用。有鑒於此，在澳門大學的支持下，我們組織相關人員，以廣西師範大學出版社影印本爲基礎，進一步收集、掃描了收藏在北京、香港的原始檔案，經過校勘比較，以轉寫方式對該檔案重新進行了整理，希望對國內外研究者有所裨益。限於學術水平，此次轉寫難免存在錯誤，敬請各位讀者批評指正！

郝雨凡　林廣志　葉農

2016年3月28日

凡 例

一、本次轉寫的檔案，系1849年6月18日至1869年12月6日期間，美國駐澳門領事致美國國務院的函件及其附件。分爲兩卷，卷一時間範圍爲1849年6月18日至1863年12月31日，卷二時間範圍爲1864年3月31日至1869年12月6日。

二、檔案共有189組。其中卷一收錄136組，卷二收錄53組。爲方便讀者閱讀，轉寫整理時對部分檔案的位置進行了調整。

三、轉寫時的檔案編號由轉寫者編定。以一組檔案爲基礎，每組檔案有一個編號。編號規則爲“卷號—組號”，如“2–053”，即卷二第53組檔案。

四、档案目錄由编者所加，目录包括4項内容：

1. 卷數。

2. 檔案組號。

3. 档案時間。爲原檔案寫作、提交的時間，表示方式爲“月—日—年（mm–dd–yy）”。

4. 檔案内容提要。外國人名採用中文通行譯法，首次出現時在譯文後附英文原名。中國人名、地名則依據相關資料予以還原。條約名、書名等，在中文譯文之後，附外文原名，並用斜體表示。

五、方括號内文字，爲收信部門所做的相關記錄。

六、當文字出現異文時，將出腳注説明，不做修改。

七、原文中單詞簡寫有多种形式，如“$1^{\underline{st}}$” “1^{t}” “2^{d}” “3^{d}” “$3^{\underline{d}}$” “4^{h}” “$4^{\underline{th}}$” “5^{t}” “23rd” “$\$37^{\underline{30}}$” “$Cap^{\underline{t}}$” “$Capt^{\underline{n}}$” “$Hon^{\underline{l}}$” “$Jan^{y}$” “$N^{\underline{o}}$” “$N^{o}$” “$Philo^{\underline{a}}$” “$Rec^{d}$” “$Rec^{\underline{d}}$” “$ult^{\underline{o}}$”等，均改為“$1^{st}$” “$1^{t}$” “$2^{d}$” “$3^{d}$” “$4^{h}$” “$4^{th}$” “$5^{t}$” “$23^{rd}$” “$\$37^{30}$” “$Cap^{t}$” “$Capt^{n}$” “$Hon^{l}$” “$Jan^{y}$” “$No^{o}$” “$Philo^{a}$” “$Rec^{d}$” “$ult^{o}$”等，不再一一注明。

八、原文中一些單詞寫法與标准寫法有異，如“HongKong” “Macáo” “Macaó” “Mācao”等，悉依原文，不予改動。

九、由於完成時間較早，撰寫人員、制作人員与制作方法，均各有異，故其標點符號、書寫格式均有不同，悉遵原文，不做改動。

十、原文中，有些單詞采用了簡寫形式，如“Ac/ct、A/ct、Ac'ct（Account）” “a/ct（account）” “Acknow^{lg}（Acknowledge）” “Acldg^{mt}（Acknowledgement）” “Amtg、Amt'g（Amounting）” “certif^{te}、certf（certificate）” “citz（citizen）” “conc'g（concerning）” “Decr、Dec^{r}（December）” “Depart^{mt}（Department）” “Desp（Despatch）” “E^{cy}（Exellency）” “End'g（Ending）” “Feby（February）” “Forw$^{d'g}$（Forwarding）” “Fst（Fast）” “Gen'l（General）” “Hnoble、Hble（Honorable）” “HKong、Hongkg、Hongk'g（Hongkong）” “M^{ch}（March）” “inclg（including）” “Ins（Instant）” “Inv^{o}（Inventory）” “Lieu$^{'t}$（Lieutenant）” “mchzde、mzde（merchandize）” “Pckgs（Packages）” “pass'grs（passengers）” “p^{r}（per）” “Recd（Received）” “Reg^{ter}（Register）” “Sect、Secy（Secretary）” “S^{t}（Servant）” “Triwkly（Triweekly）” “Dez（December）”等，仍遵原文，不予改動。

解 题

卷號	編號	發函時間	檔案內容提要	頁碼
卷首			縮微膠卷介紹說明	4
			簡介說明（Introductory Note）	5
	1-001	6-18-1849~10-9-1869	美國國務院所收到駐澳門領事函件匯總登記表	6
卷一	1-002	9-3-1823	駐聖巴塞洛繆（St. Bartholomew）領事休・斯蒂爾（Hugh Steel）的宣誓書	17
	1-003	3-1-1825	約翰・湯姆遜（John R. Thomson）等的領事宣誓書	17
	1-004	6-18-1849	駐澳門領事羅伯特・斯爾弗致國務卿約翰・克萊頓（John M. Clayton）函，報告自己獲任命爲駐澳門領事	18
	1-005	6-20-1849	斯爾弗致克萊頓函，報告其領事證書問題。附：6月18、19日致澳門總督亞馬留（João Maria Ferreira de Amaral）函及其葡萄牙文覆函	19
	1-006	8-21-1849	斯爾弗致克萊頓函，報告澳葡當局拒絕其領事證書及其原因、亞馬留被華人刺殺的消息	22
	1-007	9-29-1849	佛蘭克・斯爾弗（Frank de Silver）致克萊頓函，遞交任命斯爾弗爲駐澳門領事的任命狀，附：重複件一份	23
	1-008	10-3-1849	佛蘭克・斯爾弗自費城致克萊頓函，遞交斯爾費領事證書及附件	24
	1-009	10-26-1849	斯爾弗致克萊頓函，確認收到克萊頓1849年6月16日函，了解了限制攜帶各種生活品	24
	1-010	11-29-1849	斯爾弗致克萊頓函，確認收到克萊頓1849年8月22日函，了解了服裝費與使用海軍陸戰隊的規則	25
	1-011	3-25-1850	斯爾弗致克萊頓函，向其報告葡萄牙政府批準其領事證書的消息，已經非正式地傳來	25
	1-012	4-22-1850	斯爾弗致克萊頓函，報告其向澳門葡萄牙當局交涉其領事證書之事。附：1850年4月20日斯爾弗致澳門政務委員會（The Council for the Government of Macao）函、4月21日該委員會米蘭達（A. I. de Miranda）覆函	26
	1-013	5-20-1850	斯爾弗致克萊頓函，報告其通過澳葡當局收到了葡萄牙女王政府批準其擔任駐澳門領事的領事證書	28
	1-014	6-17-1850	斯爾弗致克萊頓函，報告在其所在地區沒有領事代理可任命	28
	1-015	7-1-1850	斯爾弗致克萊頓函，提交駐澳門領事館帳目，附：1849年第三、四季度美國船隻進出澳門港情況的領事報告	29
	1-016	10-20-1850	斯爾弗致美國國務卿丹尼爾・韋伯斯特（Daniel Webster）函，收到韋伯斯特函並代表在澳門的美國人向其就任致賀	31

卷一	1-033	4-6-1854	旗昌洋行致“樂瑪”（Lema）號船長伍德伯里（Woodbury）關於96箱“麻窪”鴉片的提貨函	51
	1-034	5-4-1854	致哈里斯關於旗昌洋行從事鴉片貿易函。附：1843年10月27日旗昌洋行關於鴉片銷售致伍德伯里船長函	52
	1-035	9-9-1854	馬西對駐澳門領事的覆函，已經給美國駐里斯本官員發出指令，讓他爲駐澳門領事向葡萄牙申請其領事證書	54
	1-036	5-8-1855	駐澳門副領事羅爾關於美國人巴特利特（Bartlett）先生所報告的、英國人詹姆斯·羅斯（James Ross）刺死美國籍船長約珥·伍德伯利（Joel Woodbury）一事的函；邊度士（J. M. S. Pintos）法官致羅爾關於其下令將伍德伯利下葬澳門基督教墳場函	55
	1-037	6-6-1855	駐澳門副領事羅爾致馬西函，報告羅斯刺死美國籍船長伍德伯利事件	56
	1-038	7-1-1855	羅爾致馬西函，提交1854、1855年第一、二季度美國船隻進出澳門情況及澳門專營權情況。附：1854年度、1855年第一、二季度美國船隻進出澳門港情況的領事報告	56
	1-039	1-1-1856	羅爾致馬西函，報告從1855年6月30日以來的美國船隻進出澳門港的情況、羅斯刺死伍德伯利案的最終審判結果	58
	1-040	2-4-1856	斯爾弗致馬西函，報告其領事薪金問題	59
	1-041	4-1-1856	羅爾致馬西函，收到來自國務院函；報告澳門港美國船隻進出情況、斯爾弗離開中國返回美國	60
	1-042	7-1-1856	羅爾致馬西函，確認收到國務院任命其擔任駐澳門領事函	61
	1-043	9-10-1856	羅爾致馬西函，報告收到由葡萄牙國王批準、由澳門總督簽署的領事證書	61
	1-044	4-1-1857	羅爾致國務卿劉易斯·卡斯（Lewis Cass）函，確認收到兩封國務院關於關稅及國會相關法律函；報告領事館收費情況，美國船隻進出澳門港情況；因第二次鴉片戰爭導致商業蕭條的狀況並要求增加領事薪金。附：1857年第一季度美國船隻進出澳門港情況的領事報告、1857年第一季度駐澳門領事館收費情況報告	62
	1-045	5-5-1857	羅爾致卡斯函，申請樹立旗桿的費用	65
	1-046	6-30-1857	羅爾致卡斯函，提交美國船隻進出澳門港的領事報告。附：1857年第二季度美國船隻進出澳門港情況的領事報告	66
	1-047	9-22-1857	羅爾致卡斯函，因身體健康原因任命麻西擔任代理領事。附：由美國駐華公使臨時代辦衛三畏（Samuel Wells Williams）爲麻西簽署的見證書	67
	1-048	10-14-1857	羅爾致卡斯函，提交1857年第三季度美國船隻進出澳門港情況的領事報告	68
	1-049	1-13-1858	羅爾致國務卿卡斯函，提交帳目表等文件、美國船隻進出澳門港情況的領事報告、麻西辭去代理領事的職務及暫未任命其他人士擔任此職、處理美國人在澳門從事苦力貿易的事務、戰事導致澳門商務蕭條等。附：1857年第四季度美國船隻進出澳門港情況的領事報告、1857年第四季度駐澳門領事館收費情況總表、1857年第四季度駐澳門領事館收費明細表	69
	1-050		“一位著名醫務傳教士訪問日本信件摘錄”	73

卷一	1-051	1-26-1859	1858年第二季度駐澳門領事館收費情況季度報告	74
	1-052	6-30-1858	1858年4月1日至7月1日駐澳門領事館收費情況報告	74
	1-053	7-2-1858	吉迪恩致卡斯函，提交新任欽差大臣與兩廣總督黄宗漢上任時所發佈的告示。附：由法蘭西先生（Geo. B. French）翻譯的告示與中文原文	76
	1-054	7-2-1858	羅爾致卡斯函，任命吉迪恩爲代理領事，後者的見證書即將獲得	77
	1-055	8-17-1858	吉迪恩致函美國駐華特命全權公使列衛廉（William Bradford Reed），回覆其就英法與中國關稅與貿易事項進行的談判中如何保護美國商業利益的徵詢，並坦陳其對美國產品進口等問題的意見	78
	1-056	9-3-1858	吉迪恩致卡斯函，報告前任領事逝世，享年70餘歲；並陳述澳門領事薪金低廉，申請將澳門領事納入受薪領事範圍，年薪1000美元；從澳門領事的政治、商業重要性及其代理領事以來所做工作等方面，提出加薪及昇任領事之理由；報告長老會傳教士法蘭西先生妻子在澳門街頭被華人用石頭打死之案件、第二次鴉片戰爭期間的一些重大事件（葉名琛被俘、毒麵包事件等）、柏貴的告示、澳門港務局長在澳門外港發現礁石之報告。附件：法國與西班牙在交趾支那的行動、法國革命對修約的影響、廣東巡撫柏貴告示（法蘭西先生英文譯文）	80
	1-057	9-3-1858	澳門港務局局長馮塞卡（Jozé Marca da Fonseca）所通告的新礁石——“富蘭格林礁石”情況、致吉迪恩的函（葡萄牙文本與英文譯本），該礁石先後有英國船“富蘭格林夫人”（Lady Franklin）號與美國船“瑪利拉”（Marilla）號觸碰	85
	1-058	9-3-1858	副本：吉迪恩致卡斯函，報告前任領事逝世，享年70餘歲；並陳述澳門領事薪金低廉，申請將澳門領事納入受薪領事範圍，年薪1000美元；從澳門領事的政治、商業重要性及其代理領事以來所做工作等方面，提出加薪及昇任領事之理由；報告長老會傳教士法蘭西先生妻子在澳門街頭被華人用石頭打死之案件、第二次鴉片戰爭期間的一些重大事件（葉名琛被俘、毒麵包事件等）、柏貴的告示、澳門港務局局長在澳門外港發現礁石之報告。附件：法國與西班牙在交趾支那的行動、法國革命對修約的影響、廣東巡撫柏貴告示（法蘭西先生英文譯文）	87
	1-059	9-15-1858	“E. PLURIBUS UNUM.”與“UNITED WE STAND-DIVIED WE FALL”致《德臣西報》（*The China Mail*）的聯名信，從西方列強的政治商業利益考慮在廣州選擇租界的問題	91
	1-060	9-25-1858	吉迪恩致卡斯函，關於英國額爾金勳爵（Lord Elgin）與中國簽訂條約及中國政治事務的改善、廣州貿易重開、哈里斯與日本簽訂條約（*Treaty of Ieddo*）、法國海軍總司令抵達交趾支那費倫灣（Bay of Ferron）及法國與西班牙遠征軍攻占交趾支那要塞等、法國傳教士加利（Monsieur Galy）先生逃來澳門與交趾支那的排教運動	97
	1-061	9-25-1858	副本：吉迪恩致卡斯函，關於英國額爾金勳爵與中國簽訂條約及中國政治事務的改善、廣州貿易重開、哈里斯與日本簽訂條約、法國海軍總司令抵達交趾支那費倫灣及法國與西班牙遠征軍攻占交趾支那要塞等、法國傳教士加利先生逃來澳門與交趾支那的排教運動	98

卷一	1-062	9-27-1858	吉迪恩致卡斯函，報告其收到法國全權特使本月23日函及法國與西班牙聯軍總司令關於封鎖交趾支那費倫灣及附近地方的通告。附：法國駐華全權特使布爾布隆（A. Bourboulon）23日關於封鎖交趾支那河道及費倫灣函、法西聯軍總司令發出上述封鎖通告的英文譯本	101
	1-063		關於"廣州商館區"（Factory）問題的系列文獻：1. 副本："E. PLURIBUS UNUM."與"UNITED WE STAND-DIVIED WE FALL"致《德臣西報》的聯名信，從西方列強的政治商業利益攷慮在廣州選擇租界的問題（文字略有不同）；2. 1858年10月2日由"CONCILIATE AND CONSERVE"著"THE GREAT 'FACTOR' QUESTION AND THE PROSPECTIVE SUFFERINGS OF THE 'OPERATIVES'"；10月4日由"CONCILIATE AND CONSERVE"著"THE 'FACTORY' QUESTION"及其附錄"*Suggestions of a Scheme of conciliatory treatment and temporary local Settlement at Canton, with a view to the permanent re-establishment of the Foreign 'Factories' upon recognized and broader foundations*"（與"1-059"重複，爲殘件）	102
	1-064	10-19-1858	吉迪恩致蒸汽船"火花"（Spark）號船長利卡貝（A. Ricaby）函，調停其侮辱澳門葡萄牙當局事件	111
	1-065	10-13-1858	列衛廉致吉迪恩函，任命吉迪恩爲駐澳門副領事	113
	1-066		吉迪恩於1858年9月13日致列衛廉函，報告其被已故領事羅爾任命爲代理領事及其任職過程；10月25日駐澳門副領事吉迪恩致卡斯函，報告其任代理領事期間所完成的工作及澳門領事一職的重要性	114
	1-067	11-13-1858	吉迪恩致卡斯函，提交蒸汽船"火花"號船長利卡貝侮辱澳門葡萄牙當局事件的領事報告記錄。附：關於由利卡貝船長簽署的該事件的領事報告記錄	117
	1-068	12-28-1858	吉迪恩致卡斯函，提交1858年第三季度駐澳門領事館領事收費情況報告，並提出了增加薪金或改變收費方式的要求	118
	1-069	12-29-1858	吉迪恩致卡斯函，報告三桅帆船"瑪迪爾達"（Matilda）號貨船爲英國政府送往煤炭至上海途中在巴士海峽失事、損失巨大與船員獲救經過	119
	1-070	2-22-1859	吉迪恩致卡斯函，提交駐澳門領事館領事收費情況、美國船只進出澳門港情況；指出英國僅將澳門視作珠江口外運輸中國產品的外港。附：1858年第四季度駐澳門領事館收費情況報告、1858年第四季度美國船只進出澳門港情況的領事季度報告	121
	1-071		摘自《香港政府憲報》（*Hongkong Government Gazette*）下列通告：1. 1859年2月18日威廉堅（William Caine）簽署的"政府公告"，關於英國駐廣州領事阿禮國（Rutherford Alcock）致在廣州港英國商人社區關於開設中國海關函；2. 1859年2月15日阿禮國在廣州發出的、開設廣州海關公告；3. 阿禮國發出，致在廣州港英國商人社區函	126
	1-072	2-15-1859	1859年2月《香港記錄報與船頭貨價》摘錄	128

卷一	1-073		美國船“艾瑪”號被扣押事件的過程與相關系列文件，包括：1858年6月14日澳門港務局局長馮塞卡致“艾瑪”號船長查爾斯·吉爾（Charles Gill）函，發出扣押“艾瑪”號的命令；吉爾赴駐澳門領事館所做的口供；6月15日馮塞卡給吉爾的覆函；11月3日副領事吉迪恩致吉爾函；11月6日扣押“艾瑪”號的書面證書；吉迪恩簽署的“艾瑪”號船長吉爾聲明書；11月10日吉迪恩致列衛廉函；11月13、15、22、26、27日吉迪恩函。1859年3月12日吉迪恩致卡斯函，報告駐澳門領事館收費情況、“艾瑪”號事件及清咸豐皇帝1月31日頒布關於中國和西方列強關係上諭等。附：上諭（英文譯本）及“一位著名醫務傳教士訪問日本信件摘錄”	157
	1-074	2-18-1859	副本：摘自《香港政府憲報》下列通告：1．1859年2月18日威廉堅簽署的“政府公告”，關於英國駐廣州領事阿禮國致在廣州港英國商人社區關於開設中國海關函；2．1859年2月15日阿禮國在廣州發出的、開設廣州海關公告；3．阿禮國發出，致在廣州港英國商人社區函	177
	1-075	3-12-1859	吉迪恩致卡斯函，報告領事館收費情況、“艾瑪”號事件進展。附：1858年第一季度駐澳門領事館收費情況報告、1858年第二季度駐澳門領事館收費情況報告	178
	1-076	3-28-1859	吉迪恩致卡斯函，提交領事館收費情況報告及“艾瑪”號事件“第32至50號文件副本”	183
	1-077	4-8-1859	吉迪恩致卡斯函，提交領事館收費情況報告，報銷救助“瑪迪爾達”號船只之費用、領事薪金等問題	194
	1-078	4-8-1859	吉迪恩致卡斯函，表彰中國帆船船長Cheung-ah-ng救助失事船只“瑪迪爾達”號及其幾個攷慮。附：從1859年第二季度美國船只進出澳門港情況的領事季度報告	195
	1-079	7-20-1859	吉迪恩致卡斯函，報告領事館收費情況、自己的薪金問題、“艾瑪”號事件、澳門總督訪問暹羅（Siam）、英法聯軍抵達白河河口等。附：1859年第二季度駐澳門領事館收費情況報告、葡暹關係及澳門總督吉馬良士訪問暹羅、1859年葡暹會議記錄、《葡萄牙與暹羅友好、商業、航海條約》（*TRATADO DE AMISADE, COMMERCIO E NAVEGAÇÃO ENTRE OS REINOS DE PORTUGAL E SIAM*）葡文版及其附件	197
	1-080	8-8-1859	吉迪恩致卡斯函，提交“艾瑪”號事件的相關文件，包括澳門法院對“艾瑪”號事件的處理。附：稟文、宣判書、審判記錄、“艾瑪”號買賣的相關帳務等	226
	1-081	9-24-1859	吉迪恩致卡斯函，報告根據向澳葡官員、駐香港領事基南（Keenan）打探、報紙消息判斷，美國人馬丁·湯普森（Martin Thompson）未被關進澳門監獄；英國駐澳門領事代理要求在美國船隻“電火花”號上搜查海軍逃兵。附：9月3日基南給吉迪恩的覆函、英國領事代理克利弗利致吉迪恩要求搜查“電火花”號上英海軍逃兵函	238

卷一	1-082	10-27-1859	吉迪恩致卡斯函，提交駐澳門領事館收費情況報告、美國船隻進出澳門港情況報告。附：1859年第三季度美國船隻進出澳門港情況的領事季度報告、1859年第三季度駐澳門領事館收費情況季度報告、1859年第四季度美國船隻進出澳門港情況的領事季度報告	241
	1-083	1-12-1860	吉迪恩致卡斯函，報告日益猖獗的苦力貿易及對苦力施虐導致群情激憤，影響美國利益。附：11月28日吉迪恩就苦力貿易致美國全權特使、駐華公使華若翰（John E. Ward）函、11月25日吉迪恩致華若翰函（報告其營救被綁架華人苦力）、1859年12月18日吉迪恩致華若翰函	243
	1-084	3-27-1860	吉迪恩致卡斯函，提交1859年第四季度駐澳門領事館收費情況報告。附：1859年第四季度駐澳門領事館收費情況報告	248
	1-085	6-5-1860	吉迪恩致卡斯函，提交領事館收費情況報告。附：1860年第一季度美國船隻進出澳門港情況的領事季度報告、1860年第一季度駐澳門領事館收費情況報告	249
	1-086	7-6-1860	吉迪恩致卡斯函，提交駐澳門領事館收費情況報告。附：1860年第一季度駐澳門領事館收費情況領事報告	252
	1-087	10-4-1860	吉迪恩致卡斯函，提交駐澳門領事館收費情況報告、美國船隻進出澳門港情況報告。附：1860年第三季度駐澳門領事館收費情況報告、1860年第三季度美國船隻進出澳門港情況的領事季度報告	254
	1-088	1-30-1861	吉迪恩致卡斯函，提交美國船隻進出澳門港情況、領事館收費情況報告。附：1860年第四季度美國船隻進出澳門港情況的領事季度報告、1860年第四季度駐澳門領事館收費情況的領事報告	255
	1-089	4-3-1861	吉迪恩致國務卿西沃德函，提交美國船隻進出澳門港情況、駐澳門領事館收費情況報告。附：1861年第一季度美國船隻進出澳門港情況的領事季度報告、1861年第一季度駐澳門領事館收費情況報告	257
	1-090	5-1-1861	吉迪恩致西沃德函，報告由於果阿（Goa）最高法院失職導致“艾瑪”號事件長期懸而未決、損失補償不足等，希望國務院給澳葡當局施壓。附：與澳門總督來往信函、當事人律師函、大法官致澳門總督函、澳門地方法院部分庭審記錄、果阿最高法院決議書、調解函、仲裁書、當事人抗議函等	259
	1-091	7-2-1861	吉迪恩致西沃德函，提交駐澳門領事館收費情況報告。附：1861年第二季度駐澳門領事館收費情況報告	285
	1-092	10-3-1861	吉迪恩致西沃德函，提交駐澳門領事館收費情況、美國船隻進出澳門港情況報告。附：1861年第三季度駐澳門領事館收費情況報告、1861年第三季度美國船隻進出澳門港情況的領事季度報告	287
	1-093	11-25-1861	西沃德爲愛德華·哈特（Edward Harte）簽發的外交通行證	288
	1-094	1-3-1862	吉迪恩致西沃德函，提交美國船隻進出澳門港情況、駐澳門領事館收費情況報告。附：1861年第四季度美國船隻進出澳門港情況的領事季度報告、1861年第四季度駐澳門領事館收費情況報告	289
	1-095	2-26-1862	吉迪恩致西沃德函，報告其已經準備向哈特移交領事館檔案與資產及對此次更換領事的個人看法	290

卷一	1-113	3-31-1863	瓊斯致美國財政部長薩爾蒙·蔡斯（Salem P. Chass）函，提交自2月25日至3月31日止的薪金帳目及其憑證	333
	1-114	3-31-1863	瓊斯致西沃德函，提交從2月25日至3月31日的領事館帳目，包括郵費、文具、遷移旗杆的費用等雜項帳目及憑證	334
	1-115	3-31-1863	瓊斯致西沃德函，提交從2月25日至3月31日的領事館房租等項及憑證	335
	1-116	3-31-1863	瓊斯致西沃德函，提交自2月25日以來雜項、房租、書架等帳目，各項領事報告，並提請國務卿關注其調任汕頭領事的申請。附：1863年第一季度駐澳門領事館收費情況報告、1863年第一季度駐澳門領事館官方信函收發登記表、1863年自2月25日至3月31日駐澳門領事館收費情況報告摘錄、自2月25日至3月31日駐澳門領事館官方信函發出登記表	336
	1-117	3-31-1863	瓊斯致西沃德函，報告爲駐澳門領事館購買書架及其憑證	340
	1-118	5-9-1863	瓊斯致西沃德函，提交其對“艾瑪”號事件澳葡當局處理的看法。附：相關文件（果阿最高法院判決書、仲裁函、法庭宣判書及有關帳目等）	341
	1-119	6-30-1863	瓊斯致西沃德函，提交1863年第二季度領事報告，報告美國南方邦聯私掠船可能來襲，澳門總督吉馬良士卸任及阿穆恩（José Rodrigues Coelho do Amaral）繼任、查爾斯·拉素（Edward Russell）在澳門去世。附：1863年第二季度駐澳門領事館收費情況登記表摘錄	348
	1-120	6-30-1863	瓊斯致西沃德函，提交1863年第二季度駐澳門領事館雜項開支報告及其憑證	351
	1-121	6-30-1863	瓊斯致西沃德函，提交1863年第二季度駐澳門領事館開支帳目及其憑證	351
	1-122	9-20-1863	瓊斯致美國總統林肯（Abraham Lincoln）函，因其妻之健康原因請假16天。在此期間，由前任副領事吉迪恩代理職務。附：彼特醫生（V. de P. S. Pitter）的醫療證明書	352
	1-123	9-30-1863	瓊斯致西沃德函，提交1863年第三季度駐澳門領事館房租帳目及憑證	354
	1-124	9-30-1863	瓊斯致西沃德函，提交1863年第三季度駐澳門領事館雜項帳目及憑據	355
	1-125	9-30-1863	瓊斯致西沃德函，提交駐澳門領事館1863年第三季度各項領事報告，報告澳門舉行的美國國慶活動，美國“鯉魚門”（Lyeemoon）號船長弗蘭克·布里斯克（Frank Blisk）在澳門死亡。附：1863年第三季度在澳門死亡的美國公民名錄	356
	1-126	10-24-1863	瓊斯致西沃德函，其薪金已經無以爲生，緊急申請加薪至3000美元。其陳述列明在澳門的各種開支情況、僅依靠薪金爲生、在華其他領事薪金情況、領事應系收入充足而非奢華的工作、澳門領事館的重要性。附：全體居穗美國傳教士致總統林肯的聯名簽署函（陳述駐澳門領事對傳教事業的重要性，請求總統建議國會將其薪金由每年1500元加至3000美元）	357
	1-127	11-25-1863	瓊斯致總統林肯函，申請提高薪金至3000美元	361
	1-128	11-27-1863	瓊斯致總統林肯函，申請盡快提高薪金。附：11月12日全體居穗美國傳教士致總統林肯要求給瓊斯加薪的聯名簽署函	362
	1-129	12-31-1863	瓊斯致西沃德函，提交1863年第四季度駐澳門領事館雜項帳目及憑證	364
	1-130	12-31-1863	瓊斯致西沃德函，提交1863年第四季度駐澳門領事館房租帳目及憑證	365

卷二	2-014	12-31-1864	瓊斯致西沃德函，提交1864年第一季度駐澳門領事館房租及憑證	413
	2-015	12-31-1864	瓊斯致西沃德函，提交1864年第一季度駐澳門領事館雜項帳目及憑證	414
	2-016	12-31-1864	瓊斯致西沃德函，提交其在1864年呈交國務院報告目錄。附：1864年寫給國務院信函報告	415
	2-017	12-31-1864	瓊斯致西沃德函，提交1864年第四季度美國船只進出澳門港情況的領事報告	416
	2-018	1-30-1865	瓊斯致西沃德函，確認收到1864年4月5日發出、國務卿的第11號函，提請西沃德注意其申請提高薪金的函	419
	2-019	1-30-1865	瓊斯致西沃德函，糾正1864年第12號函件中關於中國進出口貿易額之錯誤	420
	2-020	2-27-1865	瓊斯致西沃德函，報告“艾瑪”號案件的最新進展及對其領事工作的現狀［美國地理統計學會（American Geographical and Statistical Society）召開大會、瓊斯在會上發表其最近一次赴中國內地的旅行］、出售其領事館賬本等	421
	2-021	3-31-1865	瓊斯致西沃德函，提交1865年第一季度駐澳門領事館房租及憑證	423
	2-022	3-31-1865	瓊斯致西沃德函，提交1865年第一季度駐澳門領事館雜項帳目及憑證。附：1865年第一季度美國在澳門的航運與商務表、1865年第一季度美國船只進出澳門港情況的領事報告、1865年第一季度駐澳門領事館收到的官方信函登記表等	424
	2-023	6-26-1865	瓊斯致執行國務卿威廉·亨特（William Hunter）函，對總統林肯等遇刺深表哀悼、報告與澳葡政府就此事的官方往來信函及他們表達的同情及降半旗活動等	428
	2-024	6-26-1865	瓊斯致西沃德函，希望其及其家人從林肯被刺時所受傷害中恢複過來	430
	2-025	6-30-1865	瓊斯致亨特函，提交1865年第二季度駐澳門領事館房租及憑證	431
	2-026	6-30-1865	瓊斯致亨特函，提交雜項帳目及憑證。附：1865年第一、二季度在澳門的中國帆船進出口情況的領事報告，1865年第一、二季度美國在澳門港航運與商業表	432
	2-027	7-1-1865	瓊斯致亨特函，提交美國船只進出澳門港情況報告。附：1865年第二季度美國船只進出澳門港情況的領事報告	436
	2-028	7-20-1865	瓊斯致亨特函，報告美國公民雅各布·霍斯（Jacob W. Hawes）因病去世及相關問題	438
	2-029	9-1-1865	駐馬塞約（Maceio）領事代理博斯特爾曼（J. Borstelmann）致領事小托馬斯·亞當森（Thomas Adamson Jr.）函，報告馬塞約港出口情況。附：1864年7月1日至1865年6月30日馬塞約港出口情況的領事報告，1865年第一、二季度馬塞約港出口統計	439
	2-030	9-30-1865	瓊斯致西沃德函，提交美國船只進出澳門港情況的領事報告等。附：1864—1865年澳門商品的平均價、1865年第三季度死於澳門的美國公民登記表	442

卷二	2-047	12-4-1867	瓊斯致西沃德函，報告其將駐廣州領事館的檔案與印章交給了鲁伊斯（E. M. Ruis），並返回澳門領事崗位	476
	2-048	5-29-1868	瓊斯致西沃德函，報告其2月1日離開廈門，經廣州與澳門回到華盛頓	477
	2-049	6-7-1868	瓊斯致西沃德函，通知國務卿不再返回澳門領事崗位，並陳述原因	477
	2-050	6-8-1868	瓊斯就其自廈門至華盛頓的薪金問題致西沃德函，指出其調任廈門的原因，要求支付其遷居廈門的費用，報告其從澳門至廈門，從廈門返回華盛頓的費用。附：由美國駐華公使蒲安臣致瓊斯函（同意瓊斯調任廈門）	478
	2-051	6-10-1868	瓊斯自華盛頓致西沃德函，指出其自廈門回國的費用屬於應付範圍。附：總檢察長對此事的看法	481
	2-052	10-9-1869	額必勒致國務卿漢密爾頓·菲什（Hamilton Fish）函，辭去駐澳門領事館執行副領事，將領事館的檔案與傢具轉交駐香港領事之手	483
	2-053	12-6-1869	賈斯伯·史密斯（Jasber Smith）報告稱：額必勒辭職，因無報酬、貿易微乎其微、不宜由外國人擔任、緊鄰香港，建議不再任命駐澳門領事	484

美國駐澳門領事館報告
（1849—1869）

Despatches from United States Consuls in Macao（1849-1869）

卷·首

·

Frontispiece

縮微膠卷介紹說明

Frontispiece: Introductory Note of the Microfilm

In this microcopy are reproduced two volumes that consist, for the most part, of despatches addressed to the Department of State from United States consular representatives at Macao between June 18, 1849, and December 6, 1869. These despatches, with their enclosures, are arranged, with very few exceptions, in chronological orders; their contents are registered on the first roll of the microcopy. The volumes, each of which has been photographed on a separate roll, are distributed as follows:

Roll	Volume	Inclusive dates
1	1	June 18, 1849–Dec. 31, 1863
2	2	Mar. 31, 1864–Dec. 6, 1869

Macao, opened as a consular agency in the Canton consular district, was made a consulate in 1848. The post was closed in 1869. During the period when Macao was a consular agency, reports were made to the consulate at Canton.

A number of these consular despatches are covering letters for enclosures of a routine nature forwarded by the consul to the Department of State. Some of these are tables of consular fees received, of arrivals and departures of American vessels, and of other data collected in the ordinary course of consular duty.

In Record Group 59, General Records of the Department of States, in the National Archives there are several series of volume containing additional material on the relations between China and the United States. Complementary to the despatches from Macao and other American consular posts in China are instructions to United States consuls in China. Also related to these, though less directly, are despatches from Unite States Ministers in China （File Microcopy 92）, instructions to United States Ministers in China （part of File Microcopy 77）, notes from the Chinese Legation in the United States to the Department of State （File Microcopy 98）, and notes from the Department of State to the Chinese Legation in the United States （part of File Microcopy 99）.

INTRODUCTORY NOTE

The volume microcopied on this roll has the following backstrip title: "1/ Macao/ September 3, 1823/ December 31, 1863/ Department/ of State." It contains despatches, with enclosures, addressed to the Department of State from United States consular officials at Macao between June 18, 1849, and December 31, 1863. Bound at the front of the volume, apparently by error, are two consular bonds; one for Hugh Steel, consul at St. Bartholomew, dated September 3, 1823, the other for John R. Thomson, consul at Canton, dated March 1, 1825.

The volume is part of a body of records in the National Archives designated as Record Group No. 59, General Records of the Department of State. It is volume 1 of a series generally referred to as Consular Despatches, Macao.

At the front of the roll are reproduced parts of volumes, constituting registers of despatches received by the Department of State from United States consuls at Macao from 1848 to 1869. These volumes in their entirety comprise registers of consular despatches received by the Department from all parts of the world from 1828 to 1906.

美國國務院所收到駐澳門領事函件匯總登記表

Registration and Collection of Despatches from United States Consuls in Macao Addressed to the Department of State

[1-001]

□□□ Macao 183

Pierce WP.	March 30 1848 July 13 Has heard of his app[l]. declines it. See page 343

Macao from page 183

Whom from	No.	Date		Received	Import.
		*see Below			
Rob[t]. P. De Silver	1.	June 18	1849	Septem: 8	Received appointment in absence of Exequatur the Governor permitted him to act per forwarded his bond to the U. States – wants a Flag etc. Send them to Frank De Silver. Philadelphia
Rob[t]. P. De Silver	2.	June 20	1849	Septem: 8	In relation to assuming consular duties–Correspondence with the Governor of Macao–asks instructions with Agent to 2nd Section of Act of Congress
Frank De Silver Philadelphia		Sept: 29	1849	Septem: 30	Enclosing bond of R. P. de Silver, appointed U. S. C. at Macao, (returned disapproval)
		Octo: 3	1849	October 4	Enclosing bond of R. P. de Silver
R. " P. De Silver	3.	Augt: 31	1849	Novem: 18	Receipt of letter of Department concerning his Exequatur his course concerning it. The French and Spanish Consuls given Exequaturs by Gov't: of Portugal. –The Government of Macao will forward his Commission with the signs of to grant an Exequatur – Notice of the assassination of the Governor of Macao by the Chinese – The Council will carry out the wishes of the late Governor concerning his Exequatur– Portugal pays 500 Tales annually to the Chinese for the Use of the portion of land in which Macao is located – Their Claim and tide to it. Jurisdiction over the Laws etc.
R. " P. De Silver	4.	Octob: 26	1849	Jany 17, 1850	Receipt of Circular of 16[0] June 1849.
"N.P.Pierce" Shang Hai, China		*March 30	1848	July 14th, 1848	Has received from Hon. G. W. Hopkins U. S. Minister at Portugal notice an appointment as Counsel for Macao. Has not received the despatches said to have been sent him – As he has not resided in Macao for 3 years, and has no intention of returning. He begs to decline the honor of the appointment, tho'with a deep □□□ of the kindness conferred.
R. P. De Silver	5.	Novem 29	1849	March 9/50	Receipt of Circular of 22 Aug: 1849
R. P. De Silver		March 25	1850	June 14	Speaks of former despatches; States that he has unofficially been informed that the Portuguese Government approved of the late Governor's recognition of him, but has not received his Exequatur as yet.

R. P. De Silver	8.	May 20	1850	Aug 10	Has this day recd □ his exequatur from Queen This Port Gov.
R. P. De Silver	9.	June 17	1850	June 17	Recd Circular of March □□□ □□□
R. P. De Silver	7.	Ap. 22	1850	Sept. 24	Recd letter of St Joze. & copy of letter of 38" may correspondence with the Consul of Macao related to his exequatur copies sent no 1 & 2 enclosed.
R. P. De Silver	11.	July 1	1850	Jan. 7	Enclosed accounts & Balances. □□□ of dfts.
				Feb. 17	Reports the blowing up of the Portuguese ship Donna Maria and commends the accident of the officers of our U. S. Ship Marion on the occasion.
R. P. De Silver		Oct 26	1850	Feb. 17	Received Circular of July 23[d]; gratifying information.
	13.	Jan 3	1851	July 21	De Silver R. P. Janu. 1 Returns ; Feb. 1. & 56
	14.	May 26	1851	Aug. 7	Reports the death of □□□ □□□ Effects will be sold and placed to the credit of the U. S.
			1851	1851	
De Silver R. P.	15.	July 16th	1851	Oct. 13	Rec[d] Despatch of May 1st--, Replys to the letter of the P. M. Gen[l] of U. S.-Has sent Fees.-
De Silver R. P.	16.	Jany 1st	1852	April 3[d]	Rec[d] despatch of Sept 4th, Can give no account of John Smith – encloses his account – no American Vessels put in during the year-Fees $32 for 1851.
De Silver R. P.	17.	July 5th	1852	Dectr 1	Encloses Returns of Fees ($201) & accounts.
De Silver R. P.	19.	July 20th	1853	October 17th	Returns and fees.
De Silver R. P.	20.	July 20th	1853	October 17th	Gratified with receipt of despatch of March 9th.

Macao 505

Name	N°	Date	Year	Received	Import.
De Silver R. P.	21	Jany 28th	1854	April 28th	Resignation of Consular office. Appointed S. B. Rawle an American Actg. Consul.
De Silver R. P.	22	Jany 30th	1854	April 28th	Advice of Draft.
Rawle S. B.	22	June 6	1855	Sept. 21st	Murder of Capt. J. Woodbury
Rawle S. B.	22	May 8"	1855	Sept. 21st	Further information respecting Capt. Woodbury's death
Rawle S. B.	2	July 1"	1855	Sept. 21st	Returns fees. Macao, a free Port. detail concerning it
			1856		
De Silver R.	–	Nov. 5	1855	Jan. 24	Resigns the office – reasons assigned. – Recommend the appt. of S. B. Rawle a citizen of U. S. – Relinquished all claim to salary
Rawle S. B.	–	Nov. 12	1855	Jan. 24	Transmits Mr. De Silver's despatch tendering his resignation-asks for the appt.-Lived in China 13 years-Refers to various respectable gentleman – Is a citizen of U. S. – Born in Philadelphia
Rawle S. B.	3	Jan. 1	1856	Mch. 21	Enclosed Returns for the last half of 1855. Death of Joel Woodbury. Sentence of the murderer.

De Silver R.	–	Feb. 4	1856	Apl. 26	Advice of Dft.
Rawle S. B.	–	July 1	1856	Sept. 16	Recd notice of appt. Thanks – Has sent Bond – Born in Penn. –Has been engaged in the China trade 20 Years. – Has resided 3 years in Macao.
Rawle S. B.		Apl. 1	1856	June 24	Recd despatch of Nov. 7 – Not recd. fee book nor instructions–Enclosed returns – Departure of Mr. De Silver –
Rawle S. B.		July 1	1856	Sept. 16	Recd notice of appt. –Has sent bond – Born in Penn.
Rawle W. H.		Oct. 22	1856	Oct. 23	Transmits bond of S. B. Rawle
Rawle S. B.	6	Sept. 10		Oct. 23	Recd Commission and Exequatur Instructions.
Rawle S. B.	9	Apl.	1857	June 19	Recd tariff of fees, Statutes of 1st & 2d. Sessions of Congress & c, Transmits and returns to 21st Mch. Complain of the cessation of his salary. Refers to his services. Wants salary allowed.
Rawle S. B.	–	May 5	1857	July 21	Advice of draft for flag staff
Rawle S. B.	11	Aug. 8	1857	Oct. 24	Returns to 30 June – Blockade of Canton
Rawle S. B.	–	Sept. 22	1857	Dec. 3	Has appd W. A. Macey of N. Y. Depy Consul.
Rawle S. B.	15	Oct. 14	1857	Dec. 22	Transmits returns to Sept. 30th
Mustin T.	–	Jan. 13	1858	Jan. 13	Information wanted as to the appt. of S. B. Rawle
Rawle S. B.	16	Jan. 13	1858	Mch. 29	Returns to 31st. Dec – Trade Report.

506 Macao

Name	No.	Date		Recd.	Import.
Rawle S. P.	–	July 1	1858	Sep. 18	App.d Gideon Nye Acp. Consul asks its approval.
Nye Gideon	–	July 1	1858	Sep. 18	Translation of a Chinese proclamation rel. to foreigners with remarks thereon.
Nye Gideon	–	Sep. 3	1858	Nov. 17	Death of S. B. Rawle – Inadequacy of the freq – Con'. duties Disposition of the Chinese – Proclamation of the Gov. Letter to Mr. Reed.
Nye Gideon	2	Sep. 25	1858	Dec. 1	Remarks on the Treaties between No. 8. China & Japan, with copy of Brit. Treaty.
Nye Gideon	3	Sep. 27	1858	Dec. 1	Enclosing letter of the French Minister rel. to the blockade of Cochin China.
Nye Gideon	2	Sep. 25	1858	Dec. 28	Duplicate
Nye Gideon	3	Sep. 25	1858	Dec. 28	ditto
Nye Gideon	4	Sep. 29	1858	Dec. 28	Instructions wanted rel. to sailing licenses.
Nye Gideon	5	Oct. 26	1858	Dec. 28	Has been recognized as V. Consul. Enclosing printed letters rel. to matters at Canton, & the steamer "Spark", & correspondence with Mr. Reed.
Nye Gideon	5	Oct. 26	1858	Jan. 20	Duplicate

Nye Gideon	6	Nov. 13	1858	Jan. 20	Termination of the "Spark Controversy"
Nye Gideon	7	Dec. 28	1858	Feb. 28	Returns to Sep 31. Inadequacy of the fees. Must resign unless a salary is granted.
Nye Gideon	8	Dec. 29	1858	Feb. 28	Loss of the Bark "Matilda".
Nye Gideon	9	Feb. 22	1859	Apl. 30	Returns to Dec. 31. Inadequacy of the fees. Seizure of the Ship "Emma". – Printed Custom House notices – Hostility to Christianity in Japan.
Nye Gideon	4	Sep. 29	1858	Jan. 6	Duplicate
Nye Gideon	9	Feb. 22	1859	May 12	do
Nye Gideon	10	Mch. 12	1859	May 12	Cir. No. 9 rec[d] Remarks ás to his returns– Case of the "Emma", with correspondence. Cons[l]. edict – Christianity in Japan – Exports & imports in Japan.

Macao. 507

Name	No.	Date		Rec[d].	Import.
Nye G.	10	Mch. 12	1859	May 30	Duplicate
Nye G.	11	Mch. 28	1859	May 30	Further correspondence rel. to the "Emma".
Thompson Mrs. M.	11	June 21	1859	June 24	Rel. to imprisonment of her husband & son in Macao.– Wants them relieved.
Nye G.	13	Ap. 8	1859	June 28	Ref. to 8 & 12. Merits of Cheung–ah–ng. in rescuing crew of Matilda.
Calvert Charles		June 25th		June 27th	Rel: to supposed imprisonment of Capt. Thompson at Macao or a charge of carrying coolies, as to interposition of deport to effect his release &c.
Nye G.	14	July 20	1859	Sept. 27	Ret & fees. To June 30: Case of the Emma Capt Gill's letter. Printed rep. in Siam. Mark in the Picho
Nye G.	4	Sep. 29	1858	Jan. 6	Wants instructions as to licenses.
Nye G.	4	Sep. 29	1858	Jan. 6	ditto
Nye G.	7				
Nye G.	12	Apl. 8	1859	Apl, June. 27	Returned inadequacy of fees. Case of the Chinese Junk.
Nye G.	17	Oct. 27	1859	Jan. 10	Fees.
Nye G.	13	Apl. 8	1859	July. 27	Rescue of Seamen of the "Matilda"
Nye G.	15	Aug. 8	1859	Oct. 19	Rel. to the "Emma"
Nye G.	–	Sep. 24	1859	Dec. 3	Rec[d]. des. of June 24–Information as to Capt. Thompson.
Nye G.	18	Jan. 12	1860	Mch. 15	Coolie trade
Nye G.	19	Mch. 27	1860	May. 31	Returns
Nye G.	20	June. 5	1860	Aug. 23	Returns
Nye G.	21	July. 6	1860	Sep. 14	do
Harrison W. H. S.	–	Oct. 1	1860	Oct. 5	Rel. to the Ship "Emma" & wants his claim attended to.
Nye G.	22	Oct. 4	1860	Dec. 20	Returns.
Nye G.	23	Jan. 30	1861	Ap. 6	Returns.

Nye G.	24	Apl. 3	1861	June 14	Returns.
Gideon Nye	25	May 1	1861	Aug. 9	Relating to the case of the American Ship. "Emma" and respects to be instructed on the subject some respondences
Gideon Nye	26	July 2	1861	Sept. 19	Quarterly Returns.
Gideon Nye	27	Oct. 3	1861	Nov. 24	Quarterly Returns.
Gideon Nye	28	Jany 3	1862	Mar. 21	Qrly Returns.
Gideon Nye		Feby 26	1862	May 5	Receives with pleasure the notice of Mr. Harts: appt.
W. P. Jones		June 12	1862	June 14	Has seen confirm in papers. Ignorant of nomination. Asks con□□□
W. P. Jones		June 19	1862	June 23	Asks to delay dep for pvat till 10th Sept.
W. P. Jones		June 25	1862	July 1	Bond enc^{d} Bowen P^{a} appt^{d} form Ill.

508

Macao

Name	No.	Date		Rec^{d}.	Import.
G. Nye	30	April 11	1862	June 14	Qrly Ret.
G. Nye	31	May 8	1862	July 17	Grants passports to two citizens, Report.
G. Nye	32	July 8	1862	Sept. 12	Qrly Ret.
5th Aud		Sept. 30	1862	Sept. 30	Instruc. period of Consul Jones
A. A. Sargent		Dec. 26	1862	Dec. 27	Is consulate vacant. Has O. Sullivan been now for Singapore
G. Nye		Oct. 2	1862	Dec. 22	Qrly Ret.
G. Nye		Oct. 12	1862	Dec. 22	Receives notif of Consul Jones appt. Translation of late Port. treaty with China. Consular address to Min of Portugal. Reply of His Excy. Loyal expressions
G. Nye	35	Jany 2	1863	Mch. 23	Qrly Ret.
G. Nye	36	Feby 13	1863	May 4	Departure of Gov. Gen. Guimaraes
W. P. Jones	1	Feby 25	1863	May 4	Arrived Feb 24. Entered on duty July 25. 1863. Invty.
G. Nye	37	Feby 24	1863	Feby Apl^{d} 18	Ret. for fractional qr. Invty. Gov Genl pardons an Am. prisoner at his suit. Hopes he has done his duty.
5th Aud		May 13	1863	May 13	Transit period of Consul Jones?
W. P. Jones	1	Mch. 27	1863	June 4	Condition of Constes at Macao & Swatow. Wants appt to latter place.
W. P. Jones	2	Mch. 28	1863	June 4	Pub. of exeq. Rect of flags arms &c & Circ 25 Pardon & release of Jas Davis.
W. P. Jones		Mch. 27	1863	June 17	Asking transfer to Swatow. (Bartle)
W. P. Jones to Sec. Treas.	2	Mch. 31	1863		Salary a/c. (to Sec. Treas.)
W. P. Jones	3	Mch. 31	1863	June 12	Misc. exp.
W. P. Jones	4	Mch 31	1863	June 12	Rent a/c.
W. P. Jones	4	Mch. 31	1863	June 20	Qrly Rep. Calls attention to apply for transfer to Swatow
W. P. Jones	5	Mch. 31	1863	June 12	Bill for Bookcase.
5th Aud		June 20	1863	June 20	Past period of Consul J.

W. P. Jones	7	May 9	1863	Aug. 4	As to unlawful seizure & sequestration of ship Emma.
W. P. Jones	9	June 30	1863	Sept. 9	Misc a/c.
W. P. Jones	10	June 30	1863	Sept. 9	Rent a/c.
W. P. Jones	8	June 30	1863	Oct. 5	Certh Qrly Reports. General remarks.
5th Aud		Oct. 19	1863	Oct. 19	As to cert transit of Consul J. His explang dis encld.
W. P. Jones	11	Sept. 30	1863	Dec. 15	Rent a/c.
W. P. Jones.	12	Sept. 30	1863	Dec. 15	Misc a/c.
W. P .Jones to Prest		Sept. 20	1863	Dec. 28	Concerning absence from Consulate.
W. P. Jones	13	Sept. 30	1863	Dec. 19	Qrly Ret.
5th Aud		Dec. 15	1863	Dec. 16	With Nos 4 & 7 of NSC. May his compense be allowed?
Comptroller		Jany 11	1864	Jany 11	Infg Dept of Balance to credit of late V. C. Nye to be presented to Sanitary Com. as per his dis of July 20. 1863 (soakn)
W. P. Jones	14	Oct. 24	1863	Jany 2	Importance of Consulate. Inadequacy of salary.
H. N. Congar & G. Nye		Oct. 29	1863	–	Vouching the cost of living in China & inadequacy of Consl. Salary
W. P. Jones	15	Nov. 27	1863	Feby 5	Petition of Am. Missionaries at Canton as to Macao Consulate
W. P. Jones to President	2	Nov. 25	1863	Feby 13	Calling attention to Petition above noted as to increase of compensation
W. P. Jones	16	Dec. 31	1863	Mch. 19	Rent a/c.
W. P. Jones	17	Dec. 31	1863	Mch. 19	Misc a/c.

Macao 509

Name	No.	Date		Recd.	Import.
W. P. Jones	18	Dec. 31	1863	Apl. 4	Corres with Govr Respg "Alabama". Qrly Reports.
W. P. Jones	19	Dec. 31	1863	Apl. 4	Enumeration of Dispatches.
W. P. Jones	1	Mar. 31	1864	June 16	Accts 1 Qr, 64,
W. P. Jones	2	Mar. 31	1864	June 16	Miss Acct, 1 Qr, 64
W. P. Jones	3	Mar. 31	1864	June 16	Condition of our Commerce, &c The "Alabama". Movements of our "men of war". Naval depot transferred to Macao, Receipts from the Dept. Paralization of Am. trade. & condition of trade generally. Quarterly Reports. /sta./
W. P. Jones	8	July 9	1864	Sep. 19	Failures of Portuguese Treaty negotiations. Denial of sovereignty at Macao.
W. P. Jones	5	June 30	1864	Nov. 18	a/cs for 2d qr' 64 (mis)
W. P. Jones	6	June 30	1864	Nov. 18	do do (mis)
W. P. Jones	11	Sep. 30	1864	Dec. 30	Ret of arrival Am. Dep of A□□ □□□.
W. P. Jones	4	June 8	1864	Aug. 20	Asks books, stationery, &c.

Name	No.	Date	AD.	Received	Import.
W. P. Jones	12	Sep. 30th	1864	Jan. 30th	Arrival Report for qr ending Sep 30th 1864
W. P. Jones	9	Sep. 30th	1864	Mch. 10th	Miscel. expense.
W. P. Jones	10	Sep. 30th	1864	Mch. 10th	a/c for office rent
W. P. Jones	13	Dec. 14	1864	Mch. 10th	ask inc salary. enc. petition of ministers &c
W. P. Jones	1	Jan. 30th	1863	Apr. 10th	Comp. of loss of time in rec. dup.
W. P. Jones	2	Jan. 30the	1863	Apr. 10th	Corr. error in Com. Ap. 1864
W. P. Jones	14	Dec. 31st	1864	Mch. 24th	a/c for off. rent.
W. P. Jones	15	Dec. 31st	1864	Mch. 24th	a/c for misc exp
W. P. Jones	$15\frac{1}{2}$	Dec. 31st	1864	Mch. 24th	Quar. returns
W. P. Jones	16	Dec. 31st	1864	Mch. 24th	Rep of □□□ for 1864
Asst. Pm. Gen	16	Mch. 28th	1864	Mch. 29th	Trans. dead letter.
W. P. Jones	5	Mch. 31	1865	June 2d	a/c for office rent &c.
W. P. Jones	4	Mch. 31	1865	June 2d	a/c for misc. exp.
W. P. Jones	6	Apr. 27	1865	July 27	Settlement of the estate of Edwd. Russell – deceased.
W. P. Jones	7	June 30	1865	Sept. 18	Return of Off. Rt. a/c 2d qr 1865.
W. P. Jones	8	June 30	1865	Sept. 18	Return of miscel, exp. a/c for 2d qr 1865.
W. P. Jones	10	July 20	1865	Oct. 20	Refers to death Am. Citz. J. W. Hawes of Mass.
W. P. Jones	11	July 20	1865	Oct. 20	Req. Copy "Con. Manual" .
W. P. Jones	15	Sept. 30	1865	Jan. 22	Annual Com. Report for 1865 (Sr.)
W. P. Jones	3	Feb. 27	1865	May 2	Case of the "Emma" at Lisbon, Conlr Employment,
W. P. Jones		June 26	1865	Sept. 5	Official Corres with colonial Govt. of Macao, on death of President Lincoln.
W. P. Jones		June 26	1865	Sept. 5	Letter of condolence
W. P. Jones		July 1	1865	Oct. 5	Returns for 2d qr 1865,
W. P. Jones	12	Sept. 30	1865	Dec. 14	Accounts 3d qr 1865.
W. P. Jones	13	Sept. 30	1865	Dec. 14	Miscel exp a/c 3d qr 1865.
W. P. Jones	14	Sept. 30	1865	Dec. 14	Returns for 3d qr 1865.
W. P. Jones	16	Oct. 28	1865	1866 Jany 22	Takes charge of Consulate at Amoy, appoints Vice Consul.
W. P. Jones	17	Oct. 28	1865	1866 Jany 22	Acct, for Off. Rt. part 4th qr 1865.
W. P. Jones	18	Oct. 28	1865	1866 Jany 22	Acct for Miscel exp, part 4th qr 1865.
5th Auditor		Jany. 24	1866	Jany 24	Inq, for what time W. P. Jones be allowed salary.
J. Q. Barton	1	Dec. 31	1865	Mar. 19	Office rent a/c for part 4th qr 1865.
J. Q. Barton	2	Dec. 31	1865	Mar. 19	Miscel. exp for part 4th qr 1865.

J. Q. Barton	3	Dec. 31	1865	Mar. 19	Returns for 4th qr. 1865.
J. Q. Barton		Jan. 26	1866	Apr. 6	Ackg. Deps No. – dated 21. Nov. 1865, rel, to change of comp, from Salary to Fees, $Recv^{d}$ at date.
Auditor		Apr. 16.	1866	Apr. 11	Inqs. for what time J. Q. Barton may be allowed salary at his post.
		May 17	1866	May 18	Same as above.
W. P. Jones	6	April 20	1866	June 29	Miscel exp a/c & Returns for part 2^{d} qr. 1866,
W. P. Jones	7	April 20	1866	June 29	Office Rent for 1st qr. 1866.
W. P. Jones	8	April 20	1866	June 29	Removal to Amoy, Appoint of Vice Consul,
W. P. Jones	9	April 20	1866	June 29	Return of Fees for 1st & 2^{d} qrs. 1866.

Macao, (China.) 215

NAME.	NO.	DATE.	A. D.	RECEIVED.	IMPORT.
H. Ebell	1	Feb. 27th	1867	Apr. 27th	Returns for year 1866.
	2	Feb. 27th	1867	Apr. 27th	Cef'g to his No. 8. of 1866 rel. to Salary.
W. P. Jones	1	Dec. 4	1867	1868. Mar. 6	Inf'g. Dept. of his arrival at his post after having delivered the archives of the Canton Consulate to E. M. King Esq. as per instructions.
W. P. Jones	–	May 29	1868		Reports his return to the U. S. on the 28" instant.
W. P. Jones	–	June 7	1868	June 9	Req^{r}. to withdraw his Desp. of Dec. 4" 1867 announcing his return to Macao & giving his reasons why.
Fifth Auditor	J.	June 8	1868	June 9	Inq^{r}. rel. to acct. of W. P. Jones for transit to Amoy & home.
W. P. Jones	–	June 8	1868	June 9	Rel. to his claim for salary while making his transit from Amoy to this city.
W. P. Jones	–	June 10	1868	June 11	Rel. to his claim for salary while in transit; Ref'g to the opinion of the Atty. Genl. & c.
H. Ebell(V.C.)	–	Oct. 9	1869	Nov. 30	Resigning position as V. C. States that he has sent the Conslr. Archives to the Consulate at Hong Kong.

卷·一

VOLUME ONE

卷一介紹說明

Introductory Note of Volume One

File Microcopies of Records in the National Archives: No.109

Roll 1

DESPATCHES FROM UNITED STATES CONSULS IN MACAO, 1849–1869

REGISTER, 1848–1869

and

Volume 1

June 18, 1849–December 31, 1863

THE NATIONAL ARCHIVES

Washington: 1947

[1-002]

[46451
2755
R □□
54]

KNOW ALL MEN BY THESE PRESENTS,

That we Hugh Steel, Cornelius Gooding and James B. Moore are held and firmly bound to the United States of America, in the sum of two thousand dollars, money of the said United States, to the payment whereof we bind ourselves jointly, and severally, our joint and several heirs, executors, and administrators. Witness our hands and seals, this Third day of September 1823.

The condition of the above Obligation is such, that if the above bounden Hugh Steel bear appointed consul of the United States in certain foreign parts, shall truly and faithfully discharge the duties of his said office, according to law, and also shall truly account for all moneys, goods, and effects, which may come into his profession by virtue of the laws of the United States, or of his said office, then the above obligation to be void; otherwise to remain in full force.

SIGNED, SEALED, AND DELIVERED
IN THE PRESENCE OF
David Ditch
Paicathan Lynch

Hugh Steel Seal
Cornelius Gooding Seal
James B. Moore Seal

□□□□□□□□□□□□□□□□□
□□□□□□□□□□□□□□□□□
□□□□□□□□□□□□□□□□□
□□□□□□□□□□□□□□□□□
□□□□□□□□□□□□□□□□□

[Hugh Steel
Consul at S^t^. Bartholomew
Dated 3 September, 1823.

Penalty $2,000.]

[1-003]

KNOW ALL MEN BY THESE PRESENT,

That we John R. Thomson and Edward Thomson of the City of Philadelphia Merchant are held and firmly bound to the United States of America, in the sum of two thousand dollars, money of the said United States, to the payment whereof we bind ourselves jointly, and severally, our joint and several heirs, executors, and administrators. Witness our hands and seals, this first day of March 1825.

The condition of the above obligation is such, that if the above bounden John R Thomson Appointed Consul of the United States in certain foreign parts, shall truly and faithfully discharge the duties of his said office, according to law, and also shall truly account for all moneys, goods, and effects, which may come into his possession by virtue of the laws of the United States, or of his said office, then the above obligation to be void; otherwise to remain in full force.

SIGNED, SEALED, AND DELIVERED
IN THE PRESENCE OF

Rodney Fisher
Edw[d]. R. Thomson
Peter Mackie
Cha[s]. Mackie

To the signature of Edw P. Thomson
To the signature of John R. Thomson

Jno R. Thomson
Edw Thomson

Certify my opinion that this Obligation is sufficient secured. C. I. Ingurall, dirt. Atty–5. July 1825

[of J. R. Thomson,
Consul at Canton
dated do 1. March, 1825.
Penalty $2,000.]

[1-004]

[Re'd 8 Septr.
N°. 1 Mr. Hoffs r
R.]

Consulate of the U. S. of America
Macaó, June 18th, 1849

Sir,

I have the honor to acknowledge the receipt of my appointment as U. S. Consul for the Port of Macao, and in the absence of the usual Exequatur his Excellency the Governor of Macao has recognised me officially and granted me permission to act.

I beg leave to state that I have signed my Bond and forwarded it to the United States to be duly executed which when done it will be immediately sent to you.

I respectfully request that I may be furnished with a Flag Consular Seal & U. States Con[l]. of Amer. If they are sent to M[r]. Frank De Silver Philadelphia he will forward them to China per first opportunity.

I am Sir
With great respect,
Your Obd[t] Ser[t]
Robert P. De Silver
U. S. Consul

[To the Hon.[l]
John M. Clayton
Secretary of States
Washington City]

[R. P. de Silver
U. S. Consulate
Macao
June, 18th, 1849]

[1-005]

[R
N°. 2]

Consulate of the U. S. of America
Macao, June 20th, 1849

Sir,

I have the honor of addressing you on the 18th int. after an interview I had with his Ex. the Governor of Macao, since which and at his request, I made my application for permission to commence my Official Duties in the absence of the usual Exequatur in writing, a Copy of which I enclose marked N° 1 as also sent him a Copy of my letter of appointment. I enclose a Copy of his reply marked N° 2 as also mine marked N° 3 which I trust will meet your approbation.

I respectfully ask for your instructions in reference to the 2nd Section of the act of Congress alluded to.

I am Sir
With much respect
Your Obd[t]. Ser[t].
Robert P. De Silver
U. S. Consul

[To the Hon.[l]

John M. Clayton
Washington
City]

/Copy/

Consulate of the U.S. of America
Macáo, June 18th, 1849

Sir,

I have the honor to enclose you a Copy of my appointment by the President of the U. States, as "Consul of the United States for the Port of Macao", you will perceive that my Commission has been paid to the Legation of the United States at Lisbon with instructions, I apply to the Portuguese Government for the usual Exequatur, in the absence of which I respectfully request that your Excellency will recognise this appointment and grant me permission to enter upon my duties.

I am Sir,
With great respect
Your Obd.t Ser.t
/sign/ R. P. de Silver
U. S. Consul

[To His Excellency
The Governor
of Macáo]

[R. P. de Silver
U. S. Consulate
Macao
June, 20th, 1849]

/Copy/

Consulate of the U. S. of America
Macao, June 19th, 1849

Sir,

I have the honor to acknowledge the receipt of your letter of this day.

In reference to that portion of it relating to the Consular Bill as passed by Congress and approved by the President of the U. States August 11th, 1848, I respectfully state that in the absence of any instructions on this period, I acceed to your proviso, and shall not act on that section of the Bill relating to Macáo, until I receive orders from the United States Government.

With sentiments of the greatest respect,

I am Sir,
Your Obd.[t] Ser.[t]
/Sign/ R. P. de Silver
U. S. Consul

[To His Excellency
João Maria Ferreira de Amaral
Governor of Macáo]

[N. 8
Gouerno da Provincia
Macau Timor
Solor

□□□ediente Geral
□□]

/copy/

Itlm[o] Senhor Robert P. de Silver

Tenha a honra de accuzar a recepção de vosso officio, com data de hontem, no qual, vos me envias a copia da vossa nomeação de Consul do Estados unidos da America em Macáo, pela qual se vé, que o vosso governo passa a solicilar o Exequatur do meu Governo, e ao mesmo tempo que vou mostra no mesmo officis dezejos de comerçar desde já, de entrar no exercicer de vossas funcçoens Consulares.

Congratulo–mo connosco da ler escolha q. o vosso Governo fez nomeando–o go para este lugar, e na certeza que tenho que o Exequatur não vou será negado, nenhua duvida se me offerecer a tomar sobre minha responsabilidade, o Consenter, que, deste ja, entruo no exercicio de vossa funcçoẽs, com a condição que vos não fareis por pretesto algum uzo da Secção 2[a], na parte que diz respeito a Macau, do acto de Parlarmento approvado pelo vossa Prezidente, aos 11 de Gosto de 1848, que diz assim. And be it further enacted…… commited in the dominions of China, including

Macao

Podindo aprovar vou que o Governo de Sua Magestudo Fidelhpina bon desigido reclamaçõens do vosso sobre este objecto.

Desde que vos mo desejaes hum documentos official da nossa parte, neste sentido nenhuma objecão tirus da minha parte, con □□□ao□□□ Consulares, ate que □□□ receba nosso ordens do □□□ Governo.

Deus guarde a US[a] Macao 19 de Junho de /49c

/sign/ Joáo M. F. do Amaral

Itlm[o] S[r]. Robert P. de Siver

[1-006]

[Rec. 18th Nov. Mr. La Reintire
N° 3
R:]

Consulate of the U. States of America
Macao, August 21st, 1849

Sir,

I have the honor to acknowledge the receipt of your despatch dated 28th May 1849, covering my appointment as U. S. Consul for this Port, and giving me the information that the Government of Portugal had declined granting me an Exequatur, "on the grounds that her Majesty's Government had not exercised such right or power in favor of any nation for the Island of Macao" and that if said Government pays to China an annual fee for the "usufruct" of the Island, I may possibly procure a recognition by the Chinese Authorities through M[r]. Davis our commissioner.

The fact is clearly established that the Portuguese Government do pay an annual fee of 500 Tales to the Chinese for a certain portion of land on which this Port is located not withstanding, which they, the Portuguese, claim right & title to it, & will not permit any nation to excises judicial Authority here, therefore although an application to the Chinese Government for an Exequatur would be immediately successful, in fact they would be too happy that by such a request, it would have the non recognition of the right of Portugal by the U. S. Government, yet the present Governor would on no account permit me perform my consular duties, nor the American Flag to be hoisted under such circumstances. Immediately after the receipt of your despatch, I conferred with our Commissioner Mr. Davis who suggested my calling at once upon his Ex. the Governor, unofficially, but with the view of obtaining a proper understanding of the matter, for his Excellency a few days after the arrival of Mr. Davis in Macáo had written him officially, that her Majesty's Gov.[t] would be pleased to grant an Exequatur to Consuls from any nation, I accordingly had an interview with his Excellency, who expressed great surprise that the Exequatur had been declined particularly on the grounds as set forth, which are not correct, for they have granted such power both to France & Spain, he begged that I would leave my Commission with him that he might forward it to his Government, with a request that an Exequatur should be granted, which he had no doubt would be complied with. In the meantime I would continue to perform my duties as heretofore; with his object I have left my commission with him to be forwarded.

I am Sir
With great respect
Your obd.[t] Ser.[t]

Robt P. De Silver
U. S. Consul

August 27th

P. S. Since writing the within a most barbarous act of atrocity has been committed by the Chinese, the assassination of the Governor of Macáo, on the outskirts of the Town, but within its limits, whilst riding with his Aul de Camp; our commissioner Mr. Davis informed me that he has given you all the particulars. –I have seen some of the numbers of the Council & they inform me that the late Governor's wishes （which they were aware of） with regard to my Exequatur, shall be fully carried out & my commission be forwarded to the Portuguese Government at Lisbon.

Robt P. De Silver
U. S. Consul

[To the Hon.[1]
John M. Clayton
Secretary of States
Washington
City]

[Consulate of the U. States
□□□□□
August, 21st, 1849]

[1–007]

[Rec.d 24 Sept.'49 & C Mr. □□□]

The Honble John M. Clayton
Secretary of State
Washington City

Sir,
I have the honor to hand with the enclosed bond being surety for R. P. De Silver as consul in Macao.

With Great Respect
Your Obd.[l] Ser.[t],
Frank De Silver
Philadelphia September 29th 1849

□□□□□□

[1-008]

[Rec'd, d 4 Oct'd 49 Macao

Bond appends & sent to
□□□□□
Se chy of Fuaiy 4 Oct'49]

The Hon[ble] John M. Clayton
Secretary of State
Washington City

Sir,

Be pleased to find enclosed bond of R. P. de Silver Consul Macao, with an additional surety attached, certified by the District Attorney I was ignorant of the fact that two Trusties were required, or they should have been appended in the first place.

With Great Respect
I have the honor to be
Your Obd.' Servant
Frank De Silver
Philadelphia Oct. 3 1849

[1-009]

[Ack 17 Jany'50 Mr. La Reintire
R:
N° 4]

Consulate of the U. States of America
Macao, October 26th, 1849

Sir,

I have the honor to acknowledge the receipt of your Consular dated June 16th 1849. The contents I have carefully noted and the various provisions shall be strictly attended to.

I am Sir
With great respect
Your Obd.' Ser.'
Robt. P. De Silver
U. S. Consul

[To the
Hon.[l] John M. Clayton
Secretary of States
Washington
City]

[1-010]

[Rec'd 9 March
Mr. La Reintire
N°.5 R]

Consulate of the U. S. of America
Macáo November 29th 1849

Sir,

I have the honor to acknowledge the receipt of your Consular dated August 22nd 1849 and have carefully noted the rule with regard to the expenditure of Clothing & to destitute Mariners.

I am Sir
With great respect
Your Obd.[t] Ser.[t]
Robt. P. De Silver
U. S. Consul

[To the
Hon[l] John M. Clayton
Secretary of State
Washington
City]

[1-011]

[Rec'd
Mr. La Reintire]

Consulate of the U. States of America
Macao March 25th 1850

Sir,

I had the honor to address you under date August 21st & 27th 1849 （dispatch N°3） in reference to the steps

I took with regard to my Exequatur.

I now deem it my duty to inform the Hon.[l] Secretary that notwithstanding my Commission was returned to the Portuguese Government by the Hon.[l] Council of Macao last October with a request for an Exequatur, yet up to this time I have not received it.

I have however been unofficially informed that the Portuguese have approved the act of the late Governor by my recognition by him.

I am Sir
With great respect
Your Obd.[t] Ser.[t]
Robt. P. De Silver
U. S. Consul

[To the
Hon.[l] John M. Clayton
Secretary of State
Washington
City]

[1-012]

[Rec.d 24 Sept.–

Mr. La Reintire

N°7 R.]

Consulate of the United States of America
Macáo April 22nd 1850

Sir,

I have the honor to acknowledge the receipt of your dispatch of 2[d] January last, giving me institutions relative to the 2[d] section of the act of Congress of 11th August 1848, and covering copy of yours of 28th May 1849. Immediately on the receipt of which I enclosed a copy to the Hon.[l] The council for the Government of Macáo. (see N°1)

I, this day, received a reply /see N°2/ all of which is respectfully submitted.

I have the honor to be
With great respect
Your Obd.[t] Ser.[t]
Robt. P. De Silver
U. S. Consul

[To the
Hon[l] John M. Clayton
Secretary of State
Washington
City]

[N°1]

Macáo April 20th 1850

Honorable Sir,

I have the honor to enclose you a copy of a despatch which I have received from the Honorable the Secretary of State of the United States of America.

I respectfully request to be informed if my Commission has yet been returned by Her Most Faithful Majesty's Government of granting me the usual Exequatur.

I am Sir,
With great respect
Your Obd.[t] Ser.[t]
/sig/ R. P. de Silver
U. S. Consul

[To the Honorable
The Council for the
Government of Macao–]

[Rec'd 24 Sept.
N°2]

The Honorable the Council for the Government of this Province requests me to acknowledge the receipt of your Official Dispatch of yesterday's date covering copy of dispatch received by you from the Government of the United States of America relating to your appointment at Consul for this Port.

The Honorable the Council are of opinion that by this time the Home Government of her Most Faithful Majesty will have received the explanation which was necessary to expedite the Royal Sanction in favour of your appointment.

The Hon[l] Council hopes in a short time to have the satisfaction to deliver to you the respective Diplomas.

God Preserve You

Macáo April 21st 1850
/sig/ A. I. de Miranda

Secretary

[To
R. P. de Silver Esqr
U. S. Council
Macáo]

[1-013]

[R.
Rec.'d 10 Augt.
Mr. La Reintire
N°8]

Consulate of the U. States of America
Macáo May 20th 1850

Sir,

I have the honor to report that I have this day received from his Majesty's the Queen of Portugal's Government, through the Colonial Government of Macáo my Exequatur as U. S. Consul for this Port.

I am Sir
With great respect
Your Obd.l Ser.l
Robt. P. De Silver
U. S. Consul

[To the
Honl John M. Clayton
Secretary of State
Washington
City]

[1-014]

[Rec'd 8 Sept.
Mr. La Reintire
N°9 R.]

Consulate of the U. States of America
Macao June 17th 1850

Sir,

I have the honor to acknowledge the receipt of your Circular of 4th March 1850.

I respectfully inform you that there are no Consular agents in my district, and no port to render such appointments necessary.

I am Sir
With great respect
Your Obd.[t] Ser.[t]
Robt. P. De Silver
U. S. Consul

[To the
Hon[l] J. M. Clayton
Secretary of State
Washington
City]

[1-015]

[Rec'd 6 Jan[y] '51
Mr. Abbott
N°.10]

U. S. Consulate
Macáo July 1st 1850

Sir,

I have the honor to enclose you herewith two separates accounts current, one showing balance due me of $49.50 being for Amounts paid for the relief of distressed American Seamen at this Port, & the other for $135.01 being for actual necessary expenses of this Consulate.

I have drawn two bills on you for the respective Amounts of the above, at thirty days sight, in favour of Mess[es] De Silver and Thomas of Philao[a] which I respectfully beg you will protect. You will observe that I have charged no percentage for disbursement, nor difference of Exchange, not knowing whether it would be allowed.

I have the honor
to be Sir,
With great respect
Your Obd.[t] Ser.[t]
Robt. P. De Silver
U. S. Consul

[To the Hon.[1]
John M. Clayton
Sec. of State
Washington
City]

[□□□□□□□□
□□□□□□□□
U. S. Consul
Macao]

□□□□□□□□
of American Vessels Arriving at and Departing from Macao from 1st July 1849 to the 31st December inclusive

Date of Arrival	Class	Name	Tonnage	Master	Where from	Where bound	Cargo	Date of Departure	Fees	
									Deposits & Delivery of paper	Noting Protest
1849								1849		
July 20th	Ship	Janthe	414	Johnson	Singapore	Whampoa	Rice	July 26th	$4	
August 2d	Ship	Great Brittain	700	Dumansque	Whampoa	Shanghai	Sundries	August 22d	$4	
August 17th	Brig	Eagle	328	Lovett	Calcutta	Whampoa	Opium	August 19th	$4	
August 27th	Brig	Eagle	328	Lovett	Whampoa	Calcutta	Balast	August 29th	$4	
September 29th	Ship	Helican	1113	Gose	Boston	Whampoa	Sundries	October 5th	$4	
October 17th	Ship	Sea Witch	907	Walesman	Calcutta	Whampoa	Opium	October 20th	$4	$4
December 4th	Brig	Frolie	212	Taucon	Whampoa	Bombay	Balast	December 6th	$4	
December 8th	Bark	Inea	316	Buxton	Liverpool	Whampoa	Sundries	December 11th	$4	
December 15th	Brig	Eagle	328	Lovett	Calcutta	Whampoa	Opium	December 17th	$4	
1850								1850		
April 19th	Ship	Santas	593	Johnson	Boston	Whampoa	Sundries	April 25th	$4	

Received for Certificates of Shipments of Invoices to California per Portugues①
Barque "N. S. das Dores" May 22d 1850 — $18
Received for Certificates of Shipments of Invoices to California per Portugues②
Brig Amizade May 30th 1850 — $20
Total amount of fees received from 1st July 1849 to 1st July 1850 — $82

U. S. Consulate — Robt. P. De Silver
Macao, July 1st, 1850 — U. S. Consul

① Sic.
② Sic.

[1-016]

[Rec'd 17 Feb.'51

Mr. Abbott]

U. States Consulate

Macáo October 20th 1850

Sir,

I have the honor to acknowledge the receipt of your circular dated July 23rd, last informing me that the President by and with the advice and consent of the Senate has appointed you Secretary of State of the United States and that you had that day entered on the duties of that office.

Permit me to assure your Sir that this information is most gratifying to myself and to your fellow countrymen at this Port.

I am Sir

With great respect

Your Obd.t Ser.t

Robt. P. De Silver

U. S. Consul

[To the Honl

Daniel Webster

Secretary of State

Washington

City]

[1-017]

[Rec'd 17 Feb.r'51

Mr. Abbott]

United States Consulate

Macáo November 25th 1850

[□□□□□□□□□□ secretary of the navy.]

Sir,

It becomes my painful duty to apprise you of the total destruction of the Portuguese Frigate "D. Maria 2d".

I have the honor to report that on the 29th ultimo about half past 2 o'clock P. M., she blew up at her anchorage in the Taipa which is at a distance of some two & a half miles from this Port, & fully in sight, with upwards of two hundred souls on board, including Captain de Assis e Silva. The U. S. Ship "Marion" Capt. W. M. Glendy, laid within 200 yard of her, and it may only owing to her very close proximity, that she was not lost, also, or serious damage done to her, and her crew, for Spaw, masses of heavy limber & Guns were blown clear over her, whilst light articles only, fell on deck and rattled along the Ships side. Caplain Glendy being on Shore, their Command dissolved on Lieu[t] A. M. Pennock; too much praise cannot be bestowed on him, his officers & Crew for the prompt & energetic measures taken to save their own Ship from fire （for at one time it was feared the burning much might drift on to her） and fearless activity displayed in saving life.

The only one injured was one of her men who was tending boat on the off side of the Ship, a falling iron bolt struck him on the arm, glanced on to his knee and gave him a severe wound, the damage sustained by the Ship was having one of her boats stove.

The Marion's boats were man'd at once, & the much braved, & from beneath smouldering timber & fragments of Spars, several mutilated & blackened but live persons were taken, several also were taken from the water, in all ten, & placed on board the "Marion", the further such attempt was only given up after sundry explosions, presumed of shells, the smoke becoming enveloped in flames, and the fear of a second explosion of the after Magazine, for the stage of the Vessel was left, whilst the forward part was entirely blown away. But subsequently it was ascertained that all of her powder 300 Barrels had been forward; of the persons taken on board the "Marion", several died almost immediately and after they were removed to the Portuguese Hospital on shore, only three of them are now alive.

There were many Chinese on board of the Frigate at the time of the explosion, shoemakers, tailors, bumboat people & wash women. Of the persons attached to the Ships, but not on board of her at the time, there were a party of eight men on duty at the Taypa Port with an officer, on shore at Macáo was the Captain's son, a midshipman, the Chaplain, Purser, Surgeon, Captain Clerk and some few at the Hospital, in all including the three men now alive, some 33 were spared. The day was the anniversary of the Birth of the King Consort of Portugal, both Ships were dressed & salutes has been fired at 12 o'clock, when we first heard of the disaster, it was thought that accidently some fire might have reached the magazine, but I learn now from the Senior Naval Officer, on the Station that the Gunner was a very bad fellow, had been under arrest several times for drunkenness, the day previous to the explosion the Captain had pulled his beard and the afterwards amongst his messmates had vowed revenge, saying that he had not much longer to live that he was sixty years of age & had been forty in the services, that he would not live under such an indignity, it is therefore presumed that he blew the Ship up himself & all hands. A few days after, Capt[n]. Assis bury □□□□nd & buried with every honor for days bodies □□□ parts of bodies, were found in great number, and buried in Masses, for they could not be identified.

This melancholy event has again quit a gloom over this apparently fated Colony.

I am Sir
With great respect
Your Old.[t] Ser.[t]
Robt. P. De Silver
U. S. Consul

[To the
Hon[l] Daniel Webster

Secretary of State
Washington
City

Returied by Navy □□□□
22 Feb.r 51]

[1-018]

[Rec'd 21 July

Mr. Abbott

N°13]

United States Consulate
Macao 3rd January 1851

Sir,

I have the honor to enclose you herewith Consular Return of American Vessels arriving at and departure from Macao from 1st January to the 31st December 1850 inclusive, with statement of fees received.

I am Sir
With great respect
Your Old.t Ser.t
Robt. P. De Silver
U. S. Consul

[To the
Honl Daniel Webster
Secretary of State
Washington
City]

Consular Return
of American Vessels Arriving at and Departing from Macáo from 1st January
to the 31st December 1850 inclusive

Date of Arrival	Class	Name	Tonnage	Master	Where from	Where bound	Cargo	Date of Departure	Fees	
									Deporting of delivery of papers	Noting protest
1850								1850		
September 25	Ship	Ariel	877	Brewster	Boston	Whampoa	Sundries	September 29	$4	
December 15	Bark	Nautilus	283	Page	Whampoa	New York	Tea & Matting	December 20	$4	
Consular Seals at Various times $28:										

Robt. P. De Silver
U.S. Consul
Macao May 20th 1851

[1-019]

[Rec'd 7 August

Mr. Abbott.

N°14]

U. S. Consulate
Macáo May 20th 1851

Sir,

I have the honor to enclose to you a translation of a declaration made in reference to the death of John Smith, an American Sailor, who died on his passage on board the Portuguese Vessel "Sophia" on a voyage from Manila to this Port. His effects will be sold at auction & the proceeds placed to the credit of the U. States Government should no/no per claim be made for them here.

I am Sir
With great respect
Your Old.' Ser.'
Robt. P. De Silver
U. S. Consul

[To the
Hon' Daniel Webster
Secretary of State
Washington
City]

[Translation]

Declation

In the year of our Lord 1851 on the twenty six days of month April on board the Bark "Sophia", under, my command, Feliz Lourenço Pinna, proceeding in her voyage from Manila to Macao in Latitude N15, 12 long E. of Greenwich 120 of 6 o'clock p.m. died on board the said Bark an American passenger named John Smith, who embarked in Manila on the previous day apparently in a sound State of death. The cause of the death was a severe Cholie or Indi-□□□we were not able in any way to alliveate, the □□□ having administered all the medicine on board, but without success. I immediately after the death of the said, I, the Captain Pinna, ordered me to make this declaration □□□ take an inventary of every thing the man possessed □□□ memo annexed for the truth of this, I do hereby signed my name as well the Captain & two other witnesses.

/sig/ Pedro Lopes
/sig/ F. L. de Pinna

Witnesses
/sig/ George Poppe
/sig/ George Willam

Inventary
3 White Shirts
1 Wollen do
2 Pcs drawers
1 Valvet Wiscoat
2 Pcs Pantalons
1 Red Scarf
5 Pcs Socks
1 Pcs Razors
1 Shaving Brushes
2 Combs
1 Housewife
3 Hair Brushes
1 Disely Bag
6 Books
1 Cloth Bag

Witnesses
/sig/ George Poppe /sig/ Pedro Lopes
/sig/ George Willam /sig/ F. L. de Pinna

[1-020]

[Recd 13th Oct. Mr. Abbott.

N°.15]

United State Consulate
Macáo July 16th 1851

Sir,
I have the honor to acknowledge the receipt of your despatch of May 1st 1851 enclosing a copy of a despatch

from the Port Master General of the United States in reference to postal communications with China and at your request I respectfully state as follows.

All merchants Vessels from San Francisco with but few exceptions anchor at HongKong,[1] at which place the English Gov[t] have a well organized Post Office from which mails are made up for the five Chinese open Ports and Macao. No Vessels put into this Port, from San Francisco, and very few touch at Shanghai. I would therefore suggest that the Mails of Merchant Vessels be made up for HongKong.

Should it be in contemplation to establish a line of Steamers from San Francisco to China, I would then recommend the Mails be made up for this Port, as for the terminus, Macao is latter adpted than either of the five Chinese Ports. The inner Harbour is one of the safest in the world, possessing good holding ground and completely sheltered from the effects of Typhoons, Vessels can lay close to landings & fine large Government Store Houses well adopted for Goodes & Coals, formerly Custom House ware Houses may be procured at very moderate Rents, Vessels drawing over 15 feet cannot go into the inner Harbour, but are compelled to lay in the Roads, the Mails could be addressed to my care & by me forwarded to the various Points of Distination. Contracts can be made for any quantity of good Coals delivable here from Formosa at from seven to eight dollars per Ton.

I have the honor to report that under Date of January 3[d] last, I forwarded to you statement of fees received at the Consulate for the last half year of 1850.

I am Sir
With great respect
Your Old.[t] Ser.[t]
Robt. P. De Silver
U. S. Consul

[To the
Hon[l] Daniel Webster
Secretary of State
Washington
City]

[1-021]

[Recd 3d April Mr. Abbott.

No.16]

Consulate of the U. State of America
Macáo January 1st 1852

Sir,

I have the honor to acknowledge the receipt of your despatch of September 4th 1851.

---

① Sic.

I regret that I can give you no information of the friends or relations of John Smith seaman who died on the voyage from Manila to this Port. You will find the auction sale of his effects enclosed.

I respectfully enclose account current and vouchers for the year ending 31st December 1851.

I have the honor to report that no American Vessels have put into this Port during the past year & that the fees at the Consulate have amounted to $32 for certifying Invoices of Shipments to San Francisco & Powers of Attorney.

I am Sir
With great respect
Your Old.' Ser.'
Robt. P. De Silver
U. S. Consul

[To the
Hon' Daniel Webster
Secretary of State
Washington
City]

[1-022]

[Rec'd Dec. 1st

Mr. Abbott.
a/cs sent to Agent

N°17]

Consulate of the United States of American
Macao July 5th 1852

Sir,

I have the honor to enclose you a return of American Vessels which have put into the port during the past six month, also account current with vouchers for expenditures on account of distressed American Seamen.

I am Sir
With great respect
Your Old.' Ser.'
Robt. P. De Silver
U. S. Consul

[To the
Hon' Daniel Webster
Secretary of State

Washington
City]

Consular Return
of American Vessels Arriving at and Departing from Macao from 1st January
1851 to 1st July 1852 inclusive

Date of Arrival	Class	Name	Tonnage	Master	Where From	Where Bound	Cargo	Date of departure	Fees	
									Deporting of delivery of papers	Noting protest
February 27	Ship	Amity	504	Pearson	New York	Whampoa	Ballet	March 7	4	
March 27	Bark	Chio	373	Ranpack	S. Francisco	S. Francisco	Passengers	May 21	4	2

For Surveying Passenger Ships bound to San Francesco & verifying Invoices $201

Robt. P. De Silver
U. S. Consul

[1-023]

[Recd apl. 7th

Mr. Abbott.

No18]

United State Consulate
Macáo 1st January 1853

Sir,

I have the honor to enclose you herewith Consular Return of American Vessels, arriving at, and departing from Macao, from 1st July to the 31st December 1852 inclusive with statement of fees received.

I am Sir
With great respect
Your Obd.t Ser.t
Robt. P. De Silver
U. S. Consul

[To
The Honorable
The Secretary of State
Washington
City]

Consular Return

of American Vessels Arriving at and Departing from Macao from 1st July 1852

to 31st December inclusive

Date of Arrival	Class	Tonnage	Name	Master	Where from	Where bound	Cargo	Date of Departure	Fees	
									Deporting of delivery of papers	Noting protest
1852 November 27	Ship	696	"Lelanns"	Hale	New York	Whampoa	Coal & Sundries	December 19	$4	–

For Consular Seals at Various times $ 10.

Robt P. De Silver
U. S. Consul

[1–024]

[Recd 17. Oct. Mr. Abbott.

N°19]

Consulate of the United States of American
Macao July 20th 1853

Sir,

I have the honor to enclose you herewith Consular Return of American Vessels arriving at and departing from Macao from 1st January to the 30th June 1853, inclusive with Statement of fees Recd.

I am Sir
With great respect
Your Old.t Serv.t
Robt P. De Silver
U. S. Consul

[To the
Honl W. L. Marcy
Secretary of State
Washington
City]

Consular Return

of American Vessels Arriving at and Departing from Macao from

1st January to 30th June 1853 inclusive

Date of Arrival	Tonnage	Name	Class	Master	Where from	Where bound	Cargo Inward	Cargo Outward	Date of departure	Fees
										Deporting of delivery of papers
January 2	783	Gertrude	Ship	A. Winsor	New York	Calcutta	Coals	Balast	February 10	$4
January 14	370	Mary Adams	Bark	J. Harding	Califorrnia	California	Passengers	Passengers	January 22	$4
April 9	270	Dragon	Bark	Andrew	Cumsingmoon	Shanghai	Rice	Rice	January 11	$4

Consular and Notarial Fees

Verification of Copies of Original,
Certificates of Market value of Goods, } $151
Extending Protest with Copies

Robt. P. De Silver
U. S. Consul

[1-025]

[Recd 17. Oct.

Mr. Abbott.

N°.20]

Consulate of the United States of American
Macao July 20th 1853

Sir,

I have the honor to acknowledge the receipt of your Circular dated March 9th last informing me that the President by and with the advice and Consent of the Senate had appointed you Secretary of State of the United States, and that you had that day entered on the duties of that office.

Permit me to assure you Sir that this information in most gratifying to myself, and to your fellow Countrymen at this Port.

I am Sir
With great respect
Your Obd.t Serv.t
Robt. P. De Silver
U. S. Consul

[To the
Hon.l W. L. Marcy
Secretary of State

Washington
City]

[1-026]

[Recd 18 April

Mr. Abbott.

□□□, 10 May
N°21]

Consulate of the U. S. of America
Macao January 28th 1854

Sir,

I have the honor to report that the Honorable the Secretary of the Navy having ordered the transfer of the U. S. Naval Depot from this place to Hongkong & accordingly the removal of all Public Property and supplies for the East India Squadron which for a number of years has been under my charge as Naval Storekeeper, and which, for the safe keeping, preservation, and expenditure. I am held accountable, under these circumstances renders it necessary that I should accompany it, the fees of this Consulate being totally inadequate to my support. But in order that the United States Government might still have diplomatic agent here. I have taken the liberty of appointing appointing during my absence. S. B. Rawle by a Citizen of the United States, although a long resident of China and a gentlemen in those capability & integrity I have every confidence, to act as U. S. Vice Consul. I sincere by trust Honorable Sir, that this appointment will meet with your approval, and awaiting which, his Excellency the Governor of Macao has been pleased to recognize.

I respectfully enclose to you a copy of my letter to his Excellency Governor Guimaraes N°1 a copy of his reply N°2 also a copy of my letter of Appointment N°3 to Mr. Rawle.

I have the honor
to be Sir
With great respect
Your Obd.' Ser.'
Robt. P. De Silver
U. S. Consul

[To the Honorable
W. L. Marcy
Secretary of State
Washington
City]

Copy N°1

Consulate of the U. S. of America
Macáo January 26th 1854

Sir,

The U. S. Government having ordered a transfer to HongKong of the public Stores under my charge and to establish at that place the U. S. Naval Depot, I being responsible for the safe keeping, & preservation of the Public Property, under it necessary & imperative that I should accompany said property, under these circumstances, it becomes necessary that I should appoint same responsible person to perform the duties of my Consulate during my absence & whose acts will meet with an approval and recognition from you until I can communicate with my own Government, may I respectfully offer, & beg that you will recognize as U. S. Vice Consul for the Port of Macáo. S. B. Rawle Esq. a gentleman with whom you are well acquainted and in whose capability and integrity, I have every confidence.

I did my self the honor to call upon you this morning with Mr. Rawle and regret that you were not at home.

I am Sir
With great respect
Your Obd.t Ser.t.
(sig) R .P. De Silver
U. S. Consul

[To
His Excellency
The Governor of Macao]

(Copia)

[N°2
Governo da Prov.a de
Macáo, Timor Solor
Expediente Geral
N°1]

Itlmo Snr:

Aceusando reecebido o officio de U. S. a datado d'hontem tenho a responder que sentindo que U. S. a tenha de se ausentar de Macáo onde U. S. a permanececo por tão longo tempo e onde merecer a estima geral de seus habitantes, não tenho duvida em que Mr Rawle fique encarregado do Consulado dos Estados Unidos da America em quanto o Governo dos mesmos Estados não determinar mais regularmento o que deve ter lugar.

Deus Guarde a U. S. a Macao 27 de Janeiro de 1854.

(asigd) I. F. Guimaraes①

① Sic.

[Itlm[o] Sr. R. P. d' Silver
Consul dos Est. Un. d'America
em Macáo]

Copy N[o].3
Consulate of the U. States of America
Macáo January 2[d] 1854

Sir,

Having every confidence in your integrity & capability, I hereby appoint you U. S. Vice Consul for the Port of Macao to act for me during my forced absence which I trust will meet with the approval of the Government of the United States.

I enclose to you a copy of a letter which I addressed to his Excellency the Governor of Macáo notifying him of my intention and requesting for you his recognition. I am most happy to inform you that his Excellency has responded to my wishes most cordially, and consents that you should act as U. S. Vice Consul during my absence, and awaiting the more formal & regular appointment from our own Government. I enclose you a copy of his Excellency's letter to me with this you will receive the Record of the Consulate, Circular from the Department of State, and Instruction to Consuls, to all of which I refer you for your guidance in the performance of your Official duties my seal of Office and a fly Press U. S. Con[l] of Arms and an American Ensign.

I sincerely trust Sir that your intercourse with the authority of Macáo may always prove of that satisfactory & pleasurable a nature, which I have experienced at their hands during the past six years. I am sure that you will always find them disposed to afford you every facility in the discharge of your duties when you may find it necessary to call upon them.

You will be pleased to write to the Department of State and inform the Honorable Secretary when you may have entered upon the Duties of your Office.

I am Sir
With much respect
Your Obd.[t] Ser.[t]
/sig./ R. P. De Silver
U. S. Consul

[To
S. B. Rawle, Esq.
U. S. Vice Consul
Macao]

[1-027]

[Recd 18 April

Mr. Abbott

N°22]

Consulate of the U. S. of America
Macao January 30th 1854

Sir,

I have the honor to report, that from the first of July 1853 to the thirty first of December of the same year, no American Vessel has put into the Port, and had my Consular fees for verifying Invoice and Powers of Attorney during that period have amounted to $22.

I respectfully state that I have this day drawn on you in favour of Mr. Frank de Silver of Phila.d at thirty days sight for the sum of Ninety Three Dollars & ninety six cents being balance due me by the United States Government as p. my books, with five p. cent added.

I have the honor to be Sir
With great respect
Your Obd.t Ser.t.
Robt. P. De Silver
U. S. Consul

[To the Honorable
W. L. Marcy
Secretary of State
Washington
City]

[1-028]

(Mr Abbott.)

□□□ 12th June
□□□□ 8 Aug

Mr Flagg. It will scarcely be proper
to publish portions of New District.

/Confidential/

Macao March 24th 1854

Sir

Having turned my attention to the Island of Formosa, and being much struck with its capabilities and importance to the United States, not only as a Naval Dépôt, but from Political and Commercial reasons, I take the liberty of giving you an abstract of some of the considerations which may be urged in favor of its acquisitions.

B The first settlement on this Island was made by the Dutch, about 1620, and they continued to occupy a portion of the west coast, up to 1661, when a body of Chinese headed by Coxinga, having vainly contended against the Tartar invasion, left the Province of Fo–kien, and sought refuge in Formosa, and after a short struggle, conquered the Dutch, and remained in quiet possession up to 1683, when they were brought under the Tartar rule, by the Emperor Kang–hi.

Formosa is situated between 21°54' & 25°20' North Latitude and on the meridian of 121° East Longitude, being about 80 miles from the main–land, and contains some 18,000* geographical square miles.

[The]

*See Mr Harris' despatch dated 4th May 1854, reducing the area to 10,000 square miles

[The Hon[l] W[m] L Marcy
Secretary of State
Washington]

The climate is very agreeable; the summer heat is moderate by the Southern monsoon, while the freezing wind, which in winter sweeps from the Arctic, and chills the inhabitants of the mainland is te□□□ in crossing over the sea which separates Formosa from China.

The soil, like that of all volcanic countries is very fertile, and the products are as abundant as they are various:–Rice and sugar are exported in enormous quantities, and the Camphor of the Island supplies nearly the whole export to the Western worlds. The orange, peach, papaya, guava, coconut and arecapalm （betet nut） & c & c flourish, and most of the fruits of the Tropics and the temperate zone can be produced on its plains, or the acclivities of its mountains; Tea is raised for an use of the inhabitant, and if Coffee was cultivated as largely as it may be, it would furnish the U. S. a variety of fine woods for cabinet work, and ship timber are also found here; hogs and poultry are in great abundance; the buffalo is chiefly used in agriculture; some neat cattle and a few horses are raised, and large numbers could be bred, as the climate is favorable and the natural pasture is excellent.

That great essential of modern navigation, Coal of an excellent quality is found in abundance at the north end of the island, and happily a good harbour exists near to the coal–mines, which naturally points this out as the place for a Naval Dépôt: –The cost of bringing coats from Europe, the United States, Borneo or Sabuaw; the danger of capture during war; the many accidents which attend all seaborne coals, by which a steam fleet might become useless,

[are]

are too obvious to require any argument here, and render a supply of coals at a naval dépôt, invaluable.

In addition to the ship–timber of Formosa, Teak of the best quality, can be cheaply procured from Samarang in Java, and the Chinese would soon become expert and cheap workmen in a ship–yard: Sulphur is found in large quantities and Salt–petre is to be cheaply had from Bengal, and a large market would be found in China, for powder property manufactured.

The essential food for the supply of an army or fleet is already produced, and the so-called small stores of a ration, could soon be supplied by the Island.

The Chinese, drilled by American officers would be superior to the Seapoy troops of India, as they have more physical strength, are docile and obedient, and have no moral fear of death; they bear pain with more stoicism than any people on Earth, and drilled by competent officers, they would only be inferior to white troops. The words of command would be given in English, and the recruits learn with great quickness the meaning of all orders, the pay and ration of a Chinese as a soldier would be between $50 & 75$ per annum.-

The population of the island is variously estimated, and in giving the sum of two to three millions, it must be understood as being an approximation only, as no data exist, on which to base a correct opinion.

It is difficult to estimate the value of Formosa, as a dépôt for the merchandize of the United States, for exchange with the Chinese, or the extent to which manufactures of machinery and implements of agriculture could be carried; or, what is of greater importance still,

[the]

the moral influenced of Christianity which would radiate from thence.

The principal ports of China can be reached by steam from Formosa in 10 to 36 hours only, and the civilized power that may hold it, can control the commerce by Sea, between the northern and southern provinces of that mighty Empire.

The United States are the nearest civilized power to China, and in view of the rapidly increasing population of California and Oregon; the probable completion of a rail-way from the Mississippi to San Francisco, by which the United States will become the high-way between Europe and the north of Asia; the people of the United States must felt a deep and increasing interest in all that may concern that Empire, and they could not, with indifference, see any other power establish itself in Formosa, for it is almost the gate by which the commerce of the first coast of America must pass to China.

The coasts of Japan are within 48 hours steaming from Formosa, and it is a note-worthy fact, that the Dutch influence in Japan, states its decline from the period of their expulsion from that Island.

Its revenue of but little value to the Imperial Treasury, altho' enormous sums are said to be extorted from the inhabitants, by the chicane of its rulers, beginning with the Viceroy and ending at the lowest employé.

The Chinese possess the west side and the north end of the shore, while the centre and Eastern side is occupied by the aboriginal inhabitants, who are sparse in numbers, and closeby assemble the Indo-polynesians in their persons and habits, and are in constant state of warfare with the Chinese.

[The]

The west coast is a nest of Pirates, who are a scourge to the while of the mainland, from Quan-Tung in the South to Shan-Tung in the North. E

The considerations to be urged on the Imperial government to induce it to part with the island, among others, would be:

1st The eradication of Piracy from the coasts and Islet of Formosa.

2[d] The payment of a sum of money; and the present juncture is peculiarly favorable for the reception of money offer.

3[d] Precedent: The Chinese ceded HongKong to the English who were them at war with them, and gave them no consideration for it; while the Americans have always been friendly, and moreover offer to pay for what they desire.

4th The cession of Macao to the Portuguese.

5th That Formosa is distant from the mainland; that it is only in part held by the Chinese, that it yields but little revenue; and that it would inevitably be lost to them, in their first war with any of the western powers.

6th Hint as negociations how with the aborigines, and the possibility of purchasing their little to the West coast & c.

To the inhabitants of Formosa, the rule of the United States would be a blessing, for they could no longer be

[subject]

subject to intolerable exactions, but enjoy security in their persons and property, while a very moderate Tax would defray the expenses of the Government, and a discreet land system would repay the sum expended in the purchase of the Island.

If the foregoing shall not be considered as of any value by you, I trust to your kindness to find an apology for me, in my wish to be of service to my Country.

I am only on a visit to this place, and should you wish to write to me, you will please advise me care of Messe[s], Armstrong & Laurence Hong Kong.

I have the honor to be
With Sincere respect
Your ob.[t] and humble Servant
Townsend Harris

[Respectfully referred
for the perusal of the
President, by direction
of the Secretary of State
Department of State
July 31st 1853
R.□□□□□□□]

[Harris Townsend
1854 Rec[d] 12th June.]

Macao, Mar. 24th

Gives description of the Island of Formosa, its capabilities & importance to the U. States, not only as Naval Depot, but for political & comm[l]. reasons.

Above despatch sent to The President by function of Secretary of States, July 31st, 1853.

[1-029]

[Macao]

Department of State
Official Business

[G. Ryan Deoyel Esq.
U. S. Consul
Mozambique]

[1-030]

[Recd 14 July
Recd 31 Aug.

Mr. Abbott]

Macao May 4th 1854

Sir

I had the honor of addressing you on the 24th of March last, & I now beg to correct an error contained in that letter:- The extent of the island of Formosa was stated to be 18,000 geographical square miles; a subsequent examination of better authorities reduces the area to 10000 square miles.

In my letter to you of 26th October 1853, I charged the American Consul at Canton with participating in the Opium traffic: --It is almost impossible for private person like myself to procure legal proof of a fact which is patent to all, inasmuch as such proof can only be procured from parties who are themselves engaged in the illegal traffic, and of course they will not volunteer any testimony of their own misconduct.

On the 11th of April last, I had an interview with Mr. McLane, when I stated to him the facts connected with the Opium question in China, and charged the Consul at Canton with participating in it, and also told him he could procure full proof of the truth of any allegations, provided he would institute an inquiry:--in reply, Mr McLane stated,

[that]

[Honl Wm. L. Marcy
Secretary of State
Washington]

that he had received two letters on the same subject, and that he would receive any document that might be offered to him, but that he should not open any investigation: I do not pretend to give Mr. McLane's exact words, but I believe the above to be the sum of what he stated to me.--Mr. McL. was suddenly called to Shanghai by the events which transpired there, which prevented my further communications with him on the subject.

It has become a question of veracity with me to establish the charges made by me, in my letter of October

1853, and I could wish that the President would order an investigation by M[r]. McLane;--In the interim, I take the liberty of transmitting some papers on the subject , and beg to call your attention to the same, viz.--

N[o] 1. Letter from Rusell & Co. to C. Woodbury concerning Opium

N[o] 2. do do do concerning a voyage along the coasts of China for the sale of their Opium & c & c

N[o] 3. Verified copy of account sales of Opium, made in pursuance of orders contained in Letter no 2

N[o] 4. Letter from Heerjeebhoy Rustomjee a respectable Parsee stating that he has draft with Rusell & Co. for Opium

The last paragraph on page 3 of No 2 of the inclosures shows that the parties were conscious of the illegality of the proceeding, for the person instructed is told to avoid American men of war.

The opening of Japan to American commerce

[will]

will create a new Consulate, and I respectfully solicit the appointment, promising, not only a faithful performance of the duties of the office, but also my best endeavors to procure and transmit to you all obtainable information concerning Japan, its products, wants of the people, & c & c.

Should you wish to write to me, please address me to the care of Mess[rs] Reveley & Co.

Pulo Penang
Straits of Malacca

I have the honor to remain, with great respect.
Your Ob[t]. Servant
Townsend Harris

[1-031]

[With May 9]

Account Sales of 142 chests Malwa Opium on boards Schooner Swallow–East Coast China 1843 & 1844 on Account of Messes Russell & Co. Macao.

c. Lot No 1														
K	#	6791.99①	6^{T}	#	6830.98^{C}	12^{T}	#	6886.99^{C}	11^{T}	#	6936.98^{C}			
IH	#	6800.99	–	#	6903.98	15	#	6814.99	12	#	6924.99	2^{T}		
AN	#	6914.98	12	#	6905.98	12	#	6823.99	4	#	6794.99	4		
	#	6935.99	8	#	6944.99		#	6805.99		#	6825.100			
	#	6916.98	14	#	6831.99	6	#	6931.100		#	6941.99	8		
	#	6892.99	8	#	6922.98	12	#	6489.97	10	#	6212.99	4		
	#	6197.99	12	#	Total 2478 Catties. 12 Taels @$ 805.$\frac{52}{100}$								19966	33
K&C	#	5539.98	12	#	5806.99	8	#	5807.98	14	#	5818.99	6		

①本欄中單位均爲“c”，轉寫時不再一一標注，本表其它欄，均同。

	#	5809.98	12	#	5816.100		#	5535.99	9	#	5815.99	6		
	#	5545.98	8	#	5812.99	4	#	5546.99	6	#	5543.99	10		
	#	5297.98	13	#	5817.99		#	5808.99	2	#	5182.99	12		
	#	5181.99	7	#	5188.98	8	#	5536.99	6	#	1813.97	14		
	#	5534.98	11	#	5124.99		#	5978.98	7–					
	#		Total 2279 Catties 2 Taels @ $ 805.50										18358	36
KK	#	3732.98	4	#	6420.99	4	#	6419.98	12					
	#		Total 29.6 Catties 4 Taels @ $										2386	31
◇A J	#	7220.98	12	#	7200.99	4	#	7184.99		#	7225.99	6		
	#	7215.97	4	#	7198.98	10	#	7204.98	3					
	#		Total 590 Catties 7 Taels @ $										5581	48
RRA	#	4999.100	Catties										805	50
KM	#	7827.99	6	#	7822.97	10	#	7524.97	6	Total 294.6 @$			2371	20
◇R	#	99 1 98 15 99 1 99 3 99 6 Total 495 Catt 16 Taels. @ $											3992	21
□R	#	99 10 100 Toal 199 Catties 10 Taels @ $											1607	98
J	#	3726.99	3	#	3729.98	10	#	Total 197 Catt. 13 Taels @ $					1593	38
◇A	#	4562.98	14	#	4572.16	3	#	ullage Total 118 Catt 1T @ $ 865.50					926	84
□□	#	6215.99		#	6212.98	10	#	3123.98.7		#	6217.98	4		
	#	8217.98	11	#	Total 493 Catties @ $								3971	13
D	#	425.100		#	436.97.9		Total 197 Catt 9 Taels @ $						1591	37
G	#	2434.98	12	#									795	43
□J														
□G	#	6202.97	13	#	6197.98	2	#	6205.97	18	Total 293.14 @ $			2367	17
DGN	#	7588.98	12	#									795	4□□
□R	#	2033.99	6	#									800	47
													67890	61
							W Lot No 2							
PA	#	5264.99		#	4995.98	10	#	5811.100		#	5537.99			
					Total 396 Catties 10 Taels @$								3197	87

W. Lot No 2.

					Amount brought over –									
NM	#	3941.97[1]	6[T]	#	3937.99[C]		#	4338.98[C]	10[']	#	3939.98	12		
	#	3942.99	8	#	3741.99	5	Total 592 Catties 12 Taels @ $						4774	59
MK	#	5841.98	12										795	43
DJR	#	409.99	7	#	356.98	15	#	404.99	11	#	377.99	3		
	#	408.98	10	#	4111.98	12	#	321.99	1	#	382.99	9		
	#	403.100		#	3258.98	8	#	384.99		#	3273.98	8		
	#	386.98	10	#	335.98		#	372.98	5	#	333.99			
	#	325.99	3	#	Total 1682 Catties @ $								13548	57
DHD	#	1945.99	2										798	45
HHSRH	#	50.98	3										790	90
DJ	#	5783.97	14	#	4220.100		#	5782.98	12	#	4212.98	15		
DGS	#	5788.98	8	#	4214.99	8	#	5787.99	9	#	4217.99			

①本欄中單位均爲“c”，轉寫時不再一一標注，本表其它欄，均同。

	#	4206.99		#	4216.99	8	Total 990 Catties 10 Taels @ $					7979 45
WB	#	5361.99	12	#	6365.99	8	#	6361.99	1	#	6363.98 6	
	#	6367.99		#	6359.99	8	#	3364.97	13	#	3332.99 6	
	#	6368.99	1		Total 891 Catties 7 Taels @ $							7180 52
						R Lot No 3.						
NH	#	657.99	4									799 45
MGB	#	531. 98.	12	#	573. 99. 9 # 518. 98. 10 # 512. 99. 4 # 521. 99. 7							
	#	516. 18.	15.		Total 594 Catties 9 Taels @ $							4789 20
D&B	#	2023.98.	8.									795 41
										Total		113335 44

May 7th 1844. E. & O. E.

Charles Woodbury

[1-032]

Amount Sales 11 Chests 15 Balls Patna Opium on Board Schooner Swallow East Coast China 1843 & 1844 on account of Messes Russell & Co. Macao.

R Lot No.3

	$ cts
M/P 10 Chests @ $ 950	9520 00
P 1 Chest @ $	752 50
M/P 15 Balls	243 75
	$10496 25

May 7th 1844 E & O.E E E.

Woodbury

[1-033]

[No. □□□□

Enclosure from T. Harris

of Opium on board Sch Swallow from Jan 15th 1844 to May 1844]

[With May 4th]

Canton Oct 6th 1843.

Capt. C. Woodbury

Ship Lema.

Dear Sir,

We have you herewith the following orders, for 96 chests Malwa Opium which you will please receive on board the Lema and hold ready for shipment into the such Swallow. The drug is to be of first quality & full weight

& you will please look particularly to the same.

993 Thompos & Co 11 Sept 1843 in the Tenolia for				7 chests
185 D & M Ruatony & Co 6th Oct. 1843 in the Juan Gozina				45 "
186	do	do	do	21 "
187	do	do	do	21 "
188	do	do	do	2 "
			Malwa	96 chests

Your Obt. S

Russel & Co.

P. S.

We also hand you Thompson & Co. on Tenolia

no for 50 chests

no for 50 chests

100 one hundred chests

Malwa to be recd as above. Yrs Ro & Co.

[Captain Charles Woodbury

Ship Lema

Whampoa

EM Meses Russell & Co. □□□ Oct 6th 1843

Messes Russell & Co.

Recies Oct 6th 1843

No □

Inclosure from T. Harris]

[1-034]

[With May 9th]

Macao 6th April 1854

My dear Harris,

I have received your letter of this 3rd Instant and feel much pleasured answering your question contained therein.

I have been residing for the last years in China as a Merchant, and do acquainted with the firm of Messes Russell & Co, and which firm has always dealed in opium, and □□□ □□□ great deal of business with them in opium, some time buying & some time selling to or through the said firm.

I hope the above answer will be satisfactory.

Your Very Truly
Heerjeebhoy Rustomjee

[T. Harris Esq.]

[N° 1 with May 4th]

Macao Oct 27. 1843.

Capt. Charles Woodbury
Schooner Swallow
Macao
Dear Sir,

Herewith
We have memorandum of Opium, we have shipped on board the "Swallow", and for which we give you the following limit,– below which you will not sell, without farther order from us.

Patna 950
Benue 920
Malwa 850

we are □□□ hopes that you will be able to get something considerably above these rates and at $1000 □□ Patna of $900 for Malwa should do us immediate sales of should not with you to be □□ absent more than three month for the sake of getting something above our limits, that is, we should prefer to have you
[come]

come down to them, rather than be absent more than 3 mos from noon of today when your humane begins – You will bear in mind that one day difference in your arrival here, makes a month difference □□□ the humane of Calculate accordingly – We expect you to proceed put to China then to use your payment in selecting the best place of sales.– You may perhaps meet the "Sarah Abijail" in which case Capt. Prescott Olen perhaps give you some valuable information on the point, and should it seem to yourself and him expedient our vessel might transfer to the other and the empty one return to Macao, but of course it would be cleavable that this should be the Swallow, as she could put up □□□ better in the winter than the "Sarah Abijail" – We enclose a copy of the form of the Policies effected on your Cargo, for your information and you will see that in shipping down. Return which you are authorized to do by any port vessel, you must not put about $20,000 in one bottom.– The Shroff who goes with you has received two months advance and will have $1 per bhat on his return if his a/cs of money prove all right. The small Bars of gold are worth here about $220 each, weighing 9T. 7m. 5c.–– Car□□□ Sycee will probably keep at 3 @4% prem and Mexican cotton 4% @5% duty – Sycee is likely to be the least return –– and gold the next –– in fact gold at $210 would be as good as Sycee but great care would be required in receiving it on the part of the Shroff.

We shall probably have opportunity of writing you so as to be able to vary on instruction if we wish to do so and you will write in as after as you can.

We do not care to have you join the way of American Vessels of war, though we have no reason to apprehend any interference from them. The Chinese who, goes up with you interested in the 100 Chests Malwa have no authority to interfere in any way with our instruction regarding sales, but as pres□□□ is to affect in finding Buyers & c – you will keep carefully weight of each chest delivered （of Malwa） so as to show the sho□□□ weight belonging to each parcel.

To compensation as Captain of the schooner & attending to the □□□ you are to have $150 per month, and we furnish Cabin.

Wishing you good luck & safe return.

We are

Yours

Russell & C

[N° 2

Inclosure from T. Harris

Russell & Co

Oct 27/43.]

[1-035]

Department of State

Washington Sept. 9. 1854.

G. Ryan Deoyer Esq.

U. S. Consul

Mozambique

Sir,

Your despatches to no 6 inclusive have been received.

In compliance with your request, instructions have been sent to the U. S. minister Resident at Lisbon to renew the application for the issue of your Exequatur.

I am Sir, respectfully

Your obedient servant

W. L. Marcy.

[1-036]

[Rec.^{d} 21st Sept.

Mr. Abbott R]

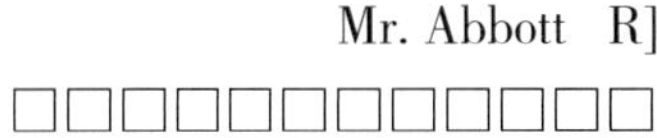

Consulate of the United States
Macao, May 8th 1855

This morning a Mr. Bartlett who called himself an American, from the state of New Hampshire, called on me, with the following information viz:– he said he was a stranger in Macao.– That he came over from Hong Kong yesterday in a Lorcha （small vessel） that an Englishman named James Ross came over by the same vessel as a passenger that he has not personally acquainted with Ross previous to their meeting on board the Lorcha that he Bartlett never having been here before. – Ross who knew the City undertook to show him a place where he could obtain lodgings – that while walking together for this propose on the Praya Grande or public walk a certain Captain Joel Woodbury, who calling himself an American from one of our Eastern States. I believe Massachusetts, and who I believe was an American, landed from a Boat on the Said Praya Grande– that Ross immediately on seeing him left Bartlett and advanced towards him––that he Bartlett walked on, and have not proceeded many yards, before he heard some person say that Ross and Woodbury have had "a scuffle" and that Ross had stalked Woodbury – he Bartlett immediately returned and found it to be the case – that Ross after having committed the act followed Woodbury who took refuge in the Guard House, a few steps off – that Ross was taken into custody by the "Guard" and that Woodbury was taken to the Public Hospital." –

Captain Woodbury died on the 9th Jan – shortly after his decease, on the same day I received a note from the Judge of this City of which the following is a true translation.

"Sir" Having departed this life early this morning in the Hospital of S^{t}. Raphael, the American Joel Woodbury, in consequence of the wound perpetrated by the Englishman James Ross yesterday––it is now necessary that you should give proper instructions for the interment of the deceased."

Macao. May 9. 1855
Sign.^{d} { The Judge
J. M. S. Pintos

To S. B. Rawle Esq.

Vice Consul of the United States of America Upon the receipt of the above I gave the necessary orders and had Captain Woodbury buried in the Protestant Cemetery of this place.

S. B. Rawle
United States Vice Consul
for Macao.

[1-037]

[Rec.[d] 21st, Sept.

Mr. Abbott]

United States Consulate
Macao– June 6. 1855

Sir

I have the honor to inclose you a "note" of the death of – Captain Joel Woodbury an American, caused by a wound received by him from James Ross an Englishman in an affray which arose from an old quarrel between the Parties––Ross remains in prison awaiting his trial which will take place upon the arrival of the Governor––who is at present absents but is expected to return in the come of next month.

I have the hnor
to be very respectfully
Your obed.[t] Sevt
S. B. Rawle
United States Vice Consul
for Macao

[To the Honorable
W. L. Marcy
Sec.[y] of State
Washington
D. C.]

[1-038]

[Rec.d 21st Sept.
N[o] 2.

Mr. Abbott]

Macao, July 1. 1855

Sir,

I have the honor to inclose you the Consular returns of the arrivals and departures of American Vessels to and from this port in the year 1854, 1855 to date––Macao being, entirely free Port and having no Custom House – no entry of Either inward or outward, Cargoes is required – so that it is difficult if not impossible to ascertain the particulars of them–neither are there any tonnage or anchorage dues levied – The Expenses of the Government, also of a Garrison of about four hundred men are maintained the mother country, Portugal, and by the monopolies of various articles of consumption – aided by a direct Tax upon Real Estate – The marine force consists of one frigate of Twenty guns and one Lorcha or Schooner rigged vessel carrying six guns--The mercantile marine consists of one hundred Lorchas and a few small Barques and Brigs which trade to the neighboring Ports--The Lorchas are formally employed in the coasting trade on the Chinese courts--the Recent Governor Isidoro Francisco Guimarães, who is also Plenipotentiary from the Court of Portugal to China, is very popular and much esteemed.

[E]

I have the honor to be
very respectfully
From obed.' Ser.'
S. B. Ralwe
United States Vice Consul
for Macao

[To the Honorable
W. L. Marcy
Secretary of state
Washington City
D. C.]

No.1– Consular Returns of American Vessels arriving and departing from the Port of Macao from 1854 1855 to date

Date of Arrival	Class	Name	Tonnage	Master	Where from	Cargo	Date of departure	Where bound	Outward Cargo	Fees for Deposit and delivery of papers	Noting Protest and Estimating sums
1854	No arrivals or departure during this Year--Received in Consular Seals										$14 – fourteen dollars
1855											
February 1	Barque	Siri	407. $\frac{85}{95}$	J. D. Carlisk	Manila	Rice	January 9	Manila	Sundries	$ 4.–	$12–
Feburary 10	Barque	Jaime	385. $\frac{20}{95}$	J. P. Pierce	Whampoa	Sundries	Feby 26	Whampoa	Rice	$ 4.–	
March 6	Barque	Maria	274. $\frac{35}{95}$	L .A Peterson	Manila	Sundries	March 9	Singapore & Calcutta	Sundries	$4.–	
March 6	Ship	Howard	713	A. Peak	Manila	Salt provisions & fruits	April 4	Havanna	Chinese Coolies	$4.–	

Received for Consular seals $6.– $22. –
Total Receipts for 1854 & 1855 Dollar 48.–
Say Forty Eight Dollars

"note" Macao–beings free Port, having no Custom House
The particulars of Cargoes – are difficult to be ascertaining

Macao. July 1, 1855
S. B. Rawle
United States Vice Consul
for Macao

[4th Mr. Rawle No.2]

[1-039]

[Rec.d 21 March
No.3

Mr. Abbott]

United States Consulate
Macao January 1, 1856

Sir

I have the Honor to inclose to You the Consular Returns for the year 1855– since the 30th June at which date the new Law relative to Consuls took effect with reference to my respects under date of Jane 6, 1855– with note inclined detailing the account of the death of Joel Woodbury by the hands of the Englishman James Ross, I have the honor to report that after/some delay the trial of Ross took place and the verdict was homicide – the sentence two years imprisonment or banishment from this place of course Ross chose the latter and left this place immediately. You will please understand that the authorities here are not permitting to execute any culprit whatever his offence may be but must state the offence to the Government at Goa and receive their authority from thence.

I have the Honor to be
Sir with respect
I'm Obed.t Ser.ts
S. B. Rawle
United States Vice Consul
for Macao

[To the Hble
M. L. Marcy
Secy of State
Washington
D. C.]

[Macao
□□□

June/55 to
copy
（a small about）]

Consular Returns
of American Vessels arriving and departing from the Port of Macao since 30 June 1855

Date of Arrival	Class	Name	Tonnage	Where from	Master	Inward Cargo	Where bound	Outward Cargo	Fees for receiving and returning paper	Remarks
1855 August 1	Ship	Alhusbu Rough	615 $\frac{45}{95}$	Singapore	Thos Woith	Sundries	Hong Kong	Balast	$4	lost by collision with another vessel put out of port

Recd – for Consular Fees to sundry certificates of
Amount correction of invoice of exports to San Francisco 20.–
To the credits of the United States secretary to the （Dolls） 24.–
new Law – Respecting Consular fees –

Macao July 1st 1856
S. B. Rawle
United States Vice Consul
for Macao

[1–040]

[Rec.d 26 April
Mr. Abbott]

Consulate of the U. S. of America
Macáo February 4th 1856.

Sir,

Referring to my letter addressed to you under the date of November 5th 1855, I now have the honor to advice you that I have this day drawn on you at Thirty Days sight in favours of Mr. S. B. Rawle, Esq. U. S. Vice Consul Macao for the sum of Six hundred and Twenty five Dollars said amount being for my salary as U. States Consul at this Port with difference of Exchange added （see Vouchers annexed to the Bills） from the 1st July 1855 to 31st December 1855, which I respectfully beg that you will protect, and trust that the same may meet with your approval.

I have the honor to be Sir
With Great Respect
Your obd.t Serv.t
Robt. P. De Silver

U. S. Consul

[To the Honorable
W. L. Marcy
Secretary of the State
Washington]

[1-041]

[No 4
Rec.d 24. June

Mr. Abbott

Macao]

Consulate of the United States of America
Macao. April 1' 1856

To the Honorable
W. L. Marcy
Secretary of State
Washington City
Sir,

I have the honor under date of the 1' of January inclosing Consular Returns for this port – since which I have had the honor to receive a dispatch from the Department under date of the 7h November 1855 concerning that a Book had been sent to my address 11/12 the Record of Treasury fees, "which are to be enferred or prescribed in sections 201 and 202 of the Instructions," I regret to say that neither the Book or the "Instruction" have yet been received – when they come to hand I shall be most happy to know the instructions of the "Department".

I beg to inclose the Consular Returns for this Consulate ending the 31' March last – Observing that the steamer "Spark" therein maintained – now plying between this port, Canton and Hong Kong is used as a River Boat to carry passengers when in occasionally, merchandise one of her owners Mr. James B. Endicott an American Citizen, resides, here with his family.

Robert P. de Silver Esq., late Consul for this Port left China by the last overland mail steamer on the 15 March last –for the United States.

I have the honor to be
Sir – with great respects
Your most obedt Sert
S. B. Rawle
United States Vice Consul

[1-042]

[Recd 16. Sept.

Mr. Abbott R]

Consulate of the U. S. of America
Macao July 1st 1856.

Sir,

I have the honor to acknowledge the receipt of your communication under date of 17th March ultimo, advising me of my having been appointed by the President of the U. S. to the post of Consul for this port, also handing various Documents as communicated, all of which has received my careful attention; and in tendering my thanks to the Department for the high power cou □□□ 'd upon myself I would state, that by the present mail, I have sent forward the required Bond duly signed by myself to be executed as required by Law, and forwarded at once to the Department, and in the interval which must elapse prior to the receipt □□□ my commission & continue to carry on as □□□ the functions of U. S. Consul at this port. □□□ previously requested by the Department.

In reply to the formal queries continued in your dispatch now under reply, I would respectfully state, that I was born in the City of Philadelphia, state of Pennsylvania,

[and]

and having been commercially engaged between my own Country and China for a period of time extending over twenty years, I have during those years resided many times at this port, and have been a permanent resident during the past three years, and I have not resided in any other dependencies of Portugal or in that Country.

I have the honor to be
Sir,
Very Respectfully
Your Most Obedient Servant
S. B. Rawle

[To the
Honorable
W. L. Marcy
Secretary of State for the U. S.
Washington D. C.
U. S. A.]

[1-043]

[Rec.d 2nd Novr.

Mr. Abbott

N°.6]

U. S. Consulate
Macao
September 10 1856

Sir

I have the Honor to acknowledge the receipt for last mail of my commission as Consul of the United States for this Port also of the Exequatur of His Majesty the King of Portugal approving of the same. The Governor of this place has counter signed the Exequatur which I presume is correct. I have also received the General Book Instructions issued by the Department to all Consuls and its directions shall be followed.

I have the Honor
to be Sir, with
the highest respect
I'm obed. Ser
S. B. Rawle
U. S. Consul for Port of
Macao

[To the Honorable
W. L. Marcy
Secretary of State
Washington City
D. C.]

[1–044]

[Recd 19. June
act 24 June
and □□□□□

Mr. Abbott.

N°9]

United State Consulate
Macao, April 1 1857

[J. □□□ And □□□ June 24]

Sir,

I have had the honor to receive from under date Nov 8. 1856 also the dispatch of the Hnoble J. A. Thomas Assistant Secretary of State dated 28 Decr 1856 together with a tariff of fees and a Copy of the 1[1] and 2[d] Sessions of the 34th Congress of all of which I have hither due note. I now have the honor to inclose a list of the fees received at this Consulate for the last quarter commencing the 1t January 1857 and Ending the 31 March last amounting to Dollar Sixty Eight also the Returns of American entries and departures to & from this port during the same period. I may have remark that the trade of this place has increased & will increase considerable in consequence of the destruction of Canton, many of the shopkeepers and Merchants & c. of that place have removed here–the receipts of Raw

[+dispatch]

Silk & Oil（for burning in lamps）& a variety of China produce have become much down in price in consequence of the drive and for Export – these articles used to be sent to Canton and be shipped from thence previous to the present war–which has put a stop to the Commerce of Canton entirely – It has with much regret that I found that by the last Consular Bill. The Salary, for this consulate, had been chopped first in the place is beginning to be of consequence for the tension above mentioned, the destruction of Canton. – The Bill gives the Consul here the fees and allows him to trade, but the trade of the place is almost entirely monopolized by the Portuguese & the Chinese to that any foreigner has very little chance to compete with them – The fees of the official not remunerate the Consul for the trouble and Expense he has with American Vessels and Sailors, many American Vessels will have for pilots and for orders without discharging or taking any cargo consequent by there has no fees according to the Consul. I hope the Department will take the above into consideration and recommend the renewal of the salary viz. $1000 – Within Consulate or at least a part of it. My appointment by R. P. De Silver the previous Consul was end and confirmed 14 Feby 1856 and my appointment as Consul by the President is dated March 17. 1856. Since my appointment by Mr. de Silver, my Consular Returns have been regularly provided, but with the exception of the acknowledgement of my Official Bond, no notice has ever been taken of my dispatches or my Bills for my Salary. I have not rcd one cent of my Salary––since I have been in office.

I have the honor
to be Sir, very respectfully
I'm obd St
S. B. Rawle
U. S. Consul Macao

[To the Hble
The Secretary of State
Washington City
D. C.]

□□□□□□□□□□

of American Vessels arriving & departing from the Port of Macao since 31 Dec 1856 to state of this Report

□ o □□□ of this report

Date of Arrival	Class	Name	Tonnage	Master	Where from	Inward Cargo	Where bound	Outward Cargo	Date of sailing	Fees Received
1857 January 3	Bark	Witch	419. $\frac{54}{95}$	Hultman	Amoy	Chinese produce	□□□	Chinese produce	Jany 10th	$2.05

February 28	Ship	Helen Mar	510. $\frac{92}{95}$	Lowe	Singapore	Rice	Rangoon	do		$2.55
February 28	Ship	Black Prince	1061. $\frac{25}{95}$	Brown	Hongkong	Do	HongKong Indt. port of inward Cago			$5.30
April 1	Steamer	Spark	100	Burry	Recd for 43 Inhus and departures to & at this port. When 31 Decr 1856 to date on 72a cent p Ton each time					21.50
April 1					Steamer Willamette Conic Recd for 24 Inhus & departures at & from this port tonnage 414 tons @ 72a cent p Ton each time					50.08

"Note" The steamers Willamette and Spark ply between HongKong and this place carrying passengers and cargo. Dolls 81.48

Macao April 1. 1857
S. B. Rawle
United States Consul
for Macao

Consular Returns of Fees recd at the Consulate at Macao since the 31 Decr 1856 to date of this report being the last Quarter

1857			
April 1	Recd from W. S. Wetmore for Consular Seal to private document	$2	
	Recd from W. C. Hunter for 4 Consular Seals to private document	8	
	Recd from Mr Devwis for Consular Seal to private document	2	
	Recd from Assignor of G. Nye for 2 Consulate Seals to private documents	4	
	Recd from James Pardon for 2 Consular Seals to private document viz. valuation of Property loss in Canton	4	
	Recd from Mess Gruner & Galliuns for 2 Consular Seals to private documenting viz property loss in Canton	4	
	Recd from Ring & Co for 2 seals to private documents property loss in Canton	4	
	Recd from S. W. William & others for 4 seals to private documents viz valuation of property loss in Canton	8	
	Recd from Wo[l] Walph for 2 Seals to private document	4	
	carried forwd.	$40	

Brought forward $40
Recd for Consular Seal to duplicate
of private document $2
Recd from D. N. Spooner for Seal
to private document 2
Recd from the captain of this port for
2 Seals to private documents 4
Recd from Mr. M[c]Cormick for Seal
to private documents 2
Recd from Mr Johannes for 2 Seals
to private documents (losses at Canton) 4
Recd from Rec.[d] S. W. Bonney for
2 Seals to private document viz
loss of property in Canton 4
Recd from W. C. Hunter for Seals

to private document	2
Recd from J. B. Endicott for Seal to private	
document	2
Recd from N. Grew for Seals in duplicate	
to private document loss of property in Canton	4
Recd from the assignees of G. Nye	
for Seal to private document	2
The above amount was all received	680
during the quarter ending 31 March last.	

Macao April 1, 1857
S. B. Rawle
U. S. Consul for Macao

[1-045]

[Macao Sept 30, 1857
Transferred to
Report
（dft） H]

[Mr. Abbott
□□□□□□□]

Consulate of the United States
Macao, 5h May. 1857

Sir,

I have been advised by Mr. Wm. M. Cornell, auditor of the Treasury Department under date of 14h February, 1857, that I must draw upon the Secretary of State for the disbursements made at this Consulate for the erection of a flagstaff.

I have accordingly drawn upon the Department for the sum of Twenty three dollars for that purpose, under this date, my bill of exchange at fifteen days sight, to which I beg you to give due honor, and herewith also inclose the proper voucher.

I have the honor to be,
Sir,
Respectfully your obdt Servant
S. B. Rawle
Consul for U. S. A.

[To the Honorable

The Secretary of State
Washington]

[Respectfully referred
To State Depart
G. Rodhan
T. Dept
July 21/57 C. C

Ina 214 July 21/57]

[1-046]

[Rec.[d] 24.Octr.

Mr. Abbott.

No.11 Ref Sent to Mr. Fla□□□ Oct 24]

U. S. Consulate
Macao 8 Aug. 1857

Sir,

In accordance with the Book of Instruction, I have the honor to enclose the Returns of American Vessels at this Port for the quarter ending 30th June 1857.

As affecting the opening trade at this place, I have to announce the declaration by the British Admiral, Sir Michael Seymour, of a strict blockade of the Port of Canton to take effect from the 7th August instant.

I have the honor to be
Sir,
Yours respectfully
S. B. Rawle
U. S. Consul
for Macao

[To the honorable
The Secretary of State
Washington D. C.]

□□□□□□□□□□□□□□
of
American Vessels arriving at, and departing from, the port of Macao,
during the quarter from the 1st of April to the 30th of June 1857, inclusive

No	Date of Arrival	Class	Name	Tons	Master	Where from	Inward Cargo	Date of Sailing	To Where Bound	Outward Cargo	Fees	Noting Protest
	1857							1857				
1	April	Ship	Black Prince	1061	Browne	Singapore	Rice		Singapore	Ballast	$5.30	
2	26 April	Brig	Escort	474	Schebye	Singapore	Rice	16 May	Singapore	Ballast	2.50	
3	12 May	Ship	Norseman	811 $\frac{89}{95}$	Haskell	HongKong	Rice	30 May	Singapore	Ballast	4.25	
4	29 May	Ship	Kensington	494 $\frac{43}{95}$	Thrane	Singapore	Rice		Singapore	Ballast	2.47	2.00
5	31 May	Bark'n	Penguin	583 $\frac{81}{95}$	Wheeler	Singapore	Rice				2.97	2.00
6	1 June	Ship	Ariadae	799 $\frac{24}{95}$	Knight	Calcutta	Rice		Bombay	Sundries	4.25	2.00
7	19 June	Ship	Yalatea	1041 $\frac{24}{95}$	Barber	Hong Kong	General				5.25	
8	22 June	Ship	Starr King	1170 $\frac{81}{95}$	Turner	Singapore	Rice		Macao		5.85	2.00
9	26 June	Bark	Helen Mar	570 $\frac{92}{95}$	Lowe	Rangoon	Rice		"		2.55	
10	30 June	Steamer	Willamette	414	Currie	Between Hongkong & Macao					39.33	
11	30 June	Steamer	Spark	100	Woodruffe	Between Hongkong & Macao					24	
12	22 June	Bark	Quickstep	524	Smith	Pinang	Rice	17 July	Hong Kong		2.64	2.00
											101.36	10.00

S. B. Bawle
U. S. Consul
for Macao

[June 30 1857
Transferred to
Report
(dft) H]

[1–047]

[Recd 3d Decr.
Ansd 10 Decr

Mr. Abbott]

U. S. Consulate
Macao 22d Sept. 1857

To the Hon. Lewis Cass Esq
Secretary of State

Sir,

I have the honor to inform you that in consequence of continued ill–health and infirmity, I have availed myself of the power conferred upon Consuls by Section 36, Chapter 4 of the Consular Regulations of 1856 to appoint as Deputy Consul for this place Mr. Wm. A. Macy, a native of the State of New–York. His Testimonials signed by the chargé d'affaire of the United States is herewith enclosed.

As enjoined by Section 38 of the Regulations, I shall await the action of the Department before taking any farther step.

I have the honor to remain
Sir,
Your obedient & humble Servant
S. B. Rawle
United States
Consul for Macao

Macao, 22[d] Sept. 1857

I hereby certify that William A. Macy, a native of the State of New York, is known to me, and I regard him as a suitable person for, and competent to the discharge of the duties of the Consulate in this colony.

S. Wells Williams
Changé d'affaire, ad int.
U. S. A. in China

[1–048]

[Recd 22nd Decr. Mr. Abbott
Enclosed sent same day to □□□
No.16]

Consulate of the United States
Macao 14 October 1857

Sir,

I have the honor in accordance with the regulations, to forward the quarterly returns of vessels arriving at and departing from this port during the Quarter ending 30th September 1857. The number of Americans vessels is on the increase, and a few are loading for the United States.

I have the honor to remain.
Sir
Very respectfully

Your obedient servant
S. B. Rawle
U. S. Consul
for Macao

[To the honorable
The Secretary of State
Washington]

[1-049]

[Recd 29 March

Mr. Abbott

Rec.[d] Stat. Off. July 19th
No 16]

Consulate of the United States
Macao 13 January 1858

Sir,

I have the honor to enclose my accounts for the quarter ending 31st December 1857, embracing a transcript of the Fee Book and a tabular statement of American Vessels for the above mentioned period and also an Account Current for the same period.

I have the honor to notify you that the services of Mr. William A. Macy being no longer available and he having handed in his resignation, he ceases from this date to act as my Deputy and for the present I shall not appoint another.

During the past quarter two vessels have loaded with coolies for the Havana.

[and]

[To the honorable
The Secretary of State]

and another is now under despatch. The attention of H. E. Mr. Reed has been directed to this matter, and as he informs me that he is about to communicate with the Department on the subject, I do not deem it necessary to repeat the steps which as his direction were taken by me to endeavor to check or prevent this business as carried, on under the American Flag, from this port.

The trade of the Port is very much diminished, both in consequence of the commercial revulsion in America and of the assault upon the City of Canton, which was successfully attacked on the 28th, 29th and 30th December 1857, and is now in the possession of the English and French forces who have also succeeded in seizing the persons of all the high officers) . The

[farther]

farther steps of the allies are not known. But it is thought that business will soon be resumed at that Port.

I have the honor to remain
Sir,
Your obedient servant
S. B. Rawle
U. S. Consul for Macao.

Macao

During the Quarter ending 31st December 1857.

No.	Date of Arrival	Class	Name	Tons	Master	Where From	Inward Cargo	Date of Sailing	Where Bound	Outward Cargo	Fees received	Noting protest	Remarks
0	28 Sept	Ship	Contest	1098	Steele	Hong Kong	Rice	12 Dec	New York	Tea &c	$17.80	$1.	
1	3 Oct	Ship	John Jay	494	Mendall	Hong Kong	Teas	24 Oct	New York	do	4.47		
2	5 Oct	Ship	Kate Hooper	1488	Jackson	do	Ballast		Havana	Coolies	7.44		
3	9 Oct	Ship	Hydra	499	Parker	Batavia	Rice	29 Dec	New York	Tea &c	14.50	1.	
4	9 Oct	Ship	Endeavour	1137	Doane	Batavia	do	16 Oct	Shanghai	Rice	5.68	1.	
0	25 Sept.	Ship	Beaver	727	Smith	Penang	do		Hong Kong	Ballast	.50		No.5 Formerly under New Granadian Colors. No.6 Was remeasured on account of having had a new deck added since her register was made out.
0	23 Sept	Barque	Comet	536	Burn	Hong Kong	Ballast	19 Oct	New York	Tea & c	3.50		
5	10 Oct	Ship	Emma	444	Gill	do	do	8 Nov	Siam	Ballast	20.72	1.	
6	5 Nov	Ship	Ticonderoga	1679	Boyle	do	do	3 Dec	Havana	Coolies	14.90		
7	13 Nov	Schooner	Linda	36	Chris tian	do	do		Siam	Sundries	.68		
8	16 Nov	Ship	Ocean Eagle	596	Cheever	do	Rice				2.98		
9	10 Dec	do	Indiaman	1164	Smith	do	do	23 Dec	Singapore	Ballast	5.82		
10	24 Dec	do	Chilo	413	Hollis	Fuhchau	Teas				2.06		
11	31 Dec	Steamer	Spark	100	Woodruffle	50 Arrivals and Departures					25.		
12	31 Dec	Steamer	Willamette	414	Currie	2 Arrivals and Departures					4.14		
											$130.19	$4.	

Total Fees from Shipping $134.19

Macao 13th January 1858

S. B. Rawle
U. S. Consul
for Macao

[Macao
2. Return
Dec 31/57

Rec.[d] at State Office
April 22d 1858

Suspended D]

□□□□□□□
From 1st October to 31st December 1857

Dr. Cr

1857					1857				
Dec	31	To Fees from Vessels as per a/c rendered Fees from all other sources	$134 54	19	Dec	31	By Fees appropriated in lieu of Salary	$188	19
			$188	19				$188	19
					E. E. S. B. Rawle U. S. Consul for Macao				

United States Consulate at Macao

Fees received during the quarter ending 31st December 1857

Date	No.	Name of Vessel	Name of the party paying the fee.	Nature of service rendered	Amount of fees paid	
					$	cts
1	87		S. Robertson	Affixing 2 Consular seals	4	
2	88	Contest	Jas Steele	Noting Protest	1	
3	89	John Jay	R. B. Wade	Tonnage fees	2	47
5	90	Kate Hooper	J. J. Jackson	do do	7	44
	91	Hydra	Jas. H. Parker	do do	2	50
6				Noting Protest	1	
9	92	Endeavour	Trueman Doane	Tonnage Fees	5	68
				Noting Protest	1	
10	93	Beaver	G. J. O. Smith	Certificate of desertion		50
13	94	Contest	Jas. Steele	Extending Protest & copy	12	80
17	95	Comet	H. P. Burr	Shipping 6 men	3	
				Decl. not able to procure Am.		50
20	96		M. Ferran	Affixing 2 Cons seals	4	
	97		W. C. Hunter	‘’ 1 do do	2	
21	98		S. Robertson	‘’ 2 do do	4	
23	99	John Jay	J. T. Mendall	Certif. of new master	1	
				Shipping 1 & Disch’g 1	1	
24	100	Emma	Charles Gill	Papers granting Am. Flag	8	
				Tonnage fees	2	22
				Noting Protest	1	
27	101		W. C. Hunter	Affixing 1 cons. Seal	2	
				amount continued	67	11

Date	No	Name of Vessel	Name of the party paying the fee	Nature of service rendered	Amount of fees paid
			Amount continued		$67
Oct 29	102	Hydra	Jas. H. Parker	Warrant for survey	1
				Extending Protest	
				Certificate to signatures	
Nov 2				Shipping 1 man	7
				Certificate to desertion	1
	103		W. C. Hunter	Affixing Cons. seal	2
3	104		S. Robertson	do 4 do do	8
5	105	Emma	Charles Gill	Shipping & Disch'g seamen	10
				Decl. not able to proc. Am.	
	106	Ticonderoga	N. P. Boyle	Tonnage Fees	8
6	107		R. Carlowitz	Cons. Certif. to signature	2
10	108		L. Carvalho	Affixing 2 Cons. seals	4
13	109	Linda	W. T. Christian	Tonnage fees	
				Shipping one man	
16	110	Ocean Eagle	W. J. Cheever	Tonnage fees	2
23	111		M. Bourjan	Affixing 2 Cons. seals	4
	112	Ticondaroga	N. P. Boyle	Shipping 7 men	3
				Papers for remeasuring ship	3
24	113		H. N. Macomb	Affixing Cons. seal	2
25	114		S. Robertson	do 2 do do	4
				Amount Continued	132

Date	No	Name of Vessel	Name of the Party paying the fee	Nature of sevice rendered	Amount of fees paid	
			Amount Continued		$132	cts 17
28	115	Contest	Jas. Steele	Shipping 11 men	5	
	116		W. C. Hunter	Affixing Cons. seal	2	
8	117	Hydra	Jas. H. Parker	Shipping 4 men	2	
10	118	Indiaman	W. W. Smith	Tonnage fees	5	82
	119		S. Robertson	Affixing Cons. seal	2	
11	120		W. C. Hunter	do do do	2	
14	121		W. C. Hunter	do do do	2	
	122		L. Carvalho	do do do	2	
15	123		W. C. Hunter	do do do	2	
24	124	Chilo	Lewis. G. Hollis	Tonnage Fees	2	06
31	125	Spark (str)	Woodruffe	Tonnage fees on 50 trips	25	
				do do on 2 trips		
	126	Willamette (str)	Currie		4	14
Total Amount for the Quarter					$188	19

Amount of Fees from Vessels	$134
Amount received from all other sources	54
Total of Fees for the Quarter	$188

Macao 13th January 1858

S. B. Rawle
U. S. Consul for Macao

[No.16
Macao
Jan. 13/58
Port office July 19]

[1-050]

Extract of a letter from a distinguished Medical Missionary visiting Japan.

NANGASAKI[①], JANUARY 26TH 1859.

"I had the pleasure of receiving a letter from you just before I left and as your are not in the habit of receiving letters from the 'Rising Sun' I embrace an occasion of sending this from Dezima, a 'Factory' pretty well known in mercantile and–alas–in other annals.

Mr. sent a steamer built for the folks, to Nangasaki to find a purchaser and kindly gave me a passage in her. To see a new country when on the eve of returning for a time to my native land is no small privilege;–and such a country!–It is truly a puzzle to the political economist as to the moralist, to the merchant and to the naturalist.

I do not know enough how or what to observe in order to satisfy the curiosity of a merchant, and can only say in general that this land seems to want little, but is has more for Exports than is supposed abroad. Considerable profits have been made of late, which has caused a sort of Japan fever at Shanghae–a glut of foreign articles and a rise in native produce are the consequences: – All this will of course settle down in time, when, the real value of the Commerce of the port can be estimated.

I am pained to report that hostility to Christianity suffers no abatement: The chief object of my visit has been to ascertain how far there was a prospect of successful missionary effort, but at present the prospect is discouraging. I made the acquaintance of some intelligent officials who speak Chinese and they gladly accepted Testaments in Chinese and English, but were soon compelled to return them at the peril of losing their heads, they said. Their eagerness to adopt foreign Arts and the like augurs well, however, and it may yet be that the gospel will accomplish ere long its peculiar changes in the land."

[June 30/58]

① Sic.

[1-051]

Quarterly Returns of
Fees received at the Consulate of the United States at Macao
From the 1st of April to the 30th of June 1858

Date	No.	Name of Vessel	Name of the party paying the fee	Nature of Service rendered	Amount of fees paid	
1858					$	
June 30	47	Spark	J. B. Endicott	Tonnage Fees	24	50
June 30	48	Rose	J. B. Endicott	Tonnage Fees	14	43
					$38	93

S. B. Rawle
U. S. Consul for Macao

[1-052]

[Recd From
G. Nye
U. S. Vice Consul
Macao]

Fees received at the United States Consulate at Macao
from the 1st of April to the 1st of July 1858.

Date	No.	Name of Vessel	Name of the party paying the fee	Nature of service rendered	Amount of fees	paid	Remarks
April							
1858					$		
6	23	Wm. Spraque	Bowers	Tonnage Fees	3	86	
6	24	Hymph	Wm. T. Clarke	Tonnage Fees	2	34	
	25	Anlelope	Clark	Tonnage Fees	3	29	
				Discharging 9 men	5		
				Shipped 8 men	4	50	
				Seals 2	4		
	26	Argonaut	Dunbar Horton	Tonnage Fees	3	13	
April				Desertion 5 men			
April				with seal & oath	2	25	
20	27	Eurika	Lane	Tonnage Fees	6	28	
20	28	Crystal Palace	B. Simmons	Tonnage Fees	2		
				Discharged 4 men	2		
				Seal and oath	2	25	
‘’	29	Game Cook	Osgood	Tonnage Fees	6	95	
		□□□	□□□	□□□	6	65	

Date	No	Name of Vessel	Name of the party paying the fee	Nature of service Rendered	Amount of fees paid		Remarks.
				Discharging 1 man		50	
				Seal & oath	2	25	
	31	Frank Johnson	Lothrop	Tonnage Fees	2	64	
				Noted a Protest	2		
				Extending Protest	6		
	32	Loo Choo	Horton	Tonnage Fees	4	20	
	33	Manry	Fletcher	Tonnage Fees	3		
	34	Myrtle	Mottspora	Tonnage Fees	2	99	
				Noted a Protest	2		
				Extending Protest	5		
				Shipped 6 men	3		
				Seals & oaths	4	50	
				Copy of Protest & Seals	2	50	
May 24	35	Two	Plummer	Tonnage Fees	4	49	
May 28	36	Early Bird	Cook	Tonnage Fees	2	72	
				Noting a Protest	1		
				Discharged 8 men	4		
			(July 1/58)		$120	82	

Date	No	Name of Vessel	Name of the party paying the fee	Nature of service Rendered	Amount of fees paid		Remarks.
1858					$ brought forward		
May 24	37	Emma	Gill	Tonnage fees Noting Protest	120	82	Hot sailed
May 31	38	Arcadia	S. Sherman	Tonnage Fees			Sold
June 3	39	Crystal Palace	Simmons	Tonnage Fees			
				Tonnage Fees	4	96	
				Discharging			Consuls hands
				Steward & Wife	35		Advance waged
June 3	40	Helen Mar	Low	Tonnage Fees	2	55	
				Dischared 1st Mate		50	
June 18				Shipping 8 men	4		
June	41	Northern Light	S. Doane	Tonnage Fees	5	10	
June 23	43	Jennette	S. Q. Barclay	Tonnage Fees			Hot Sailed Sold to J. M. Endicott
June 26			J. Sherman	Discharging 5 Men	2	50	
				3 Seals 3 oaths	6	75	
June 29	44	Spirit of Times	John Klecin	Tonnage Fees			Hot Sailed

June 29	45	Palmello	John. B. Kenny	□□□ Noting Protest			
June 30				Discharging 6 men			
	46	Spirit of Times	John. B. Kenny	Discharging 3 men			
					$181	98	

S. B. Rawle

July 1. 1858

U.S. Consul for Macao

[1-053]

□□□□□□□

Macao July 2d 1858.

Having been requested by Mr. Perry, the Consul of the United States for Canton to obtain from the Reverent Mr. French a translation of a Proclamation of H. E. Hwang, the newly arrived Imperial Commissioner and Governor General, or at least of that portion of it wherein allusion is specially made to the Americans, for transmission to your Department by the outgoing mail, and the delays of collation with the various versions of it in circulation having rendered it impracticable to place it in Mr. Perry's hands in time to enable him to so transmit it to you. (he being at Canton or Whampoa), I interpret his wish to be, in the contingency that I should address it to the Department of State direct.

I have the honor, therefore, to hand you the translation of the Reverent Mr. French of the portion alluded to, as well as a copy of the most accepted version, of it; – that Gentleman (in whose judgment I place perfect confidence) deeming it unadvisable to attempt a full

[translation]

[Honorable
Lewis Cass
Secretary of State of the
United States of America
City of Washington]

transaltion of the "Chop" until one of the original placarded copies can be obtained for reference.

As the circumstance of the official transmission of this Document and particularly the selection of the portion now quoted might appear to you to imply a confidence in its professions of special regard for Americans to which it is not entitled and hence impart to it undue importance Mr. French, in handing it to me, expressed the hope that no such interpretation of the sentiments of the Mandarins would be accepted by the Government or people of the United States,– as such expression are entitled to very little weight being intended for a temporary purpose and chiefly to gain the support of the Chinese people to the hostile measures of the Government against Foreigners. He added that we must not infer from such plausible professions that our □□□ are at this conjuncture any □□□ upon our shoulders!

I have the honor to be,
Sir,
Your Obedient Servant
Gideon Nye Jnr.

An extract from the Proclamation of （黄宗漢） Hwáng Tsung-hán, Chinese Imperial Commissioner, and Gov. Gen. of the Provinces of Kwáng-Tung & Kwáng-Sí, issued at Canton on the 19th June, 1858, the time of his entering, upon the duties of his office.

"The Province of Canton has held commercial relations with the people of foreign countries for more than two centuries. The Americans, officers & Merchants, have always diligently attended to their own affairs, not proudly relying on their wealth and power. The people of China delight in them & foreigners of all countries respect them, the Heavenly Dynasty also has bestowed upon them the highest praise. All other nations have been just & upright in their commercial dealings, not practising the least deception.

If the English Barbarians had not thus wantonly and commenced hostilities & cruelly & violently oppressed men, above provoking the wash of heaven & below forfeiting the good will of men, how would it have come to this that scarcely a single brick of the Foreign Factories now remains, every thing being entirely crushied; & how would it have happened that the merchants of all nations should thus be cut off from the privileges of trade, for several years not a single mercantile establishment being opened? Truly this interruption of the trade of all nations, & this loss of pecuniary capital is entirely owing to the misdeeds of the English."

A true translation,
Geo. B. French

Macao, July 1st 1858.

Extract from the Chinese Proclamation

粤東與外國人通商二百餘年矣。花旗官商向來安分謹守，不恃富強，華民歡悅，各夷矜式，天朝實深為嘉尚。其餘各國亦均公平交易，毫無相欺。苟非暎夷無端召釁，兇餤迫人，上干天怒，下失人和，十三行洋樓，何至一片瓦礫，玉石俱焚？衆商人豈至斷絕買賣數年之久，不聞開艙？故各國之貨物阻滯，資本損折，實暎夷階之厲也。

[1-054]

[Recd 18. Septr.

Mr. Abbott]

Consulate of the United States of America
Macao, July 2d 1858.

Sir,

I have the honor to inform you that in consequence of continued ill-health and physical infirmity, I have availed myself of the power conferred by Section 36 chapter 4 of the Consular Regulations of 1856 to appoint as Deputy Consul for this place Mr Gideon Nye J^r a native of the Massachusetts, long a resident Merchant in China and Consul of the Republic of Chile for Canton from 1845 to his resignation of that Office in 1855.

His temporary testimonial will probably be obtained from Mr Consul Perry and Mr Acting Consul Roberts pending the return of the Legation of the United States to the South of China, when I expect to be favored with the approval of his appointment by His Excellency Mr Reed. According to Section 38 of the Regulations, I

[await]

[The Honorable
Lewis Cass
Secretary of State of the United States
City of Washington]

[await]
the action of the Department before taking any further steps.

I have the honor to be
Sir
Your Obedient Servt
S. B. Rawle
U. S. Consul
for Macao

[1-055]

[copy]

Macáo, 17th August 1858.

Sir,

I was favored with your Excellency's letter of the 31st ult° a few days ago; but severe illness has precluded a reply thereto until now.–

You do me the honor to intimate to me that their Excellencies, the Imperial Commissioners and the Governor-General of the Province, have communicated their intention to proceed shortly to Shanghai to confer with your Excellency and the Ministers of England & France upon the details of the (proposed) Raised Tariff; and you are pleased to invite from me any suggestions which I may be disposed to make respecting the Commercial interests of the United States.

I thank you Excellency for this mark of courtesy: – And in reply to the invitation. * (I beg to say that considering the former Tariff a moderate one and in its general provisions conducive to the enlargement.

[To His Excellency

The hon.[ble] William B. Reed

Envoy Extraordinary & Minister Plenipotentiary of the

United States of America

& c. & c. & c.]

[Shanghae.–]

*Suggestions of Consul Nye Jr. relative to China Tariff

2

of Commence, I do not perceive the necessity or the scope for any radical or important change therein.–

If, however, there shall have been exacted any material modifications of the Tariff in respect to the British Flag or Goods, it will be but right that our peculiar products and manufactures should participate in the benefits of such ameliorations.–

In such case, I would specially suggest a reduction of the duty upon our peculiar root–Ginseng, and of that upon our heavy cotton fabrics, Drillings, Sheetings, and Jeans: – which manufactures are specially entitled to any relaxation of Government imports from their being specially adapted for the use of the poorer classes of China. The increases of their consumption has formed the most remarkable feature of our American trade the past twelve years; and I esteem it of the utmost importance, alike to China and to our own country, to facilitate the introduction of these excellently – durable fabrics among a people so regardful of economy as the lower classes of Chinese are.–

Lead, of our native production is no longer an article of importation from the United States, as it was when the former Treaty was made; but foreign Lead now forms a portion of the cargoes of our ships from our own ports; so that we have a reason to obtain a relative reduction of the duty upon it.–

Neither is Cotton – of which several cargoes came out from Mobile and New Orleans soon after the former Treaty was made – any longer

3

an article of import from the United States; but mindful of the revolutions to which commence is subject and that our Country is the largest producing one of that great Staple, we are not totally unconcerned in the question of the duty upon it.––

Quicksilver is already an important item in our imports from California and one upon which the former duty bore rather heavily, leading to a very general smuggling of the metal.––

Mindful that a dearth of food not infrequently occurs in China and that California and Oregon are greatly productive of wheat and other grains and of vegetables, I would suggest that such should be admitted free, in common with Rice, and entitle the vessel bringing them to similar exemptions from port charges.)

Such are, briefly, suggestions which occur to me.–

For any want of clearness in conveying them, as well as for my omissions of important topics within the scope of Your Excellency's invitation, I must beg your indulgence an account of the severe illness with which, I am still afflicted.–

I have the honor to be,
With great respect,
Your Excellency's
Most obedient Servant
(signed) Gideon Nye Jnr.–

[1-056]

[Recd 17 Novr, Mr Abbott]

Consulate of the United States of America
Macáo, 3[d] September 1858.–

Sir,

I regret to inform you of the death of the estimable M[r]. Samuel Burge Rawle, the Consul of the United States at this Port.

He died yesterday morning:––His age was somewhat beyond seventy years.–

I avail of this occasion to apprize you of the inadequacy of the recompense for Consular Services at this Port; and I beg respectfully to express the hope that, instead of such recompense being restricted to the amount of the Fees recoverable under the last low Scale or Tariff of the Department of State, that you will readmit Macáo into the Category of Salaried Ports, thus restoring to the family of the late M[r]. Rawle the expected Salary of one thousand Dollars per annum.––

[The honorable
Lewis Cass
Secretary of State of the United States of America
City of Washington.––]

2.

I beg leave to express the doubt whether any respectable or reputable American, other than some person of very advanced age, who finding himself in a position similar to that of the late M[r]. Rawle (which of course is quite an exceptional and accidental circumstance,) would accept the appointment at even the fixed Salary of One Thousand Dollars.

(The past eighteen months have been quite exceptional in respect to the number of American ships frequenting this port, by means of the closing of the Port of Canton; and yet the amount of Fees during this whole period has not, I believe, exceeded $1000.–)

Under ordinary circumstances, with the Port of Canton Opened, there is no probability that the fees at this Port hereafter will amount to more than $400 p[r] annum.

As this Favorite Colony of Portugal is an important political point of this part of the World; the permanent

Residence of the Minister of France and of the Consul General of Spain; the occasional residence of the American Minister; the almost Constant Residence of several American families; the heads of which are usually Merchants at Canton; the frequent resort of British and other Government Officers and of the vessels of War of Our Own and other nations; it will be obvious to you, Sir, that the Representative of the United States should be a person at least of respectability, if not of some pretentious

3.

to personal Dignity.– His position should certainly be one of such relative respectability as would entitle him to an interchange of courtesies with the Royal Governor–General of Portugal and the several Dignitaries of other Powers resident here: – Indeed, without such Status any Representations which he might have occasions to make to the Authorities wrote be tinged with a prejudice derived from his personal character which would greatly impair the force of them.

Occasions for the intervention of the Consul are likely frequently to arise in a Community of such mixed elements as this presents, the more especially that there exist here certain anomalies of Law & Custom arising from the Somewhat uncertain tenure by which the place is held from the Chinese – the gradual growth of somewhat more than three centuries.––

As an instance in point, I may mention that a few days after I accepted the appointment of Deputy–consul an American Missionary and his wife were assaulted by Chinese with Stones, on returning to their home through one of the principal Streets of the city in the evening––My personal relations with H. E. the Governor–General enabled me to immediately represent the circumstances to him direct; whereupon H. E. took prompt steps to investigate the case and to report the result to the family in question.–

A person differently circumstanced would,

4.

of necessity; have had to proceed upon a certain routine, which might have consumed so much time as would have defeated any attempts at investigation, in this fluctuating community of Chinese, offenders being enabled to escape from Justice by fleeing into the interior of China or to the neighboring Islands.––

I have deemed it my duty thus to apprize you of the requirements in respect to the Consular Office at this Port, the more especially that any future incumbent might not be in so independent a position as myself. –– I have no desire to hold the office with a view to its emoluments, nor should I accept the appointment of Consul here if such bound me to a stated period of residence, even were the Salary equal to that of the Consul for Shanghai: –– But from a willingness to be of Service to my Country, whilst circumstances of a personal nature induce me to remain here, I am disposed to retain the office of Deputy–Consul or to accept that of Consul in the place of the late M[r]. Rawle, should you be pleased to nominate me to the President.–

You will be good enough, therefore, to view the opinions which I have expressed as purely impartial and unbiased.–

In July I had occasion to address you, in behalf of M[r]. Jerry the Consul for Canton, to transmit a translation of the portion of an

5.

important Proclamation of H. E. Hwang, the Imperial Commissioner–which alluded especially to Americans. I then thought it expedient to state a Caution of the Rev.[d] M[r]. French, our Countryman, a missionary of the Presbyterian Board, with whom I concurred in the importance of guarding against a too favorable interpretation of the compliments which it had pleased the Mandarin to pay the Americans.–

The caution was well–timed, as we very soon found; and the circumstances which I am about to proceed to state will serve to impart to it a permanent value.–

I allude to the subsequent, but almost simultaneous, issuing of the most stringent order of the Authorities of the Canton Province, holding delegated authority of the Emperor–Known as "Chiefs of the Shun–Rum" – enjoining upon all Chinese resident with Americans, Portuguese, Germans, & Spanish, as well as those living with English & French, to leave the houses of their employers within a very limited period, under threats of penalties of the greatest severity:––

Thus showing that in any measures of hostility there is no practical distinction made by the Chinese Authorities between different foreigners, but on the contrary, that they are, as we have seen on all former occasions,–– (viz[t] in the instance of the imprisonment of all Foreigners alike in 1839 at Canton

6.

and the more recent atrocities of Yeh in the capturing of steamers, rewards for heads, poisoning bread & c) –– perfectly reckless as to the consequences which may befall others among foreigners than those with whom they may be at war.–

(I beg to hand you copy and translation of a letter of the Captain of the Port of Macao of this date, informing me of the discovery of a Rock in the Outer Roads of this Port, a Note of the bearings of which he also transmitted to me; and as the existence of this danger is important to Navigation, I hasten to report the discovery of it to you with a view to the widest Authoritative publication in the United States.)

I was recently favored with an official request of H. E. M[r]. Reed, addressed to me in my private capacity as a merchant, for my suggestions that I might deem it expedient to make in aid of the Revision of the Tariff and Trading Regulations; and as the reply which, I had the honor to make to the application of H. E. may be of interest to you, I herewith transmit you a copy of it.–

I am,
Sir,
With great respect,
Your obedient servant.–
Gideon Nye Jnr.
Deputy– Consul of the United States of America.–

7.

Postscript. 4th September 1858._

I have now the satisfaction to hand you a translation of the Proclamation of Peace by Peh–Kwei Lieutenant

Governor of the Province of Canton – Governor of the City &c. &c., dated the 31st ult°. which is of so remarkable a tenor as induces me to call your particular attention to it.–

Accepting its expressions as the inspiration of Good–Faith, we may well regard it as signalizing the inauguration of a new era in our intercourse with China; and foreign residents, for whose heads rewards have so recently been offered （not without some victims）–and from whom all servants had just been peremptorily withdrawn, not without sinister reports or further evil intentions, may well contrast the phrase––" From this time let the Chinese and Foreigners be one family; let them for ever be at peace" –– with the usual form of Official Proclamations in which they have been stigmatized as Barbarians.––

I have reason to know that the French Navel Commander in Chief, Admiral Rigault de Genouilly has already passed this place on his way to Cochinchina and Tonquin to fulfill the enterprise with the execution of which his charged.–

The force under his orders is being augmented by a considerable number of Spanish

8.

troops from Manila.–

The primary object of the Governments of France and Spain appears to be to obtain redress of recent injuries and to assert the rights of their Co–Religionists:––The Spanish Bishop was executed last year by the authorities of Tonquin, and other Priest have from time to time suffered a similar fate, whilst the native converts, who are very numerous–some computations place the number as high as 400,000 – in the whole Empire of Cochinchina, have suffered in great numbers.–

It is understood, that France will also renew her claims on that Government derived from grants made during the last century to certain French citizens or officers which were confirmed by a Treaty of Alliance Offensive and Defensive.––

The Revolution having intervened in France and prevented the ratification of the Treaty in question and the fulfillment of certain stipulations, by France, it has been assumed that the rights of the aforesaid citizens and officers had lapsed in consequence; but I apprehend that those prior grants, which were in reward of personal services, still form a legitimate basis of Governmental action in vindication of private rights.–

I am & c,

Gideon Nye, Jnr.

Translation of a Proclamation of H. E. Peh （Peh Kwei） Governor of Canton & Lieu't Governor of the Province

（by the Revrd Mr French.）

"Peh, Lieu't Governor of the Province Canton, & c., & c. issues the following Proclamation for the purpose of quieting the minds the people.

"I have lately received a communication from H. E. Hwang Governor General &c, &c, informing me that he had respectfully received an Imperial Edict communicating the intelligence that a Treaty of Peace had been concluded at Teen–tsin between China, England and France; that has had already sent a communication on this subject to the Tartar General, the Major General, and the Hoppo, and also to the Military Association at Hwá–üne, all of which officers had complied with the Imperial Will; he furthermore stated that he had addressed a similar communication to the officers of Foreign Countries informing them that a Treaty of Peace, & c, & c.

"Since then communication have also been received from their Excellencies Ló, Lung, & Soo–（the three heads of the Gentry at Hwá–üne, acting under Imperial appointment）（quare–authority □□□□? ）––addressed respectively to myself, the Tartar General, the Major General, and the Hoppo, stating that as peace had been concluded at Teen–tsin, they should immediately restrain the Braves, and not allow them to enter

[the]

the City again to make trouble; that if any persons in the city or suburbs, or on the river, should hereafter injure Foreigners in any way, such persons were not connected with the Braves, and it behaved the local officers to have them arrested & punished. These things are on record.

"I have examined and find that before peace was definitely concluded, the Braves from the different villages assembled at the Provincial City. Now however that the two countries（i.e. the two parties to the War）it is my bounden duty being entrusted with the office of Government, to carry out the Will of Emperor, to preserve inviolate the peace and to quiet the minds both of the Chinese and Foreigners.

Besides therefore having commanded the different officers, Civil and Military, to return to the City and perform their duties, as formerly, I issue this official Proclamation that all the people of the Province, troops and civilians, may thoroughly understand. You ought to know that a Treaty of Peace has been concluded at Teen–Tsin; hereafter there will most assuredly be mo more fighting. If any vagabonds, pretending to be Braves, should again enter the city & injure foreigners, or take advantage of existing circumstances to plunder the people, I have strictly commanded the local officers to have such persons at once arrested and punished. It is also permitted to every one without distinction, troops and civilians, to seize（these vagabonds）and hand them over for punishment. If upon examination they are really found to be guilty, the persons seizing them shall be liberally rewarded; if any resistance should be made to these being seized, they may be killed without ceremony.

[Let]

3.

"Let all the merchants both Chinese & Foreigners resume their business as usual; let the families & merchants who have removed from the City, at once returned and live in quiet & peacefully pursue their avocations. From this time let the Chinese & Foreigners be one family; let them forever be at peace.

"Let the merchants cheerfully engage in trade & enjoy together the blessing of peace."

"This is truly my earnest desire."

"A Special Proclamation"

"7th Moon 23[d] day" –（August 31st 1858）

"A True Translation

（signed）J. R. A."

Macao Sept 3d 1858.

[A true copy of Mr French's
Translation from his imperial
Witness my hand
Gideon Nye Jur.
Deputy Consul of the United Untied of America
for Macao
□□□ 4h 1858]

[Proclamation of Peace
By the Lieu't Governor
(Pehkwei)
of
The Province of
Canton
Governor of
The
City
×××

Macao Consulate]

[1-057]

Pedra da "Lady Franklin"
(Rada de Macao)

Esta pedra é de configuração proximiamente circular, tendo de 3 a 4 braças de diametro.–

Aprsenta no centro huma elevação de 4 pés (ingleses) àcina do fundo e vai drinimindo gradualmente de altura para a circumferencia.

Em baixamar de aguas vivas há 14 pés inglezes dagua sobre o cume da pedra.

A sua posição e determinada pelas seguintes Marcaçõens.–Rumos magneticos

Ponta de Kahó	S. 9⁰ E.
Ilha da Tylok (cume)	S. 56 E.
Pico de Lantáo	N. 75 E.
Satcháo (pequeno ilhote em forma de botão, que fica ao S. da 1ª do N. das Nove Ilhas)	N. 9. E.
Guia (Fortaleza)	N. 54. O.
Penha Igreja	N. 71. O.

Ponta da Taipa quebrada	
és meis da Ilha Mong cháo	S. 78. O.
Ponta de Kai-Kiang	S. 48. O.

Translation

Sir,

I have the honor to transmit to you, herewith the bearings which determine the position of a rock recently discovered in the Macao Roads, on which the English Ship "Lady Franklin" struck about the end of June last, and lately the American Ship Marilla.–

I hope that you will be good enough to give to this communication from me, the necessary publicity.–

God preserve you.–

Harbour Master's office–Macao 3[d] September 1858.
(Signed) Jozé Maria da Fonseca
Harbour Master

(□□□)

[To the Honble
The Consul of the United States of America
at Macao–]

[copy]

Translation

"Lady Franklin" Rock
(Macao Roads)

The shape of this rock is nearly circular, having a diameter of 3 e 4 fathoms– In the center it is elevated about 4 English feet=from the bottom and gradually lessens toward the circumferences.

At low tide–during Spring tides–there are 14 English feet of water upon it.–

Its position is determined by the following bearings. (Bearings by Compass)

Kahó Point	S. 9[0] E.
Summit of Ty lok Island	S. 56 E.
Lantao Peak	N. 75 E.
Satchao (a Small Island having the form of a button–lying South of the 1st Northerly of the nine Islands	N. 9 E.
Guia Fort	N. 54 W.
Penha Hermitage	N. 71 W.
Taipa– Quebrada Point and midway of the Island Mongcháo	S. 78. W.

Kai-Kiang Point S. 48. W.

Additional Land Marks

Taipa Quebrada point in one with the middle of the Island of Mong chao:-

The Small Island of Satchao nearly touching the South point of the 1st Northerly of the Nine Islands.-

Itl[mo] Snr:

Juntas tenho a honra de reinetter á U. S.ª as marcaçoens que determinam a posição de uma pedra, recentemente descoberta na rada de Macáo, e sobre a qual tocaram a galera Ingleza "Lady Franklin" in fins de Junho de corrente anno e há pouco tempo a galera Americana Marilla Espero que U. S.ª de sirva dar a esta minha communicação a commiente pubicidade.-

Deus Guarde a U. S.ª

Capitania do Porto de Macao 3 de Setembro de 1858.--

□□mo h Consul dos Estados Unidos da Amanica

em Macáo

(asig[do]) Jozé Maria da Fonseca

Capitão do Porto.-

[Macao

Sept. 30. 1858

No.2

No.30

Port Office

□□□ 18]

[1-058]

[Duplicate

No.1]

Consulate of the United States of America

Macao 3d September 1858.--

Sir,

I regret to inform you of the death of the estimable Mr. Samuel Burge Rawle, the Consul of the United States at this Port.--

He died yesterday morning--his age was somewhat beyond seventy years.-

I avail of this occasion to apprize you of the inadequacy of the recompense for Consular Services at that Port;

and I beg respectfully to express the hope that instead of such recompense being restricted to the amount of the Fees recoverable under the last low–Scale or Tariff of the Department of State, that you will readmit Macao into the Category of Salaried Ports, thus restoring to the family of the late M^r^. Rawle the expected Salary of One thousand Dollars per annum.–

I beg leave to express the doubt whether any respectable or reputable American, other than some person of very advanced age, who finding himself in a position similar to that by the late M^r^. Rawle（which of course is quite an exceptional and accidental circumstance,）would accept the appointment at even the fixed Salary of One thousand Dollars.––

The past eighteen months have been quite exceptional in respect to the number of American Ships frequenting this Port, by reason of the closing of the Port

[Honorable

Lewis Cass

Secretary of State of the United States of America

City of Washington]

of Canton; and yet the Amount of Fees during this whole period has not, I believe, exceeded $1000.–

Under ordinary circumstances, with the Port of Canton open, there is no probability that the fees at this Port hereafter will amount to more than $400 p^r^ annum.

As this Favorite Colony of Portugal is an important political point of this part of the World; the permanent Residence of the Minister of France and of the Consul General of Spain; the occasional residence of the American Minister; the almost Constant Residence of several American families, the heads of which are usually merchants at Canton; the frequent resort of British and other Government Officers and of the vessels of War of Our Own and other nations;– it will be obvious to you, Sir, that the representative of the United States should be a person at least of respectability, if not of some pretentious to personal Dignity.––

His position should certainly be one of such relative respectability as would entitle him to an interchange of courtesies with the Royal Governor General of Portugal and the several Dignitaries of other Powers resident here: Indeed, without such States any Representations which he might have occasion to make to the Authorities would be tinged with a prejudice derived from his personal character which would greatly impair the force of them.––

Occasions for the intervention of the Consul are likely frequently to arise in a community of such mixed elements as this presents, the more especially that there exist here certain anomalies of Law and Custom arising from the somewhat uncertain tenure by which the place is held from the Chinese – the gradual growth of somewhat more than three centuries:––

As an instance in point, I may mention that a few days after I accepted the appointment of Deputy–Consul an American Missionary and his wife was assaulted by Chinese with stones on returning to their home through one of the principal streets of the City in the morning. – My personal relations with H. E. the Governor General enabled me to immediately represent the circumstances to him direct; whereupon H. E. took prompt steps to investigate the case and to report the result to the family in question.––

A person differently circumstanced would of necessity have had to proceed upon a contain routine which might have consumed so much time as would have defeated any attempts at investigation in this fluctuating community of Chinese,–offenders being enabled to escape from Justice by fleeing into the interior of China or to the neighboring Islands.––

I have deemed it my duty thus to apprize you of the requirements in respect to the Consular Office at this Port, the more especially that any future incumbent might not be in so independent a position as myself.–I have no desire to hold the office with a view to its emoluments, nor should I accept the appointment of Consul here if such bound me to a stated period of residence even were the salary equal to that of the Consul for Shanghai:– But from a willingness to be of service to my Country, whilst circumstances of a personal nature induce me to remain here, I am disposed to retain the office if Deputy–Consul or to accept that of Consul in the place of the late M[r] Rawle, should you be pleased to nominate me to the President.––

You will be good enough, therefore, to view the opinions, which I have expressed as purely impartial and unbiased.–

In July I had occasion to address you in behalf of Mr. Perry the Consul for Canton to transmit a translation of the portion of an important Proclamation of H. E. Hwang, the Imperial Commissioner – which alluded especially to Americans. – I then thought it expedient to state a Caution of the Rev.[d] M[r] French, our Countryman, a Missionary of the Presbyterian Board with whom I concerned in the importance of guarding against a too favorable interpretation of the compliment which it has pleased the Mandarin to pay the Americans.

The caution was well–timed as we very soon found; and the circumstances which I am about to proceed to state will serve to impart to it a permanent value.––

I allude to the subsequent, but almost simultaneous, issuing of the most stringent orders of the Authorities of the Canton Province, holding delegated authority of the Emperor–Known as "Chiefs of the Shun Rum" – enjoining upon all Chinese resident with Americans, Portuguese; Germans and Spanish, as well as to those living with English & French, to leave the houses of these employers within a very limited period, under threats of penalties of the greatest severity.––

This showing that in any measures of hostility there is no practical distinction made by the Chinese authorities between different foreigners but on the contrary that they are, as we have seen all former occasions,– (viz.[t] in the instance of the imprisonment of all Foreigners alike in 1839 at Canton, and the more recent atrocities of Yeh in the capturing of steamers, rewards for heads, poisoning of bread &c) – perfectly reckless as to the consequences which may befall others among foreigners than those with whom they may be at war.–

I beg to hand you Copy and translation of a letter of the Captain of the Port of Macao of this date

5.

informing me of the discovery of a Rock in the Outer Roads of this Port, a Note of the bearings of which he also transmitted to me; and as the existence of this danger is important to Navigation, I hasten to report the discovery of it to you with a view, to the widest Authoritative publication in the United States.–

I was recently favored with an official request of H. E. M[r] Reed, addressed to me in my private capacity, as a merchant, for any suggestions that I might deem it expedient to make in aid of the Revision of the Tariff and Trading Regulations, and as the reply which I had the honor to make to the application of H. E. may be of interest to you, I herewith transmit you a Copy of it.–

I am,
Sir,
With great respect,
Your Obedient Servant
Gideon Nye, Jnr.
Deputy Consul of the United States
of America.–

6.

Postscript–4th September 1858.–

I have now the satisfaction to hand you a translation of the Proclamation of Peace by Peh–Kwei Lieutenant Governor of the Province of Canton, Governor of the City &c. &c., dated the 31st ult°, which is of so remarkable a tenor as induces me to call your particular attention to it.–

Accepting its expressions as the inspiration of Good–Faith, we may well regard it as signalizing the inauguration of a new Era in our intercourse with China; and foreign residents, for whose heads rewards have so recently been offered （not without some victims） and from whom all servants had just been peremptorily withdrawn, not without sinister reports or further evil intentions, may well contrast the phrase–– "From this time let the Chinese and Foreigners be one family; let them forever be at peace" ––with the usual form of Official Proclamations in which they have been stigmatized as Barbarians.––

I have reason to know that the French Navel Commander in Chief, Admiral Rigault de Genouilly has already passed this place on his way to Cochin–China and Tonquin to fulfill the enterprize with the execution of which he is charged.–

The force under his orders is being augmented by a considerable number of Spanish troops from Manila.–

The primary object of the Governments of France and Spain appears to be to obtain redress of recent injuries and to assert the rights of their Co–Religionists.–– The Spanish Bishop was executed last year by the authorities of Tonquin, and other Priest have from time to time suffered a similar fate, whilst the native converts, who are very numerous––some computations place the number as high as 400,000––in the whole Empire of Cochinchina, have suffered in great numbers.––

It is understood, that France will also renew her claims on that Government derived from grants made during the last century to certain French citizens or officers which were confirmed by a Treaty of Alliance, Offensive and Defensive.–

The Revolution having intervened in France and prevented the ratification of the Treaty in question and the fulfillment of certain stipulations by France, it has been assumed that the rights of the aforesaid citizens & officers had lapsed in consequence; but I apprehend that those prior grants, which were in reward of personal services, still form a legitimate basis of Governmental action in vindication of private rights.–

I am & c
Gideon Nye, Jur.

[□□□□□□□□
No.1
None in duplicate
Received

Death of the Consul M[r] Samuel B. Rawle,
Necessities of the Country
in respect to Consulate;
False pretences of the
Chinese as to special
friendship for Americans;
Discovery of a Rock
in Macao Roads;
Suggestions invited by
H. E. M[r] Reed as to a
revision of Tariff, & c;
Proclamation of Peace by
Pehkwei at Canton;
Movement of France
& Spain upon Cochin-
China.]

[1-059]

To the Editor of the “*China Mail*”

Macao, 15th *September*, 1858

SIR,

I have read with much interest an intelligent exposition of the subject of the future location of the British or Foreign settlement at Canton, contained in your last issue.

Your correspondent presents the several suggestions of previous writers in an evident spirit of perfect fairness, and with much perspicuity; and in very modest terms suggests the selection of another site, which, in a word, I may say combines political and commercial advantages over either of the other designated localities.

But, Sir, with all his lucidity of statement in other respects, I regret to find on the one hand, a certain degree of obscurity as to his meaning whether this selection of a site is to be made in an exclusive spirit solely with a view to British interests, or not, and on the other that he has allowed certain disagreeable reminiscences of the assertion of the relative rights of the other Treaty Powers to cast the tinge of prejudice over his otherwise attractive and truthful sketch.

To my mind, Sir, the experience of the past from the days of the East India Company to the present time, inculcates union-nay, *fraternity*-between foreign residents in China. Indeed, in every crisis in political affairs, whether of purely domestic origin or involving foreign action, the accessities of the situation have led to spontaneous mutual support on the part of foreigners at both Shanghae and Canton.

And such must continue to be our experience until the Chinese and Foreigners become as in the recent words of Pihkwei– *"one family"* .

The policy of complete isolation, therefore, is of impossible realisation.

As fellow Christians and co–workers in the spread of civilisation were it not better may wiser at this remarkable epoch to realize at Canton, in however imperfect a manner yet in some degree, the inculations of a common faith–whilst at the same time acquiescing in the treaties at Tien–tsin which although separately concluded, severally contain the principle of equal participation, finally confirmed by a conjoined ratification of the Emperor himself.

As we have seen in war the recklessly cruel. Yeh pursue his head cutting, bread poisoning, and steamer capturing policy toward Foreigners, without distinction of nationality in the victims or spoilers, so now we find his master the Emperor recognizing the same principle by classing together the four treaty nations as representatives, in common, of Christendom.

It seems to me, Mr. Editor, that any step indication estrangement would be a retrograde one from this imperially recognized common attitude of the people of the West, and that, confronting as we are a Pagan people, too much caution in preserving intact its undeniable advantage cannot be exercised.

In this spirit, therefore, I shall proceed to comment upon other points noticed by your correspondent with a hope that upon reflection he will consent to forego the exclusive preoccupations of his mind, or that the majority of the British and other foreign residents will concur with me in a course to conciliate differences of opinion or feeling and conserve union in the promotion of the objects involved which undeniable are common to all.

As the proposer of the old site, with an extension westward, □□□ pages 283 to 286 of the *Hongkong Magazine* of December 1st, 1857, it behoves me, in now declaring my preference for Kuper's Island as suggested by your correspondent, to explain what may appear as an abrupt change of opinion.

In the first place,–the "campaign at Canton" has failed. I may say in broad terms of its object and instead of producing a salutary and lasting impression of Foreign power, has resulted in greater estrangement of the people generally, accompanied by increased elation of the party inimical to foreigners.

This political default is fraught with insecurity to our future position if not with actual danger to our persons and property.

It is obvious, therefore, that we shall best conserve our future security, as well as the cause of peace between China and the Western Nations, by waiving our claims to a locality involving as in a too immediate contact with the Chinese populace.

Having experienced the violence of the mobs of the period of the former war and those subsequent to the Treaty of Nanking, I feel the necessity, in the present unsatisfactory political state of this province to guard the community against similar dangers; and herein chiefly lie in the reasons for my apparent change of choice, but a reproduction of the sketch of my aforesaid "Scheme of treatment and of temporary local settlement" will best explain the point, since it will be seen that the mode of actual treatment and the consequent untoward course of events have widely differed from my suggestions and hopes.–

Leaving said sketch, however, for an appendix I now proceed to more direct comments upon your correspondent's communication and to some additional illustrations of the advantages of the locality preferred by him.–

The political reasons for the selection of the Kuper's Island site are perhaps sufficiently indicated in the foregoing: but it is well to bear in mind in this connection the strategic advantage of its position suggested by your correspondent, who says that, "in a military point of view it is the key of the city" . This, however, presents but one of its strategic merits––Its capacity of isolation, as an island; its greater proximity to Whampoa, Hongkong, and Macao; and its general accessibility by water on all sides to vessels may be added the feasibility of the introduction and accommodation of a Military or Naval force should protection appear necessary, without the risk of producing the excitement and alarm amongst the Chinese which would attend a similar step at the sites in more immediate proximity to the people. This is a point whose importance can perhaps be fully appreciated only by those who, having witnessed both mobs and fires around the old factories, are mindful that the combustible character of their buildings is equalled by the inflammable nature of the Canton people themselves.

The dangers from conflagrations are prominent amongst the objections to the old site in particular, whether the settlement be extended West or East; and in fact any extension from it will proportionately add to the dangers previously incurred. Amongst the inflammable elements of danger incident to the old site, I may mention the superstition of the people, which on two occasions, at least, has exercised a wide influence: I allude to the mob of 1844, the exciting cause of which was declared evil influence of a new brass vane, somewhat elaborately ornamented, then recently put upon the American flag staff, which was removed as the only measure to appease the populace; and to the widely attributed sinister effect of the pointed turrets of the church tower, in more recent years–the two or three extensive fires originating at points nearly North thereof, being clearly traceable, according to Chinese imagining, to the anger of a justly outraged Joss!

The increased force of the tides opposite the old site and the enlarging traffic, as well as the immovable obstructions and dangers of access to it, the latter affording, as your correspondent says, only a clear opening of 96 feet in width, preclude any increase of size or draft of water in the steamers for passengers and traffic with Hongkong and Macao; whilst they suggest the probability of greater impediments to traffic in future. In this connection the dangers arising to life and property from the rapidity of the current require particular notice; and the future may well be viewed with apprehension in this respect, if the increased force of water, clearly observable of late years, arises from causes of gradual and permanent growth, I have myself observed a decided encroachment upon the river's breadth by the deposit of broken bricks and other heavy rubbish about midway of the city, which of course increases the evil: and with this heedless and inefficient Government, obstructions of this nature are likely to increase along the city front rather than diminish.

Amongst the objections to the old site, without entering at tedious length into particulars, I may instance the absolute necessity to close up the ferryways and landing places, hitherto existing at the foot of Old China Street, and at the foot of Mouqua Street, as well as the renewedly opened one at the foot of the old Hog Lane: – A measurable degree of security is not otherwise attainable; whereas, complete isolation is of the last importance. – Confessedly existing causes of irritation are sufficiently numerous; and if it were possible to convey, to those who have not experienced at Canton dangers of the nature alluded to, an adequate idea of them, I might assume that my suggestions on this head in the foregoing are conclusive, since nothing less than an imminent peril to the Peace that has been concluded between the four Powers and China is involved therein.

Such are the prominent and, if rightly viewed, as I conceive, over–ruling objections to the selection of the old site: – Some of them are of a permanent nature precluding removal or mitigation and the others are but too surely fraught with the dangers of aggravation.

It seems, therefore, unnecessary to further discuss this branch of the subject; but in proceeding to a further presentation of the superior advantages of Kuper's Island, I may incidentally remark here that one claim of advantage advanced in favor of the old site can hardly be admitted as involving a legitimate objection to that Island: I allude to the alleged proximity of pack houses and shops, by which it is true the old factories *were* surrounded, but to mark the former existence of which there is now hardly left one stone upon another! The Hongs where Teas were laid down and the shops where Silks were exhibited having, therefore, all disappeared, the Honam packhouses will stand in the same position relatively to Kuper's Island that the packhouses above Sha–ming did to the former Factories; and it will remain only– to complete the necessary appliances of trade–to build upon the Island itself or upon the shores opposite thereto, Tea packhouses and shops for Silks and other goods, instead of completing a like necessity at the old site. And herein it is a consideration of not a little importance that the enormous cost of building sites at and around the former factories, where it may be said they bore a fictitious value – which would no doubt be exacted again–will be avoided at Kuper's Island.

Moreover, in respect to Tea packhouses and shops, all persons who are at all conversant with and especially those directly interested in the matter, will concur with me in viewing as of the utmost important, a radical change in the system of business hitherto pursued at Canton and the adoption of that followed at Shanghae, in so far as relates to the delivery of Tea and other Merchandize upon the purchase thereof:– a change not easily effected if the foreign residences are restored at the old site with the former surroundings alluded to:– Whereas it will be competent to each Merchant established at Kuper's Island to exact the delivery upon purchase of Teas or the goods into his own godowns for examination and shipment. Too great stress cannot be laid upon the importance of this change; nor can the difficulties of completely effecting it without a change of site which shall combine a breaking up of old associations and acquisition at moderate cost of ample warehouse room for each Merchant, be too prominently brought to the notice of those who have not had lengthy practical experience of the old "Compradoric" and Hong Systems of Canton.

Incidentally, in alluding to the political and strategic advantages of position appertaining to Kuper's Island, I have instanced amongst them the greater proximity to HongKong, Macao and Whampoa, that the Foreign Community would there attain: Your correspondent has suggested this point as he has most others; but it seems to me that some considerations may yet be presented without fear of appearing prolix. In the first place:–

The General business of the whole Foreign Community would be greatly facilitated at Kuper's Island, for the following amongst other reasons: The lessening of the time required for intercommunication with HongKong, Macao and Whampoa: – 1st, by reason of lessened distance: 2d, by avoidance of that portion of the river, I may say the only portion of it, where the passage is obstructed by shoals and rocks and impeded by the rapidity of the current, by native shipping and boats and not unfrequently by fog, which, together, always compel a lessening speed, and sometimes involve the loss of a night below the junks, or collision with the native boats, and consequent difficulties of a harassing and even dangerous nature, –so that we may estimate the advantage as fully equal, on an average of a year, to an hour's time.

This saving in time, along with the greater certainty of intercommunication, constitute a very important, it seems to me almost a sufficient, reason for the selection; for it happens to involve – such are the relative situation of Canton and Hongkong – just the difference that will render practicable and assured what would be at the other sites either confessedly unattainable or at best uncertain. To illustrate: The most pressing necessity for Canton residents is their ability to obtain their mail letters in time to write of their contents by the steamers to Manila and the Coast of China ports; and an essential of security and comfort in the river traffic is the practicability of performing the passage to or from Hongkong or Macao by daylight. These gains are all based upon the capacity of the steamers at present employed upon the river; but they may be greatly enhanced by the introduction of a larger and therefore more powerful class of steam vessels whose capacity for cargo as well as speed will enable merchants, not only to compass a satisfactory arrangement in respect to their correspondence by the mails, but to store their goods at Hongkong and Macao, and selling by sample; effect delivery about as quickly as though the merchandize were stored in the more combustible packhouses of Canton: Residents in China who have experienced somewhat of the roughness and dangers of estuary of Canton river in the present class of steamers will not, either, esteem as a slight gain the greater security and comfort and the lessened period of exposure to passengers. The new class of steamers thus called into use being of somewhat greater draught, and of much more beam and length, will, with the increased ratio of power and stability, perform the passage from or to Hongkong or Macao in 5 to 6 hours; the dangers of collision and consequent irritation being thus greatly lessened if not wholly obviated by the certainty of accomplishing the voyage by daylight. Another material facility and consequent gain to all foreign mercantile interests, will be the time saved in communicating with the shipping at Whampoa, and the ability to effect the more rapid loading and unloading of cargoes, which moreover, are accompanied by an actual lessening of the perils of the passage and of the period now afforded for the perpetration of frauds.

It is not unlikely, indeed, that the shipping itself may, with the exception of the larger vessels, be brought up the river to a point considerably nearer to Kuper's Island than its present anchorage.

Added to these direct gains of the Canton Community in respect to facilitating business, I may instance one amongst those applying to Hongkong or rather to commerce in general:– that the arrival of a steamer or other vessel might be communicated to Canton with promptitude and certainty and her redespatch determined upon and effected within two–thirds if not half the time hitherto required.

The question of salubrity can only be fully determined experimentally; but as the vetilation will be complete, whilst the drainage may be rendered effective by connection with the rise and fall of the tides – the Island being directly in the tideway with the actual channel of the river close to its southern margin – we may trust that its relative advantages in this respect will equal those already set forth, – indeed, from being at least equally open to the South–west monsoon with the old site, and possessing upon the East abroad and long expanse of open water, which the latter has not, we may assume as certain a greater degree of coolness than we have been, accustomed to even in the front Factories.

Nor must we be unmindful at this point, that the increased scope for exercise and recreation to be gained over the old site, including the carriage–drive around the Island suggested by your correspondent, and the greater facilities for boating without the serious dangers incurred hitherto to deter it– the "Junk river" as well as "the Fiddler's Reach ¨ branch affording clear way and attractive scenery as well as the inducement to visit the shipping, thus brought within convenient distance, as well as the practicability of making excursions on shore without immediate contact with the populace of Canton; – that these advantages appertaining to Kuper's Island all involved the primary question of health, may well go far to determine the choice of the site in all reflective minds, – for the very current of business in our community depends materially upon the general current of health.

Adding to what I have in the foregoing adduced as shewing time reasons for my seeming change of opinion, – (the consequence of a change of circumstances.) – my concurrence in the other reasons by which your correspondent supports his suggestion of Kuper's Island, I will only say, finally, that if it be true, as I wrote last year, that – "Costly armaments cannot be annually sent to China, or repeated in brief periods of time, even if another forty years, peace prevails in Europe, " – "the first requisite, is a settlement that has the essential elements of permanency," –it assuredly behoves the community to so regard the present temper of the Canton people as to pursue a course of conciliation and adopt such plans of a permanent nature as are, on the one hand, least likely to precipitate dissensions, and on the other, best calculated to lead to an amelioration of intercourse.

In the sense of my introductory remarks and as conveying an essential maxim for foreigners in China, I subscribe myself in the motto of my country,

E. PLURIBUS UNUM.

POST SCRIPT. MACAO, SEPTEMBER 20th.

Since writing to you on the 15th instant I observe in your issue of the 16th the "note" of your new correspondent, to which you refer in some just remarks of your own, who so strenuously opposes a change of site that in his impetuosity he not only totally ignores the history of Shanghae, but is equally oblivious of the destruction of the Warehouses and shops and the general uprooting of the land marks of Trade around the former Factories, whilst he seems also to have lost all proper idea of distance, for he speaks of Kuper's Island as "a remote locality" !

Why! Shanghae is in direct point of contradiction to his whole argument, according to the basis of which the Foreign Settlement should have been established at Soo–chow.

At Shanghae, on the contrary, a relatively inconsiderable town and never a mart of Foreign Goods or for native Products of the kinds sought for by Foreigners, the *British buyer did go with his money and to him the Chinese seller has come with his Goods until now*, at the end of a period of fifteen years, we behold the most remarkable instance of the rapid expansion of Trade ever known in the World's history, as exhibited by the Returns of the last year in the following aggregates of the several branches, namely:–

Imports of legalized Merchandize, Taels 14,549,226 equal to £4,940,674 sterling.

Imports of Opium (Sold at Shanghae) – – – £4,442,385 sterling.

Total Imports of Merchandize – – – – – £9,383,059 sterling.

Total Exports of Products & Manufactures, Taels 33,344,435 or £11,323,214 sterling.

With such a result as this before us we find his logic no better in the base of his argument than we do in his classing Kuper's Island amongst remote localities; – and the applicability of his generalized remarks can only be recognized in the sense precisely opposite to his intention, since so far from *migration* being necessary in the case of Kuper's Island, so "immediate" is the "contact" with the populous city of Canton that a Bridge may be made to connect them, if deemed advisable. – There is, therefore, no "withdrawal" or "removal" in the sense suggested; and hence so far from a "defeat" being possible, we shall more fully develop the "capabilities of China" by bringing our "Ships" into more "immediate contact with" the rather populous if not "vast" city of Canton.–

Having obtained the "Register" of the 7th instant, by sending specially to purchase it, only on the evening of the 18th instant, I was happy to observe in its arguments – both editorial and communicated – a marked coincodence of opinions with those already advanced by me in respect especially to the present political objections to the old Site; – regretting only the suggestions of British exclusiveness at the close thereof – my sentiment being comprised in the here anglicised maxim of my Country.

"UNITED WE STAND–DIVIED WE FALL."

[1–060]

[Recd 28 Dec.
□□□ te.

Mr. Abbott]

Consulate of the United States of America
Macao 25th September 1858.–

Sir,

Referring to my despatch N°.1 transmitted by the last mail, I have now the satisfaction to hand you a Duplicate thereof in a form more strictly conformable to the directions of the Department than the original was, my severe illness since assuming the duties of Deputy Consul having produced the perusal of these directions in extenso.––

Confirming the tenor of my last communication respecting the indications of an amelioration in political affairs, I have now the satisfaction to hand you a printed copy in duplicate of a Chinese version of Lord Elgin's treaty received through Shanghai from Peking, whose lucid and satisfactory tenor may be taken as an evidence of peculiar value as to the sincerity of the Imperial Court, since it is improbable that with an intention not to observe them the several stipulations of the Treaty would be set forth with such particularity and evident faithful adherence to the text. But the accompanying Rescript of the Emperor ratifying the Acts of his High Commissioners in concluding the four Treaties – with England, France, Russia & America may be deemed as the most significant mark of Lord Elgin's success.

Although in this Province there has been much hesitation apparent on the part of the people to credit or acquiesce in the requirements of the Treaty, yet within the last week there are more decided indications of an intention to abide by its stipulations and there now seems a prospect of the re–opening of trade at Canton within a limited period.––

[Honorable
Lewis Cass
Secretary of State of the United States of America
City of Washington]

As the Treaty with Japan negotiated by the Consul General, M[r]. Harris, has been sent forward to you by a Special Bearer of Dispatches and its safety may thus be assumed, I do not here state the information which has reached me respecting its important moral and material acquisitions; but I may be permitted to express the satisfaction which, as an American, I feel in the reflection that the rightful position of Our Country as the nearest civilized neighbor of Japan is fully established in our relations with that Empire and its peculiar people, thanks to the indomitable spirit, signal tact, and patient conciliation of the heroic Perry and to the highly creditable perseverance of M[r]. Consul General Harris.

In reference to the intimation conveyed in the Postscript of my Dispatch N[o].1, that the French Naval Commander in Chief has already passed this place in pursuance of his Special Mission to Cochin China, I am now enabled to inform you of his having made good a landing at the bay of Ferron and the capture and occupation of its fortifications by the joint Forces of France and Spain, with no lose of life to themselves and apparently but little to the Cochin Chinese.

This footing thus made good is declared to be, so far as France is concerned, of a permanent nature, in virtue of the reasons suggested in my said Postscript.

I understand that an Expedition would be organized to start within a few weeks for an attack upon Húe the Capital.

In the meantime a French missionary, Monsieur Galy, has almost miraculously reached this place in an open boat in twenty three days from Tonquin, having escaped and embarked in ignorance of this expedition with a hope to reach Macao, where he had been some years before, for the purpose of apprizing the Authorities and the superiors of the respective Religious Missions of his Country and Spain of the relentless persecution to which the Bishops & Missionaries of France and Spain as well as the native converts are still subject.

Exhibiting in his own person proofs of this to those who had before known him as of ruddy cheek and hale person, he declares that the passion of the King has evidently reached the point of insanity to which Bishops, Missionaries and Converts have alike fallen victims.

I have the honor to be,
Sir
With great respect
Your Obedient Servant
Gideon Nye, Jnr.
Deputy Consul of the United States
of America

[1-061]

[Recd 1. Dec.

Mr. Abbott]

Consulate of the United States of America

Macao 25th September 1858.–

Sir,

Referring to my dispatch N°.1 transmitted by the last mail, I have now the satisfaction to hand you a Duplicate thereof in a form more strictly conformable to the directions of the Department than the original was, my severe illness since assuming the duties of Deputy–Consul having produced the personal of these directions in extense.––

(Confirming the tenor of my last communication respecting the indications of an amelioration in political affairs, I have now the satisfaction to hand you a printed copy (in duplicate) of a Chinese version of Lord Elgin's treaty received through Shanghae from Peking, whose lucid and satisfactory tenor may be taken as an evidence of peculiar value as to the sincerity of the Imperial Court, – since it is improbable that with an intention not to observe them the several stipulations of the Treaty would be set forth with such particularity and evident faithful adherence to the text. – But the accompanying Rescript of the Emperor ratifying the Acts of his High Commissioners in concluding the four Treaties––with England, France, Russia & America–– may be deemed as the most significant mark of Lord Elgin's success.

Although in this province there has been

[□□ The Honorable
Lewis Cass
Secretary of State of the United States of America
City of Washington]

much hesitation apparent on the part of the people to credit or acquiesce in the requirements of the Treaty, yet within the last week there are more decided indications of an intention to abide by its stipulations and there now seems a prospect of the re–opening of trade at Canton within a limited period. –)

As the Treaty with Japan negotiated by the Consul General, Mr Harris, has been sent forward to you by a Special Bearer of Dispatches and its safety may thus be assumed, I do not here state the information which has reached me respecting its important moral and national acquisitions; but I may be permitted to express the satisfaction which, as an American, I feel in the reflection that the rightful position of Our Country as the nearest civilized neighbours of Japan is fully established in our relations with that Empire and its peculiar people, – thanks to the indomitable spirit, signal tact, and patient conciliation of the heroic Perry and to the highly creditable perseverance of Mr Consul General Harris.–

In reference to the intimation conveyed in the Postscript of my Dispatch N°1, that the French Naval Commander in Chief has already passed this place in pursuance of his Special Mission to Cochin China, I am now enabled to inform you of his having made good a landing at the bay of Ferron and the Capture & occupation of its fortifications by the joint Forces of France and Spain, with no loss of life to themselves and apparently but little to the Cochin Chinese.

This footing thus made good is declared to be, so far as France is concerned, of a permanent nature, in virtue of the reasons suggested in my said Postscript.

I understand that an Expedition would be organized to start within a few weeks for an attack upon Húe the Capital.–

In the meantime a French missionary– Monsieur Galy has almost miraculously reached this place in an open boat in twenty three days from Tonquin, having escaped and embarked in ignorance of this Expedition with a hope to reach Macao, where he had been some years before, for the purpose of apprizing the Authorities and the Superiors of the respective religious missions of his Country of the relentless persecution to which the Bishops & Missionaries of France and Spain as well as the native converts are still subject.

Exhibiting in his own person proofs of this to those who had before known him as of ruddy cheek and hale person, he declares that the passion of the King has evidently reached the point of insanity to which Bishops, Missionaries and Converts have alike fallen victims.

I have the honor to be,
Sir,
With great respect,
Your Obedient Servant,
Gideon Nye, Jnr.
Deputy–Consul of the United States
of America.–

[□□□□□□□
N°.2
1 in duplicate
Received
Amelioration of Political
Affairs in China;
Mr Consul General Harris'
Treaty of Ieddo;
The French & Spanish
Forces take possession
of Forts, & c. in Cochin–
China; a Missionary
arrives at Macaō after
narrow escapes and
great hardship to
report the insane
persecutions of the
King.]

[Duplicate]

Consulate of the United States of America
Macao 27th September 1858.–

Sir,

Referring to my dispatch N° 2 already sent to HongKong for transmission by the mail, I have now the honor to hand you a copy of the letter of H. E. the Plenipotentiary of France dated the 23d inst.,（but received only this morning） accompanied by a notice of the blockade of the Bay of Ferron, and places adjacent in Cochin China used by the Rear Admiral of France Commanding in chief the Forces of France and Spain in that Country.

By the next mail, I shall forward you translations of the same.

I am
Sir,
With great respect,
Your Obedient Servant
Gideon Nye, Jnr.
Deputy Consul of United States
of America

[Honorable
Lewis Cass
Secretary of State of the United States of America
City of Washington]

Translation

Legation of France
in China

Macao 23rd September 1858

Sir,

I have just received and have the honor to transmit to you herewith a copy of the declaration of H. E. the Rear Admiral, Commander in Chief of the French and Spanish Forces in Cochin China relative to the establishment of an effective Blockade of the Bay & River of Ferron as well as of the Port of Cham–Callao.

Be pleased, Sir, to communicate this declaration to whom it may concern, and receive the assurance of my highest consideration.

The Minister Plenipotentiary of
France in China
（signed） A. Bourboulon

[To Gidern Nye Esquire, Consul ad interim of the
United States at Macao._]

Translation

I the undersigned Rear Admiral, Commander in Chief of the French and Spanish Forces, charged to obtain from the King of Cochin China reparation of grievances which is due to the Governments of France and Spain, and in virtue of the Powers appertaining to me as Commander in Chief:

Declare:--

From and after the 1st of September 1858 the Bay and River of Ferron and the port of Cham-Callao in a state of effective blockade by the Naval and Military Forces under my Command.

All vessels attempting to violate the Blockade shall be dealt with in conformity with international laws and existing Treaties with Neutral Powers.

Bay of Ferron 1st September 1858.-
(signed) C. Rigault de Genouilly-

[True copy
Macao 23 September 1858
The secretary, ad interim
(L. S.) of the Legation of France in China
(signed) Klier Rowski]

[no 14
Macao
G. Nye
Stat Office
Sept. 27]

[1-063]

The dangers from conflagrations are prominent amongst the objections to the old site in particular, whether the settlement be extended West or East; and in fact any extension from it will proportionately add to the dangers previously incurred. Amongst the inflammable elements of danger incident to the old site, I may mention the superstition of the people, which on two occasions, at least, has exercised a wide influence: I allude to the mob of 1844, the exciting cause of which was declared evil influence of a new brass vane, somewhat elaborately ornamented, then recently put upon the American flag staff, which was removed as the only measure to appease the populace; and to the widely attributed sinister effect of the pointed turrets of the church tower, in more recent years – the two or three extensive fires originating at points nearly North thereof, being clearly traceable, according to Chinese imagining, to the anger of a justly outraged Joss!

The increased force of the tides opposite the old site and the enlarging traffic, as well as the immovable obstructions and dangers of access to it, the latter affording, as your correspondent says, only a clear opening of 96 feet in width, preclude any increase of size or draft of water in the steamers for passengers and traffic with Hongkong and Macao; whilst they suggest the probability of greater impediments to traffic in future. In this connection the dangers arising to life and property from the rapidity of the current require particular notice; and the future may well be viewed with apprehension in this respect, if the increased force of water, clearly observable of late years, arises from causes of gradual and permanent growth, I have myself observed a decided encroachment upon the river's breadth by the deposit of broken bricks and other heavy rubbish about midway of the city, which, of course increases the evil: and with this heedless and inefficient Government, obstructions of this nature are likely to increase along the city front rather than diminish.

Amongst the objections to the old site, without entering at tedious length into particulars, I may instance the absolute necessity to close up the ferryways and landing-places, hitherto existing at the foot of Old China Street, and at the foot of Mouqua Street, as well as the renewedly-opened one at the foot of the old Hog Lane: – A measurable degree of security is not otherwise attainable; whereas, complete isolation is of the last importance. – Confessedly existing causes of irritation are sufficiently numerous; and if it were possible to convey, to those who have not experienced at Canton dangers of the nature alluded to, an adequate idea of them, I might assume that my suggestions on this head in the foregoing are conclusive, since nothing less than an imminent peril to the Peace that has been concluded between the four Powers and China is involved therein.

Such are the prominent and, if rightly viewed, as I conceive, over-ruling objections to the selection of the old site: – Some of them are of a permanent nature precluding removal or mitigation and the others are but too surely fraught with the dangers of aggravation.

It seems, therefore, unnecessary to further discuss this branch of the subject; but in proceeding to a further presentation of the superior advantages of Kuper's Island, I may incidentally remark here that one claim of advantage advanced in favor of the old site can hardly be admitted as involving a legitmate objection to that Island: I allude to the alleged proximity of pack-houses and shops, by which it is true the old factories *were* surrounded, but to mark the former existence of which there is now hardly left one stone upon another! The Hongs where Teas were laid down and the shops where Silks were exhibited having, therefore, all disappeared, the Honam packhouses will stand in the same position relatively to Kuper's Island that the packhouses above Sha-ming did to the former Factories; and it will remain only – to complete the necessary appliances of trade – to build upon the Island itself or upon the shores opposite thereto, Tea packhouses and shops for Silks and other goods, instead of completing a like necessity at the old site. And herein it is a consideration of not a little importance that the enormous cost of building sites at and around the former factories, where it may be said they bore a fictitious value – which would no doubt be exacted again–will be avoided at Kuper's Island.

Moreover, in respect to Tea packhouses and shops, all persons who are at all conversant with and especially those directly interested in the matter, will concur with me in viewing as of the utmost important, a radical change in the system of business hiterto pursued at Canton and the adoption of that followed at Shanghae, in so far as relates to the delivery of Tea and other Merchandize upon the purchase thereof:– a change not easily effected if the foreign residences are restored at the old site with the former surroundings alluded to:– Whereas it will be competent to each Merchant established at Kuper's Island to exact the delivery, upon purchase, of Teas or other goods into his own godowns for examination and shipment. Too great stress cannot be laid upon the importance of this change; nor can the difficulties of completely effecting it without a change of site which shall combine a breaking up of old associations and acquisition at moderate cost of ample warehouse room for each Merchant, be too prominently brought to the notice of those who have not had lengthy practical experience of the old "Compradoric" and Hong Systems of Canton.–

Incidentally, in alluding to the political and strategic advantages of position appertaining to Kuper's Island, I have instanced amongst them the greater proximity to HongKong, Macao and Whampoa, that the Foreign Community would there attain: Your correspondent has suggested this point as he has most others; but it seems to me that some considerations may yet be presented without fear of appearing prolix. In the first place:–

The General business of the whole Foreign Community would be greatly facilitated at Kuper's Island, for the following amongst other reasons: The lessening of the time required for intercommunication with Hongkong, Macao and Whampoa:– 1st, by reason of lessened distance : 2d, by avoidance of that portion of the river, I may say the only portion of it, where the passage is obstructed by shoals and rocks and impeded by the rapidity of the current, by native shipping and boats and not unfrequently by fog, which, together, always compel a lessening speed, and sometimes involve the loss of a night below the junks, or collision with the native boats, and consequent difficulties of a harassing and even dangerous nature,– so that we may estimate the advantage as fully equal, on an average of a year, to an hour's time.

This saving in time, along with the greater certainty of intercommunication, constitute a very important, it seems to me almost a sufficient, reason for the selection; for it happens to involve – such are the relative situation of Canton and Hongkong – just the difference that will render practicable and assured what would be at the other sites either confessedly unattainable or at best uncertain. To illustrate: The most pressing necessity for Canton residents is their ability to obtain their mail letters in time to write of their contents by the steamers to Manila and the Coast of China ports; and an essential of security and comfort in the river traffic is the practicability of performing the passage to or from Hongkong or Macao by daylight. These gains are all based upon the capacity of the steamers at present employed upon the river ; but they may be greatly enhanced by the introduction of a larger and therefore more powerful class of steam vessels whose capacity for cargo as well as speed will enable merchants, not only to compass a satisfactory arrangement in respect to their correspondence by the mails, but to store their goods at Hongkong and Macao, and selling by sample; effect delivery about as quickly as though the merchandize were stored in the more combustible packhouses of Canton. Residents in China who have experienced somewhat of the roughness and dangers of estuary of Canton river in the present class of steamers will not, either, esteem as a slight gain the greater security and comfort and the lessened period of exposure to passengers. The new class of steamers thus called into use being of somewhat greater draught, and of much more beam and length, will, with the increased ratio of power and stability, perform the passage from or to Hongkong or Macao in 5 to 6 hours; the dangers of collision and consequent irritation being thus greatly lessened if not wholly obviated by the certainty of accomplishing the voyage by daylight. Another material facility and consequent gain to all foreign mercantile interests, will be the time saved in communicating with the shipping at Whampoa, and the ability to effect the more rapid loading and unloading of cargoes, which moreover, are accompanied by an actual lessening of the perils of the passage and of the period now afforded for the perpetration of frauds.

It is not unlikely; indeed, that the shipping itself may; with the exception of the larger vessels, be brought up the river to a point considerably nearer to Kuper's Island than its present anchorage.

Added to these direct gains of the Canton Community in respect to facilitating business, I may instance one amongst those applying to Hongkong or rather to commerce in general: – that the arrival of a steamer or other vessel might be communicated to Canton with promptitude and certainty and her redespatch determined upon and effected within two–thirds if not half the time hitherto required.

The question of salubrity can only be fully determined experimentally; but as the vetilation will be complete, whilst the drainage may be rendered effective by connection with the rise and fall of the tides– the Island being directly in the tideway with the actual channel of the river close to its southern margin – we may trust that its relative advantages in this respect will equal those already set forth,–indeed, from being at least equally open to the South–west monsoon with the old site, and possessing upon the East abroad and long expanse of open water, which the latter has not, we may assume as certain a greater degree of coolness than we have been, accustomed to even in the front Factories.

Nor must we be unmindful at this point, that the increased scope for exercise and recreation to be gained over the old site, including the carriage–drive around the Island suggested by your correspondent, and the greater facilities for boating without the serious dangers incurred hitherto to deter it– the "Junk river" as well as the "Fiddler's Reach" branch affording clear way and attractive scenery as well as the inducement to visit the shipping, thus brought within convenient distance, as well as the practicability of making excursions on shore without immediate contact with the populace of Canton; – that these advantages appertaining to Kuper's Island all involved the primary question of health, may well go far to determine the choice of the site in all reflective minds,– for the very current of business in our community depends materially upon the general current of health.

Adding to what I have in the foregoing adduced as shewing time reasons for my seeming change of opinion, – (the consequence of a change of circumstances,) –my concurrence in the other reasons by which your correspondent supports his suggestion of Kuper's Island, I will only say, finally, that if it be true, as I wrote last year, that – "Costly armaments cannot be annually sent to China, or repeated in brief periods of time, even if another forty years peace prevails in Europe," – "the first requisite, is a settlement that has the essential elements of permanency," –it assuredly behoves the community to so regard the present temper of the Canton people as to pursue a course of conciliation and adopt such plans of a permanent nature as are, on the one hand, least likely to precipitate dissensions, and on the other, best calculated to lead to an amelioration of intercourse.

In the sense of my introductory remarks and as conveying an essential maxim for foreigners in China, I subscribe myself in the motto of my country.

E. PLURIBUS UNUM.

POST SCRIPT. MACAO, SEPTEMBER 20th.

Since writing to you on the 15th instant I observe in your issue of the 16th the "note" of your new correspondent, to which you refer in some just remarks of your own, who so strenuously opposes a change of site that in his impetuosity he not only totally ignores the history of Shanghae, but is equally oblivious of the destruction of the Warehouses and shops and the general uprooting of the land marks of Trade around the former Factories, whilst he seems also to have lost all proper idea of distance, for he speaks of Kuper's Island as "a remote locality" !

Why! Shanghae is in direct point of contradiction to his whole argument, according to the basis of which the Foreign Settlement should have been established at Soo–chow.

At Shanghae, on the contrary, a relatively inconsiderable town and never a mart of Foreign Goods or for native Products of the kinds sought for by Foreigners, the *British buyer did go with his money and to him the Chinese seller has come with his Goods until now*, at the end of a period of fifteen years, we behold the most remarkable instance of the rapid expansion of Trade ever known in the World's history, as exhibited by the Returns of the last year in the following aggregates of the several branches, namely:––

Imports of legalized Merchandize, Taels 14,549,226 equal to	£4,940,674 sterling.
Imports of Opium (Sold at Shanghae) – – –	£4,442,385 sterling.
Total Imports of Merchandize – – –	£9,383,059 sterling.
Total Exports of Products & Manufactures.Taels 33,344,435 or	£11,323,214 sterling.

With such a result as this before us we find his logic no better in the base of his argument than we do in his classing Kuper's Island amongst remote localities;– and the applicability of his generalized remarks can only be recognized in the sense precisely opposite to his intention, since so far from *migration* being necessary in the case of Kuper's Island, so "immediate" is the "contact" with the populous city of Canton that a Bridge may be made to connect them, if deemed advisable. – There is, therefore, no "withdrawal" or "removal" in the sense suggested; and hence so farfrom a "defeat" being possible, we shall more fully develop the "capabilities of China" by bringing our "Ships" into more "immediate contact with" the rather populous if not "vast" city of Canton. –

Having obtained the "Register" of the 7th instant, by sending specially to purchase it, only on the evening of the 18th instant, I was happy to observe in its arguments – both editorial and communicated – a marked coincodence of opinions with those already advanced by me in respect especially to the present political objections to the old Site;– regretting only the suggestions of British exclusiveness at the close thereof – my sentiment being comprised in the here anglicised maxim of my Country,

"UNITED WE STAND–DIVIED WE FALL."

THE GREAT "FACTORY" QUESTION AND THE PROSPECTIVE SUFFERINGS OF THE "OPERATIVES."

How far is it a question of Fact!
How far of surmise and conjecture!

The so–called "*vexed*" question of the day; – but which may more properly be called the vital question, for truth to say, it possesses "vexed" elements of a graver import than casual observers perceive or careless writers stop to ponder upon:– The question, simply defined,

Whether the foreign community shall return to the old site bearing all the indignities there suffered upon their backs and passing again, as it were, under the portals of the old Hongs find their new residences and places of business of the same *Compradoric* order, buttressed about by the old association, customs and habits, which as "second nature" shall so hold and control every one that Canton again alone shall furnish an illustration of the olden time in China – as it were by way of contrast to the freedom, security, social and other advantages presented at Shanghae and elsewhere on the coast?–

Or whether we shall in the spirit of the Treaties of Teen–tsin, assert our independence in the only remaining effective step left to us and which is moreover confessedly the practically safe one:– Namely to demand the cession of a datached and wholly new site which combines all possible attainable advantages?

Such is really the vital question, to which the *pro* and *con* in the other respects must be held subordinate.–

Several writers have essayed to "ventilate" the subject; but from some obfuscation of the mental vision or defect of olfactorial① perceptiveness have left it much in the state of the atmosphere of the old Factories of a Summer's day with a light easterly or north westerly zephyr disseminating without dispersing the odors of the place and causing a very stupifying effect. Among them is one who writes in an editorial form in the last "Register" a lengthy and in some respects interesting leader, wherein he expresses opinions (not always clearly defined, however), differing essentially from those of a previous editorial writer in the same Journal, whose reflections upon the vital points of the question were eminently just and prescient; and it is upon these–the political objections to the old site–that the two writers are most distinctly or materially at variance.

This new Champion of the old site – (his memory cannot be *refreshing* him with old *sight* and *smells*!) – introduces himself by a comparison of this example of his editorial dissidence with the similar seeming caprice or contradictions observable in writers for the "Times" – the *Great Thunderer*, as he terms it; but it may be doubted if he has approached a parallel to the brilliant and always self–consistent aberrations of that Journal. Instead of real *thunder* we have a deal of scattered, uncertain, and ineffective rumbling, giving no token of latent explosive force, and unaccompanied, as such always is, by any bright flashes or real enlightening, – unless, indeed, that flight of fancy the "Flying Bridge" which he suggests, to connect the Honam Quarter with the old site, be deemed such!–

If the "humble Journalist's" – *little Thunderer's* – object be to suggest the most impracticable course of proceeding and to contribute to the elements of confusion already existing (if we are to judge from the public Journals) in public opinion upon the subject, he has not essayed to thunder in vain; but we would that there really were a *Great Thunderer* here to drown these uncertain rumblings, and flash upon the scene some of its brilliant coruscations of genius, to disperse the murkiness of the mental atmosphere and reveal to us the future as presented in the most perfected human horoscope; – for it is the *future situation* of the Foreign community and not the present scattering of brains and bodies that a wise mercantile foresight, and much more, a Statesman–like vision will chiefly regard.

CONCILIATE AND CONSERVE.

October, 2d 1858.

THE "FACTORY" QUESTION.

It is a point of honor among the civilized States of the West to sheathe the Sword when Peace has been proclaimed and equally their custom for the respective belligerents to at once emulate each other in acts of courtesy and conciliation, – in short, to enter with alacrity upon a mutual binding–up of the wounds inflicted upon each other; and it is one of the most lamentable of the evils attendant upon a war with an Eastern people that all diplomatic and military successes are rendered more or less indecisive by, on the one hand, the inability of

① Sic.; should be "old factorial".

ignorant minds to comprehend a real defeat, and on the other, the treachery and distrust which form the inevitable counterpart of Western good-faith and conciliation.--

This is not only an evil lamentable in its moral aspects; but it constitutes, of course, also one of the greatest disadvantages under which both the Diplomatic and Military Chiefs of the West labor in any transactions requiring mutually scrupulous good-faith for their entire completion: -In war they give blow for blow, when Peace is solemnized by Treaty they would cease contention, but such cordial acquiescence is wholly wanting, on the part of the Chinese for instance; -and, inefficient if not cowardly in battle, they meanly take advantage of the Foreigner's moral disability by endeavoring to wrest from him, by piece-meal if not more audaciously the privileges stipulated for mutual advantage which have been fairly won from their stubborn obtuseness.

If the foregoing presents no unfair picture of the relative disadvantages and disabilities of Lord Elgin considered with reference to the present respective attitudes of the two parties; and we find that his hands are further weakened by the state of English affairs and the consequent disinclination of the people to prosecute coercive measures toward China, may we not well view the present aspect of local affairs as imposing the utmost caution in respect to causes of irritation and inducing a course tending to as complete a reconciliation as is possible under the circumstances?-

As nothing is more unmistakable than the present temper of the English people in their determination to ignore the lesser if not the greater grievances which their countrymen may suffer hereafter in China; so there is nothing more evident than the wish and purpose of Lord Elgin to lay the foundations of the Peace with China broad and firm.-

If, then, we find in the editorials of the "Register" of the 28th ultimo, on the one hand, the confession that there are so many inflammable ingredients in his Lordship's Treaty that it may be described as containing "ten battles" - "were there even an attempt made to carry it out;" -and on the other, the assertion that "any cession that takes place, whether by purchase or otherwise, will be granted under the menace of our troops, and not to the prayers of our merchants, and if we, the unarmed community are left to enforce its fulfillment, the present war will have been worse than useless:" -are we not justified in our hesitation to accept the writer's opinions as in any sense offering a solution of the difficulties of the question?

So far as they are decidedly expressed they imply extensive exactions and coercion to enforce them, coupled with the *Non Sequitur* that the majority of the community *will not go to Kuper's Island.*-

It obviously remains to the proven whether the majority of numbers will stay away if the weightier portion of the community decide upon the spot where durable, because safe, relations can best be established and whence the important interests in Hongkong and the ports of the Coast and in steamers, Exchanges, Opium, &c. &c., can best be conserved and fostered.-

It is a sheer "begging the question" to assert that the majority will not go to whichever site the weight of authority may incline; - and all doubters may rest assured that to the spot so indicated both Foreigners and Chinese will flock in such numbers as shall raise the value of the original purchases.-

According to the magnificent and aggressive scheme of the writer in the "Register," we are to claim the old site with an extension westerly to the Shameen creek and northerly for this whole space to thirteen factory street; to span that creek by a bridge; and appropriate for additional Factories the flats, swamps, and other "sinks of iniquity" at Shameen (at an estimated cost for "filling in" of a part only of $80,000) : - Thus completely intercepting the most important traffic of the Chinese namely, that through Old China Street, Mowqua Street, and Shameen creek, to and from most places in the interior and embracing a large portion of the passengers and business to and from Canton by the three branches of the river as well as a great deal of local traffic:– Or to occupy the old site, as above enlarged, and add to it the north west corner of Honam down to Carpenter's creek; – the connection with the old site to be "maintained by means of a Flying Bridge."

This proposed extensive acquisition on Honam embraces by far its most valuable portion and involves the removal and consequent certain enmity of thousands of its inhabitants: – In one word, such an acquisition in totally inconsistent with the preservation of Peace, if not utterly impracticable.–

Here are schemes involving present coercion such as nothing short of open War would justify or tolerate and such as would if now attempted result in the discomfiture of the "unarmed community" in some grave form or other.–

But putting aside for the moment the political reasons, has this writer attempted to estimate the pecuniary cost of the execution of either of his schemes?

The cost of the old site in the mode proposed will be something enormous, and either the Honam Quarter or the Shameen *Swamp* will sink another vast sum before one dollar is used for the Foreign Factories themselves.–

Finally, as to coercion, are we not at the length of our present tether and confessedly in need to beware of a recoil?

And as to expensive outlays in site, buildings, and ground rents, considering the amounts already invested at Hongkong and the coast ports, is there a general disposition to incur extensive liabilities of this nature at Canton?–

To these questions we may answer, that nothing solid and valuable can now be gotten by attempting coercion, whilst much of the *prestige* retainable by a course of dignified moderation would be lost; and that confidence being impaired by the irritations consequent upon the infractions of private rights and the obstructions of public thoroughfares, involved in the proposed acquisition of the old and contiguous sites, all facilities would be withheld; whereas at Kuper's Island, perfect security and political tranquillity being assured, the moderate and gradual expense involved could easily be borne.–

One course is to provoke incessant hostility and never–ending enmity;–the other is to,

CONCILIATE AND CONSERVE.

October, 4th 1858.

Appendix.

Suggestions of a Scheme of conciliatory treatment and temporary local Settlement at Canton, with a view to the permanent re–establishment of the Foreign "Factories" upon recognized and broader foundations.

(extracted from the Hongkong Magazine of December 1857).

"As in the course of the *dénouement* of the Local Question, our views of the inutility, not to say futility, of the policy of isolation––now attributed to the American Government––will be elucidated; and as the solution of it now engages the efforts of the British Officers, as well as the attention of our readers, we proceed to sketch here briefly a scheme of treatment and of temporary local settlement that we communicated to two friends on the 1st of January last, to the general features of which we still adhere.

"If America still holds herself aloof at Canton, it will be a direct disservice to the Chinese, for then the

British Authorities will be constrained, in the interest of a selfish policy thus suggested, to interdict Trade there, pending a final settlement at Peking,–which indeed, would greatly simplify the political question.–If, on the other hand, America loyally takes her place as one of the Standard Bearers of Christendom confronting a Pagan Government, England would be authorized to declare that, having redressed the insults to her flag and the cowardly massacres of her citizens by the capture of Canton, she holds it in the name of the Three Treaty Powers, in conjunction with whose Plenipotentiaries she is proceeding to demand at Peking indemnity for the past and security for the future.

"Thus, the first step after local redress, in the way of amelioration, would have been taken; and so taken that the moral effect would go far toward reconciling Mandarins and people to the further purposes of the Western Powers.

"The new relations being thus initiated at Canton, the further application of our scheme of local settlement would be practicable by a resolute, patient, and persevering course of action;–by which only will any real reform of the abuses to which Foreigners have been subjected be accomplished and secured.–

"The three Plenipotentiaries would, then, in the

First place:–Declare that, for the well-being of the Chinese People–as inseperable from the just rights of the Western Nations–the Forces of England held Canton in the name of the Three Treaty Powers, pending such a settlement with the Government of China as should obtain indemnity for the past and provide security for the future.–

Secondly:–That for the proper accommodation of all Foreigners resorting to Canton, as provisions against ill-health, against exposure to the populace, and against fire, as well as to favor an enlarged Commerce, – for these and other constraining reasons in the interest of the Chinese people, on the one hand, and of the people of the West on the other,––the Foreign Quarter shall be isolated and enlarged, under the supervision of deputed Officers of the three Powers, in the following manner:

The front of the Foreign settlement shall commence at the Shameen Creek and extend to the Jardine Creek.

This being, for sanitary as well as political and commercial reasons, by all odds the preferable site; and the incidental benefits of its extension as suggested being such as to commend the measure to the well-disposed Chinese, particularly the exclusion thus effected of the disreputable and dangerous class of people hitherto congregated at and frequenting Shameen, the creek now used by them being thus available for foreign boats.

The rear line shall be carried back 50 to 100 feet; and either (or both) a CANAL *shall be formed, to protect that line against the populace and fires, extending from Shameen to the Jardine Creek with gates to be opened and closed with reference to the tides so as to best ensure cleanliness and provide against fires,–or a* RAMPART WALL *shall be built 20 feet high and 20 feet broad on its top, to serve as a promenade and means of protection against mobs and fires.*

The land thus set apart for the Foreign Settlement to be held on a lease for a term not less than 25 years, at a moderate ground rent, in the names of the Plenipotentiaries of the Three Treaty Powers subject to renewal on equally moderate terms, the charge of the details to be vested in the respective Consuls or in at public auction,–– the proceeds of which sales to form a Fund for the general purposes of drainage, raising the level, building the wall, forming the canal, &c., &c., and deficiencies for these purposes to be made good form the annual ground rent.

Owners of Ware Houses opposite the Foreign Quarter or of other buildings or lands, to be publicly recommended and enjoined to sell or lease them to Foreigners,–that thus the discouragements to the latter to settle at Canton may not longer lead to a preference for the other ports of China."

"Such a simple and yet persevering assertion of Foreign rights and power will have a greater and much more salutary effect than the destruction of the city. Initiated and conducted, thus, upon broad principles of right and practicability, it is divested of all appearance of vindictiveness and hardship to the people,–whose direct interest in its beneficial results lends it, indeed, a conciliatory character."

[1–064]

Consulate of the United States of America
Macao October 19th 1858.

Sir,

His Excellency the Governor General of Macao &c &c has done me the favor to acquaint me unofficially – (during a call with which H. E. honored me on the 17th Inst.) – with the violence of demeanor and language with which you received and ordered out of your vessel an orderly of the captain of the Port, who in the 16th Inst. had proceeded to her to hand you a written summons from that officer to appear at his office to answer to a complaint and claim for damages brought against you by the Owner or Captain of Lorcha N° 5, in consequence of your refusing to pay for the injuries inflicted upon that vessel by the steamer "Spark" under your command.–

The circumstances were of so aggravated and unprovoked a character upon your part as to impose upon the captain of the Port the duty to represent them to His Excellency the Governor General; but the latter, in the exercise of his prerogative, has stayed summary proceedings, in order to obtain redress without a resort to the measures which a less high–minded and conciliatory chief would have deemed imperative in immediate vindication of the Laws and honor of Portugal.–

A statement of what occurred has been furnished to me, by which it appears that the Orderly bore to your vessel the usual written summons to appear at the Captain of the Port's office to answer to the complaint in question and that after making known his errand

[Captain A. Ricaby
Steamer "Spark" –]

and not finding you on board was requested by your chief officer to await your return to her in order to obtain your signature to the summons as a Customary acknowledgement of its presentation; that upon your arrival on board, the contents of the summons was translated and explained to you, – whereupon you threw said official document upon the deck and said to the Orderly that the Portuguese Authorities has no business to interfere with you or your vessel and that you wants not allow armed soldiers on board of her, commanding him to forthwith leave the vessel and declaring that if he did not do so you had arms onboard to compel him; that then the Orderly demanded of you a written declaration as to the reception of the summons by you, when you replied that he should take it back as he brought it or that you would tear it in pieces, at the same time again ordering him out of the steamer; upon which he left her. And that the witnesses of your conduct beside the Orderly were the Master of Lorcha N° 5 Gregono Rodrigues do Nascimento and the mate of the steamer, Primo dos Santos, which last acted as Interpreter for you.–

The Captain of the Port further states that after the lapse of a few hours you came to his office with the manner of a man calling to know for what you had been summoned and feigning ignorance of the damage done to the Lorcha; that upon his censuring your conduct as highly offensive to the Authorities who had sent you the summons in the usual way, you remarked that you lost yourself command at the sight □□□ soldier onboard of your vessel – that you thought that the captain of the Port was a civilian and that as such his summons should have been served upon you by a civil officer as is the usage in your own Country; that you thought you should under no pretence allow a soldier on board of any vessel under your command carrying the American flag.–

Such are the facts as represented to me and such our virtual acknowledgment of the correctness of the presentation; and however disposed I may be to palliate offences committed by my countrymen, my first duty is □□□ inculcate in them and exact from them, so far as my authority extends, perfect respect for the Government under whose protection we all live here: – This is the more incumbent because during periods characterized by grave political complications in 1854 and in the past two years the Administration of the present Governor General has successfully averted the dangers incident to such a state of things from this mere outpost upon the threshold of a Great Empire.–

To permit any of my countrymen to impair the Authority of this Government by Word or Deed would □□□ to countenance the undermining of the security which we have so long enjoyed and upon which we and those of our countrymen who may succeed us have to rely on the future: – But apart from and above all selfish considerations and as an Act of Comity and Common Right toward Portugal it is, I repeat my first duty to intervene and prevent any acts calculated to lessen the respect upon which the integrity of all Governments so much depends.

It is undeniable that your demeanor and threatened use of the arms onboard your steamer, whilst it was outrageously insulting to the Government itself, was conduct and language will calout □□ also not only to impair its authority in a general sense, but to inflame the disaffected amongst its own soldiery of such there are and to become a bad example to foreigners generally.–In fact, it was conduct of so flagrant and dangerous a nature that as His Excellency proceeded to narrate the circumstances to me, I was fain to hope to gather from them, before his recital should be completed some feature of a mitigating kind, but none appeared, and your sole explanation to the Captain of the Port is that you "lost your self command at the sight of an armed soldier onboard your vessel", which bores its force, even if admitted as in any sense a valid exercise, when it is pointed out that the Orderly had merely his customary side arms bayonet.–

You will perceive that His Excellency □□□ thus -- by presenting the care to my notice unofficially placed myself as acting Consul as well as yourself under great obligations, since it was competent to the Government to immediately take severe measures against you in vindication of its authority so insultingly set at defiance by you; – and in now awaiting my action in the matter H. E. also testifies how well affected he as toward our country.–

I will not permit myself to doubt therefore, that upon reflection you will be prepared gratefully to respond to this spirit of moderation by satisfying the requirements of the case in the most ample manner in your power, to the end that the atonement may completely obliterate the unpleasant remembrance of the offence and fully reinstate you in your own esteem as well as that of others cognizant of the circumstances.–

It is my purpose, if you thus promptly avail of the clemency of the Government, to keep the whole matter private here; but should you, on the other hand, refuse my advice, I shall in honor be compelled to acquiesce in the measures which the Government will then institute against you.--

What is required of you is only what every man of a nice sense of honor cheerfully accords to those whom he has wrongly offended and such as in your case is all the more incumbent because in the persons offended the Government of Portugal is represented.

It is that you will send or carry to the Captain of the Port an apology and expression of regret for having so far forgotten your duties and accountability as to treat his Summons and its Bearer with your disrespect and utter the menace of the use of your vessels' arms.--

I shall wish to see or hear this communication to the Captain of the Port and will accompany you if you decide to make the apology in person.

I am,
Sir,
Your Obedient Servant
(Signed) Gideon Nye Jnr.
Deputy Consul of the United States
of America.-

[enclosure
with despatch No 5
Copy of letter to
Captain A Ricaby
of Steamer "Spark"
N°3.
October 19th 1858.]

[1-065]

[Copy]

To Gideon Nye Jr. Esquire
Macao

Sir,

The exigencies of American interests at the city of Macao rendering it important to appoint some one to discharge this duties of Consul of the United States, (a vacancy having occurred by the death of the Consul), and having confidence in your integrity, prudence and ability, I do by the Authority vested in me as Envoy Extraordinary and Minister Plenipotentiary of the United States of America appoint you Vice Consul at Macao and empower you to perform all the duties and receive all the emoluments of said office until the pleasure of the President of the United States Shall be further known.

Given under my hand and Seal of office at the Legation of the United States of America, this thirteenth day of October in the year of Our Lord 1858 and of the Independence of the United States the 83d.

(signed) William B. Reed.

[(L. S.)
attest
(signed) S. Wells Williams
Secretary of Legation.–]

[□□□□□
of Mr Nye as
Vice Consul
granted by His Excellency
William B. Reed
October 13th 1858.]

[1–066]

[copy
N°.1]

Consulate of the United States of America
Macao 13th September 1858.

Sir,

Unofficial Information of the regretted death of Mr. Samuel B. Rawle, late Consul of the United states for this Port, (which occurred in the 2nd Inst.) will have reached Your Excellency prior to the receipt of this Despatch; but it has become my official duty to formally apprize you thereof and of a consignment annually, as it appears to me as respects my present official position.–

On the 2nd of July Mr Rawle appointed me his Deputy and advised the Secretary of State thereof under that date.–As according to the usage of the Department (vide Section 38 of the Regulations of 1856) a Consul is not authorized to apprize the local Authorities of a nomination of the kind or request a recognition in that capacity until a confirmation of his act by the Department of State has reached him, it now occurs–as Y. E. will perceive– that I am without proper Official status in respect to the local Authorities, whilst according to the definition of "Deputy Consul" contained in the Book of Regulations (vide Section 35. 36. 39. & 40.) my position is no less anomalous.–

According to Section 41 of the Regulations it would appear that in the fact I am at present fulfilling the conditions of a Vice–Consulship rather than those of a Deputy.–

I deem it right to present to Y. E. these Circumstances of my position deferring of course entirely to your judgement.–

I am
Sir,
With great respect,
Your obedient servant
（signed） Gideon Nye, Jnr.
Deputy Consul of the United
States of America

[His Excellency
The Hon[ble] William B. Reed
Envoy Extraordinary and Minister
Plenipotentiary of the United States
of America & c. & c. & c.
Shanghae._]

[Copy of Mr. Nye
letter of Septr, 13th 1858
to His Excellency
Mr Reed]

[Macao October 26th 1858.
Gideon Nye, Jr
Vice Consul
N[o].5
Four
Received_____
Appointment as Vice
Consul by His Excellency
M[r] Reed.
Confirmations of previous
advice of favorable
political indications.
Insult of the Authorities
of Portugal by an
American Commanding
a River Steamer.]

[Duplicate
N[o]5

Rec 20. Jany Mr Abbott.]

Consulate of the United States of America.–
Macao, October 25th 1858.–

Sir,

Referring to the Despatches N°1 to 4 inclusive, which I have had the honor to address to you in the Capacity of Deputy Consul, I beg now to hand you a Copy of a Diploma granted to me by His Excellency William B. Reed Envoy Extraordinary and Minister Plenipotentiary, whereby I am empowered to assume and exercise the duties of Vice–Consul of the United States at this City– "until the pleasure of the President of the United States shall be further known." ––

As H. E. thus noticed my communication of the 13th Ult° to him upon the subject; I beg to hand you a copy thereof in further explication of the subject.–

In further confirmation of the favorable interpretation which I put–in my despatches N°1 & 2 ––upon certain political indications, I have now the satisfaction to refer to the arrival of the High Chinese Commissioners at Shanghae and to the general tenor of the advices from that place, to which I need not further allude as you will no doubt receive by this mail full particulars thereof from the Legation.––

In illustration of that portion of my Despatch N°1 wherein I pointed out the importance & delicacy pertaining to the functions of the Consular Officer at this Port, I beg now to hand you a Copy of my letter of the 19th Inst. to Captain A. Ricaby of the "Spark", an American Steamer which constantly plies between this port & Canton, wherein I severely censured and demanded apologies for

[The Honorable
Lewis Cass
Secretary of State of the United States of America––
City of Washington.–]

certain acts and words of violence and insult toward the Authorities of this place, which H. E. the Governor General of Macao &c &c in that conciliatory spirit which characterizes him, had represented to me in person and unofficially, with a view to obtain satisfaction for a gratuitous insult, to be attributed as much, perhaps to ignorant presumption as to senseless passion. – As the circumstances are generally embodied in the inclosed letter. I have no need, at present––pending a reply from the Captain––to enter into further explanations.–

I beg to hand you Duplicate of my Despatch N° 4 and I am,

Sir,
With great respect,
Your Obedient Servant
Gideon Nye Jnr.
Vice–Consul of the United States
of America.–

[1-067]

[Rec 20 Jany Mr. Abbott.
□□16]

Consulate of the United States of America
Macao, November 13th 1858.–

Sir,

In handing to you the Duplicate of my Despatch N°5, I have now the honor and satisfaction to hand you a copy of the Minute for the Consular Records made on behalf of Mr A. Ricaby the Commander of the steamer "Spark", which, as I conceive, terminates in a satisfactory manner the question which arose from certain acts and words of insult toward the Portuguese Authorities imputed to him as set forth in my letter of the 19th Ult°. a copy of which I transmitted to you under cover of my said despatch.

I am,
Sir,
With great respect,
Your obedient servant,
Gideon Nye, Jnr,
Vice Consul of the United State of America.–

[copy]

Minute for Consular Records:––

In reference to the Charges against Captain A. Ricaby of the steamer "Spark" of violent demeanor and language in derogation of the Authority of Portugal within the harbor of this port,– which are embodied in the letter of the 19th Inst. to him from this Consulate,–the undersigned, Vice–Consul of the United States, considering the right of Mr Ricaby to have a Statement of the excuses pleaded by him, in extenuation of the conduct and language therein imputed to him placed upon the Consular Record, causes this Minute made accordingly to be attested by the Signature of the accused as followeth:–

First:––That he protests himself animated with full and proper respect for the Officers of the Portuguese Government and that hence there was nothing of the Native of Malice prepense in his demeanor or language; that, in fact, the expressions of a disrespectful character used by him and for which he now offers his regrets and apologies, were uttered in a misconception of the errand and demand of the Orderly and are to be attributed to his want of a Knowledge of the language, whereby he understood the demand of the Orderly to be for immediate payment of the Claim of the Captain of the Lorcha, who was present with him apparently in aid of the enforcement of the claim; that feeling such summary demand, without a hearing, an injustice and the presence of the Captain of the Lorcha in the capacity of assistant an outrage– the more an injustice and an outrage because neither he or any one onbroad the "Spark" were aware of having touched or in any wise damaged the Lorcha – he, as he submits naturally, get excited and used the gestures and language which he now regrets; – and as respects his action and gestures he has also to make the important correction of the charge of throwing the summons, as if in contempt, upon deck, that instead of such intention he attempted twice to hand it back to the Orderly, who refused to take it and that then he threw it toward him, when it fell upon the deck:––

That as regards the allusion to arms onboard the steamer, feeling stung by the indignity of a seeming arrest by a soldier assisted by a claimant of undefined and perhaps imaginary damages – having neither committed or imagined wrong to any man – he did say that there was no need to send soldiers to his vessel and that any call for such could be answered by the arms and men onboard for her; but he protests that he did not intend thereby to defy the authority of the Government or to assert more than his right to intimidate men whose conduct appeared to him to indicate an illegal arrest of his person onboard his vessel:––

Secondly: ––That so soon as the Orderly and captain of the Lorcha had left the steamer and he had obtained a full and correct translation of the summons he proceeded to the Office of the Captain of the Port to answer to it; that having been summoned upon a charge improper and groundless, so far as anyone onboard the "Spark" know, he naturally had the air attributed to him, but that so far from intending or feeling any disrespect for the Captain of the Port, he had in the meantime reflected upon the occurrence with a regret heightened by his appreciation of the gentlemanly character of that officer.–

Finally, that rather than cause further trouble, he satisfied the claimant, although unaware what, if any, damage was, in the darkness of the night, suffered by the Lorcha during the necessary "dropping" of the "Spark" into a berth suitable for her oaring.––

That having already in person, accompanied by the undersigned, the Vice–Consul, called upon the Captain of the Port with explanations and apologies in the sense as herein recorded, and professing himself, as he does, animated with perfect respect for His Excellency the Governor of Macao; he trusts to the exalted sense of right of these officers for his examination from further blame in the premises:–

Requesting that a Copy of this Minute may be respectfully transmitted to His Excellency by the undersigned the Vice–Consul.–

(signed) A. Ricaby

To the letter of the 19th Ult° and the above statement of Captain Ricaby the undersigned has only to add that upon a full review of the case he is quite of opinion that it forcibly illustrates the importance of the communication of important orders of Government in the language of the recipient.––

(signed) Gideon Nye Jnr.
Vice Consul of the United
States of America.––

[1–068]

[Recd 28. July, Mr. Abbott.

N°7

Red Jul 6 Art
May 7]

Consulate of the United States of America
Macao, December. 28th 1858.–

Sir,

I beg leave to hand you the account of fees received at this consulate during the Quarter ending 30th September 1858 and amounting to one hundred fifty nine Dollars and thirty nine and a half cents, which has been kept open by the neglect of some of the steam boat proprietors.–

This meagre sum will give point to my representations in Despatch N°1 of the inadequacy of the recompense to the Consular Officer at this port; and an analysis of the Return confirms my previous opinion that when Trade is fully resumed at Canton the income here will fall below $400 per annum; whereas I am compelled （a fail in my duties） to pay an Assistant $900 per annum!

Unless there is likely to be a change in respect to salary or income, I must beg the President to accept definitively of my resignation: still reserving to myself the right mentioned in said Despatch, to resign whenever my own interests call me away from Macao.–

I beg to accompany the above with a Return for the Corresponding Quarter of the arrival & departures of American vessels at this Port, which is in some minor respects of detail somewhat imperfect

[The Honorable
Lewis Cass
Secretary of State of the United States of America
City of Washington.–]

owning to my severe illness during the summer.–

I am,
Sir,
With great respect
Your obed[t] Serv[t]
Gideon Nye Jnr.
Vice Consul of the United States of
America.–

[1-069]

[Rec 28, Feby. Mr Abbott
N°.8]

Consulate of the United States of America
Macao, December 29th 1858.–

Sir,

I regret to inform you of the total loss of the Barque "Matilda" of New York, Captain Jurgen Rickmers belonging to Messrs Funck & Meinke of the said city, while on a voyage from the Port of Swansea in Wales to Shanghae, with a cargo of coals belonging to the British Government.––

She left Swansea in the 1st of May; reached Hong Kong on the 25th of September; where receiving orders to proceed to Shanghae to deliver her cargo, in terms of the Bill of Lading, she left the day after her arrival; and encountering very heavy weather on the 3rd to the 7th of October was abandoned on the latter day by her Officers and Crew, when about 150 miles Southwest of the Bashee Islands, by estimation, who saw her founder at about 10 A. M. of that day.–

The weather was still so heavy when the crew took to their boats that they were compelled to throw almost every thing overboard to keep them afloat; but, happily, by their exertions they were enabled five days afterward to reach the Island of Hainan, where, not being permitted to land, they were rescued by the Chinese Junk "Le–check–Le", Captn Cheong–ah–eh,–who agreed to bring them to Macáo for the very moderate sum of Three

[The Honorable
Lewis Cass
Secretary of State of the United States of America
City of Washington]

hundred Dollars as a recompense for this peculiar and in some respects hasardous service, to which was to be added the cost of their subsistence whilst–onboard the Junk.–

They reached this port on the 19th Inst., having thus been about seventy days on the voyage from Hainan and consumed food charges at $109 – only or but 12 1/2 cents per man per day, there being 12 men including the captain and officers.

The junk also brought two boats, which being the only things saved belonging to the ship, and no Freight having been carried up to the period of the abandonment of her, the captain ordered them sold by public Auction today to pay over the crew; and whilst writing I hear that they have produced about forty one Dollars and a half.–

During the voyage the junk was detained by the Mandarins at Shapah and the captain of her bound and imprisoned, on the ground that he was receiving "Europeans" whilst their Governments were still at war with the Chinese at Canton, the explanation that these were Americans and even the exhibition of the Flag of the United States was of no avail for their release and the sum of Two hundred Dollars was exacted for their ransom. – After two or three days detention Cheong–ah–Eh found a Junk supercargo willing to advance him this price of ransom if he wants allow forty per centum as the difference of Exchange, which was gladly availed of; as it was clear that the Mandarins were not capable or willing to distinguish between the seaman of an American Ship or those of an European Vessel – a point involved in all the more differently in this case because the captain, officers and men are without exception naturalized citizens of the United States who habitually speak with each other in their native language – the German – and then in definite detention or maltreatment might be apprehended in case of refusal to pay.

The Captain being without means and the Agents of the Owners in HongKong Mess[rs] Siemssent & C[o] a German House –not being disposed to advance him more than the stipulated price of rescue and the actual expense of subsistence, say $ 409, I have felt it my duty to assume the payment on behalf of the Government of the United States, of the further sum of $ 280. Say Two hundred and Eighty Dollars, being the price of ransom from the Mandarins of Shapah and the Exchange of 40% before named; and shall beg leave to draw for my reimbursement accordingly.–

The public grounds for this assumption seem to me of the strongest conceivable kind, indeed, I feel that I should be derelict in my duty if I allowed his worthy Junk man to suffer the loss of any portion of the very moderate recompense agreed upon with the Captain of the "Matilda" –a loss which he would incur if the sum expended to obtain the ransom of these shipwrecked men and of his Junk be not returned to him.––

The peculiar merits of this Junk captain and the considerations of a public nature which render the distinguishing of him by some mark of the favor of the President politic as well as deserved, I shall beg leave to present in a separate Despatch, in accordance with Section 340 of the General Instructions to Consular Officers.––

I am,
Sir,
With great respect,
Your obd[t] Servant
Gideon Nye Jnr.
Vice Consul of the United States of
America.–

[1–070]

[Rec 30. Ap Mr. abbott
N[o]9. May 8th]

Consulate of the United States
Macao, February 22nd 1859

Sir,

I beg leave to refer to my Despatches N[o]1 & 7 in now handing you the Account of Fees received at this Consulate during the Quarter ending on the 31st of December last passed, and amounting to $150 $\frac{22}{100}$½ say, One hundred fifty Dollars, twenty two and a half cents; which, as in a former case, has been some what delayed by the want of returns, from River Steamers.–

I beg to hand you, also, the Returns of the arrivals and Departures of American Vessels during the same quarter.

It is unnecessary to renewedly point out the inadequacy of the yearly income which this and previous Quarterly Accounts of Fees as present, or the disproportion that it bears to the actual duties of the Office here. In further illustration of this point, I may instance the amount of time consumed in the important case arising from the seizure of the Ship "Emma" upon false Declarations, which I shall have occasion to lay fully before you by the next Mail;

[although]

[The Honorably
Lewis Cass
Secretary of State of the United States of
America.–
City of Washington]

although I am happy to say that I am informed thro' the Counsellor of the Owner that the main question is no longer pending and that the remaining one of damages due the Owner of the vessel will, partially or wholly, become matter of Arbitration according to Law.

I have the gratification to say that our countrymen interested in this question – being Captain Gill the Owner and M^r^. Edward J. Sage the Supercargo – express themselves very gratefully to the service that I had done them in this case, saying that they "do not know what they could have done without my aid." ––

Having laid this case fully before His Excellency Mr Reed during his sojourn in HongKong harbor in November and December, I had no need to address the Department of State until the question entered upon a new phase; but shall beg leave to present it to you fully within the next two weeks.––

I am,
Sir,
With great respect–
Your Obedient Servant
Gideon Nye Jnr.
Vice–Consul of the United States
of America.–

P. S.

I beg to hand you a British Government Notification of the 18th inst., which may be of interest to the Treasury Department of the United States, showing as it does that Macao is viewed as merely an outlying port of the Canton river for the Shipment of Chinese produce and that hence Teas &c are subject to the regular Export duty if sent onboard ships lying at Whampoa: – A ruling by the British and Chinese Officers – which clears Teas shipped from Macao to the United States of Duty, if indeed there has ever been a question as to their exemption.–

I have the pleasure to hand you also a list of articles embraced in the Trade as at present conducted with Japan, which has reached a scale of development considerably beyond general expectations.

I hand you also printed Extracts of a letter from Japan recently received by me; and a Newspaper containing two articles of interest.–

I am

Gideon Nye Jnr.

United States Consulate at Macao

Fees received during the Quarter ending 31st December 1858.–

Date	No	Name of vessel	Name of the party paying the fee	Nature of service rendered	Amount of Fees Paid	
□□□① 5th		Levanter	Richd Pollard	Certificate to Invoice of Merchandize	$2	
6th	4	Marilla	W. B. Robinson	Deposit of papers 699 tons	$3	50
6th	4	Marilla	W. B. Robinson	Noting Protest	$1	50
6th	4	Marilla	W. B. Robinson	Discharging 2d mate & seal	$1	50
6th	4	Marilla	W. B. Robinson	Shipping 4 men & Seal	$2	50
6th	4	Marilla	W. B. Robinson	Certificate of Desertion	$1	
20th	6	Tho W. Sears	A Drew	Deposit of papers–499 $\frac{91}{95}$ tons	$2	50
23d		Levanter	Adolph Bowsjaw	Certificate to Invoice of Merchandize	$2	
23d			Jas Cunningham Jr	Passport to Manila	$1	
23d			Franklin Gibbs	Passport to Manila	$1	
23d			Thn B. Wales Jr	Passport to Manila	$1	
23d			E. V. Thwing	Passport to Manila	$1	
23d	2	Aluiatia	A. B. Richardson	Deposit of papers 472 tons	$2	36
23d	2	Aluiatia	A. B. Richardson	Shipping 4 men & Seal	$2	50
25th		Levanter	Jose Lopes	Certificate to Invoice of Merchandize	$2	
26th		Levanter	Richd Pollard	Certificate to Invoice of Merchandize	$2	
26th		Levanter	G. Raynal	Certificate to Invoice of Merchandize	$2	
26th		Levanter	do	Certificate to Invoice of Merchandize	$2	
30th	8	Mastiff	Wm O. Johnson	Deposit of papers–1030 $\frac{70}{95}$ tons	$5	15
30th	8	Mastiff	do	Certificate of discharge of the Cook	$1	
□□□② 1st	8	Mastiff	do	Certificate of discharge of the Steward	$1	
1st		Levanter	Dr. Sinclair U.S.A	Certificate to Invoice of Merchandize	$2	
4th		do	José Lopes	Certificate to Invoice of Silks	$2	
6th		do	Act de Mello &Co	Certificate to Invoice of Sundries	$2	

① should be "Octer".
② should be "Nover".

11th		do	William Peterson	Deposit of papers–$849\frac{76}{95}$ tons	$4	25
11th		do	William Peterson	Certificate of Desertion	$1	
11th		do	William Peterson	Shipping 5 men	$2	50
11th		do	William Peterson	Certificate of nothing able to procure 2/3 Crew of Americans		50
12th		Mary F. Slade	Richd Pollard	Certificate to Invo of Merchandize	$4	
13th		Levanter	G. Raynal	Certificate to Invo of Merchandize	$2	
19th		Mary F. Slade	M. A dos Runedios	Certificate to Invo of Merchandize	$2	
20th	3	Mary F. Slade	Hatzel F. Crowell	Deposit of papers $199\frac{42}{95}$ tons	$1	
20th	3	Mary F. Slade	Hatzel F. Crowell	Shipping 6 men	$3	
20th	3	Mary F. Slade	Hatzel F. Crowell	Desertion of 10 men	$5	
22th	11	Carbon	George Tyson	Certifying his Signature	$2	
22th	11	Carbon	George Tyson	application for sea letter		25
22th	11	Carbon	George Tyson	Authenticating Signature	$2	
				Amount carried forward	$75	1
				Amount brought forward	$75	1
Nover 22d	11	Carbon	George Tyson	Recording 4 Documents	$1	□□□
	11	Carbon	George Tyson	Certificate to oath of the master		□□□
24th	–	–	W.C. Hunter	Authenticating Signature	$2	□□□
29th	–	–	W.C. Hunter	Authenticating Signature	$4	□□□
Decer 11th	12	Kate Hooper	Ed. P. Johnson	Deposit of papers–$1488\frac{76}{95}$ tons	$1?	□□□
31st	14	Matilda	Jurgen Rickmers	Noting protest	$1	□□□
31st	14	Matilda	Jurgen Rickmers	Extending Protest	$2	□□□
31st	14	Matilda	Jurgen Rickmers	1236 additional words, beyond 200	$12	□□□
31st	14	Matilda	Jurgen Rickmers	Authenticating 3 Copies of same, 1/2 fee	$2	□□□
31st	14	Matilda	Jurgen Rickmers	Certificate of payt. of money to the Chinese Junk Captain		□□□
31st	14	Matilda	Jurgen Rickmers	Certifying Duplicate of do		□□□
31st	14	Matilda	Jurgen Rickmers	Certificate of sale of 2 ships boat to public auction		□□□
31st	14	Matilda	Jurgen Rickmers	Certifying Duplicate of same		□□□
31st	–	–	J. B. Endicott	Certifying Invo Sundaries & "Hydro" –1857	$2	□□□
31st	9	Arcadia	R. B. Wade	Deposit of papers–$705\frac{61}{95}$ tons		□□□
31st		Arcadia	R. B. Wade	Certificate of discharge of the Steward		□□□
31st		Spark		Tonnage dues for 4th Quarter	$12	□□□
31st		Rose		Tonnage dues for 4th Quarter	$4	□□□
31st		Cumfa		Tonnage dues for 4th Quarter		□□□

				Dollars	150	□□□

E. E. Macao December 31st 1858.–

Gideon Nye Jnr.

Vice Consul of the United States of
America for Macao

Quarterly Return of the arrivals and departures of American Vessles at the United States Consulate of Macao from the 1st of October to the 31st of December 1858.--

Date						Vessels				Cargo			
Month	Day	Class	Name	Tonnage	Where from	When built	Where built	Where belonging	Where bound	Import	Export	Owners	Masters
1858													
October	4th	Ship	Wanderer	196	HongKong	1853	Baltimore	HongKong	HongKong	Saltpetre	Ballast	John Heard	George Hardy
	16th	Barque	Aluiatia	473	do	1857	Boston	Boston	Shanghae	Ballast	General	Th[s] M. Cutter	Albert B. Richardson
	16th	Barque	Mary F. Slade	199	do	1848	Scitirate	Boston	San Fran[co]	General	do	Osborne Howes	Hatrel F. Crowell
	16th	Barque	Marilla	699	Penang	1854	Hallowell	Bath	Singapore	Rice	do	Rich: H Mills	W B. Robinson
	16th	U.S. Ship	Germantown	–	Whampoa	–	–		–	–	–	–	Captain Rich[d] Page
	20th	Ship	Thomas W. Sears	499	Penang	1845	Medford	Boston	Amoy	Rice	Rice	Dan[l] G. Bacon	A. Drew
	21th	Ship	Ladoga	867 $\frac{60}{90}$	do	1854	Portsmouth	Boston	Singapore	do	General	W[m] Ropes	W[m] Pearce Jr
	23[d]	Ship	Mastiff	1030 $\frac{70}{95}$	Batavia	1856	Boston	New York	Amoy	Rice Ratlines &c	Rice &c	Warren Dilano Jr	W[m] O. Johnson
November	1st	Ship	Arcadia	705 $\frac{61}{95}$	HongKong	1854	do	New York	Sold here	Ballast	–	J.B. Endicott	Rossitor B. Wade
	11th	Ship	Levanter	849 $\frac{76}{95}$	do	1852	Damari scotta	New York	New York	do	Teas, Silks, &c	W. L. King & others	William Peterson
	22nd	Schr	Carbon	299 $\frac{30}{95}$	do			HongKong	HongKong	do	Ballast	Geo Tyson	Manbally Moore
Decb[r]	2nd	Ship	Kate Hooper	1488 $\frac{76}{95}$	do	1853	Baltimore	Baltimore	Whampoa	Coals	do	Ja[s] A Hooper	Edw[d]. P. Johnson
	15th	Ship	Live Yankee	1637 $\frac{63}{95}$	do	1853	Rockland	New York	Havana not yet sailed	Ballast	Chinese Coolies	Loz Nickerson & others	Eben A. Thorndike
	20th	Barque	Matilda	409 $\frac{87}{95}$	Abandoned near the Bashee Islands	1849	S[t] Louis	New York	–	Coals	–	Tunck & Meineke	Jurgen Rickmers
	21th	Barque	Rosette	596 $\frac{77}{95}$	HongKong	1856	New York	New York	New York not yet sailed	Ballast	Teas, Silks, &c	Jns: H Serekley & others	Ignatius Pierce
				8952 $\frac{30}{95}$									
	River	Steamer	Spark	2400 $\frac{30}{95}$	Canton & HongKong	100 tons	24 trips				J.B. Edicott	A. Ricaby	
	River	Steamer	Rose	814 $\frac{30}{95}$	do	74 tons	11 trips				do	G. Burmester	
	River	Steamer	Aimfâ	25 $\frac{30}{95}$	do	25 tons	1 trip				do		
				12,191 $\frac{30}{95}$									
				596 $\frac{70}{95}$									
				11,594 $\frac{55}{95}$									

E. E. Macao December 31st 1858
Gideon Nye Jnr.
Vice Consul of the United States of America for Macao

[1-071]

[Dec8 /58
1st Quart.–
Rec[d] April 26/57
Dec 8/58]

FROM THE HONGKONG GOVERNMENT GAZETTE.

GOVERNMENT NOTIFICATION.

The following notification addressed by RUTHERFORD ALCOCK, Esquire, Her Majesty's Consul at Canton, to the British Mercantile Community at that Port, respecting various matters in connection with the Chinese Custom House, is herewith published for general information.

By Order,

G. W. CAINE.

Superintendency to Trade, Victoria, Hongkong, 18th February, 1859.

NOTIFICATION.

BRITISH CONSULATE, CANTON, *February* 15th, 1859.

His Excellency the Hoppo has requested the undersigned, Her Majesty's Consul, to call the attention of the British Mercantile Community at this Port to the necessity for greater care on the part of those who transmit Foreign Goods from any other Consular Port to Canton, with an exemption Chop. Unless the Chop supply fully particulars as to the Quality, Quantity, Number of Pieces, &c., – so as to give the Custom House Officials here *satisfactory means of identifying the Packages or Goods* as those upon which Duties have actually been paid, and also specify the Sum paid, the Importers cannot be allowed the exemption sought. And as much inconvenience frequently arises from the absence of such details, it would be well if Mercantile correspondents at the other Ports, were duly warned of the necessity for greater care as to the insertion of such full particulars in every exemption Chop.

Various questions have also been the subject of discussion recently, connected with a carrying trade in Chinese produce; more especially Cotton, Peas, and Beans and the transhipment of Teas at Whampoa, from Macao or other outlying Ports, and for which exemption from duty has been erroneously claimed by the Shippers.

The undersigned is further requested, therefore, by His Excellency the Hoppo, to advice the British Mercantile Community, that no Chinese produce, brought here from any other Port or Place for consumption or sale, can by Treaty be held exempt from an Import Duty, either on the plea that it has already paid an Export Duty at the place of shipment, or that it is a class of produce exempted by the Treaty – "Import Tariff," – only applicable to Foreign Goods or produce. In the case of Teas, brought from any other Port or Place for shipment at Canton or Whampoa, the Tariff Export Duty is just leviable, unless it can be shown that such Teas have already paid at some other Consular Port the legal Export Dues according to Tariff.

The duty levied on Cotton, the produce of China, brought to the Port in Chinese Vessels, His Excellency the Hoppo states to be the same as that specified in the Treaty Tariff: namely, 4 Mace per Picul. There is no distinction made therefore to the disadvantage of Foreign Ships, since this is also the amount claimed when the same produce is brought in the latter. The duty on Peas, at present rate of exchange, is about 56 Cash per Picul in Chinese Vessels, and the same rate only is claimed when brought in Foreign Vessels.

(Signed) RUTHERFORD ALCOCK,

TO THE BRITISH MERCHANTILE COMMUNITY AT CANTON. H. B. M.'s Consul for Canton.

Extract of a letter from a distinguished Medical Missionary visiting Japan.

NANGASAKI,[1] JANUARY 26TH, 1859.

"I had the pleasure of receiving a letter from you just before I left and as your are not in habit of receiving letter from the 'Rising Sun' I embrace an occasion of sending this from Dezima, a 'Factory' pretty well known in mercantile and–alas–in other annals.

Mr. sent a steamer, built for the folks, to Nangasaki[2] to find a purchaser and kindly gave me a passage in her. To see a new country when on the eve of returning for a time to my native land is no small privilege; – and such a country! – It is truly a puzzle to the political economist as to the moralist, to the merchant and to the naturalist.

I do not know enough how or what to observe in order to satisfy the curiosity of a merchant, and can only say in general that this land seems to want little, but it has more for Exports than is supposed abroad. Considerable profits have been made of late, which has caused a sort of Japan fever at Shanghae – a glut of foreign articles and a rise in native produce are the consequences: – All this will of course settle down in time, when, the real value of the Commerce of the port can be estimated.

I am pained to report that hostility to Christianity suffers no abatement: The chief object of my visit has been to ascertain how far there was a prospect of successful missionary effort, but at present the prospect is discouraging. I made the acquaintance of some intelligent officials who speak Chinese and they gladly accepted Testaments in Chinese and English, but were soon compelled to return them at the peril of losing their heads, they said. Their eagerness to adopt foreign Arts and the like augurs well, however, and it may yet be that the gospel will accomplish ere long its peculiar changes in the land."

---

① Sic.

② Sic.

[1-072]

[vide portions marked HMS #]

THE

OVERLAND  REGISTER

AND PRICE CURRENT.

NEW SERIES. Vol. 1.–No. 3. | VICTORIA, TUESDAY, FEBRUARY 15, 1859. | PRICE–$12 *per Annum in advance.*

Shipping Reports.

The brig *Lanrick* reports the *Mathilda* Atheling to□□□Fuhchau on February 3 for Liverpool.

The American ship *Daylight*: Capt. Holbrooks reports very bad weather at sea for the last 30 days: she spoke the French ship *Lucie* on January 1st, latitude 22.54 S. longitude 171.21 E. from Melbourne bound to Hongkong. 33 days. Exchanged signals with the British ship *Dove* on the same day from Melbourne, destination not known.

The British ship *Alipore*. Capt. Murdorh, on her passage from Shanghae on the 26th and 27th, she encountered very heavy gale of wind thick weather, accompanied with high seas.

The British ship *Edwin Fox* spoke the British ship *New Era* off the Island of Borou, from London bound to Shanghae, 119 days out

---

The barque *Ellen* brings the following report, that on the 4th January at 11 A. M., a ship's whale boat came alongside with 12 men in, 5 of which requested a passage: Hongkong which was immediately granted them, the remainder returned to the Island of Wangi Wangi, they reported themselves as belonging to the British vessel *Leptuna*, which had been wrecked twenty days previous, wrong Capota reef, the vessel was seeing anything; Horsburghs calculations are most probably correct, being thirty miles East of the former ; on the 28th to 29th, wind N. to N. N. E. strong, with a heavy head sea, passed to the Westward of Strong Island, one of the Caroline Group about 20 miles distant ; on the 31st, in lat. 10.10 N., and long 105.47 E., at 5 A. M., struck against a large spar, or portion of a wreck going at the time $11\frac{1}{2}$ knots, it was observed by the look-out-man though not in time to warn us of its proximity: found it necessary to pump every two hours, the vessel having sprung a seious leak, making fifteen minutes spell in that time with both pumps working; on the 1st to 3d Feb., strong steady trade nearly all the time passed the Island of Rota, one of the Marina Group, on our port beam distant fourteen miles ;on the 4th, moderate from N. to N. N. W. found the leak to have increased considerably, making twenty six minutes spell every two hours with both pumps working ; on the 5th, wind Northerly, strong, weather fine, course W. N. W., distance 220 miles; on the 9th, strong breeze to N. E., with a very high beam sea, vessel labouring at the time course Westerly N. $\frac{1}{2}$ N., distance 236 miles, in lat. 19.20 N., and long. 128.10 E. ; on the 10th, wind light and fine variable weather ; on th 11th, blowing a fresh gale. With very thick weather, and being close up to the North Bashees without seeing them, hauled on a wind till the weather cleared : under double reefs, at 7 P. M., bore away W. by N., still a fresh gale; on the 12th, wind Northerly, moderate towards midnight; on the 13th, very strong breeze with

NOTICE OF FIRMS.

NOTICE.

THE undersigned have this day established a GENERAL AGENCY and COMMISSION BUSINESS at Canton and *Hongkong* under the Firm of,

BOURJAU, HUBENER & Co.

Mr. H. O. DE VOSS has been authorized to sign our Firm per Procuration at either place.

ADOLPH BOURJAU,

C.. A. HUBENER.

Hongkong, 1st January, 1859.

3m.–3o.

NOTICE.

MR. WALTER MOURILYAN has this day been admitted a Partner in my business, which will hereafter be carried on under the Style of ELLES & Co.

JAMIESON ELLES.

Amoy, 1st January, 1859.

10w.–2o.

NOTICE.

MR. THOMAS DAVID NEAVE, is authorized to Sign our Firm.

SMITH KENNEDY, & Co.

Hongkong, 27th December, 1858.

t.f.–o.

DEATHS.

At the General Hospital, Hongkong, on the 20th January, SAMUEL MARTIN Corporal H. M. 1st Royals. Aged 29 years.

At the General Hospital, Hongkong, on the 21st January, J. BECK of H. M. N. I. 12th Regiment.

In Hongkong Harbour, on board H. M. S. *Melville*, on the 21st January, ROBERT MOORE, Corporal H. M. S. Calcutta, aged 45 years.

At the Seamen's Hospital, Hongkong, on the 23d January, R. H. MOORE, Mariner, of the *Mary L. Sutton* aged 31 years.

At Shanghae, on the 26th January, Mr. AGOSTINHO DE MIRANDA, of Macao,

---

PASSENGERS.–Per steamer *PEKIN*, to sail to-day the 15th of February, at 2' P.M :--

For Southampton,– Mr. and Mrs. Skinner and 2 children, Dr. and Mrs. Hobson, Miss. and Manter Hobson, Capts. Barker, R.N., and Mr. E. C. Nicholls, Webb's family, 2 children, and 2 nurses, Messrs, Randall, Pearse, Fox, Meller, and Aviortei.

For *Merseilles*.– Messrs. J. Dewsnap, Charles Wegner and R. Garretta.

For *Bombay*.–Messrs. C. TurMahomed, R. Habibhoy. C. C. R. Rooke, Ensign 1st Royals, H. Parpia, V. Parpia, M. Khetsey, Jaffer Moladina, and S. Dhunjee.

on her passage from Ampanam to Amboina laden with rice, she remained three days on the reef and then slipped off into deep water and sunk immediately. The remainder of the crew are upon the above mentioned Island waiting for the first opportunity of getting a passage to Singapore.

In the 3d January, the *Ellen* spoke the British barque *Roy Wench* in Bouton passage, from Sourabaya bound to Hongkong.

The *Eagle Wing* exchanged signals with the Dutch barque *Juno* just North of Formosa, on the 1st *January*.

The *Diana* from Ningpo, reports the total loss of the Bremen barque *Von Stein* Captain Herboth, which vessel sailed from here about the middle of December and she struck on the Island of North Nanbo, in the □□□ Group on the night of the 21st January, in a thick fog; we are sorry to learn that the Captain, two officers, and one seaman, attempted to land on the island in one of the small boats with only two oars, but they were drifted away by the current and had not been heard of up to the time of the *Diana*'s departure on the 29th, □□□of the crew succeeded in landing, and were menaced□□□□ the Chinese, but fortunately they had some muskets □□□ them, which kept the Chinese in check they reached Ningpo on the 27th, and took passage in the *Diana* for Hongkong.

The Bremen barque *Von Stein*, from Whampoa, with a general Cargo, was lost on the 21st instant. She struck on a rock off North Island or Nan-ho, and went □□□ in 6 fathoms. Some of the crew arrived at Ningpo in a China boat on the 25th; the Captain and remainder in one of the ship's boats were still missing on the 26th instant. – *Postcript to the North-China Herald*, Jan. 31.

---

hard squalls. moderating toward moening, and at 9 A. M., received a Chinese Pilot on board. She reports a great rush of Gold diggers to Port Curtis from Sydney and Melbourne. She also reports that the Chilian ship *Grey Hound*, sailed from Melbourne, on the 23d December, bound for Hongkong ; and the Bremen ship *Renzard* and the American ship *SierraNevada*, were both to leave on the 1st January for this port.

The *Rajah* reports intelligence to have reached Manila, of the total wreck of the Danish ship *Adele*. She was chartered by the French to take supplies from Sual to Cochinchina, and when loaded and leaving the harbour, she struck on a sunken rock at the entrance to the port. and became a total wreck.– *Hongkong Shipping List*, Feb. 14.

Cargoes.

The ship *Beaver*, from Shanghae for New York. – Tea Green, Young Hyson 375,964 lbs., Hyson 19,781, Twankay 49,956, Gunpowder 40,906, Imperial 49,784– Tota. 536,391 lbs. Black, Souchong and Congou 25,400 lbs, Raw Silk 53.60 piculs, Cassia 500 do., Rattans 330 dol Fire Crackers 2,000 boxes.– AUGUSTINE IKRAND & Co

---

Ferdinand Nies brought, 16,000 piculs Rice.

The *Kremlin* sailed from Whampoa for New York on the 30th January. She took,–

1,742 rolls Matting.
1,262 piculs Cassia.
2,720 boxes Fire Crackers.
74 picuis Raw Silk.
3,000 pieces Crape Scarfs.
836 boxes Fans.
73 boxes Sweetmeats.
10 boxes Vermillion.

RUSSELL & Co.

The *Solent* sailed from Whampoa for London on the 3rd February. She took,–

Tea, –5,526 chests }
3,721 half-chests } 810,100lbs
8,279 boxes }

NOTICE.

MR. A. BOURJAU and Mr. C. A. HUBENER having retired from our Firm, we have authorized

Mr. A. C. LEVYSOHN to sign our Firm, and Mr. T. ARNHOLD to sign per Procuration from this date.

OXFORD, & Co. of Canton.

Hongkong, 1st January, 1859. 3m.–3o.

NOTICE.

THE Interest, and responsibility of Mr. GRAHAM ANDERSON, ceased in our Firm on *31st December*, 1858.

D. W. MACKENZIE, & Co.

Canton, 1st January, 1859. 3m–3o.

NOTICE.

THE responsibility and interest of Mr. F. REICHE in our business expired, by limitation, on the *31st December*, 1858.

RUSSELL & Co.

Hongkong, 8th January, 1859.

t. f.–o.

NOTICE.

MR. G. HITZEROTH is authorized to sign our Firm per procuration.

CARLOWITZ & Co.,

Canton, 1st January, 1859. 2.m.–1 o.

EDITORIAL NOTICE.

Mr. ROBERT STRACHAN having disposed of his Interest and Property in the *Hongkong Register*, and the Printing business thereto attached: It is requested that all accounts due up to the 31st ultimo be paid to the said Mr. Robert Strachan. The Subscriptions for the ensuing year, and all papers and communications for the *Register*, *Overland Register* and *Daily* Register, and all orders for printing &c., will be received

For *Malta*.– Mr. Sherman.

For *Cadiz*.– Messrs. S. G. Salas, and F. Sta Maria.

For *Singapore*.– Mr. F. J. Secretary.

Overland Summary.

(Communicated.)

NORTH-CHINA, Jan. 22d 1859.

RAGS AND ROTTENNESS! T'is even so; and no two words could better describe the actual state of China, *Politically* considered. *Rags* and *rottenness*! If reports be true, even the emperors own household is ragged and rotten; and go where you may, amongst officials, *rags* and *rottenness* will meet you on all sides.

There is something rotten in the state of Denmark. Well it will be if there can be found anything that is sane and sound– anything that is not either ragged or rotten, or both.

At Tientsin every possible effort is making, and will be made, to keep out the *Barbarians*; and if the new Ambassador, the Hon. Mr. Bruce, reaches the Chinese capital without breaking the new Treaty, he will be a fortunate man. Time will show; at this moment, however, the disposition of the Emperor's Cabinet towards the "rebellious English" it anything but friendly– It is hard to say whether hatred or fear will carry the day. *Friendship*, between the two, there is not.

The Emperor's Commissioners, now quartered in Shanghai, have positive orders from their master, so report says, not to return to the capital until the existing troubles are at an end! It is their business, and not his, and they must finish it, or abide the consequences. Canton must be replaced, and the barbarians driven out; and if money is to be paid, it must not come from the Emperor's chest; &c., &c. When all these things are "makee finish," then Kweiliang and Hwashan□ may return to Peking.

By H. I. M. S. *Prégent*, we learn that the French fleet were to leave Touron on the 3rd February for □one, with the intention, it is stated to commence operations in that Port.

The American ship *Dirigo*, Captain Atwood, reports that in her passage from Shanghae she experienced a very heavy gale of wind from the N.E., whith thick foggy weather accompanied with a high sea which compelled her to heave too for some time.

The U. S. frigate *Mississippi* is to fit out in Hongkong previous to her departure for Washington via Japan : she takes the Japanese Ambassador and suite to that city.

The U. S. frigate *Germantown* is to take the *Mississippi*'s station.

The Str. *Yengtsze* reports the Str. *Formosa* off the Island of Gutzlaff on Sunday morning last.

The *Aden* was to leave Shanghae on the morning of the 7th.

The barque *Arthur* spoke the U. S. frigate *Niayara*, on the 10th October, in lat. 34.47 N., and long. 41.34 W.

The *Rayah* reports the *Mooresfort* to leave Manila on the 12th for London, also the *Lancushire Witch* on the 15th.

The *Star of the East* spoke the American ship *Mameluke*, on January 27, off the Island Ombay, from Cardiff bound to Hongkong, 95 days out.

A Detachment of the Royal Artillery has arrived here, by *the Star of the East*.

REPORT OF THE SHIP "HIMALAYA."

CAPTAIN BENDIXON, FROM

MELBOURNE TO HONGKONG.

On the 31st December 1858, at 1 P.M., left Hobsons Bay, and at 6 P.M., passed through the Heads, discharged the Pilot

Silk, 44 cases.

Matting, 1,100 rolls.

Canes, 16,000.

Sundries, 216 packages.

FLETCHER & Co.

The *Portena*, from Shanghae for London.– Tea, Black 149,653 lb., Green 197,551 – Total 347, 204lb. Silk, Raw 429 bales. Thrown 33– Total 462 bales. Waste Silk 4 bales, Silk Piece Goods 5 caxes.

BOWER, HANBURY & Co.

The steamer *Aden* brought,– Silk 873 bales, Sundries 143 cases, Tea 625 chests, Specie 10, Jewellery 1. Value of Specie for Hongkong $4,120, for Bombay $33,980– Total $38,100.

Per *Star of the East*, Government Stores, General and Sundries.

The *Samuel Russell*, sailed from Fuhchau for New York, on January 28, took– Congou and Sou–chong, 171,900 lb; Oolongs, 439,300 lb– Total, 611,209 lb.

The *Sorata*, sailed from Fuhchau for London, on January 31, took– 404,200 lb.

The *Earl of Mar & Kellie*, sailed from Fuhchau for the Colonies, on January 31, took– 495,200lb Tea.

The *Judge* Shaw, sailed from Amoy for New York, on February 5, took– Ning Yongs, 166,720 lb; Ankois, 258,230; Orange Pekoes, 66,420; Congous, 94,000– Total; 585,370 lb.

The *Mathilda Atheling*, sailed from Fuhchau to Cowes for Orders, took– 892,000 lb Tea.

The *A. Cross* brought 2,930 bags of Sugar.

The *Melita* brought 797 chests Tea.

only by the present Editor, Mr. LONG PHILLIPS.

The Printing business and office, have been removed to the Premises in Pottinger and Stanley Streets, lately occucpied by Messrs Angier & Co.

The Overland Register.

HONGKONG, TUESDAY, 15TH FEBRUARY, 1859.

BIRTH.

At the Oriental Bank, Hongkong, on the 9th instant Mrs Patrick Campbell of a Son.

MARRIAGES.

At St. John's Cathedral, on the 12th Feb., by the Rev. J. J. Irwin assisted by the Rev. W. R. Beach, Mr. JAMES BELL Surgeon (Amoy) to HENRIETTA MARY TURTON, only daughter of William Turton Esq., Solicitor, Stoke, Staffordshire.

At Macao, on the 2d February, Mr JOAQUIM P. DE CAMOES, to JOZEFA DA SILVA.

On the 5th February, at the Cathedral Church of Sé Macao, by the Rev. Anacelto da Silva, His Excellency. AUGUSTO R. CARVALHO, Chief Justice of Macao, to Carolina, relict of the late Mr. Monoel V. Marques.

Reports like this must have some foundation. There are other bitter ingredients in the cup of these high Comissioners. *Ten thousand coolies* are to be exported, and carried off to the French dominions; and to this traffic the Commissioners must give their consent. This is probably true; in fact, it comes through a channel that can hardly fail to be trustworthy. (?) From what ports these 10,000 coolies are to be taken, does not appear.

It is further reported, that the native carriers of "foreign physic" are determined not to give up their rightful calling. They have as good a right to it as the mandarins; and having the night they will keep the right and let the mandarins go begging.

The long–haried rebels, too, show no symptoms of decay. Thus on all sides the Imperial government is hard pressed.

X.

OUR readers are by this time aware that the "Bowring Praya" question has been disposed of by the Legislative Council. We suppose it must be considered to be finally disposed of. When a decided majority, including all the non–official members of the Council record in such an unmistakeable manner, their opinion of the inutility and needlessness of such an expenditure, it must be taken for granted that the colony wants it not. Such being the case no private feeling can be allowed to interfere with public opinion.

We are well content to take the judgement of the Public as conclusive on this matter, which we suppose is laid at rest, we will chant no re–

and stood to the Southward with a light breeze the Eastward; on the 9th January 1859. at Noon passed Norfolk Island, distant three leagues; the last seven days, alternate light winds and squalls, with a heavy swell from the N. E ; on the 13th, passed about 25 miles to the Eastward of Esonan, one of the South Hebrides Group ; on the 13th to 26th. light variable airs and calms, with sultry oppressive atmosphere, averaging about sixty miles a day ; on the 27th, wind N. E. strong and clear at 9 P. M., passed over the position of Pleasant Island assigned by Lieutenant Rapers Tables, without			

14 **The Overland Register and Price Current.**

quiem over the remains of the "Praya." neither will we raise our voice in a triumphat pæan. The community has righted itself and can afford to be generous.

We have received a communication on the subject which we publish below. It comes from a quarter of deserved influence and respect and therefore we willingly give it admission; but we must not be understood to subscribe to all the sentiments and assertions therein contained.

The discussion of Friday on the Bowring Praya must have put an end to all Sir John's hopes as to leaving behind him here a name cut in stone. His great aim in life out here, his thought in all his outgoings and incomings, in his downsittings, and in his uprising, the manner in which he thought to make his name immortal, all have been utterly overthrown in a single day, and he has found his cherished hopes dissipated by the vigorous good sense of the majority of the council.

All of the speakers for the amendment based their arguments on one ground, the want of funds, but Sir successor. At the same time we hear that it is doubtful whether France will send an Ambassador to Pekin, or whether French policy will continue to be represented by a minister plenipotentiary.

The question of the sites at Canton has already been virtually decided, as Messrs. Russell & Co. have resolved on building on the old site, not only a house for themselves, but also several houses on speculation. Two of the great European firms also are said to have the intention of acting on the same policy. The provisions of the old treaties then will be called into force to establish the rights of new settlers.

The claims of Honam to become the site of the new settlement have been easily disposed of by its insalubrity. A creek runs close to the residences of the merchants, which, by encroachment, has assumed the character of a chaked sewer. So much fever has resulted therefrom that it is considered not only dangerous to remain in its neighbourhood, but even to remove the filth now there, lest malaria, now dormant, should

rockets had the usual effect on the Chinese, who took to their heels in the most approved of style, the olders then came forward offering a ransom and brought the affairs to a conclusion. Everything have been arranged, H. M. steamers returned to Hongkong. The machinery of the *Five Brothers* can be got away, it is stated by means of divers. The wreck has been purchased by Mr. Lapraik for $ 25.

WE extract from the *Government Gazette* the following report of the proceedings of the vessels sent to Kupchi in consequence of the piratical attack on the wreck of the *Five Brothers*.

HER MAJESTY'S SHIP *Niger*,
HONGKONG, 5th *February*, 1859.

SIR, In compliance with your Excellency's instructions, I left this harbour at 2 P. M. on Monday last, the 31st ultimo. with the Steam Gun-vessel *Nimrod*, and Gun-boat *Plover*,– taking the latter in tow in the LyemoonPass, and proceeded to Cupchi, where I arrived at 4 P. M. on Tuesday.

2. I found the remains of the *Five Brothers* in the spot indicated by the Master of that Ship, a very small portion of the fore part of the vessel and her Funnel only shewing above water,– the hull having parted two,

As Mr. Anglo Barradas, a Portuguese Clerk is the employ of Messrs. Lindsay & Co., was sitting down to his dinner on Saturday evening last he was suddenly attacked by his servant, receiving a severe wound, inflicted by a knife, no doubt intended for a fatal one. Fortunately it did not prove so. Mr. Barradas got up, and after □□□severe struggle, received several wounds. He struck the servant a blow in which stunned him, the Police then interfered and secured the cowardly wretch.

WE regret to hear that the difficulties connected with the American Consulate are not yet at □ □□ end; O. E. Roberts, Esq., the late Vice Consul having been arrested here yesterday at the □□□ of General Keenan. We do not care to go into the causes that have been assigned for this act □□ we fear however, that the legal disputes consequent upon this arrest are by no means over.

BY our last advices from Canton we learn that the expedition to Fayuen had not returned. Another of much greater importance is to start with Lord Elgin

John utterly scorned such low and grovelling ideas. The want of a proper jail and of water works are things beneath his notice: if the people want them, "they must pay for them," while the whole surplus funds of the Colony are to go to erect a Praya, which however ornamental, has been shewn neither to be useful nor necessary. The argument of the Colonial Treasurer, as to the Praya being necessary for the construction of landing places, fails to the ground when confronted with Mr. Dent's statement regarding the wharves. That gentleman in his protest shews that in the entire European Frontage of Central Victoria, there is one landing place to every 50 yards, and that with new piers thrown out from the Government and Bazaar wharves, nothing more is required: and yet the Colonial Treasurer advocates the throwing away of an untold sum of money, because forsooth, he the Canton chaplain actually did fall into the sea. The cause of this was however amply explained by the Chief Magistrate.

The cost of making a few new piers, and of repairing and altering Pedders wharf, would be a mere bagatelle and would never be objected to by the most economical of the council.

The Governor in his concluding remarks maintained "that the Sanction of the Home Government had been given to the construction of the Praya on condition of there being funds in hand beyond what were *then* the requirements of the colony," but this is not the question. The *persent* and *probable* requirements of the Colony must be considered, and to begin to build the Praya with the small balance of Colonial funds, a balance be it remembered which is likely to be and which ought to be directed to the pressing wants of the Colony, would be more than unwise, be called into a more active state of existence. An application addressed to H. B. M. Consul on the subject has met with the following answer.

CANTON, February 7th, 1859.

GENTLEMEN,–On my return from Hongkong your letter of the 22nd January respecting the state of the creek called Ee–Too–Keeoo was brought under my notice, and I hasten to inform you in reply that, quite agreeing with you as to the filthy and insalubrious state of this canal, and the expediency, if it be in any way practicable, of applying a remedy before the summer heats set in, I will lose no time in communicating with the authorities on the subject, and consulting with them as to the best mode of meeting the evil. At the same time I fear much difficulty will be experienced from the nature of the nuisance and the local interests, If it be proposed to clear it out and turn the tidal waters through it, the first step necessary would be the removal of a mass of tenements built into the bed of the canal. Delays, difficulties and considerable expense are all involved in any effort of this kind. If on the other hand it should be proposed to fill it up and make a covered drain, we shall again be met by local habits and a large item of expense. I will however see the authorities and ascertain how far they are disposed to take active steps in the matter as a first step towards the end we have in view, and again communicate with you,–I have the honor to be Gentlemen your obedient servant,

(Signed) RUTHER FORD ALCOCK.

To Messrs. H. D. MARGKSSON,

A. FINCHAN,

And others.

Although the ultimate importance and being almost broken up owing to the heavy swell setting through the narrow pass.

3. I immediately directed Commander Mends to search the vicinity with an armed party, in case any of the plunder from the wreck should be in the neighbourhood; but everything taken from it had been removed into the interior, while his proceedings were watched from the heights above by a great number of Chinese, who kept aloof, and it was impossible to communicate with them before dark.

4. The following morning, after an unsuccessful attempt to get the *Plover* over the Bar, I proceeded up to the town of Cupchi with the armed Boats, and demanded an interview with the Authorities. A Military Mandarin was immediately sent to me, and on stating the object of my visit, he replied that the Authorities had already been made acquainted with the outrage committed upon the Passengers and Crew of the *Five Brothers*. and had sent a report to the Prefect of Lokfun;– that measures were bring taken to discover the perpetrators of it, but that some of the Villages were wholly beyond the control of the Mandarins, and requested I would punish them in any way I thought proper, as a warning to deter others from committing a similar offence,– the South western suburb of Cupchi itself being especially pointed out as requiring to be made an example of, being the resort of men half fishermen and half pirates.

5. Accordingly, on Thursday I landed all the Smallarm Men and Marines, with a 12–pounder Rocket Battery, marched to the Villages nearest the scene of the wreck, and demanded an indemnity from the Elders for the loss of life and property that had taken place, threatening them with the detruction of their Villages if my demand was not complied with. A similar demand was next made on the Elders of the S. W. suburb of Cupchi, but as no notice was taken of my message, I directed a few Rockets to be thrown into the place, and in person in the course of the week for the purpose of exploring the Pearl River. It is supposed that it will be absent for nearly 3 weeks Baron Gros accompanied his Lordship.

A note from Amoy, under date the 10th inst□□□–Since I wrote you last nothing of moment has occurred, excepting the following daring exploit of some Pirates. Shortly after midnight of Sunday last Feb 6,) a long piratical boat containing 70 men, entered in harbour of Amoy, and boarding a junk lying in the midist of many others off the Cornwallis Rock, killed seven men, and made off with her cargo, some of □□□being Opium. The crews of the neighbouring junk finding no measures were taken by the mandarins for the capture of the Pirates, attacked a small custom house in the vicinity, killed the watchmen, and plundered the building of the goods stored there.–*Hongkong Shipping List, Feb.* 14.

THE last mail has brought some news with regard to the Diplomatic appointments in China. The following may we believe be regarded as an accurate list of the nominations as far as it goes.

Hon. F. Bruce– Ambassador Extraordinary and Plenipotentiary.

Mr. Horace Rumbold– Secretary of Legation.

Mr. Wade– Chinese Secretary.

Mr. W. de Norman– 1st paid Attaché.

Mr. H. St. Clair }
Mr. G. Wyndham } Attachés.

Admiral Martin to the command of the China Squadron.

Mr. Green confirmed as Acting Attorney General for Hongkong.

Dr. John Ivor Murray, Colonial Surgeon.

Dr. Milne, Interpreter.

it would be arrant folly.

The question however has been settled. No arguments that Sir John's supporters can now bring forward no home influence which can be brought to bear on the question, can do away with the decision of the majority of the Council, resulting as it did from that appreciation of right and wrong, which always distinguishes sensible men, still less can any influence do away with the effect of Mr. Dent's excellent protest.

So His Excellency must rest content. We did not want the Praya and we are not to have it. His memory will remain out here in something quite as enduring as stone, and the Colonial funds will doubtless be appropristed to the proper use. The Praya "article" has been sent in to the Hongkong Magazine, but the conductors of that periodical finding it too heavy, and ill got up, respectfully decline it without the thanks.

SPECTATOR.

THE poet philosopher of ancient Rome remarks that it is excessively jolly during a storm to sit cozily at home and look at a ship-wreck from your diningroom windows. He observes that the pleasure consist not in seeing that others have got into a mess, but rather in noticing what a pickle you might have got into if you had been in their place, only you did not happen to be so. So we, cultivating the barbaric element for a few days, afer the fashion of our contemporary of the *Mail*, look back upon the stream of life that has been whirling past us, and thank our blessed stars that we have been away, and can look on the events of the last fortnight with the eyes of a comparative stranger. The question of the Bowring Praya has arisen, been discussed, and consigned to the tomb of the Capulets during our of the case may be diminished by the fact that the settlement will ultimately be on the old site, yet, as Honam must for some months, or even for two years, continue to be the residence of foreign merchants, it is most important that some attention should be paid to its sanitary condition.

We learn that an expedition of about 2,000 men with provisions for 7 days, was to start on Tuesday last. Not only was Fayuen, the head quarters of the Shun-kum, to be visited, but it waas rumored that the troops would attempt to push far into the interior by means of a creek which has not yet been explored by Europeans.

Local News.

THE steamer *Five Brothers* has been completely wrecked off Cupchi Point. The vessel ran ashore soon after mid-day, and was immediately surrounded by pirate boats who killed a considerable number of the Chinese passengers who were on board. The *Zephyr* fortunately was passing and sent in her boats to her assistance and fortunately succeeded in saving the crew, (with the exception of two Lascars, who were killed by gunshot wounds) and a portion of the Opium and Treasure.

THE following extract from her log gives a full account of the disaster.

1 P.M. strong N.E. winds and fair weather,- steering towards Cupchi passage under the Captain, when having entered the passage, steaming at the rate of $5\frac{1}{2}$ knots per hour on as Easterly course and the Soundings $5\frac{1}{2}$ and 6 fathoms, the vessel suddenly struck on a rock in the Cupchi passage- not laid down in the admiralty chart the Fishing Boats off it to be set on fire. Some resistance was offered, but these measures had the desired effect. and they came off to sue for money.

6. The result was that, after due deliberation, I accepted the sum of 2,500 Dollars from the Elders of the Suburb and Villages, which I considered sufficient indemnity under the circumstances of the case.- the statement of the Master of the *Five Brothers* having been found from reliable and corroborative evidence, to be much exaggerated, and considering also that the suburb of Cupchi, and one of the Villages, which opened a fire on our force with Matchlocks, had suffered severely from the Rockets, which were directed with great precision by Lieutenant Blake, First of this Ship.

7. During these operations. Mr. Veitch. the Master of the Niger, made a survey of the pass where the Wreck took place, a copy of which is enclosed It is impossible to took at it, without being satisfied that to attempt the passage was in the highest degree imprudent.

8. I cannot conclude without expressing my thanks to Commander Mends and Lieutenant Rason, for the manner in which they carried out my orders. We had no casualties. but I fear that the Chinese had several; and as this expedition was carried out on their New Year's day, a strong impression will have doubtless been made upon a people so superstitious, which, if it tends to cause shipwrecked mariners to receive better treatment for the future in this locality, will not have been thrown away.

9. Mr. Caldwell, whose services have been invaluable, having completed his arrangements with the Elders for the payment of the indemnity, I left Cupchi at 2.30 yesterday afternoon. and have the honour to report my arrival here with H. M. S. *Nimrod* and *Plover* at 11 o' clock A.M. this day.- I have the honour to be, &c., &c.

P. CRACROFT,

Captain.

Mr. Alcock, Consul General in Japan.

Mr. G. S. Morrison, Consul at Nagasaki

Mr. Parkes, Consul at Shanghae.

Mr. Robertson, Consul at Canton.

Mr. Gingell, Consul at Amoy.

Mr. M. C. Morrison, Consul at Fuhchau.

Mr. Medhurst, Consul at Tangchow.

Mr. Meadows, Consul at Nieuchwang.

Mr. Sinclair, Consul at Chin-keang-foo.

Mr. Harvey, Consul at Ningpo.

Mr. G. W. Caine, Consul at Swatow.

Mr. Markham, Vice-Consul at Shanghae.

Canton.

CANTON, 4th February, 1859.

On Monday last, an expedition started for Tylek, one of the largest of the 96 villages. The troops returned the same evening having met with no opposition. Only one gun was seen. There is no doubt that the villagers had carefully concealed all military preparations.

There has been considerable business done □□□ Tea within the last week, the market having been cleared of Congou with the exception of one chop which is held for an advance of 3 Taels. Two other chops are reported as arriving, but these can hardly as yet be considered to be in the market.

The issuing of passports for Fatshan, which one of our cotemporaries stated had been definitely arranged for turns out to have been a mere suggestion, none of the Commissioners having heard anything about it. However, a formal application having been addressed to them yesterday on the subject, it is more than probable that the ice will be broken and that by Monday or Tuesday, we shall be able to absence. It was an utimely death it is true regretted however by none; had we been called upon to sit on an inquest on the remains, our verdict must have been Felo de se. We believe that the cause of the Praya was lost by mismanagement alone. At the West of the town it was wanted; it was even wished for by the inhabitants. Why was it not commenced there? Had this been done, success would have been easy. Each fox that had lost its tail would have joined in the attempt to induce others to submit to the same deprivation till at last when the work had reached Pedders Wharf, Messrs. Dent and the Lindsay would have stood alone in their resistance, with the public against them. As it was, the public was on their side: they saw that the portion of the Praya to be commenced with would be a public ornament but a private nuisance, and they rejected it.

But through it was rejected we do not see that there was cause for triumph and rejoicing over him who was defeated. It was open to any one to object to the information of the Praya, but hate must have sunk low indeed when age and infirmity are deemed fit subjects of ridicule. It was indeed worthy of him who could make family bereavement a matter of ridicule, to abuse private friendship in publishing and circulating a caricature thrown off in jest, and never intended but for his own eye.

With regard to the German mission the case has been almost the same. The Government of Hongkong has bought the house occupied by that body, therefore a fraud must have been practised. The whole affair passed through the hands of the Gentleman who holds the office of Prussian Consul at Canton. Will the Prussian Consul endorse a single statement of

(Lollensons Sunny) – ordered the Engines to be reversed instantly, but before the order was executed the Engine Room was full of water extinguishing the fire immediately. The fore compartment also filled with water damaging the whole of the cargo,– got out the boats and put the ladies, children passengers and mails on them and went to the *Zephyr*, also landed a great many of the Chinese passengers on the main land at their own request, a number of them going in a China boat which came alongside.– At this time we observed the Chinese boats gathering in great numbers at the back of the rocks when suddenly they made a dash out and pulled right towards the vessel, evidently with the intention of boarding,–fired several shots in the direction of the boats of which they took no notice. About this time the Chinese on the rock had mounted guns wherewith which they kept up a constant fire, the shot falling close around us. The vessel at this time was listing over so much that our guns fore and aft were becoming useless, by firing heavy charges of grape &c., &c., we kept them off for a time but were at least compelled to have all hands at the guns and small arms.– Got the treasure (2 boxes) into one of the life boats also 3 chests of opium and sent them to the *Zephyr*. which was at anchor $1\frac{1}{2}$ miles distant. By dark the fore hold was full of water also the Engine Room, and the ship breaking up, we resolved to abandon her as we considered it impossible to hold the ship during the night from the attack of the Chinese who had gathered round us in great number also rising up from the rocks, where they had a large gun mounted. At 7

His Excellency Rearr Admiral
SIR MICHAEL SEYMOUR, K.C.B.,
Commander.in.Chief.

THE British Barque *Courser*, Captain Cowie, the property, we believe, of Mr. Rogers of Bombay, has been particularly unfortunate. At Fuh–chow–fu, a short time ago, she got into the hands of salvors, and had to sustain an action in the Admiralty Court here entailing considerable expense. Leaving this, on a voyage to Australia, she struck on a rock in Gaspar Straits two days before Christmas, had to throw all the Cargo overboard and cut her masts away. With a broken back, she is now in Batavia; and as the crew have been paid off, she has been abandoned we suppose to the underwriters. – *Friend of China*, Feb. 2.

WE hear that Dr. John Ivor Murray has been appointed Colonial Surgeon, and may be expected out shortly. Dr. Murray was an old resident in Shanghai for many years, and was much esteemed by the community. We trust the report is true.

A CIVIL HOSPITAL.

The community will rejoice to hear that we are at length to have suitable accommodation for the unfortunate strangers, who may from time to time be taken sick. The New Treaty having provided for the opening of a cemetery on the main land, the German Missionaries will reside there. The large mission house at West point; is in the consequence to be sold, and the Government have availed themselves of the opportunity to secure it for a civil hospital. The situation is one of the best in Hongkong, it is on high ground in a healthy locality and has an abundant supply of that most, valuable of all medicines, good fresh air.

---

report the first legalized expedition into the interior under the new system.

The promenades militaries which have been resolved upon are for the moment suspended owing to an unwillingness to interfere with the Chinese celebration of their New Year. It is however reported that Fa–yuen will be visited shortly.

CANTON, 5th February, 1859.

When we last wrote we stated that, acting on the intimation given in the *China Mail*, we had made application for passports to Fatshan. In reply the Allied Commissioners informed us that they were not aware of any arrangements having been made for granting such documents, and suggested that, as their only knowledge on the point was derived from the same source as our own, a formal application should be sent into them, which should be laid before the Commander–in–chief without loss of time. This was accordingly done, and as it was impossible that a reply should be received before the next evening we determined on spending the following day in a visit to Shek–tseng, to see and endeavour to understand the ground of that terrible action, in which the principal disasters, of whose occurrence we have heard were, that the commanders lost their temper. our allies feared they had lost their the *Daily Press* with regard to the sale of this building? And yet he surely is a disinterested witness. Let Mr. Murrow dare to publish his account of this affair, and he will publish the best answer to his own aspersions on the Government.

The political changes that have occurred here are also important. The departure of H. E. Sir Michael Seymour seems to have been definitively announced, and Admiral Martin named as his

P.M. let the vessel and proceeded on board the *Zephyr*.– Our cutter being a little distance from the other boats was attacked by the Chinese, plundered of every thing, 2 men being spared, the rest wounded and driven overboard.– At 8, reached the *Zephyr*, secured the boat, and at 11.30 weighed and made sail for Hongkong.

THE Cupchi expedition returned on the 4th Feb., having set fire to the above village, and surveyed the place where the wreck of the *Five Brothers* occurred.

A slight resistance was offered, but a few

The Overland Register and Price Current.

reputation, and our fat, but unhappy contemporary □□□the privilege of visiting the lines.*

Of course till the boat was fairly hired Fuh-kee□□ught the expedition not only practicable but easy, which it currently was. Very valorous were the boatmen as we passed up the river until we came to the first village beyond the barrier passed over by our Gunboats. We were then □□armed "truly my thinkee no can walkee, too muchee mandarin soldier inside that village," but □□□ suggestion of no Shek-tsing, no dollar revived □□□ fainting hearts. After about four hours □□wing and punting, we came to the village of □□a-tow, on passing which we found a stockade nearly a hundred yards in depth extending across the whole stream, with a very intricate open channel between the stakes, barely wide enough for the passage of a small flower boat. At this point the river took a sharp bend, and on a low hill immediately opposite to and perhaps half a mile distant from the further

Commissioners about the passports for Fatshan waiting for us. Here it is.

GENTLEMEN,– Having brought your application of yesterday's date to the notice of the Commanders-in-Chief, we are instructed to inform you that the arrangements made by their Excellencies for future visits to Fatshan, are applicable only to officers or other persons under their own military jurisdiction, and not to civilians non-resident within the limits under martial law. who should therefore refer for information on this subject to their respective Consuls.

We are, gentlemen &c.

To the Vice-Consul then, in the absence of Mr. Alcock, we addressed ourselves, but with no better result than before. He too was unaware of any disposition on the part of Peh-kwei to grant passports. We could get no assistance from Governments, or Consuls.

But we were not to be done so readily. After all the luxuries of passports, chops, and attendant pig-tails could be dispensed with, and as we had no great or pressing fears of diplomatic etiquette or violated treaties before our

tained by the secretary, who thanked them for their visit and expressed his regret at their retiring so early, as he could not justify himself to the prince for having allowed them to depart without making them all intoxicated.

The monthly meeting of the North China Branch of the Royal Asiatic Soecity was held at the Library on Tuesday evening the 18th instant.

The papers read were "Notes on the present state of some of the Magnetic elements in China and places adjacent" by Capt. Shadwell, R.N., C.S., and "A Journal from Shanghai to Han-kow and back," by a gentleman who accompanied the expedition.

The first paper was read by its author. After some brief observations on Terrestrial Magnetism generally, in which a cursory survey was taken of the objects of Magnetic research, and a popular description given of the instruments employed and the course of observation recently followed in the Magnetic Observatories, established a few years since for the purpose of investigating the phenomena of magnetism; the writer passed on to the record of the present state of

Art. 11. Supplies for the British navy may landed and stored at Kanagawa, Hakodadi, and Nagasaki, free from duty; but if any are sold the purchaser must pay the proper duty.

Art. 12. If any British vessel be wrecked on the coast of Japan the Japanese authorities shall render assistance to vessel and crew, and send the latter, if necessary, to the nearest consular station.

Art. 13. British merchant vessels may employ a pilot to take them in or out of port.

Art. 14. At each of the open ports British subjects may import and export, directly or indirectly, any lawful merchandise, paying the duties prescribed by the treaty. With the exception of munitions of war, which shall be sold to the Japanese government alone, they may freely buy from, and sell to, Japanese may buy and use the same.

Art. 15. Mode of determining the value of goods imported.

Art. 16. All goods imported into Japan by British subjects, which have paid the import duty, may be transported by the Japanese to any of the empire without any further duty.

Art. 17. British merchants who have imported merchandise, and paid the duty, end of the stockade were the traces of a double line of ruined earthworks, overlooked from a considerable distance □□□ a small fort on the summit of a hill in the rear of the position. Here then it was evident that the crews of the Gunboats had landed, and had the forts been held by Eurpoean troops, our troops, would indeed have had troublesome work before them. At Cha-tow the ground is nearly flat and □oo ded, whilst a narrow causeway runs between the village and the water; whilst as soon as near buildings are passed the ground sinks and □□nes a morass which extends to the foot of the fortified hill of which we have spoken, □□d runs for some little distance into the interior. The causeway skirts this marsh and□□ses it in a winding course towards its upper end being all the time under the fire of the guns. Here, if any where, the charge of the French des □□ed by our contemporary must have taken fire, not made by the troops under the command M. d'Aboville, who never were in this port of the field, but by two boats' crews who accompanied the gunboats, and who we are informed □□□ no casualties reported, and could not threrfore been guilty of leaving their wounded to be rescued by others. This fort however having been taken and destroyed, it was an easy matter □□□ keep to the level ground behind the low range □□□ hills which here skirts the river, and, after a couple of miles march, appear immediately above and behind Shek-tseng.

Proceeding onwards, another half hour or rather more brought us to this last named village which embosomed eyes, we sallied forth to put to the test the firm conviction we had formed, that patience, determination and a moderate share of good humour would enable foreigners to go to Fatshan or anywhere else without molestation. And so it proved. It is true that when we reached that city there was considerable unwillingness on the part of our servants to accompany us, and interpret our wishes. It is true that a crowd collected, but as the observations of Fanquei, Tuh-ne-ama, and other such polite requests moved us but little, we were enabled to walk through the greater part of Fatshan without any further inconvenience that the admiring shouts of small boys, who perhaps, had the circumstances been reversed, had the city been placed in *more civilized* lands, would have been influenced by the humane sentiment indicated by Punch in his sketch of the miners: "Twig that stranger Bill. Heave half a brick at him."

Of Fatshan itself we have little to say. It was New Years' time and the shops were mostly closed; several even of those that were open were closed at our approach, from fear of the mob that collected. The suburb was filthy, but not more so than that of Canton, and in the interior of the place the streets were wide and the pavement infinitely better than any which we have seen in the city of Runs. The most remarkable thing which we saw there was the long creek running between the town and one of its suburbs, through which we went for nearly two miles, along a regular street of Mandarin boats and flower boats five or six deep on one side, and two or three deep on the other; the only breaks being at those places where a ferry was kept open.

We only hope that foreigners will follow up the example of visiting these

the magnetic elements in this part of the world as deduced from his own observations.

Several interesting facts were stated, of which we call a few.

At Anjer the present value of the variation of the Magnetic Needle is 1.53 E.; while the Dip or Inclination is 27.15 S.

At Singapore the Variation is 2.8 E. and the dip 13.21 S.

At Hongkong the Variation is 0.14 E. and the Dip 31.26 N.

At Shanghai the Variation is 2.30 W, and the Dip 45.19 N.

The Line of no dip or the Magnetic Equator would seem to intersect the coast line of China in about $8\frac{1}{2}$ degrees North Latitude at the South extremity of Cochin China.

The Line of no Variation appears to intersect the coast of China a little to the Eastward of Hongkong.

By a comparison of Capt. Shadwell's observations in 1857-58 with those made by the late Sir Everard Home, then commanding her H. M. S. *North Star* in 1842-43, it would appear that at Singapore the South dip of the needle has increased 37 minutes in 15 years.

At Hongkong the North dip has increased about 40 minutes in the same time, while at Shanghae and Woosung the increase amounts to half a degree.

At Woosung lying 10 miles nearly due North of Shanghae. The dip is 45.2 N. being 17 minutes less than at Shanghae, an anomaly probably caused by some local disturbance or irregularity.

An irregularity of a similar kind is shewn by a comparison of the observations at Ningpo and Kintang.

The Secretary then read one half of "A Journal from Shanghae to Hankow and back," - the time not admitting of the whole being read on this occasion.

The journal is written in an amusing and spirited style commencing with the first start of the *Dove* on Nov. 6th, and carrying us

shall be entitled to a certificate of the payment, and may then re-export it, and land it in any other port without any additional duty.

Art. 18. The Japanese authorities at each port shall adopt proper means to prevent smuggling.

Art. 19. All penalties and confiscations made under the treaty shall belong to the Tycoon of Japan.

Art. 20. The articles for regulation of trade appended to the treaty are to be considered as part of it, and equally binding.

The British diplomatic agent, in conjunction with the Japanese government, may make such rules as may be necessary for carrying out both treaty and articles.

Art. 21. The treaty being signed in English, Japanese, and Dutch, the Dutch text shall be considered the original. All official communications from British diplomatic and consular agents to be written in English, but for a period of five years to be accompanied by a Dutch or Japanese translation.

Art. 22. Either party may demand a revision of the treaty on or after July 1, 1872.

Art. 23. The British government and British subjects shall be entitled to equal participation in all advantages granted, in Japan to the government and subjects of any other nation.

Art. 24. Ratifications to be exchanged within a year.

REGULATIONS FOR BRITISH TRADE.

Regulation 1.

The Captian of a vessel is to exhibit to the Japanese authorities, within 48 hours of his arrivial (Sunday excepted), proof that he has deposited his ship's papers at the British consulate, and shall then make entry of his ship in writing and deposit a written manifest of his cargo, stating who are the consignees, and adding a list of his stores.

Any error may be corrected within 24 hours without fee; afterwards 15 dols. must be in trees, through which it presents a long front of houses to the river, backed by □□ooded knolls. Almost at the very extremity of the village is the bridge, rising with three different levels, open at the sides but protected or rather closed at either end by a simple gate-house. Here then was the Chinese position. In front, □□□ towards the North side of the city a wide expanse of dry paddy-held crossed by a causeway, and interspersed with tufts of trees, and one or two villages, stretches nearly to the walls of Canton. Immediately around the gate house □□□the remains of a small semicircular earthwork apparently not more than three or four □□□ in height, unprotected by any ditch in front. and open to the bridge in the rear. □□□ the further, （*i. e.* the Chinese） side of the rear were to other earth works, not crossing □□□ fires but commanding the two sides of the earth works and these again had houses in their □□□ of which about half a dozen on the Chinese □□□ seem to have been destroyed. We can perceive that this would have been a most formidable position to attack *in front* if held by European troops, but even then its left flank was utterly uncovered, and the extreme right could be, in actually was turned by the force under Captain M. Cleverty, thus exposing the Chinese rear and rendering their position actually untenable. In fact no serious fighting seems ever to have taken place in this quarter. The Chinese retired before our men were within 400 or 500 yards of them, and the French forces who had been left as a reserve to guard the ambulances and the rear, were places. There may not be much to see beyond the inhabitants, but there is a work to be done. It is in their power to habituate the Chinese to the sight of Europeans, and if they will only do so now when it can be down with ease and safety, laying aside that hectoring demeanour which arises too often from never seeing a Chinaman about them who is not a servant or a tradesman, they may do far more to open up, we will not say traffic, but intercourse, with the interior of China, than the Treaty of Tientsin; if unaided, can accomplish. But at the same time a grave responsibility rest upon them. If those who make there excursions display a haughty and overbearing demeanour, hustle rudely the natives from their way, and neglect those forms of common courtesy towards them which not only decency, but fear, would compel them to observe at home, then the present temporary opening of China will have been productive of evil and not of good, for it with prove that the term of "barbarian" has been not wholly misapplied to a people among whom youthful thoughtlessness sometimes assumes the form of insolence and even violence.

In a word we cannot speak too highly of the results likely to arise from the system of "promenades militaires" that has recently been commenced; we cannot regret too deeply that they did not take place twelve months ago. Had such been the case an occasional skirmish might have been the consequence, but it would have proved to the inhabitants of the interior a fact that our *boys and compradores will not and cannot teach them, viz: that there is a higher feeling than that of mere trade among us, and that we are not, as they seem to think a nation whose whole life is spent in self indulgence, in plundering and being along with the expedition as far as the Rebel station of Wochoo which it appears was reached no Nov. 23d.

The remainder of the Journal is to be read at the Society's Meeting in February and we then purpose giving a short precis of the whole, At that time also, probably, another paper emanating from the late expedition will be brought forward and the audience may have the opportunity of spending an evening both profitably and pleasantly on the Yangtsze kiang.

NAGASAKI SHIPPING.

ARRIVED FROM,-

Jan. 4. Minna, （Am. schr.） Shanghae.

"4 Henry Ellis, （British ship.） Ningpo.

"6, Versailles, （British ship.） Shanghae.

DEPARTED FOR.-

Jan. 4, Ann, （Am. barque.） Shanghae.

" 4, Yeddo, （Japan str.,） Simabura.

" 8. Vindex, （British schr.,） Shanghae.

IN HARBOUR,-

Kwang Komar, Japan war-str.

Ninnonmar, or Japan. Japan war-str.

Nagasaki, Japan war-str.

Thérésia. Japan war-schr.

Askold; Russian str.

Strélock. Russian str.

Tribune, H. M. St.-fri.- put in for Repairs.

Charles Prices, Am. whaler.

Rapid, Am. whaler

Henry Ellis, British ship.

Minna, Am. schr.

Versailles, British ship.

THE TREATY WITH JAPAN.

（*North-China Herald*, *Feb. 5.*）

Summary of the Treaty between Her Majesty and the Emperor of Japan, Signed at Yedo, August, 26, 1858.

Art. 1.- Stipulates for peace and friendship.

Art. 2.- Stipulates for the □□□□□□ right to appoint a diplomatic agent at the paid. Any goods not entered in the manifest will pay double duty.

Any captain neglecting to enter his ship within the time prescribed shall pay a penalty of 60 dols. a day.

Regulation 2.

Japanese custom-house officers may be placed on board any ship in port, except ships of war.

No goods to be unladen between sunset and sunrise. Hatches may be secured by the Japanese officers, and any person breaking the fastening shall pay a fine of 60 dols. for each offence.

Any goods discharged from a ship without having been duly entered shall be liable to confiscation.

Packages with goods of value fraudulently concealed, and not mentioned in the invoice, shall be forfeited.

If any British ship is engaged in smuggling, she shall pay a fine of 1000 dollars, and the goods shall be forfeited.

Vessels needing repairs may land their cargo without payment of duty, under supervision of the Japanese authorities. If any part be sold duty to be paid thereon.

Cargo may be transshipped from one vessel to another, under supervision, and on proof of *bonafide* nature of transactions.

Importation of opium being prohibited, if any British vessel has more than three catties' weight on board the surplus quantity may be seized and destroyed, and any persons smuggling opium shall be liable to a fine of 15 dollar a catty.

Regulation. 3.

Mode of entering goods by the owner or consignee. The entry is to state the name of the enterer, and of the ship, the marks, contents, and value of each package.

The original invoices to be presented to the Japanese custom-house.

The Japanese officers may be examine the packages, but without expense or unreasonable delay.

If the importer or owner should find that

never within half in even three quarters of a mile of the main action, having their time occupied in manoeuvering so as to hold in check a body of braves who menaced the rear.

Such are the observations we were enabled to make on the sport. Positive details it was almost impossible to procure after the reports that have been set on foot, and it has seemed safer to us to trust to the appearance of the ground. and the probabilities, we had almost said the possibilities of the case, than to accounts often involuntarily colored. and never, from the mere nature of the circumstances complete. How much painful feeling, how much needless irritation how many a galling remark would be published in the Government Gazzete. The personal honor of the general is a more than ample guarantee for their accuracy and we cannot see why he should hestitate to give a report of these actions against plunderers on land, whilst his immediate superior, Sir Michael Seymour, reports every action fought against the pirates of the coast. There can be no strategical reason for the secrecy, and we can only regard it as a portion of the absurd official reserve towards the British public, which has characterized the conduct of all, except our gallant Admial, who have had to do with the direction of this war, or shall we call it bellicose negotiation, with the Chinese Empire.

But to return. When[1] we got back to Canton. we found the reply to our letter to the Allied

* The village of Shek-tseng being plundered.

Shanghae.

WE extract the following from *North-China Herald* of 29th January,-

The Master of the British Brig *Emma* has been award the sum of 4,000 Taels for services rendered to a Chinese junk, 3,000 for the Captain and 1,000 to cover damages incurred to the *Emma*.- H. M. Consular Court Jan. 11th, 1859.

The Chinese Imperial High Commissioners, Kweliang. Hwanhana Ming and Twan proceed to Soochow to pass the China New Year holidays, and will probably be absent until the return of the British Embassy.

We have advices from Nagasaki to the 8th instant. In another column will be found the Shipping news of that port.

Our correspondent also informs us that the Commanders and Officers of the Dutch Navy residing at Desima had lately been invited by the Prince of Frizen to visit his batteries and arsenal. They went, accommpanied by the Secretary of the prince and were shown a great number of brass and iron guns and mortats principially for 9 and 11 inch shell, with some 32 pounders, all made by Japanese workmen. The magazines and store houses are bomb-proof and there were piles of shot and shell for 300 rounds.

A splendid dinner was prepared in Eurpoean style in one of the buildings where they were afterwards enter-

open ports. The British diplomatic agent and consul general may travel to any part of Japan, and the Japanese diplomatic agent and consul general to any part of Great Britain.

Art 3. The ports and towns of Hakodadi, Kanagawa, and Nagasaki, to be opened to British Subjects on July 1, 1859.

Nee-egata, or, if that is unsuitable as a harbour, some other port on the west coast of Nipon, on Jan. 1, 1860.

Hiogo on Jan. 1, 1863.

In all those places British subjects may permanently reside, and may lease ground and purchase and erect buildings, but shall not erect fortifications. They are not to be confined by any wall or gate, and there free ingress and egress not to be impeded.

The limits within which British subjects may travel are defined. The general limit is ten ri （each ri being 4275 yards） in any direction.

After Jan. 1, 1862. British subjects may reside at Yedo, and from Jan. 1, 1863. in Osaca, for purposes of trade only. In each of those cities a suitable district for their residence, and the distance to which they may go, shall be arranged by the British diplomatic agent and the Japanese government.

Art. 4. All questions arising between British subjects in the Japanese dominions shall be under the jurisdiction of the British authorities.

Art. 5. Japanese guilty of any criminal act towards British subjects shall be punished by the Japanese authorities.

British subjeets who may commit any crime against Japanese or other foreigners, shuould be punished by the British authorities according to the British law.

Art. 6, Mode of setting complaints of British against Japanese, or of Japanese against British.

his goods have been damaged on the voyage, he may apprise the custom house, and have the damage appraised, so as to make a deduction from the value in his entry.

All goods intended for export must be entered at the Japanese custom-house beforce they are shipped. Any good shipped without having been so entered, and all packages containing prohibited articles, shall be forfeited.

No entry shall be required for supplies for ships and their passengers and crews, nor for passengers' clothing, &c.

Regulation 4.

Ships wishing to clear must give 24 hours' notice at the custom-house. If clearance be refused the captain or consignee and the British consul must be informed of the reason.

British ships of war shall not be required to enter or clear, nor shall they be visited by the customs or police.

Mail steamers may enter and clear on the same day, and shall not be required to deliver a manifest, except for passengers and goods to be landed in Japan.

Whale ships touching for supplies, and ships in distress, shall not be required to deliver a manifest, unless they wish to trade.

Regulation 5.

Any person signing a false declaration or certificate, with intent to defraud the revenue of Japan, shall pay a fine of 125 dollars for each offence.

Regulation 6.

No tonnage duties shall be levied on British ships in the ports of Japan, but the following fees shall be paid to the Japanese custom-house authorities:-

For the entry of a ship, fiftee dollars.

For the clearance of a ship, seven dollars.

For each permit, one dollar and a half.

For each bill of health, one dollar and a half.

---

[1] Sic.

situated on a creek of the main river, we resolved on proceeding by boat, as our creature comforts would thus best be cared for.		Art. 7. The authorities on either side are to do their best to enforce recovery of debts due by their own people to those of the other nation, without, however, being responsible for payment. Art. 8. The Japanese government will place no restriction upon the lawful employment of Japanese by British subjects. Art. 9. British subjects to have free exercise of their religion in Japan, and may erect places of worship. Art. 10. Foreign coin to be current in Japan; the value to be determined by weight. Coin（except Japanese copper coin）, and foreign gold and silver, may be exported.	For any other document, one dollar and a half. Regulation 7. Duties shall be paid to the Japanese government, on all goods landed in the country, according to the following tariff:– Class 1. All articles in this class shall be free of duty:– Gold and silver, coined or uncoined. Wearing apparel, in actual use. Household furniture and printed books, not intended for sale, but the property of persons who come to reside in Japan. Class 2. A duty of 5 per cent shall bepaid on the following articles :– All articles used for the purpose of buildings, rigging, repairing, or fitting out of ships. Whaling gear of all kinds. Salted provisions of all kinds. Bread and bread stuffs. Living animals of all kinds. Coals. Timber for building houses. Rice. Paddy. Steam

16 The Overland Register and Price Current.

machinery. Zinc, lead. Tin. Raw silk. Cotton and Wooollen manufactured goods. Class 3. A duty of 35 per cent shall be paid on all intoxicating liquors. Class 4. All goods not included in any of the preceeding classes shall pay a duty of 20 per cent. All articles of Japanese production, which are exported as cargo, shall pay a duty of 5 per cent, with the exception of gold and silver icon, and cooper in bars. Rice and wheat, the produce of Japan, shall not be exported from Japan as cargo; but all British subjects rendent in Japan, and British ships for their crews and passengers, shall be furnished with sufficient supplies of the same. Foreign grain brought into any open port of Japan in a British ship, if no part thereof has been landed, may be re-exported without hindrance. The Japanese government will sell from time to time at public auction any surplus quantity of copper that may be produced.	claims of England and America to the credit of "rending the curtain of ages." – 1st.– In the editorial of November 1st we read;– "Fortune favoured the boldness of the enterprise, and American astuteness helped us. Lord ELGIN reached Nagasaski on the 3d of August, and found no one there but some Japanese underlings and some Dutch officials, who naturally gave him small hopes. Thence he went, staggering through one of the tremendous gales that vex those seas, to the wretched harbour of Simoda, where the Americans are in power, and at this place he for the first time discovered the workings of the echoes of his own doings on the Peiho. It seems that. as soon as the Tien-sin Treaty was arranged, the American Commodore rushed off to Japan to take advantage of the consternation certain to be created by the first news of recent events in the Pei-ho. It was smartly imagined. He found at Simoda the American Consul General just	Whereupon the *Times* so complacently– not to any arrogantly– founds the claim of the roaring *Lion* to the well garnered harvest of the *peaceful, philosophical, husbandman*, in terms which had they been used by our countrymen whould have run the risk of being denounced by it as the grandiloquent assumptions of American self-conceit.– First, then, so far from it being "smartly imagined" by the American Commodore that by *rushing* from the Pei-ho a new Treaty might be wrested from the terrors of the Japanese, inspired by the Lion's roaring in that river, we have it from the highest authority: 1st.– That His Excellency the Commodore had not the most remote idea that Mr. Harris of our Government contemplated a new Treaty with Japan; that he went there under an express order of the Navy Department, and for a totally different purpose. 2nd.– And most material:– that Mr.	the haughty humour of Europeans, with the cupidity of the merchant, and the occasionally intemperate zeal of the missionary. However pure our intentions may be in general, we must not conceal from ourselves that they will not be regarded as such, and that the Chinese mandarins, for instance, and not quite inexcusable when they express repugnance □□eeing the rights we have acquired in the midst of the people they have to govern. It is not merely because the recognition of those rights has been imposed on them by force,（which would not, however, be so bad □□□ reason）it is also because the new *regime* has caused the immediate diminution of their authority, and the probable ruin of the moral and political order of things to which they owe their existence. In their eyes, if they are sincere Chinese– and why should they not be so?– our missionaries, with all the dogmas which they preach, and

Five years after the opening of Kanagawa, the import and export duties shall be subject to revision, if either the British or Japanese government desire it.

THE following notice of the antecedents of Mr. Harris the U. S. Consul General of Japan may not be without interest to our readers.

Some thirty years ago he began to be known in New York as an importer ef earthenware. While yet extensively and successfully engaged in that business, he took an active and efficient part in the cause of public education. He became a trustee of the schools of the ninth ward under the old system, and commissioner of schools under the new. He was twice elected President of the Board of Education. Against great opposition he navigated through the Legislature a bill establishing in New York a Free Academy for the benefit of scholars who had passed through the common schools with credit. In 1848 he withdrew from the importing business, and purchased and freighted, on his own account, a bark, with which he proceeded to California. After trading on the Pacific at various points, 1854 found him in China, holding the post of U. S. Consul at Ningpo. In 1855 he returned home, but soon after went out again as Consul-General to Japan. Before proceeding thither, he went to Siam, and negotiated a very important treaty. In less than two years after reaching his post in Japan, he worked his way into the bodily presence of the Emperor, and not only made a treaty, but also paved the way for Lord Elgin to make one. He has acquired a knowledge of the languagews of the countries he has visited, and is now preparing histeries of Formosa and Japan.

TO THE EDITOR OF THE "HONGKONG REGISTER."

SIR,– The *Times*, with a fertitlity of resource that almost anticipates public returned from Jeddo, whither he had been upon a six months' mission, vainly importuning for some commercial privileges. The Commodore immediately took him on board his ponderous steamer the *Powhattan*, and steered right away for Kanagawa, a station well known to the American men-of-war since Commodore PERRY's time, about 15 miles below the capital city of Jeddo. Terrible stories and frightful anticipations had for some time possessed the minds of the Japanese. Japan, like other countries of ancient institutions, has its conservative and progressive parties. The Prince of BORINGO had stood stontly for the ancient Japanese constitution and no foreign competition. But when the American ship-of-war appeared, and when the American version of the warlike operations in China circulated, a strong feeling gained ground in favour of the progressive party. Prince BORINGO retired, and Prince BITSU took his place. Under the new Administration Mr. HARRIS, the Consul General was admitted to an interview with the EMPEROR; ports were opened, and commercial tariffs agreed upon pretty much as is set forth in the statement we borrow from the *North-China Herald*. When Lord ELGIN arrived at Simoda he found Mr. HARRIS in high spirits at having completed his Treaty, and the precedent gave him an opportunity whereof he sadly stood in need. We must here– having recently spoken in terms of complaint of our American friends for sending their silliest men upon important Embassies– acknowledge that Mr. HARRIS acted throughout these transactions with a frankness and courtesy worthy of the representative of a great friendly Power. Harris had concluded his Treaty long prior to Commodore Tatnall's arrival at Simoda, and, if not prior to, near the period when Lord Elgin left Shanghae for the Pei-ho, in April.

For some political reason of a domestic character, a prospective date was affixed to the Treaty, which was the 1st of September, copies being held by the respective parties and a sub and secret Treaty signed and sealed by all the parties binding them to the execution of the main Treaty on the day of its date. Both had been concluded long before Commodore Tatnall reached Simoda, and long before the movements in the Gulf of Pechili.

It will be seen, therefore, that we must attribute to the favorable impressions left by Commodore Perry and the diplomatic ability of Mr. Consul General Harris, rather than to the echo of the Guns of the British Fleet at the Pei-ho, the effectual opening-up of Japan.

Undoubtedly upon reading the two Treaties at Simoda, the Commodore suggested an earlier public execution of the main one than had been designated, in view of the not-improbable visits of other Negotiators, and the consequent possible questioning of Mr. Harris's claim to priority; and, accordingly, he conveyed the Consul General to Kanagawa, where in his presence the main Treaty was fully executed by both parties, the prospective date erased and that of the day-July 29th 1858- substituted,-when the sub or secret Treaty was destroyed, also in presence of Commodore Tatnall-

But beside these Treaties, Mr. Harris had another tangible proof of his success in inspiring confidence and good-will, in the first real autograph of the Emperor himself that ever left Japan- it being an autograph letter to the President of the United States actually signed by the Emperor; whereas others had been signed only by the Ministers.

with all the new principles which they inculcate cannot be considered in any other light than as revolutionist. Officials of a Government which has never been anything but the patrimony of an excessively small minority in the midst of the mass of Chinese people, and which has never had any other vital principle than the belief which it has inspired of its power- the mandarins feel, by reasoning, by experience, and by what is still stronger, by instinct, that all the concessions made to foreigners are so many mortal wounds inflicted on their own prestige. The first war in which they were beaten by Europeans, the first treaty which ceded a small barren island to England, and opened four ports to foreign commerce, was followed, as effect follows cause, by a terrible insurrection, which succeeded in plunging the finest provinces of the empire into a state of inextricable anarchy. How can they shut their eyes to that cruel lesson? What can we expect from them but that their ordinary contempt for sworn faith, their habitual want of foresight, and the ignorance which, like all Asiatics they inbour under, of the necessities which compel our Government to take up arms to obtain reparation for the injury done to the most humble of their subjects, will impel them to endeavour to reconquer by cunning and by continual breach of treaties what they have been compelled to grant by force? The first peace with China lasted twelve years; how long will the second endure? We cannot say, but it appears to us very doubtful that it will last as long as the first, and that the Chinese will now be more capative or more desirous than before of maintaining the engagements which they have just entered into with us."

curiosity, has recently furnished to its readers a series of articles ostensibly designed to illustrate the present transition phase of politics in China and Japan preparatory to their induction into the comity of Nations; and in the course of them has, with much bestowal of just praise of Lord Elgin, and much omission of just desert of Sir Michael Seymour, launched arrows, not a little poisoned, at the American Minister to China;– whilst in generalizing its acknowledgements both of the courtesy and services of the American Consul General to Japan in a manner to ignore his just merits, it gives point to its own reflections upon the American Naval Commander–in–chief, by "smartly imaging" a fictitious basis for its inordinate appropriationof credit to England for the negotiations at Jeddo, to the relative disparagement of American diplomacy.

We regard not the China–won laurels of Lord Elgin with jaundiced eyes; we rather rejoice in them as emblematical of the common gain of Christendom;– but if, like a General flushed with victory in one field, he went to Japan to appropriate the spoils of a battle already gained by the moral intrepidity and persevering vigilance of our Countrymen, and in the height of his advantage displaces alike the early trophies of the indomitable Perry, and the green wreaths of the patient Harris, that his own standards may fill the eyes of an admiring World, we shall deny him the possession of what we are fain to attribute to him– that magnanimous sense of justice which is the characteristic of great minds.

We shall remind him that after Perry had– with consummate tact and resolute constancy– overborne the wall of two centuries' formation, the first person acquiescent in its attempted re–erection was a British Admiral; and yet, that, by subsequent presevering peaceful efforts, Mr. Harris had again turned the tide of civilization against it with effect, and finally consummated the work so admirably Mr. HARRIS acted like a man who was strong in his own knowledge of the interests of his country. Lord ELGIN departed at once for the anchorage below the capital, where he found the American, and also the Russian war steamers. The neutrals had been quick to scent the game from afar; they had run a race against us to gather not only the spoils won by our arms, but even the contributions to be exacted by the terror of our deeds. Beyond this anchorage of Kanagawa were rocks and whirlpools and perils unnumerable, all faithfully deposed to by Japanese pilots. Captain SHERARD OSBORN, who has the reputation of being confindent, and not unreasonably confident, in his own seamanship, believed in none of these things. Steaming over the anchorage he held on up the Bay of Jeddo, and, stimulated by the sight of Jeddo city, which slowly unrolled itself in the north–west angle of the gulf, he pursued his course, undeterred by a full gale of wind until he could cast anchor within gunshot of a series of well constructed batteries, which run across the shoals facing a portion of the city. Lord ELGIN's well judged confidence in his captain was thus rewarded by a position which, considering he had to deal with Asiatics, insured his success. It was a bold move made at a timely moment, for he could have done nothing at a distance. Since Mr. HARRIS obtained his Treaty there had been a reactionary movement in Jeddo, directed by the independent Princes and hereditary nobles. They had ousted the Minister who signed the Treaty, and Prince BORINGO ruled again. But the apparition of the British steam frigates *Furious* and *Retribution* intruding even upon the sacred seclusion of the capital, spread consternation throughout the camp of the obstructives. We made

It would, we think, be difficult to find in the contemporary reflections of any other periodical of the day so many *smart imaginings* to the desparagement of another Nation's claims as are ingeniously– not to say disingenuously– set before the World in these two editorials of the leading Journal of Christendom– from whose columns are hereafter to be called the materials of History– save the mark!– We are, Sir, with apologies for so considerable a trespass upon your space, your obedient servants.

SEVERAL AMERICANS.

January 31st 1859.

Batavia

（*From our Batavia Correspondent.*）

THE *Java Courant* states that the projected line of telegraph running over the entire Island had been completed, whilst only some of the smaller branch–lines were still in course of construction.

The same paper contains a lengthy and very circumstantial statement of the origin and immediate cause of the quarrel with Boni（Celebes）we are told that in a few days, the military expedition would proceed, consisting of nine war–steamers, 3 war–schooners, 6 gunboats, and 22 transports with 3 battalions of infantry, 1 detachment of cavalry, a company of sappers and miners and 2 batteries of artillery. These forces are accompanied by the former governor of Celebes, and the present members of the council of India, empowered to make a last attempt to obtain redress without recourse to extremities.

In 1824, it appears, Boni was forcibly compelled to ratify the ancient treaties, entered into with the E. I. Company, by which all the free states of Celebes were declared independent of each other, and under the protectorate of the Netherlands. Boni had often endavoured to assume a supremacy over

We give the above extract as shewing the views held on the China Question by one of the ablest journals in Europe. We may not agree with all its assertions about the universal want of principle &c., in the Chinese, but we must still remember that cunning is too often the weak man's armour. On the whole we believe that the above is a far juster appreciation of the results of □□□ war, than the unbounded self–gratulation with which the treaty of Tien–tsin has been welcomed by the English papers.

Our latest papers from China still present a fearful glut of Tonnage in the different ports Hongkong harbour alone contains about 93,000 say *ninety–three thousand* Tons of Shipping. And the other ports in proportion. We ask again, where is the slightest prospect of improvements in freights, when each succeeding Mail confirms the previous doleful accounts. As the rage for ship–building goes on at present, it seems we shall soon have more vessels that men to man them, and although the annual loss of seagoing ships is frightful, yet there come by every Mail accounts of vessels built one bigger than the other, which makes us ask the question, is the Millenium drawing near, when all the world shall run to and fro? But jesting aside, the question of overdoing it in ship–building naturally arises, and we can scarcely doubt for a moment, that in many parts of the world, ship–building is overdone. Were freights high in other parts of the world, there might be a rush to such quarter, □□□ in China we have the extraordinary spectacle of hundreds of noble vessels, going actually a begging as it were, for a mere song, and cannot even then meet with quick dispatch. Cannot some of our nautical friends give us some explanation of the causes of the bad times begun by his predecessor, so that when his Lordship arrived at Simoda it wanted little more to assure him of success than the assumption of a spirit of happy audacity, and the services of Mr. Harris's Interpreter.

We pause, however, to say that we are very far from attributing to the Noble Earl the inspiration of these depreciatory "leaders" of the *Times*– emphatically *mis-leaders* as they are of public opinion;– his whole career disproves the supposition, as his language in Parliament and on public occasions in America contradicts it, or we have widely interpreted the one and much misread the record of the other.

But the ever vigilant *Times*– that with its hundred anus compels all the ends of the Earth to tribute, and that has become the World's Herald,– we would it were more cosmopolitan in spirit.

The change would prevent the exhibition of a deal of ill humor and of much mutual recrimination, nay, it would tend to consolidate the friendships of peoples and to conserve the peace of the World.

It is quite true that it plays such a deep game of, "fast and loose" with American, that we can hardly judge from the target of one day to what point the arrows of the next will be directed, or how much poison their barbs will bear;– thus ever tantalizing even if sometimes amusing. in the jaunty air of its effrontery, in protesting innocence and transferring the blame of a quarrel to American shoulders, it is often rather the caterer to a morbid craving of reproach to republican institutions, than the intelligent reflex of sound public opinion.

If it abuses its great opportunities and perverts its high mission as the leading Press of the Word, let the Nations mark its course and the evil will sooner or later be upon its own head. At present it concerns us to rectify its perverted record of history in respect only to Japan;– the question between the two legations, as to the action of Mr. Reed in China, having been left by the no menaces and used no threats, but we fear there was something like the pressure of a force which was not altogether moral put upon these gentle Japanese. Our excuse must be that if the Americans had obtained concessions upon the strength of the terror created by the roar of the lion, it would have been hard that the lion should get nothing on his own account."

2nd.– And in the editorial of November 3d as follows:–

"We don't stand exclusiveness. We hold that the world is made to us all; and so we have gradually edged on and finally pushed our way close up to the City of Jeddo, through rows of junks, abreast of green batteries, and dropped our anchors where barbarian ship was never seen before. We took advantage of a panic, and did it with a rush. While we were concluding matters up the Peiho the Russian and American Plenipotentiaries were off with breathless haste to Nagasaki, to reap the first fruits of our harvest. They got start enough to get all they wanted, and give time for a reaction. However, Lord ELGIN was not far behind; and when he came up he capped the achievements of his brother Plenipotentiaries, and got for them more than they had ventured to ask for themselves.

So with the "Open, Sesame" of a little resolution we have rent the curtain of ages. Captain OSBORN reports that there must be a channel, and up they all steam. The mountain side opens, and European eyes rest on objects never seen before but on cups and saucers, and never to be seen, as many believed, till the consummation of all things, the Millennum, or the great mustering for the battle of Armageadon. Lord ELGIN went ahead; the bigger ships followed the day after; they bring a handsome present with them, which they wisely judge worthier to be delivered in the presence of an Imperial city that a the other independent states which was thereby done away with. Lately however, the Sultan again tried to extend his dominions at the expense of the others, and in direct defiance to the representations of the Batavian Government. Not only were hostile intentions manifested on several occasions, but even the delegates of the Government were treated with the greatest disrespect and could hardly obtain a hearing, whilst the Netherlands flag was purposely insulted by an order that it should be carried upside down through the territory of Boni. Claims for redress were met with the utmost indifference, or a pretext of ignorance.

Other news there is none; the market for tonnage is in the same depressed state as ever.

Burmah

Our readers will remember the fact of a embassy having been some time ago sent to the United States by the King of Burmah. Pominent among the matter contained in the "royal letters" was an application for an American Consul to reside at his new capital of *Mandelag*. An American paper remarks–

"The King manifests a shrewd sense of the diplomatic weakness of our party Government by stipulating that;" "such official resident shall be a man of talent and good temper." The object of the King in all this is quite obvious, it is no affection for foreigners; no desire to be brought into more intimate relations with western officials, that has promted his extraodinary request; but a clear perception of the strength of the outside pressure of British influence, and an increased sense of his own incompetency to withstand it. With the astuteness of an old diplomat he has, although at a very late hour, bethought himself of putting one influence against another. The King need complained of? We shall receive any communication on this important subject with thanks and promise to give it our earliest and most serious consideration– *Bintang–Timor*, Jan. 11

A waggish fellow has been tendering his congratulation to President Buchanan on the gratification of his desire to have the Atlantic Telegraph remain neutral in case of trouble. "The telegraph has not a word to say *on either side*."

NEW RACE OF ABORIGINES. – GOLD DISCOVERY.– Some time since a parapraph appeared in the *Empire*, relative to the discovery. in the far interior, of a new race of blacks, "who had no hair on the top of their heads, in the place where the wool ought to grow." The account of this most extraordinary discovery has, been corroborated by an eye–witness– a Mr. Thompson. who is at present residing at Mr. Whittaker's, in East Matland, who has just arrived from the vicinty where these funny aboriginal ruralise. They are of a copper color, and are tall and athletic, much superior in every respect to their darker skinned brethren. The women are also said to have more claims to beauty. They, however, are also deficient of what is generally acknowledged to be "the glory of women." Mr. Thompson, it appears, was at camp on the Upper Balonne, with others, on ground hitherto untrodden by a white man, when he was surprised by a visit from these bald pated, copper–colored beings. They appeared to have friendly intentions, and as nothing was noticed in their conduct of an aggressive nature, a conservation by signs and nods ensued. After a while a sovereign were shown to them, when one of them picking up a stone, pointed public discussion of it, in the *Times* upon one hand and the *New York Times* on the other, in a state to necessitate the notice, directly or indirectly, of one or the other of the respective Chiefs.

First, then, of the *mis-leaders* of the *Times* of November 1st and 3d,– which are so saturated with the unction of self-glorification that we can hardly make an extract of them that shall fully combine its essence– the following portions may serve our immediate purpose of initiating inquiry into the relative

distant outport; they come with peaceful bearing, except that they head no signals; they received the courteous Japanese officials with equal courtesy but the spectacle tallies so exactly with the terrible reports from the opposite shores of China, that in a moment Japan throws away its Palladium of perpetual isolation."

Now, what was this advance beyond the American and Russian ships lying at Kanagawa better than an imitation of Commodore Perry's similar movement and breaking the line of the cordon of Government boats when first penetrating toward the head of the bay of Jeddo?– What but an imitation so palpable as to suggest a comparison in favor of the moral heroism of the American Pioneer?

But we now purpose to deal with facts, rather than to suggest inferences; and proceed to disprose the statements purporting to embody the material points

feel no apprehension however: better turn his thoughts to the improvement of his people, and the cultivation of national character and he will soon find his foreign relation on □□□ satisfactory footing.

THE following article upon China is from the *Journal des Debats*.

"It is, without doubt, an excellent and desirable thing to open China to every nation, but it would be puerile not to preceive beforehand that the first effect of new system will be to increase to enormous proportions the occasions for conflicts with the natives. It is with Asiatics that we shall have to deal; with perfidy, falsehood, and that barbarian pride which universally distinguishes them; and yet they, on their side, will not perhaps be always in the wrong, when they have to struggle with

with his finger the far west, and intimated that stones of a similar description to the sovereign were to be picked up on the ground, in masses as large as the stone he held. The place was understood to be some hundred miles further in the interior, but they signified their intention of bringing some of these stones at their next

→ see Supplement.

SUPPLEMENT
TO THE
OVERLAND REGISTER & PRICE CURRENT, No. 3.

VICTORIA, TUESDAY, FEBRUARY 15, 1859.

We extract from the *North-China Herald* the following sketch of the state of trade in Shanghai during the past year–

The news of the bombardment and occupation of Canton on the 29th of December 1857, arrived in Shanghai on the 6th January 1858, and on the 1st January 1859. Lord Elgin returned from an expedition up the Yangtsze undertaken with a view to forming some idea what ports, under the new Treaty, it would be desirable to open along its banks. The result of that research we do not know; we mention the circumstance as the last of those great events that appear to have been essential to prepare the way for the completion of the treaties, on our part, by the coming Minister, when Lord Elgin shall resign the plenipotentiary powers into his hands; and these have been accomplished in the short space of nine months from the arrival of the foreign plenipotentiaries at Shanghai, which

Fancy Goods have assumed a leading place amongst our articles of Import. The deliveries for the year are unprecedently heavy, but still the supplies have been in excess of the requirements of the trade, and generally prices have not been satisfactory to Importers.

The following are the comparative deliveries of manufactured goods from 1st January to 31st December, 1858:–

COMPARATIVE STATEMENT OF DELIVERIES OF MANUFACTURED GOODS FROM 1ST JANUARY TO 31ST DECEMBER.

		1857	1858	1858	
				Incr ease	Decr ease
Grey Shirtings	pcs.	1,006,300	1,676,000	669,700	
White Shirtings	pcs.	282,500	206,000	13,300	
T. Cloth	pcs.	274,200	222,000	········	52,200
Sheetings & Drills.	pcs.	354,000	402,000	48,000	
Spotted Shirtings.	pcs.	127,600	280,300	152,700	
Brocades	pcs.	84,700	121,000	36,300	
H'kerchiefs	doz.	30,000	40,800	10,800	
Velvets	pcs.	20,256	20,100	········	156
Chintz.	pcs.	68,000	79,800	29,800	
Long Ells.	pcs.	23,500	25,300	1,800	
Woollens.	pcs.	20,600	28,000	7,400	
Camlets.	pcs.	7,200	7,600	400	
Lastings.	pcs.	1,700	3,200	1500	

During March and April we had reports of the rebels having appeared in force in the various Tea districts, that the different Tea Hongs had been plundered, and the picking of the first crop Teas much interfered with. The Teamen became alarmed, ceased to send up funds for the purchase of new Congous. and we understand that not more than 180 chops of all kinds were purchased for this market.

The additional expenses incurred in endavouring to suppress the rebellion, have induced the Mandarins to have recourse to extraordinary means to raise funds, and latterly they have imposed additional inland duties on all Teas brought here by way of Hangchow, amounting it is said in all to about 12 Tls. per pecul. Under these circumstances the commonest descriptions of Congou costing Tls. 6 a 8

they may be to appear to arrogate to themselves a superior perception– the duty to cast what light they may possess upon the right path, or at least, to throw a suggestive ray across the salient points of error.

China has, ever since the monopoly of "the Company" ceased, if not before, been a fruitful field of fallacies; and nothing is more observable in the popular opinions and press of the day than the assumption of false premises from absolute ignorance, or the deducing of erroneous inferences by the ignoring of some inexorable condition of its Trade, its finance, or its political and social state. At one period, it was held in England and America that there was always a large reserved stock of Teas in the interior of China, available for took place on the 20th to 24th of March Last. In three months from that time the Treaties of Tien-tsin were obtained, that of Lord Elgin having been signed on the 26th of June. In two months more the English Treaty of Yeddo was signed at that city, on the 26th of August from whence his lordship returned here on the 2d of September, and after waiting five weeks for the Chinese Imperial Commissioners, the Tariff and Trade Regulations were agreed upon, and signed by the American and British Plenipotentiaries on the 8th of November. On the same day Lord Elgin and suite embarked for Hankow from whence they returned on the 1st last.

That these great results, following in such rapid succession, having been so easily obtained is mainly owing to the energy and determination with which Lord Elgin has acted in all his dealings with the Chinese Officials; steadily adhering to the policy which, on his arrival here, he stated that he would pursue; "never to prefer a demand which he did not believe to be both moderate and just, and from a demand so preferred never to recede."

Whether our trade here will derive any immediate advantage from the Treaty of Teen-tsin is doubtful, for the benefits expected from the opening of additional ports on the coast are in a measure nullified by the restrictions prohibiting British vessels from bringing Peas, Beans, Bean Cake &c., from Niew chang and Tang chow, whilst the opening of the Yang-tsze Kiang depends upon the evacuation of Nanking by the rebels. Late events in that quarter may, however, expedite that desirable consummation.

The legalization of Opium is another important point gained, although probably it will not materially affect the trade.

It will of course be said in England that this concession has been obtained by the application of strong coercive measures, and to the heated imagination of the frequenters of Exeter Hall, Lord Elgin will seem a "very demon." or possibly he may figure on the

Metals.- Have been unusually depressed throughout the year, the market having been over-supplied with Iron, whilst the comsumption of Lead has fallen off materially, probably owning to a less quantity than usual having been required for the manufacture of the leads for Tea chests.

Straits Produce.- The imports have been largely in excess of the requirements, and prices have consequently been very low during the year.

Sugar.- The market has show little animation, at any period of the year, the disturbances in the country having interfered with the consumption, and prevented any advance in prices.

Rice.- Prices, ruled high during the early part of the year, but experienced a very great decline in November on the arrival of large supplies from the South.

Opium.- Notwithstanding the disturbed state of the country, the total deliveries of Opium are of 600 chests in excess of last year, whilst a moderately high range of prices has been maintained. In Febrary an arrangement was made by the local Mandarins by which Opium was allowed to be brought up from Woosung on the payment of a "squeeze" of 24 Tls. per chest, and under the new Treaty the trade has been legalized and it now appears in the Tariff as an Article of Import at a fixed duty of 30 Tls. per pecul. Malwa- The average rates have been Tls 460 a 470 for best drug, and from being comparatively cheaper it has commanded more attention than Patna, the deliveries showing an increase of 2,600 chests whilst those of Patna have decreased 2,000 chests. Patna has maintained its price entirely owing to the firmness of holders but has experienced great flucation, having been quoted in January Tls. 445 a 450 in March, Tls. 580. and in July, Tls. 495 a 500. Since then the market has been quiet with

per pecul in the country, cannot be laid down here under Tls. 18 a 20 whilst the finer kinds cost Tls. 30 a 35, consequently so long as these taxes are levied our supplies are likely to be limited to the latter, which may be sold without loss, whilst the common kinds, which are seldom worth over Tls. 12 a 14 per pecul must either be left ungathered, or has been the case this year taken for the Northern markets. The export of Black Tea for the year is 6,000,000 lbs. less than in 1857, and now the market is completely bare of stock.

Amongst the features worthy of notice connected with the Tea trade, we may, mention the departure of two ships direct for Cronstadt taking for 464,000 lbs. Tea; the arrival of 3 cargoes of Tea in foreign bottoms, from Namquan, all which were bought for the Northern markets, and finally the purchase of about 200,000 peculs Tea in the Oopack districts, also destined for the Russian inland trade.

The future dawns more hopefully on us, and we not unreasonably anticipate that the opening of the Yangtsze kiang, will again place Shanghae on her former footing as a Tea exporting port, by allowing supplies to be brought down without being subjected to the excessive inland duties now levied by the Mandarins.

The Green Tea market presents no new feature which calls for remark, the supply continuing equal to the requirements, whilst no great fluctuations in price have taken place

EXCHANGE.- The introduction of the Shanghae Tael of Sycee as the currency at this port has given universal satisfaction, as it has tenued to keep Exchange at a moderate level throughout the year, and prevented those extreme rates which occasionally ruled when the Carolus Dollar was the sole medium of payment.

any extraordinary foreign demand;- an error that nothing short of the annual re-purchase at Shanghae for the consumption of China or of Russia of the major part of the stocks of the lowest qualities of both Black and Green Teas for several years, since 1853, would have effectually dispelled.

At another period, the tone of the consuming markets was destroyed, by the success of an enterprising American House in gaining renewed access to the old Tea districts of the Bohea hills- whence "the Company" had drawn its principal supplies of a class of Tea which had in more recent times been supplanted in public favor by the new Black-leaf sorts of "Ho How," "Moning," "Woonam" and "Woopak" - and to the Ko Kew (Ooloong) districts; -and the consequent assumption of the fallancy that the coast was thus to be permanently reduced and the obstacles to supply, from the rebellion, indirectly overcome,- as through the extraordinary competition and excitement thus produced at these points were not to have their legitimate effects upon prices, or the growth of Tea could be stimulated upon a low scale of them to an extent to replace the impending deficiency in the Black-leaf kinds!

More recently, we have seen the fluctuations of the consuming markets originating from the fallacy that the lessening of the supply and permanent enhancement of the coast of Tea was more dependent upon the question of peace with the Foreigner than upon the prolongation of the civil War.- which, in fact, ever since 1853 has been striking at every roots of the stage, as in days of old, when Jardine and Dent appeared as the heroes of a melo-drama costumed as "blod smugglers." a pistol in one hand, and a bill of opium in the other cramming the latter down the threats of the unfortunate Chinamen. whilst sanctimonions Scotland will doubtless shed bitter tears, at the "awful back sliding" of her degenerate son, but it must be borne in mind, that though not previously legalized, the importation of drug, under the name of foreign medicine, had been permitted at one of the ports, whilst here the Mandarins admitted it on the pament of 23 Tls. per chest

Although the treaty with Japan has not yet come out ratified, a trade has already commenced which is likely to increase rapidly, and to be of great advantage to this place.

Whilst the past year has been eventful in the East not less marked has been its course in the West, for, monetary panic which swept away in its headlong course so many of the leading Merchantile Houses in England and America, will long be remembered as one of the most severe ever experienced. All articles of foreign Imports were more or less affected by it, but the staple productions of China probably suffered more than any others. but our trade on the whole seems already to have recovered from the effects of it.

IMPORTS.- The trade in Manufactured goods during the year, has been comparatively satisfactory to Importers, the deliveries of the staple articles shewing a considerable increase compared with the previous year.

Periods of extreme depression have occasionally occurred, when the movements of the rebels has he neighbouring provinces have prevented goods from in be sent into the interior, or when the market becomeing temporarily overstocked owing to the simultaneous arrival of large supplies, which have been forced off against produce and resold at reduced rates, thereby entailing heavy issues to the native dealers, who had laid in their stocks before the an occasional advance in price when foreigners commenced purchasing.

EXPORTS- Silk.- The Silk trade must always prove the most important feature in our commerce here, as owing to the large deliveries of China Silk in Europe, it seems not improbable but that our export may still go on increasing, provided excessive competition amongst purchasers here, does not force up prices beyond what manufacturers at home can afford to give. Should the Continental crops again prove a failure next year, the cultivation of the Mulberry may to some extent be abandoned, when Europe would be more than ever dependant on China for her supplies, but it is only by a moderate scale of prices that we can expect long to enjoy a monopoly of the trade.

The year opened with the receipt of most unfavorable accounts of the London market, which exercised a depressing influence here till the end of March, when a reaction took place consequent upon more favorable accounts being received, and large purchases were made at full prices.

In June the market was quiet in anticipation of the arrival of the new crop which was reported to be "abundant and of good quality," whilst a very large stock of old Silk was said to be retained in the country.

The new crop did not prove so fine in size as was expected, and higher prices were demanded than purchasers were inclined to give, consequently little was done till July, when purchases commenced and since then we have had a most active market, the monthly settlements averaging nearly 10,000 Bales.

The market opened at Tls. 330 for No. 3 Tsatlee, with exchange 5s. $11\frac{1}{2}$d. per tael, making the laying down price in London about 17s 4d. per lb., and since then the Silkmen have regulated their demands, advancing or reducing them,

Sudden changes have taken place, and high rates have been experienced, but these are more attributable to speculative transactions amongst the local Banks, than to an actual scarcity of Silver, or an undue pressure of Bills on the market.

From January till the middle of July the quotation for 6 months'sight Bills on England remained steadily at 5s. 11d. a 6s. 1d., and on India Rs. 280 a 290 per 100 Tls., then declined for a short time to 5s. $9\frac{1}{2}$ d. a 5s. $10\frac{1}{2}$d. per Tael, on the receipt of unfavorable advices about Silk, but rallied shortly afterwards, and repaidly advanced, till the highest point was reached in November. the quotation then being. for a couple days only, 6s. $10\frac{1}{2}$d. a 6s $11\frac{1}{2}$d. □□□□□□□□□□□□India. Since then rates have declined, and the tendency is still downwards, as transactions in produce are likely to be limited for some time.

SHIPPING. - The number of Merchant vessels that arrived in 1858 was less than in 1857, although at one time there were 140 ships in the harbour, and in no former year has the number ever exceeded 90. In 1857 there arrived 554 vessels aggregating 256,327 tons, and in 1858 the arrivals were 510 of the burthen of 285,500 tons, showing the number to be fewer in 1858, but the burthen greater. On the 1st of January in 1858 there were 58 vessels of 35.500 tons in port. and on the 31st December the number was 73 of 42,000 tons.

The above includes all foreign vessels except lorchas.

On the improvement of the settlement there is not much to observe. The New Dock on the Hongkew side, which was in course of excavation at the commencement of the year, has been completed and is in full operation after many difficulties that were presented by the failure of the caisson, the falling in of the embankments and frequent inundations.

Several new foreign buildings have Tea trade.

Such are, briefly. some of the mischievous rancies. espectiing the Tea Trade of the last five years, and which, being naturally first detected in China, have served,- along with the exceptionally- adverse extraneous influences of the period upon the markets of England and America,- to keep the scales of prices here in advance of those markets and thus to inflict upon shippers repeated losses;- losses, moreover, in inverse proportion to their deserts derived from superior perception, however paradoxical this may appear.

Similar results, although happily less disastrous in the aggregate amount of loss, have arisen from fallacious reasoning respecting the prospective consumption of Cotton and other Goods, which have become somewhat notorious from the absurdity of the estimate of some writer that 300 millions of people would each be prepared to buy a pair of Cotton Trousers of the Foreigner!-

To the various fallacies which have from time to time arisen in respect to politicaland social questions I have no need to more than recall here the recollection of my readers.

With such proneness abroad to misread the alternating signes of the times, it becomes especially important at a moment when, as now, general attention is fixed upon Chinese affairs, and when Statesmen as well as Merchants are studiously collecting and collating evidence and comparing authorities upon questions affecting the selection of new ports of trade and the regulations of future intercourse- when a new campaign of peaceful decline took place.

The market for cotton manufactures has maintained a healthy tone throughout the year, and generally the prices obtained have been remunerative to Importers. The year commenced with an active demand for Grey and White Shirtings at full prices, which were fairly supported till the beginning of June, when the commencement of hostilities at the North caused a temporary panic amongst the native dealers and a decline in prices.

Since then the market has been quiet, and prices gradually declined till November when the lowest point was reached. the quotations for $6\frac{1}{2}$ catty Grey Shirtings being Tls. 1.7.0 per piece. Latterly shipments to some extent have been made to the southern ports, where quotations were higher than those current here, and now there is a specuiative demand in anticipation of an advance taking place after China New Year. Prices have slightly improved, and have still an upward tendency. Stocks are now much reduced, and the supplies on the way out excessive so we look with confidence for a satisfactory trade in Shirtings next season.

Woollen manufactures have not experienced many fluctuation, but the disturbances which have taken place in Kiangsi, &c., have materally interfered with the development of the trade, and tended to keep prices at a low level.

as exchange rose or fell, so as to keep price of No. 3 Tsatlee rather over the rates ruling in London, each successive mail. The stock in the country is known to be large, but as the holders are not in want of money it is doubtful whether the whole will be brought down here should purchases refuse to give the rates now current.

Tea– A variety of circumstance have combined to interfere with the Black Tea trade at this port, and this season it seems certain that the supply will show a marked deficiency compared with that of the last five or six years.

The year opened with an active market, purchases being stimulated by the stoppage of trade at Canton, and the uncertainty whether the old Teas in stock there would be fit for export, whilst the total supply of new Congou was known to be short. On the receipt of the November advices from London, business was almost suspended for a couple of months, then sprung into short lived activity for a week or two, and subsequently relapsed into inactivity till the close of the season, on accounts being received of the opening of trade at Canton. and large purchases there.

been erected on both sides. A new Jail has been built on the British Consular Ground. The bund on the Soochow creek is extended to Barriet Road, as a foot path, and only requires leveling to be passable by carriages. A large lot of ground on the Road of the Soochow creek North–west of the British Consulate has been filled in, improving that quarter; a Jetty has also been completed at the end of Church street on the Soochow creek, and several of the old jetties have been repaired and raised.

TO THE EDITOR OF THE

"HONGKONG REGISTER."

SIR,– Your purpose in republishing the Review of the Year of the *North–China Herald*, in your No. 12, was no doubt conceived in the interest of your constituents, so that it would be gratuitous– to say the least– to suppose that you wish them to understand that you endorse its false reasoning or adopt the fallancies of its deductions;– however unexceptionable its narrative or useful its statistical portions may be deemed by you: And, as an annual *Résumé* of the Trade of any particular point in the Commercial World is, if correct, to be accepted as, so far, an indice and guide to its future course and proper conduct, the reliability of such a publication is of that degree of importance which, while it should restrain the pens of all who are not at once practical men and logical reasoners, likewise impose upon those who may perceive a divergence from the just line of sequence or of inference– however reluctant commerce and a wider Mission–effort for the spread of Christian truth are being inaugurated– that public writers at the great commercial and political centre of Shanghae should well weigh their opinions and words before undertaking to present a digest similar to that which you have extracted from the columns of your respect–able northern contemporary.–

"It is an axiom that 'every man is to be believed in his own art,' hence the practical man is the real lawgiver;– the Legislator and the Diplomatist must found their theory on the Merchant's experience. This is especially the case in China, for our whole intercourse hitherto may be said to be simply commercial– socially and politically we have been rigorously excluded;

Supplement to the Overland Register and Price Current No 3.

and hence an unusual responsibility attaches to those who attempt to present the practical working of commercial relations."

To the narrative or the statistics of the author of the Shanghae Retrospect I take no exception,– the less because it is obviously incomplete in these respects; but I cannot refrain from expressing regret that its just acknowledgment of Lord Elgin's services is tarnished by the puerile cavil about the petty carrying trade in *Peas* and *Beans* being interdicted from the two new northern ports of trade.– a cavil that but ill befits the ambitious claim of Shanghae to all–but–a monopoly of the foreign trade of China; and as little accords with the hopes expressed in another paragraph, as quoted below.

A more worthly cavil might have been made to some of his Lordship's proceedings, and one in which I confess to some sympathy, although as yet the grounds for it are conjectural: I allude to the Expedition up the Yang–tsze–kiang, and certain attendant circumstances prejudicial to the Rebel cause; but this were a cavil to gain very few adherents at Shanghae– now that the cause of the Patriots is decidedly on the wane, after years of neglect on the part of the Christian Nations;– for there is no mistaking the prevailing idea there that by some *coup de maitre* or other– the direct aid to the Imperialists for years not having sufficed– the Rebels were to be compelled to make way for the expansion of the Opium and other branches of the already large Trade of that favored port.–

Nothing can be more unpopular among Merchants than such a cavil; but I cannot restrain the expression of it in this conditional form pending further information of the real purposes of Lord Elgin in this regard.

No person, perhaps, has derived are very much in the way of the trade of Shanghae,– so have they, and in a greater degree, obstructed the trade of Canton, and never so much as in that very year of 1854–55.– The permanent conditions, too, of the relative situation of Shanghae must be better kept in view,– for instance, in respect to all "Common Congou," and even the bulk of what had formed the trade in Black Teas previously, that these Teas could (in 1856) be conveyed to Foo–chow at a difference in cost estimated at 15 per cent: which, if we take into account with the adverse difference of Exchange at Shanghae, more fairly accounts for the subsequent decline of the Black Tea trade of the latter port than the reasons presented in the following paragraph.

"*The additional expenses incurred in endavouring to suppress the rebellion have induced the Mandarins to have recourse to extraordinaty means to raise funds, and latterly they have imposed additional inland duties on all Teas brought here by way of Hangchow, amounting it is said in all to about 12 Tls. per pecul. Under these circumstances. the commonest descriptions of Congou, costing Tls. 6 a 8 per pecul in the country. cannot be laid down here under Tls. 18 a 20. whilst the finer kinds cost Tls. 30 a 35; consequently so long as the taxes are levied our supplies are likely to be limted to the latter, which may be sold without loss, whilst the common kinds, which are seldom worth over Tls. 12 a 14 per pecul, must either be left ungathered' or, has been the case this year taken for the Northern markets. The export of Black Tea for the year is 6,000,000 lbs. less than in 1857, and now the market is completely bare of stock.*

But I am admonished by the exigencies of time and your space that I

P. S.– Since closing the foregoing, the Steamer from Shanghae has brought to me the perspiculous reply of Lord Elgin to the address of the British mercantile Firms of the 13th instant; and with reference to my hesitation upon the question as to the right use of his Lordship's power and influence upon the Yang–tsze–kiang, as between the Rebels and Imperialists, it is only just to acknowledge the evidence which not a few of his words afford of a prevailing sense of accountability to principles– a recognition of the rightful claims of the people–("the inhabitants of these countries")– to the benefits of enlarging intercourse.

It is hardly necessary to add, in conclusion, that I am not suggesting a rivalry or instituting a comparison between Shanghae and the other ports; but endeavoring to reach a just estimate of its resources by duly regarding the conditions inseparable from its geographical position and from its actual possession of an Export Trade of about Forty millions of Dollars in Raw Silk and Green Tea.

OLD CANTON.

January 27th, 1859.

ANNUAL RETROSPECT OF THE STRAITS' TRADE FOR 1858.

The trade of the Straits Settlements for the official year 1857–58 appears from the published Statements to have amounted in value as follows:–

IMPORTS.

Singapore. . .	Rs. 67,052,939
Pinang	13,072,907
Malacca.	4,540,829
	Rs. 84,666,675

EXPORTS.

Singapore. . .	Rs. 57,835,839
Pinang.	18,554,078
Malacca.	3,244,935
	Rs. 79,634,852

The value of the trade of Singapore for 1858, brought down to the end of the year, does not show the same ratio of increase as for some previous years, there being in fact a slight falling off.– The value of the Imports in 1858 was estimated as $26,574,332 being $573,711 less than in 1857. The value of the Exports was $23,408,106 being less than those in 1857 by $1,026,382. The total value of the trade in 1858 was $49,982,438 being less than that of 1857 by $1,600,093. It may be remarked that the trade of 1857 exceeded that of the previous year 1856 by $7,525,831. The number of square–rigged vessels which arrived in 1858, was 1,168 being 14 more than in 1857. The departures of square–rigged vessles in 1858 were 1205, being 26 less than in 1857. The number of junks and native boats which arrived in 1858 was 2,549, being 152 less than in 1857. The number of junks and native boats which left Singapore in 1858 was 2657 being 387 less than in 1857. The very depressed state of trade in Europe, and the serious interruption to it in India and China, during 1858, reacted unfavorably on that of Singapore, and some heavy local failures, owing to over–trading and rash speculation, contributed to render 1858 a very unsatisfactory year for the commerce of Singapore. During the greater part of the year the harbour was crowded with shipping, as much unable here, as in China, India, and elsewhere, to find employment on any terms. Measures were adopted by the merchants to prevent over speculation amongst the native traders, by limiting the length of time for which credit had formerly been given, and the practice of giving large advances to the traders on contracts for the delivery of produce was done away with. Other measures for improving the greather gratification from the achievements of his Lordship, as no one can have more fully appreciated the difficulties overcome by his admirable perseverance and consistent firmness; but when I heard of the departure of his Expedition up the Yang-tsze I dreaded, almost, to decipher the inscription upon the Standard that his vessel bore, lest I should read these words of ill-omen for the Patriots:- *Trade is more precious than the struggle for principles.*

"*The future dawns more hopefully on us, and we not unreasonably anticipate that the opening of the Yang-tsze Kiang, will again place Shanghae on her former footing as a Tea exporting port, by allowing supplies to be brought down without being subjected to the excessive inland duties now levied by the Mandarins.*"

To these commendable aspirations no exception need be taken were there not inseparable from those who write in the special interest of Shanghae- that it is possible to concentrate the Black Tea Trade, as well as that in Raw Silk and Green Tea at that point,- a fallacy that- independently of all considerations of proximity facility of carriage and existing ways and means pertaining to the other ports- rests upon a total ignoring of an insuperable obstacle existing, by reason of its enjoying the large Raw Silk and Green Tea Trade, in the adverse ruling of the Exchanges there relatively to the other ports, produced by the general distribution of Imports over the country, in conformity to the natural law of consumption- a condition of things to which the trade in Exports must correspond and *pari passu*, adjust itself until, at least, the introduction of Railways shall so greatly overcome time and space as toindicate one common controlling point of distribution for the former and shipment must restrict myself to the alternative intimated at the close of my first paragraph, in now proceeding specially to notice the more "silent points of error" or misdirection of remark in the publication which suggested this letter; and I beg leave to do so in an interrogatory form.-

1st. Is the reasoning in the following paragraph respecting Raw Silk in logical conformity to the laws of trade?-

"*The Silk trade must always prove the most important feature in our commerce here, as owing to thhe large deliveries of China Silk in Europe, it seems not improbable but that our export may still go on increasing, provided excessive competition amongst purchasers here, does not force up prices beyond what manufacturers at home can afford to give.*

Should the Continetal crops again prove a failure next year, the cultivation of the Mulberry may to some extent be abandoned, when Europe would be more than ever dependent on China for her supplies, but it is only by a moderate scale of prices that we can expect long to enjoy a monopoly of the trade."

2nd. Is it possible by the introduction of a new *Measure of Value* to control the trade- i. e. enlarge of □□□□□□□□□ a great commercial centre, as is implied by the statement that substitution of the "Shanghae Tael" for the previous *denomination* of the Currency had tended "to keep Exchange at a moderate level thoughout the year" - as made in the following quoted paragraphs?-

"*Exchange.- The introduction of the Tael of Sycee as the currency at this port has given universal satisfaction, as it has tended to keep Exchange at a moderate level throughout the year, and prevented those extreme rates which occasionally ruled when the Carolus Dollar was the sole medium of payment.*

Imports as above...	84,666,675
Total	Rs. 164,301,527

There was an increase on both Imports and Exports at all the three places, as follows:-

IMPORTS.

Singapore···	Rs. 14,207,951
Pinang ······	1,476,446
Malacca······	591,816
	Rs. 16,276,233

EXPORTS.

Singapore···	Rs. 10,058,858
Pinang ······	2,274,775
Malacca······	431,473
	Rs. 12,765,106
Imports as above···	16,276,233
Total increase	Rs. 29,041,339

□□□□□□□□ □Singapore during the official year 1857-58, amounted to Rs. 785,294, exceeding those of the previous year by Rs. 106,754. The receipts were derived from:-

Excise Farms and Pawnbrokers Licenses···	Rs. 561,558
Fees and Fines from Court of Judicature and Court of Request···	35,339
Quit-rents, Land sold, registry fees, rent of Government markets, and houses, and difference of Exchange···	88,557
Post Office······	66,888
Light dues······	20,332
Registry of vessels, hire of Government steamer &c···	7,052
Miscellaneous.······	5,564

The disbursements for 1857-58 amounted to Rs. 868,051, exceeding those of the previous year by Rs. 247,324. The disbursements were as

Local Residency charges.. Rs. 300,327

system on which trade is conducted between the European and native merchants were also partially brought into operation but afterwards abandoned, owing to the refusal of one or two European firms to concur in them.

The rise in the value of real property which we noticed in the retrospects for 1856 and 1857 as having taken place in Singapore, was fully maintained in 1858. The increase in the price of labour and of building materials was equally great, but notwithstanding this a great many new houses were built both in the town and the country. The price of food has also undergone a material enhancement, a matter of serious inconvenience to persons with fixed and limited incomes, such as the subordinates in the Government offices.

PINANG.- From returns published in the Government Gazette we learn that the Imports into Pinang during the official year 1857-58 amounted in value to Rs. 13,072,907, showing an increase over the previous year of Rs. 1,476,466. The Exports during 1857-58 amounted to 18,554,078, being an increase over the previous year of Rs. 2,274,775. The total value of trade in 1857-58 amounted to Rs. 21,626,985. The number of square-rigged vessels, which arrived in 1857-58 was 550, being an increase of 56. The departures were 499, being an increase of 39. The arrivals of native-craft were 1,619, and of departures 2,492. The trade of Pinang in 1858, like that of Singapore, suffered from over speculation, principally on the part of the Chinese merchants. A number of failures took place and the loss was estimated at some lakhs of dollar, which chiefly fell upon the Chittys, who had advanced upwards of $800,000 to these traders.

MALACCA.- The value of the Import

for the latter;– or, till the actual increase of the consumption of Imports, relatively with the shipments of Exports, shall reverse the balance of Trade at that port.

The longing eyes of Shanghae, which so constantly revert to the great Tea year of 1854–1855, must keep in view, also, the exceptional circumstances of that year tending to what– after all has been said in its favor– proved to be *inflation*; and that to a degree which shippers thence would be glad to forget:– If the Rebels have been and

"*Sudden changes have taken place, and high rates have been experienced, but these are more attributable to speculative transactions amongst the local Banks, than to an actual scarcity of Silver or an undue pressure of Bills on the market.*"

I may remark here that I suppose there will soon be a step taken in the interest of Shanghae calculated to ameliorate the difficulties of the Currency and thus facilitate Trade; but the mere *instrument* of Currency or arbitary "*Dollar*" of Account cannot rule the Exchange low or high– its rate depending upon the balance of Trade.

Straits Settlements do..	53,136
Military charges....	400,855
Conviet do......	94,703
Straits Lights charges..	18,998

The disbursements exceeded the receipts by Rs. 82,757.

and Export trade of Malacca during 1857–58 amounted to Rs. 7,785,764, showing an increase over that of the previous year of Rs. 1,023,289. The number of square–rigged vessels which arrived during 1857–58 was 30, being one less than in the pprevious year, and the departures were 17 being 12 less than in 1856–57. These figures are exclusive of the arrivals and departures of vessels trading between Malacca and Singapore and Pinnang, and which amounted to about 230 either way, being about 30 less than in the preceding year.– *Singapore Free Press*, January 6.

visit. Mr. Thompson intends to return again to the Balonne, and to await their arrival. If this story be true, the age of wonders truly has not ceased. The incredulous may, by a visit to Mr. Whittaker's, hear the particulars as we have described them.– *Maitland Mercury*.

Hongkong Market.

(15th February, 1859.)

OPIUM.–

After the arrival of the last mail, MALWA remained steady at $602.30 a 605 until after the Chinese New Year, when it advanced to $607.50 a 610 with but moderate demand. After the arrival to the *Ottawa* prices declined to $605, a few sales being made. Holders however are firm and not inclined to sell, owing to the advanced prices at Bombay. To–day's quotations are $605 a 610.

BENGAL remained steady at $762.50 a 765 till after the Chinese New Year, when it advanced to 770, with a fair demand; on the arrival of the *Fiery Cross*, which brought only about 1,100 chests, rates further advanced to $777.50 a 780

Longkong.	Lucklow.	Kowkong.	Rereeled.
$390	$370	$350	$400

Stocks estimated at 1,000 piculs.

ARRIVALS,– From England, Bio Bio.

From U. States none.

DEPARTURES.– For London, Solent.

For U. States, Kremlin.

LOADING AND ON THE BERTH.– For London, Glendoveer, Menam, Bio Bio, Caroline Agnes.

For Liverpool, Crisis.

For New York, T.W. Sears and Myrtle (going to Whampoa) Rosette, (at Macao)

FREIGHTS.– To England £2 for tea per ton of 50 cubic feet.

To United States. $8 per ton of 40 cubic feet.

EXCHANGE.– Bank Rates quite nominal.

First Class Paper and good credits 4s. $6\frac{3}{4}$d. a 4s. 7d.

On India Rs. 217 a 218 per $100.

BULLION.– Bar Silver 10 a $10\frac{1}{2}$ per cent premium.

Gold Leaf, $23.90.

Per P. & O. S. N. Co.'s Steam–ship

OPIUM,– This market has been steady and quiet since the last mail left; from that date until the commencement of the New Year holidays there were no arrivals of Drug, and stocks became low, yet an advance in prices has not been established, our latest quotations, for actual business on the 31st Ultimo, being the same nearly as those on the 21st. Bargains, to be cleared after the holidays, were made at about 10 taels higher than cash prices and these to the extent of about 400 chests are included in the stocks below given.

The highest and lowest quotations since the 21st are,– *Malwa* Tls. 443 and 460, *New Patna*, high numbers, Tls. 543 and 558, low numbers, Tls. 528 and 545, and *Old Patna*, Tls. 523 and 530. During the last two or three days there has been no business and quotations are quite nominal.

The following is a statement of Imports, Deliveries, and Stocks:–

	Malwa.	*Patna*.
Stocks on 4th January, 1859,	3,900 Chests	2,000 Chests.
Imports since, ···	1,221 "	···310 "

SILK,– As anticipated in our report the settlements during the fortnight have been small, estimated at about 1,000 bales, making for the month 4,000. Prices have continued to rise as the stock declined and an advance of 20 taels has taken place in the month. The unsold stock at present in the market is very small, probably not much over 1,000 bales, and the quality inferior; a large accession to it is expected when business is resumed, after the holidays. The news just received of improvement in the home markets will tend to increase the firmness of dealers in their demands.

The export to date is 10,000 bales more than at the same period in last season.

QUOTATIONS.

TSATLEES– Nos. 1, a 5, (1 & 2 nom.)	Tls. 390 a 395
TAYSAAMS– Nos. 1, a 5, (No. 1, nom.)	Tls 240 a 330
Long reel. ..	Ils250 a 275
LAE YUNGS, ..	Ils220 a 235
THROWNS English twist,..	Ils 330 a 350

for old and 800 for new. From 400 to 500 chests more may be looked for by the steamer *Viscount Canning*.

BENARES. little has been done in this drug, but the prices have kept up say at $805 a 810. On the arrival of the *Fiery Cross* rates had a further advance, owing to the smallness of the stock. To-day's quotation is (nominal) are–

New Benares $840 a 850

Old do. 830

Turkey is in demand. None in the market.

COTTON,–

BOMBAY $13½ a 14¼,– BENGAL no enquiry. We have heard of a few sales of Bombay Cotton at from $13½ to 13.70 for middling kinds.

RICE,–

BENGAL CARGO $2.10 a 2¼. White $2.40 a 2½. Some small lots of Bengal Cargo changed hands at $2.15 a 2.20 and $2½ a 2.55 for White.

BULLION,–

SILVER BAR, 10 a 10¼. per cent prem:

SYCEE SILVER 8¼ a 8½ per cent.

GOLD LEAF $23.90 a 23.95 per tael

SOVEREIGNS $4.55 a 4.60. Silver Bars, have been sold 10½ per cent prem: may now be had a 10 per cent. Sycee Silver, some for sale a 8½ per cent. Gold leaf is to be had at $23.95 per tael.

EXCHANGE.

ORIENTAL BANK CORPORATION.

EXCHANGE.

On London,– 6 months' sight, 4s. 6d.

Calcutta,– 3 days' sight, Rupees 218 per $100.

Bombay,– 3 days' sight, Rupees 218 per $100.

CREDIT AND OTHER BILLS.

On England,– 4s. 7d. 6 months' sight.

"*Aden*."

(From the *North–China Herald*.)

Shanghae Market Report.

(*February 5, 1859*.)

We extract the following from the Shanghae Market Report of Feb. 5:–

The trade of the port has been satisfactory. It is now interrupted by the China New Year holidays, but will be assumed next week.

Stocks of Imports in Foreign Godowns on the 25th ultimo, have been taken by general consent of the importers. They prove to be light in most manufactured goods, and an advance in prices is expected after the holidays.

Ships continue to clear outwards for, and enter inwards from, Nagasaki.

IMPORTS–

We have again to report an active Import market, the dealers having continued purchasing manufactured goods at current rates, till the 2nd instant, when all businessceased for the Chinese New Year holidays. The native settling day on 1st instant was put over without much difficulty, money appearing plentiful amongst the traders, and an increased demand for manufactures is looked for on the resumption of business.

Grey and White Shirtings have again slightly advanced, and the market closed with an upward tendency as the northern Junks are expected to take off a considerable quantity in the course of the month.

Fancy Goods are quoted much the same as at the date of our last report, at which considerable sales have been made, and stocks of all kinds expect Chintzes are becoming reduced.

Woollens, Long Ells and Camlets continue in fair demand at former rates.

The market for Straits Produce remains inactive, and although stocks in first hands are comparatively light, prices do not advance.

Rice has still an upward tendency, and not much left in stock.

Total, .. 5,121 Chests 2,310 Chests.

Deliveries since Januany,

1,921 560

Stocks on 3rd Febry., 1859,

3,200 Chests 1,750 Chests.

EXPORTS.

TEA,– An extremely limited supply and the consequent exorbitant demands of the delaers has caused the transactions of the fortnight to be very small. The settlements are reported at 2,000 chests of fair Ningchow at 27 a 28 taels, 1,500 of good to fineat 34 a 35½, e 1,000 half chests of Oolong and old repacked Congou at 17½,– the latter for Colonies, and the Oolong for America,– and about 14,000 packages of Green, also for the United States; leaving a short supply in the market, which the Chinese assert will be but little increased by arrivals from the country during the remainder of the season.

QUOTATIONS.

CONGOU,

Ningchow, Oonam and Oopak,

Tls. 27 a 29–35

Old, do., & common Souchong & Congou,

18 a 26

Common Superior to

to Good. fine & finest

Gunpowder, & Imperial

Tls. 22 a 26 Tls. 27 a 36–35

Young Hyson,

Tls 17 a 23 Tls 24 a 34–40

Hyson,

Tls 21 a 26 Tls 27 a 45–50

Twankay. & Skin,

Tls 13 a 17 Tls 18 a 22

EXPORTS *from* SHANGHA I *from 1st July* 1858, to *dates*.

To Great Britain direct,–

Black. Green. Total.

To Jan. 21, as

per last report, lbs. 4,600,374 4,157,228 8,757,602

To Jan 30 per *Zealandia*, for London, lbs. 849,700,227 800 1,077,500

Feb. 2, per

The Export to Great Britain, the Continent of Europe, and India. direct and Coastwise, is as follows:–

To Jan. 21, as per Bales.

Last report, 54,798

Thrown. Coarse. Waste.

"23, per *Formosa*,

for Hongkong, 2,061

To Jan. 30, per *Zealandia*,

for London, 1,538*

Feb. 2, per *Portena*,

for London, 466*

Feb. 5, 1859–

Total, 58,863

inclg. 4,943 64 50

The P. & O. Co.'s Steam Ship *Aden*, for Hongkong, to–morrow morning, will take about 869 bales.

Against total Export to 5th Feb,, 1858, } 48,792 4,098 34 499

SUNDRIES,– per *Zealandia*, Rhubarb 252 cases. Silk Piece Goods 1 case, * includes 67 Throwns and 146 Coarse. Per *Portena*, Silk Piece Goods 5 cases, * includes 33 Throwns and 4 Waste. Per *Henry Harbeck*, Baw Silk 23.15 pieces, Rhubarb 19.50 pieces, Rattans 50 pieces, Matting 295 rolls, Gongs 8 caases. Per *Beaver*, Raw Silk 53,60 pecs., Cassia 500 pecs., Rattans 330 pecs, Fire Crackers 2,000 boxes. Per *Joshua Bates*, Silks,– White Pongees 2,025 pcs., Sarsnets 125 pcs., Gauzes 318 pcs., Handkerchiefs 934 pcs., Raw Silk 33.56 pecs.

EXCHANGE AND BULLION.

Business for this mail has been on a most limited scale, as usual at this season, but Bills having been rather pressed on the market, rates have somewhat advanced.

On India the demand has been very small, remittances being chiefly made in Gold.

The mail closes rather weakly at the following quotations.

On Bombay,– 3days' sight, Rupees 218.

On Calcutta,– 3 days' sight, Rupees 218.

COMMERCIAL BANK OF INDIA.

On London,– 6 months' sight 4s. $6\frac{3}{4}$d. Sight 4s. 5d.

Calcutta,– 3 days' sight, Rupees 218.

Bombay,– 3 days' sight, Rupees 218.

Canton Market Report.

(From 27th January to 12th February 1859.)

All quotation less 2 per cent.

IMPORTS.

A few speculative purchases were made just before Chinese New Year's day (3d February) in manufactured goods and business may now be said to be fairly resumerd. The demand however is not brisk, and prices remain almost unaltered for the principal staples. The following quotations are duty paid.

COTTON YARN.– 440 bales sold, Nos. 16 a 24 $37 a 40: Nos. 28 a 32 $44 a 48; Nos. 38 a 42 $39 a 42.

GREY SHIRTINGS.– 15.600 pieces sold. $5\frac{1}{4}$ a 6 catty, $2.10 a 2.40; $6\frac{1}{4}$ a $6\frac{3}{4}$. $2.65 a 2.90; $7\frac{1}{4}$ a $7\frac{1}{2}$, $3.25 a 3.40.

WHITE SHIRTINGS, –10.500 pieces sold, 56 a 60 reed, $2.55 a 2.70; 64 a 66 reed, $2.80 a 2.95; 68 a 72 reed, $3 q 3.25.

AMERICAN DRILLS.– 40–yards 1,000 pieces sold at $4.15 per piece.

SPOTTED SHIRTINGS.– 1,000 pieces White, sold at $2.55 a 2.65: 2,500 Dyed at $3.50 a 4.05.

BROCADES– 2,250 pieces White sold at $3.50 a 4.05.

CHINTE– 3,000 pieces sold, Common $1.50 a 1.85; fine $2.05 a 2.55.

SPANISH STRIPES.– None sold since our last quotation, $1.20 a 1.40.

LONG ELLS.– None sold; nominally 50 a75 c. per piece dearer.

Sugar has rather improved in value, and was in good demand at advancing prices till the close of business on 1st instant.

QUOTATIONS DUTY, PAID IN TAELS OF SHANGHAE SYCEE.

The Deliveries are for the month.

SHIRTINGS,– Grey have manufactured an advance that took place before the *Anglo Saron* arrived. Stocks in first hands are moderate. White remain as borke Grey, $5\frac{1}{2}$ to 6–catty, Tls. 1.6.5 a 1.7.5; $6\frac{1}{2}$ to 7–catty, Tls. 1.9.0 a 2.0.0; $7\frac{1}{2}$–catty, Tls. 2.3.0– Deliveries 120,000 pieces. White, common to fine, Tls. 1.5.5 a 2.2.5– Deliveries 22,000 pieces.

T. CLOTHS,– $4\frac{1}{2}$ to $5\frac{1}{2}$–catty, Tls. 1.1.0a 1.4.5– Deliveries 10,000 piecces.

SPOTTED SHIRTINGS,– White, and Assorted, are in demand, Tls. 1.7.5. a 1.8.5. and Tls. 2.2.0 a 2.5.0– Deliveries 19,000 pieces.

BROCADES,– Are sought for. White, Tls. 2.2.0. a 2.3.5; Assorted, Tls. 2.7.5 a 3.2.0– Deliveries 8,500 pieces.

DAMASKS,– Tls. 2.7.5a 3.2.0– Deliveries 2,200 pieces.

HANDKERCHIEFS,– Stocks rather large. Large and small assorted colors and patterns, mace 4.5 a 6.0 per dozen– Deliveries 6.500 dozens.

CHINTZES, Tls. 1.2.0a 1.6.5; scarlet 1.4.0– Deliveries 12.000 pieces.

AMERICAN GOODS,– Transactions small. Prices nominal. except for best marks. *Drills*, 40–yards, best goods, Tls. 2.8.5a 2.9.5; 30–yards, are proportionately less– Deliveries 25,000 pieces. *Sheetings*, 10–catty, Tls. 2.1.0; 11–catty, Tls. 2.3.0– Deliveries 1,500 pieces. *Jeans*, 40–yeards, Tls. 3.2.5– Deliveries 3,300 pieces.

WOOLLENS,– Continue to be enquired for. *Spanish Stripes*, mace 7.0 a 9.7 *Habit Cloths*; Assorted colors, best goods, Tl. 1.0.5. *Medium Cloths*; Assorted

Portena,

for London, lbs.

149,653 197, 551 347,204

Feb. 5, 1859 – Total, lbs.

5,599,727 4582,579 10,182,306

Against total Export.–

To 5th Feb. 1858. lbs.

15,956,964 2,942,499 18,899,463

To United States,–

To Jan. 21, as per

Last report, lbs. 1,535 12,649,045 12,650,580

To Jan. 27, per *Henry Harbeck*,

for New York, lbs. – 793,903 739,903

To Jan 28, per *Beaver*,

for New York, 25,400 536,391 561,791

Feb 2 per □□□ *Bates*,

for New York, lbs.

□□□ □□□ □□□

Feb 5, 1859– Total lbs.

43,722 14,532,886 14,576,588

Against total Export,–

To 5th Feb., 1858. lbs.

230,416 10,633.408 10,863,824

On *London* { Bank Bills, 6 m. st. 6s. $1\frac{1}{2}$ d. First Class Credits m 6s. $2\frac{1}{2}$d. Duet. & other Bills m 6s. 3d. a 6s $3\frac{1}{2}$d. } per Tl.

On *Calcutta* { Bank Drafts, 3d. st. Rs. 299

On *Bombay* Do. 8 d. sr. Rs. 288 } per 100 Tls.

On *Hongkong* Do. 15 d. st. $27\frac{1}{2}$ a 28 per cent disct.

CANTON SYCEE, 9.4 percent premium. ENGLISH BAR SILVER. 17 dwts. B. $11\frac{1}{2}$ per cent premium.

GOLD BARS.– *Pekin*, 98 touch Tls. 162 a 163– *Soochow*, 97 touch Tls. 160 a 161 per ten Tls *Shanghae* □□□

MEXICAN DOLLARS.– 73 cents.

COPPER CASH.– 1,390 per Tael. 16,000 to a pecu Tls, 11.2.0 per pecul.

TREASURE– Exported– Jan. 24, per Formosa, Taels 221.274.

CAMLETS.– About 300 pieces sold, English $17 a 23, Dutch $29 a32.

LEAD.– 1,050 piculs sold at $7.60 a 8.00. Tin Plates no sales $7.25.

NAIL ROD IRON.– 1.900 pieces sold at $3.00 a 3.70, Steel no sales $6.00 a 8.00.

HOOP IRON.– 25– piculs sold at $3.50 a 4.00, Spelter no sales $6.00.

IRON WIRE.– 800 piculs sold at $6.50 a 9.00

QUICK SILVER– 50 flasks $82.

COCHINEAL. 24 piculs $110 a 120.

EXPORTS.

TEA.– The market was quite cleared before the commencement of the holidays, and since then the arrivals have been very trifling. The demands of the Chinese have consequently been higher for Congous, which in some instances have been acceded to.

Sales. Stock.

CONGOU,– New and refired 7 chops at tls. 23 a $28\frac{1}{2}$; 6 cps.

– Old. 1 " " 19; 1"

To al settlemtnts of Congou since 1st July to date, New 193 chops.

Old 24 "

SOUCHONG,– No sales. Stock 7 chops.

TAYNAM CONGOU.– $900\frac{1}{2}$ chests at Tls. 19. Stock none.

SO□□ Oz. PAKOK. 11.000 boxes Tls 22 a 26 small

S□□TED CAPER. 6.000 boxes Tls $13\frac{1}{2}$ a 24 small

CAST a GUAP WDER 5,000 boxes Tls 13 a 19 mdte.

CAST IMPERAL 5,000 boxes Tls 13 a 19 mdte.

YOUNG HYSON. 700 boxes Tls 16 mdte

COUNTRY GREENS.– The sales are very small and the stock consists of about $13.000\frac{1}{2}$ chests Young Hyson and $1.200\frac{1}{2}$ chests Gunpowder.

colors, best goods, Tls. 1.7.7 a 1.8.0– Deliveries 2,200 pieces.

LONG ELLS,– Saleable at quotations. Scarlet Tls. 7.0.0 a 7.5.0; Assorted Tls. 6.8.0 a 8.0.0– Deliveries 640 pieces.

CAMLETS,– Small stock of Englis for which there is some demand. Tls. 15.5.0a 21.0.0– Deliveries 240 pieces.

VELVETS,– Neglected and 22–inch, Black, mace 1.5 a 1.6; Gentian, mace 1.4 a 1.5 per yard.– Deliveries 500 pieces.

VELVETENS,– Stock large. 18–inch, mace 0.9.0 a 1.1; 26–inch, mace 1.7 per yard.– Deliveries 500 pieces.

LEAD,– Wanted. Tls. 5.0.0 a 5.1.0 per pecul.

IRON,– Market over supplied and no demand. Square and Round, Tls. 2.4.0a 2.5.0; Nail Rod, Tls. 2.6.0 a 2.8.0 per pecul.

TIN,– Malacca and other first sort Straits, Tls. 27.0.0 a 28.0.0; Inferior, Tls. 24.0.0 a 25.0.0 per pecul.

TIN PLATES,– Tls. 6.0.0 per box.

QUICKSILVER,– Tls. 50 per pecul.

COAL,– English, Tls. 11 a 13 per Ton.

RATTANS,– Fine wanted. Banjermassing, Tls. 2.9.0a 3.2.0; Straits, Tls. 2.0.0 a 2.6.0 per pecul.

PEPPER,– Black, Siam and Singapore, Tls. 6.0.0 a 6.2.0 White, Tls. 11.0.0 per pecul.

SANDALWOOD,– Tls. 9.0.0 a 12.0.0 per pecul.

SAPANWOOD,– Stock low, large shipments having been made to Japan. Tls. 1.6.0a 2.0.0 per pecul.

MANGROVE BARK,– Mace 6.0 a 8.0 per pecul.

INDIGO,– Tls. 4.7.0a 5.0.0 per pecul.

SUGAR,– Good Brown is still in demand. Black and Brown, Canton, Swatow, Formosa, Amoy and Hainan. Tls. 3.2.5 a 3.9.0; White, Tls. 4.5.0 a 7.0.0 per pecul.

EXPORT OF TEA FROM CHINA TO THE UNITED STATES.

(From 1st July 1858 to the present time.)

VESSEL.	SAILED.	FROM.	BLACK TEAS.	GREEN TEAS.	TOTAL.
Beaver	Jan. 22	Shanghai	25,400	536,400	561,800
Henry Harbeck	" 24	do.		739,900	739,900
Joshua Bates	" 31	do.	16,800	607,500	624,300
Samuel Russell	" 31	Foochow	611,200		611,200
Judge Shaw	Feb. 5	Amoy	585,370		585,370
			1,238,770	1,883,800	3,122,570

TOTAL EXPORTS OF TEA TO THE UNITED STATES.

Season.	Shanghai.	Foochow.	Amoy.	Canton.	Total.
1858–9	14,5□□,□□0	5,903,235	3,226,444	822,170	24,528,349
1857–8	12,014,□□0	5,688,917	4,082,503	613,369	22,398,986

COMPARATIVE STOCKS OF TEA IN CHINA

	1859.		1858.	
	Black	Green	Black	Green
Shanghae	2,817,500 lbs.	4,440,000 lbs	3,527,500 lbs.	7,975,000 lbs.
February 5th,				
Foochow, " 8th,	1,648,000 "	……	4,862.000. "	……
Canton, " 10th,	348,500 "	1,174,800 "	15,700,000 "	1,719,000 "
	4,814,000 lbs	5,614,800 lbs.	24,089,500 lbs	9,634,000 lbs.

EXPORTS OF TEA, AND SILK, FROM CHINA TO GREAT BRITAIN,

FROM 1ST JULY 1858 TO 12TH FEBRUARY 1859.

VESSEL.	SAILED.	FROM	TO	TEA. (lbs.)	SILK. Bales.
	Total as	per Statement	to 25th January, 1859,	36,569,933	49,283
Solent	Jan. 31	Whampoa	London	810,100	
Zealandia	" 30	Shanghae	Do.	1,077,454	1,392
Portena	Feby. 2	Do.	Do.	347,204	462
Sorata	Jany. 31	Foochow	Do.	404,200	
M. Atheling	" 31	Do.	Cowes for Orders	892,000	
Cadiz (Steamer)	" 30	Hongkong	To Southampton, 1,296 " Mars eilles, 677 Bls		1,296
	Total Export to 12th February 1859.			40,100,891	52,433
	Do.	Do.	Do. 1858	40,520,392	48,286
	Do.	Do.	Do. 1857	49,249,002	59,242
	Total Export to Marseilles to 12th February, 1859.				5,787
	Do.	Do.	Do. Do.	1858	5,963
	Do.	Do.	Do. Do.	1857	8,772

Memorandum: "Seawfell" printed last Mail as 596,100; should have been 956,100.

CASFIA,– 300 piculs sold, $17\frac{1}{4}$. Stock 2,800 piculs. OILS AND Drugs– No sales and stocks small. SILK.– 100 piculs taken for India and prices are still high,–	RICE,– The market remains nearly as reported Arracan and Siam, Tls. 1.3.0 a 1.4.5; Bengal, Tls. 1.8.0 a 1.9.0 per pecul.	

SHIPPING INTELLIGENCE.

ARRIVED

AT	DATE	NAME	FLAG & RIG	TONS	CAPTAIN	FROM	SAILED	CARGO	CONSIGNERS
Hongkong	Jan. 30	Lanrick	Brit. bg.	290	Thomson	Fuhchau	Jan. 28	Teas	Jardine, M. & Co
"	" 30	Zephyt	Brit. sch.	148	Roper	Cupchi			Dent & Co
"	" 30	Dido	Ham bk.	272	Ipland	Siam	Dec. 9	Rice	Wm. Pustau and Co
"	" 30	Helena	Dan. bk.	260	Simoas	Singapore	Dec. 17	General	W. Pustau & Co
"	" 30	Esperanza	Ham bk.	200	Johansen	Whampoa	Jan. 29	General	Wm. Pustau & Co
"	" 31	Alipore	Brit. sh.	811	Mundoch	Shanghae	Jan. 26	Cotton	Gilman and Co
"	" 31	Daylight	Am. sh	547	Helbrooks	Sydney	Dec. 3	Ballast	Order
"	Feb. 1	Fernandes	Port. str.	214	Xavier	Macao	Jan. 31	Sundries	W., Borradalle & Co
"	" 1	Johanna Caesar	Bre. bg.	164	Becher	Formosa	Jan. 30	Sugar	Order
"	" 2	Wild Dayroll	Brit. sch.	159	Wilson	East Coast		Treasure	Dent & Co
"	" 2	Marmora	Brit. bk.	363	Lyell	Whampoa		Ballast	Master
"	" 2	Furious	H.M. Str		Osborne	Shanghae	Jan. 26		
"	" 2	Edwin Fox	Brit. sh.	835	Ferguson	Freemantle	Dec. 24	Ballast	Jardine, M. & Co
"	" 2	Asa Packer	Brit. bk.	323	Gold	Whampoa	Jan. 30	Ballast	Russell and Co
"	" 2	Edward & Julie	Belg. sh.	310	Mennan	Whampoa	Feb. 1	General	Order
"	" 2	Prospero	Ham. bg.	170	Miller	S. SeaIsland	Dec. 26	Sandal wood	Wm. Pustau & Co
"	" 2	Ellen	Brit. bk.	229	Bing	Cotie	Jan. 1	Rattans	Order
"	" 3	Toeywan	Brit. str	165	Chape	East Coast		Sundries	John Burd & Co
"	" 3	Diana	Bre bk.	320	Heesing	Ningpo	Jan. 29	Sundries	Siemssen and Co
"	" 3	Lucie	Fr. sh.	650	LeBer	Dieppe	Aug. 11	Coals	Vaucher Fieres
"	" 3	Albert	Am. bk.	359	Gregory	Boston	Aug. 30	Lumber	A. Heard and Co
"	" 3	Eagle Wing	Am. sh.	1172	Worth	Shanghae	Jan. 31	Ballast	Russell & Co
"	" 3	Roseneath	Brit. bg.	252	Grant	Ningpo	Jan. 29	Peas	Master
"	" 3	Ferdinand Nies	Prus. sh.	688	Coler	Sourabaya	Nov. 30	Rice	Siemssen and Co
"	" 3	Johanna	Dan. bg.	198	Diedricksen	Singapore	Dec. 23	General	W. Pustau and Co
"	" 5	La Place	H.I.M. Str		Kerjuge	Shanghae			
"	" 5	Niger	H. M. Str		Cracroft	Cupchi			
"	" 5	Nimrod	H. M. Str		Mends	Cupchi			

"	" 5	Plover	Gunboat		Rason	Cupchi			
"	" 6	Henry Winch	Brit. bk	713	Gaiffia	Sourabaya	Dec. 23	Rice	Order
"	" 7	Pregent	H.I.M. str		d' Osery	Touron			
"	" 8	Dirigo	Am. sh	608	Atwood	Shanghae	Feb.	Ballast	A. Heard and Co
"	" 9	German Town	U. S. S.		Page	Macao			
"	" 9	Mississippi	U. S. Str.		Nicholson	Whampoa			
"	" 9	Crishua	Brit. bk.	273	Giles	Macao			
"	" 9	Yangtsze	Am. str.	700	Dearborn	Shanghae	Feb. 6	Sundries	Dent and Co
"	" 9	Pekin	Brit. str.	1200	Bruno	Whampoa	Feb. 8	General	P. & O. S. N. Co
"	" 9	Toeywan	Brit. str.	174	Chape	Macao	Feb. 9	Sundries	John Burd and Co
"	" 9	Ravenscraig	Brit. sh.	589	Barron	Macao	Feb. 8	Ballast	Order
"	" 9	Coromandel	H. M. Str		Mitchel	Canton			
"	" 10	Aden	Brit. str.	812	Bernard	Shanghae	Feb. 7	Mails, &c.	P. & O. S. N. Co
"	" 10	Flying Fish	Brit. sh.	1500	Neal	Fuhchau	Feb. 7	Ballast	Order
"	" 10	Hesper	H. M. Str		Loane	Canton			
"	" 11	Banian	Brit. sh.	760	Graham	London	Oct. 1	General	Smith. K. and Co
"	" 11	Ottawa	Brit. str.	1974	Aldham	Bombay, &c	Jan. 16	Mails, &c.	P. & O. S. N. Co
"	" 12	Shanghai	Am. bk.	509	Hasetwood	Whampoa	Feb. 11	Sundries	P. & O. S. N. Co
"	" 12	Arthur	Am. bk.	555	Hoyt	Boston	Oct. 2	Spars	A. Heard and Co
"	" 12	Fiery Cross	Brit. str	444	White	Calcutta	Jan. 25	Opium	Jardine. M. & Co
"	" 12	Manila	Brit. str.	503	Gillson	Fuhchau	Feb. 9	Sundries	P. & O. S. N. Co
"	" 12	Gen. Wyndham	Brit. sh.	864	Harrison	Macao	Feb. 11	Coolies	Order
"	" 13	Rajah	Brit. str.	550	Noire	Manila	Feb. 9	Mails, &c.	P. & O. S. N. Co
"	" 13	Cruizer	H. M. Str		Bythesea	Shanghae	Feb. 8		
"	" 13	Himalaya	Dan, sh.	692	Bendixon	Melbourne	Dec. 31	Ballast	W. Pustau and Co
"	" 13	Star of the East	Brit. sh.	1219	Gaggs	London	Oct. 29	General	Gibb, L. and Co
"	" 13	Marmora	Brit. bk.	363	Lyell	Macao	Feb. 12	Ballast	Master
"	" 14	A. Cross	Chil. bg.	168	Hardy	Formosa	Feb. 12	Sugar	Order
"	" 14	Melita	Am. sch.	191	Strattan	Fuhchau	Feb. 12	Teas	W. Pustau and Co
"	" 14	Lily	H.I.M. str		Borelli	Canton			
Macao	" 6	Emigrant	Sp. sh.	840	Juam	Manila		Sundries	A. F. Castro
Amoy	Jan. 21	St. Lucia	Sp. bk.	132	Arragoita	Manila	Dec. 26	Sundries	Order
Shanghae	" 22	Cohota	Am. sh.	696	Day	Bangkok	Nov. 7	Rice	A. Heard and Co
"	" 26	Anglo Saxon	Brit. sh.	693	Laird	London	Aug. 24	General	Reiss and Co
"	" 30	Minna	Am. sch.	299	Smith	Nagasaki	Jan. 24	Sundries	Russell and Co
"	" 31	Aramingo	Am. sh.	716	Cassam	London	Sept. 3	Coals	W. R. Adamson & Co
"	" 31	Jacob & Anna	Dut. sch	248	Petersen	Nagasaki	Jan. 20	Sundries	W. Pustau and Co
"	" 31	Eamont	Brit. sch.	120	Geary	Nagasaki		Sundries	Dent and Co
"	Feb. 1	Nymph	Am. bk.	468	Price	Bangkok		Rice	Olyphant and Co

"	" 1	Golden City	Am. sh.	810	Seary	S. Francisco		Ballast	Russell and Co
"	" 1	Henry Ellis	Brit. sh.	412	Elmstone	Japan		Sundries	D. S. S. & Co
"	" 2	Glengariff	Brit. bk.	404	Webster	Singapore	Dec. 1	Sundries	Order
"	" 2	Young Mechanic	Am. sh.	1376	Amsbury	Hull		Coals	Wm. Hargreaves
"	" 5	Welcome	Brit. bk.		Schwalky	Singapore		Sundries	Order

SAILED.

FROM	DATE	NAME	FLAG & RIG	TON.	CAPTAIN	FOR	CARGO	CONSIGNEES
Hongkong	Jan 30	□□□	Am. str.	□□□	□□□	Shanghae	Sundries	Dent and Co
"	" 30	Cadiz	Brit. str.	900	Curling	Bombay, &c	Mails, &c.	P. & O. S. N. Co
"	" 30	Wodan	Dan. sh	300	Mathissen	Shanghae	Sundries	Order
"	" 30	Formosa	Brit. str.	750	Browne	Shanghae	Mails, &c.	P. & O. S. N. Co
"	" 31	Retribution	H. M. S.		Barker	East Coast		
"	" 31	Niger	H. M. Str		Cracroft	East Coast		
"	" 31	Nimrod	H. M. Str		Mends	East Coast		
"	" 31	Adventure	H. M. S.		Lacy	Whampoa		
"	" 31	Magicienne	H. M. Str		Vansittart	Whampoa		
"	" 31	Manilla	Brit. str.	503	Gillson	Fuhchau	Mails, &c.	P. & O. S. N. Co
"	Feb. 1	Carntyne	Brit. sh.	945	Sparke	Singapore	Sundries	Order
"	" 1	Dido	Ham. bk.	272	Ipland	Whampoa	Sundries	Wm. Pustau and Co
"	" 1	Helena	Dan. bk.	260	Simons	Whampoa	Sundries	W. Pustau and Co
"	" 1	J. Wakefield	Am. sh.	1225	Young	New York	Teas, &c.	Lyall, Still & Co
"	" 1	Pioneer	Brit. sh.	452	James	Shanghae	Sundries	F. B. Cama & Co
"	" 1	Swan	Brit. str.	240	Craig	Singapore	Sundries	John Burd and Co
"	" 1	Tereza	Chil. Bk.	189	Bollo	Calao	Sundries	J. J. dos Remedios
"	" 1	Wilhelmine	Dan. bk.	236	Thomson	Whampoa	Sundries	John Burd and Co
"	" 1	Zephyr	Brit. sch.	148	Reper	Shanghae	Sundries	Dent and Co
"	" 1	James Hartley	Brit. str.	478	Hook	Calcutta	Sundries	Dent and Co
"	" 1	Pekin	Brit. str.	1200	Burne	Whampoa	General	P. & O. S. N. Co
"	" 3	Biobio	Brit. sh.	582	Langley	Whampoa	Sundries	Gibb, L. and Co
"	" 3	Esperanza	Ham. bk.	200	Johansen	Shanghae	Sundries	W. Pustau and Co
"	" 3	Lady Mary Wood	Dut. str.	650		Samarang	Sundries	Siemssen and Co
"	" 3	Neva	Brit sch.	120	Waller	East Coast	Sundries	Gibb, L. and Co
"	" 3	Furions	H. M. Str		Osborne	Canton		
"	" 4	Kitty Simpson	Am. sh.	700	Gaufield	Bangkok	Sundries	Master
"	" 4	Roseneat	Brit. bg.	252	Grant	Whampoa	Sundries	Master
"	" 5	Diana	Bre. bk.	320	Heesing	Whampoa	Sundries	Siemssen and Co
"	" 5	Edward Charlie	Belg. sh.	540	Mennan	Shanghae	Sundries	Order
"	" 5	Johanna	Dan. bg.	198	Diedricksen	Whampoa	Sundries	Wm. Pustau and Co

"	" 6	Asa Packer	Brit. bk.	323	Gold	Fuhchau	Sundries	Russell and Co
"	" 6	Marmora	Brit. bk.	363	Lyell	Macao	Sundries	Master
"	" 6	Mercator	Dut. bk.	460	Wonde	Shanghae	Sundries	Schaeffer and Co
"	" 6	Toeywan	Brit. str.	46□	Chape	Canton	Sundries	John Burd and Co
"	" 7	Adventure	H. M. S.		Lacy	Whampoa		
"	" 8	Stag Hound	Am. sh.	1534	Hussey	Singapore	Sundries	Olyphant and Co
"	" 8	Twee Jeannes	Dut. bk.	674	V der Wendi	Batavia	Sundries	Order
"	" 9	Asia	Bre. sh.	81□	Nutzhorn	Macao	Sundries	W. Pustau and Co
"	" 9	Bellona	Dut. sh.	900	Kluin	Macao	Sundries	W. Pustau and Co
"	" 9	Joseph Shepherd	Brit. sh.	629	Phillips	Whampoa	Sundries	Order
"	" 10	Crishua	Brit. bk.	272	Giles	Sydney	Sundries	Schaeffer and Co
"	" 10	Hound	Am. sh.	560	Baker	San Francisco	Sundries	K. & Bosman
"	" 10	Johanna Cæsar	Bre. bg.	164	Becker	Formosa	Sundries	Order
"	" 12	Rajah of Sarawak	Brit. sh.	525	Kennett	Macao	Sundries	N. Duns and Co
"	" 12	T. W. Sears	Am. sh.	500	Drew	Macao	Sundries	A. Heard and Co
"	" 12	Daylight	Am. sh.	547	Hoibrooke	New York	Teas. &c.	Order
"	" 12	Yangtsze	Am. str.	700	Dearbori	Shanghae	Sundries	Dent & Co
"	" 12	La Place	H.I.M. str.		Kerjegu	Cochin China		
"	" 12	Hesper	H. M. Str		Loane	Canton		
"	" 13	Chusan	Brit. str.	750	Brooks	Manila	Mails, &c.	P. & O. S. N. Co
"	" 13	Senator	N. G. bk	400	Scott	Bangkok	Sundries	S. E. Burrows & Sons
"	" 13	Lily	H. I. M. str		Boretti	Canton		
"	" 14	Aden	Brit. str.	812	Bernard	Shanghae	Mails, &c.	P. & O. S. N. Co
"	" 14	Mississippi	U. S. Str		Nicholas	Japan		
"	" 15	Shanghai	Brit. str.	500	Haselwood	Amoy	Sundries	P. & O. S. N. Co
Macao	" 2	Pamella	Port. sh.	670	Vital	Singapore	Sundries	A. A. de Mello & Co
"	" 7	Denia	Sp. sch	230	Gil	Manila	Sundries	A. F. Castro
Whampoa	Jan. 18	Abeona	Brit. bk.	250	Seal	Liverpool	Teas, &c.	Birley and Co.
"	" 24	Cineinnatus	Brit. sh.	784	Cellars	London	Teas, &c.	Jardine, M. and Co
"	Feb. 3	Solent	Brit. sh.	732	Brooks	London	Teas, &c.	Fletcher and Co
Swatow	Jan. 23	Smyrna	Brit. bk.	240	Wood	Singapore	Sundries	Wo-Hong
"	" 30	Amy Donglas	Brit. sch	264	Pennsbury	Bangkok	Sundries	E. Waller
Amoy	" 23	Statesman	Brit. bk.	370	Wable	Singapore	Sundries	Order
Fuhchau	" 5	Game Cock	Am. sh.	1400	Osgood	New York	Teas, &c.	A. Heard and Co
"	" 19	Magniperb	Dan. sh	404	Raemar	London	Teas, &c.	Wm. Pustau and Co
"	" 22	Anna Dixon	Brit. bg.	188	Wellsman	Melbourne	Teas, &c.	Gibb, L. and Co

Shanghae	" 27	Henry Harbeck	Am. sh.	714	True	New York	Teas, &c.	Wetmore, W. & Co
"	" 28	Beaver	Am. Sh.	727	Smith	New York	Teas, &c.	A. Heard and Co
"	" 28	Avalanche	Brit. sh.	692	Scott	Guam	Ballast	Turner and Co
"	" 29	Ann	Am. bk.	641	Munro	Nagasaki	Re-exports	Russell and Co
"	" 30	Emma	Brit. Bk	121	Donglas	Nagasaki	Re-exports	Blenkin, R. & Co
"	" 30	Zealandia	Brit. sh.	1031	Fester	London	Teas. &c.	Dent and Co
"	Feb. 1	Proas	Brit. sh.	663	Holmes	Nagasaki	Sundries	Jardine, M. and Co
"	" 2	Portens	Brit. bk.	254	McGowa	London	Teas, &c.	Bower, Hanbury & Co
"	" 3	Joshua Bates	Am. sh.	620	McCallon	New York	Teas, &c.	Birley, W. and Co.
"	" 3	Inflexible	H. M. Str		Brooker	Japan		
"	" 4	Earmont	Brit. sch.	120	Geary	Nagasaki	Ballast	Dent and Co
"	" 5	Betty	Sw. bg.	260	Helmbirg	Sydney	Teas, &c.	Bower, Hanbury & Co

[1-073]

[With No.9110 □□□]

Whereas Charles Gill a native of the State of Maine – of the United States of America – at present the sole Owner and Commander of the ship "Emma" of 444 $\frac{59}{95}$ tons Register, now lying in the inner harbor of this port, being morally aggrieved and suffering pecuniary detriment by reason of certain irregular and vexations proceedings of the Authorities of Macao in respect to the said vessel and the business thereto pertaining, now seeks the protection of the Government of the United States and herely declares the circumstances and particulars of the grievances hitherto, on several occasions, and at present suffered by him as Owner and Commander aforesaid, to the end that all detriments and damages already incurred or which may be incurred in Consequence of the proceedings aforesaid may be recovered from those who have directed them.

Namely: -- 1. That, on the 14th (fourteenth) day of June last passed, when about to proceed to Shanghae with a freight already engaged for his said vessel he the said Charles Gill received a written order from the Captain of the Port of Macao, of which the following as a Copy, directing him to proceed and moor her near the War Lorcha "Amazona" and there remain until the decision of a cause at Law between the Chinese Chang Ahoi and the proprietor of the "Emma", – that the publicity

2.

of the said order of arrest, beside being a moral grievance, was so far a direct pecuniary detriment that it nearly deprived him of the freight already engaged for the said voyage to Shanghae:–

Translated Copy of said order.

"Sir,

In virtue of the orders of Government which, I have just received, you will proceed to moor the American Ship Emma under your command northward of the War-Lorcha "Amazona" where the Pilot may direct who is the bearer of this Despatch; and you will continue to lay at the moorings until the decision of the cause at Law pending before the court between the Chinese Chong-Ahoy and the proprietor of the same.

God preserve you.

"Office of the Captain of the Port of Macao.
14th June 1858.-"

Charles Gill, Esqre
Captain of the American Ship Emma

(signed) José Maria da Fonseca
Captain of the Port

2. That on the same day he the said Charles Gill proceeded to the Consulate of the United States and there before the Consul, the late Samuel B. Rawle, Esquire, protested against the said order in words and act as follows:--

I, Charles Gill, sole owner, and master of the American Ship "Emma" and so recognised by the Government of the United States of America,

3.

as per Archives in the American Consulate of this city and port of Macao; do hereby protest against an order of the captain of the port of Macao, date this day 14th of June A. D. 1858, a copy of which is deposited at the American Consulate; by which I am now commanded to move my vessel and moor her alongside the War Lorcha "Amazona". And I do protest against all and singular, the Portuguese Government, the Governor of Macao, the Captain of the Port, and all and every Authority from whom said order emanated.-

And I as an American Citizen do and shall hereby hold the said Portuguese Government, and the Officers aforesaid, for all damages, detentions, and any losses of any nature or Kind soever that may proceed from the issuing or executing said order.

(Signed) Charles Gill

Given under my hand and seal this 14th day of June A. D. 1858, at the American Consulate for the Port of Macao.

In witness to the above of have hereunto signed my name and have affixed my official seal the date above written.-

(signed) S. B. Rawle

(L. S.) U. S. Consul
for Macao.–

4.

3. That the foregoing Protest was by him transmitted to His Excellency the Governor of Macao, accompanied by a letter of the same date, (the sending of which direct was perhaps in breach of etiquette although owing to the illness of the Consul Mr Rawle) – a copy of which is hereto appended.

4. That on the following day he received the letter of which the here following words are a translation, intimating the cancelling of the order of the 14th of June and referring him for explanations upon the subject to the Civil Court of this City "at where requisition the said order was given." –

Sir,

By order of the Superior Authorities I have to communicate to you that the intimation made to you by my Despatch datetd yesterday to proceed with your vessel and moor her Northward of the War–Lorcha Amazona is cancelled and should you require any explanation on this subject, you will please to address yourself to the Civil Court of this City at where requisition the said order was given.–

I return to you, herewith the protest made by you in this matter.–

God preserve you

Office of the Captain of the Port of Macao 15th June 1858.

Charles Gill Esq.

Captain of the American Ship Emma

(signed) José Maria da Fonseca
Captain of the Port.–

5.

5. That on the first day of the present month of November 1858 he the said Charles Gill received an Official letter from M^r. Nye the Vice Consul of the United States of that date apprising him of designed received interference with the Ship Emma and the business of her lading to him pertaining, on the part of certain of the officers of the Government of Macao, the intimation thereof being conveyed in said letter in words as followeth:––

Consulate of the United States
Macao, November 1st. 1858.

Sir,

In courtesy the Captain of the Port of Macao has apprised me of an action before His Honor the Judge in Virtue of which the former officer will arrest and detain the Ship Emma now sailed by you as Owner and Commander, in default of your appearing at the office of His Honor the Judge and giving satisfactory Bonds to answer to said action according to Law; and I recommend you to avail of this overture to avoid a public arrest of your vessel by which your Own interests would suffer detriment.–

I am, Sir,
Your Obt. Ser[t].
(signed) Gideon Nye Jr
Vice Consul of the United States
for Macao–

[To Captain Charles Gill
Ship "Emma"]

6.

6. That being aware of the groundless nature of the action against his property and apprehending the purpose to draw him into litigation, he wrote a reply to the letter of the Vice–Consul under date of the 2nd instant in which he expressed his determination to sign no such Bonds as those alluded to and to abstain from any act in recognition of pretensions at once illegal, vexations and detrimental toward himself; that he is informed by the Vice Consul of the verbal communication of the contents of his said letter of the 2[d] ins[t]. to the Captain of the Port with a view to prevent further action in the premises, and that it was left with that officer in order that its purport might be stated to His Honor the Judge of Macao: 7. That on the succeeding day, the 3rd ins[t]: he received another letter from the Vice Consul of that date, apprising him that a summons to appear at Court would be served upon him the next day – i.e. – on the 4th Ins[t]. – said letter being in words as followeth:––

Counsulate of the United States.
Macao, November 3[d] 1858.–

Sir,

"The Captain of the Port of Macao has just called at this office to intimate that the present stage of proceedings in the court compels the Judge to summon you to answer to the claim

7.

of the party or parties who wish to prosecute, and that said summons will be served upon you tomorrow–morning.–

I need not tell you that you are bound to answer the summons of the court by appearing and showing why the action cannot be against you, or your ship.– I will accompany you to the Judge's Office with pleasure if you wish.–

Not to answer a summons would be to allow the action to take effect by your own default.–"

I am, Sir,
Your obt. Servt.
(signed) Gideon Nye Jr.

[Captain Charles Gill
"Emma"]

8. That no such Summons was received by him; but on the contrary, that he was on the 5th ins[t], informed by the Vice Consul that the Captain of the Port had that morning called to say that he had no further action to take in

the matter as His Honor the Judge had concluded to arrest the ship （"Emma"） at once without making the summons upon him the said Charles Gill:--

9. That accordingly later in the day of the said 5th of November 1858 five men came on board the "Emma", one being an interpreter and in the absence of the said Charles Gill the commander and Owner of the vessel ordered the chief officer to heave up the anchor and take the ship up alongside the Portuguese

8.

men of war and there remain, exhibiting to the Mate an order for the arrest of the ship, to which order to move her the Mate replied that the Captain would be onboard soon and he should do nothing of the kind before his arrival: That when the said Charles Gill did get onboard, the bearers of the aforesaid Order repeated that they bore the same from the Judge of Macao to seize or arrest the ship, and the interpreter proceeded to read it, to the effect that he Captain Gill was commanded to move her alongside the Portuguese man of war and presented a paper for his signature, requesting him also at the same time to seal up the hatches and furnish them an inventory of what the ship had onboard: Whereupon he the said Charles Gill requested the giving into his possession the said Order of the Judge and that the Bearer thereof should accompany him to his Consignee's office to determine through reliable interpretation the official character and real scope of the Order; but these requests were refused. When he the said Charles Gill told the said Bearer of the order that no interference would be offered to the seizure or arrest of the ship or the sealing of her hatches he having exhibited a seal for the latter purpose; but the Bearer refused to proceed further, replying that they wished him the said Charles Gill to arrest the vessel and take her in and that if he required a pilot and move

9.

men he would send them to the ship, whereupon the Bearer of the order went on shore to report to His Honor the Judge, as it was said, and upon returning in about an hour, and finding the others who had accompanied him onboard gone as here again left himself:--

10. That on this day the 6th of November 1858, the formal arrest of the ship "Emma" with here cargo, apparel, & c, was completed in manner and before Witnesses as detailed in the following Certificate the Original of which, together with the originals of the several other Papers referred to, are deposited at the Consulate of the United States along with the original Bill of Sale of the ship, her sailing-license and other Papers:

Copy

We the undersigned do hereby certify that we were present this day, 6th of November A. D. 1858, on board the American Ship Emma, Captain Charles Gill when two officers came onboard with a file of soldier and an order of the Judge of Macao to seize the said Ship, and with written instructions that if the ship was not given up to use force. The Captain asked them twice through their interpreter, what they came on board for – Their reply was that they came to seize and arrest the ship and that they took possession upon the spot in the name of the Portuguese Government and the Captain notified them

10.

that he abandoned the ship under protest.–

(signed) G. L. Agabeg
(signed) Edward J. Sage
(signed) Joseph Clutterbuck
(signed) George Coots: –

11. That prior to these several infractions of his rights– namely about the first of June 1857– the Captain of the Port came onboard of the "Emma" , after she had cleared outward when proceeding upon a voyage to Siam, and saying that he had an order to arrest the ship as the property of James M^c^Cormick asked to see her papers; and that when they were shown to him he remarked that captain James M^c^Cormick had no interest in her and she could not be stopped.

12. Finally: That being the sole owner of said ship "Emma" and her commander in virtue of a true Bill of Sale duty executed before the Consul of the United States in presence of M^r^. W^m^. C. Hunter in the eighteenth day of February A. D. 1857 at the Consulate thereof in Macao and having held legal possession of her during the whole intermediate period of more than twenty months, down to this day, under both the Flags of New Grenada and the United States, that is to say, from said February 1857 until the twentieth day of October of the same year 1857 under the former, and from the latter date until this time under the Flag of the United States; that thus controlled and protected she has made several distinct voyages to Shanghae, Siam,

11.

the Straits and Akyab, returning in each case to this port, -- a course of proceeding which, while it has almost constantly afforded the opportunity of legal arrest of the ship, is totally contradictory of the assumptions and pretentions of the prosecutors in this suit: And that irrespective of the serious moral grievance inflicted upon him the said Charles Gill by these repeated interferences and interruptions with and of his business and by this aforesaid seizure of his property, his pecuniary rights and liabilities involved in the arrest are represented by the following sums:

Value of the ship	$28,500
Freight to Bombay and back	$ 9,000
Stores on board	$ 2,000
Advanced to officer & crew	$ 900
3 months extra wages to discharge crew	$ 1,350
Instruments, charts &c	$ 750
	$ 42,500

to which must be added the liabilities for the valuable cargo already onboard consisting of silks, Teas, &c. for a valuable part of which Bills of Lading have been signed & forwarded by the last outward mail.

All which property he has abandoned to the Portuguese Government under the enforced orders of the Judge of Macao this day in the presence of Competent Witnesses.–

Now therefore: Know all Men

12.

by these Presents-- That on the day of the date hereof before me Gideon Nye, Jr, Vice Consul of the United States of America for Macao and the Dependencies thereof personally came & appeared Charles Gill before named, and after stating the facts contained in the foregoing premises, hath protested as by these Presents, I, the said Vice-Consul, at his special instance and request, do publicly, and solemnly protest, against all and every person whom it doth, shall, or may concern, and especially against those officers of the Government of Macao and of the Kingdom of Portugal by whose acts or under whose orders and the aforesaid grievances, detriments, damages and claims, suffered or to be suffered, have originated, hereby holding the said person or persons or Government responsible therefor.--

In testimony whereof, the said Charles Gill hath hereinto subscribed his name, and I the said Vice Consul, set my hand and affix the Seal of this Consulate at Macao this sixth day of November A.D. 1858.-

（Signed） Gideon Nye Jr
Vice Consul of the
United State for Macao.

（Signed） Charles Gill
Owner & Commander of the "Emma"

13.

[Copy]

Extract of a Despatch to His Excellency the Honble William B. Reed Envoy Extraordinary and Minister Plenipotentiary of the United States dated Macao, November 6th 1858. N°.6.

I shall beg the honor to wait upon Your Excellency again soon to instruct on important case which has arisen here, involving considerations of the inviolability of the Flag of the United States and the rights of a Citizen thereof.

I am, with great respect,
Your Excellency's
Obedient Servant,
（Signed） Gideon Nye, Jnr
Vice Consul of the United States
of America for Macao.

N°7

Consulate of the United States of America
Macao, November 10th, 1858.

Sir,

I had the honor to intimate to Your Excellency, in my dispatch N°6 of the 6th Inst, the existence of a question of gravely with the Authorities of this Colony of Portugal, involving Considerations of the inviolability of the Flag of the United States and of the rights of a Citizen thereof, then recently brought within my

[His Excellency
The Hon[ble] William B. Reed
Envoy Extraordinary and Minister Plenipotentiary
of the United States of America.–
&c &c &c]

14.

official cognizance by the person aggrieved Captain Charles Gill the Owner and Commander of the Ship "Emma", and I beg leave now to apprise you that so soon after the completion of the necessary Declaration and Protest as propriety permitted that is to say on Monday Morning the 5th Inst I respectfully claimed of His Excellency the Governor General of Macao and its Dependencies indemnity in behalf of the said Charles Gill in terms of the herewith copy of my written Communication, which appeal I delivered in person and robustly confirmed during an audience marked by great courtesy on the part of H. E.–

I now transmit, also to Y. E. a Copy of the said Declaration & Protest of Captain Gill as presenting the ostensible bases of my proceeding; and with those beg to submit the communication derived from the collective circumstances of the Case which impelled and guided my action.

1st No action exerted against Captain Gill.

2nd He held the "Emma" as his rightful Owner according to the Laws of the United States.

3rd The proceedings had been irregular and vexatious, in that he never was properly summoned to Court and yet had suffered repeated interferences and injuries from the propagation of reports of intended seizure, & finally by an informal demand for his Signing Bonds to abide the result of an action against his vessel.–

The principles of Law applicable to the case being as I conceive such as:–

1st To debar restraint of person without competent

[=tent]

15.

= tent cause in action; hence that Captain Gill could not, in strict legality, be summoned.

2[d] Equally to debar seizure of property on a ship's block acquired in the absence of visible action against the vessel and enjoyed under the flag of another Country; hence that nothing short of incontestible proof of a conspiracy to defraud in respect to the acquisition of his title in her could breach Capt[n] Gill's right of possession or arrest from him the flag she bore, the onus probandi, moreover, being with the prosecutor, and a default of proof throwing upon them all damages and detriments thus put upon a third–innocent person.

The position of Captain Gill and of his property in the whole block of the "Emma" being thus independent, although he had held himself ready to answer a summons to show cause why, an action could not be against his vessel, as abandoned her under Protest upon the acception by his Honor the Judge of the District or the summary step of seizure in her or the previously intimated one in a preliminary summons, and appealed to the protection of the Government of the United States.

That the whole exercise of proceedings by the Portuguese Authorities has been marked by illegalities will appear to Your Excellency, as I submit, from a review of the fact, which I have still to present, in addition to what is shown on the foregoing and the herewith accompanying Papers; but I am unable, for want of time, to state these facts to day.--

16.

I am, Sir,
With great respect,
Your Excellency's
Obedient Servant,
(signed) Gideon Nye Jnr.
Vice Consul of the United States of
America for Macao

N°8

Consulate of the United States of America
Macao, November 13th, 1858

Sir,

I beg to refer to my Despatch N°7 in now proceeding to state to Your Excellency some facts in the case of the "Emma" in addition to those already presented circumstantially in proof of the illegalities to which I have alluded, as well as in further elucidation of the subject in general.

1st The action against M^{r} McCormick, the former owner, was not effective until several months after the transfer of the "Emma" by proper Bill of Sale to said Charles Gill.

2nd Said action was based upon two or three items of a running account with the prosecutor Cheong Ahoy, the account comprising transactions in Hong Kong and Canton as well as Macao and said items of it being merely receipts or requests at the two former places and not within the jurisdiction of Macao, whilst, on the other hand, M^{r} McCormick was able to rebut the action by an account of payments at Macao to and for Cheong Ahoy amounting to $ 8,616.47 – I may remark

17.

also that the Account Current between the parties according to M^{r} McCormick's rendering showed Cheong Ahoy indebted to him in about $24,000 – At best, therefore the items upon which action was commenced were but a small part of a remaining, disputed account, and were portions of it which arose at other places.

3^{d} The said James McCormick was transacting business, effecting charters of Vessels &c &c and making many payments several months after the said sale and transfer of the "Emma" and I have original written proof thereof in my possession for instance, in a charter Party concluded on the 8th of April 1857 with Captain Leerbeck of the Danish Barque "Fredrick Wilhelm" through the Agency of Messrs Cartoritz & Co which charter, or by endorsement of said McCormick, became effective on the 27th of said April 1857 and upon it he paid the sum of

$1800 say eighteen hundred Dollars as is proved by the Original receipt in my possession of said Mess[rs] Cartoritz & Co in behalf of Cap[t]. Leerbeck which as a further proof of his being in good credit some time after the sale of the "Emma".

I have also an original note of invitation of M[r] J. P da Silver to him to attend a Ball at the house of said da Silver in the evening of the 14th of April 1857 this M[r] da Silver being now the Copartner of the said Cheng Ahoy in the farming of the Gambling House License this year and the active promoter of the suit against M[c]Cormick.–

And it is said, but I have not yet written

18.

proof of it, that Cheong Ahoy himself was still doing business with M[r] M[c]Cormick after the sale of the "Emma." ––

I beg now to hand Your Excellency copies of several additional Papers pertaining to this question and shall from time to time wait upon you with further information upon it.–

Referring to a list of enclosures at foot,

I am
Sir,
With great respect
Your Excellency's
Obedient Servant
(signed) Gideon Nye Jr
Vice Consul of the United States of America.–

Enclosures

N[o] 1. Translation of reply of H. E. the Governor General of Macao of November 8th 1858 to my representation of the same date.

N[o] 2. Translation of the letter of idem of same date notifying intended departure and transfer of Government charge &c.

N[o] 3. Copy letter of Captain Gill of Nov 2[d] to me to give Bonds referred to in Declaration and Protest.–

N[o] 4. Copy–portion of Log kept by chief officer of the "Emma".–

N[o] 5. Declarations of 1st & 2[d] officers of "Emma".

N[o] 6. Copy of summons to house of His Honor the Judge and of Declaration of parties

19.

present to what was said and done on the occasion.–

N[o] 7. Copy of items forming ground of action against James M[c]Cormick; and,

N[o] 8. Copy of items of payments by him at Macao to offset the above.

E. E.

(sig[d]) G. N. Jnr.

N°9.

Consulate of the United States of America
Macao, 15th November 1858.–

Sir,

Referring to the Despatches N° 6. 7. & 8, which I have recently had the honor to address to Your Excellency, I beg in continuation of the subject of the seizure of the "Emma" – to apprize you that in the course of a Conversation with His Honor the Judge of Macao (now by right "His Excellency" as President of the Council of Government, ad interim held during a call with which he honored me he expressed a desire to see the question mitigated and manifested throughout the interview the sincerity of that expression.–

He commenced by repeating what H. E. the Governor General had stated both in conversation with me and in reply which he wrote to my claim for redress,–that the question of the "Embargo" of the "Emma" was not legally within the Cognizance of the Government (meaning the chief Executive Power as I conceive,) but was in the exclusive Jurisdiction of the Civil Court; and suggested the employment

20.

of Counsel by Captn Gill to appear in his behalf before that Court.

I ventured, in reply, as I had before done during the audience of H. E. to express His opinion that the forcible act of sequestration against the property of an American citizen who is, confessedly not a party in the suit and involving also the detention (if not the less or damage) of the goods of other third parties for which he has become liable and the consequent abandonment and protest, suffered to bring it within the category of international questions; & that, therefore, Captn. Gill would prefer to await the result of the reference already made to Y. E. but that I would state the suggestion of His Honor to him.–

During the interview I urged upon His Honor's attention these vital points of defect in the prosecution;

1st That there was no visible action against the Ship at the time of transfer to her present owner and that none has attached until now, after the expiration of more than twenty months.–

2nd That the fact of the vessel being half laden, outward bound, was a legal bar to arrest.–

3rd That the basis of action against the former owner was upon items of Account occurring beyond the Jurisdiction of Macao– Said account as a whole being, also, in dispute: and

4th That the weight of presumption evidence was in Captn Gill's favor since it was in proof by original Documents in my possession that the former Owner was transacting–

21.

business here months after the transfer of the vessel, in the charter of shipping and payment of money thereupon &c &c whilst, upon Captn Gill's non part, the evidence of bona fi de appeared in his returning to Macao repeatedly with the vessel even after intimation of a desire to proceed against her.

His Honor, in reply, constantly urged the necessity of Captn Gill's contesting the action before the Court in his own name and by employment of Consul and intimated that the Plaintiff would be held for all the damages and costs incurred adding that no doubt he was competent to meet them as he was in Bonds to Government in

$80,000 as Farmer of the Gambling House Contract: In that, His Honor exhibited an evident desire to ameliorate the question, which personally, I should gladly have reciprocated to the fullest extent within my competence had I not, in expectation of Your Excellency's early return to the neighborhood already placed the question within your proper control.–

Since writing the foregoing I am informed that the discharge of the cargo of the vessel has been commended by a transhipment of it to another vessel bound to Bombay, so that it appears that the Authorities of Macao are seriously proceeding in then infractions of the rights of Captn Gill.–

I have just received Original papers containing proof, under the signature of Cheong–Ahoy, the plaintiff in the suit against M^r McCormick,

22.

that the said Chinese was on the 31st May 1857 (that is to say more than three months after the transfer of the "Emma" by a proper bill of sale to Captn. Gill) – joint owner with the said McCormick of the ship formerly called the "Levant" then the Portuguese "Estrella do Norte", which had been bought by them in the 3^d of February of the previous year 1856; and that on the said 31st May 1857 – it was mutually agreed between the parties to continue to run the said vessel or otherwise dispose of her as might be most advantageous: – which is at once presumptive proof of the highest degree that no action or intended action existed on the part of said Cheong Ahoy against said McCormick, and direct endorsed that the latter was in the enjoyment of good credit with the former and that, hence, the pretenses upon which action is now taken to invalidate a proper Bill of sale made before the United States Consul according to Law, are baseless.–

Having them submitted to Your Excellency the essential points in the case of the "Emma" in the order in which they have been presented to me, and upon which I await Y. E. instructions, I have now the honor and satisfaction to wait upon you with copies presenting a case which arose here recently with the Authorities of Macao from the offensive conduct of an American Citizen (whose name I desire to shield from public comment) and which received a satisfactory solution by the semi–official treatment disclosed in said Copies.–

Receiving as I did the repeated thanks,

23.

oral & written of His Excellency the Governor General, as well as those of the exercised person, I hope also for Your Excellency's approbation upon the manner of my procedure in the delicate case.

I beg to hand to Y. E. in conclusion, copies of four several papers N° 1 a 4 inclusive presenting the circumstances attending the Act of "Embargo", as reported by the officers of the Authorities of Macao, which reports, however, differ in some essential respects, from the Declarations of Captn Gill and his officers as communicated to Y. E. heretofore, but as the primary legal points are not affected by these discrepancies I shall not now trouble you with an attempt to reconcile them one with another or either with the truth.

I am,
With great respect
Your Excellency's

Obedient Servant,
（signed） Gideon Nye Jr.
Vice Consul of the United States
of America.

N°10

Consulate of the United States of America
Macao, November 22^d 1858–

Sir,

I beg leave to present to Your Excellency in the Bearer of this Captain Charles Gill the Owner and late commander of the American ship "Emma", whose business–forming, as it has,

24.

the subject of several of my recent Despatches Dr Williams recommends to a personal submission to Y. E.

Captain Gill would accordingly have waited upon Y. E. orders but that several days ago he was notified of an action against him in the Court for the recovery of the equivalent of 222 sovereigns; which were received by him in the capacity of Master of ship "General Blanco" in 1856 to pay off her crew, at HongKong, and for account of Mr James McCormick her Owner, as appears by the general Account Current of the last named with Cheong Ahoy the Plaintiff in this case. Captain Gill answered the summons on Saturday and is assured by his legal advisor that the Plaintiff will be non–suited, but the raising of the question now–about three years since the sovereigns were received upon baseless grounds, serves to show the nature of the expedients to which the Prosecutors of Captain Gill are driven and is another illustration of the irregular and illegal course pursued toward him.––

I beg to hand Your Excellency, herewith, copies of the Original Bill of sale; of Mr Silas E, Burrows' sailing License as Consul for New Granada; and of the papers granted by my Predecessor Mr Wm A. Macy as Deputy Consul in October 1857.–

I may remark to Y. E. that Mr. Cooper Turner Crown Solicitor at HongKong has long been the legal advisor of this Cheong Ahoy

25.

in this business.–

I have nothing else to report since my Dispatch N°9.–

I am,
Sir,
With great respect
Your Excellency's
Obedient Servant
（signed） Gideon Nye, Jr
Vice Consul of the United States

of America for Macao.

N°11

Consulate of the United States of
America.–
Macao 26th November 1858.–

Sir,

I had the honor to receive Your Excellency's Despatch of the 23d Inst on the evening of the 24th and I waited upon His Honor the Judge of Macao yesterday accompanied by Mr Van Loffelt my Consular assistant as interpreter with the purpose of further conciliating the question regarding the "Emma" and accordingly took with me several papers to submit to His Honor's inspection containing proof of the (as I esteem it) utterly baseless nature of the action.–

During the interview I intimated to His Honor, with reference to my previous statement to him at my own house that I was, awaiting the reply of Y. E. that you allowed the case to rest at present upon the steps already

26.

taken through myself; that you did so in the confidence entertained by you that the Court will do Justice to Captain Gill and that if the suit brought against him proved to be unfounded and vexations, he will be indemnified.–

I then proceeded with discussion upon the merits of the question, in the course of which His Honor stated that the actual transfer of the "Emma" and the obtaining of her New Granadian papers was in June 1857 and upon my contesting that point he brought for my inspection the original depositions of William Tarrant (Editor of the Friend of China) & George Cooper Turner (Crown solicitor at HongKong) of the 7th October 1857 in which they declare their belief that McCormick continued to be the Owner of the "Emma" and that Captain Gill came to Hong Kong on the 9th June 1857 to obtain the flag of New Granada of Mr Silas E. Burrows Jr. and to give color to this declaration they annexed thereto a note of the said Mr Burrows Jr. of the 11h June 1857 in reply to said Mr Turner which note however (being in English) upon being translated into Portuguese was found to the evident astonishment of His Honor–to convey no such idea, but rather the contrary– the essential part of it reading as follows.–

My dear Turner,

The name of Mr McCormick was in the register of the "Emma" (late counters of seafield) previous to our giving her the New Granadian flag.–

27.

Such are, I believe, the exact words, but if not they convey the exact sense of the first paragraph of the note.–

Another paragraph of it whose precise form I do not remember states that she was then (i.e. in the 11th June 1857) in Captain Gill's name and that he was then at HongKong obtaining a Crew.–

Whereas I was enabled to prove by the certificate of Silas E. Burrows Senior, attached to the Copy of the Original Bill of sale of the 18th February 1857– said certificate being dated on the 20th February 1857 and signed by him a Consul for New Granada （with the seal of that Republic attached） declaring that the "Emma" , had, then been placed under the flag of said Republic.–

As this Original Document was recently in Your Excellency's possession I have no need further to allude to it.–

It is at once conclusive upon the essential point at issue, as His Honor seemed to me to admit; and disposing as it does of the only tangible basis of the action, should exonerate Capt[n] Gill from the previously presumptive necessity to enter into litigation in the Court of which His Honor is the Chief Justice.–

His Honor, however, still insists upon the point that Capt[n] Gill must meet this–baseless and unjust suit before the Court, at the peril of an adverse decision otherwise.–

I have no more time by this steamer.–

I am
Sir,
With great respect,
Your Excellency's
Obedient Servant
(signed) Gideon Nye Jr
Vice Consul of the United States
of America.

N°12

Consulate of the United States of America
Macao 27th November 1858–

Sir,

I had yesterday the honor to report to Your Excellency by my Despatch N°11 the Circumstances attending an interview held with His Honor the Judge of Macao by which you will have perceived that the case of the "Emma" then entered upon a new phase by the discovery of and exposure to the Judge of a lamentable error or a willful perversion in the Deposition whereupon His Honor had founded the proceedings of the Court.–

As the proof of the baseless nature of the action was Conclusive by written document bearing the Consular seal and signature of Mr Burrows Senior and the perversion of the meaning of the note of M[r] Burrows Jr. was equally apparent, I confess that I cannot see how the Judge can reconcile with a proper sense of right and with the dignity of Portugal any further proceedings against the "Emma" and her Owner Charles Gill.––

29.

It appears to me more consistent with these for His Honor to annul the proceedings already taken, as not only illegal but disgraceful in the perversion used to form their basis.–

I am now enabled to hand to Y. E. a Copy of the Record of the Court in this case furnished by His Honor the Judge, which will serve to elucidate what I have hitherto communicated to Your Excellency.–

I beg to hand also several other copies of papers bearing upon the subject as enumerated below.–

Awaiting as I was indications of disposition on the part of His Honor the Judge to reinstate Captn Gill and indemnify him for the damages already suffered, I report to be compelled to apprize Y. E., at these stage of my letter that I have just heard of the circulation of reports which can only have emanated from the house of the Judge conveying a very different sense from that which my Communications were justly susceptible of respecting the intentions of Your Excellency.–

I could well understand that the Judge under the influence of a natural Amour propre should be reluctant to acknowledge the insufficiency of the grounds of his proceedings up to the period of our last interview, but that he should longer give countenance to the promoters of this action, as the reports just alluded to appear to indicate, I may

30.

justly surprize Y. E. as it does myself in view of the correct appreciation of the exposure then made of the deliberate misconstruction of a note put in as evidence supporting false declarations, evinced by his remarks that such acts would subject their authors to prosecution for perjury.––

I shall perhaps be able to transmit with this the purport of the advice of one of the most respectable counsellors at Law, the Senhor Francisco d'Assis e Fernandes, upon being consulted this morning by Captn Gill and Mr Sage.–

An exact Copy of the note of Mr Burrows Jr, alluded to in Dispatch N° 11, I am now able to append at foot, and Y. E. will perceive the perversion of meaning in the portions of the Record of the Court referring to it.–

Referring to the enclosures,

I am,
Sir,
Your Excellency's
Obedient Servant
(signed) Gideon Nye Jr
Vice Consul of the United States
of America for Macao

Copy

"My dear Turner,

James McCormick name was on the register of the Emma (formerly "Countess of Seafield") previous to our granting,

31.

her a N. Granadian register.

McCormick gave a bill of sale of her, to her present Captain Charles Gill, and she therefore now stands in his name.–

Day before yesterday Gill shipped a crew for her before me.

She is going to Siam.

Your Faithfully,
（Signed） S. E. Burrows Jr.
11 June.–

Note of Enclosures

N°1. Copy of portion of the Record of the Court, as furnished by order of the Judge of Macao.

N°2. Confidential Statement of Opinion by a distinguished Counsellor of Law, of Macao.

N°3. Letter of Mr Edward J. Sage an American Citizen, stating facts within his knowledge respecting the "Emma" as well as respecting the claims of Chong Ahoy upon James McCormick &c.

N°4. Copy Warrant of Mr Deputy Consul Macy to W. K. Cressy directing the measuring of the Emma.–

N°5. Declaration and oath to citizenship and ownership by Charles Gill.

N°6. Return to warrant for measuring the Emma by W. K. Cressy–

N°7.Copy letter of Mr S. E. Burrows Jr. of Oct 22d 1857 to Mr Samuel B. Rawle––Consul at Macao. E. E. （signed） G. N. Jr.

[N°.1]

[Recd. May. Mr. Abbott]

N°10.

Consulate of the United States.
Macao, March 12th 1859.

Sir,

I beg to hand you Duplicate of my Despatch N° 9, of the 22nd Ulto., since which––on the 3rd inst.––I have received Circular N° 9 of the Department, of Novr 15th last, reporting to me the non–receipt of the Quarterly Returns of the respective periods ending on the 31st March, 30th June and 30th September; and in reply there to beg to say that the two first named periods expired before my appointment as Deputy–Consul.–

I shall, however, proceed to make up the Returns in time for the next mail, from such Records as I find in the Consulate.

I have the impression that the two Quarters in question had been duly reported to the Government, although I inferred an error in their transmission to the Secretary of the Treasury instead of yourself, finding in the letter–book of the former Incumbent copies of his Despatches addressed to your said Colleague

[The Honorable
Lewis Cass
Secretary of State of the United States
of America.–
City of Washington]

of April 1st and July 1st purporting to cover said Returns.–

As to the period terminating on the 30th Sept^r, I have already transmitted its Returns to you, as I have also those of the subsequent Quarter.

Referring to the case of the "Emma", alluded to in my last Despatch, I regret to say that although the Judge of the Supreme Court here has decided that Captn Charles Gill's title to the vessel is valid, yet His Honor seems disposed to sanction an Appeal to the Superior Court at Goa, upon grounds which I conceive to be quite insufficient and with the imposition of conditions wanting in the essential element of reciprocal fairness.

Considering the evidences conclusive that this Appeal is evasive and totally wanting in the character of good–faith on the part of the Prosecutors, I feel it my duty to give my countenance and support to our aggrieved countrymen, as hitherto, in the defence of their rights; and as I find by the Record of the Court a newly–substituted basis of action in place of that which I exposed the unsoundness of in November (vide my letters N°.11 & 12 to His Excellency Mr Reed herewith) I confess that my confidence in the attainment of justice to our Countrymen is seriously impaired.–

Without further comment, I now beg to submit to you copies of the Protest of Captn Gill and of my official communications to H. E. Mr Reed in elucidation of the case, (pages 1 @ 31 inclusive) reserving for the next mail copies of the two Records of the Court alluded to, and of several other Papers presenting the new phase upon which the case has just now entered.–

I beg to hand you – as it is possible that the Chargé d'Affairs being in Canton at present may not be able to do so – Copy of an Imperial Edict of the 31st January, which may be characterized as, – next to the Emperor's general confirmation of the Treaties of Tiensin of last summer, if indeed the evidences of good–faith in this more outspoken acquiescence in the New Relation with Western Nations are not, as I esteem them, still more significant – as the most important public step toward an international league ever taken by an Emperor of China.–

The discovery and exposure of the double–dealing of Hwang and others – albeit the inspiration of the Imperial Court by the finding of the public Document in question and other "Chops", gave Lord Elgin a lever by which he has completely confirmed the success of his diplomacy.

I am,
Sir,
With great respect
Your Obedient Servant
Gideon Nye Jnr
Vice Consul of the United States
of Amereica.–

[Macao March 12th 1859
Gideon Nye, Jr
N°10.
2 original &c
3 duplicate

Received
Accounts & Records
"Emma" case
new Imperial Edict]

Duplicate
N°9

Consulate of the United States
Macao, February 22nd 1859.–

Sir,

I beg leave to refer to my Despatch N° 1 & 7 in now handing you the Account of Fees received at this Consulate during the Quarter ending on the 31st of December last passed, and amounting to $150 $\frac{22}{100}$ ½ say, one hundred fifty Dollars, twenty five and a half cents, which, as in a former case, has been some what delayed by the want of returns from River Steamers.

I beg to hand you, also, the Returns of the arrivals and Departures of American vessels during the same quarter.–

It is unnecessary to renewedly point out the inadequacy of the yearly income which this and previous Quarterly Accounts of Fees represent, or the disproportion that it bears to the actual duties of the office here. In further illustration of this point, I may instance the Amount of time consumed in the important case arising from the seizure of the ship "Emma" upon false Declarations which I shall have occasion to lay fully before you by the next mail; although I am happy to say

[The Honorable
Lewis Cass
Secretary of State of the United States of
America
City of Washington.–]

that I am informed thro' the counsellor of the owner that the main question is no longer pending and that the remaining one of damages due the owner of the vessel will, partially or wholly, become matter of arbitration according to Law.

I have the gratification to say that our countrymen interested in this question– being Captain Gill the Owner and Mr Edward J. Sage the supercargo express themselves my gratefully for the service that I have done them in this case, saying that they "do not know" what they could have done without my aid." –

Having laid this case fully before His Excellency Mr Reed during his sojourn in Hong Kong harbor in November and December, I had no need to address the Department of State until the question entered upon a new phase, but shall beg leave to present it to you fully within the next two weeks.

I am,
Sir,

With great respect
Your Obedient Servant
Gideon Nye Jnr
Vice Consul of the United States
of America.–

P. S.

I beg to hand you a British Government Notification of the 18th Inst which may be of interest to the Treasury Department of the United States, showing as it does that Macao is viewed as merely an outlying port of the Canton river for the Shipment of Chinese produce and that hence Teas &c are subject to the regular Export duty if sent onboard ships lying at Whampoa: – it ruling by the British and Chinese officers which clears Teas shipped from Macao to the United States of Duty, if indeed there has ever been a question as to their exemption.–

I have the pleasure to hand you a list of articles embraced in the Trade as at present conducted with Japan, which has reached a scale of development considerably beyond general expectations.–

I hand you also printed Extracts of a letter from Japan recently received by me; and a Newspaper containing two articles of interest.–

I am, &c
Gideon Nye Jnr.

[No2]

IMPERIAL EDICT.

(*From the Peking Gazette 31st January.*)

We have this day received a memorial from Kwei–leang and his colleagues to the effect that they have received, with the letters from the British, a false Imperial Edict of the kind dispatched directly from the Imperial Court, and which, they were informed, had been obtained by a Englishman in Kwan–Tung.

On perusing this, OUR surprise was extreme. From all time, China has held fast by principles of the highest justice in her benevolent measure for tranquilizing the various nations: she has never laid plans for secretly injuring them.

Subsequently to the failure of Yeh ming–shin. We appointed Hwang–tsung–han to be Governor–general of the two Kwang, and gave him the seal of Imperial Commissioner. Our territories, as to Vice–President Lo–tun–yen and his colleagues, they stimulated by patriotic ardor. enrolled braves for the defence of their country. – a perfectly rightful occupation for local gentry.

Recently, however, the amicable negotiations of Kwei–leang and his colleagues as Teen–tsin having been finished, Hwang tsung–han had to busy himself with internal military affairs only, while Lo–tan–yen and his colleagues had, in obedience to OUR commands to deal solely with native bandits. It was not in contemplation that they should engage in hostilities with the British and French. Although these nations have not yet re–delivered the capital of Kwang–tung, yet if they maintain proper order among their troops, causing no annoyance to the inhabitants, they may live together in peace, free from all troubles.

A court despatch has, however, been fabricated giving cause to difficulties between Lo–tun–yen with his colleagues on the one side and these two nations on the other, and producing doubt and suspicion in the mind of the British. We now therefore command Hwang-tsung-han to take strict measures for the seizure of the lawless fabricators, and to punish them with utmost right of the law. Thus may all nations know that China transacts her affairs in an open, rightful and liberal spirit and that, when once a settlement is arrived at. suspicions and doubts may be given up, and so no rooms be left for the instigations of false mischief makers.

As Shanghai, where the arrangements connected with the general trade are at present being made, lies at a considerable distance from Kwang-tung. WE hereby appoint the Governor-general of the two Keang. Ho-Kwei-tsing to be Imperial Commissioner of Foreign Affairs, and WE hereby command Kwang-tsung-han to send a special officer to deliver to him the seal of Imperial Commissioner now in use. Respect this.

Extract of a letter from a distinguished Medical Missionary visiting Japan

NANGASAKI,① JANUARY 26TH, 1859.

"I had the pleasure of receiving a letter from you just before I left and as your are not in the habit of receiving letters from the 'Rising Sun' I embrace an occasion of sending this from Dezima, a 'Factory' pretty well known in mercantile and-alas-in other annals.

Mr. sent a steamer built for the folks, to Nangasaki② to find a purchaser and kindly gave me a passage in her. To see a new country when on the eve of returning for a time to my native land is no small privilege;-and such a country! – It is truly a puzzle to the political economist as to the moralist, to the merchant and to the naturalist.

I do not know enough how or what to observe in order to satisfy the curiosity of a merchant, and can only say in general that this land seems to want little, but is has more for Exports than is supposed abroad. Considerable profits have been made of late, which has caused a sort of Japan fever at Shanghae – a glut of foreign articles and a rise in native produce are the consequences: – All this will of course settle down in time, when, the real value of the Commerce of the port can be estimated.

I am pained to report that hostility to Christianity suffers no abatement: The chief object of my visit has been to ascertain how far there was a prospect of successful missionary effort, but at present the prospect is discouraging. I made the acquaintance of some intelligent officials who speak Chinese and they gladly accepted Testaments in Chinese and they gladly accepted Testaments in Chinese and English, but were soon compelled to return them at the peril of losing their heads, they said. Their eagerness to adopt foreign Arts and the like augurs well, however, and it may yet be that the gospel will accomplish ere long its peculiar changes in the land."

[1-074]

FROM THE HONGKONG GOVERNMENT GAZETTE.

GOVERNMENT NOTIFICATION.

The following notification addressed by RUTHERFORD ALCOCK, Esquire, Her Majesty's Consul at Canton, to the British Mercantile Community at that Port, respecting various matters in connection with the Chinese Custom

① Sic.

② SIc.

House, is herewith published for general information.

By Order,

G. W. CAINE.

Superintendency to Trade, Victoria, Hongkong, 18th February, 1859.

NOTIFICATION.

BRITISH CONSULATE, CANTON, *February* 15th, 1859.

His Excellency the Hoppo has requested the undersigned, her Majesty's Consul, to call the attention of the British Mercantile Community at this Port to the necessity for greater care on the part of those who transmit Foreign Goods from any other Consular Port to Canton, with an exemption Chop. Unless the Chop supply fully particulars as to the Quality, Quantity, Number of Pieces, &c., – so as to give the Custom House Officials here *satisfactory means of identifying the Packages or Goods* as those upon which Duties have actually been paid, and also specify the Sum paid, the Importers cannot be allowed the exemption sought. And as much inconvenience frequently arises from the absence of such details, it would be well if Mercantile correspondents at the other Ports, were duly warned of the necessity for greater care as to the insertion of such full particulars in every exemption Chop.

Various questions have also been the subject of discussion recently, connected with a carrying trade in Chinese produce; more especially Cotton, Peas, and Beans and the transhipment of Teas at Whampoa, from Macao or other outlying Ports, and for which exemption from duty has been erroneously claimed by the Shippers.

The undersigned is further requested, therefore, by His Excellency the Hoppo, to advise the British Mercantile Community, that no Chinese produce, brought here from any other Port or Place for consumption or sale, can by Treaty be held exempt from an Import Duty, either on the plea that it has already paid an Export Duty at the place of shipment, or that it is a of class of produce exempted by the Treaty – "Import Tariff," – only applicable to Foreign Goods or produce. In the case of Teas, brought from any other Port or Place for shipment at Canton or Whampoa, the Tariff Export Duty is just leviable, unless it can be shown that such Teas have already paid at some other Consular Port the legal Export Dues according to Tariff.

The Duty levied on Cotton, the produce of China, brought to the Port in Chinese Vessels, His Excellency the Hoppo states to be the same as that specified in the Treaty Tariff: namely, 4 Mace per Picul. There is no distinction made therefore to the disadvantage of Foreign Ships, since this is also the amount claimed when the same produce is brought in the latter. The duty on Peas, at present rate of exchange, is about 56 Cash per Picul in Chinese Vessels, and the same rate only is claimed when brought in Foreign Vessels.

(Signed) RUTHERFORD ALCOCK,

TO THE BRITISH MERCHANTILE COMMUNITY AT CANTON. *H. B. M.'s Consul for Canton.*

[1-075]

Duplicate.

N°10

Consulate of the United States.

Macao, March 12th 1859.–

Sir,

I beg to hand you Duplicate of my Despatch N° 9, of the 22nd Ult°, since which– on the 3d Inst – I have received Circular N° 9 of the Department, of Novr 15th last, reporting to me the non–receipt of the Quarterly Returns of the respective periods ending on the 31st March, 30th June and 30th September; and in reply there to beg to say that the two first named periods expired before my appointment as Deputy Consul.

I shall, however, proceed to make up the Returns in time for the next mail, from such Records as I find in the Consulate.–

I have the impression that the two Quarters in question had been duly reported to the Government, although I inferred an error in their transmission to the Secretary of the Treasury instead of yourself, finding in the letter book of the former Incumbent copies of his Despatches addressed to your said Colleague

[The Honorable
Lewis Cass
Secretary of State of the United States
of America.–
City of Washington.]

of April 1st and July 1st purporting to cover said Returns.

As to the period terminating on the 30th September, I have already transmitted its Returns to you, as I have also those of the subsequent Quarter.–

Referring to the case of the "Emma", alluded to in my last Despatch, I regret to say that although the Judge of the Supreme Court here has decided that Captn Charles Gill's title to the vessel is valid, yet, His Honor seems disposed to sanction an Appeal to the Superior Court at Goa, upon grounds which I conceive to be quite insufficient and with the imposition of conditions wanting in the essential element of reciprocal fairness.

Considering the evidences conclusive that this Appeal is evasive and totally wanting in the character of good–faith on the part of the Prosecutors, I feel it my duty to give my countenance and support to our aggrieved countrymen, as hitherto, in the defence of their rights; and as I find by the Record of the Court a newly–substituted basis of action in place of that which I exposed the unsoundness of in November (vide my letters N°11 and 12 to His Excellency Mr Reed herewith). I confess that my confidence in the attainment of justice to our Countrymen is seriously impaired.–

Without further comment, I now beg to submit to you Copies of the Protest of Captain Gill and of my official communications to H. E. Mr Reed in elucidation of the case,* reserving for the next mail Copies of the two Records of the Court alluded to, and of several other Papers presenting the new phase upon which the case has just now entered.–

I beg to hand you, – as it is possible that the Chargé d'Affairs being in Canton at present may not be able to do so, – Copy of an Imperial Edict of the 31st January, which may be characterized as,– next to the Emperor's general confirmation of the Treaties of Tiensin of last summer, if indeed the evidences of good–faith in this more outspoken acquiescence in the New Relations with Western Nations are not, as I esteem them, still more significant – as the most important public step toward an international league ever taken by an Emperor of China.–

The discovery and exposure of the double–dealing of Hwang and others–albeit the inspiration of the Imperial Court – by the finding of the public Document in question and other "Chops", gave Lord Elgin a lever by

[*pages 1 @ 31 inclusive]

which he has completely confirmed the success of his diplomacy.–

I am,
Sir,
With great respect,
Your Obedient Servant
Gideon Nye, Jnr.
Vice Consul of the United States
of America.–

N°1

United States Consulate at Macao

Fees Received during the Quarter ending 31 March 1858.–

Date	No	Name of Vessel	Name of the party Paying the fee	Nature of service rendered	Amount of fees paid	
2	1	Chilo	L. G. Hollis	shipping 2 men	$1	–
				discharging 1 man （extra wages $75 less $5 debt）	–	50
	2	Flora Temple	John M Cole	Tonnage fees （coolie ship）	$9	58
	3	Ocean Eagle	W. J. Cheever	shipping 1 man	–	50
5	4	Chilo	L. G. Hollis	Certificate to deserion of 7 men	$3	50
6	5	Helen Mar	E. J. Lowe	Tonnage fees	$2	55
	6		W. C. Hunter	Affixing 2 Cons. seals	$4	–
14	7		J. B. Endicott	Affixing 1 Cons. seals	$2	–
	8	Flora Temple	John M Cole	Shipping 6 men	$3	–
20	9	Spirit of the Times	J. Klevin	Tonnage fees, certificate to desertion of 3 men – & loss of one overboard	$9	03
				Noting Protest	$2	–
9	10		H. Reinhart	Affixing 3 Cons. Seals – to private documents Wetmore	$6	75
11	11		W. C. Hunter	do 1 Cons. Seals to invoices	$2	–
1	12		W .C. Hunter	do 2 Cons. Seals to invoices	$4	–
7	13	Empress	D. R. Le Crew	Tonnage fees （cargo: Rice）	$6	50
				Noting Protest	$2	–
				Certifying Ship & discharged of 20 men	$10	–

24	14	Palmette	S. B. Kenny	Tonnage fees	$1	41
26	15	Swallow	B. W. Tucker	Tonnage fees （coolie ship）	$7	18
				Certificate shippg 6 men	$5	–
25	16	Wanderer	T. H. King	Tonnage fees	–	87
3	17	Adjuster	A. A. Enquest	Tonnage fees	$2	50
4	18		W. S. Wetmore	Affixing 1 Consular seal private documents	$2	–
□□□	19	Curlew	Stratten	Tonnage Fees （Lorcha sailing under Am' colors to Siam）	$	55
				Certifying ship 14 men	$5	–
	21	Spark	J. B. Edicott	Tonnage fees	$25	–
	22		G. Nye Jr	Affix 2 Cons: Seals & oath to private Docts	$4	50
			Roberts	Affix 1 Cons: Seals to Will	$2	–
					$124	92

Copied from the Book of the late Consul
E. E. Macao March 15th 1859.
Gideon Nye Jnr
Vice Consul of the
United States for Macao

No2

United States Consulate at Macao.–

Fees received during the Quarter ending 30 June 1858.––

Date	No	Name of Vessel	Name of the party Paying the fee	Nature of service rendered	Amount of fees paid	
□ 6	23	Wm Sprague	Bowers	Tonnage fees	$3	86
□ 6	24	Nymph	Wm F. Clark	Tonnage fees	$2	34
□ 6	25	Antelope	Clark	Tonnage fees	$3	29
				Certificate dischg 8 men	$4	50
□ 6				Desertion & dischg 2 mates – 4 seals	$4	–
□ 6		Argonant	Dunbar Norton	Tonnage fees	$3	13
				Certificate of disertion of 5 men	$2	25
□ 6	27	Eureka	Lane	Tonnage fees	$6	28
20	28	Crystal Palace	B. Simmons	Tonnage fees	$2	–
				Certificate dischg 4 men	$2	–
				Certificate seal & oath	$2	25
20	29	Game Cock	Osgood	Tonnage fees	$6	95
20	30	John Tucker	Williams	Tonnage fees	$6	65

				Noting Protest	$2	–
				Cert dischg 1 man–Sent to Hospital & died	$2	75
24			W. C. Hunter	Seals 1 oath	$2	25
24	31	Frank Jonson	Lothrop	Tonnage fees	$2	64
				Noted Protest	$2	–
				Extend protest	$6	–
	32	Loochoo	Norton	Tonnage fees	$4	20
	33	Manry	Flitcher	Tonnage fees	$3	–
	34	Myrtle	Boltsford	Tonnage fees	$1	99
				Noted Protest	$2	–
				Extend protest	$5	–
				Copied Protest	$2	50
				Certificate shipping 6 men	$3	–
				Seals & oath	$4	50
			S. B. Drinker	Private documents	$2	25
			S. B. Drinker	Private documents	$10	–
12			L. Carvalho	Power of Attorney	$6	–
17			J. B. Endicott	Affix 1 Cons Seal to Private Documt	$2	25
17			W. C. Hunter	Affix 1 Cons Seal to Private Documt	$2	25
18			W. C. Hunter	Affix 3 Cons Seal to Private Documt	$6	–
19			W. C. Hunter	Affix 3 Cons Seal to Private Documt	$6	–
24	35	Ino	Plummer	Tonnage dues	$4	49
28	36	Early Bird	Cook	Tonnage dues	$2	72
				Noting Protest	$1	–
				Carried forward	$136	29

Date	No	Name of Vessel	Name of the party Paying the fee	Nature of service rendered	Amount of fees paid	
				Brought forward	$136	29
May 28	36	Early Bird	Cook	Certificate discharging 8 men	$4	□□
June 9	39	Crystal Palace	B. Simmons	Tonnage fees – Certificate to 2 men	$4	□□
	40	Helen Mar	E. T. Lowe	Tonnage fees	$2	□□
				Certificate disch[g] 1 mate		□□
				Certificate shipping 8 men	$4	□□
	41	Northern Light	S. Doane	Tonnage fees	$5	□□

21	42		J. B. Endicott	Affix^{g} 1 Consulate Seal	$2	□□
26			J. Sherman	3 Seals 3 oaths	$6	□□
				Certificate disch^{g} 5 men	$2	□□
29	44	Spirit of the Times	John Klein	Noting protest	$2	□□
30	46	Spark	J. B. Endicott	Tonnage Fees	$24	□□
30	47	Rose	J. B. Endicott	Tonnage Fees	$14	□□
30		Spirit of the Times	John Klein	Certificate disch^{g} 3 men	$1	□□
					$2□□	□□

Copied from the Book of the late
Consul
E. E. Macao March 15th 1859.
Gideon Nye Jnr
Vice Consul of the
United States for
Macao.

[1-076]

[Rec 30. May. Mr Abott]

N°11

Consulate of the United States
Macao, March 28th 1859

Sir,

Referring to my Despatch N° 10, by the last mail, I now beg leave to hand you the Returns of this Consulate for the Quarters left in arrears by my Predecessor, as called for by the Circular of your Department N° 9.–

[N° 1 & 2]

In continuation of the exposition of the case arising from the sequestration of the ship "Emma", I beg to hand you also, pages 32 to 50 inclusive of the Copies of Documents thereto pertaining, including my official letter to His Excellency the Governor of this place communicating the Protest of Charles Gill the Owner and Master of the Ship. –

[N° 3.]

[The Honorable
Lewis Cass
Secretary of State of the United States
of America.–

City of Washington.]

As a final decision upon the Appeal of the Chinese claimant has not been notified, although the disposition to concede it is evident, I reserve comment upon the circumstances of hardship to our Countryman involved in an Appeal to another distant Dependency of Portugal until the final decision of the Judge is notified to me by our Countrymen interested.–

I am,
Sir,
With great respect,
Your Obedient Servant
Gideon Nye Jnr
Vice Consul of the United States
of America for Macao––

[N°4]

P. S. March 29th

I have just received and now transmit the enclosed letters of Captain Gill upon the subject of his grievances, as I have not sufficient time left for copying it.

The present hesitation or Vacillation of the Judge – which ever it may be – seems attributable to the want of sufficient security from the Chinese to legally warrant the actual grant of Appeal in face of the protest impending from Captain Gill – the entire sum yet paid in including a recent instalment being but $9,000 – against a value and damages of more than four times that amount.

In the meantime, and as appears probable to gain time for acquiring further security, the Judge proposes to give up the "Emma" to Captain Gill upon his giving the Bonds originally demanded of him in November.

I am &c
G. N. J

[Macao March 28/29 1859
Gideon Nye Jnr
N°11.
Four
Received
Returns
"Emma" case]

32.

[Copy]

Consulate of the United States of America
Macao, November 8th 1858.

Sir,

I beg leave to bring to Your Excellency's notice a case of very great gravity, wherein a Citizen of the United States is morally aggrieved beside suffering much pecuniary detriment, under circumstances which– as I consider and respectfully submit– demand prompt redress.

I allude to the seizure of the American ship "Emma" and the several preliminary steps thereto, taken by certain of the Authorities of Macao – in the name of Portuguese Government, which as I conceive constitute infractions of the rights of Charles Gill, the citizen above named; who is the rightful owner of that vessel and was, as he has long been, the commander of her until his formal abandonment under protest of the ship and her cargo, to the officers and armed force sent onboard of her on Saturday the sixth day of this month in the presence of Competent Witnesses.

The necessity of the case are so urgent from the moral harm suffered by Captain Gill and the amount of pecuniary damages involved as well as the responsibilities incurred to the shippers of the cargo for Bombay – that I do not extend my own remarks, holding myself prepared to give Your Excellency information

[His Excellency
Isidoro F. Guimarães
Governor General of Macao and its Dependencies
&c &c &c]

33.

in furtherance of an equitable adjustment of damages, and in the mean time referring to the herewith submitted Declaration and Protest of Captain Gill. I beg leave respectfully to claim indemnity in his behalf.

I am,
With great respect,
Your Excellency's
Obedient Servant
(signed) Gideon Nye Jr.
Vice Consul of the United States
of America.–

No29

Translation.

Sir,

I have the honor to acknowledge receipt of your Despatch relative to the "embargo" of the American Ship "Emma" which, I am informed, has been done by order and authority of the chief Judge of this district, and not by order of the Government as erroneously stated in your Despatch and Document accompanying it – the parties who appeared onboard having been constables of the said Judge accompanied by an armed Police force and not by officers (military men and soldiers) as it may be inferred from the manner in which you expressed it in the said Despatch. I am therefore in duty bound to repel all idea of such an act being imputed to this Government since it is beyond my official cognizance.--

After what I have just expounded, you

34.

will become aware that the case in question arises from an act of an Authority – which not only is not subordinate to me – but which forms part of the Executive Power of State entirely independent according to the constitution of Portugal.

I cannot therefore take cognizance of the document which accompanied your Despatch beyond transmitting it to the chief Judge along with a copy of the dispatch that he may give them that consideration which he may deem proper and to the said Judge the party interested should direct his claims and uphold the justice of his cause and not to this Government which cannot have any thing to do in the premises being forbidden to interfere in any way with the Judicial power.–

God preserve you

Macao 8th November 1858.–
(signed) Isidoro F. Guimarães.

[G. Nye Jr Esquire
Vice Consul of the United States of America at Macao.]

Translation.

Sir,

It behoves me to inform you that having to absent myself from Macao. I transferred

35.

the Government of this Colony to the Council of Government of which His Honor Augusto Henrique Ribeiro de Carvalho Chief Judge is President ad interim and to whom all official correspondence relating to affairs pertaining to the Government of Macao must be addressed.

God preserve you

Macao 9th November 1858.–
(signed) Isidoro F. Guimarães

[G. Nye Jr Esquire
V. Consul of the U.S.A. at Macao]

Macao, Nov 2d 1858.

Gideon Nye Jr. Esq

U. S. Consul

at Macao

Dr Sir,

I have just received your official note, stating that the Captain of the port had verbally intimated to you, that he held an order for the arrest and detention of the ship "Emma" owned and commanded by me; which order must take effect unless bonds were given by me to abide the issue of an action in consequence of a suit in Court of a Chinaman against her former owner.–

I fully appreciate this civility upon the part of the Captain of the Port, but I wish you officially to apprise him that, I decline to sign any such bonds,

36.

as something, I have nothing to do with, and which he cannot draw me into – also of what will be the result of such an order.–

For your information, I refer you in the first place, to the ships papers which you have in your consulate; and the certificate of the U. S. Government that it will defend me in my title; Secondly, to the enclosed Correspondence, held last June with the officials of the Portuguese Government, with an order to me to arrest my own ship, upon the same claim, and my protest against it, and my action under it, also, a last letter from the captain of the port, saying that the vessel was free.–

You will by this perceive, that this suit is no new thing, but has the last year been forced upon me, to make me appear in Court against this Chinaman, with whom I have nothing to do in all of which time, the Government has not dared virtually to arrest my vessel, but when about to sail, they have in some underhanded way, tried to give me annoyance.

The last time I was here, (last June, the publicity given to what was termed an arrest of the ship, nearly lost me the freight engaged for a voyage to Shanghae.–

The Portuguese Government fully understands the responsibility it would assume in taking possession of my vessel, when it knows that the United States Government will defend my claim against the World, but they can issue orders &c without a

37.

formal arrest to annoy me.

I wish you to make the official to whom you make your communication, fully understand that those orders can aggrieve, as well as annoy – In this order now held by the Captain of the Port I may be aggrieved and my interests damaged, if it as publicly known, as the ship is now loading for Bombay and is half loaded, with a valuable cargo of sugar, Teas, silks, &c a Bill of lading of a part of which, was sent by last mail Steamer. – If such has happened, or should happen, it would result in a heavy loss to me, as I shall not be able to get more freight, or to do any thing with the vessel.

You can clearly perceive my position in the case, and the annoyance, & prosecution, if not positive loss. I have been already made to suffer. – I am determined not to put up with it any longer, and if I am in any way aggrieved by this order I shall demand indemnity, and call upon the Government of the United States to collect it.–

I have the honor to be, Sir,
Yr. mo. obt. servt.
(signed) Charles Gill–

I, Joseph Clutterbuck, first officer of the American Ship "Emma" having left unwritten two days of the log of the said ship, viz. Those of Friday

38.

and Saturday the fifth and sixth days of November A. D. 1858 do append the following history of the said two days as I passed them aboard the said ship – viz:

On Friday the 5th day of November I was engaged taking cargo – the crew also at work taking in said cargo & setting up rigging – Stevedore stowing Cargo in lower hold – fine pleasant weather, wind N. E.

At about 4 p.m. the Captain being on shore, five Portuguese came on board the ship & representing to me that they had an order from the Judge to arrest the ship, ordered me to heave up the ship's anchors – I replied that the Captain was on shore & I should not obey their orders or raise the anchors until the Captain ordered me.

At about 5 p.m. the Captain came on board, and by dark the five men had left the ship.

On Saturday the 6th day of November I was engaged as the day before receiving cargo and preparing top gallant rigging for sea.

Fine weather wind Northerly.

At about 4 p.m. a party of men Portuguese officers, with a file of soldiers; came on board and said to me (the captain being on shore) that they came to seize and arrest the ship– I told them that the captain would be on board soon.–

When the Captain returned I was called by him to be a Witness. The officers presented a document which they said was signed by the Judge

39.

of Macao & that they came by virtue of that, to arrest & seize the ship & with written instructions to use force if the ship was not given up quietly – The Captain received a paper from them & notified them that he abandoned the ship & every thing on board to the Portuguese Government – immediately after the Captn called the crew and said that he had given the ship up and that he had nothing more for them to do and that the officers present were in entire charge & possession of the ship and that they could remain onboard only if they allowed them. The soldiers loaded their guns upon the deck and the officers sealed up the hatches & the Cabin, the Captain having left with only his private clothes – leaving the Instruments – Chronometer &c on board.

I have indited this in the office of the American Consul at Macao, in consequence of not having time to write my log up onboard, the Captain having taken it on shore with him when he left. – Macao–Nov 8th 1858–

(signed) Joseph Clutterbuck

Consulate of the United States of America.
Macao November 8th 1858.–

I, the undersigned Vice Consul of the United States of America for Macao and its Dependences, do hereby certify that on the day of the date hereof, before me, personally appeared the within named

40.

Joseph Clutterbuck and signing the foregoing two pages as a continuation of the Log Book of the ship "Emma" in my presence made oath in due form of law to the truth of the said writing in all its parts.

Given under my hand, and the
Seal of this Consulate the day &
year above written;–
(signed) Gideon Nye Jnr
(L. S.) Vice Consul of the United States
of America for Macao.––

Report

On the 6th June 1857 Cheong Ahoy a Chinese – demanded in Court the Embargo of the Ship Emma against James McCormick for a debt of $8,055.40 and presented documents relating to said debt as per fol 3. 4. 5. 6. of the suit of arrest.–The prosecutor having thus satisfied the requirements of the Law – action was taken accordingly Decreeing the Embargo as per fol 13.

The prosecutor having also signed the usual obligation of responsibility for damages prejudices as per fol 14 petitioned as per fol 15 that the Captain of the Port should be informed of the said Decree to the end that he might prevent the departure of the vessel from port.–The Captain of the Port replied on 16th June 1857 f 16 that the New Granadian

41.

ship "Emma" did not belong to McCormick and that her present owner was Captn Charles Gill – having notified the attorney of the said Chinese on the 16th June no further steps was taken by him with regard to the Embargo until the current year, however he tired to institute an ordinary suit against McCormick – as he effectually did commencing an Action on the 22d June 1857 Summons having been served to that effect on the 17th June of the said year f 5 of the file of papers that belong to that lawsuit with these papers was included a note of non–conciliation between him and the said – McCormick date 9th June 1857 the signature to which by McCormick is seen on the notice of the Summons f 3. When McComick was called before the Court in the 17th June, he signed the notice of the Summons fl 2. but he alleged nothing before the Court, nor did he constitute an attorney to defend him, the case passed by his default until the final sentence which is to be found a f 9 of the said papers of the Law suit dated 27 Oct 1857 – In October 1857 the same Chinese brought an action against McCormick to prove – 1st That the sale made by M[c]Cormick to Capt[n] Gill was fantastic and fictitious – 2nd that the "Emma" was still the property of M[c]Cormick not withstanding the certificate of sale or Bill of Sale dated Macao 18th February 1857 executed in favour of Capt[n] Gill. –

42.

He added a f 4 the declaration taken at HongKong on the 7th of the said Month of October in which – the deponents – William Tarrant and G. Cooper Turner affirmed that M[c]Cormick was the Owner of the "Emma" and not Charles Gill – for this reason that on the 9th June or thereabouts Gill came to HongKong for the purpose of obtaining from the Vice Consul of New Granada – Burrows Jr. the flag of that Republic which was granted – and in support of this they annexed a letter of the said Vice Consul dated 11th June 1857 addressed to the Deponent Turner f 7 in which the Vice Consul States that previous to the granting of said flag of New Granada the "Emma" was Mr. M[c]Cormick's property & that she was registered as such.–

As the sale of the ship (said to have been made to Capt[n] Gill) took place on the 18th February 1857 and the Vice Consul says on the 11th of June of the same year that previous to the flag of New Granada being granted the "Emma" was Registered as the property of M[c]Cormick, it follows that the said sale was fictitious and done in prejudice of his Creditors in June when he had been summoned to appear in Court to pay the debts. – Let the dates be compared – that of the Call before the Justice of the Peace – and that before the Court of Macao with the date in which the Vice Consul says he granted the flag of New Granada – the truth of the assertion

43.

will be known. The Chinese prosecutor has also endeavoured to prove by Witnesses the justifiable nature of the items (of account) as per fl 3 found but as a justification was not the competent means to account the sale of the ship, sentence was not awarded in his favour on the 4th November.

The same Chinese brought an action against Capt[n] Gill of nullity of sale of the Emma & Capt[n] Gill was summoned on the 7th November 1857. This suit is not yet concluded, and the prosecuted Captain has allowed it to proceed by his default, his unwillingness to sign the notice of the summons and refusal to receive the copy of the petition of the prosecutor or the translation of it is affirmed by the Constable and Witness who have signed a declaration therefore.

In June of the present year – Capt[n] Gill having arrived from a voyage in the Barque Emma, the Chinese prosecutor demanded a warrant of Embargo of her – and such not having been effected in the said month by reasons which are stated in the Documents of this Lawsuit, it was, however, carried into effect on the 6th Nov, 1858. It is not known when Capt[n] Gill gave up the flag of New Granada taken in June 1857 – to hoist that of the United States under which the ship sails now – nor how he is enabled to cover the different flags that the ships has had.

Capt[n] Gill having been informed of the Embargo in the 5th repelled the officer Bearer of the Warrant

44.

and the officer returning on the 6th inst with a police force then made the Embargo, and Capt[n] Gill not having had recoursed to the Court as he could have done and allege according to Law the non-application of the embargo as a third party, but he went to the Vice-Consul of the United States where he entered a protest abandoning everything and claiming 42,000 Dollars of which 28,500 as the value of the ship and the remainder as the value of the freight, charts & nautical instruments, pay of the Crew &c.

This protest was forwarded to that Government by the Vice–Consul and the answer of His Excellency the Governor has been to the effect that the Governor has no command over the Judicial Authority which according to Law is an independent one The Documents relating to this Embargo or arrest of – shows that it was only made for the ship & her appurtenances and not on the nautical instruments, charts and merchandize belonging of other parties.–

45

– Translation.

Fran^co^ d' Assis e Fren^s^ Esq:

In the action brought in by the Chinese Merchant Cheong Ahoy – prosecutor – against Charles Gill for nullity （of the purchase of the ship Emma） sentence has been awarded of which I transmit you a Copy for you information and government as Attorney for the said Gill.

God preserve You.–

Macao 22 February 1859.–
（signed） Thomaz d'Aq^no^ Miqueis–
Clerk to the Civil Court.–

Copy of the Sentence

Reviewing the documents pertaining to this Lawsuit and those attached to them, it appears that James M^c^Cormick having sold to Charles Gill the Ship "Emma" the Chinese prosecutor Cheong Ahoy contests the validity of the purchase alleging that the same was done in prejudice of the Creditors of the first named and to substantiate this charge he states at fl that the sale was done before Mr Hunter and not through the Notarial Records with an intention to evade the claims which his creditors might institute in Court – that in the month of June 1857, the very seller stated to M. V. Marques and to Mark H. Shaw that the Barque "Emma" was his and he was willing

46.

to sell her for fifteen thousand dollars, and consequently the said sale alleged to have been done to the prosecuted is null, imaginary and fantastic – That the prosecuted has no property of his own, is not in business, merely living on his pay as Captain Navigator, and therefore could never been able to dispose of the amount of twenty eight thousand dollars for the purchase of the said Barque – That James M^c^Cormick to the end of defrauding his Creditors effected the sale with the utmost simulation, – so much so that immediately on his being summoned to answer to an action he absented himself from this City; that the same thing was done by the prosecuted on his being summoned for the present action – That according to Ordinance Book 4th Title 71 – Simulated Contracts are de jure null; whence the sale of the said Barque having been a simulated one should and ought to be null and the prosecuted condemned to forego his hold on the same in order that execution might be made upon it as the property of James Mc Cormick until full payment of the debt of which the prosecutor is Creditor and furthermore the expenses and legal fine.—The Prosecutor further states that the prosecuted Charles Gill having been summoned @fl2 has not appeared in Court allowing thereby the present suit to run by default and only lately resolved to appear in Court imploring the restitution of the property, alleging the reasons stated in the Contestation and exceptions which he presents – Finally, it appears by the document appended N° 4 that during the course of the present suit of nullity in

47.

the purchase of the ship "Emma" the Chinese prosecutor Cheong Ahoy having petitioned that the prosecuted be compelled to give Bond to the Court by reason of his being on the eve of leaving this port to the end that the claim of the prosecutor might not be eluded, in terms of Ordinance Book 3rd Title 31 in princip: Accordingly the prosecuted was summoned to give a bond, which not having been done the vessel was seized notwithstanding the resistance offered by the prosecuted to prevent the carrying–out of the Warrant of this court – and it was only after he had made his claims through the Consular Agent of his Nation, the abandonment of the Ship to the Government of this Colony, and obtained a fruitless result that he took the deliberation to appear in court to protect his rights by means of embargos of nullity and third party and possessor of the said ship as shewn by the said documents appended:–

The foregoing having been fully reviewed and examined shows that the defence offered by the prosecuted by Contestation and exception @ fl invoking in his favor the advantage of restitution cannot be attended to for reason of its not having been done within the legal limit of time the prosecuted having been summoned, as shown by the certificate of the officer @ fl had an opportunity of appearing in Court in due time to defend his rights, and it he has not done so it was through his unwillingness and because he fancied that this question as well as the subsequent one of the sequestration of the vessel ought to have been treated between the two Governments as proved by the dispatches

48.

of the Government of this colony in the Archives of the court in which the case of the surrender of the ship by reclamation of the Consul of his country has been discussed – therefore, if the prosecuted has not defended his right contesting the charges of the present suit when the Law afforded him an opportunity of so doing, he must impute the blame to himself – The same is the case with the contestation of nullity and plea of third party and possessor the first as extemporaneous and the latter as incompetent – The Documents show that the ship Emma having been sequestred on the 6th of November last passed – the prosecuted only now thinks of contesting the nullity of the same: as to the incompetency of the latter, it is evident for beside that the sequestration of the ship was not made as the property of James Mc Cormick but rather as the property of the prosecuted, which not having been pledged it was only in case of its having been pledged that the alleged embargo could have been proceeded with. – As regards the principal question of the nullity of the sale of the ship the documents show that the prosecutor based his argument upon three motives to invalidate in Court the sale and purchase of the said ship viz: of its having been made before Mr Hunter & not through the Notarial Records, the testimony of M. V. Marques and Mark Shaw who affirm that her former owner James Mc Cormick was willing to sell the said Barque for the sum of fifteen thousand dollars in the month of June 1857 and the plea that the prosecuted could not dispose of the sum of twenty eight thousand dollars with

49.

which to buy her. But none of these arguments are sufficient to conclude thereby the nullity of the said sale and only serve, annexed to the evidence of the Witnesses, to establish more or less presumption of simulation in this contract between James McCormick and the prosecuted. – According to Law the necessary documents to make this sale invalid are of its having taken place after the question has been brought to litigation and the insolvency of the Debtor – but from the Lawsuit and Documents pertaining to it, it appears that the sale of the ship was verified in the 18th February 1857 and the seller McCormick was only summoned to account for his debt to the prosecutor four months after the sale had taken place – that is to say, in June of the same year; in consequence of which according to the argument in a contrary sense to be deduced from Ordinance Book 4th – Title 10th & 9th One of the essential requisites is wanting for invalidating the contract of sale. – Furthermore the insolvency of the former Owner of the ship has not been proved by the documents as it should and ought to have been done. – As to the statement of the Witness for the prosecution that he owned money to various individuals and did not pay them, it is not that kind of proof which is required at Law to establish the insolvency of a Debtor; in order that the insolvency may be proceeded with it is necessary that the circumstances required by the Commercial Code should be apparent – Moreover it is not proved by the Documents of this Lawsuit that the said James McCormick had no other property of his own besides the ship – that it may be

50.

considered as the only property bound to satisfy his debts and as such without any right of disposing freely of it. – Therefore in view of the above, exposition and further documents and the principles of Law to which I conform myself, judging valid the purchase of the Barque Emma by the prosecuted, Gill – I absolve him of the demand of the prosecutor and condemn the latter to pay the expenses and the legal fine.–

Macao 21 February 1859 –
(signed) Augusto Henrique Ribeiro de Carvalho
(signed) Miqueis
Macao 29th Mach 1859.

Dear Sir:

Since handing you the decision of the Judge of Macao, in my favor, in the case of the ship Emma dated 21st Feby last, my counsel has petitioned for the delivery of the vessel to me, and for damages for her arrest, detention, &c.

The court proposes to give up the ship in case I sign bonds to await the issue of the suit at Goa, of the Chinaman against her former owner the very bonds they tired to get me to sign before the seizure of the vessel, under the threat of arresting her.

As I shall not and cannot be forced to sign any such bonds for the benefit of another and being now kept out of my property for five months and over one month after the highest tribunal here has decided upon the validity of my title, the case now stands on the position, if I mistake not, when on the judgement of Mr Reed, our late Minister to China, the proper officer of our Government here should interpose to see me righted.

From the first as you are well aware I have been most shamefully wronged, and now when the Macao Court decides that such is the case, and that my vessel has been illegally-detained, I call upon my Government for aid and earnably desire you to apprize Commandre Jaimall of my situation, that he may takes steps, such as he may deem best, to protect my interest as an American citizen.

I trust you will urge upon him the immediate necessity of his interference.

I have the honor to be Sir,
Yr. mo. obt. servt.
Charles Gill

[Gideon Nye Jr. Esq.
U. S. Vice Consul
for Macao]

[1-077]

[Duplicate

Recd J □□ 27
Exchange □□□□□□□
auditor □□□ &c]

N°12

Consulate of the United States
Macao, April 8th 1859.

Sir,

I beg now to hand you the Returns of this Consulate for the Quarter ending on the 31th Utl°. and to call your attention to the confirmation of the Opinion expressed by me in my Despatch N° 1 as to the probable meagre amount to be expected from the Fees, now shewn by the sum of \$83 $\frac{13}{100}$ received during the period covered by this account.-

I beg also, - with reference to my Despatch N°.8 Copy herewith, to advise my Draft upon you as noted below in reimbursement of my outlays for the Relief of the shipwrecked crew of the Barque "Matilda" of New York, the peculiar circumstances of whose rescue, as stated

[The Honorable
Lewis Cass
Secretary of State of the United States of
America. City of Washington.]

in said Despatch being certified by Dr Williams, the chargé d'Affaires ad-interim of the Government as per certified copy herewith, the original of which with the original of all the required Vouchers N°1 to 26 has been handed to Captain Soule the purchaser of the Draft to accompany its presentation at the Department. I hand you the

Account Current balanced by my said Draft, and accompany it with the certificates required by the Regulations. In addition to this I take the liberty to hand you copies of the declinatures of all the principal American Houses in this part of China to purchase Drafts upon the Government and that of General Keenan the Consul at Hongkong offering the same rate at which I sold the Draft. I confess that I was disappointed and surprised to find so little inclination to buy a Government Draft; and had I not already disposed of my present small means before ascertaining the indisposition of Mess[rs] Russell & Co., upon whom as the financial Agents of the Government I had relied especially, I would willingly have subjected myself to a longer outlay of the amount by remitting the Draft for collection for my own account.–

As the matter stands you will see that I had already been under advances of this sum several months, without & charging interest of money and that I have had all the trouble connected with the disbursements without a dollar of recompense, whilst my fees for the whole Quarter do not pay one third of the salary of my Assistant!–

Meagre as is the sum of $300 to 400 per annum, and little as I coveted the office which I fill, I should be ashamed to be suspected of not being a scrupulously faithfully servant of the Government so long as I hold it, so that I venture to trouble you with these brief declinatures in addition to the usual Vouchers.––

I take leave also to place under in cover with this another addressed to the Fifth Auditor of the Treasury with copies of the accounts the Originals, as I before said, having accompanied the Draft.–

I still add D[r] William's translation of the written statement of the Junk–Captain and Copy of a letter of M[r] Weise of the House of Siemssen & Co （Consul at HongKong for Hamburgh） shewing that he fully recognized the claim of the Junk Captain to the $280 – but did not like to assume the risk of more than $409 without the means or authority of the Owner of the vessel.

I am,
Sir,
With great respect,
Your obedient servant
Gideon Nye Jnr.
Vice Consul of the United States,
of America for Macao

Memorandum

N[o] 1_Draft of March 26th 1859 – upon the Hon[ble] the Secretary of State @ 15 days sight in favor of H. J. Soule Esq of New Haven in due form, for one thousand three hundred seventy one Dollars ninety four cents.–

E. E. G. N. Jr

[1–078]

[Rec 27 July. Mr. Abbott
Duplicate.]

N°13

Consulate of the United States–
Macao, April 8th 1859.–

Sir,

I beg to refer to my Despatches N° 8 &12 in now proceeding specially to submit, in conformity to section 340 of the General Instructions -- the peculiar merits and deserts of the Junk Captain Cheung–ah–ng who with his crew rescued the officers and crew of the Barque "Matilda" of New York, which vessel foundered in a Tyfoong in October last.–

To properly appreciate the conduct of this brave Junkman and his crew, the following considerations must be kept in view.–

1st The general fact of piracy and violencec characterizing the maritime people of these Seas:

[The Honorable
Lewis Cass
Secretary of State of the United States of America
City of Washington.]

2nd The moderation of his demand upon these shipwrecked men, wholly in his power, a demand moderate alike with reference to the protracted service of 10 days from Hainan and to the usual charges of one thousand Dollars or more to convey shipwrecked people from the Prata Shoal within 250 miles of HongKong.–

3rd His fortitude in bearing the shackles of the Mandarins at Shah pah for a couple days without abandoning his charge at though denounced for assisting "Europeans" while war with them was proceeding at Canton, and his perseverance in bringing the shipwrecked men to Macao against the strength of the North East Monsoon.

Such, briefly, are the singular claims of this Chinese, to a special mark of recognition by the President; and it will not escape your observation that the nature of some of them plainly suggests that it will be eminently politic to make such bestowal.–

You will notice, by his endorsement in my Despatch N°8, the concurrence of Dr Williams, the Chargé d'Affaires of the Government in the sense of my suggestion.--

Perhaps you will permit me to suggest as a suitable present a Telescope costing $50 to $100 or a Watch costing the latter sum.–

I am,
Sir,
With great respect,
Your Obedient Servant
Gideon Nye Jnr.
Vice–Consul of the United Sttes
of America for Macao.

[Mr. Ron,

Please give me the residence below of
Mrs M. Thompson
New York
Street address not given.——
&
Charles Caloest
Washington, D. C.

Whose letters were sent to
you – dated June 21, & June
25, 1859,
Your respectfully
G. N. U.]

Quarterly Return of the arrival and Departure of American Vessels at the United States Consulate at Macao, from the 1st of April to the 30th June 1859.——

Date		Class	Name	Tonnage	Where from	When built	Vessels			Cargoes		Owners	Masters
Month	Day						Where Built	Where belonging	Where Bound	Import	Export		
April	8th	Ship	Minnehaha	1695 $\frac{9}{95}$	Whampoa	1856	Boston	Boston	Bombay 14th April	Part Cargo for Bombay	Bombay	Buy: Franklin Kendall & others	I. Beauchamp
	18th	Ship	Invincible	1768 $\frac{65}{95}$	HongKong	1851	NewYork	NewYork	NewYork 22d June	Ballast	Tea, silks &c	Jas W. Phillips & others	Henry W. Johnson & D. S. Austin
	28th	Ship	Judith	993 $\frac{6}{95}$	Shanghae	1853	Booth-Bay	New Orleans	HongKong 2d May	Cotton – goat hair	Ballast	Richd S. Brown & others	Richd S. Brown
May	21st	Bk	Cornelia L Berand	330 $\frac{68}{95}$	Penang	1846	Baltimore	Baltimore	Shanghae 30th June	Rice	Sugar, Indigos &c	Jacob-W-Hugg	Jas. Pedersen
June	18th	Ship	Dirigo	608 $\frac{12}{95}$	Foochow	1852	Bath	Boston	HongKong 18th June	Tea	Ballast	Jacob Stanwood & others	Euml. Attwood
				5395 $\frac{65}{95}$									

Gideon Nye Jnr
Vice Consul of the United States of America for
Macao.

[June 30
Macao
3rd Qts
Recd Oct 5/59]

[1-079]

[Rec 27. Septr Mr Abbott.]

N°14

Consulate of the United States.
Macao, July 20th 1859

[Fees & C cks □□□□□□□□□□)]

Sir,

Referring to my Dispatch N° 12 in which I forwarded the returns of this consulate for the previous quarter, I now beg to hand you thereof the quarter ending the 30th Ult°, the amount of fees, as you will observe, being \$ 91 $\frac{63}{100}$, and showing, with the last; that my annual remuneration is but little above \$300. –

[No1. & 2.]

Reverting to the Case of the sequestration of the ship "Emma", I beg leave to hand you a letter of her owner Captain Charles Gill of the 18th inst to your address, the purport of which

[No 3.]

[The Honorable
Lewis Cass
Secretary of State of the United States
of America –City of Washington.–]

I am enabled to substantially, confirm; and I trust that in view of the aggrieved feeling which naturally actuates Captain Gill, you will be pleased not to view its form with fastidiousness.

I beg to hand you a pamphlet presented to me by H. E. the Governor General of Macao containing a Relation of his extraordinary Mission to Siam.I hand you also an Extra Newspaper conveying the account of the lamentable collision between the English & French and the Mongol Chief in charge of the new defences at the mouth of the Peiho, which, it is understood, were exacted chiefly at his own expense.–

I am,
Sir,
With great respect
Your obedient Servt.
Gideon Nye Jnr.
Vice Consul of the United States
of America for Macao.–

United States Consulate at Macao
Fees received during the Quarter ending 30th June 1859.–

Date	No	Name of Vessel	Name of the party paying the fee	Nature of service Rendered	Amount of fees received	
□□□						

□□□ 4th			O. E. Roberts	Certificate to a Deed of writing	$2	–
	6	Uncle Toby	R. Pollard	Certificate to an Invoice of Sundries	$2	
6th		do	I. T. Soule	Deposit of papers 1,144 $\frac{52}{95}$ tons	$5	72
		do	do	Shipping 2 men	$1	–
14th	1	Minnehaha	Isac Beauchamp	Deposit of papers 1,695 $\frac{9}{95}$	$8	48
18th	7	Swallow	Thor H Morton	Deposit of papers 1,435 $\frac{42}{95}$	$7	18
20th		Mary L Sutton	Rd Pollard	Certificate to Ino Sundried from HKong	$2	–
	3	Judith	Brown	Deposit of Papers– 9,94 tons	$4	97
8th		Robin Gray	David Dick	Entry of Protest in the absence of the British Consular Agent	$1	–
		do	do	Warrant of Survey –do–	$1	–
9th		do	do	Copy of Protest noted	$	50
21st	2	Invicinible	R. Pollard	Certificate to Invo Cassin	$2	–
		Aurora	do	Certificate to sugar from HongKong	$2	–
		Georges	Brundas & Co.	Certificate to mine do	$2	–
30t		Aurora	R. Pollard	Certificate to Tea do	$2	–
16th	2	Invicinible	E. H. Green	Certificate to sundries	$2	–
□□		do	W. C. Hunter	Certificate to sundries	$2	–
20th		do	David S. Austin	Deposit of papers 1,768 $\frac{65}{95}$	$8	84
		do	do	Shipping 31 men	$5	–
		do	do	Certificate & oath of New Master & Reporting the same	$1	25
		do	do	one extra seal	-	50
		do	do	Certificate of not being able to procure 2/3d Crew of Americans	-	50
		do	Henry W. Johnson	Preparing Bill of Sale–794 woods	$4	47
		do	do	Acknowledgement of do as his free Act & Deed	$2	
		do	do	Endorsement of New Ownership as Ships Register	-	50
22d		do	Rd Pollard	Certificate to Invo Sundries	$2	–
		do	David S. Austin	Acknowledgement to Bond of hypothecation	$1	–
		do	do	2 Seals to Dup & Trip: do	$1	–
		Black Warrior	R. Pollard	2 Certf to Invoice sundries from HongKong	$4	–
30	4	Cornelia L. Bevan	J. Pedersen	Deposit of papers 330 $\frac{68}{95}$ tons	$1	65
		do	do	Noting protest	$1	–
		Willamette		Tonnage fees for 2d Quarter	$2	07
		Spark	John Endicott	Tonnage fees for 2d Quarter	$8	–
					$91	63

Gideon Nye Jnr Vice Consul of the United States of America for Macao

[Corth Nec Consul
Nye 3 Beshelet N°.14]

[Gideon Nye, Jnr, from H. E.
Governor General Guimarães.]

RELATORIO
DA
MISSÃO EXTRAORDINARIA
DE
PORTUGAL A SIAM,
DE QUE FOI ENCARREGADO
COMO MINISTRO PLENIPOTENCIARIO DE S. M. F.
O CONSELHEIRO ISIDORO FRANCISO GUIMARÃES
Governador Geral de Macao, etc. etc.

MACAO:
Typographia de J. DA SILVA, Rua Central No. 7,
1859.

RELATORIO.

No dia 8 de Janeiro de 1859 pelo meio dia Sua Exa. o Conselheiro Isidoro Francisco Guimarães, Ministro Plenipotenciario de S. M. F. na China e Siam, partio de Macao com destino a Bangkok a bordo de brigue *Mondego* do commando do 1o. Tenente da Armada José Severo Tavares, para cumprir a Missão de que S. M. Magnifica El-Rei de Siam, fazer um Tratado de Amizade, Commercio e Navegação entre Portugal e este paiz. Acompanhavam Sua Exa. o Ministro o 2o. Tenete de Armada José Maria da Fonseca, na qualidade de Secretario de Missão, □ o Alferes do Exercito Francisco de Mello Baracho, como Addido.

No fim de seis dias de viagem com monção favoravel–na tarde de 14 de Janeiro – e brigue *Mondego* entrou nas agoas do golpho de Siam, e ao anoitecer do dia 20 fundiou no ancoradouro fóra da barra de Bangkok entre varios navios mercantes de diversas nações, que alli se achavam ancorados.

No dia 21, depois do meio dia, largarm para terra o Secretario e o Addido da Missão em um dos escarleres do

Mondego, e depois das tres horas da tarde chegaram á embocadura do rio Menam ou mais propriamente Chao Pya, por quanto a palavra Menam significa em lingoa siameza mãi das agoas, e é demoninação commum a todos os rios de Siam. Pelas 4 e meia atracou o escaler ao cáes de Paknam, villa que fica obra de duas milhas acima da foz do rio e onde reside um governador, que commanda tambem tres fortalezas de mui boa apparecia, situadas uma em cada margem e outra em um ilhote no meio do rio, que defendem a entrada do porto.

Segundo as instrucções que levava o Secretario, em companhia do Addido, foi visitar o governador de Paknam e communicar-lhe que se achava fóra da barra o brigue portuguez *Mondego*, tendo a seu bordo o Embaixador de S. M. El-Rei de Portugal. O governador recebeu mui cortezmente os dois Officiaes portuguezes e mostrou-se mui satisfeito com a noticia; fez varias perguntas relativamente ás graduações dos officiaes do navio-numero da tripulação e artilheria, offereceu alguns refrescos-e tendo mandado apromptar uma embar-

-2-

cação siameza, que lhe tinha sido pedida, o Secretario e o Addido da Missão, depois de se haverem despedido desta authoridade,- e tendo mandado para bordo o escaler do *Mondego*, largaram para Bangkok n'aquella embarcação quasi no fim da tarde.

A distancia do ancoradouro a Paknamé de 12 milhas : desta povoação á cidade de Bangkok são 22 milhas seguindo o caminho pelo rio; porém algumas milhas acima de Paknam e perto de uma povoação chamada Paklat Lang ou Paklat de baixo ha um canal entre os dois pontos extremos de uma das grandes sinuosidades do rio, que diminue a distancia de 10 milhas: o canal é estreito e tem pouco fundo; é por tanto navegavel só para pequenas embarcações: aquella em que iam o Secretario e o Addido da Missão, seguio por este canal, e ás 11 horas da noite os desembarcou no Consulado portuguez, onde foram recebidos pelo Consul o Sr. Antonio Frederico Moor, em cuja caza acharam o melhor agasalho.

No dia 22 pela manhãa o Secretario da Missão, com o Consul portuguez, Addido, e o Chanceller do Consulado o Sr. Joaquim Maximiano da Silva, que, tendo adquirido muito conhecimento da lingoa siameza durante a sua longa residencia em Siam, prestou muitos serviços como Interprete da Missão, teve uma entrevista official com o Praklang ou Ministro dos Negocios Estrangeiros siamez, para communicar-lhe a chegada do Plenipotenciario de Portugal e tratar a respeito das cerimonias para a recepção de Sua Exa.

Sua Exa. recebeu com muito agrado o Secretario e o Addido da Missão, e com signaes de amisade os Srs. Moor e Silva que de ha mais tempo conhecia. O Secretario expoz ao Praklang o objecto da sua visita: o Ministro siamez respondeu em termos muito amaveis, dando os parabens aos cavalheiros portuguezes presentes pela feliz chegada de Sua Exa. o Embaixador de Portugal, e dizendo que essa noticia seria um motivo de grande prazer para S. M. El-rei de Siam, que de ha muito tempo esperava a Sua Exa.,-que á chegada de Sua Exa. a Paknam se lhe faria a recepção que é do estilo fazer-se aos Embaixado-res estrangeiros á entrada do porto, e deu as informações convenientes acerca do cerimonial a seguir, com que o Secretario concordou. Sua Exa. disse que indicava sómente o que era do estilo fazer-se e se tinha praticado com outros Embaixadores-que ainda não tinha recebido as ordens do seu soberano-porém que estava certo de que S. M. não deixaria de fazer que a recepção do Embaixador de uma nação de ha tanto tempo amiga de Siam fosse o mais explendida possivel. Sua Exa. o Praklang disse tambem que havia uma caza em terra destinada para residencia da Missão, cujos arranjos ainda não estavam termina-

–3–

dos,–para o que pedia a Sua Exa. o Plenipotenciario que demorasse de dois dias o seu desembarque em Bangkok; e que seria muito do agrado de S. M. que Sua Exa. lhe escrevesse participando a sua chegada.

Depois de algum tempo de conversação sobre diversos objectos o Secretario despediu–se de Sua Exa. o Praklang, e voltou com os cavalheiros que o acompanhavam ao Consulado portuguez. O Sr. Consul Moor incumbio–se de arranjar um vapor para rebocar o *Mondego* para Bangkok–o que se effeituou afretando–se o vapor americano *Jack Waters*, que se achava fóra, e que devia estar de volta ás 2 horas da tarde, mas que em consequencia da demora que teve na viagem chegou depois das 6 horas. Perto das 8 da noite o Secretario, Addido, e os Srs. Consul Moor e Chanceller Silva embarcaram no vapor e chegaram a bordo do *Mondego* na madrugada do dia seguinte.

Na manhãa de 23 o *Mondego* suspendeu da rada de Bangkok e a reboque do vapor *Jack Waters* seguio para a barra do Menam. Veio a bordo uma embarcação mandada pelo Governador de Paknam com alguns presentes de frutas e um pratico siamez para pilotar o navio para dentro da barra, cujos serviços foram dispensados por se achar o birgue a cargo de um piloto americano, que antes se tinha engajado. Ás 10 da manhãa fundeou o *Mondego* defronte de Paknam e salvou com 21 tiros e a bandeira siameza no tope de proa: um dos fortes de Paknam respondeu á salva com igual numero de tiros. Veio a bordo o Governador de Paknam, acompanhado de um Ajudante e varios siamezes de sua comitiva: o Governador fez os seus cumprimentos a Sua Exa. e o convidou a desembarcar em Paknam, onde Sua Exa. era esperado por um Alto Funccionario siamez （o irmão do Praklang） nomeado por S. M. para fazer–lhe a recepção do estilo:–o Governador retirou–se, e algum tempo depois Sua Exa. o Plenipotenciario acompanhado do Secretario, Addido da Missão, Consul portuguez, Chanceller do Consulado e do Commandante do *Mondego* com alguns dos seus Officiaes em escarleres do *Mondego*, largou de bordo dirigindo–se para Paknam: á sahida de Sua Exa. o brigue *Mondego* fez as honras devidas ao Plenipotenciario de S. M. F. Ao desembarcar em Paknam salvaram as fortalezas, e Sua Exa. foi recebido pelo Enviado d'El–Rei de Siam e cumprimentado por esta personagem da parte de S. M. O lugar da recepção era um pavilhão aberto, eujo tecto era sustentado por varias columnas de madeira, levantado em uma esplanada proxima de uma das fortalezas. No meio do pavilhão havia um estrado sobre o qual se achavam uma meza com varias frutas e refrescos, e cadeiras para Sua Exa. e pessoas que o acompanhavam, e para os Funccionarios

–4–

siamezes de mais alto grão,–conservando–se as pessoas do seu sequito prostradas por terra, como usam os siamezes, quando estão na presença de superiores. O Enviado siamez trajava um vestido de tela de ouro e seda, apertado na cintura com um cinto de ouro fechado na frente por uma chapa cravejada de pedras preciosas; e entre as pessoas do seu numeroso sequito havia um pagem, que lhe trasia a espada, e outro uma salva de ouro sobre a qual haviam um vaso para agoa com a competente taça, caixa para cigarros, caixa para o *betel* que os siamezes constantemente mascam, etc.,– todos estes objectos eram de ouro cravejados de pedras precíosas,–e além do uso para que são destinados servem tambem como insignias do grão da pessoa a quem pertencem: os desta especie podem sómente ser usados por pessoas de alta jerarchia. Sua Exa. o Plenipotenciario e os Officiaes, que o acompanhavam foram convidados a tomar alguns refrescos, e depois de uma breve demora a meza Sua Exa. retirou–se para bordo, tendo–lhe sido offerecidas pelo Enviado siamez embarcações do Estado para condusil–o a Bangkok, no caso de Sua Exa. não preferir fazer a viagem no brigue. O Enviado siamez acompanhou a Sua Exa.

até a bordo, onde se demorou por algum tempo, e depois de se haver retirado, o *Mondego* suspendeu novamente pelo meio dia, e seguio a reboque do *Jack Waters* para Bangkok, fundeando ás 7 horas da noite defronte da caza destinada para residencia da Missão, que fica um pouco acima do Consulado portuguez, e na mesma margem do rio.

No dia 24 veio a bordo o Praklang visitar a Sua Exa., e participar que se achava prompta a caza, destinada para sua residencia em Bangkok. Sua Exa. recebeu uma carta do primeiro Rei em resposta a outra, que tinha escripto a S. M. no dia antecedente. S. M. expressava a sua satisfação pela chegada do Embaixador de El–Rei de Portugal, e determinava o dia 27 para ter lugar a recepção official de Sua Exa. e a entrega da carta de S. M. F. Á 1 hora da tarde o *Mondego* salvou á bandeira siameza com 21 tiros; a salva foi respondida por um dos fortes da cidade. Depois do pôr do sol Sua Exa. desembarcou para a caza da Missão, onde se achava o Praklang para recebel–o:–a caza achava–se soffrivelmente arranjada, e haviam alli cincoenta e oito siamezes destinados para o serviço da Missão;–neste numero comprehendiam–se as guarnições de duas galeotas do Rei, que ficaram ás ordens de Sua Exa. durante a sua estada em Siam.

No dia 25 Sua Exa. foi visitado por S. A. R. o Principe Krom–Hluang Wongsa, irmão dos Reis de Siam, e por Suas Exas. Chao Pya Pra Kalahom, primeiro Ministro, e Chao Pya Yom–marat, Ministro

–5–

de Justiça, e pelo filho do primeiro Ministro, que é encarregado dos Negocios da Marinha. Sua Exa. foi tambem vistado pelos Consules estrangeiros, por Sua Exa. o bispo Pallegoix e Missionarios francezes, e por varios outros europeos residentes em Bangkok. Veio tambem cumprimentar a Sua Exa. o General de artilheria que tem o titulo de Pya Visset, e o nome de Pascoal Ribeiro de Albergaria: é um dos descendentes de antigos portuguezes, de que ha muitos em Siam: é homem de mais de sessenta annos de idade e de mui agradaveis maneiras; falla portuguez mui intelligivel e escreve soffrivelmente. Estes descendentes de portuguezes são em tudo siamezes, menos na religião, que seguem a christã: em lembrança dos serviços prestados por seus maiores os Reis de Siam os tem sempre tratado com particalar benevolencia.

Neste dia, bem como no antecedente, e em outros, que se seguiram, Sua Exa. foi mimoseado com diversos presentes de frutas e doces do paiz, mandados por SS. MM., pelo Principe, e pelos Ministros. SS. MM. mandaram tambem grande porção de frutas, arroz, peixe, assucar, etc., para uso da guarnição do *Mondego*.

Em 26 Sua Exa. pagou as visitas das authoridades siamezas, e jantou com o Principe Krom Hluang, sendo tambem convidados o Secretario, Addido, Consul portuguez, Chanceller do Consuldado, e o Commandante do *Mondego* com sete dos seus officiaes. A meza estava posta á europea e o jantar foi magnificamente servido.

O dia 27 era o dia destinado por S. M. siameza para a recepção de Sua Exa. e entrega de carta d'El–Rei. Pelo meio dia chegaram as galeotas, destinadas para Sua Exa. e para a carta de S. M., e varias outras, que deviam formar o cortejo. São embarcações mui compridas e razas, pintadas de diversas cores, com muitos ornatos doirados; tem a popa e a proa recurvadaas elevando–se a bastante altura: na proa tem diversas figuras, com o busto de um idolo, a cabeça de uma serpente, etc.; a popa tem a configuração da cauda de um peixe: estas embarcações são guarnecidas por um grande numero de remadores vestidos de vermelho, que remam com pás; dois remadores colocados na popa as governam por meio de remos mui compridos: no meio de cada embarcação ha uma especie de remos mui compridos: no mei de cada embarcação ha uma especie de docel forrado de panno vermelho guarnecido de ouro com cortinas e guarnições da mesma côr; debaixo deste docel ha uma alcatifa onde se sentam as pessoas que nellas embarcam, e almofadas para lhes servirem de encosto. Na galeota, destinada para a carta, o docel era de forma piramidal, recamado de ouro, e debaixo delle havia uma especie de throno todo doirado e de mui delicado lavor.

–6–

Sua Exa. o Plenipotenciario acompanhado do Secretario, Addido, Consul portuguez, Chanceller, e Commandante e Officiaes do *Mondego*, todos de grande uniforme, recebeu na caza da Missão um Alto Funccionario siamez encarregado de condusir a carta de S. M. Sua Exa. tomou das mãos do Secretario uma caixa de prata doirada, dentro da qual se achava a carta, e a entregou ao Mandarim siamez, que depois de a ter saudado segundo o uso de Siam, a poz em um vaso de oiro coberto come um panno de veludo escarlate bordado de oiro, e, acompanhado de Sua Exa. e dos Officiaes portuguezes, se dirigio para a embarcação, que lhe era destinada, onde collocou o vaso de oiro com a carta no throno, que alli havia. Ao embarcar da carta o brigue *Mondego* salvou com 21 tiros, tendo a gente nas vergas. Depois da salva largou a galeota, que levava a acarta, e apoz ella a de Sua Exa., na prôa da qual um marinheiro do brigue levava a bandeira portugueza, precedidas por diversas outras, em algumas das quaes haviam musicas do paiz, e seguidas por aquellas em que iam os Offiaes portuguezes, e por outras onde se achavam Mandarins de diversos gráos. As embarcações, que formavam o cortejo, eram mais de trinta, e de certo excederia a seis centos o numero dos remadores, que as guarneciam. O cortejo seguio em muito boa ordem pelo rio acima, e ás 2 horas da tarde chegou ao lugar do desembarque perto do palacio do Rei, onde havia um grande concurso de povo. Ao desembarcar Sua Exa. o Plenipotenciario foi recebido por um Principe de sangue real, e um parque de artilheira, guarnecido por soldados com uniformes europeos, salvou com 21 tiros. O vaso de oiro, em que ia a carta de S. M., foi posto em um andor levado por oito homens, no qual havia um throno e docel similhantes aos da galeota, que a tinha condusido: este andor cercado por grande numero de Mandarins siamezes, rompia a marcha, seguindo–se Sua Exa. em uma cadeira doirada sobre um palanquim mui adornado, levado aos hombros de oito homens, e os Officiaes portuguezes em palanquins mais singelos; um numeroso sequito de siamezes fechava o cortejo.

Pelo caminho até as muralhas do Palacio haviam alas de tropas siamezas, formadas de differentes corpos, armados cada um de modo diverso,–uns de espadas, outros de lanças, alabardas, arco e frechas, arcabuzes, e outras armas usadas em tempos antigos, e todos vestidos do modo mais extravagante. Á porta, que dá entrada para o recinto do Palacio, havia uma guarda de soldados com uniforme á europea, soffrivelmente arranjados, que appresentaram as armas quando Sua Exa. passava. Seguiam–se mais alas de tropas siamezas, e em cada uma das outras portas, por que passou o cortejo, uma guarda de

–7–

soldados vestidos á europea: de espaço a espaço haviam bandas de musica militar siameza, compostas de tambores, gougos, e outros instrumentos com que fasiam muito estrondo. O cortejo parou em um mui espaçoso largo onde se via um grande numero de edificos diversos, dos quaes uns eram os aposentos reaes, outros salas de recepção, pagodes, quarteis para as guardas d'El–Rei, etc.; haviam tambem differentes telheiros, fechados por grandes dimensões: neste largo se achavam formadas tropas com uniformes europeos, que appresentaram as armas quando Sua Exa. lhe passou pela frente: os soldados pareciam bem exercitados, e as vozes do commando eram dadas em inglez:–o numero das tropas deveria exceder a dois mil homens. Viam–se tambem diversos elefantes armados para guerra, cobertos com xaireis de panno vermelho bordado de oiro, e ornados com outros enfeites; alguns mais estimados tinham nos dentes diversos anneis de oiro.

Sua Exa. foi condusido por um dos grandes Mandarins a uma sala de espera onde havia uma meza, sobre a qual se achava uma salva de oiro com *bétel* e *aréca*, e dois grandes vasos de prata com embutidos de oiro–obra de Siam–cheios de agoa; em roda da meza haviam cadeiras para Sua Exa. e pessoas que o acompanhavam, e um pagem do rei fez servir chá e café.

Perto do lugar destinado para Sua Exa. havia uma outra meza coberta com panno bordado de oiro, sobre a qual foi colocado o vaso, que continha a carta, ficando os Mandarins que a companhavam prostrados diante della: – os siamezes costumam fazer ás cartas dos reis as mesmas honras que á pessoa do soberano.

Depois de algum tempo um Mandarim veio annunciar que S. M. se achava no throno, e desejava receber a Sua Exa. O vaso de oiro em que se achava a carta foi novamente collocado no andor em que tinha vindo, e o cortejo seguio na mesma ordem por entre alas de musicos vestidos de tunicas de panno vermelho, que tocavam tambores, clarins, e uma especie de businas, que produsiam um som roùco e prolongado. O cortejo parou perto de um edificio demoninado *Maha Prasath*, de mui boa apparencia, e onde fica a salla destinada para as grandes recepções, para a qual se sobe por uma escada de marmore. Alli se achavam collocados sobre diversas mezas, e expostos á vista dos circumstantes, os presentes que Sua Exa. tinha levado para S. M., e que tinham sido entregues de manhãa. Depois de novas saudações dos Mandarins siamezes o vaso, que continha a carta d'El–Rei, foi entregue a Sua Exa., que o tomou nas mãos e acompanhado dos Officiaes

–8–

que formavam o seu sequito entrou na salla de audencia. Esta salla é mui espaçosa e alta, e assemelha–se muito a um templo: duas fileiras de columnas de madeira lavrda com capiteis doirados sustentam o tecto, e deixam um caminho ao longo da salla: a um e outro lado deste caminho grande numero de Officiaes e Nobres siamezes, talvez mais do quatro centos, prostrados por terra e seguindo–se uns aos outros pela ordem de suas graduações até ao pé do throno, formavam a côrte d'El–Rei de Siam. S. M. achava–se no throno, que é uma especie de janella aberta na parede do fundo da salla, elevada obra de duas varas acima do pavimento, aos lados da qual ha algumas columnas doiradas, que sustentam um docel lavrado e doirado mui semelhante aos que se veem sobre os pulpitos de algumas das nossas igrejas em Lisboa: debaixo do throno ha um estrado para o qual se sobe por alguns degraos, e de cada lado uma das umbrellas de sette andares que os siamezes chamam *satt* e que são insignias da realesa: aos lados achavam–se varios pagens do rei com a espada de S. M., e outras armas, e defronte do throno os Principes de Sangue Real, e apoz estes os Nobres de primeira classe, entre os quaes tinham o primeiro lugar os Ministros:–estes Principes e Nobres estavam prostrados sobre almofadas de veludo vermelho, e tinham junto a si as suas espadas, algumas mui ricas, e as salvas com as caixas para o *bétel* e *aréca*, etc., que tambem são insignias da sua jerarchia:– todos estes objectos eram de oiro cravejados de pedras preciosas. O vestuario dos cortezãos consistia em uma cabaia de seda de cor, ou de tecido de oiro e seda para os de maior graduação, e no panno com que os siamezes cobrem a parte inferior do corpo, especie de chaile de seda, que arranjam de modo que parece uma calça larga e curta, que apenas lhes chega acima do joelho: alguns destes pannos tem grande preço. Os Principes e Grandes estavam vestidos de um modo similhante com a differença de serem os tecidos mais ricos, e de terem sobre a primeira cabaia uma tunica de renda branca bordada com palheta de oiro, que fazia mui bom effeito: a cabaia de dentro era apertada com um cinto de oiro guarencido de pedrarias, e abotoada com botões de pedras preciosas. Sua Exa. o Plenipotenciario depois de ter feito tres venias a S. M., coloeou o vaso, que continha a carta, sobre uma meza coberta com um panno de veludo verde guarnecido de oiro, que para esse fim se achava defronte do throno, e depois de ter lido um discurso, em que expunha a S. M. objecto da sua Missão, sentou-se em uma almofada de veludo verde, eolocada entre os Nobres de primeira ordem, atraz da qual se achava uma alcatifa para as pessoas do seu sequito.

-9-

S. M. exprimiu a sua satisfação pela chegada do Embaixador d'El-Rei de Portugal, informou-se da sande de S. M. e da Familia Real, e depois varias perguntas a Sua Exa. sobre diversos objectos fez signal para lhe ser entregue a carta d'El-Rei. Sua Exa. tirou a caixa que continha a carta de dentro do vaso de oiro em que tinha sido condusida, e subindo os degráos do throno a entregou a S. M., bem como o seu discurso. S. M. entregou a Sua Exa. um documento em que declarava ter recebido a carta de S. M. F. com todas as honras devidas e na presença da sua Côrte e Nobreza. Sua Exa. voltou a sentar-se no seu lugar, e S. M. leu um longo discurso em siamez, em que fazia a historia das relações do portuguezes com Siam desde o seu principio, exprimia a sua satisfação por vel-as estabelecidas de um modo mais formal e permanente durante o seu reinado:-este discurso foi depois entregue a Sua Exa. por um dos Principes. Depois da leitura S. M. retirou-se, tendo asseverado a Sua Exa. que seria tratado como os Embaixadores das primeiras nações de Europa, e que hia nomear os Plenipotenciarios siamezes para se comerçarem as negociações do Tratado.

Logo que S. M. se retirou fechou-se uma cortina de damasco vermelho, que ha adiante do throno: toda a Côrte saudou o Soberano, pondo a cabeça em terra, e elevando por tres vezes as mãos juntas acima da cabeça:-os Principes e Nobres sentaram-se sobre as suas almofadas, e os outros Mandarins começaram a sahir da sala a seu bel-prazer. Sua Exa. e os Officiaes que formavam o seu sequito foram cumprimentar a S. A. o Principe Krom-Hluang e os Ministros, e foram por estes appressentados a outros Principes e Nobres, que se achavam presentes. O Praklang veio da parte de S. M. convidar a Sua Exa. e os Officiaes portuguezes para um jantar, que lhes estava preparado, e condusio a Sua Exa. para uma salla do jardim onde se achava a meza, posta á européa, e se serviu um magnifico jantar. A alguma distancia da meza havia uma outra mais pequena, sobre a qual se achavam algumas garrafas de christal com vinho e licores, e uma salva com copos destinada para S. M., que appareceu quasi no fim do jantar, acompanhado de oito ou dez de seus filhos, de 4 a 8 annos de idade, do Principe Krom-Hluang e de alguns dos Ministros. S. M. conversou por muito tempo com Sua Exa. sobre diversos assumptos, informou-se dos nomes e posição dos Officiaes presentes, tratando a todos com affabilidade, offereceu vinho e licores pela sua mão, e deu o seu bilhete de visita a cada um dos officiaes. Terminado o jantar Sua Exa. retirou-se, sendo acompanhado até ao lugar do embarque pelo mesmo Principe por quem tinha sido recebido.

-10-

No dia 29 S. A. R. o Principe Krom-Hluang Wongsa, e SS. Exas. Cháo Pya Nayok, commandante em chefe do exercito, Cháo Pya Prakalahom, primeiro Ministro, Cháo Pya Praklang, Ministro da Justiça, e Pya Vorapong, Ministro Privado de S. M., foram nomeados Plenipotenciarios, e no dia 9 de Fevereiro:-neste intervallo Sua Exa. teve uma audiencia privada de S. M., e por essa occasião teve a honra de ser apresentado a S. M. a Rainha de Siam.

No dia 10 de Fevereiro teve lugar a assignatura do Tratado a que se procedeu com todas as formalidades no Palacio do Principe Krom–Hluang, achando–se presentes S. A. e SS. Exas. os Plenipotenciarios, o Secretario, Addido, Consul, Interprete, e o Commandante do *Mondego* com os seus Officiaes, todos em grande uniforme. Logo que se acabou de assignar e sellar a primeira copia, um forte, que fica perto do Palacio do Principe, deu uma salva de 21 tiros, que foi repetida pelo *Mondego*, que desde ás 8 horas da manhãa se achava embandeirado em arco com a bandeira siameza no tópe de prôa. A assignatura do Tratado teve lugar pelas 2 horas da tarde.

S. M. o segundo Rei, que se achava nas provincias á chegada do *Mondego* a Bangkok, escreveu a Sua Exa. no dia 10 annunciando–lhe a sua volta á capital e destinando o dia 12 para a recepção de Sua Exa., que effectivamente teve lugar nesse dia com o mesmo ceremonial que se seguiu na recepção do primeiro Rei, sómente as tropas estavam mais bem arranjadas, e a côrte era menos numerosa. Depois da audiencia o filho mais velho do Rei condusio a Sua Exa. e of Officiaes que o acompanhavam a uma caza de recreio, que ha dentro do recinto do Palacio, e que tem o nome de *Royal pleasure Hall*, onde S. M. os recebeu com toda a affabilidade. A caza achava–se perfeitamente mobiliada á européa, – na salla viam–se os bustos de Rainha Victoria e de Principe Alberto, de Napoleão 1o. e de Lord Wellington, e os retratos da Familia Real de Inglaterra, de Washington e do Presidente Pierce. No gabinete de S. M. achavam–se diversos instrumentos nauticos e de physica, e estantes com as obras dos melhores authores inglezes tanto em litteratura como em sciencias. Na salla do jantar havia uma collação que constava de grande variedade de frutas e doces, preparada para Sua Exa.: –a meza estava posta com tanta simplicidade como bom gosto.

No dia seguinte S. M. o 2o. Rei fez uma visita a Sua Exa. a bordo do *Mondego* onde se demorou mais de tres horas: vio o navio todo,–assistio aos exercicios de artilheria, de armas e de espada, feitos pela

-11-

guarnição, e examinou os chronometros e instrumentos nauticos, mostrando–se de tudo muito entendido; depois do que se despedio de Sua Exa., dizendo que tinha vindo a Bangkok sómente para recebel–o, e que partia de novo para as provincias. Na occasião da despedida S. M. presenteou a Sua Exa. com diversos objectos curiosos de manufactura siameza, pedindo–lhe que os conservasse como lembrança sua. S. M. vinha em um pequeno vapor, que lhe pertence, e que tem na melhor ordem possivel. Este vapor é tripulado por siamezes, e tem officiaes e engenheiros siamezes.

No dia 15 teve lugar no palacio de S. M. o primeiro Rei a audiencia de despedida a Sua Exa. e a entrega da carta d'El–Rei de Siam para S. M. F. A cerimonia não se podia comparar em pompa com a que teve lugar para a recepção da carta d'El–Rei. Sua Exa. foi recebido por S. M. em uma salla do jardim onde se achava o Principe Krom–Hluang, os Ministros e alguns nobres. S. M. fez varios presentes a Sua Exa., taes como se costumam fazer aos siamezes a que se confere alto grão de nobreza, e pôz–lhe pela sua mão no peito uma insignia da ordem do elefante, dizendo que desejava que sua Exa. a usasse como lembrança da sua visita s Siam. A carta de S. M. dentro de uma caixa de madeira de Siam, contida em um sacco de tecido de oiro, foi entregue a um grande Mandarim siamez, que a pôz em um andor igual aquelle que tinha condusido a carta d'El–Rei de Portugal, e que foi acompanhado até ao lugar do embarque por Sua Exa. e Officiaes portuguezes, por varios Mandarins siamezes e por uma banda de musica do paiz: ao embarcar um parque de artilheria salvou com 21 tiros. A embarcação em que ia a carta foi acompanhada por aquellas em que hiam Sua Exa. e os Officiaes portuguezes até a bordo do brigue *Mondego*, onde a carta foi entregue a Sua Exa. pelo Mandarim que a condusia: nessa occasião o brigue *Mondego* deu uma salva de 21 tiros.

Achando-se concluida a Missão, de que tinha sido encarregado, Sua Exa. partiu de Bangkok a bordo do brigue *Mondego* no dia 17 de Fevereiro, passando a barra a 19, com destino a Singapura, onde chegou no dia 8 de Março, sahindo dalli para Hongkong no dia 18 a bordo do vapor inglez *Carthage*, que chegou a Hongkong no dia 28.

No dia 29 pelas 11 da manhãa Sua Exa. embarcou no vapor portuguez *Fernandes*, que partia para Macao, e pelas 4 horas da tarde chegou á cidade do seu governo, onde foi recebido com as honras devidas á sua cathegoria.

DISCURSO
DE
SUA EXA. O PLENIPOTENCIARIO DE S. M. F.
A
S. M. EL-REI DE SIAM.
NA AUDIENCIA DE 27 DE JANEIRO DE 1859.

(COPIA) .

SENHOR!-Sua Magestade Fidellissima o Rei de Portugal meu Augusto Soberano fez-me a honra de encarregar-me junto a Vossa Magestade de duas Missões summamente honrosas e agradaveis para mim; a primeira é de, além de cumprimentar a Vossa Magestade em Seu Regio Nome, de entregar a Vossa Magestade uma Carta escripta de Seu Regio Punho, e a segunda é a de confirmar, consolidar, e estreitar por um Tratado de Commercio e Navegação as relações amigaveis, que ha seculos tem existido entre Portugal e Siam; a primeira parte acha-se a ponto de ser cumprida, porque Vossa Magestade com auqella benignidade, que A destingue para com a Nação Portugueza, se appressou em fixar o dia da minha recepção de um modo extremamente lisongeiro para mim.

Espero, Real Senhor, que a segunda parte de tarefa, que o meu Augusto Soberano me commetteu, se conclua em breve. Vossa Magestade foi O primeiro a reconhecer a necessidade de Portugal fazer um novo Tratado, que habilitasse os seus subditos a negociarem em Siam a par das nações a que Vossa Magestade tem feito tam importante concessões pelos ultimos Tratados, e foi correspondendo a esse desejo de Vossa Magestade, tam benignamente expresso na carta, que Vossa Magestade ordenou ao Seu Ministro dos Negocios Estrangeiros que me escrevesse, que Sua Magestade Fidellissima me encarregou de tam honrosa Missão junto á Real Pessoa de Vossa Magestade, Missão extremamente importante e lisongeira para mim, e de que sempre conservarei gratas recordações. Estou certo, que Vossa Magestade

dará as convenientes ordens para que sejam nomeados os Plenipotenciarios com que hei de ter a honra de tratar, a fim de dar começo as negociações.

As bençãos do Céo desçam sobre Vossa Magestade e sobre a nação, que Vossa Magestade tam benigna e sabiamente governa.

Bangkok 27 de Janeiro de 1859.

(Assignado) ISIDORO FRANCISCO GUIMARÃES.
Está conforme,
(Assignado) JOSÉ MARIA DA FONSECA,
Secretario da Missão.

DISCURSO
DE
SUA MAGESTADE O 1º. REI DE SIAM,
NÃ AUDIENCIA DE 27 DE JANEIRO DE 1859.
(TRADUCÇÃO) .

Pedimos a Sua Exa. o Sr. Embaixador de Portugal e aos Srs. Officiaes portuguezes, que o accompanham, queiram prestar attenção ao Nosso discurso, em que Relatamos as cousas desde a sua origem.

No tempo em que as cidades de *Ayuthia* e *Lavo* eram capitaes do reino de Siam havia no paiz homens de muitas nações da Europa, a saber: Francezes, Hespanhoes, e Portuguezes, que os Siamezes denominavam *farang* (francos) , porque assim lhes chamavam os estrangeiros da India, que os tinham introdusido no reino, e lhes davam esse nome desde muito tempo. Havia tambem, pelo que Temos ouvido dizer, Inglezes, Gregos, e Hollandezes; porém de todos estes europeos os Portuguezes foram os primeiros, que vieram ao reino de Siam. Nas memorias antigas de ha mais de trezentos annos consta, que havia em Siam engenheiros portuguezes, que auxiliaram o Rei daquelle tempo no traçado da estrada de Pra Bath, e no de outras estradas, bem como na abertura de canaes na linha recta, e em outras differentes obras.

Quando teve lugar a revolução, que fez passar o reino de Portugal ao dominio de uma corôa estrangeira, e que este reino se vio embaraçado com guerras exteriores e com outros revezes, os Portuguezes residentes em Siam, faltando-lhes o apoio da Mãi Patria, se tornaram subditos dos Reis de Siam, e se casaram no paiz, tomando por mulheres Siamezas, Cambojanas, Cochinchinas, e Peguanas. Os seus descendentes com a successão dos tempos assimilharam-se em physionomia aos Siamezes, mas apezar de tudo ficaram sempre firmemente ligados á Religião Catholica Romana, e conservaram o uso de se diserem Portuguezes, sob a denominação de francos: muitos conservaram até hoje alguns conhecimentos da lingua portugueza.

-16-

Na epocha das grandes guerras, que trouxeram comsigo a ruina de *Ayuthia*, antiga capital deste reino, todos os europeos residentes em Siam abandonaram o paiz, á excepção dos antigos descendentes portuguezes. Estes existem ainda em grande numero na capital actual, e estão ao serviço do Rei, uns como soldados, outros como interpretes, alguns como medicos ou como capitães de navios. Os Soberanos de Siam lhes tem permittido de se reunirem em povoação e de construirem igrejas do culto Catholico Romano.

No reinado de Sua Magestade Pra Bath Somdetch Prabuth Lobsalai Paloi Nosso Real e muito estimado Pai e segundo Rei da presente dynastia, e alguns annos antes da era siameza de 1882, Sua Exa. o Sr. Governador de Gôa e Sua Exa. o Sr. Governador de Macao enviaram um certo portuguez em deputação a Sua Exa. o Ministro dos Negocios Estrangeiros em Siam, rogando-lhe que auxiliasse este Enviado, no encargo de apresentar ao Rei um pedido, para obter na Capital um lugar, em que os negociantes portuguezes pudessem estabelecer uma feitoria, e comprar maderias para construirem navios. Nessa épocha os Siamezes estavam ainda em guerra com os Birmans, que tinham mandado por mar alguns emissarios ao Soberano da Cochinchina, para o engajarem a unir-se a elle na guerra, que faziam ao Reino de Siam. Alguns Birmans, dos que assim hiam por mar, tinham sido aprisionados pelos crusadores Siamezes, e por navios mercantes de Siam. Por este motivo o Governo Siamez tinha adquirido certa friesa para com os estrangeiros, suspeitando os Enviados Portuguezes, de serem talvez mandados pelos Birmans por estratagema para espiarem o paiz, e verem o que se passava na capital de Siam, por isso que os Siamezes tinham sabido, que no paiz dos Birmans haviam tambem muitos descendentes de Portuguezes como aqui. O Governo Siamez não quiz por tanto acceder ao pedido, que faziam os Enviados Portuguezes, e pelo contrario os persuadiu fortemente a que ashissem do paiz.

Tempos depois Sua Exa. o Sr. Governador de Gôa enviou o Sr. Carlos Manoel para fazer o mesmo pedido ao Governo Siamez. O Sr. Carlos Manoel chegando a Siam fez vêr caramente a um grande numero de membros do Estado que as Cidades de Gôa e Macao não tinham ligação alguma com os Birmans e Cochinchinas, e obedeciam sómente ao Rei de Portugal. Então os antigos descendentes des Portuguezes, que fallavam ainda um pouco a lingua dos seus antepassados, ficaram por fiadores da verdade das palavras do Sr. Carlos Manoel, e lhe serviram de meio para obter uma audiencia de Sua Alteza o Principe Krom–mamum Chetta–boddin Nosso irmão mais

–17–

velho, e depois terceiro Rei da presente dynastia, que então se achava encarregado dos Negocios Estrangeiros. Sua Alteza entendendo perfeitamente dos negocios maritimos, e tendo a certeza de que os negociantes portuguezes não pertencião ao Reino Birman, condusio o Sr. Carlos Manoel á audencia de Sua Magestade Pra Bath Somdetch Prabuth Lobsalai Paloi, e fez conhecer a S. M., que o Sr. Carlos Manoel tinha vinho a Siam da parte de SS. Exas. os Srs. Governadores de Gôa e de Macao com intenções rectas. Então S. M. convencido de que estes Portuguezes eram da mesma nação que os antigos descendentes portuguezes, conhecidos sob a denomiação de francos, que habitavam em Siam desde muito tempo, e que, ainda que seguindo uma religião differente das dos Siamezes, jámais tinham dado lugar a qualquer motivo de descontentamento, entendeu que convinha permittir aos negociantes portuguezes da Europa, da mesma nação que estes *francos* estabelecidos em Siam que fundassem uma feitoria nesta Capital, e depois concluir um Tratado de Alliança com S. M. El–Rei de Portugal. Em consequencia do que S. M. deu ordem a Sua Exa. Chao Pya Surivong Montri, que se achava exercendo o cargo de Praklang, que escrevesse as SS. Exas. os Srs. Governador es de Gôa e de Macao, communicando–lhes que S. M. El–Rei de Siam concedia aos negociantes portuguezes um lugar para estabelecerem uma caza de commercio segundo os seus desejos. Com esta noticia Sua Exa. o Sr. Carlos Manoel Consul Geral, e o mandou a Siam em um navio de guerra portuguez, para tomar conta do terreno promettido. Sua Exa. o Sr. Governador mandou pela mesma occasião a El–Rei de Siam presentes de grande valor, entre os quaes se achava o retrato de S. M. El–Rei de Portugal, e tambem um estojo de costura, outro de toilette, e uma carteira para S. M. Kromma Somdetch Si Suriyenthramath Rainha de Siam, Nossa Real Mãi. Havia tambem muitos e diversos objectos destinados uns a Sua Alteza o Principe Krom–mamum Chetta–boddin, filho mais velho do Rei, que se achava encarregado dos negocios estrangeiros, e outros para Nós mesmo, que eramos então o mais velho dos filhos do Rei, que ainda residiam no Palacio. Sua Exa. o Governador de Gôa dirigia tambem uma longa carta a Sua Exa. o Cháo Praklang, tratando de alliança com Siam, outra carta mais ourta sobre a mesma materia a Sua Alteza o Principe Krom–mamum Chetta–boddin, e uma terceira carta a Nós mesmo, a qual, por isso que eramos ainda mui joven, não tendo ainda completado 16 annos, Nos fazia sómente saber em poucas palavras que a Nação Portugueza era amiga da de Siam. O Sr. Carlos

–18–

Manoel e o Sr. Almirante, que commandava o navio portuguez de guerra, chegaram a Bangkok com as tres cartas e as quatro especies de prezentes mencionados acima no anno Pi–ma–rongthosak （anno da grande serpente） da era Siameza 1182. S. M. Pra Bath Somdetch Prabuth Lobsalai Paloi e S. A. o Principe Krom–mamun Chetta–boddin tiveram grande satisfação com a sua chegada, e os receberam com todas as honras convenientes: Nós mesmo recebemos o Sr. Carlos Manoel e o Sr. Almirante no Pavilhão Real á borda do rio em frente do Palacio com todas as honras, que estava ao Nosso alcance fazer–lhes nessa epoca, e conservamos ainda como lembrança de amizade a carta e os prezentes, que Sua Exa. o Sr. Governador de Gôa Nos mandou então. S. M. deu immediatamente ordem a S. A. o Principe, que tinha a gerencia dos negocios estrangeiros, e a Sua Exa. o Praklang para que preparassem o lugar em que actualmente reside o Sr. Consul Portuguez, e o entregassem ao Sr. Carlos Manoel com as duas docas para a construcção de navios, para alli levantar a feitoria para uzo dos negociantes portuguezes.

Então o Sr. Carlos Manoel, segundo as instrucções de Sua Exa. o Sr. Governador de Gôa se dirigio a Sua Exa. o Praklang para rogar–lhe que pedisse ao Rei de Siam que fizesse um Tratado de Amizade e de Commercio com Portugal. Sua Exa. o Praklang apresentou a S. M. os artigos do Tratado, taes quaes os propunha o Sr. Carlos Manoel. Sua Magestade tendo–os submettido ao exame dos membros da Familia Real e dos Ministros do Estado, foram approvados quasi todos, á excepção de dois ou tres de que ignoramos o theor, por sermos nessa epocha ainda mui pouco avançados na idade, por quanto isto se passou ha 39 annos, e a nossa memoria não conservou lembrança. Unicamente soubemos com o andar dos tempos que o Sr. Carlos Manoel tinha informado o Sr. Governador de Gôa de que o Governo Siamez não admittia dois ou tres artigos, a fim de que isso fosse participado a S. M. El–Rei de Portugal. Soubemos depois que tinha havido uma revolução em Portugal, que o paiz tinha mudado de Soberano e não estava em socego, de modo que não se fallou mais em Tratado.

No anno Pi–vok–xo–sok （anno da rapoza） 1186 da era Siameza, S. M. Pra Bath Somdetch Prabuth Losalai deixou este mundo, e todos os membros da Familia Real e os grandes Mandarins de commum accordo convidaram o Principe Krom–mamum Chetta–boddin, filho mais velho do defunto Rei para subir ao throno com o titulo de Pra Bath Somdetch Pra Nag Clao. O Sr. Carlos Manoel continuou a exercer o cargo de Consul, que servio por espaço de 11 a 12 annos a contar da sua chegada a Siam. Esteve sempre em boas relações

–19–

comnosco, e fez–nos frequentes visitas durante o tempo, que passou no paiz.

Tempos depois o Sr. Carlos Manoel, tendo feito as suas despedidas ao Rei de Siam, e tendo tambem vindo dizer–Nos adeus, deixou o paiz. Então Sua Exa. o Sr. Governador de Macao mandou o Sr. Marcelino da Roza para tomar conta do Consulado Portuguez em Siam, dando–lhe por adjuncto Sr. Joaquim Maximiano da Silva: estes dois Senhores sempre estiveram em boas relações de amisade comnosco.

No anno Pikum–trisôk （anno do porco） 1213 da era siamza, S. M. Pra Bath Somdetch Pra Nang Cláo Nosso irmão mais velho tendo deixado este mundo, todos os Principes e grandes Mandarins Nos convidaram a subir ao Throno, e a tomar conta do governo do Estado. No dia da Nossa coroação o Sr. Consul Marcelino da Roza e o Sr. Ajudante do Consulado Joaquim Maximiano da Silva assistiram á cerimonia, e Nos dirigiram uma carta de felicitações com muitos votos de prosperidade. Recebemos tambem uma carta de felicitação da parte de Sua Exa. o Sr. Governador de Macao. Depois disto o Sr. Maroelino da Roza foi atacado por uma longa doença, de que morreu: durante todo o tempo da sua doença mandámos por varias vezes saber como passava, e contribuimos da nossa parte para o seu enterro. Tendo morrido o Sr. Marcelino da Roza, Sua. Exa. o Sr. Governador de Macao nomeou o Sr. Antonio Frederico Moor Consul em lugar do fallecido, e o mandou para Siam: este novo Consul tinha muitos annos antes estado em Siam, e tido relações comnosco.

No quarto anno do nosso reinado muitas nações da Europa, a saber: os Inglezes, os Francezes, as Republicas ansiaticas de Allemanha, e os Estados Unidos da America eviaram Embaixadores a Siam para fazerem Tratados de Amizade e de Commercio, e desde o anno Pi–thok–saptasok （anno da lebre） 1217 da era siameza até ao presente anno tem sido feitos Tratados de Amizade com estas differentes nações: por isso o commercio de Siam com as nações estrangeiras tem tomado um desenvolvimento, que antes não tinha. Então pensámos muito nos acontecimentos anteriores, que acima referimos, porque SS. MM. Pra Bath Somdetch Prabuth Lobsalai Paloi e Somdetch Pra Suriyenthramat Nossos estimados e respeitados Reaes Progenitores e S. M. Pra Bath Somdetch Pra Nang Cláo Nosso estimado irmão mais velho, que tinham recebido presentes de Real amizade da parte de S. M. El–Rei de Portugal, tinham deixado este mundo, e que de todos aquelles, que receberam presentes nessa epocha, sómente existimos Nós, que somos actualmente o Primeiro Rei de Siam.

–20–

Mesmo Sua Exa. Cháo Pya Surivong Montri, que então fazia as vezes de Praklang, e que recebeu a carta de Sua Exa. o Sr. Governador de Goa tambem tinha morrido. O filho mais velho de Sua Exa. tem agora o titulo de Cháo Pya Si Surivong Sá Mangtá Pongsá Pisuth Maha–burut Ratanodom, e occupa o cargo de Samahá Pra Kalahom; o segundo filho tem o titulo de Cháo Pya Ravivong Maha Kosathibodi o exerce o lugar de Praklang, Ministro dos Negocios Estrangeiros; o terceiro filho tem o titulo de Cháo Pya Montri Surivong, e exerce o cargo que seu pai tinha naquelle tempo: este ultimo é que foi mandado como Embaixador extraordinario a Londres no anno passado. Pensando pois no testimunho de amizade, que tinhamos recebido então da parte de S. M. o Rei de Portugal, e vendo que entre este ultimo Reino e o de Siam não existia ainda um Tratado solido, que tivesse sido escripto e trocado entre as duas nações, como se acabara de fazer com a Inglaterra, a França, e outras nações, e tendo sabido pelas gazetas, que Portugal tinha ha alguns annos um novo Soberano, pareceu–nos ser o momento favoravel para Portugal enviar um Plenipotenciario, munido de plenos poderes para concluir um Tratado de Amizade em regra com Siam, que o illustrasse aos olhos das outras nações; coiza tanto mais conveniente á Nação Portugueza que de todas as Potencias da Europa tinha sido a primeira a ter relações com Siam. Por tanto ordenámos a Sua Exa. o Cháo Pya Praklang que fizesse com que o Sr. Consul Antonio Frederico Moor escrevesse nesse sentido ao Governo portuguez. Mais tarde sabendo que S. M. El–Rei de Portugal tinha nomeado a V. Exa. Seu Ministro Plenipotenciario munido de plenos poderes para vir fazer um Tratado de Alliança com Siam, tivemos um grande prazer. Esperámos por muito tempo a chegada de V. Exa., depois não ouvimos fallar mais em tal. Em fim V. Exa. chegou e Nos apresentou a Carta Regia d'El–Rei de Portugal. Nós a recebemos com a expressão de maior alegria, porque desta vez as relações de amizade entre as duas nações vão renovar–se de um modo digno da antiga amizade, que reina entre ambas desde o principio, como acima dissemos. Rogamos a V. Exa. que fique tranquillo a respeito da conclusão do

Tratado que vai fazer–se. Vamos nomear Ministres Plenipotenciarios munidos de plenos poderes para trabalharem de concerto com V. Exa., a fim de que o Tratado se termine em pouco tempo. Todas as vantagens concedidas aos negociantes das nações estrangeiras, que tem vindo fazer Tratados com o nosso Governo, igualmente as concederemos aos negociantes portuguezes. Este Tratado uma vez concluido será um titulo de gloria á memoria de SS. MM. Pra Bath Somdetch Prabuth

–21–

Lobsalai Paloi, e Somdetch Pra Si Suriyenthramat Nossos mui respeitados e estimados Reaes Progenitores, e á de S. M. Prabath Somdetch Pra Nang Cláo Nosso estimado irmão mais velho, que todos tres em primeiro lugar receberam os testimunhos de amizade da Nação portugueza. Para Nós tambem este Tratado será um titulo de gloria ainda maior do que o tem sido outros Tratados concluidos com outras nações, porque tambem tivemos igual parte no testimunho de amizade de S. M. o Rei, que então reinava em Portugal. V. Exa. terá tambem uma parte de gloria na conclusão deste Tratado por ter tido a vantagem, vindo a Siam como Ministro Plenipotenciario de S. M. El–Rei de Portugal, de Nos achar á testa do Reino de Siam, a Nós que fomos um dos primeiros, que tiveram parte no começo das boas relações de amizade com a Nação portugueza, e della temos conservado pleno conhecimento.

Rogamos a V. Exa. queira mandar traduzir exactamente as Nossas palavras em lingua portugueza, e as leve ao conhecimento de S. M. El–Rei de Portugal. Temos confiança em que este Tratado de Amizade e Alliança entre o Reino de Portugal e o de Siam durará eternamente.

Nós vos desejamos, Senhor Ministro e mais Senhores, toda a sorte de alegria e de venturas.

Tenho a honra de ser um distincto amigo e pela raça real um affeiçoado irmão de vosso Soberano.

(Assignado) S. P. P. M. MONGKUTUS,
Major rex Siamensium.
Reinando sobre Siam e suas dependencias ha 3815 dias.

L. S.

Está conforme,

(Assignado) JOSÉ MARIA DA FONESECA,
Secretario da Missão.

TRATADO DE AMISADE, COMMERCIO E NAVEGAÇÃO ENTRE OS REINOS DE PORTUGAL E SIAM.

Havendo Suas Magestades Magnificas o Primeiro o Segundo Reis de Siam manifestado o desejo de fazerem com Portugal um Tratado de Commercio e Navegação, que, confirmando e consolidando as antigas relações de amizade, que ha seculos existem entre os dois paizes, ao mesmo tempo habilitasse os Portuguezes a commerciarem em Siam, e os Siamezes em Portugal com vantagens iguaes áquellas, que Suas Magestades Magnificas haviam concedido a algumas Potencias Occidentaes, pelos Tratados ultimamente celebrados, e appreciando devidamente Sua Magestade Fidellissima El-Rei de Portugal tam benevolo e amigavel convite, e desejando corresponder-lhe completamente, por se achar animado dos mesmos sentimentos para com Suas Magestades Magnificas o Primeiro e Segundo Reis de Siam e seus subditos, resolveram Sua Magestade Fidellissima El-Rei Dom Pedro 5°. de Portugal, e Suas Magestades Magnificas Pra Bath Somdetch Pra Paramende Maha Mong-kut Pra Chom Clao① Chao② Yu Hua, Primeiro Rei de Siam, e Pra Bath Somdetch Pra Paramende Ramers Mahisvaresr Pra Pin Cláo Cháo Yu Hua, Segundo Rei de Siam, que se celebrasse entre Portugal e Siam um Tratado de Amisade, Commercio e Navegação, que estabeleça sobre bases solidas as relações de paz, amizade e alliança, que tem sempre existido entre as duas Nações portugueza e siameza, e assegure aos subitos dos respectivos estados as maiores vantagens commerciaes; e para esse fim nomearam como Seus Plenipotenciarios:

Sua Magestade Fidellissima El-Rei de Portugal a Isidoro Francisco Guimarães, do Conselho de Sua Magestade e Seu Plenipoten-

-24-

ciario na China, Commendador das Ordens Portuguezas de S. Bento de Aviz e da de Nossa Senhora da Conceição de Villa Viçoza, e da de Carlos III de Espanha, Cavalleiro da Ordem de Christo e da Antiga e Muito Nobre Ordem da Torre e Espada do Valor Lealdade e Merito, e Capitão de Mar e Guerra da Armada.

E Suas Magestades Magnificas o Primeiro e Segundo Reis de Siam a

Sua Alteza Real o Principe Krom Hluang Wongsa Thirat Sanith;

Sua Excellencia Cháo Pya Sri Surivong Sa Maha Prakalahom, Ministro do Reino;

Sua Excellencia Cháo Pya Ravivong Praklang, Ministro dos Negocios Estrangeiros;

Sua Excellencia Cháo Pya Yom-marat, Ministro da Justiça;

Sua Excellencia Pya Vorapong, Ministro Privado de S. M. o Primeiro Rei.

Os quaes depois de haverem communicado uns aos outros os seus respectivos plenos-poderes e tendo-os achado em boa e devida forma concordaram nos artigos seguintes:

Artigo 1o.

É confirmada e consolidada pelo presente Tratado a antiga amisade e alliança entre Sua Magestade Fidellissima El-Rei de Portugal e seus Successores, e Suas Magestades Magnificas o Primeiro e Segundo Reis de Siam e seus Successores. Os subditos de cada um dos dois paizes gosarão no outro de inteira e plena protecção para as suas pessoas e bens segundo as leis estabelecidas, e terão reciprocamente direito a todas as vantagens, que são, ou forem concedidas aos subditos de nações estrangeiras mais favorecidas.

Artigo 2o.

Continuará Portugal a ter em Siam um Consul ou Agente Consular, reconhecendo reciprocamente as Altas Partes contractantes o direito de nomearem Consules ou Agentes Consulares para residirem nos Portos dos Estados uma da outra, onde julgarem conveniente estabelecel-os.

① Sic.

② Sic.

Artigo 3o.

Estes Consules ou Agentes Consulares terão a seu cargo; –proteger os interesses e o commercio dos seus compatriotas:–fazer que

–25–

estes se conformem ás disposições do presente Tratado: servir de intermedio entre elles e as Authoridades de pais: velar pela strícta execução dos regulamentos estipulados, e fazer aquelles, que julgarem necessarios para a execução de presente Tratado.

Artigo 4o.

Os Consules não entrarão em exercicio sem o *exequatur* do Soberano territorial, e gosarão, bem como os Agentess Consulares e os Chancelleres do Consulado, de todos os privilegios e isenções, que forem concedidos na sua residencia aos Agentes de igual cathegoria da nação mais favorecida.

Artigo 5o.

Os Consules e Agentes Consulares das Altas Partes contractantes poderão içar as suas bandeiras respectivas nos lugares da sua habitação.

Artigo 6o.

Quaesquer questões, que tenham lugar entre subditos portuguezes e siamezes deverão ser appresentados ao Consul portuguez, que, de accordo e intelligencia com as Authoridades siamezas, deligenciará terminal–as amigavelmente, e no caso de o não poder conseguir deverão as questões civeis ser decididas pelo Consul ou pela Authoridade siameza, segundo a nacionalidade do deliquente ou accusado, e conforme as respectivas leis.

O Consul nunca interferirá em questões, que digam respeito sómente a subditos siamezes, nem as Authoridades siamezas em questões unicamente relativas a subditos portuguezes, salvo em casos crimes, em que os culpados deverão ser presos pela authoridade local, e entregues ao Consul para Macao para alli serem processados. Em quaesquer questões em que forem interessados subditos portuguezes ou siamezes, tanto o Consul portuguez como as Authoridades siamezas terão direito de assistir ás indagações, que se fizerem para esclarecimento do cazo, devendo–lhes ser dadas, todas as vezes que as peçam, copias dos depoimentos e mais peças do processo até a conclusão da questão.

Artigo 7o.

Os subditos de Siam não poderão apossar–se, causar damno, ou de qualquer modo entremetter–se com as pessoas de subditos portuguezes, nem com suas cazas, predios, terras, navios, ou outra qualquer especie

–26–

de bens. No caso de infracção deste artigo as Authoridades siamezas tomarão conhecimento do caso e castigarão os culpados. Da mesmo sorte os subditos portuguezes não poderão apossar–se, prejudicar ou entremetter–se com as pessoas dos subditos siamezes, nem com suas cazas, predios, terras, navios, ou outra qualquer especie de bens de que estes sejam possuidores, ficando a cargo do Consul portuguez informar–se de qualquer infracção a este respeito e castigar os culpados.

Artigo 8o.

Os subditos portuguezes gosarão em todo o Reino de Siam e suas dependencias de inteira liberdade de consciencia conforme os principios da absoluta tolerancia, podendo, como desde remotos tempos lhes foi concedido, cumprir com os seus deveres catholicos, e assistir aos cultos christãos, tanto em suas cazas, como nas Igrejas publicas, que poderão livremente construir nos lugares, que as Authoridades siamezas de accordo com o Consul para esse fim destinarem; as quaes Igrejas serão administradas por padres portuguezes, que gosarão de todos os privilegios concedidos aos padres de outras nações europeas, que tem feito Tratados com Siam. Igualmente os subditos siamezes nunca serão molestados nos dominios portuguezes por causa da sua religião, e se observará com elles o mesmo, que se pratica com os de outras nações de differente communhão religiosa.

Artigo 9o.

Todos os subditos portuguezes, que quizerem residir no Reino de Siam, deverão matricular-se no Consulado Geral de Portugal em Bangkok. As copias destas matriculas deverão ser enviadas ás Authoridades siamezas.

Artigo 10o.

Quando qualquer subdito portuguez tiver de recorrer á Authorida de siameza a sua petição ou reclamação será appresentada ao Consul portuguez, que, achando-a justa e convenientemente redigida, lhe dara seguimento, ou no caso contrario lhe fará modificar a redacção, ou recusará transmittil-a. Similhantemente os siamezes, que tiverem de recorrer ao Consulado portuguez, deverão seguir um methodo anaglogo por via das suas Authoridades, que procederão do mesmo modo relativamente á justiça e redacção das suas petições ou reclamações.

Artigo 11o.

É permittido aos subditos portuguezes residirem no Reino de Siam, e commerciarem livremente e com toda a segurança em todos os

-27-

portos do dito Reino, comprando e vendendo a quem bem lhes pareça. sem que essa liberdade seja embaraçada por algum monopolio, ou privilegio exclusivo de compra ou venda: porém só poderão residir permanentemente em Bangkok, e em roda desta cidade dentro em um circuito de raio igual á distancia andada em vinte e quatro horas por um barco do paiz. Os limites deste raio são:

1o.-*Ao Norte.*

O canal Bangputsa desde a sua embocadura no rio Cháo Pya até ás muralhas velhas da cidade de Lobpuri, e uma linha recta tirada de Lobpuri até ao cáes de Ta-pra-ngam, perto da cidade de Saraburi no rio Pasak.

2o.-*A Leste.*

Uma linha recta tirada do cáes de Ta-pra-ngam á juneção do canal Klong-kut com o rio Bang-pa-kong: o rio Bang-pa-kong desde a juncção com o canal Klong-kut até á sua embocadura; e a costa desde a embocadura do rio Bang-pa-kong até á ilha de Srimaharajah a tanta distancia para o interior quanta possa ser vencida em vinte e quatro horas de viagem de Bangkok.

3o.–*Ao Sul.*

A ilha de Srimaharajah e as ilhas de Si–chang da parte de leste do golfo, e as muralhas da cidade de Petchaburi da parte de oeste.

4o.–*A Oeste.*

A costa de oeste do golfo até á embocadura do rio Meklong, a tanta distancia para o interior, quanta possa ser vencida em vinte e quatro horas de viagem de Bangkok. O rio Meklong desde a sua embocadura até ás muralhas da cidade de Rajpuri: uma linha recta desde as muralhas de Rajpuri até á villa de Subharnapuri, e uma linha recta desde a villa de Subharnapuri até á embocadura do canal Bangputsa no rio Cháo Pya.

Artigo 12o.

Dentro dos limites marcados no artigo antecedente os subditos portuguezes poderão a todo o tempo comprar, wender, ou construir cazas, e fazer depositos ou armazens de provisões; comprar, vender e aforar terrenos ou plantações. Porém se algum subdito portuguez quizer comprar terrenos situados a menos de seis kilometros （200 sen） das muralhas de Bangkok será necessario que obtenha para esse fim authorisação especial do Governo siamez, salvo o caso de ter já residido por espaço de dez annos no Reino de Siam. Os limites do circuito de seis kilometros são:

1o.–*Ao Norte.*

Um sen ao norte de Wat Kemabhirataram.

–28–

2o.–*A Leste.*

Seis *sen* e sete braças ao sudoeste de Wat Bang–kapi.

3o.–*Ao Sul.*

Perto de dezenove *sen* ao sul da aldeia de Bang–kapeo.

4o.–*A Oeste.*

Perto de dois *sen* ao sudoeste da aldeia Bangphrom.

As marcas do lugar em que a linha do circuito corta o rio abaixo de Bangkok estão, na margem esquerda do rio trez *sen* abaixo da aldeia de Bang–ma–náo, e na margem direita perto de um *sen* abaixo da aldeia de Banglanpuluen.

Artigo 13o.

Quando algum subdito portuguez quizer adquirir bens de raiz de verá dirigir–se por intermedio do Consul á Authoridade local competente, que, de accordo com o Consul, o auxiliará no ajuste do preço da venda, e lhe entregará o seu titulo de propriedade, depois de feita a demarcação dos limites da mesma. O comprador deverá conformar–se ás leis e regulamentos do paiz, e a dita propriedade ficará sugeita aos mesmos direitos e impostos a que estão sugeitas as propriedades pertencentes a subditos do paiz. Se no prazo de trez annos a contar da data da posse o terreno não fôr cultivado o Governo siamez tem o direito de annular a venda, embolsando o comprador da quantia, que pagou pelo terreno.

Artigo 14o.

Os bens de subditos portuguezes fallecidos no Reino de Siam, e de subditos siamezes fallecidos em possessões portuguezas serão entregues a seus herdeiros ou executore testamentarios, e na falta destes ao Consul ou Agente consular da nação, a que pertencia o fallecido.

Artigo 15o.

Os subditos portuguezes poderão construir navios por sua conta nos portos de Siam, obtendo para esse fim licença do Governo siamez.

Artigo 16o.

Os subditos portuguezes residentes em Siam poderão empregar no seu serviço como interpretes, operarios, remadores, ou em outro qualquer mister, subditos siamezes que tenham a liberdade de se engarjarem como taes. As Aurthoridades locaes terão cuidado em que sejam cumpridos os ajustes feitos para esse fim. Os Siamezes empregados em serviço de subditos portuguezes gosarão da mesma protecção que

–29–

os proprios subditos portuguezes; porém se forem convencidos de algum crime; que mereça castigo pelas leis do paiz, sendo provado o crime deverão ser entregues pelo Consul as Authoridades do paiz.

Artigo 17o.

Se alguns subditos siamezes empregados no serviço de subditos portuguezes se tornarem culpados de infracção das leis do seu paiz, ou siamezes criminosos desejando fugir, se acoitarem em caza de algum subdito portuguez, taes individuos serão mandados procurar pelo Consul portuguez ao lugar do seu asilo, e provada a culpa ou fuga, entregues ás Authoridades siamezas. Do mesmo modo quaes quer culpados portuguezes, residentes ou commerciantes em Siam, ou quaesquer desertores de navios portuguezes mercantes ou de guerra, deverão ser procurados, apprehendidos, e entregues ao Consul pelas Authoridades siamezas, logo que lhes sejam requisitados. Na ausencia do Consul os desertores deverão ser entregues a requisição dos Commandantes ou Capitães dos navios.

Artigo 18o.

Nenhum subdito portuguez poderá ser detido no Reino de Siam, sem que as Authoridades siamezas provem ao Consul portuguez que existem causas legitimas para obstar á sua partida. Os subditos portuguezes, que quizerem passar além dos limites estabelecidos para sua residencia pelo presente Tratado, deverão munir–se de um passaporte, que lhes será entregue pela Authoridade siameza a requisição do Consul. Qualquer subdito portuguez casado em Siam com mulher do paiz, que deseje retirar–se com a sua familia, não soffrerá embaraço algum da parte das Authoridades siamezas.

Artigo 19o.

As Authoridades siamezas não terão acção alguma sobre os navios mercantes portuguezes, que estarão unicamente sugeitos á authoridade do Consul e do Capitão. Na falta de navios de guerra portuguezes, e a pedido do Consul, as Authoridades siamezas lhe prestarão todo o auxilio, de que precise para fazer respeitar a sua authoridade pelos seus compatriotas, e para manter a boa ordem e disciplina dos navios mercantes da sua nação.

Artigo 20o.

Se algum subdito siamez se recusar, ou tentar eximir-se de pargar alguma divida a um subdito portuguez, as Authoridades siamezas

-30-

derão a este todo o auxilio de que necessite para ser embolsado da dita divida. Reciprocamente o Consul portuguez dará todo o auxilio a qualquer subdito siamez, que tenha a cobrar dividas de subditos portuguezes, para que obtenha o pagamento das mesmas.

Artigo 21o.

No caso em que algum subdito portuguez estabelecido em Siam venha a fallir o Consul portuguez tomará conta de todos os bens do fallido, que serão devididos pelos credores, ficando o devedor desobrigado de cobrir o *deficit* com os bens, que possa de futuro adquirir. O Consul portuguez terá cuidado em que todos os bens do fallido no momento da quebra, tanto em Siam como fora, sejam postos sem reserva á sua disposição, para se fazer a divisão pelos credores, como fica dito. E do mesmo modo as Authoridades siamezas adjudicarão e administrarão os bens de qualquer subdito siamez, que fallir em transcções commerciaes com subditos portuguezes.

Artigo 22o.

Os navios de querra portuguezes poderão entrar no rio e fundear em Paknam; porém deverão da parte á Authoridade siameza antes de subirem até Bangkok, e entender-se com ella relativamente o lugar em que devem fundear.

Artigo 22o.[①]

A qualquer navio portuguez de querra ou mercante que éntre arribado em algum dos portos do Reino de Siam com avarias ou por falta de mantimento ou agoada as Authoridades siamezas prestarão todo o auxilio necessario para que se ahce em circumstancias de proseguir a sua viagem. Em caso de naufragio as Authoridades locaes darão todo o agasalho aos naufragados, subministrando-lhes o que lhe fôr necessario, e empregarão todos os meios ao seu alcance para que se salve o mais que for possivel tanto do navio como da carga, vigiando cuidadosamente que se não extravie coisa alguma dos salvados, que farão guardar em deposito para serem entregues ao Consul a quem communicarão o succedido com toda a brevidade. Os proprietarios dos ditos navios pagarão todos as desprezas, cuja conta deverá ser appresentada ao Consul para ser por elle examinada.

Artigo 24o.

Os navios mercantes e suas cargas não ficarão sugeitos nos portos do Reino de Siam a direitos alguns de tonelagem, pilotagem, ancora-

① Sic.

-31-

gem ou outros quaesquer, tanto na entrada como na sahida, mas sómentes aos direitos de importação e exportação, mencionados nos artigos seguintes, gozando os ditos navios de todos os privilegios e franquezas, que são ou forem concedidos aos juncos e navios siamezes, ou aos de qualquer nação estrangeira mais favorecida.

Artigo 25o.

Os direitos de importação de fazendas estrangeiras feita nos portos do Reino de Siam por navios portuguezes nunca excederão de trez por cento do seu valor, que serão pagos em dinheiro ou em fazenda á escolha do importador. No caso de haver desacordo entre o importador e os empregados siamezes acerca do valor, que se deve dar ás fazendas, será a questão submettida á decisão do Consul e do official siamez competente, os quaes poderão nomear cada um dois negociantes como arbitros, se assim o julgarem conveniente. Depois de pago o referido direito de trez por cento as fazendas importadas poderão ser vendidas em qualquer parte do Reino de siam por grosso ou a retalho, sem que tenham de pagar mais direito algum. As fazendas, que não forem desembarcadas, não pagarão direitos, e o importador será reembolsado dos que tiver pago pelas fazendas, que tiver de reexportar.

Artigo 26o.

Os direitos, que tem de pagar as fazendas de origem siameza, tanto antes da sua exportação em navios portuguezes, como no momento da exportação, serão regulados pela Tarifa annexa ao presente Tratado, assignada e sellada pelos Plenipotenciarios respectivos. Os productos, que tiverem pago os direitos marcados na referida Tarifa, ficarão por esse facto livres de quasequer direitos de transito ou de outros, que devessem pagar no interior do Reino. Do mesmo modo qualquer producto siamez, que tiver pago qualquer taxa interior ou de transito, não terá que pagar mais direitos, antes, ou no momente do seu embarque a bordo de qualquer navio portuguez.

Artigo 27o.

Os direitos mencionados nos Artigos 25o. e 26o., não poderão ser augmentados para o futuro.

Artigo 28o.

Com a obrigação de pagarem os referidos direitos é concedida aos subditos portuguezes a liberdade de importarem no Reino de Siam, tanto de portos nacionaes como estrangeiros, e de exportarem para

-32-

qualquer destino toda a qualidade de mercadorias, que na epocha da assignatura do presente Tratado não forem objecto de prohibição expressa ou de monopolio especial.

Artigo 29o.

No caso em que por effeito de escacez no paiz o Coverno siamez houver de prohibir a exportação de sal, arroz ou peixe, essa prohibição deverá ser annunciada um mez antes da data em que deva ter effeito, e não poderá tel-o retro-activo. Os negociantes portuguezes deverão participar ás Authoridades siamezas as compras, que tiverem feito antes da prohibição.

Artigo 30o.

O numerario, as provisões, e os objectos de uso pessoal não terão de pagar direito algum, tanto na entrada como na sahida.

Artigo 31o.

Se no futuro o Governo siamez fizer alguma reducção nos direitos estabelecidos para as fazendas importadas ou exportadas a bordo de navios siamezes, fica entendido que essa reducção será igualmente applicada aos direitos, que houverem de pagar os productos da mesma especie importados ou exportados em navios portuguezes. Reciprocamente será applicada aos navios mercantes siamezes qualquer reducção de direitos, que o Governo portuguez faça para o futuro em favor dos navios mercantes nacionaes.

Artigo 32o.

Os navios de guerra portuguezes prestarão todo o auxilio conforme ás leis internacionaes a qualquer navio siamez, que encontrem carecendo de soccorros no alto mar; e tanto os navios mercantes como os subditos siamezes terão direito, nos portos onde houverem Consules portuguezes, á protecção dos ditos Consules, compativel com as leis do paiz, em que se acharem estabelecidos.

Artigo 33o.

Se algum navio portuguez fôr roubado por piratas nas costas ou nas visinhanças do Reino de Siam, as Authoridades siamezas, logo que tenham noticia desse roubo, empregarão todos os meios ao seu alcance para a captura dos piratas, e para que se recobrem os objectos roubados, que deverão ser entregues ao Consul, ou restituidos a seus donos. Em quaesquer casos de pilhagem ou roubo, commettidos na propriedade de subditos portuguezes em terra por subditos siamezes,

–33–

as Authoridades locaes procederão do mesmo modo que para os casos de pirataria. O Governo siamez não ficará responsavel por quaesquer objectos roubados a subditos portuguezes, provando que empregou todos os meios ao seu alcance para recobral–os. As mesmas disposições são applicaveis aos subditos siamezes e seus bens, que estiverem sob o regimen do Governo portuguez.

Artigo 34o.

Os subditos portuguezes terão a liberdade de procurar e abrir minas em qualquer parte do Reino de Siam. Os interessados deverão dirigir as suas propostas ao Consul, que de accordo com as Authoridades siamezas tratará de estabelecer as condições, sob as quaes deverá proseguir a exploração da mina; condições, que deverão ser sempre compativeis com os fins, a que os emprehendedores se proposerem. Igualmente se não porá embaraço algum a que os subditos portuguezes estabeleçam quaesquer fabricas em Siam, sob condições rasoaveis estabelecidas pelo Consul portuguez e pelas Authoridades siamezas, não sendo os productos fabricados prohibidos pelas leis do paiz.

Artigo 35o.

O Consul portuguez velará por que so negociantes e capitães de navios da sua nação cumpram as disposições do regulamento annexo ao presente Tratado, dando-lhe as Authoridades siamezas o auxilio de que precisar. As multas, que forem impostas por infracção do dito regulamento, serão entregues ao Governo siamez.

Artigo 36o.

O Governo e os subditos portuguezes, gosarão de todas as vantagens não mencionadas no presente Tratado, de que actualmente gozem, ou para o futuro venham a gozar o Governo ou os Subditos de qualquer nação estrangeira mais favorecida.

Artigo 37o.

As ratificações do presente Tratado de Amizade, Commercio e Novegação serão trocadas no intervallo de dezoito mezes, a contar da data da sua assignatura, ficando o mesmo Tratado interinamente em vigor até que seja ratificado.

Artigo 38o.

Findo o prazo de dez annos a contar da data da ratificação, se qualquer das duas Altas Partes Contratantes desejar que tenha lugar

-34-

a revisao① do presente Tratado e do regulamento e tarifa a elle annexos, ou outros quaesquer, que para o futuro tenham vigor, feita a competente declaração para esse fim um anno antes de findo o dito prazo, nomear-se-hão Commissarios de ambas as partes a fim de fazer-lhes as modificações, que se julgarem convenientes e uteis ao desenvolvimento das relações commerciaes dos dois paizes.

Artigo 39o.

As duas versões do presente Tratado nas linguas portugueza e siameza, ambas do mesmo theor e sentido, e de que se tiraram trez copias exactas, farão fé igualmente para todos os fins, bem como o regulamento e tarifa, que lhes vão annexos, e igualmente escriptos nas linguas portugueza e siameza.

Em fé do que assignaram e sellaram os ditos Plenipotenciarios o presente Tratado aos dez dias do mez de Fevereiro de 1859 da era Christã （que corresponde ao oitavo dia da terceira lua do anno Pimamia-samarethissop da era siameza de 1220） na Cidade de Bangkok, Capital do Reino de Siam.

（Assignado） ISIDORO FRANCISCO GUIMARÃES.

L. S.

Lugares dos sellos e assignaturas dos seis Plenipotenciarios Siamezes.

Está conforme.

（Assignado） JOSÉ MARIA DA FONSECA.

① Sic.

Secretario da Missão.

REGULAMENTO

PARA OS NAVIOS PORTUGUEZES QUE VIEREM A SIAM.

1o.

O Capitão de qualquer navio portuguez, que venha a Bangkok para commerciar, antes ou depois de entrar o navio, conforme lhe fôr mais conveniente, deverá dar entrada na Alfandega de Paknam, declarando o numero da sua tripulação e artilheria, e o porto d'onde vem. Logo que fundeie o navio em Paknam deverá entregar á guarda dos officiaes da alfandega a sua artilheria e munições, e então lhe será mandado para bordo um official da alfandega, que seguirá no navio para Bangkok.

-35-

2o.

Todo o navio, que passar Paknam sem desembarcar a sua artilheria e munições, como se acha dito no artigo antecedente, será obrigado a voltar para Paknam a fim de cumprir com essa determinação, e será multado em 800 ticaes pela descobediencia. Depois de ter desembarcado a artilheria e munições ser-lhe-ha permittido voltar a Bangkok para commerciar.

3o.

Vinte e quatro horas depois de fundeado o navio em Bangkok, salvo o caso de se metter de permeio um domingo, os Capitães dos navios deverão ter dado entrada no Consulado de Portugal, e alli depositado os papeis de bordo, os conhecimentos da carga e um manidesto exacto da mesma: depois de serem todos estes pormenores communicados á Alfandega pelo Consul, esta dará licença para que se abram as escotilhas. Faltando a dar entrada, ou appresentando um manifesto falso, o Capitão ficará sugeito em qualquer dos casos a uma multa de 400 ticaes; porém ser-lhe-ha permittido corrigir dentro de vinte e quatro horas depois de ser entregue ao Consul, qualquer engano que possa haver no manifesto, sem incorrer na multa acima mencionada.

4o.

Todo o navio, que abrir escotilhas, e começar a descarga antes de obter a devida licença, ou que passar fazendas por contrabando, quer no rio, quer fóra da barra, será multado em 800 ticaes, e lhe será tomado o contrabando ou as fazendas desembarcadas.

5o.

Logo que qualquer navio esteja carregado para sahir, tenha pago todos os direitos, e entregado ao Consul portuguez um manifesto exacto da carga, que leva, ser-lhe-ha dado um despacho de sahida Siamez do navio, entregará ao Capitão os papeis de bordo, e permittirá que o navio parta. Um official da alfandega irá a bordo até Paknam, onde o navio será novamente visitado, depois do que lhe serão entregues as peças e munições, que alli tiver deixado em deposito.

(Assignado) ISIDORO FRANCISCO GUIMARÃES.

L. S.

Lugares dos sellos e assignaturas dos seis Plenipotenciarios Siamezes.

Está conforme,

(Assignado) JOSÉ MARIA DA FONSECA.

Secretaria da Missão.

–36–

TARIFA

DOS DIREITOS INTERNOS E DE EXPORTAÇÃO A QUE FICAM SUGEITOS OS ARTIGOS DE COMMERCIO.

		Ticaes.	Salung.	Fua.	Hun.	
1.	Marfim,	10				por pico.
2.	Gamboge,	6				,,
3.	Pontas de Abada,	50				,,
4.	Cardamomo, la. sorte,	14				,,
5.	Dito ordinario,	6				,,
6.	Mexilão secco,	1				,,
7.	Pennas de Pelicano,	2	2			,,
8.	Areca secca,	1				,,
9.	Páo Krachi,		2			,,
10.	Barbatanas de Tubarão (brancas),	6				,,
11.	Ditas, pretas,	3				,,
12.	Semente de Lukrabão,		2			,,
13.	Rabos de Pavão,	10				por 100 rabos.
14.	Ossos de Bufalo e de Vacca,				3	por pico.
15.	Pelles de Abada,		2			,,
16.	Aparas de coiro,		1			,,
17.	Cascas de Tartaruga,	1				,,
18.	Ditas molles,	1				,,
19.	Bicho de mar,	3				,,
20.	Buchos de Peixe,	3				,,
21.	Ninhos de Passaro (não limpos),					20 por cento.
22.	Pennas de Alcyon,	6				por 100 pennas.
23.	Cutch,		2			por pico.
24.	Noz vomica,		2			,,
25.	Semente de Pungtarai,		2			,,
26.	Gomma Benjamin,	4				,,

27.	Casca de Angrai,		2			,,
28.	Páo Aguila,	2				,,
29.	Pelles da Raia	3				,,
30.	Pontas de Veado velho,		1			,,
31.	Ditas de dito novo,					10 por cennto.
32.	Pelles de Veao, finas,	8				por 100 pelles.
33.	Ditas ordinarias,	3				,,
34.	Nervos de Veado,	4				por pico.
35.	Pelles de Buffalo e de Vacca,	1				,,
36.	Ossos de Elefante,	1				,,
37.	Ossos de Tigre,	5				,,
38.	Pontas de Buffalo,		1			,,
39.	Pelles de Elefantes,		1			,,
40.	Pelles de Tigre,		1			por pelle.
41.	Pelles de *Armadillo*,	4				por pico.
42.	Nacar,	1	1			,,
43.	Canhamo,	1	2			,,
44.	Peixe secco, *plaheng*,	1	2			,,
45.	Dito dito, *plasalit*,	1				,,
46.	Páo sapão （sibucáo）,		2	1		,,
47.	Vacca salgada,	2				,,
48.	Casca de arvore （mangrove bark）,		1			
49.	Páo roza,		2			,,
50.	Ebano,	1	1			,,
51.	Arroz,	4				por coyão.

–37–

SECÇÃO 2a.

Os artigos abaixo mencionados estando sugeitos aos direitos internos ou de transito aqui especificados, e que não serão augmentados, ficam isemptos de direitos de exportação.

		Ticaes.	Salung.	Fua.	Hun.	
52.	Assucar branco,		2			por pico.
53.	Dito vermelho,		1			,,
54.	Algodão, limpo e não limpo,					10 por cento.
55.	Pimenta,	1				por pico.
56.	Peixe salgado, *platú*,	1				por 10,000 peixes.
57.	Favas e Ervilhas,					$\frac{1}{12}$
58.	Lagostins seccos,					$\frac{1}{12}$

59.	Sesamo,					$\frac{1}{12}$
60.	Seda em rama,					$\frac{1}{12}$
61.	Cera virgem,					$\frac{1}{15}$
62.	Cebo,	1				por pico.
63.	Sal,	6				por cojão.
64.	Tabaco,	1	2			por 1,000 molhos.

SECÇÃO 3a.

Todas as fazendas não mencionadas nesta Tarifa ficarão livres de direitos de exportação, e sómente sugeitas a um direito de transito, que não excederá o que actualmente pagam.

(Assignado) ISIDORO FRANCISCO GUIMARÃES.

L. S.

Lugares dos sellos e assignaturas dos seis Plenipotenciarios Siamezes.

Está conforme,

JOSÉ MARIA DA FONSECA,

Secretario da Missão.

[1-080]

[Rec 19 Octr Mr Abbott

N° 15]

Consulate of the United States

Macao, August 8th 1859.

Sir,

With reference to my Dispatch N° 14 of the 20th Ult° & to that of March 28th, N° 11, I beg to hand you, in Continuation, pages 51 a 72 inclusive of the documents pertaining to the case of the Ship "Emma" .--

I beg to note that those paged 67 @ 72 pertain-- by way of Elucidation to the first Series of documents transmitted to you under cover of my Despatch N° 10.--

As upon examination of the Documents you will perceive that the actual course of this case through the Court of Macao completely sustains the position originally taken by me

[The Honorable

Lewis Cass

Secretary of State of the United States

of America City of Washington.-]

in behalf of Captain Gill--based upon the legality of his title--I earnestly desire to receive the instructions of your Department in the interest of the parties so grievously wronged in this case.--

I am,
Sir,
With great respect,
Your Obedient Servant.
Gideon Nye Jnr.
Vice Consul of the United
State of America for Macao

[Macao Consulate
Recd with Gideon Nye's)
Despatch N° 15. dated
□□□ 85, 1859]

51.

Translation

Fran[co] d'Assis e Fernandes Esq.

I intimate to you as Attorney for Charles Gill the petition of the Chinese Cheong Ahoy by the annexed copy for your Knowledge & guidance in the matter of the interposed appeal.–

God preserve you

Macao 2nd, March 1859.
(Signed) Thomaz d'Aq[no] Migueis
Clerk of the Civil Court

Copy of the Petition

To His Honor the Chief Judge.

The Chinese Cheong Ahoy showeth that he had been made acquainted with the Venerated Sentence of Your Honor pronounced against him in the suit for nullity of the Sale of the Ship "Emma" in which he is the prosecutor and Gill Captain of the same the prosecuted who says he is her Owner; and the petitioner with due respect appeals from this, otherwise venerated, sentence of your Honor to the Supreme Court of Judicature of the States of India and applies to Your Honor to be pleased to order that his request be filed – he now appoints Antonio Rangel the Accountant of the Court to be his appraiser – therefore he begs of Your Honor that his petition may be granted, and will ever

52.

pray.

(signed) J. D. C. dos Santos Attorney
Cheong Ahoy, in Chinese Character

Dispatch

Granted (Torne-se)
Macao 28th February 1859.-
(signed) Ribeiro Carvalho.

53.

Translation

To His Honor the Chief Judge

Charles Gill Owner of the Ship "Emma" showeth that in virtue of the Venerate Sentence dated 21st of the last month wherein the validity of the Sale of the said Ship was declared, there is no further motive for the said Ship to continue laying under arrest after the truth had been made know through this Court-for these and for other reasons already exhibited he applies to Your Honor to be pleased to order the relaxation of the Embargo and to surrender to him the said Ship notwithstanding the interposed appeal in view of the fact that the arrest was not decreed in consequence of the action of nullity being brought in, for in that case the sentence would have proceeded the arrest. - Therefore he begs of Your Honor that his petition may be granted, reserving his right for remaining claims and to order that the petition be filed along with the Documents pertaining to this Lawsuit of arrest & Embargo and will ever pray. - Macao 4 March 1859.- (signed) Franco d'Assis e Fernandes - as Attorney- Despatch - Let the Counter party be heard. - Macao 4 March 1859 (signed) Ribeiro Carvalho. - Answer - In virtue of the interposed appeal, the petitioner ought to give security to the Court for the Amount of the debt of McCormick after which I cannot oppose to his request. The Most Meritorious Judge will do justice (signed) as Attorney J. D. C. dos Santos - 2nd Dispatch - The Court being secured the

54.

order of relaxation of Embargo be granted.

Macao 5th March 1859 - (signed) Ribeiro Carvalho.

To His Honor the Chief Judge.
Grant it - Macao 9th March 1859
(signed) Ro Carvalho

Charles Gill Owner of the Barque "Emma" showeth that he requires, for the ends of justice, that the clerk in Charge of the Documents pertaining to the sequestration - inform him - what sum of money the Chinese Cheong Ahoy has deposited with the Court until this date as security for the bond of responsibility signed by him - also a Copy of the dispatch exacting this grantee, and of the bond in which promise is made to pay down a certain sum of money designated therein - He prays Y. E. to be pleased to comply with his request.

Macao 9th March 1859.
（signed） Francisco d' Assis e Fernandes.

Sir,

I beg to inform Y. E. that from the respective file of Documents it is shown that from the 15th December last passed to the 15th Feby ult°. the Chinese Cheong Ahoy has deposited with the Merchant Francisco Ahryas the sum of Seven thousand Dollars, & from the same file of Documents it appears the following copy of the Dispatch to which

55.

the above Petition alludes – Granted in terms of other petitions issuing a pass every fifteen days, Castro to sign the bonds of receiver of the money as he collects it--Macao 1st Dec. 1858 （signed） Ribeiro Carvalho--Copy of the bond to which the above petition alluded.--

On the Second of December, One thousand eight hundred and fifty eight at Macao – at my office appeared the Chinese Cheong Ahoy seizer of the Barque "Emma" and in conformity with the Dispatch of the Chief Judge stated in the petitions as above from fol to fol offered to grantee his responsibility as appears of the bond which he, as seizer, signed at fol to make it effective and in fact gave as guarantee a draft of one thousand Dollars drawn by Joséd Almeida & Sons of Singapore in Lourenço Pereira in favour of Joaqium Peres da Silva & endorsed by the latter in favour of the merchant Appum already accepted and payable on the 15h Current. – He offered besides the security of the Chinese Merchant Leo. Assan – generally Known as Mestrinho （the little China Doctor） owner of the Physic Shop on St Domingo's Lane called Seriano for Five thousand dollars – said Cheong Ahoy who farms the gambling houses further tendered to deposit with the Merchant D. Franscisco Ahryas on the 15th of each month the sum of two thousand Dollars until it reaches the sum of fourteen thousand dollars together twenty thousand dollars all of which was duly accepted by the said Judge – Mestrinho is to produce the Title Decd of his property within

56.

eight days, and Appom to endorse the Draft. In testimony whereof I drew up this Statement on which they signed together with me （signed） Francisco Ant° Pereira da Silveira – Cheong Ahoy – in Chinese Characters – Leo Assan – in Chinese Characters.

In testimony whereof and in virtue of the above Despatch I delivered there presents at Macao on the 11th March 1859. （signed） Thornag d'Aquino Migueis -- Clerk of the Civil Court.--

---

To His Honor the Chief Judge.–

Charles Gill showeth that in virtue of the annexed Despatch by which Y. E. having ordered the relaxation of the Embargo on the Ship "Emma" provided security is given to the Court he proceeds to declare for its due effects, that he will not give such security not only because the Petitioner, being a stranger in this Country without further business relations will not find any one who would submit himself to such a burden in order to stand guarantee for him, but also because he thinks he is not to yield to the security so arbitrarily required in order to receive his property – he not being responsible for another man's debts, nor the measures required by the Laws to proceed to the arrest have been complied with. – Such arrest being considered Odious and only in certain and determined cases permitted.

The Petitioner has already shown by

57.

means of clear laws quoted in various statements that in order to proceed to the arrest or rather to execution of a sentence against another man's property which is presumed to be involved, it is essentially necessary that either an action has been brought against the seller of which the buyer was ignorant – or that he had no other kind of property, or a sentence in a Lawsuit before the Court declaring the sale to be null and so true it is that Y. E. has recognized in the sentence of the 21st February last; when you judged vaild the purchase of the said Ship, but it is shown that the arrest has been decreed without complying with this requisite––What foundation there can be to detain another man's property for security of a debt for the payment of which the Petitioner has not pledge himself, or rather difficult to comprehend! If it be the interposition of Appeal – alluded to by the Claimant in his answer it has nothing to do with the arrest – it was a suit got up with the intention to prove the nullity of the sale and purchase which unfortunately for him could not be proved but a contrary decision has been elicited.–

Therefore the fact above of having instituted an action Cannot be productive of any result much less when nothing has been proved.

This it is obvious that neither the proposition of the suit nor the interposed Appeal can impede that the property should be restituted to its owners the latter not having incurred responsibility as it does not appear he did,

58.

when he ought to have done.

For these and other reasons already stated in various places, the Petitioner applies to Y. E. that you may also take into consideration the heavy losses which result from the detention of said property the claimant not having given guarantee to pay the losses & detriments that you may be pleased to order the said Ship be delivered up with the required condition and will ever pray.–

Macao 9th March 1859 – (signed) Franco d'Assis e Fernandes – As Attorney.–

Despatch

The Ship has not been arrested in the sense alleged by the Petitioner and her Captain was summoned as proved by the Documents pertaining to this Lawsuit to give a Bond in order that the Court might not be illuded when a Sentence should annul the Sale. – for then the property would revert to its present Owner, who by sentence of this Court has been considered to be indebted to the Chinese Cheong Ahoy therefore as the same causes subsist the order of relaxation will be granted upon security being given to the Court.––

Macau 9 March 1859 (signed) Ro Carvalho.

To His Honor the Chief Judge.–

Charles Gill showeth that in view of the annexed Despatch of the 9th Current he begs leave to state to Y. E. the following:–

59.

Admitting （as these can be no doubt after the despatch alluded to, although he does not recollect it） that he has been summoned to give bond for the debt of James McCormick to Cheong Ahoy, what follows from it? – The summons alluded to in order to confirm to the usual Course of proceedings ought to be founded on some Law in virtue of which the petitioner would be obliged to give Bond – for without Law, no one can be compelled to assume any onus whatever.––

It is necessary to examine whether or not a Law exists which compels a purchaser of the Goods & Chattels of a Debtor – who is charged with simulation, to give bond into the Court for debts of the Seller – Should any such Law exist it behoves – ex adverso – to exhibit it in order to put a stop to allegations, but the Petitioner is of opinion that such law does not exist as shown in the Contestation founded on Ord Book 4 – title 1Q–S–9 – and Y. E. has yourself, recognized it in the sentence by which the sale of the object under embargo was adjudged valid––, wherefrom it results that from the beginning – that is to say – from the moment the intimation was made, no well founded motives existed and consequently none can subsist at present––Very far from any Law being in existence which compels （the Petitioner） to give bonds under the assumed hypothesis; without a previous Sentence being passed in Court, there are Laws which prohibit the proceeding to sequestration of Foreign Ships. （art: 1311 – art –1312 & 1313 of the Portuguese

60.

Commercial Code） there are other Laws which also prohibit similar proceedings, （when the ship has onboard 20 tons of goods） Letters patent of 15 April 1757, & 24th May 1765 quoted by Ferreira Borges in his Commercial Dictionary at Word Embargo – page 174._

In view of the reasons of addressed it is shown that the grounds do not subsist from never having a real existence – therefore he applies to Y. E. that you may be pleased to cause the Ship to be delivered up to him without the condition of giving security to the Court for another man's debts however he has no objections to sign an act of responsibility with the declaration that he does it under compulsion of Circumstances and not because he considers himself in duty bound to do so.

If the act of responsibility signed by the claimant – notwithstanding his being a foreigner, for the security of a sum of money above $40,000 has been deemed sufficient, there should be no objection to the acceptance of the one by the Petitioner for a lesser amount of about $8,000. Therefore he begs, of Y. E. that you may be pleased to acquiesce in his request by taking his act. of responsibility with the stated declaration. – And will every pray – Macao 11th March 1859.–

（signed） Franco d'Assis e Fernandes–

Despatch – The hypothesis of the articles quoted derivable from the Commercial Code is very different – The ship has not been arrested because the Petitioner was indebted

61.

to the Seizer; but because of the existence in this Court of an action of nullity in the purchase & Sale of the Ship and to the end that the decision of the court be not evaded should the final sentence decide that the said contract is not subsistent, the Petitioner was summoned in terms of Ord: Book. 3 tittle① 31 – not having Real Estate to secure the Court and not having given such security the ship was meanwhile put under embargo or sequestration in terms of same ord: of the Kingdom – as to the sentence it under appeal – and has not yet produced the desired effect required by the Petitioner if the other part agrees in the act of responsibility lit the embargo be released – Macao 11th March 1859 (signed) R. Carvalho--

---

To His Honor the Chief Judge.–

Charles Gill showeth with due respect to annexed Despatch – that if the Ord: Book 3d title 31 quoted in said Despatch date the 11th Inst permits the proceeding of arrest, it exacts at the same time as a Condition Sine qua non – a proof before hand of three well known requisitions of the Law – furthermore the Newest Judiciary Reform prescribes in Art: 298 that the Embargo or arrest in the first instance. Will only take place in cases of certainty of debt (it is seen that it refers to the proceeding against the Debtor and not against the simulated Buyer against whom

62.

the course of the law is differently marked) change of social condition – the want of property or suspicion of absconding expressly exacted by Ord: Book 3 Title 31 – there is no action in Court against the petitioner to prove this before or after the proposition of the case of nullity of the sale of the Ship "Emma" – It results therefrom that if the Law exacts as a necessary condition the proof of the three requisites and such has been omitted, the proceeding of the arrest was null & granted in nullity – It will not be said that by the simple fact of there being a suit of nullity and simulation of purchase pending in Court the proceeding of the arrest is permitted – for there is no Law authorizing such a step and without Law or rather against the Law all proceeding acting offensively on the right of property is null and as a consequence the Embargo cannot stand – not even for a moment much less after the truth is known.–

Therefore it is not necessary to deliver to one one's own property, groundlessly arrested – the law of consent of the counter party – However, the petitioner does not object to the latter being heard – Y. E. ordering him by Your Despatch to answer whether or no be consents to the end that the severe consequences of new detriments & losses which will result from the non-restitution of the Ship may weigh heavier against the claimant Cheong Ahoy for want of said consent--Therefore he begs of Y. E. that you may be pleased to grant

63.

the request of his last petition of the 11th Current hereto annexed accepting the terms offered, and will ever pray – (signed) Franco d'Assis e Ferns.--Despatch--Let the Counter part reply.– Macao 12 March 1859 (signed) R. Carvalho--Reply--

---

① Sic.

At present the question of the arrest is not mooted--my Constituent does not object to the vessel being released or not what he exacts is lawful--that is to say--that the Petitioner give security into the Court to meet the interposed appeal of the Otherwise Venerated Sentence which decided on the nullity of the sale of the Ship "Emma" the most meritorious Judge will do usual Justice – (signed) J. D. Coelho dos Santos – as Attorney –

Francisco d'Assis e Fernandes Esq.

In the suit of arrest of the "Emma" sentence, of which I send you a Copy herewith, has been given – the same I communicate to you as Attorney for the Proprietor Charles Gill.–

God preserve you Macao 2^{d} April 1859

(signed) Francisco Ant^{o} Per^{d} da Silveira
Clerk of the Civil Court

Copy of the Sentence

Declaring the Sentence which judged valid the purchase and Sale of the Ship "Emma" in relation to the Embargo of Sequestration of

64.

said ship I don't admit them on the grounds exposed in same sentence – adding however with reference to the nullity – which were considered as extemporaneous for the sequestration of the ship having taken place as a Comminatory duty for want of guarantee or security of the court the arrested ought to have made use of the embargo without loss of time & not to have opposed them only after more than two months had elapsed conformably to the practice of the Forum.–

As to the effect of the said Sentence it is evident that it having been appealed from and the same causes of want of security to the court exist, the sequestration stands good and can only be relaxed when the counter party consents to it in the way it deems most convenient to its interests.--The arrested to pay the expenses of this incident.--Macao 2 April 1859 – (Signed) Augusto Henrique Ribeiro de Carvalho–

(Counter Signed) Silveira

F. d'Assis Fernandes Esq.

In The proceedings of the nullity between the parties Cheong Ahoy against Charles Gill the Despatch is given as per copy annexed which I intimate to you for your information and guidance. – God preserve You.--

Macao 15 April 1859 – (signed) Thomas d' Aq^{o} Miguis
Clerk of the Civil Court

65.

Copy of Despatch

I receive the appeal interposed fl "em ambos os effeitos" – I set the term of forty days for the Copy and of six months for the presentation to the Court of superior instance reckoning these terms as it is ordered in the Reformed Judicature.–

Macao 15 April 1859.–
(signed) R. Carvalho

Macao 26 April 1859

My dear Mr Charles Gill,

As you wish to have an explanation of the Despatch of the Judge by which he received the appeal of the Sentence which decided valid the purchase of your ship "Emma", this appeal being interposed by the Chinese Cheong Ahoy, I beg to comply with your wishes.––

The appeal is received "em ambos os effeitos" which means the same in other terms that the sentence appealed cannot take effect before its being confirmed by the Supreme Tribunal of India.–

The six months stated in the Despatch for its presentation to the Supreme Tribunal is reckoned from after the departure of the second vessel from the port of Macao to that of Goa according to the Law cited in said Despatch which is the 5. 21. of the article 681 of the Novissima Reforma Judiciarica, as follows – But if the documents pertaining to the Lawsuit in order

66.

to be presented should have to pass the sea, the term of six months will have only to commence from the date of departure of the second vessel from the place where the judgement was given to that where the Supreme Court is, after the end of the term in which is to be prepared a Copy.––

As it is known that every year perhaps one vessel leaves this port for that of Goa, consequently the claimant may delay for two years the presentation only of the documents independent of other proceedings.– However, it behoves me to remark that the Appeal can be forwarded by steamer without waiting for the two vessels if the appealant is willing to do so, but he cannot be compelled to do it.–

I return the intimation with the Despatch alluded to.–

I am, Dear Sir,
Your Obd[t] Servt.
(signed) Fran[co] d' Assis Fernandes

67.

We the undersigned First & Second officers of the American Ship "Emma" do hereby certify under oath before Gideon Nye, Jr. Esq. United States Vice Consul at Macao – that being onboard the said Ship on yesterday the 7th day of November, she then being in possession of the Portuguese officers to whom Captain Gill abandoned her the day before, the said officer said that they did not wish the crew onboard any longer, & soon after, a boat came alongside with another officer, who said that he came from the Captain of the port, and ordered the officers & crew who were shipped by Captain Gill to go out of the ship. We & the native crew left with our clothes accordingly.–

Macao Nov. 8th 1858.–
(signed) Joseph Clutterbuck
(signed) George Coots–

Consulate of the United States of America
Macao November 8th 1858.

I, the undersigned Vice Consul of the United States of America for Macao and its Dependencies, do hereby certify that on the day of the date hereof, before me appeared the two persons whose names, are above who, signing the foregoing Declaration in my presence then made oath severally, in due form of law to the truth of the whole of it.–

Given under my hand and the
Seal of this Consulate the day and
year above written.
(signed) Gideon Nye Junr
Vice Consul of the U. S. A. for Macao.

68.

Translation

Mr Charles Gill

By order of the Chief Judge I intimate to you to appear at the Residence of His Honor, without delay.–

God preserve you – Macao 9th Novr 1858–
(signed) Thomaz d Aqno Miguis
Clerk of the Civil Court–

We the undersigned do hereby certify that we accompanied Captn Charles Gill, late of the Am. Ship "Emma" to the house of the Judge of Macao this day at about 2. o'clk p.m. to answer the above summons.–

Captain Gill stated to the Judge that he then appeared before him upon the Said Summons & wished to know why his presence had been commanded.–

The Judge replied that it was in regard to the Ship "Emma" which had been seized – That a Chinaman C. Ahoy had a suit in Court against James McCormick and that the Ship Emma once owned by the said McCormick had been sold while owing him the said money––two receipts or orders to pay signed by the said McCormick were exhibited as the basis of the claim – one being a receipt or order to pay dated in Canton April 1856 – for \$6,055⁴⁰ and another receipt or order dated in Hong Kong for a smaller amount the exact sum and date not recollected–

The attention of the Judge was drawn to the fact that the whole transaction occurred at Canton and

69.

Hong Kong & Consequently no Court in Macao had jurisdiction of the Case – to which he made no reply – The judge said that there were not claims against Captain Gill, & said of Captain Gill would give bonds to abide by the decision of the Court in regard to the suit of C. Ahoy against M^c^Cormick he would release to him the ship and Cargo.–

Captain Gill replied that he had nothing more to do with the "Emma" but had abandoned her to the Portuguese Government and made his protest of abandonment at the United States Consulate and that now the American Government has charge of his claim in regard to her – That he had been prosecuted for the last year & a half in Macao at unreasonable hours of the day & night, to sign papers or do some act by which he would be holden for this claim, which he had nothing to do with, and which he had never been summoned to explain and that the reputation of his vessel had been impaired by the Chinese claimant and his friends, and by repeated acts of the Portuguese Government. The Judge several times made the same proposition viz to release the ship under bonds to which Captain Gill, made no other than the reply above.

Macao Nov 9th 1858–

(signed) John Fitzpatrick
(signed) Edward J. Sage

Consulate of the United States of America
Macao November 10th 1858

I, the undersigned Vice Consul of the United

70.

States of America for Macao and its Dependencies, do hereby certify that on the day of the date hereof, before me appeared John Fitzpatrick and Edward J. Sage and signing the foregoing certificate in which they declared what was said and done in consequence of the proceeding summons of the Judge of Macao, in my presence, also made oath severally in due form of Law to the truth of the whole of it.

Given under my hand and
the Seal of this Consulate the
day and year above written
(signed) Gideon Nye Junr
Vice Consul of the United States
of America for Macao.––

71.

Canton 8th Ap 1856–

Rec^d^ 6055 $\frac{40}{100}$ $

Yrs truly
(signed) Ja^s^ M^c^C

H. K. 25th Feby 1856.

My Dr. Ch Ahoy – I wish you to loan me $1,000, which I will return you on Monday – I wish it for a friend–

Yrs truly

(signed) Jas McC

H. K. October 27th 1855

Der Ch Ahoy One thousand Dollars borrowed Money–

(signed) J McC–

I have no wish to reconcile these a/c, I believe these amts will all appear in my a/cs.

72.

Cheong Ahoy

to James McCormick [p]

For cash advanced and paid for his a/c at Macao – Say:

1856

Aug	19	Paid for Captn Upton's a/c		
		as per Bill $600		
		less amo paid by him--158.05		442.23
		Cash paid him by Captn Upton	$10	173.14
	21	Cash paid him by Captn Da Silver on order #	11	250.14
	27	Cash paid him by Captn Da Silver on order #	1	320.14
Septr	1	Cash paid him by Captn Da Silver on order #	12	100.14
	18	Cash paid him by Captn Da Silver on order #	2	500.14
	23	Cash paid him by Captn Da Silver on order #	3	1000.14
	27	Cash paid him by Captn Da Silver on order #	4	500.14
Oct	8	Cash paid him by Captn Da Silver on order #	5	290.14
	8	Cash paid him by Captn Da Silver on order #	13	200.14
	9	Half of a/c paid for ship "Estrella do Norte" as cash this day $14333.72	2	2166.86
	14	Cash paid him by Da Silver on order	14	380.86
	17	Cash paid him by Da Silver on order	15	200.86
	22	Cash paid him by Da Silver on order	16	20.86
	27	Cash paid him by Da Silver on order	6	400.86
Nov	5	Cash paid him by Da Silver on order	7	560.86
	15	Cash paid him by Da Silver on order	8	25.86

Nov	17	Cash paid him by Da Silver on order	9	451.86
		due as Cash 4 Oct /56		$7978.23
		8 M[os] Interest on $7978 - from 4 Oct /56 to 4 June /57 1% of In"		638.24
		Due J. M[c]Cormick cash 4th June /57		8,616.47

Macao June 4th 1857.–

[1-081]

[Re 3d Decr Mr Abbott]

Consulate of the United States.
Macao– September 24[h], 1859.–

Sir

I had the honor to receive from the Department of State the Despatch of June 24th last, upon the subject of the alleged imprisonment of Captain Martin Thompson by the Government of this Colony; accompanied by a copy of a letter of said Captain's wife of the 21th June.

She had already addressed to me a similar representation by a previous mail, to which I had replied informing her that no such person is or has been imprisoned here.–

I had also, in the mean time,

[The Honorable
Lewis Cass
Secretary of State of the United
States of America,
City of Washington.–]

of my own thought, addressed inquires transmitting therewith M[rs] Thompson's letter, to M[r] Keenan, our Consul at Hong Kong; and I beg now to hand you a copy of his reply, of the 3[d] Inst:

[N°1]

Referring to what M[r] Keenan states, I may remark that M[r] James Fait, to whom he alludes, is now absent from China; but as in the prosecution of my inquires I have been informed that a Statement has appeared in some of the news–papers of the last few months to the effect that this Captain Thompson and his son had been rescued from an Island in the Indian or Atlantic Ocean, I infer that he will have returned to his family prior to the receipt of the present Despatch.–

I may however, add that upon receiving your Directions I made renewed inquires of the proper local Portuguese Officers, who in reiterating their previous Statement––that no such person had been imprisoned here, very reasonably pointed out that such circumstance as the prolonged imprisonment of an American Citizen could not exist without the knowledge of the Resident Consular Officer of the United States.--

I avail of the occasion to hand you copies of a letter of the British Resident Consular Agent and of my reply thereto, of the 25th Ult°., respecting a deserter from H. B. M. Naval Service, whose arrest--requested by the British Office--on board the American Ship "Electric Spark" then lying in these Roads, I declined to sanction; and I should be glad to be informed whether or not you approve of the course pursued by me in this case.--

[2 & 3.]

I am,
Sir,
With great respect,
Your Obedient Servant
Gideon Nye Jur
Vice Consul of the United States
of America for Macao.--

Copy

United States Consulate.
HongKong, Septr 3rd 1859.-

Sir,

In reply to your's of the 29th ult. I can only say that I have not heard any thing of Captain Martin Thompson or his vessel since his departure with a cargo of Coolies for Havana about three years ago. It is presumed by those with whom I have conversed upon the subject that she has been lost with all onboard. His son was his mate--I would refer you to Mr James Tait of Amoy as a person most likely to be able to speak knowingly about the matter. If I should chance to hear any thing in relation to Captain Thompson or his ship I will communicate it to you.

Enclosed please find the letter of Mrs Thompson.-

I remain,
Very respectfully,
Your Obt. Sevt.
(signed) James Keenan
U. S. Consul.-

[□□□
Copy]

Consulate of the United States
of America
Macao, August 25th 1859.-

Sir,

I am favored with your letter of this date requesting me to grant authority to the Bearer of it – a warrant officer of Police in H. B. M. Naval Service to visit the American Ship "Electric Spark" for the purpose of identifying and arresting a Deserter from Her Britannic Majesty's Naval Service; and I beg in reply to acquaint you that I do not deem it within my competence to issue such authority under the circumstances.–I will, however, submit your Communication to Captain Lothrop of the said Ship upon his return from Hong Kong.–

I am, Sir,
Your Obedient Servant
(signed) Gideon Nye Jr
Vice Consul of the United States
of America for Macao.–

[Osmund Cleverly Esquire
Her Britannic Majesty's Consular Agent.
Macao.–]

B. C. Agency Macao
August 25th, 1859.–

Sir,

A deserter from Her Majesty's Naval Service is reported to be onboard the American Ship "Electric Spark" You will oblige me by granting to the bearer (a warrant Officer of Police in the naval service) authority to visit the ship, identify and arrest the deserter.––

I am Sir,
Your very Obt St.
(signed) O Cleverly

[G. Nye Esq
U.S. Vice Consul
Macao.–]

[Macao
Quarter ending
September 30, 1859
Recd January 12/60]

[1-082]

Quarterly Return of the arrival and departure of American Vessels at the United States Consulate at Macao from 1st of July to the 30th September 1859.–

Date		class	Name	Tonn age	Where from	When built	Vessels where built	Where belon ging	Where bound	Cargo		Owners	Masters
Month	day									Import	Export		
1859												Am Lawrence	
July	12th	ship	Aramingo	716 $\frac{20}{95}$	Wham poa	1851–52	New York	New York	New York July 19	Teas &c	Teas &c	Chamberlain Philps & others	Lewis P. Cassan
	13th	Bq:	Albers	359 $\frac{45}{95}$	do	1844	Topsham, Maine	Boston	Swatow in port	Ballast	Ballast	Thos H Morton	Wm D. Gregory
	27th	Ship	George Hallet	420 $\frac{24}{95}$	Concao (Siam)	1842	Duxbury, Mass:	do	Amoy aug 6th	Rice fish &c	Part of same	Joseph L Bruce	Gdo: H. Chandler
Augt	15th	Ship	Electric Spark	1215 $\frac{58}{95}$	Hong Kong	1855	Medford Mass:	do	Whampoa Sept 21.	Ballast	Ballast	Tacher Magnm Jr & others	Asa Lothrop
	29th	Ship	S. Gidder–sleeve	847 $\frac{55}{95}$	Wham poa	1854	Portland Conn:	New York	New York Sept 3.	China Produce	Ch: Proce	Benj: B. Blydenburgbo & others	S. Johnson
Sept		Ship	Hotspur	862 $\frac{31}{95}$	do	1857	New York	do	New York Sept 18	do	do	Geo a Potter & others	Geo A: Potter
	17th	Ship	Flora Temple	1915 $\frac{6}{95}$	do	1856	Baltimore	Baltimore	Havana with 800 coolies in port	Ballast		Wm S. Peter Kin	Charles R Johnson
			Tons	6,336 $\frac{49}{95}$									

Gideon Nye Jnr
Vice Consul of the United States of America for Macao.

[Rec 10 Jany Mr Abbott
No 17]

Consulate of the United States
Macao, October 27th 1859
[Rec sect to St.
Jan 12]

Sir,

Referring to my Dispatch No 14 in which I forwarded the returns of this Consulate for the previous quarter – I now beg to hand you those of the quarter ending the 30th Ulto. the amt. of fees, as you will observe, being $56.81 and showing, with the last, that my annual remuneration is but little above $200.

I am,
Sir,
With great respect,
Your obedient Servant
Gideon Nye Jnr
Vice Consul of the United States
of America for Macao.

[The Honorable
Lewis Cass
Secretary of State of the United States
of America.
City of Washington.–]

United States Consulate of Macao

Fees received during the Quarter ending 30th September 1859.

Date	No	Name of Vessel	Name of the Party paying the fee	Nature of Service Rendered	amount of fees paid	
1st	2	Invincible	W. C. Hunter	Certifying 2 lists of disbursements	$1	–
2^{d}	4	C. L. Bevan	Ja^{s} Pediosen	Shipping one man	–	50
18th		Mary Whiteridge	R. Pollard	Certificate to Inv^{o} Sugar – ship at HongKong	$2	–
18th	1	Aramingo	do.	Certificate to Inv^{o} Ginger & Fans	$2	–
	1	do	Lewis P. Cassan	Deposit of papers 716 $\frac{20}{95}$ tons a 1/2 cent	$3	08
	1	do	Lewis P. Cassan	shipping one man	–	50
22^{d}			R. Pollard	acknowledgement to a Power of atty	$2	–
5^{t}	3	Geo. Hallet	Geo. H. Chandler	Deposit of papers 420 $\frac{24}{95}$ tons a 1/2 & s & tons	$2	10
	3	do	do.	discharging one man	–	50
9th	3	do	S. Robertson	acknowledgement to a Power of attorney	$2	–
2^{d}		S. Gildersleeve	John Heard	certificate to Inv^{o} Pina & fans	$2	–
3^{d}	5	do	W. S. Johnson	Deposit of papers 847 $\frac{55}{95}$ tons c 1/2 & s & ton	$4	24
3^{d}	5	do	do	Affidavit of insubordination of seam□□□	–	50
3^{d}	5	do	do	$acknowledg^{t}$ of Bond of hypothecation	$1	–
3^{d}	5	do	do	seal to duplicate of do	–	50
16^{h}			Jos: L. Clutterbuck	Affidavit of the circumstances relating to the Emma	–	50
17^{h}	6	Hotspur	Geo. A. Potter	Deposit of papers 862 tons c 1/2 &c &c ton	$4	31
			James Purdon	Certificate to Inv^{o} Sundries & Hotspur	$2	–
21^{t}	4	Electric Spark	Asa Lothrop	Deposit of papers 1,215 $\frac{58}{95}$ tons c 1/2 &c &c ton	$6	08
21^{t}	4	Electric Spark	Asa Lothrop	Certificate of Desertion of the 2^{d} mate	–	50
22^{d}			Jos: L. Clutterbuck	Affidavit of the circumstances relating to his account with the "Emma"	–	50
27			Tan key	Entry of Protest against Master and owns of Brit Ship "Pominison" in the absence of the British Consular Agent	$1	–
			do	Copy of Protest	–	50
			W. C. Hunter	Certificate to a copy of a Power of Atty	$1	–
30		River Str : "Spark"	J. B. Endicott	Tonnage fees for third Quarter	$15	–
30		River Str: Pak Yun	Russel & Co	Tonnage fees for third Quarter	$1	50
					$56	81

Gideon Nye Jnr
Vice Consul of the United State of America for Macao

Quarterly Return of the arrival and departure of American Vessels at the United States Consulate at Macao from the 1st of October to the 31st of December 1859.–

Date		class	Name	Tonnage	Where from	When built	Vessels Where built	where belonging	where bound	Cargo		Owners	Masters
Month	day									Import	Export		
October	11th	ship	Dirigo	608 $\frac{12}{95}$	Hong Kong	1862	Bath, Maine	Boston	New York 25 Nov	Ballast	Tea & produce	Jacob Stanwood & others	Gideon T. Emssy
	12th	ship	Marion	449 $\frac{89}{95}$	Singapore	1846	Portland, Conn.	do	Singapore 10 Decr	Str: produce	Ballast	Adam W. Thaxter	Fredk A. Gons
	15th	ship	Norway	2,078 $\frac{5}{95}$	Hong Kong	1857	NewYork	New York	Havana 25 Nov	Ballast	1,037 coolies	John K. Pruyen & others	Hugo B. Major
Nover	12th	ship	Flying Eagle	1,094 $\frac{10}{95}$	do	1852	New Castle, Maine	Boston	Singapore Nov 16h	Freight & passengers		Fred Nikerson & others	John W. Bates
	23d	ship	Kate Hooper	1,488 $\frac{76}{95}$	Australia	1853	Baltimore	Balti more	–	Ballast	In Port	Jas A Hooper	Ed. P. Johnson
Decr	2d	str	U.S.S. Hartford		Hong Kong	–	–	–	HongKong 10 Decr	–	–	–	Captain Lowndes
	8th	ship	Florence Nightingale	1,118 $\frac{73}{95}$	do	1856	Chelsea, Mass:	Boston	HongKong 22 Decr	Ballast	Ballast	Daniel Sharp Kindall & others	Edmund W. Helens
				6,907 $\frac{73}{95}$									

Gideon Nye. Jnr.
Vice Censul of the Uniteel states of America for Macao

[Macao
1st qt
□□□
recd at □□□ office
June 4/ 60]

[1-083]

[Rec 15. Mar Mr Abbott;
No18.]

Consulate of the United States.
Macao, 12th January 1860.

Sir,

The gravity of the present crisis respecting the coolie traffic induces me to submit to your notice copies of two recent communications to His Excellency Mr Ward--of the 28th November and 18th December--as affording timely illustrations of the abuses to which the present modes of conducting it are subject.–

The atrocities of kidnapping and subsequent torture, to compel the signature of the contract and declaration of willingness before the Authorities of Macao, are arousing, not only the just indignation of the Governer General

[The Honorable
Lewis Cass
Secretary of State of the United States
of America.–
City of Washington.–]

and other Authorities of the Province, but also the inflammable feelings of the people to a degree threatening not only the rupture of the peaceful relations between the two governments, but the personal safety of all foreigners.–

As the question is now engaging in the earnest attention of His Excellency the Plenipotentiary, I transmit the present merely as timely contributions in aid of the application of practical remedies for abuses of our Flag fraught with immediate danger to National and individual interests.–

I shall transmit the Quatertly Account––now left open for want of one return––by the next mail.–

I am,
Sir,
With great respects,
Your obedient Servant
Gideon Nye, Jnr
Vice Consul of the United States
of America for Macao.–

[Copy]

Consulate of the United States.
Macao, November 28th, 1859.–

Sir,

The consideration of Your Excellency has no doubt already been directed to the general subject of the evils of the Coolie Traffic; but––since some of these evils an incidental to and inseparable from the nature of such dealings with a people to constituted and so situated, in respect to Foreigners as the Chinese, there has arisen a contrariety of opinion respecting the extent and gravity of actual abuses and premeditated wrongs, I deem it my duty to bring to your special cognizance, as strikingly illustrative of these abuses, the circumstances of a case of grievous wrong to a reputable Chinese in which American Citizens were "becoming participants when my intervention rescued the victim from the Ship Norway, on the morning of the 26th instant."

Upon perceiving the importance of the case and the value of this man's testimony, I conceived the purpose of a fuller examination, than my regard for the sufferer's fatigue permitted me to make in the first

[His Excellency
The Hon[ble] John E. Ward
Envoy Extraordinary and Minister
Plenipotentiary of the United States.–]

instance, before Y. E. with the assistance of D[r] Williams as Interpreter; and as he intimated the intention to return to his family at Canton by the Steamer "Spark" on her next trip I postponed a second examination with the expectation that you would reach this place in the meantime.––

As however he did not understand my purpose, he left with his younger Brother, who had come here seeking him, for HongKong owing to a summons from an older Brother there. This is not perhaps important, since I have his address already and know where to find: some of his relatives also: indeed, the essential points in elucidation of the question of the wrongs inflicted upon the Chinese and of the participation of Americans therein, are already covered by my Minutes of what he told me immediately after his rescue:–which I now proceed to state.–

I should premise that the information upon which I acted in the search for this man, came from another Chinese who had escaped or been released, (the hypothesis in regard to him having light cast upon it hereafter) from a Barracoon in this City and had reached Canton; and it was of the following purport: namely:–That he– "Sae Qui Wing" "a native of Shun–tuck district, but now from Canton had been lost four months that he had been in the Barracoon of ______ in this City and being ill had not been shipped off.–"

I was at the same time applied to in behalf of another man–the former horse boy of the Crown Solicitor of HongKong, M[r] Cooper Turner–of whom there was no district trace; but who has since been found at a Barracoon here.

I, ascertained that during the previous 48 hours above 1000 Chinese had been sent on board the American Ship "Norway", already mentioned, and after sending my Deputy twice, in search of her Captain I addressed to him the following letter.

Consulate of the United States
Macao November 25th 1859.

Sir,

I am this morning applied for the recovery of two men who have been lost and one of which, at least, is believed to be on board your ship; he having been traced to one of the Barracoon's from whence your vessel has received Coolies.

I request your "best efforts in behalf of the bearers of this letter, who are the relatives of, respectively, 'Say Gui Wing' of the Shun Tuck District, 32 years of age; and 'Ah See' a Hakka of 22 to 23 years of age, for the return of their said friends to my office."

I shall desire to be fully assured that neither of these men are onboard before I can permit your ship to go to sea.

I am,
Sir
Your Obedient Servant
(signed) Gideon Nye Jr
Vice Consul of the U.S.America

in Macao.–

Some subsequent steps, which it is not necessary to state and which it might seem invidious to explain with particularity, since blame should not too directly attach to individuals, resulted in the rescue of this "Sae Gui Wing", whose story of hardship and all but miraculous escape from servitude I proceed to tell from his own lips.–

Upon his presenting himself I at once recognized his face, as he told the Interpreter he did mine. He said I am "Sae Gui Wing" a native of the Shun Tuck district but my home is at Canton, where my Wife, a Son 3 years old and a Daughter 7 years old reside at the Taiping Sha. I was in the employ of the Department of the Customs and it was my duty to assist in the examination of the cargoes of vessels, I know several of the Linguists.–

This explanation of his former employment at once account for our having seen each other before.–Since he left for HongKong, I learn from a friend of his where he lodged the other day, the he had attained one of the lower Mandarin ranks represented by a White Button.–

"But how, then, did you get into a Coolie ship"?–I asked: He replied– "I went from Canton to Fat Shan about four months ago and getting belated so that the large passage boats of the day had left, I took a small boat in company with two other persons wishing to go to Canton, and whilst sleeping we were all carried to Whampoa, when discovering that I had been kidnapped I offered the boat people Fifty Taels to release me, but they said "No for you will inform the Mandarins against us––you must go in the Foreign Vessel." Afterward the Foreigners gave me and other $6 each to gamble with to gain our liberty as they said of we had luck, but it was all a deception: their purpose being to amuse us with the fable: While still onboard the Foreign Ship I was severely hurt on the back of my head–which as you see is still sore–by falling during a Tyfoong, and I had my tail cut off by recommendation of a Portuguese Keeper in order to admit of the more ready healing of the wound; I have been ill for some time in consequence of the fall" – (A fortunate circumstance perhaps to him, as otherwise he must probably have been shipped per "Flora Temple" ––just lost with her 850 Coolies in the China Sea)

"I have been in Macao nearly three months at the Barracoon of _______: about two months ago many men were sent from it to some ship then leaving" – (The "Flora Temple".)

"Before sending the men all are mustered in the large room or compound and the Keeper cries out that those who are willing to go are to take one side and those not willing the other;–then the unwilling ones are flogged into acquiescence: I was so flogged myself: There were men of family and men of literary pretensions among the captives; these were most reluctant to go and were most flogged; men among them told me of then having houses and land of their own, of then having no need to labor. On one occasion there were four or five of the most reluctant flogged until nearly dead, and then put into a sick room and fed on Congee for weeks:–"

One of these escaped or was purposely sent away and he it was who told my family where I was:–Others in their despair committed suicide with Opium and others hung themselves.–

Many had begged to be allowed to write to their friends to raise the money for their ransom, but were told that there was no one there to write for them.–

On the morning of his rescue, when first sought he was asleep, from having been unable to sleep the night before until 3 or 4 a.m. at the thought of being carried away from China,––so that but for the second search he would not have been rescued.–

He is full of thankfulness to those who were instrumental in saving him to his family and country and I am under great obligations to a countryman of our's here for the faithfulness of the last search – who being absent at the moment, I do not name lest he should not care to have his name appear officially.–

Submitting this case as indicative of the great moral wrong involved in the Coolie Traffic, I have no need to suggest the grave political dangers which are the natural consequence,––Since they directly invoke the exercise of the wisdom of Your Excellency to avert from our country and our Flag alike, dishonor and positive danger.–

I have the honor to be,
With great respect,
Your Excellency's
Obedient Servant
（signed） Gideon Nye Jr
Vice Consul of the United States
for Macao.–

[Copy]

Macao, December 18th, 1859.

My dear Sir,

I trust that you have safely reached HongKong en route to Manila and I almost reproach myself for intruding upon Y. E.'s purpose, of pleasure in the visit, with an intimation that I have recently rescued another kidnapped man–Chun Amok–whose old mother came and stopped at my house three days. He had been onboard an American ship at Whampoa which gave order to my application for an official order from the Procurador to search for him. He tells me that he tried to leap overboard at Whampoa but was caught and threatened with death if he again attempted it. He also says that out of about 50 men in the Barracoon with him there are several who have property and families. He having returned to Canton I expect applications from their relatives for my intervention for their release in a few days.

I see no effectual means, however, to prevent the compromise of our Flag in these atrocities, but in making the search of each ship on the eve of departure imperative upon the respective Consuls:––That is to say, that every "Coolie" （so called） shall be interrogated and all who have been deceived released: The ship （or Charterer –for it will virtually come from the latter） to pay the Consul $2 for himself and his Interpreter and $1 for a fund to assist the deceived back to their homes.–

If Y. E. thinks the rescued men could be claimed without returning the outlay of the charterers upon them, the refusal of such repayment would be a still more effectual check to these enormities; but it may be doubted if the Portuguese Courts would release such men from obligations contracted before the local authorities according to their forms: So that a fund to provide for the deficiencies of means on the part of relatives to redeem the kidnapped and inveigled, would be necessary here, at least.–

As I long ago requested the Secretary of State to consider my resignation of the Consulate here definitive–as before intimated to Y. E.–I have no delicacy in suggesting a fee to the Consul.–

It has just occurred to me to allude to this vexed matter again, so that I write somewhat hurriedly for this steamer late at night.

I avail of the occasion to fulful my promise to send Y. E. the translation of the speech of the King of Siam, to the Governor General of Macao.

I am, My dear Sir,
Your's faithfully
(signed) Gideon Nye Jnr:

[H. E.
Honble John E. Ward
&c &c &c]

[1-084]

[Rec 31. May Mr Abbott

Ret sent same day to the

N°19]

Consulate of the United States.
Macao, March 27th, 1860.

Sir,

Referring to my Dispatch N° 17 in which I forwarded the returns of this Consulate for the previous quarter, I now beg to hand you those of the quarter ending the 31th December 1859 the amount of fees, as you will observe, being $102^82--These Returns have been accidentally mislead until now.

I am, Sir,
With great respect,
Your obedient servant
Gideon Nye Jnr
Vice Consul of the United States
of America for Macao-

[The Honorable
Lewis Cass
Serectary of state of the United States
City of Washington-]

United States Consulate at Macao -
Fees received during the Quarter ending 31st December 1859.

Date	No	Name of Vessel	Name of the Party Paying the fee	Nature of service rendered	Amount of fees paid	
1st	□□	Flora Temple	Chs R. Johnson	Deposit of Papers 1915 $\frac{6}{95}$ Tons & 1/2 cost p ton	$9	57
		do	do	shipping 13 men	$5	

17t	2	Albers	Wm D. Gregory	Deposit of papers 359 $\frac{45}{95}$ Tons	$1	80
		do	do	shipping 12 men	$5	
25th		Wild Hunter	W. C. Hunter	Certificate to an Invoice of Rice	$2	
27h	1	Dirigo	Gideon T. Emery	do of desertion of the 2d mate		50
12th		do	J. P. Van Loffelt	do to an Invo of spoilt– stores	$2	
			W. C. Hunter	do of origin of machinery &c	$4	
10th	4	Flying Eagle	John W. Bates	Deposit of papers 1094 $\frac{10}{95}$ Tons @ 1/2 ct	$5	47
14th		Dirigo	J. P. Van Loffelt	Dupt certificate to Invo of spoilt stores	$2	
		do	do	Certificate to an Invo of cassia oil	$2	
24th		do	do	Certificate to an Invo of Raltun chairs	$2	
		do	do	Certificate to an Invo of Cassia Oil	$2	
25th		do	S. Robertson	Certificate to an Invo of Preserved Ginger	$2	
		do	Gideon T. Emery	Deposit of papers 608 $\frac{12}{95}$ Tons @ 1/2 cal & ton	$3	04
		do	do	shipping 2d mate & 3 men	$2	
	3	Norway	Hugo B. Major	deposit of papers 2078 $\frac{?}{95}$ Tons @ 1/2 ct & ton	$10	39
28		–	J. B. Goularte	acknowledget to W. K. Crissy's signature	$2	
		–	do	Duplicate & Replicate of do	$2	
10th	2	Marion	Fredk A. Gross	Deposit of papers 449 $\frac{89}{95}$ Tons @ 1/2 &c &c ton	$2	25
		do	do	Discharging 2d mate		50
		do	do	shipping 2d mate & cook	$1	
		do	do	certificate of desertion of 5 men	$2	50
		–	Joaqm P. de Silva	certificate to 2 Invos of fire crackers	$4	
12t		–	J. B. Goularte	Acknowledgement of his signature	$2	
		–	W. C. Hunter	Execution of a Power of Attorney	$2	
20t		–	do	Certifying copy of survey report	$1	
31t		Spark	J. B. Endicott	Tonnage fees 36 tups 150 Tons cash	$18	
		Meelee	A. Ricaby	Tonnage fees 12 tups 80 Tons cash	$4	80
					$102	82

Gideon Nye Jnr

Vice Consulate of the United States of America

for Macao.

[1–085]

Quarterly Return of the arrival and departure of American Vessels ending 31st March 1860.

Date		class	Name	Tonnage	Where from	When built	Vessels		where bound	Cargo		Owners	Masters
month	day						Where built	where belonging		Import	Export		
	10th	str	U. S. S. Hartford	–	Hongkong	–	–	–	Hongkong	–	–	–	Captain Lowndes
	11th	ship	Florence Nightingale	1188 $\frac{75}{95}$	Hongkong	1867	Chelsea Mass:	Boston	Ballao Jany 19th	Ballast	Silks &c	Dan'. Sharp Kendall & others	Edmond W. Robins
	20th	ship	Isabella	1021 $\frac{61}{95}$	_do_ & Singapore	1856	Wiscasset	Wiscasset	Hongkong Jany 17th	Straits produce	Ballast	Issac H. Coffin & others	Charles W. Coffin
	31st	ship	Albers	359 $\frac{45}{95}$	Swatow	1844	Topsham Maine	Boston	In port	236 coolies	–	Thos. H. Morton	Wm D. Gregory

	9th	ship	Ritty Pumpson	196 $\frac{73}{95}$	Whampoa	1856	New York	New York	Havana 18th Feby	Ballast	315 Coolies	L. H. Simpson	Richd. Canfield
	□□□	ship	Alfred Hill	549 $\frac{49}{95}$	Hongkong	1834	Chelsea	Boston	Hongkong 26th Jany	Guns	Ballast	John E. Lodge & Dane Dana & Co	George Nagel
	□□□		Messenger	1350 $\frac{49}{95}$	Whampoa	1851	New York	New York	Havana 22d Feby	Ballast	379 Coolies	Plate Lyles & others	Bensn. D. Morton
	21st	str	U. S. Hartford	–	Hongkong	–	–	–	HongKong	–	–	–	Caktans Row ndes.
	□□□	ship	Matilda	489 $\frac{81}{95}$	Hongkong	1846	Portsmoth	New York	Hongkong & Shanghae 13th Mch.	Ballast	Sugar	Geo. Guimold & others	Richard Lee
		ship	Intrepid	1173 $\frac{45}{95}$	Hongkong	1856	New York	New York	New York Mch. 17th	Teas, Silks &c	Produce	Tho. Bucklin & others	Edwd. C. Gardner
		ship	Indepen dence	732 $\frac{70}{95}$	Bangkok	1834	New York	New York	In port	Rice	–	Francis Hath away & others	F. W. Thrane
				7762 $\frac{71}{95}$									

Gideon Nye Jnr.
Vice Consul of the United States
of America for Macao.–

[Macau
□□□
Recd August 23/60
Mar 31/60]

United States Consulate at Macao.–
Fees received during the Quarter ending 31st March 1860.–

□□	No	Name of Vessel	Name of the Party paying the Fee –	Nature of Service Rendered and Remarks	Amount of Fees paid	
	1	Flocc Nightingale	Edmund W. Robins	Deposit of papers 1188 $\frac{73}{95}$ tons @ 1/2 ct p ton	$5	94
		–do–	–do–	Certificate of desertion of H. Gibson		50
		–do–	–do–	Shipping 14 men	$5	
		–do–	–do–	Certificate of inability to povence 2/3 □□□ Crew Am		50
		–do–	–do–	Hospital Bill agt. George Monk	$3	60
		–do–	–do–	Chair Coolie line for – do – do – from Hospital		40
		–	W. C. Hunter	acknowledgement of his signature	$2	
	2	Isabella	Shs. W. Coffin	Deposit of papers, 1021 $\frac{61}{95}$ tons @ 1/2 ct p ton	$5	11
	5	Kate Hooper	Ed. P. Johnson	Deposit of papers, 1488 $\frac{76}{95}$ tons @ 1/2 ct p ton	$7	44
		–do–	–do–	Shipping 19 men	$5	
		–do–	–do–	Certificate of desertion of 24 men	$12	
		–do–	–do–	3 Invo wages due to J. W. Torrey @ 24 cts p. mt		72
		–do–	–do–	Seal to note of discharge – do –		50
		–do–	–do–	Certificate of being unable to get 2/3 do of protected □□□		50
		Ritty Simpson	Richd Canfield	Deposit of papers, 696 $\frac{73}{95}$ tons @ 1/2 ct p ton	$3	48

		-do-	-do-	shipping 8 men	$4	
		Messenger	Bang" D. Mantou	Deposit of Papers, 1350 $\frac{49}{95}$ @ 1/2 ct p ton	$6	75
	3	Alfred Hill	George Nagel	Deposit of papers, 549 $\frac{49}{95}$ @ 1/2 ct p ton	$2	75
		–	S. Wells Williams	Certifying Power of Attorney	$2	
	8	Matilda	Richard Lee	Deposit of papers, 689 $\frac{87}{95}$ tons @ 1/2 ct p ton	$3	45
		–	J. B. Endicott	Two certificates in relation to the Estate of W. Sage	$4	
	9	Intrepid	E. C. Gardner	Deposit of papers 1193 $\frac{45}{95}$ tons @ 1/2 ct p ton	$5	87
		–	J. B. Endicott	3 certificates to Invoice of personal effects （ "Intrepid" ）	$6	
		Albers	J. R. Vargas	Certificate to Bill of Sale	$1	
		-do-	-do-	acknowledgement of Deed of sale	$2	
		Black Warrior	a.a. de Mills & Co	Certificate to Invoice prepared opium from Hkong	$2	
		Albers	Edwd Gassett	Certificate of new ownership		50
		-do-	-do-	sailing a sea letter	$2	
		Spark	J. B. Endicott	Tonnage Fees 35 trips – 100 tons &c @ 1/2 ct p ton	$17	50
		Meelee	A. Ricaby	Tonnage Fees 9 trips – 80 tons &c @ 1/2 ct p ton	$3	60
				Dollars	$116	11

Gideon Nye Jnr
Vice Consul of the United States
of America for Macao.

[Macao
Fees]

[Rec 23d aug
N°20]

Consulate of the United States
Macao, June 5th, 1860.

Sir,

Referring to my Dispatch N° 19 in which I forwarded the returns of this Consulate for the previous quarters, I now beg to hand you these of the quarter ending the 31st March 1860 the amount of fees, as you will observe being 116^{11}.–

These Returns have been delayed until now by reason of the non-collection of the fees due by one of the River Steamers.––

I am, Sir,
With great respect,
Your obedient Servt.
Gideon Nye Jnr

Vice Consul of the United States,
for Macao.

[The Honorable
Lewis Cass
Secretary of States of the United States.
City of Washington.–]

[1-086]

Quarterly Return of the arrival and departure of American Vessels at the Consulate of the United States at Macao from the 1st of April to the 30th of June 1860.–

Date		Class	Name	Tons	Where from	When built	Vessels			Cargo		Owners	Captains
							Where built	Where belonging	Where bound	Import	Export		
May	23d	Ship	Tarolinta	549 32/95	Saigon	1839	New York	New York	In Port	Ph 11.037 Rui		Robert L. Taiplor & other	David O. Mordy
May	28th	Brk	Myrtle	398 26/95	Hong Kong	1856	Mystic Conn:	do	Siam May 31		Ballast	Rufus Park & others	C. J. Botsford
June	2d	Ship	Emma	444 59/95	Hong Kong	1856	Mystic Conn:	do	Saigon June 4		do	Nathan W. Lincoln	J. G. Kursch
				1392 22/95									

Gideon Nye Jnr
Vice Consul of the United States for Macao

[□□□
□□□
Jany 30/60
Recd Sep 22/60]

[Rec 14. Sept Mr Abbott.
No21]

Consulate of the United States–
Macao July 6th 1860.–
[Ret Sent same day & □□□]

Sir,

Referring to my Dispatch No 20 in which I forwarded the Returns of this Consulate for the previous quarter, I now beg to hand you those of the quarter ending the 30th June.–

I am,
Sir, with great respect
Your obedient Servant.
Gideon Nye Jnr.
Vice Consul of the United States
for Macao.–

[The Honorable
Lewis Cass
Secretary of State of the United States
City of Washington–]

United States Consulate at Macao.–
Fees received during the Quarter ending 30th June 1860.

Date	No	Name of Vessel	Name of the party paying the fee	Nature of service rendered	amount of fees paid	
□□□	3	Albers	Wm D. Gregory	Deposit of papers 359 $\frac{45}{95}$ tons	$1	80
	3	Albers	Wm D. Gregory	shipping 11 men	$5	–
	3	Albers	Wm D. Gregory	certificate of inability	–	50
□□□	10	Independence	F. W. Thrand	Deposit of papers 732 $\frac{70}{95}$ tons	$3	66
	10	Independence	F. W. Thrand	Noting Protest	$1	–
	–	Emma	Charles Gill	Official & Notarial Documents duplicate & Triplicate thereof translation, & interpreter, fees, & general services pending the case at law in the Macao Courts from November 5th 1858 to this time	$250	–
□□□	2	Myrthe	C. S. Botsford	Deposit of papers 398 $\frac{26}{95}$ tons	$2	–
□□□	3	Emma	I. G. Kursch	do do 444 $\frac{59}{95}$	$2	22
		Emma	I. G. Kursch	Bill of sale–572 words	$1	14
		Emma	I. G. Kursch	Certificate of new ownership	–	50
		Emma	I. G. Kursch	Appointment of new master & oath	$1	–
		Emma	I. G. Kursch	Sea Letter 290 words	–	58
		Emma	I. G. Kursch	shipping 20 men	$5	–
		–	Le A. Lubeck	Affidavit	$1	–
		–	J. M. Cantuariar	Certificate to Invo of Tea	$2	–
		Spark	J. B. Endicott	Tonnage fees for 2d Quarter	$18	–
		Melee	A. Ricaby	Tonnage fees for 2d Quarter	$4	80
					$300	20

Gideon Nye Jnr
Vice Consul of the United States for Macao.

[1-087]

Quarterly Return of the arrival and departure of American Vessels at the Consulate of the United States at Macao– from the 1st of July to the 30th September 1860.–

Date		Class	Name	Tons	Where from	When built	Vessels			Cargo		Owners	Captains
							Where built	Where belonging	Where bound	Import	Export		
July	5th	ship	Live Yankee	$1637\frac{65}{95}$	Hong kong	1853	Rockland	NewYork	Havana	Ballast	In Port	Max M. Lawrence & others	Eden A. Thrink
July	9th	do	J. Wareficto	$1225\frac{11}{95}$	do	1854	Thomaston	do	do	do	In Port	Hwain G. Buy & others	John H. Young
Augt	11^{t}	Bq	Rover	$358\frac{55}{95}$	do	1848	NewYork	do	Hong Kong	do	Guns	Wm Nealson & others	Albert Dupor
Augt	27th	Ship	Emma	$444\frac{59}{95}$	Whampoa	–	–	–	do	do	General	Nathan W. Lincoln	Allen Nickman
Sep^{t}	4th	do	Sea Serpent	$1337\frac{13}{95}$	Hong kong	1850	Portsmouth	do	do	do	do	W^{m}. Horland & others	J. D. Whitemore
Sep^{t}	25^{t}	do	Ocean Steel	$807\frac{45}{95}$	Whampoa	1853	Richmond	do	New York	General	do	Smith C. Cox & others	A. S. Smally
				$5810\frac{62}{95}$									

Gideon Nye Jnr

Vice Consul of the United States for Macao.

[Macao

4th qr

□□□□□1860

□□□□qr

□□□□□

□□□□]

[Rec 22 Dec Mr Abbott

N°22]

Consulate of the United States

Macao, October 4th 1860.

Sir,

Referring to my Dispatch N° 21 in which I forwarded the Returns of this Consulate in the previous quarter I now beg to hand you those of the quarter ending the 30th September.

I am,

Sir,

With great respect

Your Obedient Servant,
Gideon Nye, Jnr
Vice Consul of the United States,
for Macao.

[To the Honorable
Lewis Cass
Secretary of state of the United state
City of washington]

United States Consulate at Macao
Fees received during the Quarter ending 30th September 1860–

Date	No	Name of vessel	Name of the party paying the fees	Nature of Service rendered	amount of fees paid	
		Maksfield	Manuel Pereira	Affidavit relating to □□□ □□□	$1	50
		Emma	Actidknown	Deposit of Papers 444 $\frac{59}{95}$ tons	$2	22
		do	do	Discharging Boat□□□		50
		do	do	certificate to oath of new □□□	$1	
		Sea Serpent	J. P. Whitemore	Deposit of papers	$6	69
		do	W. C. Hunter	Certificate to 3 invoices	$6	
		□□□ Steed	Adam S. Smally	Deposit of papers 807 $\frac{45}{95}$ tons	$4	04
		do	do	shipping □□□ men		50
		Spark	J. Endicott	Tonnage fees 37 □□□ 100 □□□	$8	50
					$40	95

Gideon Nye Jnr
Vice Consul of the United States for Macao

[Macao
1st qt

Received at The States
Recd □□ Af □□□
15, 1861]

[1–088]

[Recd 6. Ap. Mr Abbott
N°23.]

Consulate of the United States
Macao, January 30th 1861.–

Sir,

Referring to my Despatch N° 22. in which I forwarded the Returns of this Consulate for the Previous quarter, I now beg to hand you those of the quarter ending the 31st December 1860.–

I am,
Sir,
With great respect,
Your obedient Servant
Gideon Nye Jnr.
Vice Consul of the United States
of America for Macao.–

[Sent to stat Ap. 9]

[The Honorable
Lewis Cass
Secretary of State of the United States
of America.–
City of Washington.–]

Quarterly Return of the Arrival and Departure of American Vessel at the Consulate of the United States at Macao from the 1st of October to 31st of December 1860.–

Date		Class	Name	Tons	Where from	When built	Vessels			Cargo		Owners	Captains
							Where built	Where belonging	Where bound	Import	Export		
1860 October	15	Brig	Progressive Age	296 $\frac{82}{95}$	Hongkong	1854	Belfast Maine	Belfast	New York Octbr 30th	Ballast	general	David Pierce Jr. & others	Beny Thompson
October	22d	Ship	Francis P. Sage	1146 $\frac{59}{95}$	do	1851	New York	New York	Havana still in Port	do		Thomas Ingersoll & others	Thos Ingersoll
October	27t	Ship	May Queen	619 $\frac{19}{95}$	do	1853	Topsham Maine	Bath	Havana Decr 29th	do	310 coolies	Francis C. Jordan & others	Francis & Jordan
Nover mber	10th	Ship	Haze	795 $\frac{20}{95}$	Whampoa	1860	Mystic	Mystic	New York Decr 22d	Sundries	Tea, Oil &c	J. W. Holnigs & others	Jos W. Holones
				2857 $\frac{85}{95}$									

Gideon Nye Jnr
Vice Consul of the United States
of America for Macao.–

United States Consulate at Macao.–
Fees received during the Quarter ending 31st December 1860.

Date	N°	Name of Vessel	Name of the party paying the fee	Nature of service rendered	amount of fee paid	
4'	2	J. Wakefield	John H. Young	Deposit of paper 1225 $\frac{11}{95}$ tons @ 1/2c	$6	13
4'	2	do	do	acknowledgement of Deed of writing	$2	–
24	1	Tarolinta	D. O. Moseley	Deposit of papers 549 $\frac{32}{95}$ tons @ 1/2c	$2	75
24	1	do	do	Discharging chief officer	–	50
24	1	do	do	Certificate to Oath of new Master	$1	–
24	1	do	do	Discharging book	–	50
24	1	do	do	Discharging Carpentar	–	50
24	1	do	do	Shiping 22 men	$5	–
29	1	Progressive Age	Beny: Thoinson	Deposit of Papers 296 $\frac{82}{95}$ tons @ 1/2 c	$1	48
29	1	do	do	Shipping 6 men	$3	–
1	1	Live Yankee	Eben A. Thorndike	Deposit of Papers 1637 $\frac{68}{95}$ tons @ 1/2 c	$8	19
1	1	do	do	Shipping 34 men	$5	
1	1	do	do	Cert. to Declaration to man lost overboard	–	50
15		Jacob Bell	Gustao Raynal	Certificate to Invoice	$2	
22	4	Haze	Joseph W. Holanca	Deposit of Papers 795 $\frac{20}{95}$ tons @ 1/2 c	$3	98
20	3	May Queen	Francis C. Jordan	Deposit of papers 619 $\frac{19}{95}$ tons @ 1/2 c	$3	10
20	3	do	do	Two Certificates to agreements	$2	–
20	3	do	do	Two Certificates to copies of same	$2	–
20	3	do	do	shipping 18 men	$5	–
31		Spark	J. B. Endicott	Tonnage fees 39 trips 100 tons tea @ 1/2c	$19	50
					$74	13

Gideon Nye Jnr
Vice Consul of the United States
of America for Macao.–

[Macao
□□□□□□ No 24
of Apl 3 1861

□□□□□□ 31/61
Received at the
Satistical Office
Jun 29. 1861]

[1–089]

[Rec 14. June Mr Abbott

N°24.–]

Consulate of the United States.–
Macao, April 3rd. 1861.–

Sir,

Referring to my Despatch N° 23––in which I forwarded the Returns of this Consulate for the previous quarter, I now beg to hand you those of the quarter ending the 31st March 1861.

I am,
Sir,
With great respect,
Your obedient Servant
Gideon Nye Jnr
Vice Consul of the United States
of America for Macao.–

[The Honorable
The Secretary of State of the
United States of America.–
City of Washington.]

Quarterly Return of the Arrival and Departure of American Vessels at the Consulate of the United State at Macao from the 1st of January to the 31st of March 1861.–

Date		Class	Name	Tons	Where from	When built	Vessels			Cargo		Owners	Captains
							Where built	Where belon ging	Where bound	Import	Export		
1861													
January	7th	Ship	Kate Hooper	1488 $\frac{76}{95}$	Amoy	1853	Balti more	Baltimore	Havana 11th Feby	Ballast	589 coolies	Jau: A. Hooper	Ed. P. Johnson
January	11th	Ship	Forest Eagle	1156 $\frac{04}{95}$	HongKong	1856	Rockland	Rockland	Havana 9th Feby	Ballast & store	500 coolies	Caphas Starrett & Alfred H. Kimball	Thos. R. Pillsbury
March	6th	Ship	Messenger	1350 $\frac{49}{95}$	HongKong	1851	New York	New York	Hongkong 19th Mch	Ballast	555 coolies	Ch° H. Slate & others	Ben: D. Manton
March	6th	Ship	Cormet	1836 $\frac{12}{95}$	Whampoa	1851	New York	New York	Hongkong 8th Mch	Teas & gl	Teas & Cassia	Thos R. Bucklins & others	Edward Todd.
				5831 $\frac{46}{95}$									

Gideon Nye Jnr
Vice Consul of the United States
of America for Macao.

United States Consulate at Macao.
Fees received during the Quarter ending 31st March 1861.

Date	N°	Name of Vessel	Name of the party paying the fee –	Nature of Service Rendered	Amount of Fees paid	
17	2	Francis P. Sage	Thos Ingersoll	Deposit of papers 1146 $\frac{59}{95}$ tons @ 1/2¢	$5	73
17		Francis P. Sage	Thos Ingersoll	shipping 34 men	$5	–
17		Francis P. Sage	Thos Ingersoll	Two Certificates to Agreements	$2	–
17		Francis P. Sage	Thos Ingersoll	Two Certificates to duplicates of same	$2	–
17		Francis P. Sage	Thos Ingersoll	Certificate of desertion of 13 men	$7	50
30	1	Kate Hooper	Ed. P. Johnson	Ackt of his Act & Deed to 1 Power of Attorney	$2	–
30		Kate Hooper	Ed. P. Johnson	Drawg up the same & Dupte of same	$2	–
31		Kate Hooper	J. R. Vargas	Authentication Invo O. Cleverly's signature to survey Report	$1	–
9	2	Forest Eagle	Thos R. Pillsbury	Deposit of papers 1158 $\frac{4}{95}$ tons @ 1/2 ct	$5	78
		Forest Eagle	Thos R. Pillsbury	shipping 3 men	$1	50
11	1	Kate Hooper	Ed. P. Johnson	Deposit of paper 1488 $\frac{76}{95}$ tons @ 1/2 ct	$7	44
11	1	Kate Hooper	Ed. P. Johnson	Discharging 5 men	$2	50
11	1	Kate Hooper	Ed. P. Johnson	Shipping 42 men	$5	–
11	1	Kate Hooper	Ed. P. Johnson	Ackt of his Act & Deed to 1 Power of Attorney	$2	–
11	1	Kate Hooper	Ed. P. Johnson	Drawg up the same & Dupte of same	$2	–
11	1	Kate Hooper	Ed. P. Johnson	Ackt of Wo_ Hang to a deed of writing	$2	–
11	1	Kate Hooper	Ed. P. Johnson	Ackt of Wo_ Hang duple triple & quardle of same	$3	
11	1	Kate Hooper	Ed. P. Johnson	Certificate of desertion of 21 men	$10	50
11	1	Kate Hooper	Ed. P. Johnson	Certificate of inability to procure 2/8 □□□ Crew		50
8	4	Comet	Edward Todd	Deposit of papers 1836 $\frac{12}{95}$ tons @ 1/2 ct	$9	18
		Comet	Edward Todd	shipping 5 men	$2	50
19	3	Messenger	□□□ D. Manton	Deposit of papers 1350 $\frac{49}{95}$ tons @1/2 ct	$6	75
19		Messenger	□□□ D. Manton	shipping 26 men	$5	–
31		Spark	J. B. Endicott	Tonnage fees 31 trips 100 tons lca @ 1/2 ct	$15	50
31		Rose	J. B. Endicott	Tonnage fees 5 trips 74 tons lca @ 1/2 ct	$1	85
					$110	23

Gideon Nye Jnr.
Vice Consul of the United States
of America for Macao

[1-090]

[Duplicatee Recd Aug 9
N°25.]

Consulate of the United States of America
Macao May 1st 1861.–

Sir,

I have the honor to address to you, in continuation of previous communications to the Department, representations upon a case long pending here,——which as involving great hardship to several American Citizens, will, I venture to believe, be viewed by you as justly meriting the earnest attention of the Government.–

I regret that upon the first occasion of this honor being afforded me, it is my duty to trouble you upon a matter of unsettled business; and I protest to you, Sir, that it is by no fault of mine that such is the case:–For, whether, at its inception–to avert the wrong to our countrymen,–or at its successive stages,–to lessen the accumulating damages,–I have availed of and exhausted upon the question every resource within my competency, as well of friendly remonstrance as of official representation.–

I have been met with suitable courtesy by the Executive Chief of this Government–Governor General Guimarães;–but, on the other hand, I am compelled to declare that the case arose from errors of the late Chief Justice of this District, and became aggravated by defaults equally attributable to His Honor.

[To the Honorable
William H. Seward
Secretary of State
&c &c &c
City of Washington.]

I allude to the sequestration of the American Ship "Emma" ; and I am thus explicit, in attributing errors of inception and defaults of insufficient security and hence of delay of redress, to the late Chief Justice of the District, in virtue of this decision–upon the appeal of the Prosecutor by the Superior Court at Goa, which ruled the incompetency of the Judge, as well as of the Record of the local Court itself.

The arrest of the ship took place early in November 1858 and the case was fully presented, as it then stood, by me to His Excellency Mr Reed, who soon after reached HongKong.–Subsequently I addressed to your Predecessor representations upon the subject in my Despatches of the year 1859, numbered respectively, 9. 10. 11. 14. 15; and transmitted copies of the Series of Documents and Correspondence upon which my expositions of the case rested, ending with pages 51 @72 inclusive under cover of the latter.–

These presented the case to your Predecessor as it stood on the 8th of August 1859; and I closed my Despatch of that date with the following appeal for Instructions:

"As upon examination of the Documents you will perceive that the Actual Course of this case through the Court of Macao completely sustains the position originally taken by me in behalf of Captn Gill–based upon the legality of his title–I earnestly desire to receive the instructions of your Department in the interest of the parties so grievouly wronged in this case."

As I have not been favored with the Instructions which I sought; and as the intervention of His Excellency Mr Ward,–to whom as well as the Counsellor Tatnall and Commodore Stribling, the case has been presented,–has not procured redress, I deem it my duty now to bring it to your notice.–

In so doing, I beg reference, firstly to my above cited Despatches of 1859 and to the accompanying Papers paged 1@72; and secondly, to the Series of Documents and correspondence which I now transmit, paged 73@118 inclusive, which–as enumerated below being passed in review seriatim disclose, I believe, as tangible points against the Portuguese Government:–

1st The incompetency of the Judge, as ruled by the Superior Court at Goa:–

2d The neglect to obtain adequate security to meet the damages.

As the Documents and correspondence are rather voluminous and will, collectively, afford you a clear insight of this somewhat complicated case, I shall refrain from attempting a résume of it wherein I might err in emphasising and should at least add something superfluous.–

I have, therefore, only to respectfully request that after a perusal of my Despatches and a full investigation of the case, you will be pleased to instruct me as to the purposes and wishes of the Government,–whether it will address itself directly to the Portuguese Government for redress or empower me to make more authoritative demands upon the local authorities of this Dependency of Portugal.

As there is a large surplus of Revenue in the local Treasury the Home Government can have us hesitation in directive a prompt adjustment of the claim.–

I have the honor ot be,
Sir,
Your obedient Servant.–
Gideon Nye Jnr

Enclosures

Pages	
73@76	My letter of August 15th 1859 to the Government of Macao.
77@80	Translation of the reply of the Governor of Macao to the above dated August 22th 1859.
81@93	My rejoinder to the Governor's reply, dated Septr 30th 1859.
94	Translation of letter of Attorney of Charles Gill of Sept 9th 1859.
95&96	Translation of letter of the governor of Macao of October 27th 1859.
97@99	Translation of letter of the Chief Justice of Macao to the governor of Macao of October 20th 1859.
100@102	Translation of Certificate to a portion of the Record of the District Court of Macao dated October 19th 1859.
103	Translation of the Decision of the Supreme Court of Goa dated New Goa 9th November 1859.
104@106	Bond of Compromise dated January 13th 1860.
107&108	Award of Umpire dated 29th March 1860.
109@111	Protest of Charles Gill of 25th June 1860.
112	My letter of July 2d 1860 to the Council of Government.
113&114	Letter of Mr Edward P. Sage Attorney of Charles Gill of April 10th 1861.
115	Account Current accompanying last letter.
116&117	My letter to the Governor of Macao dated April 16th 1861.
118	Translation of reply of the Governor of Macao of Apl 18h 1861.

E. E. G. N. r

PS. Macao May 13th 1861.

Wand no duplicate Documents as the Cert q postage

□□□□□□□□□□□□□ G. N. J.

[Recd 19 July Mr. Abbott.]

Consulate of the United States of America.
Macao, May 1st 1861.–

Sir,

I have the honor to address to you, in continuation of previous communications to the Department, representations upon a case long, pending here,–which as involving great hardship to several American Citizens, will, I venture to believe, be viewed by you as justly meriting the earnest attention of the Government.

[Seizure of Ship Emma.]

I regret that upon the first occasion of this honor being afforded me, it is my duty to trouble you upon a matter of unsettled business; and I protest to you, Sir, that it is by no fault of mine that such is the case:–For, whether at its inception,–to avert the wrong to our Countrymen,–or at its successive stages,–to lessen the accumulating damages,–I have availed of and exhausted upon the question every resource within my competency, as well of friendly remonstrance as of official representation.

I have been met with suitable courtesy by the Executive Chief of this Government–Governor General Guimarães;–but, on the other hand, I am compelled to declare that the case arose from errors of the late Chief Justice of this District and become

[To The Honorable
William H. Seward
Secretary of State
&c &c &c
City of Washington]

aggravated by defaults equally attributable to His Honor.–

I alluded to the sequestration of the American Ship "Emma"; and I am thus explicit, in attributing errors of inception and defaults of insufficient security and hence of delay of redress to the late Chief Justice of the District, in virtue of the decision–upon the appeal of the Prosecutor–by the Superior Court at Goa, which ruled the incompetency of the Judge, as well as of the Record of the local Court itself.

The arrest of the ship took place early in November 1858 and the case was fully presented, as it then stood, by me to His Excellency Mr Reed, who soon after reached Hongkong.– Subsequently I addressed to your Predecessor representations upon the subject in my Despatches of the year 1859, numbered respectively, 9. 10. 11. 14. 15; and transmitted copies of the series of Documents and Correspondence upon which my expositions of the case rested, ending with pages 51@72 inclusive under cover of the latter.–

These presented the case to your Predecessor as it stood on the 8th of August 1859; and I closed my Despatch of that date with the following appeal for Instructions.

"As upon examination of the Documents you will perceive that the actual course of this case through the court of Macao completely sustains the position originally taken by me in behalf of Captn Gill--based upon the legality of his title--I earnestly desire to receive the instructions of your Department in the interest of the parties as grievously wrong in this case."

As I have not been favored with the Instructions which I sought; and as the intervention of His Excellency Mr Ward to whom as well as to Commodore Tatnall and Commodore Stribling, the case has been presented,--has not procured redress, I deem it my duty now to bring it to your notice.–

In so doing, I beg reference, firstly, to my above cited Despatches of 1859 and to the accompanying Papers paged 1@72; and secondly, to the Series of Documents and correspondence which I now transmit, paged 73@118 inclusive, which--as enumerated below--being passed in review, seriatim disclose, I believe, as tangible points against the Portuguese Government:--

1st The "incompetency of the Judge," as ruled by the Superior Court at Goa:–

2d The neglect to obtain adequate security to meet the damages.–

As the Documents and Correspondence are rather voluminous and will, collectively, afford you a clear insight of this somewhat complicated case, I shall refrain from attempting a résumé of it, wherein I might err in emphasising and should, at least, add something superfluous.–

I have, therefore, only to respectfully request that after a perusal of my Despatches and a full investigation of the case, you will be pleased to instruct me as to the purposes and wishes of the Government,–whether it will address itself directly to the Portuguese Government for redress, or empower me to make more authoritative demands upon the local authorities of this Dependency of Portugal.–

As there is a large surplus of Revenue in the local Treasury, the Home Government can have no hesitation in directing a prompt adjustment of the claim.–

I have the honor to be,
Sir,
Your obedient Servant
Gideon Nye Jnr

Enclosures.

pages

73@76 My letter of August 18th 1859 to the Governor of Macao.

77@80 Translation of the reply of the Governor of Macao to the above, dated August 22d 1859.

81@93 My rejoinder to the Governor's reply, dated Septr 30th 1859.

94 Translation of letter of Attorney of Charles Gill of September 9th 1859.

95&96 Translation of letter of the Governor of Macao of October 27th 1859.

97@99 Translation of letter of the Chief Justice of Macao to the Governor of Macao of October 20th 1859.

100@102 Translation of Certificate to a portion of the Record of the District Court of Macao, dated October 19th 1859.

103 Translation of the Decision of the Supreme Court of Goa dated New Goa 8th November 1859.

104@106 Bond of Compromise, dated January 13th 1860.

107@108 Award of Umpire, dated 29th March 1860.
109@111 Protest of Charles Gill of 25th June 1860.
112 My letter of July 2d 1860 to the Council of Government.
113&114 Letter of Mr. Edward J. Sage Attorney of Charles Gill of Apl 10th □□□
115 Account Current accompanying last letter.
116&117 My letter to the Governor of Macao, dated April 16th 1861.
118 Translation of reply of the Governor of Macao of April 18th 1861.

73.

[Copy]

Consulate of the United States
Macao, August 18th 1859.

Sir,

It will be in Your Excellency's recollection that I waited upon you early in November of last year to present a Protest and Claim redress in behalf of Captain Charles Gill the Owner and Commander of the American Ship "Emma", which had then just been sequestrated by order of the Court of this Colony.

I took that formal step in the light of my Conviction that the sequestration was an illegal invasion of Captain Gill's rights; and with the sincere purpose of averting, as well an accumulation of damages as a possible

[His Excellency
Isidoro F. Guimarães
Governor General of Macao
and its Dependencies–
&c &c &c]

74

breach of the good understanding between our respective Governments, to the Continuance of which, happily–subsisting, relations it was no less my personal inclination than my official duty to contribute to the uttermost of my ability.––

Your Excellency––then on the eve. of departure upon special duties elsewhere–received my Communication for transmission to the Judicial Department of the Government.–

In the Course of the subsequent prosecution of this case I have, so far as official etiquette has not imposed reserve,– in the same spirit and to the same end,––striven to impress my Convictions upon the mind of His Honor the Chief Justice.–

Although I succeeded in exposing to His Honor the Judge the false basis of the action and was led to infer that the same evidence in rebuttal would suffice before the Court to immediately reinstate Captain Gill in his rights, it subsequently appeared

75.

that my informal communications were availed of, instead, to substitute a new basis of action; and the forms of procedure, generally, which have characterized the case and had for result the prolonged withholding of justice from my Countrymen* interested, show that I failed to evoke, at the hands of His Honor; that spirit of reciprocal fairness to which equals before the Law are entitled.–

After such protracted, irregular, and vexations proceedings as an inquiry into the course pursued by the Court and a scrutiny of its Record will disclose and in view of the full virtue & proper effect of the Protest presented by me at the period already indicated, my Countrymen* seek now to ascertain through me the intentions of Your Excellency's Government toward them*.

---

* I include Mr Sage the Supercargo, who represents the interests of a Gentleman in New York in the business of the Ship.–

76.

since if its purpose is to longer postpone a full restitution and reinstatement of their rights, it will only remain for them to make their effective appeal to the Executive Officers of the Government of the United States.–

Holding myself disposed to discuss the modes of restitution and re–instatement whenever it may suit Your Excellency's Convenience to summon me for such purpose,

I am,

With great respect,
Sir,
Your Excellency's
Obedient Servant
(signed) Gideon Nye Jnr
Vice Consul of the United States
of America for Macao.–

77.

[No9]

Translation

Sir,

In acknowledging receipt of your Despatch dated the 18th Current about the embargo of the American Ship "Emma" it behoves me to say to you that when in November last you addressed me officially upon the subject, I replied to you repelling the idea of his Government's responsibility in an act purely and entirely of the Judicial Power to which I am a stranger and with whose functions I am forbidden to interfere, for the reason that it is an Independent Power by the Constitution of the Portuguese Monarchy: I stated to you that I would transmit to the Chief Judge of this Colony the documents which accompanied your Despatch as the proper authority to take cognizance of the same;–I then had the honor to add that it was before the said Judge that the interested party should make his claims.–

Afterward, as you know, Mr Gill

78.

gave the necessary power to an Attorney to conduct his case in Court––where it took its course––Mr Gill obtaining a sentence of the Chief Judge in his favor（in so doing this Magistrate certainly showed his impartiality.）

The China man Ahoy––prosecutor of the suit at Law appealed from the Sentence to the higher Tribunal of Goa（Rellação de Goa）according to law––Mr Gill afterward also interposed his recourse toward the same Tribunal.–

It is clear, therefore, that both parties have to conform themselves to the decisions of the Judicial Power, before which, alone they ought to enter into any Conciliations, Compromise or liquidations for loses and damages which Mr Gill had to exact from Ahoy: I am informed, however that the Chief Judge had already ordered the surrender of the vessel to Mr Gill some time since.––

It will be seen from the above Statement that there is no question between American and Portuguese Authorities nor even between these and a subject of the

79.

United States but only a question between two private individuals––One a Chinese resident in this Colony and the other an American Captain of a ship at anchor in this port––that said question was carried before the Civil Court of Macao legally and properly Competent by laws & by Treaties to take it up––that before said Court this suit has had its course, that before the same it ought to be finally decided & all propositions and reclamations laid.––

This principle has been recognized by H. E. Mr Reed Plenipotentiary of the United States when he said that he left this business as it was in the hands of the Chief Judge of Macao relying upon his impartiality.–

I regret that the nature of this question does not permit me to treat of its termination with you, as you propose in your Despatch, because I am certain that I would meet on your part spirit of Conciliation, justice and equity which distinguish you.–

I avail of this occasion to renew the assurance of my distinguished Consideration.––

80.

God preserve you–

Macao 22^d August 1859.

（signed）Isidoro F. Guimarães.

[Gideon Nye, Jr, Esquire.
Vice Consul of the United States of
America in Macao.]

81.

[Copy]

Consulate of the United States
Macao, September 30th 1859.–

Sir,

I have been favored with Your Excellency's reply of the 22d ulto to my renewed representation (of the 18th of the same) of the grievances of Captain Charles Gill Owner and Commander of the American Ship "Emma"; and I beg to acknowledge the marked Courtesy of its form, whilst I am compelled, respectfully, to demur to its terms and to contradict its most material fact.

As the tenor of my said Despatch shows, it was not my purpose to discuss the merits of a question faithfully and sufficiently presented, as I conceived, in November last year, and since established to the apprehension of all persons by the searching and protracted investigation before the local court, but to elicit, instead, at the hands of Y. E. an examination into the Record of the Court and the course of proceedings followed in the case, which could not but result--under the enlightened scrutiny of Y. E.--in full redress of the injuries suffered by my Countrymen,--since it would serve to expose not only the utter inadequacy and intrinsically-defective nature of the grounds of the Original action, but the strange substitution-- after I had exposed

[His Excellency
Isidoro F. Guimarães
Governor General of Macao and
its Dependencies.–
&c. &c. &c.]

2./82.

those defects--of another legally-worthless basis for the continuation of the case. It was at this point, when the case was entering upon a new phase and when, as at every previous stage of it, the original Protest and Declaration had obtained renewed validity and vitality, that my countrymen again sought by the interposition of my Official Appeal to Y. E. to avert further complications and increasing damages.--

I see, however, as well from the general tenor of Y. E. reply as from the misstatement of a fact already alluded to, that no full investigation has been had; whilst in the mean time no reasonable proposition of redress has been made to Captn Gill.–

It is therefore in the necessities of the case that I find an imperative duty, in the absence of those who would sustain the rights of my Countrymen with greater authority to offer the present exposition of its merits to the serious consideration of Your Excellency.

The case from the beginning has involved to me most unwelcome responsibilities and personally disagreeable duties; and although my original position was sustained at every point of investigation and by the Decisions of the Chief Justice – whereby Captn Gill became entitled to full damages–yet I would fain see the whole question terminated by an equitable compromise.

It is in this spirit, although without authority to propose a compromise, that I shall proceed to expose the inherent defects of the grounds of action and of the consequent as well as incidental wrongs

3./83.

inflicted upon my countrymen.–

But before so doing I beg leave in the first place, to demur to the validity of the doctrine upon which Y. E. bases the Disclaimer of responsibility on the part of the Government of which you are the Executive Chief; and in the second place, to correct an error of fact.–

Y. E. is pleased to exempt your Government of responsibility in the case on the ground that it is between two Aliens,– "One a Chinese resident in this Colony and the other an American Captain of a ship anchored in this port," –but, in brief, the Chief Executive Power is surely answerable for the acts of its subordinates, which, in practical effect are its own.–

To say, "that there is no question between American and Portuguese Authorities no even between these and a subject of the United States but only a question between two private individuals" ––is in this case practically to impose by the hand of Power disabilities upon one party with no corresponding direct recourse against the other.–

That the Civil Court of Macao is competent to take up such cases, resting upon adequate legal grounds no one can pretend to dispute;–so that it was not necessary that H. E. M[r] Reed should recognize this principle:–The points, however, of his reply to my application were that he saw no reason for his interposition at that stage of proceedings and that if Capt[n] Gill's case was as good as I thought it, it would be a pity if it were prejudiced by his not meeting it in Court.–H. E. added:– "I have no objection, if you

4./84.

"deem it expedient, to having this decision made known to the Portuguese Authorities, at the same time saying to them that I am not a little influenced by my confidence that the Courts will do justice to my Countrymen; and that if the suit brought against him prove to be unfounded and vexations, he will be indemnified. Of course the Government of the United States reserves, in this as in all other cases, to itself the right to pursue a very different Course in the improbable event of Courts refusing to redress the wrongs of its Citizens." –

When, however, the grounds of action are found to be inadequate, and as H. E. M[r] Reed says,– "The suit brought against the party proves to be unfounded and vexations, – he will be indemnified" .––

Secondly, as to the point of fact referred to in the following paragraph of Y. E.– "the Chinaman Ahoy prosecutor of the suit at Law appealed from the Sentence to the higher Tribunal of Goa （Rellação de Goa） accoding to Law–Mr Gill afterward also interposed his recourse toward the same Tribunal." I beg to say that Captn Gill has from the first and perseveringly resisted the appeal to Goa, as Y. E. will perceive by reference to the enclosed translation of a letter of his Attorney Mr Francisco d' Assis Fernandes of the 9th Ins[t], meeting this special point, and instead of acquiescence in it has interposed his solemn protest against it.–

[vide page 94.]

Moreover he resisted, and with final success, upon the very ground that Ahoy's appeal was not, as Y. E. supposes, "according to Law," --the actual default being

5./85.

a want of adequate security on his part.–

It is thus that at this point I am brought to regard the features of the case, which, as my Countrymen feel,– with, I submit to Y. E., very good reason,–give to it the character of persecution, in the first instance, and of evasion of their just rights in the second.–

What, then, are the circumstances which verify these impressions of my countrymen and so completely establish the responsibility of Your Excellency's Government for the injustice inflicted and persisted in that I cannot dissemble my astonishment at the absence of overtures of equitable compromise?

They have been partially set forth in the Original Declaration and Protest and wrongs as they were at the inception. They have become doubly wrongs by the continuation of the prosecution:--It were enough, surely, to put upon a man material and moral disabilities,–to despoil him of his property by implication of fraud, and having apparently rendered him helpless, then call upon him to defend himself! But no,–the pursuance of a course marked by vacillation and procrastination has subjected my countrymen, beside these direct consequences, to incidental wrongs; whilst the Prosecutor has been allowed to bring independent actions against them, with no possible purpose but that of persecution.–

With what purpose may be conjectured; but with what possible legal result?–

There was but one result possible from the inception of the case, as Y. E. will perceive, as I briefly state the actual circumstance; and as I proceed I beg you

6./86.

to mark the verification of my complaint, of the want of reciprocal fairness in the conditions imposed upon the two parties:–

1st The sequestration of the ship "Emma", bearing the American Flag as the property of Captain Charles Gill her commander, was effected (in the manner stated in the Protest) when she was under charter to Bombay and nearly half laden with the goods of various parties, for which Bills of Lading had already gone forward per mail for a valuable portion; and upon which Charter $4,000. Four thousand Dollars was payable to the ship here, within about a week: Her officers and Crew were shipped & her outfit for the voyage provided.–

There was thus directly involved a pecuniary interest including the cost of the ship of some Forty thousand Dollars, beside the responsibility attaching to Captain Gill's Charter to Bombay and execution of the Bills of Lading of property estimated at $50,000 – say Fifty thousand Dollars value.–

Thus the material stake aggregated near One hundred thousand Dollars, irrespective of damages from detention, deterioration, expenses attaching to the ship &c. &c.–

But, beside this, was the more serious feature of the implication of fraud,–which, moreover, had a double significance in that, it would not only dispossess Captn Gill of his title and of the American Flag along with that, but that it involved an impeachment of the sufficiency of the Laws of the United States relating to navigation, in virtue of which the Flag had been granted to him.--

7./87

Such were the responsibilities assumed by the Court in the seizure of the "Emma" .--

What-upon the other hand-were the grounds deemed sufficient thus to Dispossess an American Ship Owner and Commander of his Vessel, with the coexistent and pertaining rights and responsibilities,-an Owner by a proper Bill of Sale and by possession and exercising these rights in this place for nearly two years?

Simply that a Chinese previously carrying on extensive joint Commercial business at Hongkong, Canton and Macao with a former part-Owner of the "Emma" , then absent; with whom he had quarrelled,-had found some loose papers implying, rather than acknowledging the receipt of about $7,000 say Seven thousand Dollars by said absent party,-being items of an unadjusted and disputed general account between the parties, wherein other items existed on the other side more than sufficient to offset these: a claim in itself, even susceptible of dispute, for want of jurisdiction in the Court, and which upon being met, since, by the Defendant through a Power of Attorney, has been accorded its legitimate Appeal to Goa.

Thus the necessary conditions precedent to seizure do not exist; and the case has presented the anomaly of a forcible retention of the property of a third party with no judgement in Court to satisfy.--

Moreover, the seizure was made in the face of a knowledge, on the part of Captain of the Port Fonseca, of the existence of the clearest documentary proof of Ownership resting in Captain Gill,--the validity of which he had admitted, after due inspection upon

8./88.

a former occasion, and so reported to the Court, as appears from its own Record.-

It became effective, however, after some vascillation upon the part of the Court or other department of the Government, on the 6th of November 1858.-

2nd It was at this point that I waited upon Your Excellency with Documents in my hands of a legal sufficiency to bar the Action; but you did not deign to invite from me an exposition of the merits of the case beyond what the Protest embodied.-

Subsequent to your departure to Shanghae, I had several interviews with His Honor the Chief Justice, with the same purpose; and, finally, on the 25th of November, with my Consular Assistant Mr Van Loffelt as Interpreter, I called upon him and entered so earnestly into merits of the case and presented such incontestible proofs of the validity of Captain Gill's title, in written Documents, that His Honor justified his proceedings by producing to me the Record of the Court (of which he subsequently furnished me a Copy) and the Original Depositions of William Tarrant and Geo. Cooper Turner of Hongkong; as forming the Basis of Action--Whatever disposition I might have had to question the adequacy of a simple deposition of belief, that Captain Gill was not the rightful Owner of the "Emma" but that James McCormick was still the Owner, from parties however much entitled to declare themselves judges in the premises; I had no need to lay stress upon the point, for I discovered, in perusing the Document, that it was utterly worthless from inhorent Defect, or, indeed, worse than that, in that it raised

9./89.

a suspicion of deliberate deception of His Honor:–For to sustain the false declaration that Captain Gill was at Hongkong on the 9th of June 1857 to obtain the Flag of New Granada for the "Emma", they had put in as documentary proof an Original note of Mr Silas, E. Burrows Jr. of the 11th June 1857, the real purport of which was just the contrary, and conclusive against themselves, instead of giving force to their declarations against Captn Gill; and I have original written proof in my possession that this purport was made known to the Prosecutor on the 17th of June 1857 by a friend of his at Hongkong who employed Mr Cooper Turner to make the investigations, indeed a part of the proof is in the handwriting of Mr Turner himself and signed by him.–

The exposure of this perversion of the meaning of the English language to His Honor evidently astonished him; and although he said that it was still necessary for Captain Gill to meet the case in Court with the Documents submitted by me, yet I inferred from the evident impression made by this discovery of the deceptive nature of the Depositions, upon which, as he told me, he had chiefly relied as his basis of action, and by the documentary proof of the validity of Captn Gill's title on the other hand,–that as the Record of the Court, thus based, was form inherent defect, so to speak, susceptible of self-annulment, if it was not, indeed, to be regarded as ipso facto void, he would take the necessary measures himself to reinstate Captain Gill in his rights.–

At the same interview – I inquired as to the security held by the Court from the Prosecutor, when His Honor said it was above

10./90.

Twenty thousand Dollars; and intimated that the Court was further protecting itself: I put the question because from what I had heard I was led to think that adequate security had not then been obtained, although at a previous interview His Honor had said to me that the Prosecutor would be held for all the damages and costs incurred; adding that no doubt he was competent to meet them as he was in Bonds to Government in Eighty thousand Dollars as Farmer of the Gambling-House Contract.

The result that I had hoped for as the fruit of my strenuous endeavors to conciliate the question, was not realized; but on the contrary, reports of an opposite nature were soon after circulated about town purporting to be based upon the opinion of His Excellency Mr Reed.–

3rd The case then entered upon a new phase; but upon what possible bases the prosecution was being carried on I could not imagine;–nor was the reality found to be less strange than the prior conception had been difficult and the protracted delay unaccountable,–when, on one of the last days of February, the decision of His Honor the Chief Justice was announced in Captn Gill's favor.–

Then was revealed the substituted ground of action upon which the case had been continued after I had destroyed, by exposing its own rottenness, the original basis of the Court's proceedings in the seizure of the Vessel; and Your Excellency having now seen the character of that, will, yet, be astonished to hear that the substituted bases of action for the prolongation of this grievous prosecution of my countrymen □□□ hearing testimony of two men who had

11./91.

long been dead–Mr. V. Marques and Mark H. Shaw, and the false statement that the Bill of Sale was executed before Mr Hunter His Honor's decision in February was that this was insufficient; and I respectfully submit that in another portion of the Sentence he virtually acknowledges in words, as he had already done by his act, in granting the appeal to Goa in behalf of McCormik as already stated, that the condition–precedent to sequestration did not exist, in that the insolvency of said McCormik had not been proven;– his words being as follows:– "According to Law the necessary elements to make this sale invalid are of its having taken place after the question had been brought to litigation and the insolvency of the Debtor (proven) but form the Lawsuit and Documents pertaining to it it appears that the sale of the ship was verified on the 18th February 1857–and the Seller McCormik was only summoned to account for his debt to the prosecutor four months after the sale had taken place–that is to say in June of the same year,–in consequence of which according the argument in a Contrary sense to be deduced from Ordinance Book 4th Title 10th S 9th– one of the essential requisites is wanting for invalidating the Contract of Sale.–

"Furthermore, the insolvency of the former Owner of the Ship has not been proved by the documents as it should have and ought to have been done:–as to the statement of the Witness for the prosecution that he owed money to various individuals and did not pay them, it is not that kind of proof which is required at Law to establish the insolvency of a Debtor; in order that the insolvency may

12./92.

be proceed with it is necessary that the circumstances required by the Commercial Code should be apparent. Moreover it is not proved by the Documents of this Lawsuit that the said James McCormik had no other property of his own besides the Ship – that it may be considered as the only property bound to satisfy his debts and as such without any right of disposing freely of it."

Such, as His Honor perspicuously states there, are the principles of Law which should have sufficed to debar action against the "Emma".

With what infraction, then, of all logic as of all right,–after rendering such decision, has His Honor witheld restitution and indemnity to my Countrymen not only; but entertained, for a considerable period, the prayer of the Prosecutor for Appeal to Goa, and even persisted in the demand for Bonds of Captn Gill?–An appeal, moreover, that was obviously not made in bona fide; because the delays and expenses incident thereto would have exceeded any probable ultimate value of the Vessel.–

This demand of Appeal was finally refused; but the logical and legal consequence of the tardy refusal: Namely:–the proceeding to adjudge the damages and execute judgement in favor of the prosecuted,–and as Y. E. will now be in a position to acknowledge–also persecuted Party, is still unannounced to him.–

In thus–with due respect–impeaching His Honor's logic, in fulfilling what I deem my Official duty to my Countrymen and to my Predecessor, who granted the American Flag to Captn Gill for the "Emma", I now reach the point

13./93.

where what I conceive to have been the real difficulty, debarring practical effect to his own convictions, may be stated:–namely:–the inadequacy of the security obtained by the Court, which as Y. E. may be surprised to learn, amounted, up to the 15th of February, to but seven thousand dollars, according to the Official Report in reply to Captn Gill's application, and that no security whatever had been obtained up to the last interview that I had the honor to hold with the Chief Justice.–

I should be very glad to be assured that this impediment of His Honor's progress, in redress of the injuries suffered by my countrymen, accounts for the appearance of particality toward the Prosecutor, to which I have alluded; and that they may now rely upon Y. E.'s exalted sense of right to promote a prompt and full requital of their wrongs.

The satisfaction that would thus be afforded them, would be fully participated in by,

Sir,
Your Excellency's
Obedient Servant
（signed） Gideon Nye, Jr.
Vice Consul of the United States
of America for Macao.

94.

Translation

Macao 9th September 1859.–

My dear Mr Gill,

I have the satisfaction to return to you copies of two despatches–from the Vice Consul of the United States of America and from the Government of this City – concerning the business of your ship "Emma" now laying here.–

Whoever is not acquainted with this business may perhaps infer from H. E.'s Despatch that Mr Gill also interposed his recourse as well as the Claimant Cheong Ahoy and that both parties have to conform themselves with the Decision of the Superior Tribunal of India.

In order to avoid all interpretation in this sense I inform you that on your part no Recourse had been submitted to said Tribunal you have only interposed a Recourse of Grievance （de Agravo de Instrumento） according to a Judicial phrase in Consequence of the Judge having enforced the sequestration which Recourse has become useless and without effect in view of a More recent dispatch of the same Judge relaxing the sequestration of said Ship.–

There is no other Recourse pending but the above one–which has become useless the reason for the complaint having ceased which I intimate to you for your understanding as requested by you, being your attorney.–

I am,
Your Obdt Servt

(signed) F de Assis Fern^{s}

95

Translation.

N° 13.

Sir,

Having received on the 15th Current your Despatch dated the 30th of the past month of September, and the contents relating to the embargo of the American Ship "Emma" to which this Government is a stranger (estranho) , as I have repeated by shown to you, I sent a copy of your Despatch to the Chief Judge of this district who replied to me as by the copy which I have the honor to send herewith as well as of the document annexed to it which responds to your question and proves that I was not ill informed when I said to you in my dispatch of the 22^{d} ult^{o} that Captn Gill had appealed to the higher Tribunal of Goa (Relação de Goa)

The wish expressed by you that this question might be treated between us is pleasing to me, but I regret that I was not fortunate enough to make myself understood when I affirmed that this question of the "Emma" is in no way connected with me or within my competence, that I am unable to discuss its merits or the mode in which it has been treated in the Court of this City, which is a tribunal independent of me the Judge being in no way my subordinate.–

These were the principles that I express to you in my dispatches of the 8th of November 185□ and of the 22nd August of the Current year which I now confirm.–

96.

When the question would have to take another form and would have to pass from the Judical power to the Government, it will appertain to His Majesty's Government to treat it–not only because it is thus determined by the treaties between Portugal and the United States, but also because to the Government alone it belongs to investigate the acts of Judges in Conformity with the Law.–

I again express to you the regret I have at not being able to treat this question with you and to have to repeat it is to the Chief Judge of this city, to whom it is intrusted, that the interested parties will have to address all representations relating to it.––

I avail of this occasion to renew to you the assurances of my distinct Consideration.

God preserve you – Macao 27th October 1859

(Signed) Isidoro F. Guimarães––

[Gideon Nye Jr Esquire
Vice Consul of the United States of America
at Macao.–]

97.

Translation.

Sir,

I have the honor to acknowledge the Dispatch of Y. E. of the 18th Current enclosing another from the Vice Consul of the United States relating to the pending question of the embargo of the American Ship "Emma" –

Beginning by saying to Y. E. that I am very sorry it is not allowable to me to throw back directly intact the injurious expressions to my honor as Magistrate of this Colony contained in the final paragraph of the Vice Consul's dispatch addressed to Y. E. and with the dignity becoming to my personal character and the office I exercise, make him feel not only that I do not allow the honors of Comparison between the impartiality with which this question has been ventilated in Court and the impartiality, good faith and masterly manner with which it has been treated and supported by the noble Vice Consul, but also the courteous and becoming manner with which the arena of official discussion is to be entered upon between Public Functionaries of two independent nations.–

I shall proceed to signify to Y. E. that I do not either discuss the merits and mode by which this question has been treated in this Court as I have the warranty of independence in the quality of Magistrate of a Constitutional Government, at the same time I do not fear the responsibility

98.

of my acts not only in this question between all those which have been judged in this capacity.–

The law does not designate this as the place suitable for me to give an account of my proceeding and for this reason alone I abstain from entering into discussion of this subject. I confine myself to give the information which Y. E. wishes to obtain whereupon to base your reply to Mr Nye.–

The prosecutor in this case signed, in conformity with the Law, a bond of responsibility (termo do responsabilidade) for the embargo of the said ship: the enclosed certificate will show to Y. E. the manner in which this security has been verified.– In my information directed to Y. E. I stated that Captn Gill had interposed a recourse towards the higher Tribunal of Goa (Relação de Goa) the same as Y. E. stated to Mr Nye in your dispatch of the 22 August last and as proof of the correctness of which I then stated. I refer to the same certificate.– –It matters not whether this recourse had taken place by means of Appeal or of the Aggravo d' Instrumento, or whether it took effect or not the fact is that recourse was interposed and is signed by the Counsel Francisco d'Assis Fernandes attorney for Captn Gill before the Court.–

I conclude my dispatch by saying to Y. E. that some of the communications

99.

which the Vice Consul says I made to him in the interview which took place between me and him, are not only without the quality of verisimilitude but also foreign to truth.–

God preserve Y. E. Macao 20th October 1859.–
His Excellency the Counsellor Isidoro Franco Guimarães Governor of this Province–
The Chief Judge of Macao – signed – Augusto Henrique R. Carvalho.–

True Copy

(signed) José Carlos Barros.

100.

Translation
Certificate.

Francisco Antonio Pereira da Silveira Clerk of the Civil Court acting Notary Public by the grace of His Most Faithful Majesty whom may God preserve.–

I certify that on inspection of the copies of the documents pertaining to the Case of Nullity of the Sale of the Barque "Emma" there appears @L 4 the sentence of the 21st February of the present year given by the Chief Judge by which the purchase of the said barque by Captn Gill was judged valid–said Sentence having been intimated to Captain Gill by a petition of 42 he signified that on account of certain expressions used therein, relating to embargoes he could not conform himself to it and desired that the said petition might be annexed to the documents pertaining to the Lawsuit, the Dispatch to this petition was given on the first of March to annex it to the other documents in the sense that he disagreed with that portion of the sentence to which it alludes.

By the original Documents of embargo or arrest @ L 59 it appears that Captn Gill asked the Judge for a declaration of the said Sentence which was granted in the following tenor: Declaring the sentence which the judged valid the purchase and Sale of the ship "Emma" in relation to the Embargo of sequestration of said ship I don't admit them on the grounds exposed in same

101.

Sentence–adding however with the reference to the nullity – which were considered as extemporaneous for the sequestration of the ship having taken place as a comminatory duty for want of guarantee or security of the court the arrested ought to have made use of the embargo without loss of time – and not to have opposed them only after more than two months had elapsed conformably to the practice of the Forum attested by Pereira e Souza.–

As to the effect of the said Sentence it is evident that it having been appealed from and the same causes of want of security to the Court exist, the sequestration stands good and can only be relaxed when the Counter part Consents to it in the way it deems more convenient to its interests. The arrested to pay the expenses of this incident.–

Macao 2d April 1859. (signed) Augusto Henrique Ribeiro de Carvalho

In view of this Dispatch Captn Gill's Attorney interposed a Recourse towards the higher tribunal of Goa （Relação de Goa） and the same attorney signed the Act of Aggravo d' Instrumento towards the Relação on the 6th of April of this year.–I further certify that it appears from the same series of documents of 75 that on the twenty seventh of May the embargo or arrest of the "Emma" was released but until the present time Captn Gill has not wished to take charge of her. It appears also from the

102.

same papers of 44 that on the 2^{d} of December eighteen hundred and fifty eight the Chinese arrester signed in confirmity with the law the Bond of responsibility for a sum of twenty thousand dollars of which five thousand under guarantee and fifteen thousand to be paid by the arrester into the treasury （Deposito） but he having only paid down seven thousand dollars and omitted the payment of the remainder, he has been imprisoned in the Jail according to the dispatch of the Procurador of this city of the 17th Current to the end of completing the payment for which he bound himself.–

In testimony whereof and by order of the chief Judge I have granted the present （certificate） Macao Nineteenth of October eighteen hundred and fifty nine–Done and signed by me the said Clerk.–

（signed） Fran^{co} A. P^{a}. da Silveira.––

True Copy
（signed） José Carlos Barros.–

103.

[Defeat of Prosecutor's Appeal to Goa,]

Translation of the decision of the Supreme Court of Judicature of the States of Portuguese India at Goa.–

It has been awarded in conference, that the present question relating purely to a commercial object––such as the validity or invalidity of the purchase of a ship, it is manifest that it should have been entered upon as a commercial question in view of the express and definitive provision of Art: 204 and following of its N° 4th–and of Art: 1029 of the Commercial Code–which not having been done, the case was brought before an incompetent Judge, therefore the present process is wholly annulled by the reasons of the incompetency of the Judge in question––the expense to be paid by appealing Prosecutor.––

New Goa 8th November 1859.–
（signed） Ferreira Pinto = Faustino Crespo =Vasconcellos.–

104.

Bond of Compromise

On the 13th January 1860 at Macao before the substitute of the Juiz de Directo Mr João Baptista Gomes– appeared the Chinese Cheong Ahoy and Captain Charles Gill for the purpose of signing a compromise in order to adjust the question of the Barque "Emma" by means of Arbitrators appointed by the two parties who have agreed upon the following points.–

1° That Captn Gill acquiescing in the proposition of Cheong Ahoy, agrees with him to submit to three Arbitrators the liquidation of damages and losses and stoppage of earnings which he has suffered by the sequestration of the Barque Emma required by Cheong Ahoy against which prejudices and loss of earnings he protested in due time.

2° That Captn Gill's right to freight of $4,000 already earned, as by the Documents submitted, will not become a matter of question for the reason that he would have received this freight before the voyage if he had not been impeded in consequence of the arrest of the Emma.–

3° That the interest on this freight is reduced to one half of the rate under protest that this is to say–@6% according to argument without prejudice to the right of Captn Gill to a higher rate of interest, in accordance with his Protest, on further amounts of his claim.

4° That the said freight & interest will be paid on the occasion of taking back the ship Emma–which Captn Gill will receive after survey and Inventory shall have been made to the end of ascertaining the deterioration by

105.

comparing its present state with the anterior one at the time of the arrest, more than a year ago, and it is desirable that the same be proceeded with in the presence of the 3 arbitrators presently named.–

5° That for the liquidation of the Damages and losses aforesaid, as well as for the deterioration of the vessel above alluded to, Captn Gill appoints for his Arbitrator James B. Endicott, Esqre–Cheong Ahoy appoints Franco Joaqm Marques Esqre and the Baron de Cercal to be the Umpire–Chosen by Cheong Ahoy and approved by Captn Gill; to the decision of the appointed Arbitrators the compromising parties will be obliged to submit to without complaint or Appeal or any other recourse whatever–which by these presents they renounce.–

6° That the 3d Arbitrator will not be obliged precisely to choose one of the two awards when they clash integrally but will be allowed to scrutinize each point of liquidation no matter whether it be from one or the other of the arbitrators or even to modify or alter some of the points should he deem it advisable provided he keeps within the limits of the two awards.

7° That Captn Gill will submit to the Arbitrators the points of his reclamation for liquidation with the Documents and Witnesses that he may have, which may be contested by Cheong Ahoy––who will offer those on his side, waiving other formalities prescribed by the Laws, unless the parties require them and the arbitrators deem it useful to the case.

8° That the expense of the Process or Processes of the Emma will be paid after sentence from the amounts deposited subject to the order of the Court.–

106.

In testimony, therefore, to what they said, and agreed upon, I drew this Bond which after being read to them, they signed with me, the clerk who drew it up.–

(signed) Franc° Ant° Per[a] da' Silveira
(signed) Charles Gill
(signed) Cheong Ahoy – in Chinese characters
(signed) Silveira

(signed) Gomes–

107.

[Award of Umpire]

Having seriously and conscientiously examined the documents in relation to this Lawsuit, and conferred with my co-arbitrators Fran[co] Joaq[m] Marque and J. B. Endicott for the better understanding of the question, by way of discussion, I came to the conclusion that the Chinese Cheong Ahoy ought to indemnify Charles Gill, Captain and Owner of the ship "Emma" for all damages and losses expenses & disappointments to him caused in consequence of the lawsuit attempted by the said Cheong Ahoy against him– Apart from the expense incurred with the American Consulate, with the Attorney of the Prosecuted, & with the legal costs, the sum of $14,665 – say,

Besides the $4,300 paid at folio–94 as freight of the ship to Bombay, and interest agreed upon,–Cheong Ahoy shall pay in compensation for the time during which the ship has been under embargo reckoning from the 15th February 1859 when the termination of her voyage to and discharge at Bombay is calculated as having taken place, since the prosecuted has already been indemnified for the time elapsed in the interval, with the $4,300–which he recessed also the estimated amount necessary for the repairs to put the ship in the state in which she was at the time of the embargo,…… $5,200

As subsidy to the Captain for the time he was on shore–350 days from the 15th Feby, 1859 to 31 January 1860–@ $40 p[r] Month…… $466

To repair various destruction and deterioration sustained by the ship, inclusive of difference in the Inventory···$9,000

Furthermore, I think the Chinese Cheong Ahoy

108.

is to have the option to undertake the repair of the ship and to fill up the wants of the Inventory for his own account should he wish it, and in that case he is to decide within 5 days from this date–the work done to be subject to the inspection and approval of the surveyors of the Underwriters of Hongkong.–

Should the repairs be made for account and at the expense of Cheong Ahoy – I judge that a sum of $9,000 should be deducted from the above specified $14,665 – arbitrated for those repairs.–

As regards the relaxation of the arrest of the ship, I don't deem it advisable to allude to–– it being a subject beyond my competency, –the compromise which restrains the decision of the arbitrators to the liquidation of losses and damages, says, that in the appreciation of the said losses and damages, the deterioration of the ship in its present state as compared with that anterior to the time of the arrest upwards of a year – will be made apparent.––

(signed) Barão do Cercal

Macao 29 March 1860.–

109.

In the name of God. Amen – Know all those to whom this Instrument shall come that in the year of the birth of O. L. J. C. 1860 on the 25th of June at Macao before me F. A. P. da Silveira Clerk & Notary Public appeared Captn Charles Gill a native of America, known by me, who stated in presence of the Witness undersigned, that he wanted to protest before me, the Notary Public––against the Chinese Cheong Ahoy & against all those whom be ought to protest against, for the new damages & stoppage of earnings already happened or to happen by default of payment of the sum awarded by the arbitrators. Whereas he should have been paid the total sum in which the said Cheong Ahoy was condemned after the ratification of the sentence––he has barely received $3,942$\frac{666}{1000}$ on virtue of the Judical Marasmus leaving a balance of 11,973$\frac{634}{1000}$ to be paid––which he supposes does not exist in the Deposit of the Court or he would have been paid at the same time.

That the said Chinese Cheong Ahoy having signed in Court a bond by which he was obliged in form of Law in order to effect the sequestration of the ship "Emma" –binding himself for the damages, losses & stoppage of earnings, the Court should be secured with the necessary guarantees required by the Law in order to prevent the said responsibility from becoming fictitious–for reason of the said Cheong Ahoy being a foreigner–he has not paid into the Deposit–at least as Charles Gill supposes–having not been paid up to this date after a lapse of two months since the proferring of the sentence.–

110.

That in consequence of this want of payment, he has been obliged to remain in this City incurring exorbitant expenses & that he is now obliged to leave appointing an Attorney in his stead––who will likewise be obliged to incur expenses–all of which must be borne by those who have given occasion for them.–

That the present Protest being a sequence of the former one which he entered on the occasion of the sequestration of the "Emma" & based upon the same principles––he refers himself to it – of which the present is a part and parcel. Therefore he declares to protest against all whom he can by right do.–

1st for Commercial interest on the balance due him fixed at the rate of 1%@ Mo for malicious delay.–

2d for losses sustained or that may be hereafter sustained for his maintenance, dwelling & so forth or those of his Attorney or his substitute–when said Attorney shall absent himself–all reckoned from the date of the ratification of the sentence of the Arbitrators until its effective reimbursement.–

said Protest he declared to be not only against the above mentioned Cheong Ahoy–but against all those whom it may concern in terms of his first Protest & requested of me the said Notary–that this Protest might be intimated to Cheong Ahoy & that Two Copies be given to him the said Charles Gill.

Thus done & Protested–which after being read over to the appearer & witnesses Jozé Joaqm Borjes & Francisco de Paula they signed together with me the said Notary who drew it out & subscribed to it.

111.

In testimony whereof–signed F. A. P da Silveira–C. G. Jozé Joaqm Borjes, Franco de Paula–True Copy of the Original Protest entered at page 87 of my Notorial Register to which I refer.–

Done & subscribed by me the said Clerk & Notary–In Testimony of Truth.––

（signed） F. A. P. da Silveira.

112.

[Copy]

Consulate of the United States.
Macao, July 2nd 1860.–

Excellent Sirs,

In obedience to the dictates of my Official duty, I waited upon His Excellency Governor General Guimarães on the 8th of November 1858 and presented the Protest of Captain Charles Gill, a citizen of the United States, against the seizure of the ship "Emma" at the suit of a Chinese known as Cheong Ahoy.–The subsequent decision of His Honor the Chief Justice vindicated the rights of Captain Gill in the premises; but the extraordinary witholding of the full redress which is his due now compels him–after the expiration of a period of about twenty months–to again Protest and Claim the damages incident to this delay of justice.–

It becomes my Duty, therefore, to present his formal Protest as made in due form before the Public Notary of this City on the 25th Ulto and again at the Consulate of the United States of America before myself, and to claim for him the prompt execution of the sentence in the case and the Damages thence accrued and accruing, as set forth in the said Protest.–

Respectfully requesting your attention to those Documents,

I have the honor to be, Excellent Sirs,
Your obedient Servant
（signed） Gideon Nye, Jr.
Vice Consul of the United States

for Macao.--

[□□□ Honorable
The Members of the
Council of Government of Macao.--]

113.

[Copy]

Macao, 10th April 1861.-

Dear Sir,

I have to trouble you again in regard to the case of the ship "Emma".

Following the instructions of our Minister Mr Ward; who also informed me that it was the wish of His Excellency the Governor of Macao, I placed in the hands of the procurador of this city, the prosecutor Chinaman, Cheong Ahoy, and his bondsman, Mestrino, the former on the 7th of February last, and the latter some weeks before that date, by presenting to that officer an order of the Judge to imprison both the said Chinamen, if they should fail to pay what was due, or give good security for the amount, within twenty four hours after the receipt of the order.

I have made two petitions to the procurador, to know what he has done in the case. He has given no answer to either and told me yesterday that he had no reply to give that one of the men had gone out of town week or two since, and the other had said to him that he had paid all he could to the Judge. He has in fact disobeyed both the orders of the Judge, now two months in his hands, although I have sent twice a week to know what diligence had been made, and although he had the orders before the Chinese new year, the time when a Chinaman would make greater efforts to be free than at any order.

I have waited until now to have the shops sold, which were taken as security for $6,500. They are sold at last, after ten months delay, and for a sum that is less than one half my expenses waiting during that time,

114.

namely for $401.-

As I am not inclined to lose any more time, I enclose you my claim including interest and my expenses here, made up to the 1st Current. It is made out according to a protest before the Court, made last June, and includes the $401, which I have not however yet received.

I wish you to make an official demand upon the proper Authorities, for the payment of the amount.-

Should they not see fit to pay it, I have no other alternative but to send the case as it stands to the Secretary of State at Washington, who has already notified me that the government will act upon it, so soon as I furnish him with the remainder of the papers.

Mr Ward advised me not to delay sending the necessary documents to Washington, after the sale of the shops, should the Macao government not pay the claim, as there was in his mind no question about the recovery of it, and I had also the word of the Secretary of State. He however thought that they would not, in looking to their own interest, let a debt go to Portugal which they will eventually have to pay, one that is increasing so fast, and one so illegal in all its features. He said moreover that His Excellency the Governor took quite an interest in the case, and he left assured that he would arrange it in some way.–

Leaving it in your hands,

I have the honor to be
Sir, yo. mo. obt. Servt.
（signed） Edwd. J. Sage

[To
Gideon Nye, Jr. Esq.
U. S. Vice Consul
for Macao]

Dr. Memorandum of sum due by Prosecutor in the case of the ship "Emma", transferred to E. J. Sage. atty. Dr.

1860 Jany	31	To award of damages	14,665	00	1860 June	6	By Cash received from Court	3,942	36		
		To award of Court, Consul fees, etc.	1,250	00			By Cash Int to 1st Apl /61. 10 mos @ 1%	394	23	4,336	50
		Interest to 1st Apl / 61 14 mos @ 1%	2,228	10	Sept.	17	By Cash rec^{d} from Fantan	400			
Dec 1861	10	To Court fees paid Mr Silveira	19	43			Int 6 1/2 mos	26	00	426	00
□□□	1	To Expenses of attorney from 29 March 1860 the date of the award unt^{o} date, as per protest made before the Court 25 June /60 viz. 12 mos @ $150	1,800	00	Nov.	5	By Cash rec^{d} from Court	890	70		
							Int 5 mos	49	53		
					Dec.	8	By Cash from Mestrino	1,000	00		
							Int 4 mos	40	00	1,040	□□
							By Cash sales houses (not received)	401			
							To Bal a/c			12,818	□□
			$19,962	53						$19,962	
	1	To Bal of a/c	$12,818	71							

116.

[Copy–]

Consulate of the United States.–
Macao, April 16th 1861.–

Sir,

It has again become my duty to appeal to Your Excellency in behalf of my countrymen interested in the case of the seizure of the ship "Emma"; and that I may not fail to convey a precise idea of the helpless situation in which they now stand, I beg leave to submit to Your Excellency's notice a copy of the communication of Mr Edward J. Sage–who represents the aggrieved parties–of the 10th Inst, setting forth the circumstances which have transpired since His Excellency Mr Ward last drew Your Excellency's attention to the case, in November, and referring to an accompanying Statement of the pecuniary Account of the present position of the claim, shewing the sum of $12,818 $\frac{71}{100}$ say, Twelve thousand eight hundred eighteen and $\frac{71}{100}$ Dollars due on the 1st instant.–

Mr Sage is now apprised by his Attorney that every requirement and recourse of the Law has been exhausted by him, so that he is absolved– as he is debarred–from further prosecution of the case through that channel.–

It is at this point, that I beg have to submit the claims and to, respectfully, ask, in his bame, for their prompt liquidation.

[His Excellency
Isidoro F. Guimarães.
Governor General of Macao
and its Dependencies.–
&c &c &c]

117.

The consideration that a period exceeding two years has expired since the decision of the Court in favor of my countrymen and that the claims are becoming rapidly augmented by damages, imposes upon me the duty to renewedly crave Your Excellency's attention to them.––

I have the honor to be,
With great respect,
Sir,
Your Excellency's
Most obedient Servant
(signed) Gideon Nye, Jr:
Vice Consul of the United States
of America for Macao.–

118.

[relation.–
Governo de Macao.–
diente dos □□□ Estrangros
No. 11]

Illtmo Snr.

I have the honor to acknowledge the receipt of your Despatch respecting the indemnities which Cheong Ahoy was sentenced to pay for the arrest of the ship Emma.–

This matter being strange (i. e. beyond the competent cognizance of) to this Government I sent your

Despatch and other Documents to the Chief Justice of this District, and I will hasten to report to you what he informs in response thereto.–

I avail of this opportunity to renew to you the assurances of my distinct consideration.–

God preserve you.– Macao 18th April 1861.––

（signed） Isidoro F. Guimarães–

[Itlmo Snr G. Nye–
□□□ Consul of the United States.–]

Quarterly Return of the Arrival and Departure of American Vessels at the Consulate of the United States at Macao from the 1st of April to the 30th of June 1861.

Date		Class	Name	Tons	Where from	When Built	Vessels			Cargo		Owners	Captains
							Where built	Where belonging	Where bound	Import	Export		
April	10th	Brig	Orbit	154 47/95	Saigon	1845	Dorchester	Portland	HongKong Apl 13th	Rice	Ballast	H. C. Leonard	F. A. Sherman
May	8th	Ship	Southern Cross	938 48/95	Saigon	1851	Boston	Boston	Bangkok June 12th	Rice	Ballast	Chs J. Morrile	Banj. P. Howea
June	15th	Ship	Norseman	811 89/95	Saigon	1856	Boston	Boston		Rice		A. Cunningham	Wm Peterson
				1904 89/95									

Gideon Nye Jnr.
Vice Consul of the United States
of America for Macao.–

[Macao 3d
Returns 2d J. 1861
With despatch No 26.]

[□□□ received at the States
local office □□□ 23d 1861

□□□]

[1-091]

[Rec 19 □□□ Mr. Abbott
Return to State Bureau
No26.–]

Consulate of the United States
Macao July 2nd 1861.–

Sir,

Referring to my Desatch Nº 24 in which I forwarded the Returns of this Consulate for the previous quarter, I now beg to hand you those of the quarter ending the 30th June 1861.

I am,

Sir,

With great respect

Your obedient Servant

Gideon Nye, Jnr

Vice Consul of the United States

of America for Macao.–

[The Honorable

William H. Seward–

Secretary of State of the United States

of America–

City of Washington–]

United States Consulate at Macao.

Fees received during the Quarter ending 30th June 1861.

Date	Nº	Name of Vessel	Name of the party paying the fee	Nature of service rendered	Amount of fees paid	
5th		Albers	Yturraldi	Certifying Copy of Certificate of New Ownership	$2	
13th	1	Orbit	F. Sherman	Deposit of papers $154\frac{47}{95}$ tons @ 1/2 ct:		77
17th		Orbit	F. Sherman	Discharging two men	$1	
12th	2	Southern Cross	Beny: P. Howes	Deposit of papers $938\frac{48}{95}$ tons @ 1/2 ct:	$4	69
		Southern Cross	Beny: P. Howes	Noting Protest	$1	
		Southern Cross	Beny: P. Howes	Government charge of one Month's wages for each seaman discharged say 3 men @ □□□ 12	$36	
		Southern Cross	Beny: P. Howes	Discharging three men	$1	50
		Southern Cross	Beny: P. Howes	Shipping 11 men	$5	
24t		–	Franco de Pe Sá	Authenticating 4 signatures	$5	
□□□		Spark	J. B. Endicott	Tonnage fees 37 trips 100 tons ca @ 1/2	$18	50
		Rose	J. B. Endicott	Tonnage fees 1 trips 74 tons ca @ 1/2		37
					$74	83

Gideon Nye Jnr

Vice Consul of the United States

of America for Macao–

[1-092]

Quarterly Return of the Arrival and Departure of American Vessels at the Consulate of the United States at Macao from the 1st of July to the 30th of September 1861.–

N^{o}	Date	Class	Name	Tons	Where from	When Built	Vessels			Cargo		Owners	Captains
							Where built	Where belonging	Where bound	Import	Export		
1	July 27^{t}	Bark	Penguin	$583\frac{81}{95}$	Hongkong	1854	New York	New York	New York Augt 14th	Rice & Tea	Rice & Tea	C. H. R. Squian & others	Joa. Brereton
2	Augt 30th	Bark	Curlew	$495\frac{41}{95}$	Hongkong	1860	Fairhaven	Boston	Shanghae Sept 12th	Ballast	Sugar	W. O. Cowstock & others	H. A. Ballard
3	Augt 30th	Bark	Hollander	500	Hongkong	Did not enter		Boston	Bangkok	Ballast	Sugar	W. O. Cowstock & others	L. P. Ward
4	Septr 3^{d}	Bark	Cossack	$586\frac{33}{95}$	Singapore	1854	Boston	Boston	Hongkong Sep^{t} 17th	General	Ballast	Sawl. F. Daua	H. N. Gray
				$2165\frac{60}{95}$									

Gideon Nye, Jnr
Vice consul of the United States
of America for Macao

[Macao
4th qr

Received at the
Statistical Office
Dec 24 1861]

[N°27. Recd 29 □□□]

Consulate of the United States
Macao, October 3rd 1861.–

[Rct □□□ □□□]

Sir,

Referring to my Despatch N° 26 in which I forwarded the Returns of this Consulate for the previous quarter, I now beg to hand you those of the quarter ending the 30th September 1861.–

I am,

Sir,
With great respect,
Your obedient Servant
Gideon Nye Jnr
Vice Consul of the United States
of America for Macao.–

[The Honorable
William H. Seward–
Secretary of State of the United States
of America.–
City of Washington.–]

United States Consulate at Macao.–
Fees received during the Quarter ending 30th September 1861.–

Date	No	Name of Vessel	Name of the party paying the fee	Nature of service rendered	Amount of fees paid	
□□1st	–	–	Fran^co de P. e Sá	Authenticating four signatures	$4	–
□□8th	3	Norseman	Wm Peterson	Deposit of Papers 811 $\frac{89}{95}$ tons @ 1/2 ct:	$4	06
□□"		Norseman	Wm Peterson	Shipping 18 men	$5	
□□"		Norseman	Wm Peterson	Certificate of inability to get 2/3 □□□ Am Crew		50
□□"		Norseman	Wm Peterson	Certificate of desertion of 20 men	$10	
□□13th	–	Estrelle & Reine	C. L de la Chapelle	Noting Marine protest –	$1	
□□15t	1	Penguin	J. Brereton	Deposit of Papers 583 $\frac{81}{95}$ tons @ 1/2 ct:	$2	92
□□"		Penguin	J. Brereton	shipping 2 men	$1	
□□"		Penguin	J. Brereton	Cert: of discharge of J. Gardner		50
□□"		Hollander	L. P. Ward, Master	No fee – Vessel did not enter	$0	00
□□12th	2	Curlew	H. A. Ballard	Deposit of Paper 495 $\frac{44}{95}$ tons @ 1/2 ct:	$2	48
		Curlew	H. A. Ballard	Shipping 10 Men	$5	
□□	3	Cossack	H. N. Gray	Deposit of Papers 586 $\frac{33}{95}$ tons @ 1/2 ct:	$2	93
		Cossack	H. N. Gray	Noting marine protest –	$1	
□□□0th		Spark	J. B. Endicott	Tonnage fees 27 trips 100 tons @@ 1/2 ct:	$13	50
					$53	89

Gideon Nye, Jur
Vice Consul of the United States
of America for Macao.

[1–093]

United States of America,
Department of State.

To all to whom these presents shall come greeting:

Know Ye, that the bearer hereof, Edward Harte, Esquire, Consul of the United States, at Macao, China, is now proceeding therein.

These are therefore to request all whom it may concern, to permit him to pass freely without let or molestation, and to extend to him all such friendly aid and protection as would be extended to Consul of Foreign Governments, resorting to the United States.

In testimony whereof, I, William H. Seward, Secretary of State of the United States of America, have hereunto signed my name, and caused the Seal of this Department to be affixed at Washington, this twenty–fifth day of November A. D. 1861, and of the Independence of the United States the 86th.

Will. H. Sewd.

[1-094]

[Macao
1st qr
4th qr

Received at the
Statistical Office
□□□ 25 18/12Dec 31/ 61]

[Rec 21, Mar. Mr Abbott
N°28.-]

Consulate of the United States
Macao January 3rd 1862.-

Sir,

Referring to my Despatch N° 27 in which I forwarded to you the Returns of this Consulate for the previous quarter, I now beg to hand you those of the quarter ending the 31st of December 1861.-

I am,
Sir,
With great respect
Your Obedient Servant
Gideon Nye, Jnr
Vice Consul of the United States
of America for Macao.-

[The Honorable
William H. Seward
Secretary of State of the United States of
America
City of Washington.]

Quarterly Return of the Arrival and Departure of American Vessels at the Consulate of the United States at Macao – from the 1st of October to the 31st of December 1861.-

Date		Class	Name	Tons	Where from	When Built	Vessels			Cargo		Owners	Captains
Mon,	Day						Where built	Where belonging	Where bound	Import	Export		
	2d	Ship	Marion	449 $\frac{59}{95}$	Hongkong	1846	Portland	Boston	In Port	Ballast	–	Adam W. Jhacter Jr. and Joker D. Batic	Fredk A. Gross

	24'	Bark	Hollander	498 54/95	Bangkok	1849	Newbury	Salem	In Port	Rice	–	Henry L. William & other	L. □□□ Sheid
				948 18/95									

Gideon Nye Jnr.
Vice Consul of the United States
of America for Macao

United States Consulate at Macao.–
Fees received during the Quarter ending 31st December 1861.

Date	N°	Name of Vessel	Name of the party paying the fee	Nature of service rendered	Amount of fees paid	
□□29th			G. W. Mellen	Authenticating signatures of Judge & Clerk, Consequal of Lorcha □□□	$2	–
□□27th			A. A. de Mells & Co	Acknowledgements to 2 Powers of Attorney	$4	–
□□27th			A. A. de Mells & Co	Certificate to a Copy of Bill of Lading	$2	–
□□31th		Spark	J. B. Endicott	Tonnage fees 41 trips @ 100 tons @ 1/2 ct	$20	50
					$28	50

Gideon Nye Jnr.
Vice Consul of the United States
of America for Macao

[1–095]

[Recd 5 Mch]

Consulate of the United States of America.
Macao February 26th 1862.–

Sir,

I was favored with the duplicate of your Despatch of the 25th of November on the 16th instant, apprising me that the President had appointed Edward Harte of California Consul of the United States at Macao, and requesting me to deliver to him the Records and archives of the Consulate, the Seal, Flag, and arms, together with the Statutes at Large, and such other books and property as is in my possession belonging to the Government.–

I have the honor, in reply, to intimate that I shall have great satisfaction in complying with this request;–as I cannot permit myself to doubt that the choice of the President has fallen upon a Gentleman worthy to represent our Country, at this period of peril.

So far as I hear, Mr Harte has not yet arrived in China; but I hope soon to be relieved of an office which was unsought by me and which has involved responsibilities and

[The Honorable
William H. Seward

Secretary of State of the United States
of America.
City of Washington.]

vexations, as well as pecuniary sacrifices, which as yet, have only been compensated by a consciousness of faithfully and successfully serving my Country.——

I have the honor to remain,
Sir,
Your very obedient Servant
Gideon Nye, Jnr
Vice Consul of the United States
of America for Macao.–

[1-096]

[Recd June 14
N° 30.–]

Consulate of the United States.
Macao, April 11th 1862.

Sir,

Referring to my Despatch N° 28, in which I forwarded to you the Returns of this Consulate for the previous quarter, I now beg to hand you those of the quarter ending the 31st of March 1862.–

I am,
Sir,
With great respect
Your obdt Servant
Gideon Nye Jnr.
Vice Consul of the United States
of America for Macao.–

[The Honorable
William H. Seward
Secretary of State of the United States
of America.–
City of Washington.–]

United States Consulate at Macao

Fees received during the Quarter ending 31st March 1862.

Date	N°	Name of Vessel	Name of the party paying the fee	Nature of service rendered	Amount of fees paid	
□□25	2	Hollander	L. Peirson Ward	Deposit of Papers 498 $\frac{54}{95}$ tons @1/2 cent	$2	49
	2	Hollander	L. Peirson Ward	Noting Marine Protest	$1	–
	2	Hollander	L. Peirson Ward	Extending Marine Protest	$2	–
	2	Hollander	L. Peirson Ward	701 add^s words beyond the 200	$7	01
	2	Hollander	L. Peirson Ward	Discharging 12 men	$5	–
	2	Hollander	L. Peirson Ward	Paper Bill of sale of the "Hollander"	$1	
	2	Hollander	L. Peirson Ward	Additional words beyond 100	$1	50
	2	Hollander	L. Peirson Ward	Certified Copy of Power of Attorney	$1	50
	2	Hollander	L. Peirson Ward	Cancelling Register of "Hollander"	50	–
	2	Hollander	L. Peirson Ward	Declaration of desertion of 6 seamen	$3	–
□□16	1	Marion	F. H. Gross	Deposit of papers 449 $\frac{85}{95}$ tons @1/2 cent	$2	25
16	1	Marion	F. H. Gross	Shipping 12 Men	$6	–
□□5	3	Cornelia L. Bevan	James Pedersen	Deposit of Papers 330 $\frac{65}{95}$ tons @ 1/2 cent	$1	65
5	3	Cornelia L. Bevan	James Pedersen	Cancelling Register of "Cornelia L. Bevan"		50
□□10	1	Emma	Ab^m Stuarman	Deposit of Papers 444 $\frac{59}{95}$ tons @ 1/2 cent	$2	22
10	1	Emma	Ab^m Stuarman	Shipping 15 Men	$5	–
□□27	6	Soo Loo	J. B. Eamse	Deposit of Papers 629 18/95 tons @ 1/2 cent	$3	15
□□28	5	Kate Hastings	Seth K. Hingman	do do 448 $\frac{12}{95}$. do. do	$2	24
□□1	4	Contest	Joseph Steele	do do 1,098 $\frac{92}{95}$. do. do	$5	49
1	4	Contest	Joseph Steele	Discharging 1 Man	$	50
□□4	7	Rover	G. W. Mellen	Recording Bill of Sale of Lorcha N°16 1,942 words @ 20¢ p^r each 100 words–	$3	90
4	7	Rover	G. W. Mellen	Certificate of Ownership	$	50
□□10	2	Raven	Crocker Nye	Deposit of papers 711 $\frac{82}{95}$ tons @ 1/2 cent	$3	56
10	2	Raven	Crocker Nye	Discharging 1 Man	$	50
10	2	Raven	Crocker Nye	Certificate of desertion of 2 men	$1	–
□□18	8	Sea Serpent	Same^l W. Pike	Deposit of Papers 1,337 $\frac{13}{95}$ tons @ 1/2 cent	$6	69
18	8	Sea Serpent	Same^l W. Pike	Shipping 2 men	$1	–
□□21	9	Spec	Peter Hussey	Deposit of papers 302 $\frac{40}{95}$ tons @ 1/2 cent	$1	50
□□21	9	Spec	Peter Hussey	Sea Letter	$2	–
□□21	9	Spec	Peter Hussey	Recordg the same 293 words @ 20 cents p^r @ 100	$	59
21	10	Soo Loo	J. B. Eamse	Deposit of papers 629 $\frac{12}{95}$ tons @ 1/2 cent	$3	15
21	10	Soo Loo	J. B. Eamse	Shipping 5 men	$2	50
21	10	Soo Loo	J. B. Endicott	2 certiftes to Invo of Perst. Effect of Sea Serpent	$4	–
21	10	Soo Loo	J. B. Endicott	One Passport	$1	–
				Amount carried over	$85	89

Date	N°	Name of Vessel	Name of the party paying the fee	Nature of service rendered	Amount of fees paid	
				Amount brought over	$85	89
Mch 24	–	–	F. D. Williams	Authent[g] 2 copies of letters of credit	$2	
Mch 31	–	Spark	J. B. Endicott	Tonnage fees 33 trips 100 tons ea @1/2 ct	$16	
					$104	

Gideon Nye, Jnr

Vice Consul of the United States of America

for Macao

Quarterly Return of the Arrival and Departure of American Vessels at the Consulate of the United States at Macao from the 1st of January to the 31st of March 1862.–

N°	Date	Class	Name	Tons	Where from	When Built	Vessels			Cargo		Owners	Captains
							Where built	Where belonging	Where bound	Import	Export		
☐	Jany 14th	Ship	Emma	444 $\frac{59}{95}$	Hongkong	–	–	–	Batavia Feby 11th	Ballast	General	–	Ab[m] Shearman
☐	Jany 31st	Ship	Raven	711 $\frac{82}{95}$	Hongkong	1851	Somerset	New York	Hongkong March 10th	Rice	Ballast	Eben B. Crocker & others	Crocker Nye
☐	Feby 6th	Bark	Cornelia L. Bevan	330 $\frac{68}{95}$	Hongkong	1846	Baltimore	Baltimore	sold here	Ballast	–	James Pedersen	James Pedersen
☐	Feby 13'	Ship	Contest	1092 $\frac{92}{95}$	Hongkong	1852	New York	New York	Hongkong March 1st	Ballast	Ballast	E. Lyman & others	Joseph Steele
☐	Feby 22[d]	Bark	Kate Hastings	448 $\frac{12}{95}$	Hongkong	1847	Newbury	Boston	Hongkong Feby 28th	Ballast	Ballast	Henry Hastings & others	Seth K. Kingman
☐	Feby 24'	Bark	Soo Loo	629 $\frac{18}{95}$	Hongkong	1861	Bath– St: of Maine	Boston	Hongkong Feby 27th	Coal &c.	Coal &c.	S. D. Nickerson	J. B. Eames
☐	Mch 4th	Lor cha	Rover	100 $\frac{20}{95}$	Hongkong	1855	Macao	–	Shanghae	–	Ballast	G. W. Mellen	G. W. Mellen
☐	Mch 11'	Ship	Sea Serpent	1337 $\frac{13}{95}$	Whampoa	1850	Portsm outh N. H.	New York	New York march 20'	Tea &c.	Tea &c.	Rob[t] C. Minturn & others	Saml W. Pike
☐	Mch 13'	Brig	Spec	302 $\frac{40}{95}$	Whampoa	1850	–	–	Saigon March 21st	Ballast	General	James B. Endicott & James P. Cook	Peter Hussey
☐	Mch 13'	Bark	Soo Loo	629 $\frac{20}{95}$	Hongkong	1861	Bath– St: of Maine	Boston	Ningpo March 22[d]	Ballast	Rice	S. D. Nickerson	J. B. Eames
				6041 $\frac{44}{95}$									

Gideon Nye Jnr.

Vice Consul of the United States

of America for Macao.

[March 31 – 1862

Macao

rd qr.

Received at the

Statistical office

July 10, 1862]

[1-097]

[Rec 17 July, Mr Abbott
N°31.-]

Consulate of the United States.-
Macao May 8th 1862.-

Sir,

I have the honor to report to the Department my leaving granted Passports to the undermentioned （two） citizens of the United States: 1st-To Mr Edward J. Sage, a native of NewYork and resident in this city several years past, dated October 1st 1861;-whose description is as followeth:-

Age, 37 years
Stature, 6 feet
Forehead, ample
Eyes, blue
Nose, prominent
Mouth, regular
Chin, prominent
Hair, dark
Complexion, fair
Face, long.

2nd - To Mr James Bridges Endicott, a native of Massachussetts, long resident in China, on the 19th day of March 1862 whose

[The Honorable
William H. Seward
Secretary of State of the United States
of America.-
City of Washington.]

description is as followeth:-

Age, 44 years-
Stature, 5 feet- 7 inches-
Forehead, high-
Eyes, blue-
Nose, small-
Chin, large-
Hair, Auberne-
Complexion, florid-
Face, large-

I have the honor to be,
Sir,
Your obedient Servant
Gideon Nye Jnr.
Vice Consul of the United States
of America for Macao.

[1-098]

□□□□□□□□□□□□□□
Ack N. W. Female College
Evanston, Qu
June 12, 1862

Hon. W^{m}. H. Seward,
Sect. of State – Washington–

An announcement in the Chicago Journals of my confirmation as Consul to Macao is the first and only intimation received by me that I have been even so much as nominated for that position, please inform me whether the telegram is correct and if so have the goodness to state what will be the compensation, also whether the Government pays the expenses of the voyage, and give such other information as may guide my completion of the honor.

Yours for the Union & the Adminstration
Most loyally
W. P. Jones.

[1-099]

[Recd 23 Mr. Abbott
North Western Female College
Evanston, Ill. June 19, 1862]

Ho. H. Seward
Secretary of State
Washington D. C.

Dear sir, I wish to leave whether I may be allowed until the tenth of September to make arrangements for my departure to Macao. My connection with my College and the great length of the voyage will render it difficult for me to leave the United States before that time, if the Government will not permit such a length of time □□□ □□□ I wish to □□□ the □□□ it.

Respectfully
W. P. Jones
□ ffice of Consol to Macao.

[1-100]

[Recd 1 □□□ □□□ Esq.
Evanston, Ill, June 25,18 □□]

Hon. W. H. Seward
Department of State.
Washington

Dear Sir: Herewith I transmit my consular bond executed under direction of the U. S. Sect viz.

I am a native of Philadelphia, Penn, am appointed from Boston and have never resided in Portugal or any of its dependencies.

Respectfully
Your Obedient Servant
W. P. Jones

[1-101]

O BOLETIM DO GOVERNO DE MACAO.

[B submitted
Ev]

OL. VIII — SABBADO 5 DE JULHO DE 1862. — No. 31

"O BOLETIM DO GOVERNO DE MACAO." □TA Folha □□ publicada na Imprensa do abaizo, □gnado em todos os Sabbados, e a sua responsibilidade á face da Lei é só na parte não official. □mitte toda a especie decorrespondencias, com-□to que seja respeitada a moral publica, e o □erno, e que não ataquem a vida privada de □oa alguma, e que não dem lugar a polemicas agradaveis, e enfadonhas: os correspondentes não responsaveis pelos seus escritos, sendo co□cidos da redação, e naõ o sendo habilitar-se competentemente; saô admittidos todos os □os, editaes e noticias relativas á compras, e □das &c.

Preços de Assignatura

Por Um anno, - - - - - $8
Por Seis Mezes, - - - - - 5
Por Tres Mezes, - - - - - 3

Avisos:

Não excedendo de 10 linhas, - - - $1

MAPPA DOS DOENTES TRATADOS NO HOSPITAL DA MIZERICORDIA.
JUNHO. 3a. DECADA. (1862.)

Movimento dos Doentes		SEXO Mascu-linos	Femi-ninos	CLASSE Indi-gentes	Não indigentes	Total
Existiam		7	5	10	2	12
Entraram		1	5	5	1	6
Sahiram	Curados	3	-	2	1	3
	Fallecidos	-	-	-	-	-
Ficam existindo		5	10	13	2	15

Hospital de Sm. Rafael, 1 de Julho de 1862.
Dr. Lucio Augusto da Silva,
Cirurgião-mór

MORTALIDADE EM MACAO No 2o. Trimestre do anno 1862.

Classificações	Freguezia da Sé	Freguezia de Sm. Lourenço	Freguezia de Sto. Antonio	Total
Homens	8	-	2	10
Mulheres	6	7	1	14
Menores d'ambos os sexos	4	2	3	9
Francezes (no seu Hospital)	-	-	-	-
Totalidade	18	9	6	33

Macáo Secretaria do Governo 2 de Julho de 1862.
Gregorio José Ribeiro,
Secretario do Governo.

Celestino Gomes d'Oliveira.- Pe. *Antonio Miguel A. dos Remedios.- Miguel Pereira Simõens. -Gonsalo da Silveira.- Lourenço Marques.*

No. 27.

O CONCELHO do Governo de Macao determina o seguinte:-

Tendo-nos representado o Leal Senado da Camara á cerca da sua intenção de irigir no Campo, um monumento em memoria da felecissima victoria alcançada por esta Cidade em 23 de Junho de 1622, sollicitando para isto uma loteria de quatro mil patacas, para com a porcentagem della occorrer ás despezas para levar a effeito este plano, havemos por conveniente, conceder, isemplo do pagamento do sèllo, a mencionada loteria de quatro mil patacas, ao sobredito Leal Senado da Camara. seguindo-se o

Excedendo de 10 linhas, 10 avos por linha pela □eira publicação, e 5 avos por cada subsequen-□ publicação. Publicações de interesse particu- são pagas.

J. DA SILVA.

PARTE OFFICIAL.

JUNHO. (1862) 3a. DECADA.

Movimento dos Doentes		CORPO OU ESTAÇAÕ A QUE PERTENCEM.							Total
		Batalhão Macao	Batalhão Nacional	Lorcha Amasona	Policia do Leal Senado	Corpo de Policia	Moços da Fazenda	Prezos da Cadeia	
Existiam		37	-	1	-	1	2	1	42
Entraram		10	-	-	1	1	-	-	12
Sahiram	Curados	23	-	-	-	-	-	1	24
	Mortos	-	-	-	-	-	-	-	-
Ficam existindo		24	-	1	1	2	2	-	30

Hospital Militar 1 de Julho de 1862.

Dr. Lucio Augusto da Silva,
Cirurgião-m ó r

O CONSELHO do Governo de Macao.

Faz saber aos habitantes Chinas de Macao que na conformidade do já annunciado pelo Edital da Junta do Lançamento de 31 de Maio ultimo, se ha-de abrir amanhã 1o. de Julho, e continuará aberto até 31 do mesmo mez, o Cofre da Recebedoria para a cobrança á bocca do mesmo, da Decima Predial, e dos fóros, incluindo a illuminação, em que foram collectados os predios Chinas sitos dentre a fóra dos muros da Cidade relativos ao anno ecconomico de 1861 a 1862; devendo as collectas ser pagas por inteiro, não tendo lugar pagamento por conta, e bem assim que aos contribuintes que não pagarem á bocca do cofre dentro d'aquelle prazo serão cobrados mais 6 por cento sobre a importancia das suas collectas, tudo na forma das ordens e regulamentos relativos.- Macao 30 Junho de 1862.- *João Ferreira Pinto.- Ivo*

mesmo methodo que se tem adoptado com outras Loterias que por este Governo tem sido concetidas. As Authoridades a quem o conhecimento e execução desta pertencer assim o tenham entendido e cumpram.- Macao 2 de Julho de 1862. *João Fereira Pinto.- Ivo Celestino Gomes d'Oliveira.-* Pe. *Antonio Miguel A. dos Remedios.- Miguel Pereira Simões.- Gonsalo de Silvera.- Lourenço Marques.*

No. 28.

O CONSELHO do Governo de Macao determina o seguinte:-

Attendendo ao que nos representou o Cabo do Corpo de Policia de Macao Antonio Vaz, No. 12, e a informação dada pelo Commandante do respectivo Corop, havemos por conveniente dar ao mencionado cabo Antonio Vaz baixa do serviço Nacional e Real. As Authoridades a quem o conhecimento e execução desta pertencer assim o tenham entendido e cumpram. Macao 5 de Julho de 1862.- *João Ferreira Pino.- Ivo Celestino Gomes d'Oliveira.-* Pe. *Manoel Lourenço de Gouveia.- Miguel Pereira Simões.- Gonsalo da Silveira.- Lourenço Marques.*

PARTE NÃO OFFICIAL

MACAO 5 DE JULHO DE 1862.

HONTEM- 4 de Julho- anniversario da indepedencia d'America, tevemos a honra de assistir a uma bilhante *soirée*, no Consulado Americano.

Na verdade a noite se passou agradavelmente, não só pela escolhida sociedade que n'aquellas lusidas sallas se encontrou, como pela attenciosa bondade, e cordial acolhimento, que com todos seus hospedes repartia o Illmo. Sr. Gideon Nye, Vice-Consul dos Estados Unidos d'America em Macao. A delicadeza fina, o tacto e gosto ni Pompei, cantor comico e professor de Obóe.

Tinhamos assistido no dia 30 de Junho passado, no theatro de D. Pedro 5o., ao concerto que por este professor ali foi dado, e se então, gostamos e sympathisamos com o artista Romano, hontem podémos melhor avaliar o seu merito, como maestro.

De Madame de Leagre, é tão conhecida a sua excellente execução no piano, e a suavidade de sua voz, que acrescentarêmos agora, que mais uma vez sentimos verdadeiro praser em a ouvir, e apreciar seus talentos sempre acompanhados de genio, alegre e bondoso, e da modestia que a caracterisa como professora.

tornar a ouvir o "Elixir d'Amur," onde hontem estava divino; dueto, cujo effeito nos agradou mais n'aquella magnifica salla do que em 30 de Junho no theatro.

Como professor de Obóe achâmos que o artista merece o titulo, porque sendo aquelle instrumento ingrato como são todos os de palheta, o Sr. Pompei faz que elle obdeça á escalla, sem apresentar uma nota falsa. Em quanto ao instrumento, seus sons são melodiosos e expressivos, porém pareceu-nos mais proprio para ser acompanhado pela orchestra do que por piano, ainda que nada ha que notar nos acompanhamentos de hontem; porem figurou-se-nos que grandes esforços estes eximios artistas faziam nas suas execuções.

especiaes deste cavalheiro, é conhecida de todos os habitantes desta Cidade, que como nós temos a honra de avaliar, além das suas boas qualidades, a intelligencia da escolha nos objectos de arte, que se encontram nas suas sallas guarnecidas com requintado primor.

A reunião da noite de hontem estava pois brilhantissima, e ali se encontravam as primeiras authoridades e os principaes cavalheiros do paiz, e ainda que pequeno o numero de senhoras, capricharam estas, pela simplicidade e gosto de suas toilettes, com a simplicidade do lugar que lhes foi reservado para recepção–larga e extensa varanda, onde as flores naturaes, adornando os portaes e janellas, com as bandeiras nacionaes de America, Portugal, Brazil, Inglaterra, França e Hespanha se abraçavam. Esta varanda elegantemente ornada, deitava sobre outra sobranceira ao jardim, illuminado caprichosamente, que recreava a vista, e onde se gosava agradavel frescura, pelo facto de olhar esta parte da casa para o lado do vento que actualmente reina, acontecendo além disto estar a noite summamente fresca e bella.

Esta illuminação de estrellas assentando sobre o fundo escuro das arvores que orlam aquelle quasi parque, reflectindo a sua luz sobre a verdejante relva que atapéta aquelle vasto espaço, e a divisão do divertimento que Mr. Nye nos convidou a gosar em sua casa, dizem mais do que as nossas palavras a respeito do gosto delicado deste cavalheiro.

Primeiramente um concerto teve lugar, desempenhado por Madame de Leagre, e o Sr. Giovan–

O concerto dividio–se em duas partes:– 1a., Solo de Obóe da opera "Lucrezia Borgia, acompanhado a piano por Madame de Leagre; a linda aria "Le Lac," a cavatina de D. Magnifico da opera "Cennerentola," um dueto da opera "Puritanos," e um solo de Obóe da opera "Traviata," a companhado por toda a banda de musica do Batalhão de Macao.

A 2a. parte foi dividida, n'um solo do Miserere da opera "Trovatore" por Obóe; uma aria da excellente opera "Martha," por Madame Leagre, desempenhada com a expressão necessaria; a bella e sempre enthusiastica cavatina– Largo e Factotum. da opera do Baberio de Sevilha; um dueto da interessante opera "Elixir d'Amur," e alfim o rondó final da "Lucia" por Obóe, acompanhado pela musica do Batalhão.

Todo o concerto correu marivilhosamente, e gosto houve na escôlha d'aquelles fragmentos de operas tão excellentes, que lagrimas de saudade nos trouxeram aos olhos, avivando recordações patrias de dias da infancia que ali correram tão lêdos.

O Sr. Pompei tem uma bella voz, porem o seu caracter principal como cantor é nas peças comicas. Gostámos de o ouvir nos Puritanos, pelo enthusiasmo de que se possuio, porém gostámos muito mais da sua voz no Dom Magnifico, e foi–nos agradavel o Factotum, apesar da restricção a qe era obrigado, por se achar desempenhando este papel n'uma salla e não no theatro, onde o Sr. Pompei é senhor do palco, porém achámos muito praser em lhe

Acabado o concerto, uma surpresa teve lugar, aparecendo no parque a dança militar, que nas festas populares de S. João e S. Pedro, com bastante ordem e decencia visitou as casas d'alguns moradores. Acolhêmos bem a ideia porque n'aquella hora, a dança camponesa estava em caracter.

Serviu–se em seguida abundante e variada ceia, na qual foi incansavel nos obsequios o dono da casa; e depois della houve na fresca varanda, um baile bastante animado, por quadrilhas e polkas, que fez esquecer a fadiga, pelo praser que causava. Nesta parte final da *soirée* a varanda, tornada em salão dançante, apresentava uma vista deslumbrante, e o Sr. Nye, para não faltar á mais leve etiqueta, apesar do Grande Washington, recostado na bandeira dos Estados Unidos, presidir á festa que com enthusiasmo se desenvolvia, offereceu o seu retrato em photographia a todas as damas do saráo.

A festa terminou quasi de madrugada, saindo todos contentes e satisfeitos da reunião agradavel com que o Sr. Nye mimoseára seus hospedes, neste dia de tão doces e gratas recordações para o seus paiz natal.

A VINGANÇA D'UMA DEFUNTA.

POR AMEDÉE ACHARD.

(*Traducção livre.*)

III

(*Continuação do numero antecedente.*)

Caminharam assim até Jara, quazi sem trocarem uma palavra, nem mesmo

[This was written by the Government Secretary Mr Ribeiro when card unclosed.

Ev.]

um olhar. Graves pensamentos pezavam em suas lembranças. Talvez que o amor não fizesse palpitar o coração de Henrique, porem o que é certo é que tinha horror a outro amor. O ciume que dominava, revoltava–se contra a ideia de lhe esacpar o poderio sobre sua mulher, e as reacções desta alma impetuozo e movil appresentavam todas as apparencias d'uma paixão, sem elle a possuir em verdade.

ção e reconhecimento. Olharam–se, e os olhos commovidos da pobre mulher se cobriram de lagrimas. Tomou a mão de seu marido e disse–lhe:

– Henrique, temos feito mal, muito mal um ao outro, quereis perdoar–me como eu vos perdôo?

– Nada tenho que perdoar, Esther, porque te amo.

Ella saccodio tristemente a cabeça.

– Não é preciso, meu amigo, fazer allusôsa

Depois baixando os olhos para Allones, accrescentou com voz resignada.

– Estou prompto, Snr., partámos.

Ao chegarem perto de Jara a tempestade principiou a bramir pelo meio das montanhas; os primeiros rigores d'um inverno prematuro tinham enchido as estradas de neve, e sobre as cristas longiquas dos montes, começava e descer uma nêgra cortina de espessa nuvens.

Um accidente que sobreveio ao vehiculo, obrigou-os a demorarem-se por algum tempo n'uma aldeia a algumas leguas de Poligny.

Tinham chegado apenas havia minutos a um mau alvergue, quando o chicote d'um postilhão se ouvio na estrada e no mesmo instante o Snr. T... entrar no alvergue. Á sua vista Esther não poude conter um grito de surpreza, e T.. tremeu. Este movimento de parte a parte não escapou ao marido; o nome que tinha procurado saber em vão, sabia-o agora. Um largo suspiro lhe encheuo peito e dirigio-se a T...

– É o acaso, sem duvida, disse-lhe comprimentando-o, que vos trouxe a esta estrada?

– Não, em verdade, replicou T ..., vou para Milão, e esta missão inesperada me obrigou a partir d'improviso.

O Conde enfiou-lhe o braço e conduzio para a porta; fóra de casa, parou.

– A sua missão será tão apressada, lhe disse, que não possa conceder-me pelo menos cinco minutos?

T ... olhou-o e comprehendeu tudo.

– Tenho despachos que levar, Snr. Conde; na minha volta estorei a vossa disposição.

– Não Snr., replicou Allones, apertando fortemente a mão do Secretaio: um ministro pode esperar, um marido não pode!

T ...não replicou, e inclinou-se.

Havia n'esta occasião na Aldeia, de passagem, uma companhia de granadeiros que ia destacada para Polygni: os dois adversarios pediram a dois soldados para os acompahar, e munindo-se das pistolas que T ... tinha na sua carruagem, dirigiram-se para um pequeno bosque perto da estrada.

Quatro minutos depois, ouviram-se dois tiros; Allones sabio só do bosque: sua casaca vinha furada na golla por uma bala. Entrou no alvergue e subio ao quatro onde um criado lhe disse que sua mulher se tinha recolhido.

Esther estava em pé perto da janela, com a cara encostada aos vidros; quando se voltou para seu marido, seu rosto estava triste, mais triste que a paizagem izolada que se apresentava em frente da caza, na qual o vento brincava com as fôlhas seccas e mortas.

– Pelo que vejo, vós vos batêstes?

dessas; ellas são terriveis ao accordar. Vós não me amaes, e eu, meu Deos! Nunca mais vos hei de amar ...

– Ainda!? atalhou elle.

– Escutai-me, replicou, apartando-lhe a mão. Ousareis affirmar que esse amor de que me fallaes, é semelhante áquelle dos nossos primeiros dias? ... Esse, é que eu chóro, e é o unico que me lembra. Ah! .. elle morreu e para sempre .... Não vos reprehendo meu amigo, as vossas injurias, se as houve, foram filhas da idade ... mas eu sou assim formada, e nada me pode avivar o que a desgraça extenguio; entre nós a confiança está perdida .... Henrique, separêmos-nos!

– Nunca, disse o Esposo apertando entre as suas, a sua mão.

– Meu Deos! disse Esther, esta vida é amarga, semeada de lagrimas, suspeitas e desordens: gostaes della? ... Os que soffrem o descanço da campa, não serão mais felizes? ... Só havendo entre nós um adeos, é que mutuamente nos poderemos perdoar .... Hoje, estou só ... A esperança do futuro, anniquilada, replicou abafando um suspiro: Minha mãe morreu, era eu ainda creança, meu bom e velho pae morreu tambem .... Já não tenho que fazer cá neste mundo.

– Entáo eu nada sou?

– Sereis para min um irmão, quando nos separar-mos ..... perto um do outro, Henrique, accreditai-me, não pode ser ... porque eu me lembrarei sempre ..... Hei de orar por vós, deixae assim que as portas d'um convento se fechem sobre mim.

– Um convento! exclamou o marido.

– Sim- um convento, replicou Esther com um doce sorrizo. Tenho grandes faltas a expiar .... O que eu fiz. foi uma falta, agora o sinto, porem a causa foi ter o coração ulcerado.... Penço ás veses em me matar, porem tão joven ainda, falta-me a coragem ... Henrique, sereis desgraçado comigo, deixai-me pois partir! ...

– Esther, não te abandonarei!

– Oh! meu Deos! .. Henrique não tendes piedade!? .. Mas não comprehendeis, continuou com o olhar influmado, que uma mulher que já não ama, arrasta a desgraça, e muitas veses a vergonha ao lar domestico!? .. Não comprehendeis que o que vos peço com as lagrimas nosolhos, é por ter mêdo de mim? Piedade! . . piedade! . . disse juntando as mãos, não me obrigueis a fazer o mal! Que me

O postilhão fêz ver o estado do Ceo a Allones, porem este a quem o repouso era impossivel, depois da sena que já descrevemos, fêz-lhe signal de continuar: mudaram-se os cavallos e o vehiculo entranhou-se pelas montanhas.

Pelo meio dia chegaram ao ponto mais elevado d'uma planura, onde o vento empurrava a neblina. Os cavallos espinotavam sobre a neve endurecida e arquejavam.

O postilhão saltou abaixo, e o mesmo fizeram Esther e seu marido, para alliviarem a acarruagem. Via-se dos lados das montanhas, as nuvens a correrem cortadas pelo vento impetuoso, e lugubres lamentos sahiam do fundo das cavernas, por onde a agoa fervia em torrentes: torbilhões de fina neev passavam no ar, cobrindo como mortalha as massas arrepiadas dos pinheiros. A cem passos, na estrada, tudo era trevas e confusão; andava-se n'uma atmosphera tépida e escura, que a prestesa da tempestade movia apressadamente.

Esther cambaleava pela estrada, onde o gêlo lhe estalava debaixo dos delicados pés. Henrique aproximou-se e deu-lhe o braço para a ajudar a caminhar.

Seguiram assim lentamente, e o vehiculo depressa desappareceu perante as cortinas fluctuantes da serrançåo; os creados o iam impellindo pelas rodas, levando o postilhão os cavallos á redea.

Havia um quarto d'hora que a carruagem rodava sobre a neve endurecida, quando de repente um grito terrivel se fez ouvir no espaço, um outro ainda mais terrivel lhe respondeu, entrando em seguida tudo n'um silencio profundo e assustador.

IV

Aprezar da distancia a que já estavam os criados e o postilhão, estes ouviram os dois gritos terriveis, e correndo voltaram a traz, encontrando seu amo accocorado na estrada, mergulhando seus olhos avidos no abismo onde o nevoeiro fluctuava.

A neve que tinha cahido formava á roda delle um rêgo que se perdia nas vagas profundezas d'aquelle barranco.

– Ai! meu Deos! disse o postilhão, a Snra. cahio ... vè-de, sem duvida lhe faltaram

– Oh! não temeis nada por elee, Snra, respôndeu o Conde, com um sorrizo amargo; a balla encontrou–lhe dinheiro na algibeira, cahio com o tiro, porem apenas contuzo.

Ella sacodio a cabeça.

– Hoje, que m' importa que morra ou não .... Porem vós, Henrique, para que vos expozestes a serdes morto? Olhai! . . será preciso commover–vos? Que vos tenho eu feito para quereres ajuntar o remorço á minha tristeza?

Ao dizer isto, Esther cambaleou; Henrique correu a seu lado e susteve–a nos braços. Ha momentos que a alma enfraquecida accorda misturada de affei–

importa vosso amor? ignoraes acazo que tenho medo de ser mãe segunda vêz?– A voz de Esther tornou–se surda, e seu olhar encheu–se de brilho ao proferir estas palavras. Henrique estava pallido e n'um estremecimento nervoso; a paixão porem fez calar a voz da sua consciencia.

– Esther! seguir–me–has, exclamou somente.

Ella levantou para o Ceo as suas mãos, n'um lançe de desespero, dizendo:–

– Elle assim o quer, oh meu Deos!

os pés ...

Os criados assustados andavam á roda do Conde, que se pendurava sobre o abismo: um delles o segurou pelo braço dizendo–lhe:

– Tomai sentido Snr. Conde, vôs ides cahir tambem.

Allones levantou a cabeça; seu rosto perturbado pelo espanto, causava horror á vista, seus dentes batiam uns d'encontro aos outros, e seus beiços estavam lividos.

– Cahio! .. Ella cahio ! .. disse então debruçando–se no precepicio onde boiava a nebrnia.

Ouvia–se subir do fundo daquella massa opaca, o rudio da agoa precepitando–se sobre um leito de rochas. De repente o cão, que andava farejando e grunhindo, d'um para outro lado, approximou–

no da borda da estrada. colle□□□ o fa□□□ sobre a neve, e □□□ □□□ o ar; raspes na terra por alguns minutos a □□□–os pelo solo, regulado e rège, redireitou–se n'um □□□ sober as □□□, □□□, e desapparecam. Allones fez seção de seguir, porem os criados o detiveram.

– V. Exa. matar–se–ha e não conseguirá cauza alguma, lhe disse e postilhão.

– Cordas então, disse o Conde, cordas para eu descêr.

Correram á carruagem; havia alli uma porção dellas. Enrollaram–as ao corpo do Conde, e segurando pela extremidade o postilhão e mais criados, assim elle foi descendo seguindo os traços do cão, do qual se ouviam os latidos como pedindo soccorro: Aquella vereda inclicade e coberta de neve ia acabar a'uma praia de larga torrente, onde as agoas fogozas caminhavam sussurrando.

O cão atirou–se á torrente, seguio o fio da agoa, abordando aqui e alli, mergulhando e dando gritos pezarosos e lugubres.

Sobre os ramos d'uma arvore espinhosa, pendia um boccado de fazenda do vestido de Esther. Allones afastou–se d'este boccado de seda e entrou e correr ao longo da praia tão depressa quanto o podiam as suas forças.

□□□□□□□□□□□□□□□□□□□□□□□
□□□□□□□□□□□□□□□□□□□□□□□
□□□□□□□□□□□□□□□□□□□□□□□
□□□□□□□□□□□□□□□□□□□□□□□
□□□□□□□□□□□□□□□□□□□□□□□
□□□□□□□□□□□□□□□□□□□□□□□
□□□□□□□□□□□□□□□□□□□□□□□
□□□□□□□□□□□□□□□□□□□□□□□
do dia corria pelo Jardim e do noite dor–
□□□□□□□□□□□□□□□□□□□□□□□

(Continúa.)

SEGUNDA LOTTERIA.

PLANO da Lotteria de 6,000 Bilhetes @ $2 per bilhete– $12,000, á beficio do Theatre de D. Pedro 5o.

1 Premio de ----	$2,000
1 Do. de ----	1,000
2 Dos. de $500 ----	1,000
4 Dos. de 200 ----	800
10 Dos. de 100 ----	1,000
20 Dos. de 50 ----	1,000
2 Dos. de 50, os dois numeros brancos anteriores mais proximos do 1o. premio ---	100
2 Dos. de 50, os dois numeros brancos posteriores mais proximos do 1o. premio ---	100

2 Dos. de 50, o numero branco anteriore posp–

PLANO DA LOTERIA.

DE $4,000, era 2,000 Bilhetes, a $2 por Bilhete, para a orecção de Monumento em Lisboa ao grande Luiz de Camões.

1 Premio de ----	$1,000
1 Do. de ----	500
1 Do. de ----	200
4 Dos. de $50 ----	200
10 Dos. de 20 ----	200
20 Dos. de 10 ----	200
180 Dos. de 4 ----	720
1 Branco da 1a. Extracção	100
1 Ultimo Branco da Ultima Extracção ----	100
O Numero antecedente, e subsequente do Numero que sahir Primeiro Pen io terá $50 ----	100
O Numero antecedente, e subsequente do Numero que sahir Segundo Premio terá $25 ----	50
O Numero antecedente, e subsequente do Numero que sahir Terceiro Premio terá $15 ----	30
225 Premios	$3,400
1,775 Brancos @ 15 por cento sobre $4,000	600
2,000 Bilhetes @ $2	$4,000

Cançado de fadiga cahio sobore um monte de pinhascos e ficou silencioso, passeando á roda de si olhares sem expressão e que nada viam. Os bramidos da tempestade faziam-o tremer.

Os criados fartos de esperar, desceram tambem ao fundo d'aquella cova por uma brécha que descobriram, alguns centenares de passos mais adiante, e foram encontrar seu amo immovel, occultando a cabeça entre as mãos. Á chegada destes estremeceu, levantou-se e seguio-os. Estava descorado, e suas faces agitavam-se por um movimento convulço.

– Como elle a amava! disia um dos criados com geral approvação.

No fim d'um quarto d'hora de caminho pela praia fóra, perceberam uma pelissa pendurada nos ramos d'um pinheiro derrubado á borda da torrente. Perto do tronco sobre um leito de calháos jasia o cadaver d'uma mulher. O cão agachado ao pé da arvore, uivava.

As pernas de Allones curvram-se ao descobrir isto e apenas teev forças para se arrastar até ao leito agreste onde dormia o cadaver. O ròsto desta mulher estava disfigurado e desconhecido, porem seu cabello era comprido e castanho como o de Esther, e seus vestidos espedaçados tinham a forma e còr do que ella trasia. Henrique cahio sobre os joelhos e desmaiou. Transportaram o cadaver para uma cabana proxima, e dois dias depois, debaixo da declaração do Conde e de seus criados, o corpo da Snra. d'Allones foi pregado n'um caixão, condusido a Norville, sepultando-se perto do tumulo do Barão.

Henrique ficou 6 semanas no castello, passando metade do dia ao pé deste tumulo, no qual se liam em pedra de marmore negro, estas unicas palavras:

"Esther d'Allones- morta aos 20 aonnos" !

O resto do dia passeava no parque, aó, e silencioso, e não queria ver ninguem. A'noute retirava-se ao seu quarto.

No fim deste tempo voluou a Pariz, e 4 ou 5 mezes depois começou este trato de vida bisarra no qual o luto e a extra-

terior mairs pioximo do 2o premio----	100
4 Dos. de 50, os numeros brancos anterior e posterior mais proximos dos dois premios de $500 -- --	200
56 Dos. de 10 --	560
435 Dos. de 4 --	1,740
1 Penultimo branco -	100
1 Ultimo branco --	500
541 Premios ----	$10,200
5459 Brancos 15 por cento @ beneficio ---	1,800
6,000 Bilhetes @ $2 --	$12,000

Macao 30 de Junho de 1862.

M. PEREIRA,

Presidente da Commissão Directora.

PLANO DA LOTERIA

DE $8,000 em 4,000 bilhetes a $2 por bilhete, que a Santa Caza da Mezericordia desta Cidade vai fazer n'este anno em beneficio das obras Pias a seu cargo.

1 Premio de	$2,000
1 Do. de	500
5 Dos. de $100 . .	500
10 Dos. de 50 . .	500
20 Dos. de 25 . .	500
30 Dos. de 20 . .	600
200 Dos. de 10 . .	2,000
1 Do. de 1o. Branco .	50
1 Do. de Ultimo Branco	150
269 Premios	$6,800
3,731 Brancos.	
15 por cento em beneficio de Obras Pias ...	1,200
4,000 Bilhetes @ 2 . .	$8,000

A extracção desta Lotaria terá lugar logo que ficarem vendidos todos os Bilhetes, com previo avizo ao publico.

A venda dos Bilhetes começará no dia 15 de Julho.

Macao Cartorio da Santa Caza 30 de Junho 1862. JOSÉ DA SILVA. *Membro e Secretario.*

A Extracção desta Loteria terá logar logo que ficarem vendidos todos os Bilhetes; os quses deverão ser pagos a pezo de 7.1.7., e os premios serão pagos da mesma sorte.

NOTICIAS MARTIMAS.

CHEGADA.

Junho 3 – *Novo Constante*, de Pangasinan.
" 9 – *Carl Ritter*, de Hongkong.
" 11 – *Scandia*, de Hongkong.
" 14 – *Nepuno*, de Sual.
" 17 – *Dolphin*, de Hongkong.
" 17 – *Anna Catharine* de Saigon.
" 23 – *Malwin*, de Saigon.
" 23 – *Europa*, de Saigon.
" 23 – *M. Howes*, de Pinang.
" 26 – *Homer*, de Pinang.
" 27 – *Fiam-Po-Soy*, de Batavia.
" 28 – *Luchow*, de Hongkong.

PARTIDA.

Junho 1 – *Rauma*, para Ningpó.
" 1 – *Odin*. para Hongkong.
" 1 – *King-man*, para Hongkong.
" 2 – *Palmetto*, para Hongkong.
" 3 – *Macao*, para Ningpó.
" 4 – *Telegraph*, para Bangkok.
" 4 – *Afreque*, para Hongkong.
" 11 – *Crowch Brothrs*, para Hongkong.
" 11 – *William Mitchell*, para Vampú.
" 12 – *Raeconnessence*, Hongkong.
" 14 – *Carl Ritter*, para Ningpó.
" 14 – *Novo Constante*, Pangasinan.
" 15 – *Greta*, para Saigon.
" 18 – *Bencluch*, para Hongkong.
" 19 – *Seandia*, para Ningpó.
" 20 – *Dolphin*, para Ningpó.
" 21 – *Acquitaine*, para Manilla.
" 21 – *Zoe*, para Amoy.
" 29 – *Neptuno*, para Hongkong, e Manilla.
" 29 – *M. Howes*, para Hongkong, e Amoy.

Macáo: Impressa na Typographia de J. DA SILVA.

[1-102]

[N°32.– Recd Sept 12.]

Consulate of the United States.
Macao July 8th 1862.–

Sir,

Referring to my Despatch N° 30, in which I forwarded to you the returns of this Consulate for the previous quarter, I now beg to hand you those of the quarter ending the 30th of June 1862.–

I am,
Sir,
With great respect,
Your obedient Servant
Gideon Nye Jnr
Vice Consul of the United States
of America for Macao.

[The Honorable
William H. Seward
Secretary of State of the United States of
America.
City of Washington.–]

Quarterly Return of the Arrival and Departure of American Vessels at the Consulate of the United States at Macao – from the 1st of April to the 30th of June 1862.

N°	Date	Class	Name	Tons	Where from	Vessels			Where bound	Cargo		Owners	Captains
						When Built	Where built	Where belonging		Import	Export		
1	April 2d	Ship	Levanter	$849\frac{76}{95}$	Whampoa	1852	Damariscolta State of Maine	New York	New York April 5th	General	General	L. Linitte & others	John A. Brown
2	April 3d	Ship	Herbert	$586\frac{20}{95}$	Bangkok	1848	Medford–State of Boston–	Boston	Hongkong Apl 14th	Rice	Ballast	Issac Thacker & others	Geo. Crocker
3	April 22d	Ship	S. H. Talbot	$593\frac{35}{95}$	Hongkong	1854	Machias–State of Maine	New York	New York May 23d	Ballast	Tea &c	Peter H. Copland & others	A. C. Sears
4	May 5th	Ship	Fortuna	$659\frac{47}{95}$	—·—	1857	Boston	Boston	Ningpo May 14th	—·—	Rice	Geo. Whitney & others	F. W. Hansen
5	May 10th	Brig	Spec	$302\frac{40}{95}$	Saigon	–	–	–	Hongkong May 20th	Rice	Ballast	Jas. B. Endicott & Jas. P Cook	Peter Hussey
6	May 14th	Bark	Palucetto	$341\frac{06}{95}$	Hongkong	1849	Kennebunkport state of Maine	Boston	Hongkong May 31st	Timber	—·—	Geo M. Barnard & others	Wm F. Upton
7	May 14th	Str:	Meteor	–	–	–	–	–	–	–	–	–	Woodward
				$3332.\frac{34}{95}$									

Gideon Nye Jnr
Vice Consul of the United States
of America for Macao.–

[June 30––1862
Macao 3d qr]

[1-103]

[Recd Dec 22]
N°33.–

Consulate of the United States.
Macao, October 2nd 1862.

Sir,

Referring to my Despatch N° 32, in which I forwarded to you the Returns of this Consulate for the previous quarter, I now beg to hand you those of the quarter ending the 30th of September 1862.–

I am,
Sir,
With great respect
Your obedient Servant
Gideon Nye, Jnr
Vice Consul of the United States
of America for Macao

[The Honorable
William H. Seward
Secretary of State of the United States of America.
City of Washington]

United States Consulate at Macao.
Fees received during the Quarter ending 30th September 1862.

Date	N°	Name of Vessel	Name of the party paying the fee	Nature of service rendered	Amount of fees paid	
□□21st	1	Comet	F. D. Williams	Certificate to Invoice Sundries	$2	–
□□26th		Comet	Edward Podd	Deposit of Papers 1,836 $\frac{12}{95}$ tons @ 1/2 cent	$9	18
		Comet	Edward Podd	Shipping 12 men	$5	–
□□□□th	2	Lotus	John Leckie	Deposit of Papers 660 $\frac{14}{95}$ tons @ 1/2 cent	$3	30
□□14th			Lun Woo	3 Certfes to Invos Opium pr "Lotus"	$6	–
			Hee Wah	3 Certfes to Invos Opium pr "Lotus"	$6	–
			Chong Woo	1 Certfes to Invos Opium pr "Lotus"	$2	–

			Chun Chong Wing	2 Certf^tes to Inv^os Opium p^r "Lotus"	$4	–
			Piu Kee	1 Certf^tes to Inv^os Opium p^r "Lotus"	$2	–
			Cum Sing Lung	1 Certf^tes to Inv^os Opium p^r "Lotus"	$2	–
			Tung Chun	1 Certf^tes to Inv^os Opium p^r "Lotus"	$2	–
			Wing Chong	1 Certf^tes to Inv^os Opium p^r "Lotus"	$2	–
			Leng Wun	1 Certf^tes to Inv^os Opium p^r "Lotus"	$2	–
□□19th	4	Calliope	G. H. Taylor	Deposit of Papers 280 $\frac{06}{95}$ tons @ 1/2 cent	$1	40
□□30th		Spark	L. d' Almeida	Tonnage fees on 100 tons @ 1/2 cent		50
					$49	38

Gideon Nye Jnr
Vice Consul of the United States
of America for Macao.–

Quarterly Return of the Arrival and Departure of American Vessels at the Consulate of United States at Macao from the 1st of July to the 30th of September 1862.–

No	Date		Class	Name	Tons	Where from	When Built	Vessels		Where bound	Cargo		Owners	Captains
								Where built	Where belonging		Import	Export		
1	July	16th	Ship	Comet	1836 $\frac{12}{95}$	Canton	1851	New York	New York	New York July 28th	General	General	Tho P. Burklin & others	Edward Podd
2	Aug^t	12th	Ship	Lotus	660 $\frac{14}{95}$	Hongkong	1852	Chelsea	Boston	S. Francisco Augt 12th	Rice	Rice	John Leckie & others	John Leckie
3	Aug^t	29th	Str	U. S. S. "Wyoming"	–	Manila	–	–	–	Amoy Septr 11th	–	–	–	Comd^ore Mc Dougal
4	Sept^r	17th	Sch	Calliope	280 $\frac{6}{95}$	Hongkong	1856	Boston	Boston	Hongkong Septr 29th	Tea	Ballast	Robert B. Forbes	G. St.Taylor
					2776 $\frac{32}{95}$									

Gideon Nye Jnr
Vice Consul of the United States
of America for Macao

[1–104]

[Sept 30–1862

Macao
Ret 4th qr]

[Recd Dec. 22.
Ans Jan 22
Mr □□□]

Consulate of the United States
Macao October 12th 1862.

Sir;

I have had the honor to receive the Despatch of the Department of June 9th, apprising me of the appointment of Mr W. P. Jones of Illinois as Consul at this place; and I beg to refer to my reply to a former similar intimation from the Department, of the appointment of Mr Edward Marte of California to the office which I have filled the past four years, in now merely stating my cordial

[The Honorable
William H. Seward
Secretary of State
Washington]

acquiescence in whatever step the President may take in the premises.

Desirous as I ever have been to serve our beloved Country to the best of my ability as opportunities have been presented to me, I am especially mindful--at this period of peril to our noble Nationality, of the importance of conciliating and ameliorating our relations with other nations and peoples:--

Such was the inspiration of the address to His Excellency Governor General Guimarães, upon his return from Peking after the negotiation of the Treaty of the 13th of this port, whereby the sovereignity over Macao and its Dependencies is conceded to Portugal.

I have since assisted in translating this Treaty from Portuguese into English; and in now handing you a copy of it（in both English & Portuguese）, I beg your reference to the three more important or special clauses of it, those numbered respectively as articles 2d, 9th & 53.--

I hand you also a copy of the address referred to which I prepared by the wish of the gentlemen representating, respectively, Great Britain, France, Netherland and Peru;

[in]

in addition to whom, Mr William Speiden Naval Store Keeper of the United States, and several other Foreign Residents, signed the address.--

I send to you the original of the reply of His Excellency as conveying the marked gratification of an officer who is very high in the favor of his own soverign; and who in addition to the numerous dignities and honors already conferred upon him, is likely to be made a Viscount, if I am well advised.--

Trusting that what I have thus, in my humble sphere, done will meet the approval of the President,

I am, Sir,
with great respect,
Your obedient Servant
Gideon Nye Jnr

[Copy.–]

To His Excellency
The Counsellor Isidoro Francisco Guimarães
Ambassador of Portugal to the Court of Peking–
&c &c &c

We have come to offer to Your Excellency our congratulations:–We congratulate you upon the success of your mission to Peking in no mere words of forces; but with a real sympathy in the rejoicing which we see around us,–which fills our ears and salutes our eyes on every side;–a rejoicing as legitimate as it is spontaneous and full–hearted. We desire to render homage to the marked ability and prudence which have characterized Your Excellency's approach of the Court of Peking;–it was as well tuned as it was cautiously essayed:–The way was beset with difficulties, if not with danger to preexisting relations and your sole force was that of reason: The states quo was were undefined, so that we may say that the point of departure was wanting, and yet, Sir, you, like a skilful navigator, have avoided the shoals and quicksands and reached the desired haven. Aye! the haven of repose for the people of Macao, for you leave set all doubts at rest;–and whereas, before there was complete incertitude and a critical question ever loomng in the distance, if not were provocatively threatening, were the future relations are assured by positive and eventually beneficial engagements.

Well may all men rejoice' Chinese as well as Portuguese and all who enjoy Your Excellency's protection here, for it is a settlement which commends itself to all.––

It is thus that, after effecting Treaties with Siam and Japan, you leave given completion to your work and justly earned the gratitude of your own countrymen and the applause of other nations:–But we refrain from longer trespassing upon time which belongs rightly to Your Excellency's own countrymen, although we claim a participation in the appreciation which they service of Your Excellency's services.––

[We]

We are,
With great respect,
Your Excellency's
Obedient Servant
(signed) Gideon Nye, Jr
V. C. U. S. America for Macao
(signed) E. L. Lauça
British Consula Agent
(signed) J. dos Amoric Van der □□□
Nederland Consul for Panto in □□□
(signed) N. G. Peter
Vice Consul for France
(signed) J. M. Cantaurian

Consul del Peru em Macao

(signed) Wm Speiden

U. S. Naval Store Keeper

(signed) Gustar Raynal

(signed) C. E. Baeddingham

(signed) Jozé Mª Del Ri□□□

(signed) A. U. Gay

Macao September 9th 1862.

[□□□
□□□
□□□]

Ilt^{mo}. Snr^{s}

Tendo tido a honra de receber a falicitação que US^{a} e outros Cavalheiros Estrangeiros me dirigirão por occasião do meu regrefro a esta Cidade, depois de haver desempenhado do milhor medo que coube em minhas forças a Missão de que o Governo de Sua Magestade Fidelissima me encarregou junto a Corte de Peking não tenho expressões com que possa agradecer condignament, mais esta prova da sympathia de US^{a} e mais signatarios pela prosperidade desta Colonia, e da sua benevolencia para commigo.

Dique-se pois US^{a} aceitar os portestos do meu eterno reconhecimento pelo bom acolhimento que encontrei da parte de US^{a} e mais Cavalheiros que assignaram a felicitação, e pelo a preço em que mostram ter o pequeno serviço que prestei.

Deus Guarde a US^{a}
Macao

Macao 12 de Setembro
de 1862.

Isidoro Guimarães

[Pu^{nco} Snr^{e} Gideon Nye
Vice Consul dos Estados
Unidos d'America.]

[Recd from the
U. S. Consul
Macao
Dece. 22]

[Mr Jones.
Please note in insertion in your next report. Mns
Treaty G. I. A.]

TRATADO
AMIZADE E COMMERCIO
ENTRE SUA MAGESTADE FIDELISSIMA
EL-REI DE PORTUGAL
E SUA MAGESTADE
O IMPERADOR DA CHINA.

MACAO:
TYPOGRAPHIA DE J. DA SILVA.
1862.

TENDO nós conseguido obter uma copia do Tratado de amisade e commercio entre Portugal e a China, que S. Exa. o Governador de Macau na qualidade de Plenipotenciario de Sua Magestade, com tamanha gloria para a corôa portugueza concluíu em 13 d'agosto ultimo, e sabendo que só depois da ratificação dará o Governo publicidade official ao mesmo Tratado, pois que só então lhe dará vigôr: tivemos por agradavel dever reproduzir extra-officialmente a nossa copia, correspondendo assim aos freneticos desejos de toda uma população, que, enthusiasmada e jubilosa, festejava hontem com as mais patrioticas demostrações o brilhante reconhecimento dos antigos direitos dos portuguezes na China.

Se, na extencia das nações, a apathia póde jamais ter uma desculpa, não é decerto a tradição de um passado glorioso que a dá. A nobreza da historia obriga, e para a invocar como titulo á consideração de extranhos não basta que um paiz se reveja n'ella indolente, mas que, exercendo sempre a sua actividade nos limites que as condições da epocha lhe impoem, preste digno culto aos fastos de que se ufana. A nação que, tendo sido grande em adquirir, descuidar na indifferença as conquistas d'esse passado brilhante, não só se arrisca a tornar-se esquecida, mas auctorisa a que a julguem degenerada.

Quando pois todas as potencias da Europa tanto se empenham em consecuções n'estas partes do oriente da Asia, Portugal, que sobre todas tem o direito de uma prioridade illustre, não podia deixar de entrar, de uma maneira clara e digna, na communhão dos grandes interesses que recentes acontecimentos teem desenvolvido cada dia mais.

Mas facilitava-nos esse direito a empreza?

A par do Tratado que ahi tendes (conseguido ha dias por um Ministro portuguez, sem desdobramento de bandeiras, nem apparatos de força) consultai o passado do nosso estabelecimento na China, e vereis que, a despeito de toda a gloria d'elle, é esta a primeira vez que os direitos e privilegios da corôa de Portugal aqui se definem de uma maneira clara e digna,- isto quando de ha muito a poderosa competencia de nações mais fortes nos veio tirar o prestigio que os nossos maiores bem souberam conquistar com denôdo, mas mal poderam guardar com firmeza. Analysando detidamente o nosso passado glorioso, que a miúdo, invocàmos com justo orgulho, mas que não obstante tinha de ser a principal difficldade na disputada negociação do Tratado, póde até dizer-se que só agora as duas nações se collocaram reciprocamente n'um pé d'igualdade;– porque, ainda que sempre nos respeitaram, mais nos tiveram por subditos fortes que por nação independente e alliada. Das brilhantes embaixadas que mandámos á China, sendo as principaes a de Metello, no reinado de D. João V, e a de Sampaio, no de D. José, é incontestavel que todas foram recebidas com mais subida consideração do que as d'Inglaterra, da Russia e da Hollanda obtiveram por aquelles mesmos tempos, mas não é menos certo que nem um só documento nos deixaram em que se assegurassem relações internacionaes, e que limitaram as suas negociações ao ceremonial mais ou menos humilde que deveriam observar na presença do Imperador, e á entrega dos presentes, que os chins apellidavam tributos. Nos unicos documentos que temos d'aquelle genero, trocados entre as auctoridades de Macau e o Governo Chinez, e que tão felizmente no Tratado são dados por não existentes, só se vê, de um lado a humildade de supplicas e pelições, e do outro a arrogancia de ordens e decretos, terminando algumas vexes pela bem conhecida formula chineza de *Tremam e obedeçam*.

Com este passado era forçôso luctar tanto mais fortemente quanto estavam de todo mudadas as circunstancias que até certo ponto o desculpam, porque, ainda que antigamente sempre estiveram mal difinidos os nossos direitos na China, certo é que eram elles tão exclusivamente nossos que a falta de competencia não só os tornava tão lucrativos como se estivessem bem estabelecidos, mas até lhes dava uma grande apparencia de dignidade e solidez. Esse exclusivo, porem, que por tão absurdamente o julgarem eterno, impediu que esses direitos fossem claramente reconhecidos n'aquelles tempos, terminou afinal como era inevitavel, e as nações que bem depressa vieram dispcctar-nos a inexgotowel partilha d'eite como mercio, souberam a todo o custo estabelecer em bazes solidas os seus direitos, recorrendo umas á força, como ainda ha pouco vimos a Inglaterra e a França, e conservando-se outras nos limites da diplomicia, mas luctando ahi com persistencia não menor, como a Russia e os Estados Unidos.

Mas se, por nos vermos assim collocados quasi em ultimo lugar nas relações dos póvos do Occidente com a China, mais urgía conseguir o que no tempo em que occuparamos o primeiro não soubemos obter,– a cessão clara e definida dos direitos ha seculos adquiridos,– é incontestavel tambem que essa mesma differença de posições devia centuplicar agora a difficuldade d'uma negociação que antes fôra julgada impossivel;– porque, obrigando-nos a muito a recordação do passado, constrangiam-nos a pouco as circunstancias do presente. E facil é de reconhecer que a essa difficuldade, que resultava naturalmente de se haver diminuido o nosso prestigio para com o Governo Chinez, acrescia outro não menos importante; porque,– pedindo a singular situação de Portugal na China que não só se definisse como direito o que antes se obtivéra de facto, como tambem que nos fossem concedidas todas as vantagens politicas e commerciaes que nações menos antigas do que nós no trato e commercio com a China teem sabido obter,– estas exigencias, a que tanto obrigava a dignidade nacional, eram de sobejo para acordar rivalidades, que muito cumpria serenar.

Taes seriam em resumo os enomes obstaculos que S. Exa. o Plenipotenciario portuguez teve de vencer; e, considerando-os, mal se crê como em tamanha lucta nos coube tão gloriosa victoria.

Mas o Tratado ahi está, e, como mostra-l'o, abstemo-nos de uma analyse que só poderia ser inferior á eloquencia d'elle. Dizer que nenhum houve por estas partes de maior gloria, nada mais é do que repetir o que tão claramente se prova em toda a lettra dos seus artigos, porque não só nos iguala, quanto ao presente, com a China, mas vae até nos tornar superiores ao que fômos quando mais podiamos do que hoje, reconhecendo formalmente o que sempre com altivez nos foi contestado:– tudo isto sem outras armas do que a profunda intelligencia de um Plenipotenciario de Sua Magestade, e o seu tão provado amor a esta colonia de Macau, que, para tudo lhe dever, até lhe deve hoje a sua completa e legal independencia portugueza.

O que torna ainda mais digno e honroso o Tratado, quanto ao reconhecimento d'esta independencia, é não sacrificar os nossos pretendidos direitos do passado á verdadeira consecução do presente, e admittir tacitamente como de ha muito existente a situação que estabelece com solidez no futuro. O reconhecimento simplesmente enunciado nada mais por certo ganharía em clareza e far-nos-hia perder muito em dignidade, porque, argumentando-se na exigencia com o passado, não convinha que desmerecesse depois na consecução o proprio argumento que se invocára. Para quem não ignora quanto, apezar da sua excessiva tolerancia, o Governo Chinez se mostra sempre resistente a quaesquer concessões que definida e claramente confirmem direitos que o lesem, embora de facto elle os haja admittido ha longo tempo, facil será avaliar quão trabalhoso seria a lucta em que não só se obteve que a colonia de Macau deixasse afinal de ser julgada territorio chinez por aquelle Governo, mas até que esse reconhecimento se enunciasse de forma que nem por isso a mesma colonia fosse considerada menos independente durante um largo passado, cuja historia mais nos arriscava a exigencia do que a favorecia ou corroborava.- Podia conseguir-se mais? Era d'esperar que se obtivesse tanto?

Logo que officialmente se dè á luz o Tratado, é provavel que, por um relatorio minucioso, o publico seja largamente informado das difficuldades que houve a combater e de todas as interessantes peripecias d'esta gloriosa negociação.- Admirar-se-ha em tal narrativa a grandeza da lucta. Por agora só podêmos manifestar com a publicação do Tratado o resultado d'ella.

Tendo presenciado as inequivocas demonstrações com que os extrangeiros residentes n'esta cidade tão espontanea e delicadamente se associaram ao regosijo publico, na volta de S. Exa. o Governador, julgámos cumprir um dever juntando á nossa copia uma traducção em inglez, devida á habil penna e á obsequiosa dedicação de um distincto cavalheiro, que estima e deseja cordealmente as glorias de Portugal.

A.-M. P.

Macau, 11 de Setembro de 1862.

TRATADO

DE

AMIZADE E COMMERCIO

Entre Sua Magestade Fidelissima

EL-REI DE PORTUGAL

E Sua Magestade

O IMPERADOR DA CHINA.

— —

SUA MAGESTADE FIDELISSIMA EL-REI DE PORTUGAL e SUA MAGESTADE O IMPERADOR DA CHINA, querendo fixar bazes solidas, por meio de um Tratado solemne, as relações de amizade e commercio que ha seculos existem entre o Reino de Portugal e o Impreio Chinez, nomearam para esse fim como seus Plenipotenciarios, a saber:

SUA MAGESTADE EL–REI DE PORTUGAL a ISIDORO FRANCISCO GUIMARãES[①], do Seu Conselho, Governador Geral de Macáu, Plenipotenciario na China, Commendador da Antiga e Mui Nobre Ordem da Torre e Espada do Valor, Lealdade e Merito, e das de S. Bento de Aviz, Nossa Senhora da Conceição de Villa Viçosa, Carlos 3o. de Hespanha, e do Elefante de Siam, Cavalheiro da Ordem de Nosso Senhor Jesus Christo, Capitão de Mar e Guerra da Armada, etc., etc., etc.;

E SUA MAGESTADE O IMPERADOR DA CHINA a HANG–KI, Alto Commissario Imperal da Dynastia Ta–Tsing, Membro do Ministerio dos Negocios Extrangeiros e do Tribunal dos Ritos, Condecorado com a Insignia do Primeiro Gráu, General das tropas da Divisão da Bandeira vermelha bordada, Conselheiro d'Estado dos Honorario, etc., etc., etc., e Chung–Hou, Conselheiro Privado, Ministro do Tribunal dos Ritos, Superintendente do Commercio Extrangeiro nos tres Pórtos de Tang–chou, Tien–tsin e Neu–choang, General interino da Provincia de Tchi–ly, etc., etc., etc.:

Os quaes, depois de haverem trocado os seus respectivos plenos poderes, que acharam em boa e devida forma, concordaram nos seguintes artigos de Tratado:

ARTIGO I.

Continuará a existir constante paz e amizade entre Sua Magestade Fidelissima El–Rei de Portugal e Sua Magestade o Imperador da China, cujos respectivos

–2–

subditos gosarão igualmente, nos dominios das Altas Partes Contractantes da mais completa e decidida protecção para com as suas pessoas e propriedades.

ARTIGO II.

É inteiramente annullado e tido como nunca existente por este Tratado tudo o que até hoje, em qualquer lugar ou epocha, possa haver sido escripto, ou impresso, ou verbalmente convencionado com respeito ás relações entre Portugal e o Imperio da China e entre o Governo da cidade de Macau （antes na provincia de Cantão） e as Auctoridades chinezas:– vistoque d'ora em diante servirá de unico regulamento válido para as mesmas relações o presente Tratado, concluido e assignado pelos Plenipotenciarios dos dois Estados, devidamente munidos das suas respectivas credenciaes.

ARTIGO III.

O Governador Geral de Macau, na sua qualidade de Plenipotenciario de Sua Magestade Fidelissima na China, poderá vir á Corte de Pekim todos os annos, quando importantes negocios lh'o exijam.

Se no futuro o Governo de Sua Magestade o Imperador da China dér faculdade para residir permanentemente em Pekim ao Plenipotenciario de qualquer outra nação extrangeira alem das que já hoje ali teem Representantes, o Enviado de Sua Magestade Fidelissima poderá considerar essa permissão como sendo–lhe extensiva e aproveitar–se d'ella, se o julgar conveniente.

① Sic.

ARTIGO IV.

Os Agentes diplomaticos gosarão nos lugares das suas residencias de todos os privilegios e immunidades que lhes concede o direito das gentes: isto é, as suas pessoas, as suas familias, as suas cazas e as suas correspondencias serão inviolaveis.

ARTIGO V.

As despezas das Missões diplomaticas de Portugal na china serão pagas pelo Governo Portuguez. Os Agentes diplomaticos que Sua Magestade o Imperador da China se dignar acreditar junto á Corte de Sua Magestade El-Rei de Portugal, serão recebidos com todas as honras e prerogativas de que gosarem todos os mais Agentes diplomaticos extrangeiros d'igual gerarchia, acreditados n'aquella Córte.

ARTIGO VI.

As correspondencias officiaes, enviadas pelas Auctoridades Portuguezas ás Auctoridades Chinezas, serão escriptas em portuguez e acompanhadas da traducção chineza.

Do mesmo modo será o presente Tratado escripto em portuguez e china depois de confrontado devidamente, e servirá de documento a cada Nação a versão escripta na sua propria lingua.

ARTIGO VII.

As formulas das correspondencias officiaes entre as Auctoridades portuguezas e chinezas serão reguladas pelas gerarchias e posições respectivas, tendo por base a mais completa reciprocidade. Entre os altos funccionarios portuguezes e os altos funccionarios chinezes, na capital ou em qualquer outro lugar, estas correspondencias terão a forma de officio ou communicação: entre os funccionarios portuguezes subordinados e as primeiras Auctoridades de provincia usar–se–ha, para aquelles a forma de exposição （*Chau–Hoei*） e para estas a de declaração （*Xen–Cheu*）; e os officiaes subordinados de ambas as nações deverão corresponder–se em termos de perfeita igualdade.

Os negociantes, e geralmente todos os individuos não investidos de caracter official, seguirão para com as Auctoridades a formula de representação （*Pin–Cheng.*）

Quando qualquer subdito portuguez tiver de representar á Auctoridade chineza do districto, deverá primeiramente levar a sua representação ao Consul. que, não a

–3–

achando inconveniente, a fará entregar, e no cazo contrario mandará escreve–l'a n'outros termos, ou recusará transmitti–l'a. Igualmente quando um subdito chinez haja de representar ao Consul de Portugal, só poderá faze–l'o por via da Auctorida de chineza, que procederá da mesma forma.

ARTIGO VIII.

Em todos os pórtos da China abertos ao commercio poderá Sua Magestade El–Rei de Portugal estabelecer Consules para tratarem dos negocios commerciaes e vigiarem pela observancia de todos os artigos d'este Tratado.

Os Consules e As Auctoridades locaes deverão tratar–se reciprocamente com polidez e corresponder–se em termos de perfeita igualdade.

Os Consules e Consules interinos terão honras de *Tau-tai*, e os Vice Consules, Agentes Consulares e Interpretes traductores as de Perfeito. Os seus poderes serão iguaes aos das Auctoridades consulares das demais nações.

Estes funccionarios deverão ser verdadeiros agentes do Governo portuguez, e não commerciantes. O Governo chinez nenhuma objecção fará porem a que Portugal, não julgando necessario enviar um verdadeiro Consul para qualquer dos pórtos, encarregue interinamente o seu Consulado n'esse porto a um Consul de outra nação.

ARTIGO IX.

Sua Magestade El-Rei de Portgual e Sua Magestade o Imperador da China, desejando manifestar as suas amigaveis intenções reciprocas, concordam expressamente no seguinte:

Todos os subditos dos dois Estados, em qualquer parte do territorio portuguez ou chinez, serão sempre tratados reciprocamente como amigos.

Sua Magestade El-Rei de Portugal ordenará ao Governador de Macau que preste a mais decidida coadjuvação a evitar tudo o que, n'aquelle ponto, se possa tornar prejudicial aos interesses do Imperio Chinez.

Sua Magestade o Imperador da China poderá nomear pois, se lhe convier, um agente para residir em Macau, e ali tratar dos negocios commerciaes e vigiar pela obserbancia dos regulamentos. Este agente porem, deverá ser Manchú ou China, e ter a graduação de quarta ou quinta ordem. Os seus poderes serão iguaes aos dos Consules de França, Inglaterra, America, ou d'outras nações, que residem em Macau e Hongkong e ali tratam dos seus negocios publicos, arvorando a bandeira nacional.

ARTIGO X.

É permettido a todos os subditos portuguezes e ás suas familias habitarem ou frequentarem os pórtos e cidades de Kuang-tchou （Cantão）, - Chan-chou （Suatau）, Amoy, - Fu-chau, - Ning-po, - Shang-hai, - Chen-kiang, Kien-kiang, e Han-kau （no rio Yang-tsi）, - Tang-chou, - Tien-tsin, - Neu-choang, - Tan-shoei e Tai-van （na ilha Formosa）, - e Kiung-chou （na ilha de Hai-nan）, e ali commerciarem ou empregarem-se livremente. As suas embarcações poderão ir e vir sem embaraço, e as suas mercadorias importar-se ou exportar-se em qualquer tempo illimitadamente.

ARTIGO XI.

O Governo Chinez não obstará de forma alguma a que os subditos portuguezes empreguem os subditos chinezes em qualquer occupação que as leis permittam.

ARTIGO XII.

É permittido a todo o commerciante Portuguez, que no desembarque das suas mercadorias em algum dos pórtos abertos tiver satisfeito aos direitos que dever, e tambem a quaesquer outros subditos portuguezes, viajarem por todas as partes do interior da China, quer por conveniencia do seu commercio, quer por simples diversão, comtanto que andem munidos de passaportes, que serão dados pelos Consules e assignados pelas auctoridades locaes. O portador de um passaporte deverá apresental'o nos lugares por onde passar, quando por elle se lhe pergunte; e, estando o seu passaporte regular, ninguem poderá pór–lhe embaraço a que allugue embarcações ou carregadores para a conducção das suas bagagens ou mercadorias. Se um viajante for encontrado sem passaporte, ou se commetter alguma offensa contra a lei, será entregue ao Consul mais proximo para que o castigue, não se podendo usar para com elle de outra qualquer medida de repressão.

São desnessarios passaportes ás pessôas que percorrerem as visinhanças de qualquer dos pórtos abertos ao commercio, dentro da distancia de 100 *lis* （12 leguas） e do prazo de cinco dias.

As estipulações d'este artigo não dizem respeito ás equipagens dos navios, porque para estas os Consules e as auctoridades locaes farão os convenientes regulamentos.

Para Nankim, ou outras quaesquer cidades que estiverem em revolta contra o Governo, não serão dados passaportes até que as mesmas cidades hajam sido retomadas.

ARTIGO XIII.

Quando nos portos ou n'outros lugares, algum subdito portuguez quizer construir ou abrir cazas, armazens, egrejas, hospitaes ou cemiterios, o contracto de compra ou aluguer d'essas propridades será feito segundo as condições mais geralmente usadas entre o povo, com equidade, e sem pagamento d'imposto algum por qualquer das partes.

Entende–se porem que só nos pórtos abertos ao commercio é permettido o estabelecimento de armazens.

ARTIGO XIV.

Os subditos portuguezes poderão fretar quaesquer embarcações que desejem para transporte de carga ou de passageiros, e o preço de taes fretamentos será determinado unicamente pelas partes, sem interferencia do Governo Chinez.

O numero das embarcações não poderá ser limitado, nem tampouco se permittirá a quemquer que seja fazer monopolio d'ellas, ou dos *cules* que se empregam em carregar mercadorias.

Descobrindo–se que n'alguma das embarcações se mette contrabando, os culpados serão immediatamente pundios conforme a lei.

ARTIGO XV.

Todas as questões que se suscitarem entre subditos portuguezes, com respeito a direitos quer de propriedade quer de pessoa, serão submettidas á jurisdicção das auctoridades portuguezas.

ARTIGO XVI.

Todos os subditos chinezes que se tornarem culpados de qualquer acto criminoso para com subditos portuguezes serão presos e castigados pelas auctoridades chinezas, segundo as leis da china, precedendo participação das auctoridades portuguezas.

Os subditos portuguezes que commetterem qualquer crime na China serão julgados pelo Consul, ou por outro funccionario publico portuguez auctorisado para esse fim, segundo as leis de Portugal, precedendo participação das auctoridades chinezas.

ARTIGO XVII.

Todo o subdito portuguez que tiver soffrido offensa de um china deverá fazer a sua queixa perante o Consul, que se informará devidamente da questão e empregará todos os esfórços para a terminar amigavelmente. Do mesmo modo quando um subdito china tiver a queixar–se de um portuguez, o Consul não dexiará de attender á sua queixa e de fazer todo o possivel para restabelecer a boa harmonia entre as duas partes. Se porem a disputa fôr de tal natureza que se não possa ter–

–5–

minar por esse modo, então o Consul pedirá ás auctoridades chinezas o seu comparecimento na inquirição do cazo, para que juntamente o decidam com equidade.

ARTIGO XVIII.

As auctoridades chinezas deverão prestar a mais inteira protecção ás pessoas e propriedades dos subditos portuguezes, sempre que estas corrão perigo de soffrer qualquer insulto ou prejuiso. Nos cazos de roubo ou incendio as auctoridades locaes tomarão immediatamente as medidas necessarias para se rehaver a propriedade roubada, para que a desordem termine, e para que os criminosos sejam presos e punidos conforme a lei.

ARTIGO XIX.

Acontecendo que um navio mercante portuguez seja roubado por piratas ou ladrões nas aguas da China, as auctoridades chinezas deverão empregar a maior diligencia para prender e castigar os mesmos ladrões e rehaver a propriedade roubada, que por mediação do Consul será restituida a quem pertencer.

ARTIGO XX.

Se algum navio portuguez naufragar na costa da China, ou fôr obrigado a refugiar–se em qualquer dos pórtos do mesmo imperio, as auctoridades chinezas, logo que recebam noticia do facto, tomarão as providencias necessarias para o soccorrer e proteger, acolhendo amigavelmente a equipagem e prestando–lhe, se preciso fôr, os meios de se transportar ao Consulado mais proximo.

ARTIGO XXI.

Se quaesquer criminosos, subditos da China, se refugiarem em Macau, ou abórdo dos navios portuguezes surtos n'aquelle porto, serão entregues ás auctoridades chinezas, precedendo requisição e provado o crime.

Da mesma forma, em qualquer dos portos abertos da China, todo o subdito chinez provadamente criminoso, que buscar asylo na habitação ou abórdo do navio de um subdito portuguez, não será acolhido nem occultado, mas logo entregue ás auctoridades chinezas, precedendo requisição ao Consul portuguez do mesmo porto.

ARTIGO XXII.

Se qualquer subdito chinez, tendo contrahido uma divida para com um subdito portuguez, se negar a parga–

lh'a, ou fraudalosamente se esconder d'elle as auctoridades chinezas empregarão todos os esforços para o prender e obriga-l'o-hão a pagar, depois de provada a divida e verificada a possibilidade do pagamento. Igualmente procederão as auctoridades portuguezas para com o subdito portuguez que dexiar de pagar uma divida a qualquer subdito chinez.

ARTIGO XXIII.

Todo o navio mercante portuguez, que tiver mais de 150 toneladas, pagará os direitos de tonelagem a rasão de 4 *mazes* de prata por cada tonelada. Tendo 150 toneladas, ou menos, pagará a rasão de 1 *maz*. O Superintende de Alfandega deverá passar um attestado com declaração dos direitos de tonelagem que tiverem sido pagos.

ARTIGO XXIV.

Os subditos portuguezes pagarão sobre todas as mercadorias que importarem ou exportarem os direitos marcados na tarifa adoptada para com as outras nações, e em nenhum cazo lhes serão exigidos direitos mais elevados do que os que pagarem os subditos de qualquer outra nação extrangeiras.

ARTIGO XXV.

Consideram-se pagaveis os direitos d'importação no acto do desembarque das mercadorias, e os d'exportação no do embarque das mesmaas.

–6–

ARTIGO XXVI.

Qualquer das duas Altas Partes contractantes poderá, no fim de dez annos, pedir um revisão da tarifa ou dos artigos commerciaes d'este Tratado, entendendo-se que, não sendo feito esse pedido dentro de seis mezes contados sobre os primeiros dez annos, continuará em vigor a mesma tarifa durante mais dez annos contados sobre os precedentes dez; e assim de dez em dez annos.

ARTIGO XXVII.

O Capitão de um navio portuguez poderá, quando assim lhe convenha, desembarcar uma parte sómente da sua carga em qualquer dos portos abertos, pagando os devidos direitos das fazendas que desembarcar.

ARTIGO XXVIII.

Todo o subdito portuguez que transportar para o mercado do interior do paiz mercadorias, de que já tenha pago os competentes direitos d'importação em qualquer dos pórtos abertos, ou que comprar no interior fazendas para as levar para os portos do Yang-tsi-kiang, ou para os portos extrangeiros, deverá observar o regulamento novamente adoptado para com as outras nações.

Os escrivães e mais empregados da Alfandega que não cumprirem o regulamento, ou que exigirem mais direitos do que devem, serão castigados segundo as leis chinezas.

ARTIGO XXIX.

Todo o navio portuguez que fôr despachado de um dos pórtos abertos da China para outro qualquer dos mesmos pórtos, ou para Macau, tem direito a um certificado da alfandega que o exempte de novo pagamento dos direitos de tonelagem, durante um periodo de quatro mezes contados sobre a data do despacho.

ARTIGO XXX.

O capitão de um navio portuguez tem faculdade para, dentro de quarenta e oito horas contadas da chegada do seu navio a qualquer dos pórtos abertos da China, mas não mais tarde, decidir-se a partir sem abrir as escotilhas; e n'esse cazo não terá a pagar direitos de tonelagem. É comtudo obrigado a dar parte da sua chegada para o competente registo logo que entrar no porto, sob pena de multa quando o não faça no espaço de dois dias.

O navio está portanto sujeito aos direitos de tonelagem quarenta e oito horas depois da sua chegada ao porto, e nem então, nem á saída, lhe será exigido outro qualquer imposto.

ARTIGO XXXI.

Serão livres de pagamento de tonelagem todos os barcos empregados por subditos portuguezes na conducção de passageiros, bagagens, cartas, provisões, ou de qualquer outra carga livre de direitos, entre os pórtos abertos da China. Todos os barcos de carga, porem, que conduzirem mercadorias sujeitas a direitos, pagarão tonelagem todos os quatro mezes, a razão de um *maz* por tonelada.

ARTIGO XXXII.

Os Consules e os Superintendentes das alfandegas deverão consultar-se, quando preciso fôr, sobre a construcção de torres de faról e collocação de boias e navios-faróes.

ARTIGO XXXIII.

Os direitos serão pagos aos banqueiros auctorisados pelo Governo Chinez para os cobrarem, em *saicí* ou em moeda extrangeira, conforme o ensaio feito em Cantão aos 15 de Julho de 1843.

–7–

ARTIGO XXXIV.

Para assegurar a uniformidade dos pezos e medidas e evitar confusões, o Superintendente das alfandegas entregará ao Consul portuguez de cada um dos pórtos abertos um padrão conforme ao que é dado pela Repartição da cobrança publica á alfandega de Cantão.

ARTIGO XXXV.

Todo o navio mercante portuguez, ao aproximar-se de qualquer dos pórtos abertos, terá a liberdade de tomar um prático que o faça entrar; e igualmente o poderá tomar para saír, quando assim lhe convenha e haja satisfeito no pórto a todos os direitos que dever.

ARTIGO XXXVI.

Todas as vezes que um navio mercante portuguez chegar a qualquer dos pórtos abertos da China, o Superintendente da Alfandega mandar-lhe-ha um ou mais guardas, que poderão ficar na sua embarcação ou passar para bórdo do navio, segundo melhor lhes convenha. Estes guardas receberão da Alfandega a comida e tudo o mais que precisarem, e não poderão aceitar propina alguma do capitão do navio ou do consignatario, sob pena proporcional á importancia do que aceitarem.

ARTIGO XXXVII.

Vinte e quarto horas depois da chegada de um navio mercante portuguez a qualquer dos pórtos abertos, os papeis do mesmo navio, os conhecimentos e mais documentos deverão ficar entregues ao Consul, o qual deverá tambem, dentro de vinte e quatro horas, communicar ao Superintendente da Alfandega o nome do navio, o registro das suas toneladas e qual a carga que transportou. Se, por negligencia, ou qualquer outro motivo, quarenta e oito horas depois da chegada do navio, se não tiver cumprido com o que fica estipulado, o capitão ficará sujeito á multa de cincoenta *taeis* por cada dia mais de demora: não excedendo porem o total da pena a duzentos *taeis*.

O capitão do navio é o responsavel pela exactidão do manifesto, no qual deverá declarar a carga minuciosamente e com toda a verdade, sob pena de multa de quinhentos *taeis* no cazo em que o manifesto seja achado inexacto. Não incorrerá porem na pena quando, no espaço de vinte e quatro horas depois da entrega do manifesto aos empregados da Alfandega, queira corrigir algum erro que possa ter descoberto no mesmo manifesto.

ARTIGO XXXVIII.

O Superintendente da Alfandega permittirá que o navio descarregue, logo que tenha recebido do Consul a nota feita nos devidos termos. Se o capitão do navio começar a descarregar sem permissão, será multado em quinhentos *taeis*, e os objectos que tiverem sido descarregados serão confiscados.

ARTIGO XXXIX.

Todo o negociante portuguez que tiver carga para embarcar ou desembarcar, deverá obter para isso uma permissão especial do Superintendente da Alfandega, sem o que toda a fazenda embarcada ou desembarcada ficará sujeita a ser confiscada.

ARTIGO XL.

Não se poderá baldear fazendas de um navio para outro sem licença especial, sob pena de confiscação de todas as fazendas baldeadas.

ARTIGO XLI.

Quando o navio tiver satisfeito no porto a todos os direitos que dever, o Superintendente da Alfandega passar-lhe-ha um attestado e o Consul restituir-lhe-ha os papeis, para que possa seguir viagem.

-8-

ARTIGO XLII.

Quando houver duvidas sobre mercadorias que, segundo a tarifa, pagam direitos *ad valorem*, e o negociante portuguez não pudér combinar com o empregado da alfandega no valor d'essas mercadorias, cada uma das partes chamará dois ou tres negociantes para as vêrem, e o preço mais alto que qualquer d'elles offerecer para as comprar será o valôr d'ellas.

ARTIGO XLIII.

Os direitos serão pagos pelo pezo de cada mercadoria, depois de deduzida a tara. Se entre o negociante portuguez e o empregado da Alfandega houver duvidas no fixar da tara, cada uma das partes escolherá um certo numero de caixas ou de fardos d'entre cada cem da mercadoria em questão, tomar-se-ha o pezo bruto d'esses volumes, fixando depois a tara de cada um d'elles, e a tara media que resultar será a adoptada para todos.

No cazo de qualquer outra duvida ou contestação, aqui não designada, o negociante portuguez poderá appellar para o seu Consul, o qual communicará a questão ao Superintendente da Alfandega, e este fará por conclui-l'a amigavelmente. A appellação, porem, só poderá ser attendida quando seja feita dentro do prazo de vinte e quatro horas; e, n'este cazo, até que a duvida seja resolvida, não se poderá fazer nos livros da Alfandega assento algum relativo ás mercadorias em questão.

ARTIGO XLIV.

As fazendas avariadas terão uma reducção de direitos proporcional á sua deterioração. No cazo de haver dufida, será resolvida como na clausula d'este Tratado relativa ás mercadorias que pagam direitos *ad valorem*.

ARTIGO XLV.

Todo o negociante portuguez que, depois d'importar mercadorias em algum dos pórtos abertos da China e de satisfazer os competentes direitos, as quizer reexportar para qualquer outro dos mesmos pórtos, deverá fazer d'ellas uma relação que entregará ao Superintendente da Alfandega, o qual, para evitar faudes, mandará examinar pelos seus empregados se os direitos foram pagos, se as fazendas deram entrada nos livros da Alfandega, se conservam as marcas originaes e se os assentos dos livros estão em harmonia com o referido na relação. Achando tudo conforme, declara-l'o-ha no certificado do despacho, mencionado tambem o total dos direitos pagos, e de tudo isto dará conhecimento aos empregados das alfandegas dos outros pórtos.

Chegado o navio ao pórto para onde conduz as fazendas, ser-lhe-ha permittido desembarca-l'as sem pagamento de direitos alguns addicionaes quando no exame d'ellas se reconheça serem as mesmas. Quando porém n'esse exame se descubra fráude, as fazendas poderão ser confiscadas pelo Governo Chinez.

Se algum negociante portuguez quizer reexportar para paiz extrangeiro fazendas que tenha importado com pagamento dos competentes direitos, deverá fazer d'ellas uma relação satisfazendo ás mesmas condições exigidas na reexportação para os pórtos da China, pelo que se lhe dará um certificado de restituição de direitos (*drawback*) que será aceito em pagamento de direitos d'importação ou d'exportação por qualquer das alfandegas chinezas.

Os cereaes extrangeiros, que tiverem sido trazidos a algum dos pórtos da China por um navio portuguez, poderão ser reexportados sem embaraço, quando se não haja desembarcado porção alguma d'elles.

ARTIGO XLVI.

As auctoridades chinezas adoptarão em todos os pórtos as medidas que julgarem mais convenientes para evitar a fraude e o contrabando.

ARTIGO XLVII.

Os navios mercantes portuguezes só poderão frequentar aquelles pórtos da China que por este Tratado são declarados abertos ao commercio. É–lhes, portanto, defeso entrarem n'outros pórtos, bem como fazerem commercio clandestino nas

–9–

costas da China, e o que violar esta diaposição ficará sujeito a ser confiscado pelo Governo Chinez com toda a carga que tiver abórdo.

ARTIGO XLVIII.

Se algum navio mercante portuguez fôr encontrado a fazer contrabando, toda a carga, seja qual fôr o seu valôr ou natureza, ficará sujeita a ser confiscada pelas Auctoridades chinezas, que poderão mandar saír do pôrto o navio, depois d'elle saldar todas as suas contas, e prohibi–l'o de continuar a negociar.

ARTIGO XLIX.

O producto das multas e confiscações, infligidas, na conformidade d'este Tratado, a subditos portuguezes, pertencerá ao Governo Chinez.

ARTIGO L.

Todos os navios de guerra portuguezes que vierem com intenções amigaveis, ou que andarem em perseguição de piratas, terão plena liberdade de visitar quaesquer pórtos dos dominios do Imperador da China, e de n'elles fazer aguada ou comprar mantimentos, para o que lhes será prestado todo o auxilio, bem como para fazerem reparações quando preciso seja. Os commandantes dos navios deverão tratar com as Auctoridades chinezas em termos d'igualdade e cortesia.

ARTIGO LI.

Nenhum commerciante e nenhum navio portuguez poderá levar a rebeldes ou piratas quaesquer mantimentos, armas, ou munições.

No cazo de contravenção, o navio será confiscado juntamente com a carga, e o culpado entregue ao Governo Portuguez para ser processado e punido com todo o rigor da lei.

ARTIGO LII.

Serão extensivas ao Governo Portuguez todas as vantagens e immunidades que o Governo Chinez conceder a qualquer outra nação. Da sua parte o Governo Portuguez, quando outra nação conceder á China quaesquer vantagens, mostrar–lhe–ha tambem, do modo possivel, a sua amisade.

ARTIGO LIII.

Sendo possivel, não obstante existir paz e amisade entre Portugal e a China, que venha no futuro a suscitar-se qualquer duvida que as duas Altas Partes Contractantes não possam facilmente decidir de cummum accordo, é expressamente estipulado que, n'esse cazo, cada um dos dois Governos convidará o Ministro de qualquer das nações extrangeiras que têem tratado com a China para decidir a questão, e que, se os dois Ministros não combinarem, se nomeará, por accordo dos dois Governos, um terceiro, cuja decisão será definitiva.

ARTIGO LIV.

As ratificações do presente Tratado, por Sua Magestade Fidelissima El-Rei de Portugal e Sua Magestade o Imperador da China, serão trocadas em Tien-tsin, no prazo de dois annos, contados da data da assignatura.

Trocadas as ratificações, o Governo Chinez dará conhecimento do Tratado ás Auctoridades superiores de todas as provincias para que o ponham em completa execução.

Em fé do que os Plenipotenciarios assignaram e sellaram o presente Tratado.

Feito em Tien-tsin no 13o. dia do mez de agosto do anno de Nosso Senhor Jesus Christo 1862, que corresponde ao 18.º dia da 7.ª lua do primeiro anno de Tung-che.

(Assignados) - IZIDORO FRANCISCO GUIMARÃES.
HANG-KI.
CHUNG-HOU.

L. S.

Lugar do Sello dos dois
Plenipotenciarios Chinezes.

[1-105]

[Recd 23 March
Nº35.]

Consulate of the United States.-
Macao, January 2d 1863.-

Sir,

Referring to my Despatch Nº 33, in which I forwarded to you the Returns of this Consulate for the previous Quarter, I now beg to hand you those of the Quarter ending the 31st of December 1862.-

I am,
Sir,
With great respect
Your obedient Servant
Gideon Nye Jnr

Vice Consul of the United States.
of America for Macao.–

[The Honorable
William H. Seward.
Secretary of State of the United States
of America.–
City of Washington]

[1–106]

[Recd May. Mr Abbott
N°36.]

Consulate of the United States.
Macao, February 13th, 1863.

Sir,

I have the honor to inform you of the departure of His Excellency Governor General Guimarães by the last English mail steamer en route to Lisbon; and to hand you copies of my official correspondence with His Excellency consequent thereupon.–

This enlightened Nobleman has always evinced a real friendship for the United States, and I am sure that you will be glad to hear that my anticipations– (in my letter N° 34 of Oct° 12th last.) –of some marked recognition of his public services by His Sovereign Dom Luis the 1st, have been realized, His Majesty having conferred upon him the title of Viscount of Macao.

I confidently expect, indeed, to hear of His Excellency's further advancement within no remote period, as a Member of the Cabinet or otherwise.–

I am, Sir,
With great respect
Your obedient Servant
Gideon Nye Jnr

[The Honorable
William H. Seward.
Secretary of State of the United States of America
City of Washington.]

[1]

[□□□ de Macao
□□□ Estrang°
N° 6.
Circular.]

[Copia.]

Ilt^{mo} S^{r}

Cumpre– me participar a U.S.^{a} que entrego hoje o Governo desta Colonia ao Consellio do Governo, retirando–me para Portugal.

Em quanto não alugar o meu successor, nomeado por Sua Magestade Fidelissima, toda a correspondencia Official relativa a negocia da competencia do Governo de Macao deve ser dirigida ao Ilt^{mo} Sr Juiz de Direito João Ferreira Pinto, como Presidente do Consellio do Governo.–

Aproveito esta occazião para significar a U.S.^{a} os meus sinceros votos pelas prosperidades da Naçao de que U.S.^{a} é digno Representante nesta Colonia.

Deus guarde a U.S.^{a} Macao 29 de Janeiro de 1863.–

(ass^{do}) Isidoro F. Guimarães

[Il^{mo} Sr Gideon Nye–
Vice Consul Americano em Macao.–]

[2]

[□□□ of Macao
Department
Foreign affairs
N° 6
Circular.]

Translation.

Sir,

It is my duty to apprise you that on my depature for Portugal– I now deliver the Government of this Colony to the Council of the Government.–

While my successor, named by His Most Faithful Majesty, is not arrived, all the official Correspondence relating to affairs within the competency of the Government of Macao, should be addressed to His Honor the Chief Justice Mr João Ferreira Pinto, as President of the Council of the Government.

I avail of this opportunity to express to you my sincere wishes (vows) for the prosperity of the Nation of which you are the worthy Representative in this Colony.–

God preserve you

Macao January 29th 1863.–
(signed) Isidoro F. Guimarães.

[Gideon Nye, Esq
Vice Consul of America at Macao.]

[3]

[Copy.]

Consulate of the United States of America
Macao, January 29th 1863.–

Sir,

I have the honor to acknowledge the receipt of Your Excellency's letter of this date, apprising me that being upon thepoint of departing for Portugal, you have delivered to the Council of Government the charge of the Government of this Colony; – and further, that pending the arrival of your Successor, named by this Most Faithful Masjesty, all official correspondence relating to affairs within the competency of the Government of Macao, should be addressed to His Honor The Chief Justice Mr João Ferreira Pinto, as President of the Council of Government.–

Your Excellency is pleased to add to these intimations, the expression of your sincere wishes for the prosperity of my country, in a form complimentary to myself as its Representative.–

In taking due note of the foregoing intimations and acknowledging the Courtesy of the close of your communication, I should as ill perfom, my official duty as conform to my own feelings, if I failed to acknowledge the uniform consideration with which my representations in behalf of Citizens of the United States have been received by Your Excellency.–

It is, therefore, in a spirit of great, cordiality that, as the humble Representative of my country here, I respectfully reciprocate your good wishes for its prosperity, and invoke,–with all my heart,–a happy reign for His Most Faithful Majesty and the Queen of Portugal and for yourself a career as fortunate as your deserving is great.

[I]

[His Excellency
The Viscount____
Governor General of Macao–
&c &c &c]

I am,
Sir,
Your Excellency's
Most obedient Servant
(signed) Gideon Nye, Jnr
Vice Consul of the United States
for Macao.

[1–107]

[Recd 18 Feb]
N°37.

Consulate of the United States

Macao, February 24th 1863.–

Sir,

Referring to my Despatch N° 35 in which I forwarded to you the Returns of this Consulate for the previous quarter, I now beg, in conclusion of my official duties, to hand you those of the fractional quarter beginning January 1st and ending February 24th 1863.–

I beg to hand you also a copy of the Inventory of the Archives &c delivered this day to Mr W. P. Jones my successor, whose signature is thereto affixed.––

I have the satisfaction to apprise you that at the eve of the depature of His Excellency Governor General Guimarães, last month, I obtained a favorable answer to my application for the pardon of James Davis an American Citizen who has been a Prisoner in Gaol here, under sentence to three years transportation to Africa.––

Trusting that my Correspondence, since September 6th 1858, has evinced to the Government the desire I have felt to worthily serve my country, although the office was unsought by me

[Honorable
William H. Seward.
Secretary of State of the United States of
America.–
City of Washington.]

and has entailed considerable pecuniary sacrifices,

I am,
Sir,
With great respect
Your obedient Servant
Gideon Nye Jnr
Vice Consul of the United states
of America for Macao.–

[1–108]

[Recd Aug 4.]

U. S. Consulate
Macao, Feb. 25. 1863.

To the Honorable Sect. of State
Washington D. C.

Sir:

I have the honor to report that I arrived at this port on yesterday, the 24th inst, was cordially received by my predecessor, Vice Consul, Gideon Nye. Esq; and entered upon the duties of my office this morning.

Herewith I transmit an inventory of the Archives of this Consulate transferred to me by the late incumbent.

Please observe that there is no bookcase or safe for preservation of records.

[No 1. Inventory of Archives.]

I am, Sir,
Your Obedient Servant
W. P. Jones
Consul for Macao.

Inventory of Archives and other articles belonging to the Consulate of the United States at Macao delivered the day by the undersigned Gideon Nye, Jr to the undersigned W. P. Jones.–

---

1 Seal Press with wooden stand
1 Solid Brass Seal of the U. S. Arms (large)
1 Solid Brass Seal of the U. S Arms (small)
1 Mother O'Pearl Seal of the U.S. Arms for Sucks
1 Ivory Seal of the U. S. Arms – for Suks
1 small Flag staff, with several fragments of Flags
1 Escutcheon of the United States
1 Book of Regulations and Forms for Consuls (bound)
1 Pamphlet list of consular Fees
5 Volumes of statutes at Large (unbound)
2 Volumes of "Commercial Relations." (bound)
3 Reports of the Secy of state with public Correspond^{ce} (unbound)
2 local Letter Books (bound)
2 Miscellaneous Record Books (bound)
1 Government Despatch Book (bound)
1 Fee Book (bound)
1 package of Official Letters, Despatches, Government printed Circulars, and various necessaries.
1 package of Pamphlets, – comprising "List of Diplomatic & Consular officers." "Message of the President" &c &c.
1 package containing remaining blank printed forms for office use in the future.–

Consulate of the United States
Macao, February 24th 1863.
Gideon Nye, Jnr
W. P. Jones.

[Enclosure
With dispatch No.1

Inventory of Archives
No.1.
Feb, 24, 1863.]

[U. S. Consulate.
Macao. Feb 25,1863.
W. P. Jones
No.1.
1 Enclosure.
Received
Announcement of arrival at
Macao and Entrance upon
duty; – with enclosure
of inventory.]

[1–109]

[copy]

U. S. Consulate
Macao, March 6th 1863.

My dear sir,

The consular archives transferred and the official introductions concluded, I open my portfolio to apprise my brother Consuls of neighboring ports, that I have entered upon duty.–

But first, allow me, by this written expression, to attest to yourself, as my predecessor, my hearty appreciation of the manner and spirit, in which you have in everything official, honored every claim of either duty or courtesy; and to convey my thanks therefor.–

Had you restricted yourself to these formal services, I would not have to add my still more fervent thanks for that cordial welcome extended to me upon the morning of my arrival;–those hospitalities, which for more than a week made your house a very house for my voyage––weary family; and those counsels and kindly offices, which have contributed so much to my comfortable establishment in my own dwelling.––

Be assured, dear Sir, that I shall always hold these favors in lively and grateful remembrance, and be only too happy to reciprocate, should occasions ever offer.–

In conclusion, allow me to express the hope that the worthy officer, the Christian gentleman, the friend and counselor of the brief acquaintance past, will conntinence my friend and advises in the future.

Very cordially,
Your obdt: Servants
(signed) W. P. Jones.

(L. S.)
[Gideon Nye, Jr: Esq.
Late U. S. Vice Consul
Macao.]

Inventory of Archives and other articles belonging to the Consulate of the United States at Macao delivered this day by the undersigned Gideon Nye, Jr: to the undersigned W. P. Jones.–

---

1 Seal Press with wooden stands
1 Solid Brass Seal of the U. S. Arms (large)
1 Solid Brass Seal of the U. S. Arms (small)
1 Mother o' Pearl Seal of the U. S. Arms for Sucks
1 Ivory Seal of the U. S. Arms for Suks
1 small Flag staff, with several fragments of Flags
1 Escutcheon of the United States
1 Book of Regulations and Forms for Consuls (bound)
1 Pamphlet list of consular Fees
5 Volumes of statutes at Large (unbound)
2 Volumes of "Commercial Relations." (bound)
3 Reports of the Secy of state with public Correspond^ce (unbound)
2 local Letter Books (bound)
2 Miscellaneous Record Books (bound)
1 Government Despatch Book (bound)
1 Fee Book (bound)
1 package of Official Letters, Despatches, Government printed Circulars, and various necessaries.
1 package of Pamphlets, – comprising "List of Diplomatic & Consular officers", "Message of the President" &c &c.
1 package containing remaining blank printed forms for office use in the future.–

Consulate of the United States
Macao, February 24th 1863.
Gideon Nye, Jnr
W. P. Jones.

[1–110]

United States Consulate at Macao.

Fees received during the fractional Quarter beginning Jany: 1st & ending Feby: 24th 1863.

Date	N°	Name of Vessel	Name of the party paying the fee	Nature of service rendered	Amount of fee paid	
□□ 3th		–	Charles Comeron	acknowledge of his Wills	$2	–

□□ 6th		–	F. D. Williams	2 Certfes to Invo Merchdes Sr "Enrek"	$4	–
	2	Agnes	Thos H. King	Deposit of papers 397 21/95 tons @ 1/2 cent	$1	99
		–	L. D. Almeida	Certificate to service coal to Whampoa per two Chinese Boats	$2	–
□□ 3d	1	Nagasaki	G. Leonard	Deposit of papers 549 09/95 tons @ 1/2 cent	$2	75
		–	G. Nye, Jr.	Certificate to Invoice Contributions to the soldiers' Relief Fund per sureka in duplicate	$4	–
□□ 10th	4	Mountain Wave	Josiah Hardy	Deposit of papers 635 05/95 tons @ 1/2 cent	$3	17
□□ 21th		–	L. d' Almeida	Certificate to Invoice coal to Whampoa per 3 Chinese Boats	$2	–
					$21	91

Gideon Nye Jnr
Vice Consul of the United States
of America for Macao

Fractional quarterly Return of the Arrival and Departure of American Vessels at the Consulate of the United States of America at Macao, beginning January 1st & ending February 24th 1863.––

No	Date	Class	Name	Tons	Where from	When Built	Where built	Where belonging	Where bound	Cargo		Owners	Captains
										Import	Export		
1	Jany: 6th	Bark	Nagasaki	549 09/95	HongKong	–	–	–	Saigon Jany:18th	General	General	Jas Pedersen	G. Leonard
2	Jany: 6th	Bark	Agnes	397 21/95	–do–	1857	New York	New York	Shanghae Jany: 9th	Rice	Rice	Chas W. King	Thos. H. King
3	Jany: 15th	Str:	U.S.S. Wyoming	–	Whampoa	–	–	–	Manila Jany:27th	–	–	–	Comdre McDougal
4	Jany: 28th	Ship	Mountain Wave	633 05/95	Manila	1852	Charle stown	Boston	–do– Feby 11th	Rice &c	Ballast	Alphens Joshua & Hardy Sesrs	Josiah Hardy
5	Feby: 16th	Schnr	James Lawrence	313 19/95	Bangkok	1855	Portland	New York	Hongkong	–do–	Rice	Wm W. Wakeman & others–	C. T. Botsford
6	Feby: 22d	Str:	U.S.S. Wyoming	–	Manila	–	–	–	Whampoa	–	–	–	Comdre McDougal
				1892 54/95									

Gideon Nye Jnr
Vice Consul of the United States
of America for Macao.

[1-111]

[Recd Jun 4]
[Ack Jun 5]

Consulate of the United States of America,
Macao. March 27, 1863.

Hon. William H. Seward,
Secretary of States of the United States,
Washington, D. C.

Sir:

I beg to call your attention to the subjoined facts concerning the Consulates at this port and at Swatow, China. corroborated by the subscribed testimony of gentlemen officially well known to the Honorable Secretary–and thereupon to solicit my transfer from this Consulate to that.

First–My brief experience here, proves that in the plainest republican style of living, my salary of Fifteen Hundred Dollars, (under bonds not to transact business) , will not support my little family; and the state of the country at home has so affected my small property there, as to forbid my dependence upon it for the deficiency. At the same time, the amount of Consular business at this port would not–I am in honor

[Inadequacy of Salary at Macao.]

bound to report – warrant an increase of the salary.

[Absence of Consul.]

Second–Mr. Brick, Consul at Swatow, has, as you have no doubt been advised, left that post for the newly opened ports of Kiukiang and Hanhow, on the Yang–tsi; where he is now acting Consul, under authority–from His Excellency, Minister Burlingame; whereby the administration of the Consulate at Swatow is devolved upon Mr C. W. Bradley, of the mercantile firm of Bradley & Co.–either as Deputy Consul or Vice Consul.–a state of things to which the Chinese Government and the American residents are both opposed, and which it was understood the elevation of Swatow to a salaried Consulate was intended to obviate. I am advised that the complaint on the port of the Chinese is not a new one. This Government has on various occasions expressed its strong dislike to the employment of merchants as Consuls. It is always suspicious of the office's be–

[Administration of Consulate by Mr Bradly as Vice Consul. Dissatisfaction of Chinese & American residents. Complaints of the Chinese Gov.]

ing used, when in interested hands, to the disadvantage of the Imperial revenue.

The trade at Swatow, last year, amounted to 8,000,000, and is rapidly increasing, so that the financial interests of our countrymen, point to the importance of having an independent consular officer in charge thereof. But probably the strongest reason for a change, urged by Americans, and especially our American Missionaries, is that the Judicial functions of this port demand to be exercised by a Consul unembarrassed by mercantile entanglements.

[Reasons for a change urged by Americans]

Besides my being thus unembarrased, the following facts may be deemed, by the Honorable Secretary, as considerations for my transfer from Macao to Swatow.

[Reasons for the appointment sought]

That district offers a less explored and more interesting field than Macao, for Geological, Mineralogical & Botanical discover, to employ any moments of recreation

which my duties might allow. Here hills and mountains of disintegrating granite make the whole face of the country, **and** not a fossil – nor a mineral of any interest – invites our search; while the Botany of this vicinity has already been diligently explored. As Swatow the production of Chinese sugar – questions upon which has already been addressed to me by the editors of two of our home Agricultural Publications – might be throughly investigated; and much other valuable material exists wherewith to respond to the Departments Circular No. 21. of 1862 demending the Am. Geographical and Statistical Society to the good offices of Consuls,

[Opportunities for scientific discoveries and to respond to circular No. 21. from the Dept.]

These were all subjects to the investigation of which my natural tastes and education as well as the public interest attract me.

Lastly– I am engaged in the study of the Chinese language, and would carry to the Consulate, should I receive the appointment, a qualification not gen–

[Qualification, from acquaintance of with the Chinese language.]

erally enjoyed by our countrymen when entering upon office among these strange people – and the possession of which by the representatives of rival nations often gives them an advantage over ourselves.

Hoping therefore, that it may be found consonant with the public interests to grant my solicitation––,

I have the honor to be, Sir,
Your Obedient Servant
W. P. Jones.–
U. S. Consul at Macao.

We cheerfully corroborate the remarks of Mr. Jones respecting the desirableness of having a United States' Consul at Swatow, and think that his appointment to the station will promote the public service,

[and]

[The Corroboration and recommendation of Dr. Williams of U. S. Legation & Ex. Vice Consul, Nye.]

and furnish him with facilities for making investigation of much value.

S. Wells Williams
Chinese Interpreter, &c., to
U. S. Legation

Gideon Nye Jnr
late Acting Consul
of the United States for
Macao.

[Enclosure
with dispatch No 2.

Condition of Consulates of
Macao & Swatow and
request for the appointment
of W. P. Jones to Swatow.

No. 1.

Macao March. 27. 1863.]

[1-112]

[Recd Jun 4
Ack Jun 9]

Consulate of the United States of America,
Macao, March, 28, 1863.

Sir:

I have the honor to report that since my despatch to the Department, under date of February 25, wherein I gave notice of my arrival at Macao, and the transfer of the Consular Archives, my exequatur has been duly published, and all those official courtesies usual on such occasions have been interchanged.

[Publication of Exequatur]

Your despatch of Oct.1 addressed to me at New York is received and I have to acknowledge – the safe arrival of the two cases containing flags, arms, stationery, blank forms and other articles for the use of the Consulate–but not containing seal, press and record–books. These last, however I received with the archives, from my predecessor.

[Receipt of Flags, Arms &c from the Dept.]

The Departments Circular, N°. 25. is received and will be observed, in the spirit of the same.

[To Hon, William H. Seward,
Secretary of State for the United States.
WashingtonD. C.]

At my entrance upon the duties of this Consulate, I found the American, James Davis, whom my predecessor had several times mentioned in his dispatches to the Deparment, still suffering imprisonment in the Macao jail. Mr. Nye received a promise from Chief Justice Pinto, last January, that this man should be pardoned at the next sessions of the Criminal Court. Two sessions had been held when I arrived and the promise had not been fulfilled. Upon knowledge to these facts, I recalled the attention of His Excellency to his promise and respectfully pressed its immediate fulfillment. I have now the satisfaction to inform you of the prisoners Pardon and release.

[Pardon of James Davis.]

Herewith I send you–（Enclosure No 1.） a statement of facts respecting the Consulates at this port and at Swatow–suggested and subscribed to by Dr. S. Wells Williams, Chinese Interpreter & Sect,

[Enclosure No 1. Facts Concerning the Consulates at Macao & Swatow &c.]

to the U. S. Legation at the Court of Peking, now residing at Macao, and Ex. Vice Consul, Gideon Nye, to which statement and the request therein contained, I beg leave to call your favorable attention.

I remain, Sir,
Your Obedient Servant,
W. P. Jones.
Consul for the United States
of America at Macao.

[U. S. Consulate,
Macao. March. 25, 1863.

W. P. Jones Consul.

No. 2.

Enclosures–1.]

[Publication of Exequatur – Receipt of Flags, Arms &c. Receipt of Circular No 25. Pardon & Release of James Davis.–]

[1–113]

Consulate of the United States
Macao, March 31. 1863.

To the Honorable Salmon P. Chase,
Secretary of the Treasury–
Washington, U. S. A.

Sir ~

I beg herewith to transmit my account for salary for the fractional quarter beginning Feb. 25, 1863.–at my entrance upon the duties of this consulate and ending March 31–as per. Enclosure No. 1..

[Acd N°1. Account for Salary.]

Enclosure No 2 & No 3. are the legally required exchange Vouchers–therewith.

[N°2 & N°3. Exchange Vouchers.]

I am, Sir.
Your Obedient Servant.
W. P. Jones.
U. S. Consul.

[U.S. Consulate
Macao. March 31. 1863.

W. P. Jones. Consul–

No. 2.

No. of Enclosures –3.

Received

Account for Salary.]

[1–114]

[Recd 12 Jun]

Consulate of the United States
Macao, March 31, 1863

To the Honorable William H. Seward,
Secretary of State for the United States,
Washington D. C.

Sir:

I beg herewith to transmit the account (Enclosure No.1.) of this Consulate with the State Department, for the fractional quarter, beginning, February, 25, at my entrance upon the duties of this post, and ending, Mar, 31. 1863.––for Postage, Stationery, and removing Flag staff, amounting in the aggregate to 19^{09},

Enclosures Nos. 2. 3. & 4, are Vouchers sustaining the several charges in account.

Enclosure Nos. 5. & 6. are the legally required exchange Vouchers.

I am, Sir. Your Obedient Servant
W. P. Jones.
U. S. Consul.

[U. S. Consulate
Macao. March 31. 1863.

W. P. Jones. Consul.

No. 3.

No. Enclosures, 6.

Received._____

Miscellaneous Expense Ac/ct,
with Vouchers.]

[1-115]

[Recd Jun 12]

Consulate of the United States
Macao, March 31, 1863.

To the Honorable William H. Seward,
Secretary of State for the United States
Washington. U. S. A.

Sir:

I beg to transmit the account of this consulate with the State Department, for office rent incurred during this fractional quarter beginning February, 25, at my entrance upon the duties of this post– and ending to day, Mar. 31, 1863– as per Enclosure No. 1. and attached Voucher, Enclosure, No. 2.

[N°1. Act Offuce Rent N°2. Act Voucher for rent.]

Enclosures Nos 3. & 4, are the legally required exchange vouchers.

[□□□ □□□ □□□]

[Nos 3. & 4. Exchange Vouchers]

I am, Sir, Very Respectfully
Your Obedient Servant.
W. P. Jones.
U. S. Consul.

[U. S. Consulate,
Macao. March. 31. 1863.

W. P. Jones Consul.

No. 4.

No. of Enclosures Sent – 4.

Received.

Account for Office Rent.]

[1-116]

[Recd June 22]

Consulate of the United States
of America, Macao, March 31. 1863.

To the Honorable William H. Seward,
Secretary of State for the United States,
Washington, U. S. A.

Sir:

Referring to my No. 3. of even date herewith, containing my account for Miscellaneous Expenses, Rent & Bookcase, I now beg to transmit Enclosures Nos. 1. 2. 3. 4. 5.–being respectively my "Returns of Arrivals & Departures of Am. Vessels", "Fees not contained in Enclosure No.1.". "Register of Letters Rec.", "Register of Letters Sent", and "Quarterly Return of Fees" –for the fractional Quarter beginning Feb. 25, at my entrance upon the duties of this port, and ending March. 31. 1863.

[Nos 1. 2. 3. 4. 5. Quarterly Reports]

Hitherto the books of this Consulate have not been so kept as to furnish materials for the

Navigation and Commerce Report (Form No. 130,) In the future all details will be strictly recorded and duly reported.

[Why no Nangation & commercial Report.]

Reports ordered to be made to the Secretary of the Treasury and to the Fifth Auditor are all in readiness and will go forward by this mail.

I venture to recall the Honorable Secretary's attention to the Enclosure with my No. 2. wherein S. W. Williams. S. L. D.––Chinese Interpreter & Secretary to the U. S. Legation at Peking, and Gideon Nye, Jr. Esq. Ex. Vice Consul at Macao, corroborate certain statements, concerning the Consulate at Swatow, and recommend my appointment thereto. Hoping that this subject may receive your favorable attention– and awaiting your reply––

[Recalling attention to Pespateh No.2]

I have the honor to remain
Your Obedient Servant
W. P. Jones.
U. S. Consul at Macao

[To save Postage I have put all in one envelope as they all contain fractional weights.
W. P. J.]

[U. S. Consulate
Macao. March 31. 1863.

W. P. Jones. Consul

No. 4.

5 Enclosures

Received

Enclosing Quarterly Reports–
and recalling attention to
Despatch No.2.]

[Form No. 130.]

Return of Fees received at the Consular Agency of the United States at Macao, from January 1st to March, 31st, 1863, inclusive.

Name of Consular Officer.	Where located.	Quarter Ending March 31. 1863.	Quarter Ending June 30, 185.	Quarter Ending September 30, 185.	Quarter Ending December 31, 185.	Remarks.
Gideon Nye. Jr Vice Consul from Jan 1st – Feb 25.	Macao	$21	91			The Forms in the Gen'l Instructions of 1856. the latest furnished me, conclude with Form No 1. 2. 3. This form is not therefore mentioned. There seems to be no calculation made for specifying the Fees – so I have given the aggregate amount.
W. P. Jones Consul from Feb 25. – March 31	Macao	$8	07			
Total for the Quarter		$29	98			

[Enclosure No.5.
With Dispatch No. 4.–

Quarterly Return of Fees
Form No 130.

No. 5.

Macao. March, 31. 1863.]

REGISTER of Official Letters and Despatches received at the U. S. Consulate at Macao for the □□□ Quarter □□□ ending March, 31, 1863.

NAME OF THE WRITER.	NO.	PLACE AND DATE OF LETTER.	WHEN RECEIVED.	ON WHAT SUBJECT.	No. of Enclosures.	REMARKS.	POSTAGE PAID.
First Comptroller of Treas. Dept.	1	Washington Oct.8.'/62	Feb. 24.'/63.	Salary a/c–	–	Foundin P. O. on my arrival	.32
Hon. James E. Harvey	2	Lisbon Aug. 14. 1862.	" " "	Transmitting Exequatur	/	Foundin P. O. on my arrival	1.50
H. E. João Ferreira Pinto	3	Macao Mar.6, 1863	Mar. 6.	Appoving Exequatur	/		
Gideon Nye. Jr.	4.	Macao Mar. 7. 1863.	Mar. 7.	Congratulatory			
Navy Department to Com. Mc Dougal of U. S. S. Wyoming	5	Washington	Mar. 8.	Circulars		Sent to W[m] Speiden U. S. Naval Store Keeper Hongkong. to be forwarded to Manilla kept till his arrival.	.72
Navy Dept_to Capt. C. Price U.S. S. sl. of war Jamestown			Mar. 8.	Circulars			.72
H. E. João F. Pinto acting Gov. &c. &c.	7	Macao. Mar. 16. 1863.	Mar. 16.	Concerning pardon of J. Davis			
Oliver H. Perry Consul–Canton	8	Canton Mar. 12, 1863.	Mar. 16.	Reply_notice of my arrival.			
O. B. Bradford– Consul–Amoy	9	Amoy Mar. 1863	Mar. 18.	Reply_notice of my arrival.			
Wm Speiden U. S. Naval Store Keeper Hongkong	10	Hongkong Mar 19, 1863	Mar. 20.	Acknowleding receipt of Despatch to McDougal to be forwarded to Manilla.			
H. E. João F. Pinto acting Gov. &c	11	Macao Mar 21, 1863.	Mar. 21	Enclosing pardon of J. Davis.	1		
Department of State. Ass't. Sect.	12.	Washington Jan. 6. 1863.	Mar 28.	Notifying me of dispatch of "Amer. Flags" &c.			.16
							$2.92

W. P. Jones U. S. Consul.

NOTE.–Consular officers are not authorized to pay postages or other charges on letters or packages addressed to them, with a view to charge them to the United States, unless they bear on their envelopes evidence of official character, as emanating from some of the Executive Departments, or from some of the legations or consulates of the United States in foreign countries. Such charges or postages, if paid by consular officers, are not to be included in their accounts for postage against the Department of State. This form, with the blanks properly filled, is to be sent, with the despatch enclosing each quarterly postage account, to the Secretary of State. Care should be taken to note the amount of postage paid on each letter.

[Enclosure, No. 3.
with Despatch No. 4,

Register of Letters Rec,

No.3.

Macao. March 31, 1863.]

Extract from transcript of fee book of those fees not enumerated and contained return of fees prescribed in Form No. 44, received at the U. S. Consulate at Macao, from February 25, to March. 31. 1863.

No.	Date		Name of Vessel.	Party paying the fee.	Service rendered.	Amount.	
6	1863 March	12	Per "Monsoon".	A. A. de Mello.	Certif. to Invoice	2	00

W. P. Jones–
Consul

[With despatch No. 4.

Fees not contained in
report Form No. 44.
Enclosure No. 1.

No. 2.

Macao. March. 31, 1863.]

Official Letters Sent

From the United States Consulate at Macao, from February 25 to March 31, 1863.

Date		No.	To whom and what place sent.	On what subject.	No of Enclosure	
1863						Postage Fee.
□□	25	1	To Secretary of State. Despatch No 1.	Announcing arrival and entrance upon duty	1	3.84
□□	25	2	To Secretary of Treasury Despatch No.1.	Transmitting ac/ct for salary during transit &c.	5	
□□	6	3	To Gideon Nye, Jr. Macao.	Acknowledging courtesies &c		

□□	6	4	To Horace N. Congar. U. S. Consul Hongkong	Giving notice of my entrance upon duty		
□□	6	5	To O. H. Perry U.S. Consul Canton	Giving notice of my entrance upon duty		
□□	6	6	To Geo. F. Seward U.S. Consul Shanghai	Giving notice of my entrance upon duty		
□□	6	7	To W. H. Carpenter U.S. Consul Foochaou	Giving notice of my entrance upon duty		1.36
□□	6	8	To A. B. Bradford U.S. Consul Amoy	Giving notice of my entrance upon duty		
□□	6	9	To W. P. Magnum U.S. Consul Ningpo	Giving notice of my entrance upon duty		
□□	6	10	To W^s Breck U.S. Consul Swatow	Giving notice of my entrance upon duty		
□□	6	11	To C. D. Williams U. S. Consul Hanhow	Giving notice of my entrance upon duty		
□□	7	12	To João Ferreira Pinto. Act. Gov. Macao	Reply to his approval of and remittance of Expense		
□□	7	13	To Hon. James E Harvey U. S. Miss. Lisbon	Acknowledging receipt of Exequatur & c.		
□□	14	14	To João Ferreira Pinto. Act. Gov. Macao	Inq. why promise of pardon to J. Davis is not fulfilled		
□□	16	15	To Wm Speiden U. S. Nav. St. Keeper Hongkong.	Asking him to forward enclosed despatch from Navy Dept to Com. Mc Dougal of Manila	1	
□□	17	16	To Com. David Mc Dougal. U. S. S. Wyoming Manila	informing him of above action		
□□	20	17	To João Ferreira Pinto. Act. Gov. Macao	Concerning pardon of J. Davis enclosing petition from Jones.	1	
□□	23	18	To João Ferreira Pinto. Act. Gov. Macao	Acknowld receipt of order of Council releasing J. Davis		
□□	28	19	To Secretary of State Despatch No. 2	Giving notice of release of J. Davis – receipt of Circ. No 25. and enclosing a petition for transfer to Consulate of Swatow.	1	3.20
				Total postage		8.40

U. S. Consulate at Macao.
March. 31. 1863.
W. P. Jones. Consul.

[Enclosure No. 4.
With Despatch No 4–

Register of letters Sent.

No.4.

Macao. March 31. 1863.]

[1-117]

[Recd Jun 12]

Consulate of the United States
Macao. March 31. 1863.

To the Honorable William H. Seward,
Secretary of State for the United States,
Washington. U. S. A.

Sir:

Referring to the inventory of the effects of this Consulate delivered to me by Mr. Nye, which I forwarded in my first despatch to the State Department, under date of February 25,–to show that no provision has hitherto been made for keeping the consular records. I herewith forward the bill for purchase of book–case–enclosure No. 1. and voucher for the same, Enclosure No. 2.

[□□□ N°1. Bill for book–case N°2. Voucher–]

Enclosure Nos. 3 & 4. are the legally required exchange Vouchers therewith–

[N°3. & 4. Exchange vouchers]

I am, Sir, Your Obedient Servant.
W. P. Jones
U. S. Consul.

[U. S. Consulate
Macao. March 31. 1863.

W. P. Jones. Consul.

No 5.

No. of Enclosure –4.

Received

Bill for Book–case
with Vouchers]

[1–118]

[□□□□□□□ □□□□□□□upon the application of the partion which
Recd Aug 9. + Mr Abbt
Ack ¢8]

Consulate of the United States of America,
Macao, May 9. 1863.

Sir:

Referring to despatch No. 25, of the year 1861, and its Enclosures, addressed to the Department by my predecessor, I now beg to recall the attention of the Honorable Secretary to the representations therein set forth touching the case of the seizure and sequestration of the American Ship "Emma", by the authorities of this

Colony. The case has been so fully and lucidly presented in the documents referred to, extending from the inception thereof, in November, 1858, to the present status of the same, that I deem it needless for me to attempt a resumé. Such an attempt is the more uncalled for

[Seizure &c of ship "Emma" Referrence to former despatches]

[To the Honorable William H. Seward,
Secretary of State for the United States,
Washington, D. C.]

as the "Decision of the Supreme Court of Goa," and the "Award of Umpire" had thereafter (Copies whereof will be found among the Enclosures with the despatch referred to, and duplicate copies of which are herewith transmitted, for more ready reference) declare the illegality of the sequestration, and decree the damages due Capt. Gill; so that a perusal of the lengthy documents of dates anterior to those decisions can now serve no-end save to illustrate the aggravatingly arbitary and tedious proceedings of the Portuguese authorities in this long protracted injury to our country man:

Allow me then to present the case as it now stands, and invoke the immediate attention of the Government thereto:

[Present Status of the Case.]

1st By decision of the supreme Court of Goa, dated Nov. 8, 1859, the entire proceedings of the Macao courts are declared illegal. (Vide Enclosure No.1.)

[Enclosure N°1. Decision of Sup. Court of Goa.]

2d By Award of Umpire dated 29th March, 1861, the amount of damages is established at Fourteen Thousand six hundred and sixty five Dollars ($14,665^{00})

[Enclosure No. 2 Award of Umpire]

3d By neglect on the part of the Judge to demand adequate security for damages, this amount, after the lapse of more than three years since the award, remains unpaid.

[Neglect of Judge to take adequate of Security.]

Herein then the responsibility of the Portuguese Government seems evident viz: in the total illegality of the proceedings of the court in the first place, and secondly in the total neglect for some months after Captain Gill had abandoned his ship to the custody of the authorities, to require any security whatever for damages; and afterwards, the acceptance of an almost irresponsible Chinaman as bondsman in the shamefully inadequate amount of Five Thousand Dollars, and this, it would seem from the course pursued,

[Responsibility of the Portuguese Government]

more for the purpose of securing the payment of costs in court than for the payment of damages to the owner of the ship.

As a consequence, after having exhausted the security—the principal of the amount awarded, (vide Statement of the Court–Enclosure No. 3.) remains undiminished, the Chinaman lies in jail powerless to produce anything further in liquidation of the claim against him, and a worthy American Citizen, despoiled of his property, still suffers hardship, and naturally appeals to his Government to demand redress from the authorities, who by their illegal proceedings have thus wronged him.

[Enclosure No. 3. Statement of the Court. Condition of the debt and the security.]

My predecessor having exhausted all mean of redress within his competence applied more than once to the former Administration of the Department for further instructions, but failed

[Failure of previous applications to the Dept. for advice.]

to elicit a reply. His despatch above referred to addressed to this Administration, also, for some reason remains unanswered.

After careful review of all the records in the case, the foregoing facts appeared to me to indicate that there was no recourse left to Capt. Gill for justice in the matter except through demand to be made by the Home Government upon the Government at Lisbon, I have therefore obtained the statement of the Court, (vide Enclosure No.3), that nothing further can be collected from the security, as being the only document needed to complete the statement of the claim, and having made this presentation of the case to the Department. I await advices. It may not be amiss for me to add that it is the hope not only of the plaintiff, who, having vainly waited nearly five years

[N°3. "Statement of Court". Desire of the plaintiff & other Americans to have a demand made upon the Gov^t at Lisbon.]

for his redress, despairs of obtaining it in any other way, but of the Americans in this city and vicinity generally, that in the wisdom of the Government it may be found expedent to forward the papers at an early day to our Minister at Lisbon, with instructions to demand that this Colony may be required, out of its present large surplus of revenue, to discharge this long standing debt of damages to our injured countryman: thus verifying the intimation conveyed to the Portuguese authorities, in the inception of the suit, by H. E. Mr. Reed, (vide Mr. Nye's extract from Mr. Reed in his rejoinder to the Governor of Macao. Sept. 30, 1859,), that if the suit brought against Capt. Gill should prove to be unfounded and vexations he would be indemnified, and that in the very improbable event of the court's failing to redress the wrong the United States Government would interfere.

I have the honor, Sir. To be
Your Obedient Servant
W. P. Jones.
Consul of the United States
of America at Macao.

[Macao. May. 9. 1863,

W. P. Jones. Consul.

No. 7.

4 Enclosures
Received,

Touching the Case of the
unlawful seizure and
sequestration of the ship
"Emma"]

Consulate of the United States
of America, Macao. May 9, 1863.

I, the undersigned, Consul of the United States of America for Macao, do hereby certify that the foregoing translations of, severally designated. Enclosure No.1. "Decision of the Supreme Court of Goa", signed, Ferreira Pinto=Faustino Crespo=Vas concellas;–Enclosure No. 2. "Award of Umpire", signed Barão de Coreal;–and Enclosure No. 3. signed, Francisco Ant[o] Per[a]. [da] Silveira &c &c,– being a "Statement of Court" – are true and faithful copies of documents filed in this Consulate and duly attested as copies of their several originals; the same having been carefully examined by me and compared with the said documents filed in this Consulate and found to agree therewith word for word and figure for figure.

Given under my hand and the seal of the Consulate at Macao, this ninth day of May, [AD] 1863.

[seal]

W. P. Jones.
Consul for the United States of
America at Macao.

[Enclosure No. 4,
With despatch No.

Certificates of authentication
of the foregoing
Enclosures.

No. 4,

Macao. May. 9. 1863.]

[Enclosure No. 4,
With despatch No. 7.

Certificates of authentication
of the foregoing
Enclosures.

No. 4,

Macao. May. 9. 1863.]

Translation of information given, petitioned for by annexed petition.

The most Illustrious and most Excellent Judge of the District.

I inform Your Excellency that in the question of the ship "Emma" the Chinaman Cheong Ahoy, and his □□□ty the Chinaman Mestrino, have paid the fodening sums, viz:

Dollars.

3942.336 Three thousand nine hundred forty two dollars, and three hundred sixty-six thousandths.

400.000 Four hundred dollars.

890.700 Also Eight-hundred ninty dollars, and seven hundred thousandths.

351.866 Also Three hundred fifty-one dollars, and eight-hundred sixty six thousandths with proceed of houses sold.

400.000 Also Four hundred dollars, that Mestrino introduced.

1200.000 Also One thousand two hundred dollars, that Mestino introduced last.

6384.932 There is no more property known to belong to the said Chinaman. Macao. May 9. 1863.

(signed) Francisco Ant^o Per^a da Silveira
Notary of District--Judge.

1000.000 I also inform Your Exq. that Mestrino has paid beside, the sum of one

7384.932 thousand dollars, as the petition declared in the audience of □□□ Dec 1860, =Macao 9 May 1863.

(signed) Francisco Ant^o Per^a da Silveira
Notary of District Judge

Dr. Memorandum of Sum due by Prosecutor in the case of the Ship "Emma", transferred to E. J. Sage. atty. Cr^f

1860 Jany	31	To award of damages	14,665	00	1860 June	6	By Cash received from Court	3,942	.36		
	31	To do of Court, Consul fees, etc.	1,250	00			Interest to 1st apl/ 61. 10 mos. @ 1%	394	.23	4,336	.59
		Interest to 1st Apl/ 61. 14 mos @ 1%.	2,228	10	Sept	7	By Do received from Fantan	400	.00		

Dec 1861	10	To Court fees paid Mr Silveira	19	40			Interest 6 1/2 mos	26	.00	426	.00
Apl	1	To Expenses of attorney from 29 March 1860 the date of the award, unto date, as per protest made before the Court 25 June 1860. – viz: 12 mos @ $150.	1,800	00	Nov	5	By Do received from Court	890	.70		
		This account up to 1st apl. 1861. showing a balance due of 12,818^{71} was transmitted at that date to the Governor of Macao by the American Consul.					Interest 5 mos.	49	.53	940	.23
			$19,962	50	Dec	8	By Do received from Mestrino	1,000	.00		
							Interest 4 mos.	40	.00	1,040	.00
					1861 Apl	1	By Do sales houses (not received)			401	.00
							To Balance a/c.			12,818	.71
										$19,962	.53
1861 Sept	1	To Balance of a.	$12,818	70			$1600. received by the Court has not yet been paid over, therefore is not credited in this account.				
		To Amount retained by Court from $400 credited apl 1st for expenses selling houses (Nett proceeds being $351.86)	49								
1862 apl	1	To Interest on $12,867^{85} from 1st apl 1861. 12 mos @1%	1,544								
1863 apl	1	To Interest on $14,411^{99} from 1st apl 1862. 12 mos @1%	1,729								
		due 1st apl. 1863.	$16,141								
		$161^{41} monthly interest to be added thereafter.									

[Enclosure No. 3.
with Despatch No. 1.

Statement of Court showing the amounts received from the security and Prosecutor, and declaring that no more can be collected.
Also account interest with the Court.

N° 3.

Macao May 9th 1863]

Having seriously and conscientiously examined the documents in relation to this law suit, and conferred with my co-arbitrators Fran^{co} Joaq^{m} Marquis and J. B. Endicott for the better understanding of the question, by way of discussion, I came to the conclusion that the Chinese Cheong Ahoy ought to indemnify Charles Gill, Captain and owner of the ship "Emma" for all damages and □□□ expense, and disappointments to him consist in consequence of the law suit attempted by the said Cheong Ahoy against him apart from the expenses incurred with the American Consulate, with the attorney of the prosecuted, & with the legal Acts the sum of $14,665.-- say, Besides the $4,300 paid at fol □□□, as freight of the ship to Bombay and interest agreed upon,--Cheong Ahoy shall pay in Compensation for the time during which the ship has been under embargo reckoning from the 15th February 1859. when the termination of the voyage to and discharge at Bombay is calculated as having taken place, since the presented has already been indemnified for the time elapsed in the interval with the $4,300. which he received also the estimated amount necessary for the repairs to put the ship on the state in which she was at the time of the embargo, dollars– $5,200.

As subsidy to the Captain for the time he was on shore–350 days–from the 15 February 1869 to 31st January 1860. @ $40 p month– 466.

To repair various destruction & deterioration sustained by the ship, inclusion of difference in the Inventory– $9,000.

Furthermore, I think the Chinese Cheong Ahoy is to have the option to undertake the repair of the ship and to fill up the wants of the Inventory for his own account should he wish it, and in that case he is to decide within 5 days from this date--the work done to be subject to the inspection and approval of the surveyors of the Underwriters of Hong Kong. Should the repairs be made for account and at the expense of Cheong Ahoy. I judge that a sum of $9000 should be deducted from the above specified $14,665 arbitrated for repairs.

As regards the relaxation of the arrest of the ship, I don't deem it advisable to allude to--it being a subject beyond my competency– the compromise which restrain the decision of the arbitrators to the liquidation of losses and damages, says, that in the appreciation of the said losses & damages, the deterioration of the ship in its present– state as compared with that anterior to the time of the arrest upwards of a year will be made apparent.

Macao, 29 March 1860.
(signed) Barão da Coreal.

[With dispatch No. 7.

Award of Umpire.

No. 2.

Macao. May. 9. 1863.]

Translation of the Decision of the Supreme Court of Jurisdiction of the States of Portuguese India at Goa.

It has been awarded in Conference, that the present question relating purely to a commercial subject, such as the validity or invalidity of the purchase of a ship, it is manifest that it should have been entered upon as a commercial question in view of the express and definite provision or art. 203 and following of its □th, and art. 1029 of the commercial code--which not having been done the case was brought before an incompetent Judge--therefore the present process is wholly annulled by reason of the incompetency of the Judge in question–the experssess to be paid by the appealing prosecutor.–

New Goa, 8th November, 1859.

(signed) Ferreira Pinto Faustino Crespo=Vasconcellas.

[With dispatch No. 7.

Decision of the Supreme
Court at Goa.

No 1.

Macao, May 9, 1863.]

[1–119]

[Recd Oct 5.
Statistical Office]

U. S. Consulate, Macao, June 30, 1863.

Sir:

Referring to my Despatch, No. 6. for the Quarterly Reports of this Consulate for the Fractional Quarter, Ending, March, 31, I now beg to present my Reports for the Quarter Ending. June, 30. 1863.–: Vice Enclosures Nos. 1. 2. 3. 4, being respectively, my "Report of Arrivals and Departures of Am. Vessels"; "Extract of Fee Book, per. Form No. 45"; "Navigation and Commerce Report"; and "Names and effects of Deceased Am. Citizens" –comprising all the materials for reports which this quarter has furnished.

[Nos.1.2.3.4, Quarterly Reports]

I should here report that the rumors, (calculated to act prinicipally upon the easily alarmed native merchants of the East) of the presence or expected presence of Confederate privateers east of the Cape, which are ever and a non fabricated by the unprincipled

[Effect of Rumors of Privateers &c. on Am. Commerce.]

[The Honorable – William H. Seward,
Secretary of State for the United States,
Washington, D. C.]

English publications at Calcalta, Singapore, Hongkong, and Shanghai, added to the exaggerated accounts of the sum which these privateers are really accomplishing in the Atlantic, are having the effect, in confunction with the high house duties on Eastern imports, and the Exorbitant and unsettled rates of exchange–to quite dishearten American Ship Owerns[①]–Moreover the Insurance, Companies, which have taken advantage of an unfortunate increase of Marine disasters to American Vessels to advance insurance on goods in American bottoms, have added grievously to the embarrassments of our carrying trade. As a consequence our vessels are fast going under other flags.

I have the honor to Communicate to the Government, that whereas the late Excellent Governor, Guimarães, after an exceedingly happy administration of the government of this Colony, for about eleven years, was in February last past, at his own request, relieved therefrom, H. E. José, Rodrigues, Coelho dos Amaral, has within the present for a night, arrived as his successors, and was, as such duly inaugurated, on Monday the 22[d], inst. H. E. was for many years Governor of the Portuguese Colony of Angola where he acquired the reputation of an upright, astute and energetic Executive. He is represented as actively possessed with the purpose to institute great improvements for the business interests of Macao, among which are the projected deepening of the inner harbor entrance, and the encouragement of a company which has already entered upon the construction of a dockyard. Should these projects succeed, they cannot fail to revive somewhat the trade and importance of this once opulent port. Americans cannot fail to desire the prosperity of Macao, since the time when it bestowed the first welcome our flag had ever received in

[Inauguration of Governor Amaral Profected Improvements]

these waters--vide letter of Mr. Samuel show to Mr Secretary Jay, dated May 19, 1785）--down to the present time, it has not failed I believe to treat that flag with all honor, and those who have been privileged to claim its protection with marked courtesy and goodwill.

During the Quarter, I have received,（April 25.） from the Hon. Asst. Secretary a dispatch addressed to my predecessor, Gideon Nye Jr. Esq, in reply to his of Oct. 12, /62,--and conveying to that excellent officer a well merited expression of the Government's appreciation of his faithful services. This acknowledgement was the more acceptable to Mr. Nye since during the entire period of the administration of Mr. Buchanon, he failed to receive reply to any of his many dispatches. I have also had the honor to receive,（April 21, via Shanghai）, the Dept's circulars Nos 28 & 29 of 1862, the President's Message of Dec 1st/62 & Blk Form No. 130--and by other routes, 2 vols. of the Ex. Document No 38, and the

[□□□ good feeling between Americans & Portuguese. Despatches &c from Dept. Rec[d] during the Quarter.]

vol of Commercial Reports for 1861.

I have furthermore to communicate that Ed[w]. Russell, late a resident of the Freemantle, England,--where his father Charles Russell, Esq., probably now resides--died in the outer Roads of this Port, on the 18th of May last past, on board the American Ship, "E. F. Mason", whereon he was acting 2[d] mate, I have received his effects with $167^{36/100}$, balance of wages due him–and hold the same subject to orders–having addressed his father at the place above mentioned, setting forth the circumstances of his sickness & death and inclosing an inventory of his effects.

[Death of E[dw] Russell 2[d] mate of Ship "E. F. Mason" –Effects &c]

---

① Sic.

Permit me to conclude my Report for the Quarter just ended—with the sentiment that has no doubt become the engrossing thought and the most sacred part of the daily life of every patriot abroad or at home— "God Save the Union!"

I have the honor to be
Your Obedient Servant,
W. P. Jones

[U. S. Consulate
Macao. June 30, 1863.
W. P. Jones Consul
No. 8.
Enclosure 4.
Received

Quarterly Reports &c]

[Form No. 45.]

Extract from Transcript of Fee—book of those fees not enumerated and contained in returns of Fees prescribed in Form No. 44, received at the Consulate of the United States at Macao, from April.1. to June 30./ 1863.

Date	No.	Name of Vessel.	Party paying fee	Service Rendered	Amt of Fees	
1863.						
April 29	51	Per "Europa"	S. W. Williams.	Invoice Certif. of Chinaman K.	2	00
June 4	7		E. J. Sage	Auth. Signature of Judge	2	00
					4	00
					W. P. Jones □□□□□□□□□	

[Enclosure No 2.
with Despatch No. 8.

Extract of Fee book
per Form No. 45,
No. 2.
Macao. June 30, 1863.]

[1-120]

[Recd Sept 9
Despatch No. 9.]

Consulate of the United States
of America, Macao. June 30, 1863.

Sir:

Permit me herewith to transmit the miscellaneous expense account of this consulate with the United States for the Quarter ending June. 30th 1863. amounting in the aggregate to $35^66--Enclosure No. 1.

[N°1 Enclosure No 1. miscel a/c & vouchers.]

Enclosures Nos. 2 & 3 are the legally required Exchange vouchers.

[Nos 2 & 3 exchange vouchers]

I am, sir,
Your Obedient Servant
W. P. Jones.
U. S. Consul.

[The Honorable
William H. Seward.
Secretary of State of the United States
Washington D. C.]

[Macao June, 30. 1863
W. P. Jones. U. S. Consul.
No. 9.
3 Enclosures
Received,
Miscellaneous Expense
a/c,
n,]

[1-121]

[Recd Sept 9.
Despatch No 11.]

Consulate of the United States

of America. Macao. June. 30. 1863.

Sir:

I beg herewith to transmit the account of this Consulate with the United States for office rent, during the Quarter, Ending June. 30th instant （Vide Enclosure, No. 1. and voucher）

[N°1. Office Rent a/c & voucher.]

Enclosure Nos. 2 & 3 are the legally required exchange vouchers.

[Nos 2 & 3. Exchange Vouchers.]

I have the honor to be, sir,
Your Obedient Servant,
W. P. Jones
U. S. Consul.

[To the Honorable
William H. Seward.
Secretary of State for the United States.
Washington, D. C.]

[Macao. June. 30. 1863.
W. P. Jones. Consul.
No. 10,

3 Enclosures–
Received–
Office Rent, a/c,
n.]

[1–122]

[Recd 28th Decr]

Consulate of the United States of Am,
Macao, Sept, 20, 1863

Sir,

I crave the Presidents indulgence for having infringed Section 84 of my Consular Instructions under the corecion of reasons set forth in the medical certificate herewith Enclosure No. 1. Upon the recommendation of this Certificate I was absent from my Consulate for a longer period than the ten days allowed by regulation, say from the 21st of August to the 8th of September––16 days.

During this period the Consulate was not closed, the late Excellent Vice Consul, Gideon Nye, Jr, Esq – having consented to act as my deputy with the written approval of His Excellency the Governor of Macao.

[N°1. Medical Cert.e]

[To Abraham Lincoln,
President of the United States.
&c &c &c]

I cannot doubt that a perusal of the enclosure testifying that this absence was essential to the restoration of my wifes health after she had been long prostrated by the effects of the climate, will induce the President to execuse my breach of regulation in not having delayed to ask his permission as I should assuredly have done, would the circumstance have permitted.

I may further add that this is the only instance in which I have been absent from my post for even a single day since my arrival at Macao.

In conclusion allow me to apologize for not having written this communication at an earlier date, by stating that until after I had set forth it was not certain that I could not make some arrangement to leave Mrs. Jones abroad and return, myself, with in the ten days legal limit.

With these representations,

I have the honor to be
Your Obedient Servant,
W. P. Jones
U. S. Consul at Macao.

This is to certify that Mrs. W. P. Jones has been under my medical advice and treatment for some months past, while suffering from a disease of the climate, viz; the Billions Intermittent Fever, during which she was confined to her room for about eight weeks. To regain one's strength fully in this climate, travel and change of air are of the highest importance, if not even absolutely necessary. I therefore advice Mrs. Jones to adopt these remedies at once.

Macao 8th of August. 1863.
V. de P. S. Pitter
M. S.

[Enclosure
Medical Certifte
of Dr Pitter.
to Occasion for absence
of Consul from his
post.
Macao. Sept 20, 1863.]

[Macao. Sept 20, 1863.

W. P. Jones, Consul.
Despatch to President,
No. 1.
1 Enclosure--
Received,
Concerning absence
from Consulate.]

[1-123]

[Recd Dec 15. N°11.]

Consulate of the United States of America,
Macao Sept. 30. 1863.

Sir:

Allow me herewith to transmit the a/c of this Consulate with the United States for Office Rent, during the Quarter Ending, September 30th instant: Vide Enclosure No.1.

[No.1. Rent. a/ct]

Enclosures Nos 2 & 3. are the legally required Exchange Vouchers,

[Nos 2& 3. Exchange vouchers act]

I am, Sir.
Your Obedient Servant.
W. P. Jones.
Consul of the U. States of Am
at Macao.

[The Honorable
Wm H. Seward,
Secretary of State for the United States,
Washington, D. C.]

[Macao. Sept. 30, 1863,
W. P. Jones. Consul.
No. 11.
3 Enclosures
Received,

Account for Office Rent
for Quarter End'g Sept. 30.]

[1-124]

[Recd Dec 15. No. 12.]

United States Consulate–.
Macao, Sept. 30. 1863

Sir:

Herewith I beg to transmit the Miscellaneous Expense a/c of this Consulate with the United States for the Quarter Ending, Sept. 30, 1863--amounting in the aggregate to 33^{25} Vide Enclosure, No. 1.

[N°1. Miscel – a/c.]

Enclosures Nos 2 & 3 are the legally required vouchers Nos 4 & 5 Letter Registers.

[Nos 2& 3. Exch. Vo chers Nos 4 & 5 Letter Registers]

I am, very Truly, Sir,
Your Ob^t. Servant
W. P. Jones
U. S. Consul, Macao.

[To the Honorable
William H. Seward
Secretary of State &c &c
Washington, D. C.]

[Macao. Sept. 30. 1863.

W. P. Jones. Consul.

No. 12.

5 Enclosures.

Received

Miscellaneous Ex. a/c
for the Quart. End'g Sept. 30
1863.]

[1-125]

[N°13. Recd Dec 19.
□□□□ □□□□]

United States Consulate
Macao, Sept. 30. 1863.

Sir

Referring to my No. 8. for the Reports of last quarter, I now forward the reports for the Quarter Ending, Sept. 30, 1863,--being, besides the letter Registers already enclosed with the Miscellaneous expense ac/ct, only two in number-i.e. My report of the Arrivals & Departure of Am. Vessels, Fees Cargoes &c per Forms Nos 44 & 45--and my report of Names &c of Deceased Am. Citizens Vide, Enclosures Nos, 1 & 2.--

[Nos. 1 & 2 Quart. Reports]

I have the honor to report that the National Anniversary was creditably abserved at this port, by the firing

[To the Honorable, W. H. Seward
Secretary of State for the United States
Washington, D. C.]

of a National Salute from the Citadel and also from the U. S. sloop of war "Jamestown", then in port. The Governor and Chief officers of the government, and consular representatives of the several powers here represented further observed the day by calling to present their compliments. Instead of that ignoble spirit manifested in some other Quarters this Government seems rather disposed to multiply its evidences of suspect in this day of our National trial.

[Observance of 4th of July]

I beg to acknowledge the receipt of the following despatches &c. from the state Department, during the past Quarter, viz: From Asst. Sect. under date of May 7. notice of his having sent "Wheaton's Interna

[Despatch form State Dept. recd.]

tional Law"; from Despatch Bureau, Blk, Forms No. 138.

I regret to have to announce the Death of Capt. Frank Blisk, late of the Am. Bark, "Lyeemoon", who died at the Hotel Royal, in, this place, Sept. 26, 1863. His wife resides at New Orleans, and his mother and Brothers at Tidsbury, Mass., I have opened communication with these friends. In the meantime the effects have been duly inventoried &c &c as the law directs more full details will go forward by the next mail.

[Death of Capt. F. Blisk.]

I have the honor to be, Sir,

Your Obedient Servt,
W. P. Jones.
Consul of the U. States @ Macao.

Form No. 21.

Names of all deceased American Citizens &c at Macao, from July 1st to Sept 30, 1863.

Date of Decease	Names of Persons	Native of where	Vessel	Where deceased	Value of effects	Disposition of effects.
1863.						
July 16.	Chas Kline	Prussia	"Nagasaki"	Macao Hospital	Nothing	–
Sept. 26	Capt. F. Blisk	–Mass–		Macao, Hotel,	$264^{00} besides clothing of little value	Awaiting orders from his wife, Sarah A. Blisk, New Orleans. La.

W. P. Jones

[Enclosure No. 2
With Despatch No. 13.
Names of Deceased
Am. Citizens
K____
No. 2.
Macao. Sept. 30. 1863]

[Macao, Sept. 30, 1863.
W. P. Jones. Consul,
No. 13.
2 Enclosures
Received,
Quarterly Reports &c]

[1-126]

[Recd □□□ Jan 2]

U. S. Consulate
Macao, Oct. 24, 1863.

Hon. Wm H. Seward,
Secretary of State for the United States,
Washington, D. C.

Sir:

Whether the feeling be a reasonable one or not, I will not venture to say, but certain it is that a feeling exists among Consuls, that they have a kind of clients right to look to their honored chief at Washington for something not unlike a patrons sympathy in their personal trials and interest in their welfare. I know it is not "so nominated in the bond," neither do such words as "kindliness," "humanity," &c, ever appear in such instruments, and yet it is understood that the honorable secretary possesses both, and interprets law and exercises office as if the functions and those sentiments were not altogether opposed.

[Reliance of Consul upon the Secretary for sympathy in their personal trials, in the service of the Dept.]

To illustrate my preface, I have felt impelled for several weeks past to tell the Secretary that I cannot live on my salary, just as though he would take an interest in that fact, and having satisfied himself by perusal of a few lines that it is so, with=

out any cant or deception on my side, would recommend the addition of at least another thousand to my salary.

Here are the facts: My Rent costs $400 per annum, servants (two less than any other foreign family in Macao keeps) $350^{00}, Physicians yearly attendance $100^{00}, and, as the Dept. has just informed me, I am to be charged with the mint premium on Mexican and Spanish dollars (the only dollars here known), which together with my tax amounts to another $100^{00}, leaving me for food, clothing and all incidentals and the charities and hospitalities, unavoidably connected with the Consulate, $550^{00}, in a country where flour is $15 per barrel, butter 70 cts per. lb, meats 20 cts per. lb, wood $20^{00} per card and other things in proportion.

So live on such a salary is impossible. I have been assured so from the first of my arrival here, and have now proved it by the actual experience. Yet I am here, money out of pocket for my transit, for all my furniture after my arrival, and now a daily deficit for the current expenses of living – yet under bonds not to transact business, if even there were opporturnity to help myself in that way, which with

[Proof of the inadequacy of His salary.]

out heavy capital, there is not.

Please note that no other salaried Consul in China has less than $3000^{00} besides Court fees, of which I have none. Certainly living is no more expensive in most of these ports than it is in Macao.

Fair dealing between the Government and Consul seems to me to require that, the question having been settled that it is important to have a consul at this port, he should be allowed sufficient for a plain, respectable style of living. It is not necessary that he should ape these merchant princes, drive a coach, keep a bevy of servants, garnish his table with wines, or even employ a clerk. But when he does all the want of his office and confines himself to strict temperance and economy in everything, he should not be compelled to sit in the shadow of a daily growing mountain of debt.

[The Consul should have a sufficient but not luxurious employment]

As to the question of maintaining a Consul at Macao, when increased salary is called for permit me to say, that when looking merely at the Commercial Returns, as I did upon my arrival, I doubted the expediency of the establishment, but my observation and experience since have taught me otherwise. This is virtually our Naval Station

[Importance of the Macao Consulate.]

for the coast of China. Since the recognition of the rebels as belligerents and the order not to allow our men of war to remain in English ports more than twenty four hours, our war-vessels have come here for stores and received them per. ship from Hongkong or bought them here. This is the only port on the coast where the men can be allowed to go ashore, and the good offices of the consul are essential to adjust the difficiulties which they occasion and to secure prompt action for the arrest of deserters. During the Crisis of the Trent difficulty the importance of Macao to our commerce, as the only Christian neutral port on this Coast in case of war, was forcibly illustrated, as on that occasion, when it was anticipated that the mail would bring tidings of a rupture, and the English gunboats in Hongkong harbor actually went under steam as soon as the mail-steamers was descried on the horizon, threating to make instant prizes of all American vessels within reach, some scare or more of Am. ships came into Macao for protection.

[Our naval Station &c. Only neutral Christian port, in case of war with Eng. Fr, &c Importance of illustra'd during Trent affair]

In case of war with either France or England the importance of this port for refuge and sale of prizes would be almost incalculable. It is at all times the greatest sanitarium in China. As such it has many temporary American residents every year, to whom a consul's presence is often a great comfort. I mention these as extraordinary reasons for our governments maintaining a consul at this port.

[The great sanitarium of this Coast]

What Hongkong is to England, Macao is, in may respects, to the United States, without any of the expense of a great colonial establishment. Of course all the ordinary occasions for the services of a consul exist here in conjunction with the foregoing reasons--so far as the commerce of the port demands.

[What Hongkg is to Grt. Britain, is Macao to the U. S.]

With this presentation of facts I respectfully submit to the Honoarble Secretary my urgent petition that he will recommend to Congress on increase of the salary of this Consulate to 3000^{00} or at least 2500^{00}, which latter sum would be a bare support, without provision for any unfortunate contingencies or reward for my services beyond present maintenance. It ought to be nothing less than 3000^{00}.

[No. 1. Endorsement of above by Consul at Hongkong &c]

With all respect,
I have the honor to be your Obt, Servant,
W. P. Jones.
U. S. Consul at Macao.

P. S.- Please see enclosure.

[Macao. Oct. 24, 1863.
W. P. Jones. Consul.
No. 14.
Enclosure 1,

Received,

Importance of the Macao
Consulate; for peculiar reasons
and necessity for
a more liberal support.]

[Mr Abbott]

Canton November 12. 1863,

To Abraham Lincoln,
President of the United States of America.
Washington, D. C.

Sir,

We, the undersigned Citizen of the United States, and American Missionaries at Canton China, would respectfully represent to the President, that, besides the ordinary occasion for Consular services at Macao, the peculiar importance of that Port to our persons, and to the Commerce of the United States, as being the only Christian neutral Port on this coast, to which we can resort in the event of such antiforeign outbreaks as have heretofor frequently occurred in this Empire, or in case of rupture of friendly relations with Great Britain, leads us heartily to approve the action of the Government in maintaining a salaried Consul at said Port.

At the same time we beg leave further to represent, that, our knowledge of the great cost of living on this coast convinces us that the present Salary of Fifteen Hundred Dollars is insufficient for said Consular Establishment. We do therefore petition the President to recommend to Congress an increase of the Salary of the Consul for Macao to the sum of Three Thousand Dollars--say-$3000[00] being, we believe lowest salary of any other U. S. Consul in China, and no more than a necessary and suitable support. We do therefore most cheerfully enclose an application for said advance of salary, which, together with certificates from the U. S. Consul at Hongkong, G. Nye Jr. Esq, late acting Consul at Macao have already gone forward to the State Department under date of Oct. 24_1863.

We remain, Dear Sir
Most respectfully.

D. Ball

Sam[l] W. Bonney

G. C.Kevin
Arthur Folsom

C. F. Preston
J. G. Schillin

John D. Nevins

J. H. Kerr.
Joa M. Condit

A. P. Happer.
Daniel Vrooman

[□□□□□□□□
at Canton China.

Nov. 12. 1863,
Request the President to
recommend to Congress
an increase of the Salary of
the Consul at Macao. from
$1500 to $3,000.

Respectfully referred by
the President to the Hon.
Secretary of State
Jno. G. Nicolay
Priv. See,
Feby 12, 1864.
Rec from the Pres^{d}
13. Feb]

[1-127]

[Despatch to the President.
No. 2.
Mr. Abbott

Recd from the President 13 Jul]

United States Consulate,
Macao. Nov. 25. 1863.

Sir:

Permit me to call your attention to a letter addressed to you on the 12th inst, signed by all the American Missionaries at Canton, China, setting forth the importance of maintaining the present Consular establishment at this port of Macao, but the great inadequacy of the present salary of $1500^{00} per. an. to support the incumbent, (at the high cost of living on this coast) even in very temperate and economical style; and petitioning the President to recommend to Congress an immediate increase of the said salary to the sum of $3000^{00}, the smallest amount paid such offices at any other salaried port in China. The petitions add, that, they thus cheerfully endorse a letter from the undersigned making statements and appli–

[To Abraham Lincoln,
President of the United States of America,
Washington, D. C.]

cation for the same object and forwarded to the Secretary of State, Oct, 24 (ult) , with the endorsements of Mr. Congar, U. S. Consul at Hongkong and Mr. Nye, late Consul at Macao.

It would be easy to obtain similar letters from all the American Merchants of Macao, Canton and Hongkong were not the above certificates &c, by the well known up right, Christian characters of the endoresers rendered sufficient to satisfy the President of the facts of the case.

Have the goodness therefore, I beg you, to kindly grant the petition and so to recommend, at Your first opportunity & convenience; that I may be relieved as soon as possible, from the unpleasant condition of living in a strange land, under bonds not to transact business, upon a greatly inadequate salary,-- to the exhaustion of my limited private resources.

I have the honor to be, sir,
Your Obedient Servant,
W. P. Jones.
Consul of the United States of America
at Macao, China.

[Macao, Nov. 25, 1863.
W. P. Jones_Consul_
No. 2.

Respecting Petition of
American Missionaries
at Canton, &c]

[1-128]

[No. 15. Recd 5 Feb]

United States Consulate
Macao. Nov. 27, 1863.

Sir:

Permit me herewith to transmit a copy of a letter addressed, per last post, to the President, by the American missionaries at Canton, setting forth the great importance of this Consulate, for peculiar and weightly economic and political reasons additional to the ordinary commercial occasions therefor, and approving the action of the Government in appointing a salaried officer thereto; but certifying that the great cost of living in China, renders the present salary of 1500^{00} greatly inadequate to the incumbents support and petitioning that his salary be increased to the minimum at other ports on this coast--say 3000^{00} per. an. as only a "necessary and suitable" maintenance. The letter also declares that the memorialists fully endorse an application to effect the same end, previously forwarded to the Secre-

[No. 1. Petition fr. Am. Mission at Canton]

[To the Honorable W. H. Seward,
Secretary of State for the United States,
Washington, D. C.]

tary of State:–thus referring to my No 14. of the 24th ult. to the Honorable Secretary, together with the emphatic endorsements made thereto, by Mr. Congar, U. S. Consul at Hongkong, and that liberal–hearted & patriotic Am. merchant, G. Nye. Jr. Esq, late Consul here.

Although it would be easy to obtain the signatures of all the Am. Merchants at Macao, Hongkong and Canton, to a similar petition, it is presumed that nothing more is necessary to assure the President and the Department of the facts in the case, than the certificates and endorsements of the distinguished and scrupulously conscientious gentlemen whose names are now before you.

Let me therefore, with an earnestness emphasized by the threatened exhaustion of my hunted private resources, beg the Honorable Secretary to kindly grant this petition his immediate and favorable attention.

I remain–Your Obedient Servant,
W. P. Jones
U. S. Consul @ Macao

[Macao. Nov. 27. 1863.
W. P. Jones – Consul.
No. 15.
Petition of Am. Missionaries
at Canton – respecting
Macao, Consulate.

1 Enclosure.
Rec[d]]

[Copy]

Canton November 12, 1863–]

To Abraham Lincoln,
President of the United States of America.
Washington D. C.

Sir,

We, the undersigned, Citizens of the United States and American Missionaries at Canton China, would respectfully represent to the President that, besides the ordinary occasions for Consular services at Macao, the peculiar importance of that Port to our Persons, and to the Commerce of the United States as being the only

Christian neutral Port on this coast, to which we can resort in the event of such antiforeign outbreaks as have heretofore frequently occured in this Empire, or in case of rupture of friendly relations to Great Britain, leads us heartily to approve the action of the Government in maintaining a salaried Consulat at said Port.

At the same time we beg leave further to represent, that, our knowledge of the great cost of living on this coast convinces us that the present salary of Fifteen Hundred Dollars is insufficient for said Consular Establishment. We do therefore

[Enclosure No. 1.
With Despatch No. 15
Macao, Nov, 27, 1863.]

petition the President to recommend to Congress an increase of the salary of the Consul for Macao to the sum of Three Thousand Dollars_say $3000^{00}, being believe the lowest salary of any other United States Consul in China, and no more than a necessary and suitable support. We do therefore most cheerfully endorse an application for said advance of salary, which, together with certificates from the U. S. Consul at Hongkong, and G. Nye. Jr. Esqre, late acting Consul of Macao, have already gone forward to the State Department under date of Oct. 24 1863.

We remain, Dear Sir,
Most Respectfully

D. Ball

Saml W. Bonney

G. C.Kevin
C. F. Preston
Joa M. Condit
John D. Nevins.
J. H. Kerr.
A. P. Happer.

Arthur Folsom
J. G. Schillin

Daniel Vroornan

[True Copy–signed
A. Folsom]

[1–129]

[Rec^d March 19: 64.]

Consulate of the United States of America.
Macao, December. 31. 1863.

Sir:

Permit me herewith to send you my statement of the a/c of this Consulate with the United States for Miscellaneous Expenses – amt'g to $34^{52} – vide Enclosure No. 1.

[No. 1. mis. Ex. a/c]

Enclosures Nos. 2. 3. &4 – are the legally required Exchange & other vouchers.
[No. 2. 3. 5 Vouchers.□□□]

I have the honor to be, Sir,
Yours Respectfully
W. P. Jones
U. S. Consul for Macao

[The Honorable
William H. Seward
Secretary of State for the United States
Washington. D. C.]

[Macao. Dec, 31. 1863.
W. P. Jones. Consul
No. 17.
4 Enclosures–
Rec[d]
Miscellaneous Expense
a/c.]

[1–130]

[No. 16.
Rec'd March 19. 64]

Consulate of the United States of America,
Macao, December 31, 1863.

Sir:

Enclosed please note the ac/ct of this Consulate with the United States for office Rent during the Quarter Ending at the date above given. Vide Enclosure. No 1--amt'g to 37^{50}
[No.1 Rent a/c.]

Enclosures Nos 2. 3 &4 are the usually required vouchers.
[Nos. 2. 3. 4 Enelose]

I am, Sir,
Your Obedient Servant,
W. P. Jones
Consul of the U. S. of am at Macao.

[The Honorable
Wm H. Seward
Secretary of State for the United States
Washington, D. C.]

[Macao. Dec. 31. 1863.
W. P. Jones. U. S. Consul
No. 16.
Enclosure 4.
Recd
Office Rent a/c,]

[1–131]

[No. 18.
Rec'd apl 4, 64.]

Consulate of the United States of America
Macao, December 31. 1863

Sir:

Referring to my Nos. 16 & 17 of even date herewith for the miscellaneous Expenses and Rent a/c. of the Quarter ending as above, I now beg to hand you enclosures Nos 1. 2. 3. 4. &5. being seveverally my "Navigation & Commercial Report", "Return of Arrivals & Departures &c", "Annual Aggregate of Fees", "Register of Letters Recd" and "Registers of Letters Sent" all for said Quarter.

I regret to report that the Rebel Corsair "Alabama" is now pursuing her career of ruthless destruction against our Commerce in the Indian and China Seas. You will doubltless have been furnished with the particulars of the destruction of the Am. Bark

[Amanda]

[Nos 1. 2. 3. 4. 5. Quarterly Returns Privateering (E) in China Seas]

[The Honorable
Wm H. Seward
Secretary of State for the United States,
Washington. D. C.]

"Amanda" and the splendid Clipper Ship "Winged Racer" in and off the Straits of Sunda, the fine Clipper "Contest" in the China sea, and the Am. Ships "Sonora" and "Heighlander" and the British Ship "Mastaban" in the Straits of Malacca–by agents of the Gov't nearer the scenes of destruction, and before this reaches you. But it is proper that I should allude to these wanton acts of barbarous hostility before stating the change in Foreign opinion which is now plainly observable here--so that men who were once either lauding or excusing "Capt. Semmes" are now ready to exclaim, as a company of them did in my presence the other day" – we are ready, every one of us, to illuminate as soon as we hear of the destruction of this rascally privateer."

Semmes' audacious act of burning the "Martaban", upon the assumption that her British Register was fraudulently obtained has excited great in=

[Favorable change in Foreign sentiment – versus the "Alabama"]

dignation among most of the Corsair's English Confreres and promises to prove for him a piece of mad impolicy; which we can but hope will put a stop to much of the sympathy and assistance hitherto as shamefully accorded him at British Ports~although it must be admitted that there are some Englishmen who would even excuse this atrocity.

In this connection I beg to forward to the Honorable Secretary of State, copies of a correspondence held with the Governor of Macao, touching the character of the "Alabama" and the treatment to be accorded her in the event of her appearing off these Roads, with desire to enter – vide Enclosure Nos. 6. 7. & 8.~

You will observe that besides the usual argument against the claims of any of the Confederate Corsairs to rights of Ocean-Belligerency, I was enabled to employ against this particular desperado an argument locally much stronger, by referring to the outrage of the "Alabama"

[at]

[Nos. 6. 7. 8. Correspondence with Gov. of Macao – respect'g the "Alabama"]

at the Portuguese Port of Terceira in the Azores. Also, in His Exc'cys reply you will please note that he evinces no disposition to evade the force of the King's Decree by assuming the rebel craft to be a "man-of-war", but freely expresses his convinction that she belongs to the class "Corsarios", named therein, and should be interdicted the Port, except in case of distress, I have since learned in private conversation with some of the authorities that it is His Exc'cys resolution to order her away the instant she appears off the Harbor.

I should not omit to mention that, in acknowledging the receipt of the Governor's Communication, after expressing my confidence that His Exc'cys would permit no evasion of the declared interdiction to inure to the benefit of the "Alabama" through a fictitious plea of the exception- I ventured to add my ardent hope, "that, in the event of the Alabama's actually touching in these Roads,

[The Alabama interdicted the Port]

"His Exc'cy might discover it as within his prerogative and eminently worthy of his usual jealous regard for the National honor to arrest and hold to strict accountability this lawless offender of the King's Dignity at Terceira; since His Majesty acknowledges no government that can be held responsible for the vessels' conduct;" and I closed by declaring "my conviction, that His Exc'cy would not fail to exert every power believed to be within his competency to rebuke this irresponsible and destructive Corsair and vindicate in the same instant both the sovereign dignity and good faith of Portugal against that audacious act whereby the 'Alabama' violently armed herself within His Majesty's domain to burn and destroy the Commerce of the United States."

His Exc'cy replied, as I must confess I deemed it more than likely he would, that he had received no official notice of the affair at Terceira, and without special orders could not avenge an offense to the national.

[honor]

[The arrest of the Alabama suggested – in retaliation for her violation of the Portuguese Sovereignity at Terceira. Gov. Amaral's reply to the above.]

perpetrated beyond his jurisdiction – and closed with the reiteration of his intention to interdict the "Alabama" as per his former communication on this same subject. Thus terminated a correspondence in which I hope that my language was such as may meet your approval, and the results all that could have been accomplished by any merely consular addresses that could have been adopted.

I have had the honor to receive from the State Department during this Quarter, on Oct 10, Circular No. 37 of 1863, on Nov. 10, Statutes at large 1862–63, on Dec. 3, Circ. No. 40, also a volume of Wheaton's Elem[ts] of International Law, and on Dec. 24, a communication from Asst. Sect. Seward, replying to my No. 7 in the Case of the ship "Emma".

Replying to Circ. No. 40. Sect. 12 – I am happy to state that I am not required to pay taxes at Macao, in view of the fact that I am not engaged

[Despatches &c Rec[d] of the Dept. 4th Quar[r] Reply to Circ. No 40. Sec 12.]

in trade in which is understood to be agreeable with the Treaty stipulatious between Portugal & the United States for consular privileges.

Touching the subject of exchange alluded to in the same circular – permit me to say, that I truly regret the impossibility of negotiating Government Bills on more favorable terms than those vouched for in my exchange certificates at various times during the year – viz: for drafts payable in gold seventy five cents to the dollar on their face, at all times, and for drafts payable in currency fifty to sixty cents to the dollar according to the rise or fall of London exchange in New York per our latest quotations at selling, You have already been informed that my salary is inadequate to my support which will explain how I have had full opportunity to learn, to my bitter cost, that a New York acceptance of the first grade would produce,

[during]

[logo per exchange]

during last summer, no more than fifty cents to the dollar. I cannot therefore believe that I am one of those for whome the rebuke in Sect. 15 of this Circular was intended ~ although I am aware that our loss per. exchange in the China ports, when Consuls make the best negotiations possible, must seem to the Department exorbitant. However we have to deal with facts: when Londons Bills sell for \$1[61] in New York, and are at a discount here – and money can be used to such great advantage on this coast as to frequently command hooper cent per mensem, you can hardly be astonished at the loss on our bills so oppressively felt at home. Myself and brother Consuls can but wish that some plan could be devised for us to draw on Baring Brothers & Co; but only the Department knows whether this is possible.

Wishing our Country and the Honorable Secretary a Happy–Glorious New Year,

I have the honor to be
Your Obedient Servant
W. P. Jones

Consul of the United States @ Macao.

[FORM No. 12.]

REGISTER of Official Letters and Despatches received at the U. S. Consulate at ········ for the Quarter ending ············. 18

NAME OF THE WRITER.	NO.	PLACE AND DATE OF LETTER.	WHEN RECEIVED.	ON WHAT SUBJECT.	No of Enclosures.	REMARKS.	POSTAGE PAID.
His Ex. Gov. Jose Rodrigues Coelho	1	do Amaral, Macao, Oct 1.	Oct 1	Exempt. Consuls for Taxes.			ct
State Dept	2	Washington. D.C. July 1st	Oct 10	Circr No 37 for 1863.			0.48
Fourth Auditor	3	Washington. D.C. Aug. 22	Oct 22	For Asst Payres Wade		of U. S. S. "Jamestown"	0.34
State Dept	4			Statutes of 1862 –5			
J. M. Cantuasias	5	Peru Consul, Macao, Nov 21	Nov 21	Announcing discharge of		Am. Mole of Peru. Ship on request	
Gov Amaral	6	Macao Dec, 24	Dec 24	Invite to Te Deum		for birth of Prince Royal	
Gov Amaral	7	Macao Dec, 24	Dec 24	Response to my official		& interdictn'y "Alabama" of this Port.	
Chief Clerk Navy Dept	8	Washington D. C.	Dec 26	To David Mc Dougal		U. S. S. "Wyoming"	0.32
Chief Clerk Navy Dept	9	Washington	Dec 26	For Capt. C. Price		U. S. S. "Jamestown"	0.32
Dept of State	10	Washington D. C.	Dec 26	Concern'g "Emma Case"			0.16
First Comptroller Treas.	11	Washington D. C.	Dec 26	a/c Current			0.16
							$1.68

W. P. Jones U. S. Consul.

NOTE. – Consular officers are not authorized to pay postages or other charges on letters or packages addressed to them, with a view to charge them to the United States, unless they bear on their envelopes evidence of official character, as emanating from some of the Executive Departments, or from some of the legations or consulates of the United States in foreign countries. Such charges or postages, if paid by consular officers, are not to be included in their accounts for postage against the Department of State. This form, with the blanks properly filled, is to be sent, with the despatch enclosing each quarterly postage account, to the Secretary of State. Care should be taken to note the amount of postage paid on each letter.

[Macao. Dec. 31. 1863.
W. P. Jones. Consul.
No. 18.
8 Enclosures.
Recd
Correspondence with Gov.
Amaral respect'g "Alabama"
Quarterly Reports]

[Enclosure
With Despatch No.
Regter of letters Recd
No. 4
Macao. Dec. 31. 1863.

[1-132]

[Copy.]

Consulate of the United States of Amerca
Macao, Dec, 23, 1863.

Sir:

I beg to address your Excellency upon a subject of very marked international importance and involving for the Government of Macáo a question of grave responsibiliy, the decision of which may be called for at any moment--I allude to the character of the so called "Confederate privateer" "Alabama", whose arrival upon this Coast is daily expected, and to the question whether your Excellency will permit or forbid her to enter this Port.

The delicate sense of International honor which has characterized Portugal throughout the present sedition in America scarcely leaves room in my mind for a doubt as to the answer that will be returned to this question; Nevertheless, while I have all confidence in the rectitude of your Excellency's purposes, it is still my duty to set before you certain facts of mutual concern and invoke thereto Your Serious attention in the consideration of this subject.

First. I have most respectfully to remind

[His Excellency,
The Counselor
José Rodrigues Coelha do Amaral.
Permanent Member of the Board for Colonies,
Governor of Macáo
&c &c &c.]

Your Ex[cy] that the government of the United States emphatically denies that Neutral Powers can by any impartial interpretation of International Law rightly concede belligerent privileges to that organization of rebels in arms against their government called the "Confederate States of North America."

And I am happy to see that His Faithful Majesty-Your Sovereign leige, by his eminently upright resolution not to imitate the discourteous haste of less considerate Powers, has thus far acquiesced in the justice of the opinion of my government. If therefore, Your Excellency's sovereign government has not deemed it proper to concede the rights of Ocean Belligerency to the conspirators who have sent forth this lawless incediary to burn, sink, and destroy the Commerce of a nation at peace with Portugal, and in some measure injure all commerce, then surely the notorious "Alabama" can be regarded by the Authorities of Macáo in no other light than a pirate -the forensic definition of that marine brigand being- "a vessell that commits depredations upon the high seas without being authorized by any sovereign State."

Second- It is my duty to refer Your Excellency to the fact that this ocean marauder, after having escape from her English birthplace in violation of British law and without clearance or register entered in this illegal-I may say piratical character the Portuguese Port of Terceira in the Azores and there in a neighboring bay of the same island, took on board her guns and most of her crew from two other British ships or vessels-in violation of the Sovereignity of Portugal and in audacious defiance of the Authorities of Terceira, who in vain ordered her away. Knowing as I do, that Your Excellency is keenly sensitive to anything that in the least degree compromises the national honor and how unlikely you would be to forget an outrage upon the sovereignty of Portugal until some manner of atonement had been made, I cannot deem it necessary for me to do more than allude to the affair of Terceira--and remark that my government fully expects that both in vindication of the affronted dignity of His Most Faithful Majesty's Government, and in attestation of the sincerity of its avowed opposition to the hostile use made of its territory in the instance referred to, Your Excellency will at least prohibit the said "Alabama" from all intercourse with this Port, if indeed you do not hold her to strict account for her outrage. Surely you can do no less than the government of Brazil has done for a much slighter offense--as witnessed in its decree of June 23. 1863.–in which it interdicts all the self styled "Confederate cruisers" from any intercourse whatsoever with any of the Ports of that Empire.

These two arguments–first, that the said "Alabama" is not entitles to Belligerent privileges--Second that she has insulted the sovereign dignity of Portugal, seem to me reasons sufficient for my believing that your Excellency will not disappoint the expectation of my Government by allowing this lawless despoiler of our Commerce and irresponsible destroyer of the property even of penetrate, to enjoy the privileges of the Roads and Harbor of Macao. Permit me in conclusion to ask your Excellency to receive and consider the memorial transmitted herewith, signed by the several Americans, resident in Macao, and addressed to you upon this same grave subject. You will find therein, an amplification of some of the arguments used above, together with **proofs** I deem unanswerable, against the right of the said "Alabama" to be treated as a belligerent--even had Portugal conceded belligerent privileges to the so called "Confederate Goveevernment--which I understand is not the case--otherwise I should here dwelt upon the same subject myself--

This memorial may serve to show in some slight degree the intense interest with which Your Exc[y] decision in this matter is looked for by the Americans in China generally--who rely upon your high sense of International honor for a rebuke to this unlawful desperado of the seas. Allow me finally to remark that such honorable action of your Excellency as is here sought will not only command the general admiration and applause of law abiding men every where, but will elicit the ardent special appreciation of the Government of the United States.

With very great Respect.
I have the honor to be
Your Excellency's Obedient Servant
(signed) W. P. Jones
Consul of the United States of America
at Macao, China–

[To Gov. Amaral. Respt'g "Alabama" No. 6.]

[Government
of Macao
□□□eign Department
N[o] 86.]

Translation–

Sir,

I have had the honor of receiving your Despatch of the 23^{d} Instant accompanying a Memorial signed by various American Citizens residing at this City with reference to the **Corsair** "(Corsario)" "Alabama" of the Southern States in Rebellion against the Government of the United States of America.–

Foreseeing the event of the said coming to Macáo you express to me the hope you entertain that she will not be permitted to enter the port nor be recognized in the character of a belligerent vessel.

Upon this subject I must refer myself to the Decree of the 29th July 1861–of which the annexed is a Copy–wherein His Majesty's Govevernment prescribes the course to be pursued in the ports of the Realm with respect to **Corsair** of any country whatever.–

In view of article second of the said Decree, there can be no doubt about the interdiction to the entrance of the **Corsair** "Alabama" into this port, save in the case prescribed in the special exceptive clause of

[To W. P. Jones Esquire
Consul of the United States of America at Macáo]

of the said article by which she could only be admitted under the restrictions therein expressed.–

God preserve you – Macáo 24th December 1863.–

(signed) J. R. Coelho do Amaral.
Governor.

[With Despatch No.
Reply of His E^{cy} Gov. Amaral
Interdicting the Alabama,
from this Port &c.
No. 7.

Macao, Dec. 31, 1863.]

[1–133]

[Government
Macáo
Copy.]

Translation.

Department of Foreign Affairs –

It being expedient, in view of the circumstance presented by the course of events in the United States of America, in execution of the principles set forth in the Paris declaration of the 16th of April 1856 made by the Representation of the Powers subscribers of the Treaty of peace of the 30th March of the said year, to which my Govevernment adheres, and likewise to adopt towards the same end such measures as I may deem useful, I have been pleased,--after hearing the Counsil of State–to decree the following:–

Article 1st: Hereby is prohibited, in the ports and in the waters of this Kingdom, in the continent as well as in the adjacent Islands and in the Colonies, to Portuguese subjects and Foreigners to arm vessels intended for Privateers.

Article 2nd: In and at the above said ports mentioned in the proceeding article,--is equally prohibited the entrance to Privateers and to prizes made by the said Privateers or by armed Transport（？）

Special exceptive paragraph:--There shall be an exception to this prohibition in cases of forca majoria, in which, according to the Law of Nations it will be indispensable to extend hospitality to them, without in the least allowing to them the sale of articles resulting from their prizes.--

The Ministers and Secretaries of State of Every Department will take notice accordingly and cause it to be carried into effect.–

Palace of Necessities on the 29th of June 1861.（signed）The King--Marques of Loulé--Alberto Antonio de Maraes Carvalho--Viscount de Sá da Bandeira--Carlos Bento da Silva--Thiago Augusto Velloso de Horta--Antonio José de Avila.--

True Copy.
（signed）Gregorio José Ribeiro
Secretary of the Government.

[Enclosure
with Despatch No.
Copy of the King's Decree
alluded to in Enclosure No. 7.
No.8.
Macao. Dec. 31. 1863.]

[With Despatch. No.
Aggregate Returns of Fees.
No. 3.
Macao, Dec. 31, 1863.]

[1–134]

[No. 19 Recd 4th qtr
V.]

Consulate of the United States of America,
Macao. Dec. 31. 1863.

Sir:

In conformity with Section 100 of the Gen'l Instructions I have to report that I have addressed – the Honorable Secretary of State--since my entrance upon duty Feb. 25, 1863 – at times and in Nos as follow; to wit:

No. 1--Feb 25--No 2. March 28,--No 3. Mar 31.

No 4, Mar 81--No 5, Mar 31--No 6. Mar. 31,

No 7, May 9--Nos. 8. 9. & 10--June 30--Nos 11. 12 & 13, Sept 30--No 14. Oct 24. No 15 Nov 27.

Nos. 16. 17. 18& 19, Dec 31.

I have the honor to be,
with great Respect,
Your Obedient Servant
W. P. Jones
U. S. Consul,

[The Honorable
Wm H. Seward
Secretary of State for the U. S.
Washington D. C.]

[Macao. Dec. 31. 1863.
W. P. Jones. U. S. Consul.
No. 19

Recd

Report per Sect of
Instructions No. 100.
Despatches during the year.

Macao–end–]

[1–135]

Official Letters Sent.

From the U. S. Consulate at Macao from Oct. 1. to Dec. 31. 1863.

Date		No.	To whom & what place sent	On what subject.	No. of Enclosures	Postage
1863						c. cts

Oct	15	1	President Lincoln, Washington	Concerning absence from Post	1	0.[92]
Oct	15	2	State Dept.	Quarterly Reports	3	3[32]
Oct	15	3	U. S. Consul, Singapore,	Forw[dg] to Capt. McDougal □□□20□□		
Oct	15	4	Mrs. Sarah A. Blisk New Orleans	Death of Husband,		1.40
Oct	24	5	Sect of State, Washington	Advance of Salary–endorsed and letters to Geo Cowie 5th Aud,	2	3[52]
Oct	24	5	Sect of State, Washington			
Nov	10	6	President LincolnWashington	Petition from Am. Mission Canton,	1	1.17
Nov	10	7	Sect of Treasury Washington	Forw[dg] 1/2 register of Parliament,	1	1.80
Nov	20	8	Capt. C. Price, Japan,	Forw[dg] letter to J. M. Wade payments		0.64
Nov	20	9	J. M. Cantuarias, Macao	Peru. Consul asking discharge of sailor		□□□
Nov	24	10	Ju Ed. Scurmolna, Macao	Capt. of Port, Sale of ship "Carrington"		
Nov	25	11	President Abraham Lincoln	Respect[g] petition of Canton Missions		3[12]
Nov	27	12	Sect. of State, Washington	Respect[g] petition of Canton Missions	1	2[16]
Nov	27	13	Geo. Cowie, Fifth – Aud. Dept	Respecting Salary	1	
Dec	5	14	Rear Admiral Com[dy] Pacific Luadron	Announc'g arrival of "Alabama" in the Indian Seas		2[16]
Dec	5	15	Collector SanFrancisco	Announc'g arrival of "Alabama" in the Indian Seas		
Dec	12	16	L. E. Chittenden Washington	1/2 Register Bark "Alabama."	1	2[00]
Dec	12	17	James Mc Bride Minister Honnohelu	Respecting "Alabama"		1[16]
Dec	23	18	His Ex. Jose Rodrigues &c Governor of Macao	Respecting "Alabama"	1	
Dec	26	19	His Ex. Jose Rodrigues &c Governor of Macao	Accept'g invitation to □□□ YE Demer		
Dec	26	20	His Ex. Jose Rodrigues &c Governor of Macao	Ach[t] receipt to reply concern'g Alabama – interdict'g her entrance		
Dec	31	21	Sect of State, Washington	a/c for Miscellaneous ex	4	
Dec	31	22	Sect of State, Washington	a/c for Office rent	3	
Dec	31	23	Sect of Treasury Washington	a/c for salary	5	
				There is a balance of $1[20] for local postage on–one of the above.		1[20]

W. P. Jones
□□□□

[Enclosure--
With Despatch No.
Reg[ter] Letters Sent.
No.5.
Macao. Dec. 31. 1863.]

[1–136]

From No. 138

AGGREGATE RETURN of all Fees received at the Consulate of the United States at Macao, China, and the Consular Agencies connected with it, from February 25. to December 31. 1863, inclusive.

NAME OF CONSULAR OFFICER.	OFFICE.	WHERE LOCATED.	Fees for the quarter ending March 31.	Fees for the quarter ending June 30.	Fees for the quarter ending Sept. 30.	Fees for the quarter ending Dec. 31.	TOTAL.	REMARKS.
W. P. Jones	U. S. Consul	Macao.	8⁰⁷	13³⁸	63⁸¹	81⁴⁸	166⁷⁴	Please observe that the 1st Quarter is Fractional.
							Total $	166⁷⁴

CONSULATE at Macao.

December 31, 1863. W. P. Jones

United States Consul.

NOTE.--This Form is to be transmitted to the Department of State, with the blanks properly filled, at the close of every year, in order that the information may communicated to Congress, as required by law. The amounts are to be given in American currency, and the total amount to be stated.

[Macac. Dee. 31.1863.
W. P. Jones, U. S. Consul
No. 19
Rec.d
Report per Sect of
Instruction No. 100.
Despatches cluring the year.

Macao–end.]

[END
THE NATIONAL ARCHIVES OF THE UNITED STATES * 1934 *]

卷 · 二

· VOLUME Two

卷二介紹說明

Introductory Note of Volume Two

File Microcopies of Records in the National Archives: No.109

Roll 2

DESPATCHES FROM UNITED STATES CONSULS IN MACAO, 1849–1869

Volume 2

March 31, 1864 – December 6, 1869

THE NATIONAL ARCHIVES

Washington: 1947

INTRODUCTORY NOTE

The volume microcopied on this roll has the following backstrip title: "2 / Macao / Mar. 31, 1864 / Dec. 6, 1869 / Department / of State." It contains despatches, with enclosures, addressed to the Department of State from United States consular officials at Macao between March 31, 1864, and December 6, 1869. The contents are registered on Roll, 1 of the microcopy.

The volume is part of a body of records in the National Archives designated as Record Group No. 59, General Records of the Department of State. It is volume 2 of a series generally referred to as Consular Despatches, Macao.

[2-001]

[□□□□□□□□□□]

Consulate of the United States,
Macao, Mar. 31, 1864.

Sir,

Permit me to hand you the account of this Consulate with the United States for Office Rent for the Quarter Ending as above.

I bide encloses, No.1 & Amg to \$37.[30], Enclosures No's 2, 3 & 4 are the usually required and changed vouchers, &c.

I remain, Sir
Your Obedient Servant,
W. P. Jones
U. S. Consul

[The Honorable
W. H. Seward
Secretary of State for the United States
Washington, D. C.–]

[□□□□□
Macao March 31st 1864
W. P. Jones Consul
No 1
Four Enclosures
Received
Account for Office Rent]

[2-002]

[Reced 16 June
No.2]

Consulate of the United States
Macao, March, 31, 1864.

Sir:–

Herewith I beg to hand you the Accounts of this Consulate with the State Department of the United States, for miscellaneous Expenses, during the Quarter Ending as above, （see Enclosure No.1.） amt'g to. \$37.[20].

Enclosures, Nos. 2. 3, 4. 5, 6. 7 & 8, are the several required vouchers.

[act] Mis. Ex. a/c vouchers

I am, Sir,
Your Obedient Servant
W. P. Jones
U. S. Consul

[The Honorable
Wm H. Seward,
Secretary of State for the United States,
Washington, D. C.]

[U. S. Consulate
Macao, Mar. 31, 1864
W. P. Jones, Consul.
No.2,
8 Enclosures,
Received
Miscellaneous Expense
a/c.]

[2-003]

[Recd June 16
No.3.]

United States consulate,–
Macao, March 31, 1864.

Sir,

I have to report that the unhappy spell upon our Commerce, wrought by the presence of the "Alabama" in the Indian Seas, her fleet movements and well disguised intentions, has been strikingly evident at this Port, during the past Quarter, within which, although the trade has been more than usually bush for the season, no Am. merchant vessels have appeared in harbor, except our steamers plying hence to Canton and Hongk'g. However, our latest duties from this nefarious craft are nearly three months old, when she was said to be cruising off Bombay, and since nothing reliable has been brought by the last four semimonthly mails, we begin to hope that her career in these waters is ended and are looking for some revival of our carrying trade during the ensuring quarter. This, hope

[Conclusion of Commerce]

[The Honorable Wm H. Seward,
Secretary of State for the United States,
Washington, D. C.]

[Public indignation against the "Alabama"]

borrows further encouragement from the ill feeling towards the "Alabama" which has been evicted among most of her former sympathizes and abettors by her ruthless disregard of neutrals–as manifested in her distinction of the "most abase" , (previously reported) and the spoliation of neutral goods found in her other prizes. We must regret that the instincts of universal justice had not prompted public indignation against the marauder in the very inception of the her lawless career, but nevertheless cannot fail to hail this tardy condemnation now that it is aroused, with heart felt satisfaction, even though we must refer it mainly to selfish considerations. From the conversation of officers of merchant ships who have been prisoners Upon the "Alabama" , I gather that she is, beyond doubt, in serious need of repairs, and as I can hardly believe that in the present state of public feeling and under the late orders believed to have come out from England to the several East India and China Ports, she will be allowed to make through repairs of any of these ports, I share the opinion of the Senior Naval officers on this station, that she has probably turned prow for the Atlantic again. Nevertheless if is not greatly improbable that she is passing around the Dutch East Indies and may soon appear off Shanghai or Nagasaki and thence run to the Pacific Coast. Accordingly Capt. Price with the Sloop of War "Jamestown" left this on the 24th ult. with intention of crossing between Manila and the North while the St. Sloop "Wyoming" , after settling. the late difficulties of Foo Chow, entered this to Coal and passed out on the 20th for Singapore. The "settlements" for the □□□ at Hongk'g show some improvement for our shippers, and if the "Alabama" does not soon reappear in our neighborhood, the improvement will rapidly advance. Furthermore as other nations have reaped commercial advantage from our □□□ so we are promised

[movements of our men of war signs of improvement]

[change of Naval Depot from Hongk'g to Macao]

some advantage from the unchivalric & melancholy war begun in Europe; Danish, German and English □□□ being now almost the sole ocean–carriers in the East.

Thus among the ashes of Quarter just concluded, we find embers that our hopes would fain cherish into flames of prosperity for the quarters that must follow. A few more victories at home and our flag shall flaunt on the monsoons as proudly as of old.

I have the honor to report that since my last regular Quarterly dispatch, the U. S. Naval Depot for the China and East India Squadron has been removed from Hongkong and returned to Macao, where I now have its duties temporarily joined with those of the Consulate; the former naval Officer, Mr. Speiden, having returned to the United States in feeble health. During the Consular Administration of Mr. De Silver at this Port, he held the office of Naval Store Keeper in permanency. The late General Keenan, Consul at Hong Kong was also for a time Acting U. S. Naval Storekeeper, from which I agree that my acceptance of the charge named will not be considered by the Department as irregular.

The transfer of the Deport from Hongkong to this, was made chiefly upon consideration of the unfriendly operation of the Queen's neutrality – proclamation whereby the stores, while remaining at the former place were rendered inutile. I may remark, that greater requisitions have been made upon the Depot by our vessels of war, since the removal, than during the entire year antecedent thereto.

I have the honor to acknowledge receipts--from the Department during Quarter as follows; Jan 26, reply to my No. 7. of 1863--in the "Emma" Case, Feb. 27, Circ. No.43, 1863, ~ , The "Presidents Message" , and the eloquent oration of Mr. Everett at Gettysburg.

The records of the Quarter being generally

[Receipts from Department]

in blank, I have nothing further to communicate.

With Very High Consideration
I remain
Your Obedient Servant
W. P. Jones
U. S. Consul at Macao.

[W. P. Jones Consul
No. 3.
Received
Quarterly Report
Condition of Our Commerce
&c. &c. &c.]

[2-004]

[Rec[d] Aug 20
Ane Aug 26
Mr. □□□
See enc.
No.4]

U. S. Consulate
Macao, June 8, 1864.

Sir,

I beg to hand you herewith a list of articles required for the use of this Consulate and generally supplied most economically by the proper Bureau at Washington.

The Blanks found in this office when I look possession were of the cheapest kind--all except the Fee book having been manufactured in China, and the various records being most heterogeneously thrown into three paper Bound volumes. I have subdivided these into-- "Protest Book" -- "Commercial Returns" so as to attain order until I could receive a creditable set of Books from the Department. I brought a few ordinary blank forms when I came to China, （or rather received them upon a requisition made while in Washington） but the number will cost me but a few months more, in most kinds, so I call for a full list of all forms required at a consulate.–

I am, Sir,
Most Respectfully
Your Obedient Servant
W. P. Jones
U. S. Consul at Macao

[To the Honorable
W. H. Sewards
Secretary of State for the United States
Washington, D. C.]

Original

Consulate of the United States,
Macao, May, 27th 1864.

Sir,

There are required at this Consulate for Office use the following Articles viz:–

1 Passport	Book	Seals and Wafers
1 Despatch	Book	Tape and Pencils
1 Letter	Book	Envelopes
1 Miscellaneous Record	Book	1 Resin Dispatch Cap Paper

1 Commercial Return* Book
1 Quarterly Acct. Current Book
1 Entry of Protests Book
1 Extended of Protests Book
1 Daily Journal
A full set of Consular Blanks–Forms
4 Doz. Blank Treasury drafts.
Please send by first opportunity.

Respectfully,
Your Obedient Servant
W. P. Jones
U. S. Consul.

Approved.

*arrived & depart □□□□□□□

Duplicate

Consulate of the United States,
Macao, May, 27th 1864.

Sir,

There are required at this Consulate for Office use the following Articles viz:--

1 Passport	Book	Seals and Wafers
1 Despatch	Book	Tape and Pencils
1 Letter	Book	Envelopes
1 Miscellaneous Record	Book	1 Resin Dispatch Cap Paper

1 commercial Return Book
1 Quarterly Acct. Current Book
1 Entry of Protests Book
1 Extended Protests Book
1 Daily Journal
A full set of Consular Blanks-Forms
4 Doz. Blank Treasury drafts.
Please send by first opportunity.

Respectfully,
Your Obedient Servant
W. P. Jones
U. S. Consul.

Approved.

[2-005]

[No.5. Rua □□□28,]

U. S. Consulate – Macao
June, 30, 1864.

Sir:

Allow me to hand you herewith, the Account of this Consulate for Office Rent as Charged by the permission against the United States for the Quarter ending as above –: say $37^{\underline{60}}$ – vide enclosure No.1.

Nos 2, 3. and 4 are the proper vouchers therewith.

[No 1 a/c for office rent. Nos 2, 3, & 4, vouchers]

I am, Sir, Very Truly
Your Obedient Servant
W. P. Jones–
U. S. Consulate of Macao

[To the Honorable
Wm H. Seward
Secertary of State for the United States
Washington D. C.]

[June 30, 1864
W. P. Jones––Consul
No.5.
4 Enclosures
Received–

Account for Office
Rent]

[2–006]

[Rec^{d} Nov.18
No.6]

Consulate of the United States of Am.
Macao, June 30th 1864.

Sir,

Permit me to hand you, enclosed, the Accounts of this consulate with the State Department of the United States for miscellaneous Expenses, during the Quarter ending as above （see Enclosure, N°1） Amounting to \$41$^{\underline{65}}$.

Enclosures N° 2, 3, 4, 5, 6, 7 & 8 inclusive are the several required Vouchers.

[□□□□□□□]

I remain Sir,
Your Obedient Servant
W. P. Jones
U. S. Consul at Macao.

[The Honorable
Wm H. Seward.

&c. &c. &c.]

[Macao, June 30, 1864
W. P. Jones, Consul,
No.6.
8 Enclosures
Received

Miscelleneous Expense a/c
2[d] Quarter]

[2-007]

[Rec[d] Sept 19.

Mr. Shurk

No.7
□□□]

United States Consulate
Macao, June 30, 1864.

Sir,

I regret to have to report, that, except the National Sloops of war "Wyoming" and "Jamestown", we have had no Am. Vessels in Port during the past Quarter; owing wholly, no doubt, to the check that has been put upon our Commerce by the late appearance of the "Alabama" in the Indian Seas.

The "Jamestown" has been in harbor most of the Quarter, occasioning some few calls for my official services, and several Invoices of goods shipped at Hong Kong have been verified before me, but otherwise there has been little besides the calendar exchanges of courtesies and occasional official soirees, to break the monotony

[of]

[Paralyzation of our Trade]
[To the Honorable,
W.[m] H. Seward,-
Secretary of State for the United States,
Washington, D. C.]

of "A Life in the Tropics and Nothing to do".

It is now generally hoped that, since the "Alabama" has passed around the Cape, the few of our vessels which still retain thus true colors and have been lying idle along this East and Southward, will be soon employed, (The trade of this Port has been rather brisk for several months, and I have heard many regrets expressed that the state of our commence prevented or discouraged freighters from taking American Charters. There is no-questioning the fact that, cateres paribus, American Carriers are the favorites on the China Coast; and we may well hope to regain one former ascendancy, after the present domestic troubles are concluded, as fast as our ship–builders and owners can come forward to occupy the field.

[Condition of General trade in Macao.]

It is the prevailing impression in this community that the Taiping Rebellion is doomed to recede into the Southwest – the ancient house and never failing retreat of nearly all Chinese insurgency and that before another summer the export trade of China will experience a great revival, whether Macao will share very largely in this expected revival is highly–problematical; yet with the present encouraging policy of its authorities, and the marked energy and ambition of our new Governor, the general trade of China will scarcely advance without an accompanying tide of prosperity for this ancient Port. [end]

His Excellency, Governor Amaral is now as at Tientsin to exchange ratifications of the recent Treaty, negotiated by the late Governor

[Brief in the dispersion of the Taiping Rebellion   Exchange of ratifications of Portuguese Treaty]

which secures for this Colony a formal recognition at Peking of the Independence which it has long assumed and for a few years back virtually enjoyed.

In conclusion I beg to hand you my Abstract of Passports for the Quarter （Enclosure No1）, also my Abstract of Fees--（Enclosure No2）,

[Nos 1. & 2. Returns]

And Remain, Very Truly,
Your Obedient Servant
W. P. Jones
U. S. Consul at Macao.

[Macao, June, 30, 1864
No. 7.
W. P. Jones. Consul.
2 Enclosures
Received

Condition of Trade
&c Quarterly Reports]

[2–008]

[Rec[d] Sept 19

Mr. Shunk

No.8]

U. S. Consulate, Macao,
July 9, 1864

Sir,

I hasted to inform you by the mail which leaves this today, that H. E. esq. Gov. Amaral, who as my No. 7, stated, was then at Tientsin to exchange the ratifications of a Treaty negotiated in August of 1862, wherein the long assumed independence of Macao (from Chinese jurisdiction) was virtually conceded, has arrived, this P. M., announcing that this Treaty has been, most unfortunately rejected, by the authorities at Peking.

The principal ground of refusal was definitely stated, as being the article involving the most coveted concession above noted. This long disputed question was fondly believed to be forever

[set]

[Rejection of the Portuguese and Chinese Treaty of 1862 & Denial of the Portuguese sovereignty of Macao]

[To the Honorably
Wm H. Seward
Secretary of State for the United States,
Washington, D. C.]

at rest, when at the very moment the Portuguese envoy extended his hand, as it were, to receive the fully expected seal and signature of its perfect conformation, the Commissioners are reported to have said–in substances–; "The Treaty is all very satisfactory and fully ratified Except Article–. This we must insist upon your changing, as by providing that the Emperor shall have the sight to send a consul to Macao, who shall be received upon the same terms and be enacted to like privileges with the Consuls of European nations, Our Sovereign is made to concede the Sovereignty of Macao to the Portuguese, whereas he has never ceased to regard it as a position of his imperial domain."

However frequently it may have been assented that "the Portuguese are entitled to the dominion of Macao through an imperial Edict", issued about three centuries since, "in return for certain services rendered by them against the pirates of this coast, surely no copy of such an Edict can now be produced–and it is well known that until even after 1840 this Colony had continued, from the first records, to pay a ground rent of 500 Taëls per annum. to the Chinese Government–also that until about 1848, when they were forcibly expelled by the Gov. Amaral of that day, the Chinese Mandarins of the neighboring district of Hiangshan claimed and rigidly exercised jurisdiction over the Chinese inhabitants of this city–only the Portuguese themselves being exempt from their government. The annunciation of the present Commissioners evinces no disposition to yield to the presumption upon which the Portuguese have lately exercised absolute and undivided control within their asserted limits.

What will be the consequences of this rejection of the Treaty upon which so many hopes and plans have been based it is impossible now to say. The Chinese population of the Colony has lately increased with great rapidity owing to the protection here found against mandarin oppression and with this increase the revenue of the Colony has naturally advanced. Will not the better class of immigrants now turn to Hongkong, where thus mandarins can never claim jurisdiction? If so, this will certainly diminish one of the present sources of encouragement for the growth of Macao. Only observation can prove results but of this I am already certain, that the Portuguese will yield no jot of their pretensions or control until compelled to do so––and there is no probability of that being attempted for some years to come, in the meantime we may hope that new negotiations will be more successful.

I have the honor to be
your Obedient Servant
W. P. Jones
Consul at Macao

[Failure of Portu. Treaty Neg.]

[2-009]

[N°. 9.

Recd. Mch. 10]

U. S. Consulate, Macao
Sept 30, 1864.

Sir:

Enclosed please receive the Accounts of this Consulate with the United States Government for Miscellaneous Expenses during the 3d Quarter of the current year amt. to – $30 13/100 –vide Enclosure No.7.

Enclosure Nos. 2 to 6, enclosure, are the several duly required vouchers.

Please note that I have had all the official letters received at this Consulate since its establishment （and which have hitherto lain in almost promiscuous disorder） properly bound, with–indexes for easy future reference. In a climate like this, which by its great humidity, during at least four months of each

[agt No 1 Miscel expense Ap Nos 2–6 Vouchers Importance of finding Official Letter &c]

[The honorable William H. Seward,
Secretary of State for the United States.
Washington D. C.]

year, requires that books and papers be exposed to frequent airings to deferred or preserve them from mould and destructive insects, – it is more than usually important that all important papers be so secured as to prevent their being lost or displaced in the handling. The lash has been a tedious one, but if the result meets your approval, as I hope, I shall be quite satisfied.

I have, only within a few weeks, procured the address of our Despatch Agent, at London, to whom I shall hereafter address most of Washington covers for economy in postage.

I am, Sir, Very Respectfully
Your Obedient Servant
W. P. Jones
U. S. consul at Macao

[2-010]

[Rec.[d] Mch. 10.
N°10.]

U. S. Consulate Macao
September 30, 1864.

Sir,

I bet to hand you herewith the account of this Consulate with the United States for so much of my Office Rent as is allowed by law for the Quarter ending as above. (vide Enclosure No.1.) –amity to 37^{50}

Enclosures Nos 2 & 3 are the legally required vouchers therewith.

[a/c for Office Rent vouchers]

I am, Sir,
Your Obedient Servant
W. P. Jones.
U. S. Consul at Macao

[The Honorable
William H. Seward
Secretary of State for the United States
Washington, D. C.]

[U. S. Consulate
Macao, Sept. 30, 1864
W. P. Jones, Consul.
No.18.
3 Enclosures
a/c for Office Rent]

[2-011]

[Rec[d] Dec. 20
N°11.]

U. S. Consulate,
Macao, Sept. 30, 1864.

Sir,

I have the honor to hand you herewith my Return of Arrivals and Departures of American vessels at this Port during the 2[d] and 3[d] Quarters of the Current year–– (Enclusure No[1]) , and my Returns of Fee is not contained in No.1––as per Form No. 2 & 5–– (Enclosures Nos. 2 and 3.) –

You will observe that the stagnation of our Commerce in these waters still continues--as evinced doubtless by the Returns from Hongkong and Ports south of this as well as by my own disheartening Report.

With unshaken faith in the Right and our Country's Future.

I remain, Sir,
Your Obedient Servant
W. P. Jones.
U. S. Consul
at Macao

[The Hon.
Wm H. Seward
Secretary of State for the U. S.
&c. &c. &c.]

Copy of

Reports to Treasury Department on Excharge, Discounts, Commissions, Port Charges &c. at Macao

Exchange	Of all kinds is regulated by the price of kinds in London, at Hongkong, where all our oilis are sold. The Consul General of the Netherland informs me that bills on Amsterdam & Hamburg are taken even there, only as an accommodation. At the present writing bills on London are selling at $4^{\$}$ 10^{c}, six mis .s□□□t.
□□□□test	Exports & Imports are generally bought for Cash.
□□□□□ts	The usual rate of interest in China is 1 percent per month.
□□□ties	Are not known either in law or regular trade Brokerage 1% but this charge seldom appears in a/c.
Port duty	None.
Habor Dues	Outer Roads $ 8^{50} } We have no docks.
Habor Dues	Inner Harbor $$20^{50}$
□□□□ago	A boat carring from 500~800 piculs $2 & 3, p^{er} □□□.
□□□□ago	Carrying rice to Inner Harbor ^{06} per ten piculs. Carrying rice to Outer Harbor ^{01} per picul 133 lbs.
□□□	Coolie hire 25 cts. per day.
□□□age	Medium packages medium distance ^{01} per picul
□□□ing	Ten $$1.^{40}$ per 50 lbs, for Box, Mats, lead, Lining Packing and marking. Cassia ^{80} per 1/2 picul box. Anise seed $1.^{00}$ per picul Golangal root ^{30} per picul bag Essental Oibs $$6^{50}$ per picul of boxes containing 8 canisters.

Weighing	\$1^{00} per day in the Inner harbor \$2.^{00} p^{r} day in the road \$2^{00} per large boat & \$1 for Small boat, larger boats than 40 Tons can seldom reach the wharf.
□□□ imports	There are none levied on trade directly. Every resident pays 10 per cent on his rent to the Government.
□□□	All the expenses and risks of this are incurred by the Chinese Sellers.
transportation	Almost all articles in this market are brought in junks from the creeks, rivers and bayous of the "East Coast" or the immediate provinces and are doubtless subject to transit duties--but it is impossible to ascertain what these amount to, as they very in every locality--and are everywhere irregular, owing to the dishonesty of the mandarins.
	Storage is exceedingly cheap in Macao, being at the rate of 300 piculs of rice per dollar--and other goods, in proportion to bulk--in substantial stone ware rooms. At Hong Kong the rate is 50 to 100 piculs per dollar.
Water Side	The Expenses attending the shipment of Mchzde, are usually paid by the Sellers of goods.

[Copy of Report to Treas.
Dept. on Exchange,
Commission, Port. Charges a/c.

No.10

Macao, Sept, 30, 1864

[2-012]

[Recd. Jan. 30.
No.12.

Statistical]

U. S. Consulate Macao,
Sept. 20, 1864.

Sir,

I have the honor to submit my Annual Report for the year closing as above; simply premising that it has involved even much greater labor than my previous acquaintance with the incomplete & obscure public statistics of this Colony gave me reason to expect. As a consequence this communication goes to mail some thirty days after date.

So far as the Records of this Consulate show no such report as is called for by section 153 of the Consular Instruction has been hitherto compiled at this office. It may be fitting therefore for me in the inauguration of what the government has a right to expect will be a regular series of annual reports from this time forward, to expend a few sentences upon the History and Geography of this ancient Colony–; both of which illustrate themselves somewhat in its Commercial Statistics.

History

As early as 1516 the Portuguese under the command of Admiral Perestrella made their appear

[The Honorable

Wm H. Seward.

Secretary of State for the United States.]

[2]

once at Canton, bearing the first European flag that had ever floated in these waters. The adventure proving successful, it was followed, the succeeding year, by the gallant Perez de Andrade in command of eight vessels, with two of which he was permitted to pass up the river to Canton, where he concluded favorable negotiations for a regular trade. Subsequently a part of this fleet returned to Malacca, well laden, while the remainder, passing up the coast to the province of Fokien, established a colony at Ningpo. This, in 1545, they were compelled to abandon; an event which afterwards concluded all their own attempts and those of other nations to gain any foothold upon Chinese territory, except that required upon this beautiful, little promontory of Macao; for centuries the golden gate of China.

This recupation began in 1537. By subsidizing the local mandarins the Portuguese, about this time, obtained permission to erect sheds, for drying goods injured in their voyage hither. By repeated bribes, they maintained this privilege, and began to build substantial dwellings and ware-houses. A few years later and by the influx of traders and priests they had planted here an extensive central missionary establishment for all China and Japan, and organized and internal government.

From this time until 1848, (say three Centuries) , the Portuguese paid the Chinese Govt. an annual ground rent of 500 Taels (say $694-) and for this consideration, and occasional services rendered against the pirates, infesting this Coast, were left comparatively undisturbed in their recupation and self-government--: although the Emperor still claimed original jurisdiction over the territory and exercised it upon all the Chinese residents; who were governed and taxed by the mandarins of the adjoining district City of Caza Branca, on the main island. On the last year above named, the spirited Governor Amaral--disgusted and enraged by the insufferable extortion exercised not only upon the Chinese at Macao, but through them upon the Macaenses (for whom they were not suffered by the mandarins to do any sort of work or facilitate trade without "Chops" , or licenses, bought at extravagant and continually increasing rates) , and moreover ambitious for the glory and independence, (subject only to his King) , of this ancient and renowned Colony--refused to pay any longer the above stated ground rent, and ejected the mandarins from all control over the Chinese within its limits. For this and other energetic conduct whereby he excited the hatred of the Mandarins and certain other Chinese, this daring governor was assassinated--; but his assumptions were never forcibly resisted by the Chinese Government and still prevail. The leading Commercial nations have apparently acknowledged this revolution as fait accompli; appointing Consular Officers thereto, as upon this admission--; although even with in the current year the Authorities at Peking have refused to ratify a Treaty with Portugal which rather covertly sought to extort a similar acknowledgment from the Emperor.

[Begin]

Geography.

Macao is a short, irregular, narrow peninsula of the great island of Heang Shan--constituting almost the entire South--Western Shore of the gulf of Lintin, （the estuary of the Canton or Pearl River）. A flat, sandy isthmus, more than a mile long though scarcely 40 paces broad, connects it with the main island. Across the middle of this isthmus lie the ruins of an ancient barrier--wall marking the Portuguese limits. The City is situated in N. Latitude 22^{0}12'--Lon, 113^{0}31' E. from Greenwich, and is thus almost due South from Canton, distant about ninety miles, and due west from Hong Kong come forty miles. Immediately West of it the great West River （Si Kiang） enters the sea, freighted with immense traffic, which should find here its

[Table No.1.]

Trade in Foreign Vessels.

Tabular Statement showing the Imports into the port of Macao, distinguishing the countries whence imported, quantities and value for the first & second quarter of 1864.

Names of Articles	From China	From Straits	From Manila	From Hongkong		Total Value
Artillery		No. 300				8674
□□□Drill				Bales[1] 35°		2500
□□□		*Piculs 616				1318
Black wood			Piculs 307			310
Broken glass			Piculs 61			400
Chinese medicines		Pekgs 57	30			381
Beans			No 13516			78
Cinnamon	Box 370					2682
Cinnamon Oil	Box 3					321
Cinnamon Flowers	Box 80					4870
Coffee			Piculs 80			1280
Chinaware	Box 4					60
Cotton	Piculs 1912	64	326			184880
Cochineal		Vol 2	6			800
Coal				Tons 140		1400
Cardamomum		Vol 40				2640
Copper		Boxes 20				480
Camphor Trunk				No 51		277
Dried Shrimps		Piculs 297				2403
Dried Fruits		Piculs 38 $\frac{1}{2}$				5299
Different Sundries	Pak^{gs} 2130	214	17	716		

① 表格中單位首字母，有時爲大寫字母，有時爲小寫字母，現均采用大寫字母。

Elephant tooth		No 2 $\frac{1}{2}$				300
Fish wings （or fins）		Piculs 375	58			10613
Furniture				No 42		200
Gunpowder		Ibls 502				2008
Guns			Piculs 18			252
Indigo	Piculs 25					100
Lamp Oil	Piculs 168					1512
Leather		Piculs 228	691	40		3827
Lead			Piculs 1590	370		16550
Lacquered				Jars 34		428
Money	Dollars 57892			315977		573869
Nutmegs		Piculs 11				231
Opium				Chest 4165		1911630
Paddy-vice in Hugh			Piculs 8291			15731
Paper	Pak^{gs} 27					63
Pearl Shells			Piculs 40			157
Pepper		Piculs 1050				6500
Quicksilver		Tin 813		79		5530
Rattan		Piculs 813	756			6161
Rice		Piculs 148854	37542			485746
Saltpetre		Piculs 155				860
Soap			Piculs 20			614
Seaworm		Piculs 157	216			7140
Silk	Pak^{gs} 281			26		91277
Seaweed	Piculs 9	350				1261
Sugar	Piculs 30	2320	871			14176
Sapanwood		Piculs 5357	3894			8577
Sulphur			Piculs 9			180
Shark skin		Piculs 254				816
Salt Fish		Piculs 1254				8175
Tin		Box 1261				1250
Tobacco	Piculs 100					525
Tree skin		Piculs 1000				1140
Tea	Box 300	900		184		9674
Tallow	Piculs 50					425
Wine				Ibls 36		1080
Wax		Piculs 157				5655
						$3336296

*1 Picul is 133 and $\frac{1}{3}$ lbs

[Table No.2.]

Trade in Foreign Vessels,

Tabular Statement Showing the Exports from Macao, during the 1st & 2nd Quarter of the 1864, designating the Countries to which exports were made, and the articles, quantities & value.

Names of Articles	To Hongkong	To Straits	To Manila	To Hamburg	To France	To England	To Australia	To China	To Japan	Total Value
□□□Stars	Box① 257									7448
□□□Oil	Box 1028	3	114			54				82266
□□□ Flower	Box 209	6	38	960	70	180		597		28979
□□□		tubs 10								70
□□□			*Piculs 20							100
□□□								Piculs 58		114
□□□						Canes 15000				600
China wood	Piculs 120	100						115		1650
□□□		Boxes 4782	1519							11329
□□□		Boxes 21						35		2710
□□□	Pak[gs] 6							2		800
Camphor trunk	No 250	52	342							6911
Copper rattles			Boxes 14							120
Copper			Piculs 12							1070
Cotton	Bales 250									9100
□□□	Piculs 50					145		60		3935
Chalk								Piculs 28		560
Cinnamon	Boxes 9717	911	310	2075	2200	3400				143413
Cinnamon Oil	Boxes 115				14					11577
Cinnamon Flower	Boxes 70									4060
□□□Sundries	Bales 477	1660	177			24		93	315	
Dried Fruits	Piculs 61	619								1897
Dried garlicks		1583								7961
Empty bags		N° 50	1042							5935
□□□cases		N° 1800								900
□□□								Vol. 1050		1050
□□□ Crackers	Boxes 314	1580						161		16908
□□□		Boxes 8								59500
□□□ pressured		230	200							1328
□□□		Piculs 217						98		1910
□□□			Piculs 6							650
Indigo	Piculs 603	8						3980		78920
□□□cry		Boxes 3								1000
□□□ sticks		Boxes 1104	96							6446

① 表格中單位首字母，有時爲大寫字母，有時爲小寫字母，現均采用大寫字母。

Leather		Piculs 4	23						1	631
Lacquered			Jars 3					600		4600
Lamp oil	Piculs 143	147						340		7072
□□□	Piculs 61	614	5							1897
□□□	Boxes 21	551	13					38	77	79453
□□□	Pieces 4	446	529							2838
□□□		Rolls 100								500
□□□	Dollars 793275	10100	4798					44500		852673
□□□	Check 99							18		39870
Pepper	Piculs 195									1365
Potatoes		Piculs 1577	5604					34		2671
Pickles		Jars 2907	19							2922
Paper		Vol 2759	85							22480
Quicksilver	Tins 99									7128
□□□ chairs			Nº 369							552
Sugar	Piculs 200							1700		27500
□□□								Piculs 85		340
□□□	Boxes 166									1162
□□□ turtle,								1		350
□□□	Boxes 526	97	188					25		294609
□□□	Piculs 1420	2573								75750
□□□	Boxes 2715	53121	304			13919	3130	4		332249
□□□		Nº 56000	9000							750
□□□		Boxes 1248	3					105		22082
□□□	Boxes 332	2				260				26036
□□□ celli		Bales 61	8							796
□□□		Piculs 24	773							1594
□□□	lbls 25									750
□□□			Piculs 73							240
□□□ Lead		Piculs 5								130
										$2,312,097

* 1 Picul is 133 and $\frac{1}{3}$ lbs.

Average Market Prices at Macao, during 1864.

Imports

Opium New Patna	$502	New Benares	$440
Malwa	$626	Turkey	$524
Cotton Shanghae	$27^{50}	Ningpo	$28
Rice Bengal New Cargo	$3	Old Dº	2^{82}
Java and Saigon	$2^{95}	Old Dº	$2^{97}
Sloco	$2^{95}	Old Dº	$2^{78}
Siam	$2^{85}	Old Dº	$2^{90}

Bassien Rangoon & Arrocaw	$\$2^{80}$	Old D°	$\$2^{65}$
Pepper white	$12	Black D°	$\$7^{25}$ per picul
Octelnut new	$\$3^{40}$	Old D°	$5 per picul
Rattan Benjemissing	$\$3^{50}$	Straits	$\$3^{10}$ per picul
Lapanwood Siam	$\$2^{95}$	Manilla	$\$1^{75}$ per picul
Sulphur	$2	Saltpetre	$11 per picul
Gunpowder Superfine @ 20 cents per lb.			
Gunpowder Coarse @ 3.50 per 20 lb. keg			
Tin pauca & □□□	$28	D° Straits	$27 per picul
Tin Lead	$6	Quicksilver	$68 per picul
Alum	$\$2^{60}$		per picul
Tea	$\$32^{70}$ to 37^{5}		per picul
Flour Callifornia	$\$8^{80}$ p^{r} Barrel		
Beef	$16 to 20 p^{r} Bbl		
Pork	$25 to 30 p^{r} Bbl		
Yellow Peas	$\$2^{30}$ p^{r} picul		
Black Dates	$\$5^{75}$ p^{r} picul		
Silk	$420 p^{r} picul		
N° 16 @ 24 Cotton yarn 2.5			
N° 56 white shirts	$\$4.^{50}$		
Turkey red	$3		
Plane Crape	$\$6^{20}$		
Asst^{d} D°	$\$14^{50}$		
U. S. Asst^{d} Carnlets	$\$22^{50}$		
D°. lasting	$\$19^{50}$		
H. H. Long Ells	$\$8^{50}$ p^{r}. bolt Black veloet of 22 in 30^{c} □□		

Export

Sugar White N°1.	$\$8^{50}$ per picul
Sugar White N°2.	$\$7^{25}$ per picul
Cassia	$\$16^{25}$ per picul
Cassia Oil	$206 per picul
Star Anisseed	$ 19 per picul
Star Anisseed Oil	$ 150 per picul
Gallangel	$\$1^{85}$ per picul
Vermillion	$ 35 per 50 ctts box
Capper Cash	$ 17 per picul
Gold Leaf	$\$22^{70}$ per tael weight

[Table No. 11
Average Market Prices
for 1864.

No.11.

Macao, Sept 30,1864.]

Map of Ships dispatched in the Port of Macao, during the year 1863, with Chinese Emigrants contracted in comformity with regulations in power.

Date		Ships	Tons	Agents of Emigration Consignees	Destination	Passangers
Jany.	3	Peruvian Clipper "Westward Ho"	1120	P. F. de Castro & C°	Callas Lima	665
Jany.	12	Chilean Schooner "Theresa"	240	Joaz Bolls	Idem	130
Jany.	23	Portuguese Bark "Eliza"	219	Manuel A. da Ponte	Idem	130
Jany.	24	French Bark "Malabar"	512	Vossen & Siches	Havana	256
Feby.	4	French Brig Persévérant	242	Idem	Idem	121
March	17	Chilean Clipper Mercedez	746	Idem	Idem	373
April	5	Peruvian Clipper Cezar	499	Fran^co^ Mr da Cunha	Callas Lina	317
August	1	Peruvian Brig Maria	219	Ramos	Idem	132
Oct^r^	18	Peruvian Clipper "Westward Ho"	1120	P. F. de Casks and C^a^	Idem	700
Oct^r^	30	Portuguese Clipper Luicita	685	Vossen & Siches	Havana	342
Oct^r^	30	Portuguese Clipper D. Mª da Gloria	592	Idem	Idem	296
Nov.	2	Portuguese Clipper Camoes	836	Idem	Idem	418
Nov.	15	Portuguese Clipper Vasco da Gama	1016	Idem	Idem	508
Nov.	30	Portuguese Clipper D. Maria Tia	774	Federics Lauallette	Callás de Lima	424
Dez.	9	Peruvian Clipper Camilo Cavour	1326	L. A. Leushold	Idem	700
Dez.	11	Portuguese Clipper □□□ Ditlbay □□□	621	Vossen & Sickes	Havana	310
Dez.	20	Spanish bark Aresona	597	P. F. de Castro and C°	Idem	298
Dez.	21	Peruvian brig Theresa	240	Poas Rolls	Callás de Lima	140
		Peruvian Clipper Perseverancia	648	L. A. Leushold	Idem	400

Total Contracted Passengers······6660

Macao, Superintendency, of Chinese emigration, Jany, 18, 1864.

(Signed) A. Marques Pereisa.

Superintendent.

[The Coolie Trade of Macao,

No.4.

Macao, Sept. 30, 1864]

□□□□□□□□□

Trade at the port of Macao, in the 1st and 2nd Quarters, 1864.

Nationality	Entered						Cleared					
	Direct trade		Indirect trade		Total		Direct trade		Indirect trade		Total	
	Vessel	Tons	Vessel	Tons	Vessel	Tons	Vessel	Tons	Vessel	Tons	Vessel	Tons
Austrian			/	763	/	763			/	763	/	763
Bremen			/	314	/	314			/	314	/	314
Belgian			/	832	/	832						
Chilean			/	301	/	301			/	301		301
Dutch			7	1616	7	1616	4	1035	3	932	7	1967
Danish			7	1781	7	1781			6	1316	6	1316
English	6	3086	11	4602	17	7688	9	4147	3	677	12	4824
French	4	1490	5	1829	9	3319	3	1077	4	1292	7	3369
Hamburg			16	3822	16	3822	1	300	12	3067	13	3367
Oldenburg			2	662	2	662			2	662	2	662
Peruvian			6	3617	6	3617	2	622	7	3449	9	4071
Portuguese			6	1608	6	1608			3	2181	3	2181
Prussian			2	580	2	580			1	200	1	200
Siamese			1	250	1	250	1	297			/	297
Sweden			2	474	2	474			/	206	/	206
Spanish	12	3349	12	3050	24	1399	10	2726	7	1638	17	4364
Total	22	7925	81	26,101	103	34,026	30	10,204	52	16,998	82	27,202

[Table No. 8.
Direct or Indirect
Trade of Macau

No.8.

Macao. Sept, 30, 1864.]

□□□□□□□□□□□□□□□□□□□□□

during the 1st and 2nd Quarters, 1864, together with tonnage and crews

Nationality	Entered									Value
	With Cargo			In ballast			Total			
	Vessels	Tons	Crews	Vessels	Tons	Crews	Vessels	Tons	Crews	
Austrian				1	763	19	1	763	19	
Bremen	1	314	14				1	314	14	18,421
Belgian				1	532	21	1	832	21	
Chilean				1	301	11	1	301	11	

Dutch	3	729	74	4	887	69	7	1616	143	30,109
Danish	5	1327	57	2	454	18	7	1781	75	55,916
English	13	5217	205	4	2471	137	17	7688	342	2,515,359
French	6	2237	93	3	1082	25	9	3319	118	96,473
Hamburg	11	2626	124	5	1196	64	16	3822	188	207,708
Oldenburg	1	322	12	1	340	14	2	662	26	22,000
Peruvian	1	1215	24	5	2402	78	6	3617	102	95,000
Portuguese	4	912	88	2	696	17	6	1608	105	65,886
Prussian	1	380	11	1	200	10	2	580	21	10,700
Siamese	1	250	20				1	250	20	111,242
Sweden	1	268	11	1	206	11	2	474	22	20,102
Spanish	20	4988	371	4	1411	73	24	6399	444	87,380
					In China Junks			379,358		
Total Entered	68	20785	1104	35	13,241	567	103	34,026	1671	3,715,654

[Vessels of All Nations

"Entered"

No.6.

Macao Sept. 30, 1864]

[Table No. 3]

The Junk Trade of Macao for the 1st & 2nd Quarters of 1864.

Names of Articles	Imports Quantity		Value	Exports Quantity		Value
Apples	Piculs*	47	$126			
□□□Drill	Piculs			Bolts	6586	30513
□□□ misseed	Piculs	212	2291			
□□□ misseed Stars	Piculs	4130	26034			
□□□ misseed Oil	Piculs	10	1341			
□□□ misseed Flowers	Piculs	15	1157			
Bamboo	Canes	583200	4142			
Bamboo sraping	Bales	17	48			
Bags empty	No.	145,000	6230			
Beans	Piculs	1905	2891			
Bulls horn	Piculs	994	780			
Cloth				Bales	39	2365
Cotton				Bales	656	20860
Cinnamon	Piculs	1907	19602			

Cinnamon Oil	Piculs	17	6943			
Camlet				Pcs	244	1609
Cattle fish	Piculs	165	3046			
Cocas	N°	189900	1989			
Cardamomum	Piculs	52	512			
China wood	Piculs	125	25			
Copper	Piculs	6	156			
Different Sundries	Pekgs	25335	16,063	Pakgs	130	4342
Dried fish	Piculs	347	5953			
Fish entrail	Piculs	6	42			
Flour	Piculs	1802	4170			
Glue	Piculs	74	640			
Hogs	N°	1077	10317			
Indigo	Piculs	3625	14923			
Lacqured	Jars	34	428			
Leather	Piculs	366	3934			
Lard	Piculs	6	60			
Lamp-oil	Piculs	12965	122772			
Matting	Pcs	329360	5379			
Nan kin				Pcs	5205	14086
Opium				Chest	822	112034
Paddy	Piculs	700	1844			
Paper	Bales	1993	8602	Bales	246	629
Rice	Piculs	7404	21818	Piculs	5745	13219
Rattan	Piculs	91	426			
Rattan split	Bales	3	34			
Red wood	Piculs	385	464			
Sesame	Piculs	96	380			
Sugar	Piculs	3334	23819			
Salt	Piculs	18484	12598			
Serge silk				Pieces	1580	4542
Soap	Piculs	22	71			
Salt Eggs	No.	4000	22			
Tea	Bales	928	4333			
Tallow	Piculs	257	3148			
Tree shin	Piculs	335	1967			
Tin	Piculs	79	2210			

Tobacco	Piculs 36	182	Piculs 400	3260
Tobacco leaf	Piculs 778	4577		
Velvet			Boxes 48	525
Wood	Pieces 205	570		
Total		$379358		$207982

* a picul is 133 $\frac{1}{3}$ lbs.

most natural communication with foreign commerce. Under present restrictions but a small portion of it comes hitha and that for the most part illicitly. This grand island of Heangshan, lying between the wealth laden Canton and West Rivers, and upon the sea, should certainly, under good government, become the Manhattan of Southern China.

Climate

Situated barely within the northern tropic, a picturesque premonitory projecting boldly into the seen and fawned by the south west and Northwest Monsoons, Macao enjoys a salubrious and generally delightful climate, that renders it the Sanitarium of China. The capability of the temperature is remarkable; the mercury never, so far I have experienced, rising to above Fahrenheit 100°, in the shade, or falling below 36°. The mean maximum （in a series of years） for July, the warmest month, was 87°; the minimum, for January, the coldest month, 46°.

Geology

Geologically Macao, like all the Southern Coast of China, belongs to the primitive formation; presenting seven unwooded, barren–faced hills, composed of a coarse, disintegrated feldspathic granite, cut vertically by numerous parallel quartz reins of form one to fifteen inches thickness, crossing the entire penninsula in right lines from N. E. to S. W. This rotten granite is easily dug with pickaxe and spade and gullied by the rains, which latter carrying down the decaying feldspar into what was once no doubt a tidewater–bay have, with the joint action of the West River depositing here its rich allusion, created a low basin, of perhaps 600 acres area, of exceedingly fertile land; which until very lately has been for centuries the one spot for European garden produce in all China.

[6.]

Population

The entire population of the Macao peninsula, by calculation based on a late census, is estimated at 105,800––classed as: Europeans 800; Creoles and Meztizes 5000; Chinese 100,000.

Agriculture

With such a Climate and such a system of Manoring as produce four crops per year it is still wonderful what an amount these frugal and industrious natives gather from the small area of arable land within this petty territory. It is extremely difficult, if not impossible, to obtain any reliable statistics from Chinese, as they are always suspecting ulterior designs where the least inquisitiveness is manifested. Had it been otherwise I might have furnished an exhibit of the products of a Chinese garden for one year that would be at least instructive. Their art of fertilizing will be made the subject of a future paper; at present I can only remark that any one who has observed the ingenuity, industry and frugality of this people ceases to wonder how China continues to sustain her teeming hundreds of millions.

Of course Macao is too insignificant in extent to render its agricultural products of any Commercial importance. Like Hongkong this is a consuming not a producing colony; a mere coast station for distribution units and collection of exports from China proper.

As such its market abounds with all the fruits and staples of this fertile tropical clime, from the neighboring shores and inland, while its own gardens, supply it bountifully with European vegetables, and contribute of the same to the markets of Hongkong and the open Ports North.

Manufactures

The industrial energies of Macao are employed principally as follows, viz: In drying, sorting, firing and boxing Tea, （a large business）; preparing Anise seed and Cassia and their Oils for exportation, （bottling, and casing it）; in Gold beating and Sugar–refining; in making Chinese Cigarettes for the Coast and Straits trade, （a large business）; making vermilion;

[□□□□□□□]

[9]

making umbrellas, Fire Crackers, Incense Sticks, Camphor wood trunks, decks and bureaus, and bamboo & rattan–work. It is impossible to ascertain the amount of Capital invested in these employments, but it is safe to say they engage fully 1/5 of the Chinese population, or about 20,000 persons.

Commerce

In the early part of the seventeenth Century, immediately preceding the exclusion of foreigners from Japan, the Commercial prosperity of Macao excited the wonder and envy of all Europe. Many of the mansions of the merchant–princes of those days, almost palatial in their extent, still remain to attest the opulence of their first masters and maintain some air at least of the City's ancient importance and glory. Even after their expulsion from Japan the Portuguese at Macao continued to amass astonishing wealth out of the China, East India and European trade. But with a shortsightedness characteristic of the age quite as much as of their race, they suffered a contemptible jealousy to set them against other nations seeking trade in China; and the mutual misrepresentations and exhibitions of hate and avarice among the contending aspirants for special privileges, together with the machinations of the papal missionaries, is disgusted and alarmed the Tartar Emperors that China grew almost as exclusive at Japans. The effect on Macao was serious; nevertheless, as being still the only place in China where foreign traders; were permitted to reside, the trade, although much restricted, was still sufficient to excite the envy of other powers, whose trade dealings were confined to their ships decks; until the rapid increase of the trade of these powers during the past half century, with the opening of the northern parts and the establishment of the overshadowing English Colony of Hongkong, even within sight, have so thoroughly sapped the prosperity of Macao as to render it, by comparison, one of the least important China ports; although even yet by no means insignificant.

[□□□]

It cannot be denied that the impolicy of the Macao Authorities, in persistently demanding heavy import and Export levies long after they had good reason to know that these very duties were impelling the English and other traders to run the risks of smuggling rather then submit, had much to do with hastening and aggravating their misfortune. On the other hand the existing abolition of all imports, the extreme liberality of the present authorities, together with low rents and exemption from taxes, the much greater security to life and property here than in the other China Ports– (under the superior police force and regulations

[10]

of this Colony) are now promising to effect a favorable reaction in its favor.

Since the closing of the Custom House little or no effort has been made to collect the statistic of trade, until since the accession of the present Governor––:a sufficient reason, I hope, for the failure of my Commercial Report last year. Since the first of January last, all masters of vessels have been required to furnish the Captain of the Port manifests of inward & outward cargo, with estimated value. Of course while the Macao Government has no direct pecuniary interest in the correctness of these figures, and the jealousies of merchants induce them to conceal their transactions, from each other, the manifests can be regarded as mere approximations, much below the actual values.

From these data, to which the truth would, I am fully persuaded, add at least a third, we learn that the Imports during the first Six months of 1864 amounted to–:

In foreign––rigged vessels	$3,336.296
In Chinese Junks	$ 379,358
Total Imports for the Half Year	$3,715,654

or an average rate of Seven and a half Millions, per Annum; being three times the Imports of all China in 1815~16, and twice the same of 1825~6.–

The Exports for the same period amounted to–:

[11]

In foreign rigged vessels	$2,302,097
In Chinese Junks	$ 207,982
	$2,520,079[1]

or an average rate of above Two Millions per Annum–: being more than the Exports of all China in 1830, or any year previous that I find tabulated, except for 1815, which were about the same.

So that were the profits of this trade what they once were, Macao might still be opulent.

The following tables Nos, 1, 2 & 3, compiled with much tedious labor from the crude data in the Captain of the Ports, office, exhibit not only the above aggregates but the quantity and value of each important import and export.

Tables 1. 2 & 3.

Thus it appears that the principal imports (see Table 1 & 2) are, in the order of Amount, Opium, Specie, Rice, Lamp Oil, Cotton, Silk, Sugar, Aniseseed, & oil, Rattan, Cinnamon, Fish, Indigo, Tea, Salt, Pork and Lead;

① Sic.

almost all of which are brought hither, for Exchange and re–exportation: the Anise, Cinnamon, Tea, Lamp–oil, Indigo, Sugar and Salt coming principally from the west Coast and inland, in native vessels.

[12]

The principal Exports, in order of value, are Opium （though not so appearing in the tables）, Specie, （much of it being copper "cash", cast here）, Tea, Silk, Cinnamon, Anice Seed and Oil, Chinese Medicine, Tobaccos, Indigo, Gold–leaf, Arm. Drills and Nankin, Cotton, （most of the imports are in store for future Shipment or Cotton would rank next after Anise）, Sugar, Vermilion, Paper, Umbrellas, Fire Crackers, Rice, Chinaware, Garlick, Quicksilver, Lamp–Oil, Camphor–wood Trunks &c. Incense Sticks（joss–sticks）, and lacquered ware.

[□□□□]

Comparisons of the Opium （$172,000）& Exported （into the interior）, and Opium Imported （1,911,000）, also of the Anise （31,000）, Cinnamon （33,000）, Silk （95,000）, Tea （16,000）, Indigo （15,000）––imported from the interior, and the Anise （118,500）, Cinnamon （160,000）, Silk （299,000）, Tea （332,000）, and Indigo （79,000）, Exported––illustrate how extensively the Chinese customs are evaded; the Opium being smuggled into and the other articles smuggled, out of the Country to avoid the duties and exactions of the mandarins. Of Course after evading their own Cunning Officers––they are not disposed to voluntarily report their smuggling here at the more request of the Captain of the Port––: Hence & inconsistencies of the above tables, to one who merely considers that this is not a producing colony and therefore cannot Export Tea, Silk &c, which it does not receive.

Table N° 4.

Presents the coolie traffic out of Macao during the year 1863. The barbarities of this traffic are reduced to very nearly a minimum is far as sanitary conditions for the passage––could be required and enforced at any port: and I may add that I believe that comparatively few instances of forcible abduction now occur. But in view of the utter ignorance of their cruel fate beyond the sea, which prevails among the natives, and the deceptive promises held out to them, as well as the drugging arts used with them until their consent is gained¯we have great season to rejoice that our flag is no longer shamed by the traffic.

Table No 5.

In my Navigation & Commercial Report for the four Quarters ending with date. The unhappy influence of rebel privateering is partially shown by an examination of the Quarter ending Dec. 31st and a comparison of the same with subsequent quarters.

Table Nos 6 & 7.

Show the Nationality, Tonnage and Crews of the several vessels entering or clearing from this Port during the First & Second Quarters of 1864. Please observe that no American vessels appear; as, save our triweekly steamer running to Canton, and the occasional visit of a Steamer from Hong Kong, and the calls of our Men–of–War, the flag has not entered our port–during the year; although last year we had seventeen American entries （ten hinging Cargo.）

Table No 8.

Shows the number of vessels and tonnage employed in Direct or Indirect trade.

[□□□□]

Table N° 9.

Presents the only comparison I am able to furnish of the trade for the five years ending Dec. 31, 1864. The increase of Entries for this year favors a statement of the secretary of Government assuring me that this year trade manifests a general improvement over that of the preceding three years.

Table No. 10.

In a Copy of my Report to the Treasury Department on Exchange, Discounts, Commissions, Port Charges &c.

Table No. 11.

States the average market Prices, during the year, of some of the principal, Exports & Imports.

[15]

[□□□]

The Harbor

The Inner Harbor of Macao is one of the safest havens on the China Coast, being perfectly land, locked, but unfortunately a sand bar renders its entrance impossible to vessels of heavy burthen. The Macao Roads are entirely safe and commodious but some four miles distant, which when a high sea is running proves a serious disadvantage H. Ex., the present Governor, promises to dredge the bar hindering entrance to the Inner Harbor–which it is hoped will be accomplished at an early day.

Employment of Amr. Capital.

There is no American Capital employed at Macao except in merchandizing–and this is done at present principally through agents of Firms at Hongkong, what direct Amr. Trade may have hitherto existed at Macao having been totally arrested by the accidents of war. The purchases of American Houses made at this Port during the year preceding this date probably reached the sum of $350,000––entirely for European trade, or if for shipment to the United States, to be delivered at Hongkong––whence they were invoiced. I have no doubt that would several enterprizing American firms, taking advantage of the present liberal policy of this Government, resolve to establish houses at Macao they might transact a very profitable business.

[and]

Hoping that my next report will exhibit an improvement of our own trade at this Port.

I have the honor to remain

Your Obedient Servant
W. P. Jones
U. S. Consul
at Macao.

[Macao Sept. 30. 1864.
W. P. Jones U. S. Consul
No.12,
11 enclosures
Commercial Report
for 1863–4]

[Macao, Sept. 30 1864
W. P. Jones, U. S. Consul
No.12.]

[□□ □□□□□□□□□□□□□□□□□□□□□□□□□]
during the 1st and 2nd Quarter, 1864, with the aggregate value of cargoes

Nationality.	Cleared.									Value.
	With Cargo			In ballast			Totals			
	Vessels	Tons	Crew	Vessels	Tons	Crew	Vessel	Tons	Crew	
Austrian	1	763	19				1	763	19	
Bremen				1	314	14	1	314	14	
Chilian	1	301	11				1	301	11	
Danish	3	539	30	3	777	33	6	1316	63	
Dutch	6	1617	106	1	350	15	7	1967	121	
English	8	3707	210	4	1117	46	12	4824	256	
French	5	1581	69	2	788	29	7	2369	98	
Hamburg	6	1935	83	7	1432	75	13	3367	158	
Oldenburg	2	662	26				2	1162	26	
Peruvian	9	4071	148				9	4071	148	
Portuguese	3	2181	73				3	2181	73	
Prussian	1	200	10				1	200	10	
Siamese	1	297	32				1	297	32	
Sweden	1	206	11				1	206	11	
Spanish	9	2400	174	8	1964	179	17	4364	353	
Total Cleared	56	20460	1002	26	6742	391	82	27202	1393	3,517,051

[Table No.7.
Vessels of all Nations
"Cleared"

No.7.

Macao. Sept. 30, 1864.]

[2-013]

[+ Mr. Jones.
Recd Mch, 10.
Ack Mch. 11.]

U. S. Consulate
Macao, 14. Decr 1864.

Sir:

I beg to recall the attention of the Honorable Secretary to the certificates & petitions contained in my No. 14, of 1863, copies of which are herewith enclosed (See No.1) and once more assure you that it is impossible with the utmost economy, for your consul to subsist upon the present salary of this consulate. My simple family expenses during the year ending Feb. 23. 1864. including rent at only \$400^{00} were \$2409.44. Fortunately we were not afficted with protracted sickness or subjected in any way to extraordinary expenses or my deficit would have been beyond my means. It is not evident therefore that, if the consular establishment at Macao is to be maintained, the salary should be increased to the minimum sum paid at the other China Ports–say \$3000?

[The consular salary at this Port]

That a consular representative ought to be here maintained seems to be granted: (first because of the use made of this Port by

[The Honarable
Wm H. Seward.
Secretary of State for the United States.]

Our men-of-war (a U. S. Store Ship being now stationed here and this being the rendezvous of our East India Squadron upon China Coast) ; second, because of the refuge Macao always has furnished and always will furnish our citizens during seasons of foreign difficulty with China proper and third for the ordinary commercial reasons existing when our commerce is unembarrassed.

Pardon me therefore if I once more over that none but a merchant can afford to officiate here on the present salary and that no merchant now here is willing to accept the position.

I remain
Your Obedient Servant
W. P. Jones.
U. S. Consul
Macao.

[U. S. Consulate Macao
Dec. 14, 1864.

W.P. Jones. U. S. Consul

No. 13.

1 Enclosure,

The Consular Salary
at this Port.]

Copies of Original Papers
sent to the Secretary of State in Despatch N° 14 of 1863.

Consulate of U. S. of America,
at Hong Kong, Oct. 24, 1863.

Sir,

I have the honor to state that I am acquainted to the fullest extent with the cost of living in China, and that I am fully assured, from such knowledge that it is impossible for the Consul at Macao to live, with his family, on the present salary of $1500 per Annum, and I am confident that $3000, would give him no more than a bare support.

With the highest respect,
I remain your Ob[t] Servt,
(Signed) H. N. Congar
U. S. Consul.

[Hon[l] W. H. Seward.
Secretary of State
Washington]

Macao, Oct. 30, 1863.

I beg leave to fully confirm what Mr. Congar says within, and may refer to my first dispatch to the department of State (of Sept–Oct. 1858) in confirmation; and for the Paramount, reasons for the retention of a respectable man as Consul here. Moreover, my opinion after about 30 years experience in China, will be concurred in by all well informed persons.

(Signed), G. Nye J[r].
Late Acting Consul at
Macao, from 1859 @1863.

Canton, November, 12, 1863.

To Abraham Lincoln,
President of the United States of America,
Washington D. C.

Sir:

We the undersigned, Citizens of the United States, and American Missionaries at Canton, China, would respectfully represent the President, that besides the ordinary occasions for Consul Services at Macao, the peculiar importance of that Port to our P□□□□ and to the commerce of the United States as being the only Chi□□□ neutral Port on this Coast, to which we can resort in the event of such antiforeign outbreaks as have heretofore frequently occurred in this e□□□□ or in case of rupture of friendly relations with Great Britain le□□□ us heartily to approve the action of the government in maintaining a salaried consul at said Port.

At the same time we beg leave further to represent, that □□□□□ knowledge of the great cost of living on this Coast convinces us that the present salary, of Fifteen Hundred Dollars, is insufficient for said consular establishment. We do therefore petiti□□□ the President to recommend to congress an increase of the sal□□□ of the Consul for Macao to the sum of Three Thousand Dollars say ($3000) being, we believe, the lowest salary paid any ot□□□ United States Consul in China, and no more than a necessary suitable support.

We do therefore most cheerfully endorse an application for said advance of salary, which, together with certificates from the U. S. Consul at Hong Kong, and G. Nye J[r] Esq, late acting Consul at Macao, have already gone forward to the State Department, under date of Oct. 24, 1863.

We remain, Dear Sir,
Most Respectfully.

(Signed) D. Ball,
(Signed) J. C. Kevin,
(Signed) C. J. Preston,
(Signed) Lra, M. Conoit,
(Signed) John L. Nevins
(Signed) J. G. Harr,
(Signed) A. P. Happer
[Reverends]

(Signed) Saml. W. Ronney,
(Signed) Arthur Folson,
(Signed) J. G. Schilliny,
(Signed) Daniel Vrooman.

U.S. Consulate,
Macao, Dec. 12, 1864,

I certify that the above are true copies of the original papers sent by me to the State Department in my No 14, of 1863.

W. P. Jones,
U. S. Consul.

[Certificates and petitions
No.1.
Macao Dec, 14, 1864.]

[2-014]

[N°14

Recd Mch, 24]

United States Consulate
Macao. Dec. 31, 1864,

Sir,

Permit me to hand you enclosed, the Account of this Consulate with the United States for so much of my office rent as is allowed by Law for this Quarter Ending as above – (Vide Enclosure No 1.) , amtg to 37^{50}–

Enclosure Nos. 2 & 3 are the usual vouchers.–

[Account for Office Rent Vouchers]

I remain, Sir,
Your Obedient Servant,
W. P. Jones.
U. S. Consul at Macao.

[The Hon. Wm H. Seward
Secretary of State for the United States
Washington D. C.
U. S. of America]

[□□□□□□□□□□□
W. P. Jones. Consul.

No. 14.

---

3 Enclosures–
Received–

Account for Office Rent]

[2-015]

[N°15

Recd Mch. 24]

U. S. Consulate
Macao. Dec. 31. 1864.

Sir;

Herewith please find the Accounts of this Consulate with the United States for Miscellaneous Expenses, during the Quarter Ending as above, Amtg to 21^{26} as per Enclosure No. 1.–

[Ac'ct for miscel. Expenses]

Enclosure Nos 2–5 inclusive are the required vouchers.

[□□□do]

[2, 3, 4, 5 v'ouchers]

I am compelled, as in times past, to sell for seventy five cents to the dollar on the fares of my draft which is therefore for 28^{35}.

[Exchange]

I remain
Your Obedient Servant
W. P. Jones.
U.S. Consul at Macao.

[The Hon.
Wm H. Seward,
Secretary of States for the United States.
Washington D. C.]

[W. P. Jones. U. S. Consul

No 15.

---

5 Enclosures
Received

Miscellaneous Expense
a/c.]

[2-016]

[No. 16

Recd Mch 22,]

United Stated Consulate
Macao, Dec. 31. 1864.

Sir,

In obedience to Sect. 100 of the Consular Instructions I beg to report that during the year now closing I have addressed the Hon. Secretary of States at times and in Nos as follows, to wit:

Nos 1, 2 & 3, March 31. Quart. Returns;
No 4– Requisition for Stationary June 8;
Nos 5, 6 & 7. June 30th Quart. Returns;
No. 8. July 9. on failure of Port. Treaty at Peking;
Nos. 9. 10. 11, Sept. 30, Quart. Returns;
No. 12. Sept. 30. Annual Com. Report;
No. 13. Dec 14, Concerning Salary;
Nos 14 & 15, Dec. 31, Quart. Returns–
No. 16–as above & enclosing Return of fees for the four Quarters of 1864 as see Enclosure No. 1.
[No.1 Return of fees]

I remain, Sir,
Yours Obediently,
W. P. Jones,
U. S. Consulate
Macao.

[The Hon. Wm H. Seward,
Secretaty of States &c.
Washington D. C.]

[Macao. Dec. 31, 1864
W. P. Jones, U. S. Consul
No. 16,
Left out of its envelope
1 enclosure––which went in last mail with enclosure No 1.
Received
Report of despatches
written to State Dept,
During 1864.]

[2-017]

[No.6] [Form No. 6—Continued.]

Return of the Arrival and Departure of American Vessels, &c., and Statement of Fees received at the United States Consulate at Macao during the quarter ending Dec. 31 1864.

DATE.		VESSELS.										CARGO. INWARD.					CARGO. OUTWARD.				
Month.	Day.	Class.	Name.	Tonnage.	Where from.	When built.	Where built.	Where belonging.	Where bound.	Owners.	Masters.	Where produced.	Where manufactured.	Description.	Quantity.	Value.	Where produced.	Where manufactured.	Description.	Quantity	Value.
Nov	19	Steamer	"Hankow"	725	Hong Kong			HongKong	SanShan	Messrs Russell and Co.	Bennet		Excussion Party.					Excussion Party			
Nov	21	Steamer	"Hankow"	725	San Shan			HongKong	HongKong	Messrs Russell and Co.	J. H. Brady		Excussion Party.					Excussion Party			
Oct–Dec	1–31	Steamer	"Spark"	100	Canton			New York	Canton	J. H. Endicott		Triweekly	Passenger & Fst. Steamers Gen'l Stores & mdse			$160,000	Tri.	Passenger & Fst Gen'l mdse			$145,000

TONNAGE FEES.		FEES FOR												DECEDENTS' ESTATES FEES.		TOTAL OF FEES.		DATE OF CLEARANCE.	
		Noting protest	Certified copy of same.	Extending protest.	Certified copy of same.	Orders of survey and recording.	Amounts paid to surveyors	Certified copy of surveys.	Arrest and release.	Certificates to crew list and articles.		Other certificates and services.							Note. United States Consuls are especially instructed to state in additional columns, to be prepared by them, the amount of any and every fee received by them for receives other than those above specified. This form is to be followed by U. S. consuls residing at ports, and to be transportted quarterly to the Department of States.
Dollars.	Cents									No.	Amount.	No.	Amount.	Dollars.	Cents.	Dollars.	Cents.		REMARKS.
																7	25	Nov. 19	There have been no other fees recd during the Quarter.
7	25																	Nov 21	
																1	00	Triwkly	
1	00															$8	25		

U. S. Consulate, Macao.
Dec. 31. 1864.

W. P. Jones.
U. S. Consul

[Enclosure with
No. 15½ 1 pt
Arrivals & Departure
For 4th Quarter.
No.1.
China
Macao Dec. 31, 1864.
□□□]

Table No. 10.

Average Market Price

For the year 1864–5.'

Tea Chiusson	@	41 to 45 tails	@	picul
Tea Congou	@	31 to 32 tails	@	picul
Cotton Shanghai	@	26½ to 30 $	@	picul
Cotton Ningpo'	@	27 to 29 tails	@	picul
Cotton Culcutta	@	23½ to 25 tails	@	picul
Rice Bengal	@	2^{90} to 3^{10} tails	@	picul
Rice Saigon	@	2^{80} to 2^{90} tails	@	picul
Rice Singapore	@	2^{70} to 2^{75} tails	@	picul
Cinnamon	@	16^{75} to 19^{25} tails	@	picul
Cinnamon Oil	@	186 to 189 tails	@	picul
Star Aniseed	@	23 to 23½ tails	@	picul
Aniseed Oil	@	174 to 178 tails	@	picul
Gallangal	@	1^{80} to 1^{90} tails	@	picul
Vermillion	@	$\$^{32}$ to 0^{33} tails	@	box
Quick Silver	@	$\$^{61}$ to 0.63 tails	@	picul
White pepper	@	11^{58} to 12 tails	@	picul
Black pepper	@	6^{75} to 7 tails	@	picul
Cinnamon Flower	@	48 to 49 tails	@	picul
Sugar No. 1.	@	8^{25} to 8^{75} tails	@	picul
Sugar No. 2.	@	7^{25} to 8 tails	@	picul
Sugar No. 3.	@	6 to 6^{10} tails	@	picul
Brown Sugar	@	5 to 5^{25} tails	@	picul

Tin	@	22 to 25 tails	@	picul
Lead	@	5^{80} to 5^{90} tails	@	picul
Rattan	@	3^{80} to 3^{90} tails	@	picul
Beatle nut	@	3^{40} to 3^{50} tails	@	picul
Sandal wood	@	8^{00} to 8^{25} tails	@	picul
Lamp Oil	@	12^{25} to 12^{75} tails	@	picul
Tobacco	@	5^{50} to 6^{00} tails	@	picul
Indigo	@	2^{75} to 2^{80} tails	@	picul
Peas	@	2^{75} to 2^{80} tails	@	picul
White Beans	@	2^{25} to 2^{60} tails	@	picul
Flour	@	1^{25} to 2 tails	@	bag of 50lbs
Silk	@	$480 to 482 tails	@	picul
Salt Petter(saltpeter)	@	8^{25} to 8^{50} tails	@	picul
Opium Patna	@	685 to 690 tails	@	chest
Opium Benares	@	665 to 670 tails	@	chest
Opium Maloa	@	820 to 225 tails	@	chest

[□□□

Recd. April 10.

No. 15½ Statistical]

[□□□□]

U. S. Consulate

Macao, Decr 31/64

Sir:

Please receive herewith my Report of Arrivals & Departures for the Quarter ending as above – I have no other Returns to make for this Quarter – my principal business being to secure the deserters from our Sloop of war now in Port; but I abide in hope of better days to come.

Yours Obediently

W. P. Jones Is,

U. S. Consul at

Macao.

[The honorable

William H. Seward

Secretary of State for the United States

Washington D. C.]

[Macao Dec, 31. 1864
W. P. Jones – Consul
No. 15½
1 Enclosure–
Received
Quarterly Returns

China
Portugal]

[2-018]

[No. 1. Recd Apr 10,
ack 18]

U.S. Consulate. Macao,
Jan. 30, 1865.

Sir:

I have the honor to acknowledge the receipt of your No. 11. of 1864 – bearing date at Washington of April 5 – but London Postmark of Nov. 28 and HongKong postmark of Jan. 25, 1865.

I therefore write immediately to beg the Honorable Secretary to take note why I have not hitherto complied with the new regulation for payment of Consular salaries; and for this reason communicate with the Treasury Department so as to secure prompt payment of my draft for salary due Dec. 31st; Otherwise I shall be innocently subjected to much loss and embarrassment in addition to what I must necessarily suffer in waiting six months after the current Quarter's salary falls due before I can receive any farther payments from the Government.

[No. 11 Recd after long delay in the mail. N. B. Concerning draft of Dec 31. Please give immediate alternation]

[The Honorable
W[m] H. Seward.
Secretary of State for the United States
Washington D. C.]

I must not humiliate myself by making more complaint about the difficulty of sustaining myself on my present inadequate salary. What has been already communicated upon this subject will enable you to understand how this unforeseen alteration of the plan of paying salaries will temporarily embarrass me; and will, I am satisfied, induce you to direct the immediate payment, （if it is not already paid）, of my last Quarter draft – sold to Messes Olyphant & Co. a month since.

Should this latter draft revert to, for non-payment, I know not how I shall be able to meet it in addition to the two quarters' maintenance of my family which I must henceforth pay in advance of salary.

[□□□□]

I remain, Sir,
Your Obedient Servant
W. P. Jones,
U. S. Consul at Macao.

[U. S. Consulate
Macao Jan, 30, 1865.
W. P. Jones – Consul.
No. 1.

Delayed receipt of State Depts No. 11 and concerning – my draft of Dec 31.]

[2-019]

[No.2 Recd Apr, 10, Statistical]

U. S. Consulate
Macao. Jan. 30, 1865.

Sir:

I have ascertained that the table showing the exports and imports of China during certain past years referred to in my No. 12 or annual Commercial Report of 1864, does not include the trade of the East India Company and my comparison is therefore incorrect.

[Error in Com. Report of 1864]

I request then that the words: "being three times the Import of all China, in 1815–16, and twice the some of 1825–6" –

Also the words: "being more than the exports of all China in 1830 or any year previous that I find tabulated, except, for 1805, which were about the same." – be eliminated from any said Report.

The words quoted will be found under the head of Import & Exports in the body of the Report, before Tables Nos 1, 2 & 3.

]The correction]

I am, Sir,
Yours Faithfully
W. P. Jones
U. S. Consul at Macao.

[The Hon,

W[m] H. Seward
Secretary of State & c
Washington, D. C.]

[Macao Jan 30, 1865.
W. P. Jones Consul
No. 2.

Received

Correcting Error in my Commercial Report of 1864 – No. 12.]

[2-020]

[Recd 2[d] May.
No.3. □□□]

United States Consulate. Macao,
Feb. 27, 1865,

Sir:

I have the satisfaction to receive by today's mail a teller from Minister Harvey, Lisbon, informing me that he has lately obtained damages in a case similar to that of the sequestration of the Ship "Emma" at this Port, and respecting which my predecessor and myself have addressed the Department on several occasions, (vide Mr Nge's Nos 5, 1861 and my No 7 of 1863) ; and inclosing copies of his correspondence with the Duke of Loulé.

Our minister remarks that he has as yet received nothing from the States Dept. at Washington respecting this case: suffer me therefore to beg the Honorable Secretary's attention to this matter while it is being agitated at Lisbon, with the hope that the exclamation instituted by the Minister may receive the immediate countenance of the Govern

[The "Emma" Case of Lisbon.]

[The Honorable
W[m] H. Seward
Secretary of State for the United States
Washington D. C.]

ment. I again assure you that we have no further judicial resort–no further appeal except to our own Government; as a careful examination of the papers sent to Washington will service. The judges last reply to the claimant being to the effect that, as the securities accepted by the Court to cover the damages of sequestration had proved insufficient, there is nothing more that the court can do to satisfy the judgment for damages. Our claim is, that when the Portuguese Government sends a platoon of soldiers on board an American vessel and sequestrates the same it is responsible for the damages, should its action prove to be illegal, as its own supreme Court of Goa has long since decided this seizure to have been and the more especially in this particular case since the injured party warned them at the time of taking bonds for damages that the securities were insufficient. Please see the papers above referred to.

Although the official duties of this Consulate requiring fees are at present reduced to almost nothing. I have, the gratification of knowing that, as in the above case, （involving several thousands of Dollars）, and in service to our men of war – and in such manner as is indicated by the inclosed card from the Am. Geographical and Statistical Society, I am able to be of some service to my country men, while drawing from my country a portion of my daily support. At the same time I would cheerfully be still more actively engaged.

With congratulations upon the cheering domestic prospects of the country and （large thanks to the Secretary） its generally happy foreign relations.

[Respecting my present consular employment]

I have the honor to remain
Your Obedient Servant
W. P. Jones
U. S. Consul at Macao.

COMPLIMENTARY
AM GEOGRAPHICAL AND STATISTICAL SOCTETY
A MEETING WILL BE HELD AT □□□ HALL □□□ ON THIS
DAY, THE 10TH NOVEMBER 1864 AT □□□ O'CLOCK P.M. ON WHICH
OCCASION THE SECRETARY WILL BY SPECIAL REQUEST OF
COUNC□□ – REPEAT THE HANDING OF A PAPER
DESCRIPTIVE OF A RECENT VOYAGE INTO
THE INTERIOR OF CHINA BY
W.P. JONES ESQ..
U. S. CONSUL AT MACAO – □□□ SO MUCH SATISFACTION AT THE
LAST MEETING OF THE SOCIETY.
Wm. Coventry H. Waddell.
R□□□ SECRETARY
A branch office of the Society will hereafter be open at 11 Pine Street.

[Macao. Feb. 27, 1865.
W. P. Jones. Consul.
No.3.

The "Emma" Case at Lisbon–
also
Reference to my present
Consular employments]

I have carried the balance due me one the former Account forward to next Quarter and venture to draw upon the Honorable Secretary of State for Office Rent as per old instructions, which forbid me to confound Rent or other Miscel Ac/cts with Accounts at the Treasury Dept.

I have therefore sold my Dft made this day upon the Secretary of State for Office Rent, amounting to 50^{00} for the sum of $37.^{50} nett– (being at the rate of 75 cents to the Dollar on its face) – to Gideon Nye. Jr. Esq. and trust that the said Dft will be duty honored.

I have the honor to remain
Your Obedient Servant
W. P. Jones.
U. S. Consul at Macao.

[Macao, March 31, 1865.
W. P. Jones. Consul.
No. 5.
3 Enclosures.

A/ct for Office Rent.]

[2–021]

[No.5.

Recd June □□□□□]

U. S. Consulate, Macao.
March, 31. 1865.

Sir:

Enclosed please find my A/ct for Office Rent at this Consulate, for the Quarter Ending to day. Amtg to $37^{50} as per Enclosure No 1.

[agt]

Enclosures N°s 2 & 3 are the legally required vouchers.

[No.1. Act for Rent Nos 2 & 3 Vouchers]

As per your latest instructions respecting the payment of Consular Accounts, communicated in the Hon. Secretary's No 11 of 1864 receiued of this office Jan. 26. 1865–I have applied the total official fees of the Quarter (amounting to $6.35) upon my Miscel. Ex. A/ct of this date–and now await the authority of the Secretary of Treasury to draw upon Baring Bros & Co, London for my unpaid salary – but no provision having been stated in the new instructions for a case where the Fees for an office do not pay Miscel. Expenses and Office Rent.

[Reason Selling direct the Se□□□]

[The Hon
Wm H. Seward
Secretary of State for the United States
Washington D. C.]

[2–022]

[U. S. Consulate. Macao,
March. 31. 1865,
W. P. Jones.–Consul.
No. 4.
6 Enclosures + 3 Vouchers

Miscel. Ex A/ct.
for First Quart. 1865.]

[No.4.

Recd June 7.]

U. S. Consulate. Macao.
March. 31. 1865.

Sir:

Permit me to hand you herewith my miscellaneous Expense Ac/ct for the First Quarter of 1865 – Amt'g to $29^65 and leaving a balance due me, after applying thereon the Total Consular Fees of the Quarter, – of $23^33 which I carry to next Quarter Ac/ct. (Vide Enclosure No.1. Herewith)

[agent]

V^s Nos 1, 2, 3 and the Returns of Letters sent or received accompany the above as vouchers.

[No.1. Miscel. Ex. Vochers Nos 1, 2 □□□ & .]

I have the honor to be
Your Obedient Servant

W. P. Jones.
U. S. Consul at Macao.

P. S. Enclosures Nos 2, 3 & 4– are Quarterly–G returns 2d Arrivals & c, 3d St of Fees, 4th Nov. 9 sept
St. And. St.

[The Hon,
Wm H. Seward,
Secretary of State for the United States,
Washington D. C.]

No.130.

NAVIGATION AND COMMERCE of the United States at the Port of Macao, during the quarter ending March, 31. 1865.

□□□ □□□	VESSELS–			CARGOES–							
	ENTERED.	CLEARED.		INWARD.				OUTWARD.			
□□□ □□□	WHERE FROM–	No. of vessels.	WHERE FOR–	No. of vessels.	DESCRIPTION.	VALUE. Dollars.	Cents.	No. of vessels.	DESCRIPTION.	VALUE. Dollars.	Cents.
/	Hong Kong	/	Hong Kong		(Passengers)				(Passengers)		
/	Canton (Triweekly)	/	Canton. (Triweekly)		Gen'l mdse	$112950	00		Gen'l mdse	$36214	00
	Except Feburary when laid by for repairs.										

□□□□s of vessels entered 2 steamers W. P. Jones
□□□□s of vessels cleared 2 steamers U. S. Consul.
□□□□gregate tonnage entered 535 Tons over and 100 Tons Triweekly

[Enclosure with
Despatch No.4.
Navigation & Comal Report
No.4.
Macao Mar. 31. 1865,
Portugal]

[Form No. 14.
Quarter Return of American Vessels]

ARRIVALS And DEPARTURES OF AMERICAN VESSELS at Macao, from the 1st of January to 31st of March 1865.

DATE.		VESSELS.										CARGOES.													
18												INWARD.						OUTWARD.						DATE OF DEPARTURE	
Month.	Day.	Classes.	Names.	Tonnage.	Where from.	When built.	Where built.	Where belonging.	Where bound.	Owners.	Masters.	Where produced.	Where Manufactured.	Description.	Quantities.	Values.		Where produced.	Where manufacture.	Description.	Quantities.	Values.		Month.	Day.
Jan–March		Sloop of War	"Relief"		In Port				In Port															In Port	
Feb	27	Sloop of War	"Kinshan"	535	Hong Kong	1863	New York	Hong Kong	Hong Kong	Heard & Co.	F. Haskell	Passengers						Passengers						Feb.	28
March	31		"Spark"	100	Canton	–	New York	Hong Kong	Canton	J.Endicott	J. W. Brady	Reg. Triweekly – Gen'l mdse				$112950	00	Gen'l mdse				$36714	00	Triweekly	

U. S. Consulate, Macao. W. P. Jones

March. 31. 1865. U. S. Consul

[FORM No. 12.]

REGISTER of Official Letters and Despatches received at the U. S. Consulate at Macao for the Quarter ending March 31st 1865.

NAME OF THE WRITER.	NO.	PLACE AND DATE OF LETTER.	WHEN RECEIVED.	ON WHAT SUBJECT.	NO. OF ENCLOS URES.	REMARKS	AMOUNT OF POSTAGE PAID ON EACH PARCEL.
C. Price	1	Washington Navy Dept.	Jany 14.	For comder of U.S. Relief.			.32
	2	Washington Navy Dept.	Jany 14.	For Paymaster U.S. Relief.			.16
	3	Yohohama, Japan 9th	Jany 25.	About store ship Relief			.32
Dept of State	4	Washington	Jany 26	No 11 To draw on Baring Bro			.32
Dept of State	5	Washington June 2d	Feby 9.	No 12 Respt'g New Seals			.32
First Compt.	6	Washington Nov. 26	Feby 9.	Conc'g Salary 2d Quart: /64			.80
Fifth Aud.	7	Washington Nov. 26	Feby 9.	Conc'g Salary 2d Quart: /64			.80
Despatch Agt.	8	London Octr 7	Feby 9.	Conc'g Despatches Missing			
Sect of Macao Govt.	9	Macao, Feby 22	Feby 22.	Conc'g a man in jail claiming to be an Am Citz.			
H. Ex & H. S. Harney	10	Lisbon Jan. 4	Feby 24.	Conc'g "Emma" Case President Message Dec /64			.32 .08
Treas Deptr	11	Washington Apl. 25	Mch: 13.	Respect'g Relief a/c.			.32
						Amt. carried forward. $	2.96

U. S. Consul.

REGISTER of Official Letters and Despatches received at the U. S. Consulate at Macao for the Quarter ending March 31st 1865.

NAME OF THE WRITER.	NO.	PLACE AND DATE OF LETTER.	WHEN RECEIVED.	ON WHAT SUBJECT.	NO. OF ENCLOSURES.	REMARKS.	AMOUNT OF POSTAGE PAID ON EACH PARCEL.
						Amt. brought forward	$2.96
State Dept'	12	Washington Nov. 11	Mch. 13	Cir. No. 53.			.32
State Dept'	13	Washington Nov. 28	Mch. 13	Cir. No. 54.			.32
State Dept'	14	Washington without date	Mch. 13	Cir. Respect'g Passports			.32
State Dept'			Mch. 21	Box of station'y & books Dead letters for men of war.			.80
						Total	$4.08

W. P. Jones U. S. Consul.

Note.–Consular officers are not authorized to pay postages or other charges on letters or packages addressed to them, with a view to charge them to the United States, unless they bear on their envelopes evidence of official character, as emanating from some of the Executive Departments, or are upon official business, or from some of the legations or consulates, or officers of the United States in foreign countries. Such charges or postages, if paid by consular officers, are not to be included in their accounts for postage against the Department of State. This form, with the blanks properly filled, is to be sent, with the dispatch enclosing each quarterly postage account, to the Secretary of State. Care should be taken to note the amount of postage paid on each letter. (See circulars Nos. 33 and 37 of 1863)

From the U. S. Consulate Macao from Jan. 1–Mar 31 1865

Date 1865		No.	To whorn and what place,	On what subject.	No. of Seal	Paid.
						1 ¢
Jan	1	1	Sect. of State, Washington,	Return of Fees report fees 100	1	.54
Jan	1	2	Sect. of State, Washington,	Rent a/c via South	3	
Jan	1	3	Sect. of State, Washington,	Miscel, a/c via South	5	5.30
Jan	1	4	Sect. of Treas, Washington,	Salary, a/c via South	3	
Jan	1	5	Sect. of State, Washington,	Quart, Repost Arrivals &c.	1	
Jan	30	6	Sect. of State, Washington,	Correction of An, Com Report		
Jan	30	7	Sect. of State, Washington,	Concerning Draft of Dec 31		3.18
Jan	30	8	First Comptroller & 5th Aud.	Concerning Draft of Dec 31		
Feby	22	9	Sect of Macao, Govt.	Deny'g the assumed citizenship of a man in jail, Macao		
Feby	27	10	Seat of State Washington	"Emma" Case at Lisbon		1.06
Mch	13	11	H. E. James E. Harvey, Lisbon	"Emma" Case at Lisbon	13	6.56
Mch	23	12	First compt Washington	Relief a/c	3	1.06

Total $ 17.70

U. S. Consulate, Macao.
March. 31, 1865

W. P. Jones U. S. Consul.

[Despatch No.4
Official Letters Sent
No.4.
Macao, March 31. 1865.]

[2-023]

[Oct. 5 Sept. Mr. Jones]

United States Consulate,
Macao, June 26, 1865.
[Ack Sep 8th]

[□□□□□
□□□□□
□□□□□]

Sir:

It would be utterly futile for me to attempt to express the contending emotions of grief, shame and indignation with which not only myself but all Americans here received the heart-sickening intelligence of our great National bereavement and the dastardly attach upon the illustrions chief of the State Department and his sons.

Although cultivated intelligence and the moral sense may not approve the purely passionate expressions of grashing the teeth and clenching hands get these were the almost universal signs that American hearts were well nigh wrong to madness by this last, most diabolical scheme and stroke

[of]

[The Honorable W. Hunter.
Acting Secretary of State for the United States,
Washington. D. C.]

of ingrate treason. Pardon me; I grant that I cannot even yet write calmly upon this soul – harrowing subject. Our great and good president Lincoln is no more! Were this all the thought would go wailing from heart to brain and brain to heart continually; he was so filled with that which loved us and made we love him; and at the same time as inspired with that which made us, willing to submit to him as a counselor and leader in these days when lead and counsel are so needful to us. But this is not all – or we would reverently fold our hands over our grief and say: he is not for God took him. No! sadly for us and our republican pride and devotion, this is not all--he was assassinated! Even while his head was bowed down with thoughts of mercy too engrossing for the scenes about him, which he only seemed to see (and even that for kindness sake merely), which he was deaf to the stepping of murder because absorbed in planning forgiveness and conciliation for men whom justice and the spirits of half a million fallen patriots declared forfeit to impoverishment and death, at such a time the dear, greet soul that could not spare a thought to guard his own life, so busy was he in devising ways to spare the lives of others （all his enemies） was struck to the earth by a friend! Doubtless God reigns over all the earth and can make the deeds even of devils aid the good they seek to destroy and so praise Him– but it is impossible that men should see the devils seeming triumph and not feel enraged against them.

So grief and rage mingled and struggled in our breasts here as in yours at home and we had no heart to rejoice over even the glorious triumphs of our enemies. All men, of all civilized nations, about us, proved themselves human, and nearer a kin than they have assumed in all the last sad four years, by uniting heartily in condemnation of the deed and sorrow for what is now felt to be more than a national bereavement.

Nor has sympathy been restricted to the account of the good President's martyrdom only; the fiendishness of the attack on our noble secretary and the Assistant Secretary of State has been fully apprehended, and reflecting how the great premier has preserved the nation from foreign collision, and at last correctly valuing his services as beyond all estimation we and all around us have mourned for his sufferings and thanked God that although the president is taken from us the First Secretary is spared. I beg you to transmit to our suffering chief the enclosed personal note of sympathy and affectionate regard.

Enclosed I have the honor to hand you the correspondence between His Excellency, the Governor of this colony, and myself concerning our bereavement and the wounding of the Secretary of State; and you will surely be gratified to perceive how feelingly this government has manifested its sympathy.

I should further observe that the programme indicated in this correspondence was even more than fully executed. The U. S. S. "Relief" set its ensign at half–mast and fired its first gun at sunrise, the Portuguese flags on all the five forts and in front of Government house and a gun from the lofty Guia Fort responded. All the other consular flags and these of the shipping in harbor, including the outgoing American Steamers to Canton and Hong Kong, drooped in unison with our ensign at the consular. The front of the consulate was festooned with flags, which, with the coat of arms, were appropriately draped. Throughout the day every half–hours the solemn guns from the Roads and the tone answering guns from the fort reminded the whole city that the day was sacred to the memory of a potent, wise and loving ruler passed from earth, and of whom the entire civilized world, now that he is indeed gone, feels bereaved.

At 12 o'clk, noon, His Excellency, Governor Amaral called in person to express the sincere grief and sympathy not only of himself but of this people, who with himself hold the memory of our fallen chief magistrate in honor and the crime that has bereaved us in utter abhorrence and detestation.

In conclusion it seems not unfitting for me to add that while we lament the death of our martyred President Lincoln we hail the past political career and recent speeches of President Johnson as evidence that, despite the remorseless hate and fury of vengeful traitors, our country's life and honor are still safe.

Wishing the honorable Acting Secretary all possible honor and success in the discharge of his onerous awesome duties.

I have the honor to be
Your obedient servant
W. P. Jones.
U. S. Consul for Macao.

[June 26. 1865.
W. P. Jones. Consul.
3 enclosures

Official Correspondences
with the Colonial Gov't
of Macao, upon the
decease of president
Lincoln, and respects
paid to the presidents
memory]

[2-024]

[Rec 5. Sept[r] Mr. Jones □□□

Consular Bureau Received

SEP 5 1865
W. MARTIN JONES.]

United States Consulate,
Macau, June 26, 1865.

Hon. W. H. Seward,
Secretary of State for the United States,
Washington, D. C.

Dear, revered Sir:

I cannot esteem it necessary to enjoy personal acquaintance with one, whose public services have rendered him so will known to me and all his countrymen, before feeling at liberty to express that sincere sorrow and daily sympathy I feel for you and your suffering family in this painful season of affliction, endured for your devotion to freedom, truth and justice.

If the assurance that you have so discharged the momentous duties of your exalted office during the past four critical years as not only to lead and satisfy the judgments of your countrymen but so as also to win their deep affection, can afford you solace and heartfelt satisfaction in the midst of your sufferings, then permit me to assure you thus much for all our countrymen and especially the consular brotherhood upon this coast.

It is my continual hope, dear Sir, and most earnest prayer to Almighty God, that you and your wounded sons may all be restored to perfect good health and to us.

I have the honor to the

Most Affectionately
Your Obedient Servant.
W. P Jones.
U. S. Consulate Macao.

[2-025]

[No. 7. Rec 18, Septr. Mr Jones]

U. S. Consulate, Macao
June 30, 1865.

Sir:

I am privileged to hand you herewith my Account for Office Rent for this consulate, for the Quarter ending to day, June. 30, 1865 Amt'g to \$ $37^{\underline{50}}$ as per enclosure No. 1.

Enclosures Nos. 2 & 3 are the usual vouchers.

[□□□ No.1 Ac/c for Rent do Nos. 2. & 3. Vouchers]

Per favor of the Tuesday of Secretary of State under date of April 13 – which privilege I gratefully acknowledge – I am now permitted to draw directly upon the State Department for this amount, and have therefore sold J. da Silva, Esq. of this City my draft for Fifty–Dollars to cover the same – being at the

[Sale of df't]

[Hon. William Hunter
Acting Secretary of State
Washington, D. C.]

rate of seventy five cents to the dollar on the draft's face.

I am, Sir,
Your Obediently
W. P. Jones.
U. S. Consul.

[June. 30 1865.
W. P. Jones. –Consul
No. 7
3 enclosures
Received
Account for Office Rent.]

[2-026]

[Recd Sept. 18.
No.8.]

U. S. Consulate Macao,
June, 30, 1865

Sir:

Referring to my N° 4 for my last quarter's ac/ct, I beg to hand you enclosed my miscellaneous Expense ac/ct for the 2^d Quarter of 1865, Amt'g, (with the unpaid balance due me on previous Quarter) to \$ 70⁵⁵ less U. S. Fees for the Quarter \$16⁵⁶ – or net balance of \$ 53⁹⁹ (see Ac/ct herewith, Enclosure No. 1 together with vouchers Nos 1, 2, and lists of letters Received and sent.)

[□□□ No.1. miscel. Ex. Sept do Vouchers 1 & 2 & letter lists.]

By permission granted in a Asst. Secretary Seward's despatch of April 13, 1865, I have this day drawn upon the Honorable Secretary of State, direct, for \$71⁹⁸ to cover the above balance, being at the rate of .75 cents to the dollar on the face of the draft; – the most favorable terms obtainable on this coast.

No. 3 is the required exchange vouchers

[Voucher No. 3. for Exchange.]

[The Honorable
W. Hunter.
Acting Secretary of State,
Washington, D. C.]

I have the pleasure to call the Secretary's attention to the fact that until April of this Quarter I have had no flag since the two received from the state Department in February 1863.

I have the honor to be.
your Obedient Servant.
W. S. Jones.
U. S. Consul.

[U. S. Consulate Macao
June, 30, 1865
W. S. Jones Consul,
No.8.
6 Enclosures

Missed, Ex. a/c 2^d Quarter.]

[Table No.3. With An. Report of 1865.]

Consular statement showing the Imports & Exports of Macao in Chinese Junks for year Ending June 30, 1865.

Names of Articles	Importation			Exportation		
	Quantity		Value	Quantity		Value
□□□seed	Piculs	3774	21277			
□□□seed Oil	Piculs	420	7529			
□□□seed □□□	Piculs	274	2650			
□□□tz	Piculs	72	4400			
□□□ Drill				Bales	9117	47511
B□□□				Bales	350	2545
Beans	Piculs	1707	3457			
Bags Empty	No.	157616	3003			
Cotton	Piculs	60	1740	Bales	5075	118578
Copper	Piculs	20	398			
Cinnamon	Piculs	2286	37969			
Cinnamon Oil	Piculs	210	13892			
China–Medicine	Bales	64	825	Bales	100	3500
Cows Horn	Piculs	2807	4943			
Cloth				Bales	423	3064
□□□tz				Bales	850	3880
Cocoa Nut	No	62600	551			
Cocoa	Piculs	2314	2415			
Cash	Piculs	35	360			
Camphor	Piculs	229	189			
Dried shrimp	Piculs	25	775			
Dried Fish	Piculs	381	8331			
Dried Cuttle Fish	Piculs	4	68			
Drugs				Piculs	108	1554
□□□ Cocoa	Piculs	1724	4967			
□□□	Piculs	44	1689			
□□□Oil	Piculs	4	570			
Flax	Piculs	236	1218			
Fish wings	Piculs	114	305			
Flour	Piculs	718	1912			
Flax Seed	Piculs	54	248			

Gum	Piculs	213	1078			
Hogs	No.	1344	21127			
Hams	Catties	162	62			
Ivory	Piculs	2	400			
□□□ Stick	Piculs	123	123			
Brown Sugar	Piculs	5553	7698	Piculs	48	144
Indigo	Lubs	35196	142527			
Kernel	Piculs	941	3425			
Lamp Oil	Piculs	30050	133686			
Feather	Piculs	279	3285			
Lard	Piculs	80	938			
Lead	Piculs	50	1000			
Lacquered	Piculs	53	575			
Meats	Piculs	23212	2115			
Ma-cú	Pieces	53487	102889			
Green Peas	Piculs	1062	2845			
Amount carried forward			$554854			$179,706

(Next page)

	Quantity	Value	Quantity	Value
Amount brought forward		554854		□□□
Nan kin	576	784	12480	□□□
Opium			540	□□□
Puddy	4696	11085		
Paper	1387	7318	40	□□□
Pima (medicine)	14	120		
Rice	46466	52854	3060	□□□
Rattan	413	2200		
Red wood	485	417		
Sugar	8656	46358		
Salt	109758	58127		
Silk	44	15830		
Silk common			80	□□□
Silk yellow	62	8007		
Sesame	4511	6328		

Sesame Oil	203	3229		
Sucan	61	671		
Salt-fish	355	1023		
Sticks	1380	24		
Tallow	1065	8127		
Tin	2033	7727		
Tea	1644	15486		
Tobacco	2319	16716	1280	□□□
Tree Skin	474	510		
Unicorn	5	100		
Varnish	123	1213		
Vilvet			2	□□□
Wood	95	606		
Wax	140	1690		
Wood Oil	30	502		
Sundries		19709		13□□□
Total		$840,915		$500□□□

(*in an empty form) [Table No 5. with Dispatch N° 15]

NAVIGATION AND COMMERCE of the United States at the Port of Macao, during the year ending June 30, 1865

VESSELS				CARGOES-							
ENTERED.		CLEARED.		INWARD				OUTWARD.			
				No. of vessels.	DESCRIPTION.	VALUE.		No. of vessels	DESCRIPTION.	VALUE.	
No. of Vessels	WHERE FROM-	No. of vessels	WHERE FOR-			Dollars.	Cents			Dollars.	Cents.
For the Quarter Ending Sept. 30.1864.											
2	Canton	2	Canton	2	General Cargo-besides pass'grs	308,000	00	2	Gen'l Cargo-besides pass'grs	186,000	00
For the Quarter Ending Dec. 31. 1864											
1	Hong Kong	1	San Shan	1	General Cargo-besides pass'grs				Gen'l Cargo-besides pass'grs		
1	Sanshan	1	Hong Kong	1	General Cargo-besides pass'grs				Gen'l Cargo-besides pass'grs		
1	Canton Triweekly	1	Canton Triweekly	1	General Cargo-besides pass'grs	160,000	00		Gen'l Cargo-besides pass'grs	145,000	00
For the Quarter Ending March 31. 1865.											
1	Hong Kong	1	Hong Kong	1							
1	Canton Triweekly	1	Canton Triweekly	1	General mdse besides passengers	112,950	00		General mdse besides pass'grs	36,214	00

For the Quarter Ending June 30. 1865.											
1	Hong Kong, Daily	1	Hong Kong, Daily	1	Gen'l mdse besides passengers	110,286	00		Gen'l mdse besides pass'grs	48,300	00
2	Canton	2	Canton	2	Gen'l mdse besides passengers	131,855	00		Gen'l mdse besides pass'grs	56,288	00
10		10		10		$815131	00			477,752	00

□asses of vessels entered 10 Steamers in 1st Quart. 2; 2d Quart. 3; 3d Quart. 2; 4th Quart 3. W. P. Jones

□asses of vessels entered 10 Steamers in 1st Quart. 2; 2d Quart. 3; 3d Quart. 2; 4th Quart 3. U. S. Consul

□ggregate tonnage entered

[Table No. 5. with annual report of 1865]

[Macao
Rept yrl June
30, 1865

Portugal]

[2-027]

Form No.14
Quarterly Returns of American Vessels

ARRIVALS AND DEPARTURES OF AMERICAN VESSELS at the United States Consulate at Macao China, from 1st April to the 30th June 1865.

DATE. 18		VESSELS.										CARGOES.													
												INWARD.					OUTWARD.								
Month.	Day.	Classes.	Names.	Tonnage.	Where from.	When built.	Where built.	Where belonging.	Where bound.	Owners.	Masters.	Where produced.	Where manufactured.	Description.	Quantities.	VALUES.	Where produced.	Where manufactured.	Description.	Quantities.	VALUES.	DATE OF DEPARTURE Month.	DATE OF DEPARTURE Day.	Tonnage Fees	Total Fees.
April	1	S of War	U. S. S. "Relief"		In Port																				
April	15	Str.	"White Cloud"	520 $\frac{57}{95}$	Hong Kong		N. York	N. York	Hong Kong	Russell & Co.	J. N. Sands	Passengers & Gen'l Cargo, Daily					Passengers and Gen'l Cargo, Daily							$5.20	$5.20
April	28	Str.	"Rinshan"	535	Canton	1863	N. York	Hong Kong	Canton	Heard & Co.	F. Hashell	Passengers & vessel in tow					Passengers and Gen'l Cargo, Daily					April	28	$5.35	$5.35
April	28	S of War	U. S. S. "Jamestown"		Japan				San Francisco													June	16		
June	30	Str.	"Spark"	100	Canton		N. York	Hong Kong	Canton	J. B. Eudicott	J.W. Brady	Passengers & Gen'l Cargo Triweekly.				$131,895.00	Passengers and Gen'l Cargo Triweekly.				$56238.00			1.00	1.00
																									$11.55

W.P. Jone s　　W. P. Jones.
U.S. Consul.　　U.S. Consul

(*in an empty form)

[Enclosure with Despatch No.9.

Arrivals and Departures, 2d Quarter
No.1.
Macao, June. 30. 1865.
Statistical.
Portugal]

Navigation and Commerce of the United States at the Port of Macao – Quarter ending June 30, 1865.
Besides two Men of War the only American Vessels in port this Quarter have been

1 Daily Steamer from HongKong & to HongKong
bringing Gen'l mdse taking away Gen'l mdse
1 Triweekly Str from & to Canton
bringing Gen'l mdse taking away Gen'l mdse
1 Steamer Str from & to Canton
bringing ship in tow & passengers taking away passengers.

3 Steamers.

[Enclosure
With Despatch No.9.

Navigation & Commerce
2d Quarter

No 2.

Macao. June 30, 1865.
Statistical]

[□□□□□□
No.9

Recvd. Oct. 5.]

United States Consulate, Macao,
July 1, 1865,

Sir:

I have the pleasure to hand you, enclosed, my Returns of "Arrivals & Departures," "Navigation & Commerce", & Statement of Fees "forms No. 45 & 44" the latter attached to "Arrivals and Departures" – (see Enclosures Nos. 1. 2. 3). Quarterly Returns to the Sect. of the Treasury and to the Fifth Auditor will be forwarded in the same mail.

[Nos. 1. 2. 3. Quart. Returns,]

I am, Sir,
Your Obedient Servant
W. P. Jones.
U. S. Consul

[The Honorable
William Hunter
Act'g. Secretary of State.
Washington, D. C.]

[□□□□□, 30, 1865,
W. P. Jones. Consul.
No. 9.
3 Enclosures,
Received,
Quarterly Returns of 2[d] Quarter, 1865.]

[2-028]

[□□□□□□□□□□□□□□□]
[Ding advertiser,]

[N° 10.

Recd. Oct. 20.
Ack Oct 26]

United States Consulate.
Macao. July, 20. 1865.

Sir:

It is my sad duty to report to you as follow:

Died of Cholera at Macao, China, July, 9. 1865, Jacob W. Hawes, presumed from letters found in his trunks to be a son of Mrs. Sylvia Hawes of Hyannis Massachusetts.

The effects were taken possession of by the Authorities and the mortal-remains of the deceased, decently interred in the New Protestant Cemetery of this City.

I have addressed Mrs. Sylvia Hawes at Hyannis, Mass., communicating all the particulars of her son's death, so far as I have been able to learn them, – and, as soon as the Portuguese law allows, will procure and forward to the same address an inventory and statement of the settlement of the local ac/cts of the deceased.

[Death of J. W. Hawes]

I have the honor to be
Your Obedient Servant
W. P. Jones.
U. S. Consul, Macao.

[The honorable
W. Hunter,
Acting Sectary of State for the United States.
Washington, D. C.]

[July 20. 1865
W. P. Jones. Consul
No. 11.

Requisition for New.
Vol. of Consul's Manual.]

[2-029]

[Copy]

United States Consular Agency at Maceió
September 1st 1865–

Thomas Adamson Jr, Esq.
United States Consul
□□□.

Sir:

I beg leave to hand you enclosed "Note of Exports during last year and Summary of exports during the last five years".

By the former you will see that no United States vessels have arrived at or sailed from this port, and that only one cargo of sugar has been shipped from this to the United States.

The fees received during the time I have had charge of this Agency amount to $3^{\underline{00}}$.

All tonnage duties and other port dues, warehouse and other regulations, remain without any modifications.

I remain, Sir
Your most obd^t servant
(signed) J. Borstelmann
Consular Agent.

[From U. S. Consular □□□
Copy of Amount and goods of
Consular Ag[t], at Maceio]

[□□□] Exports from Port of Maceio from 1st July 1864 to 30th June 1865.

□□□□□		Names of Vessels	Flag	Rig	Destinations	Cottons		Sugar			Hides
						Bags	□□□	Bags	□□□	Tons	Nos
	4	Margaret	Brit.	Barg	Liverpool	1500	7826				
	6	Sattellits	Brit.	ship	do	1204	21834	3577	21478	307	785
	1	□□□	Brit.	ship	do	2724	14381				
	1	Mary's □□□	Brit.	ship	do	2405	12468				
	4	Iris	Brit.	Barg	Channel			4300	23476	335	
	9	Olainda	Brit.	Barg	Liverpool	1150	5442				
	13	Eclipse	Brit.	Sloop	do	2167	11469	1953	10761	154	
	24	Blessed	Brit.	Brig	Channel			3129	16755	240	
	1	Raphael	Brit.	Sloop	Liverpool	1958	9857				
	17	Main□□□	Brit.	Barg	Channel			4019	23058	329	
		Dallas	Brit.	Barg	Liverpool	2552	13103	7000	37828	540	1215
	26	□□□	Brit.	Barg	do	2386	12674	2600	14368	205	
	21	Lady Elisabeth	Brit.	Barg	do	2031	10476	2200	12257	177	
	29	Fil□□□	Brit.	Brig	do	812	4124	1549	8661	124	
	15	Huinston	Brit.	Brig	do	1056	5084				
	26	Lord□□□	Brit.	Sloop	do	4378	21531	2781	14969	214	1032
	21	Eleanor □□□	Brit.	Brig	Channel			4665	28547	365	
	22	Constance	Brit.	Barg	Liverpool	1302	14943				
	31	Endy□□□	Brit.	Barg	as	3064	6433				
	5	Henrietta	Brit.	Brig	Channel			3911	21706	310	
	13	Arbitrator	Brit.	Barg	Liverpool	3138	15729	2540	14780	211	
	25	Arthurs	Brit.	Luggar	do	1100	5568	1234	7000	140	
		Jasse	Brit.	Brig	do	1150	5842				
	26	Isa	Brit.	Barg	Channel			2800	14945	213	
	3	Queen	Brit.	Barg	Liverpool	1220	6150				
	14	Raleigh	Brit.	Barg	do	1447	7576	1125	7006	100	
	14	□□□ of Spool	Brit.	Brig	do	1516	7878	2000	11089	159	
	22	□□□	Brit.	Sloop	do	1175	6190	2000	11385	162	
	30	□□□	Brit.	Sloop	do	250	1275				
	1	□□□ Fell	French	Bg.	Havse	834	4265				
	6	Cantona & □□□ Brid	Brit.	Bg.	Liverpool	2442	12723				
	9	□□□	Brit.	Yaks	Channel			3080	17406	280	
	15	Oliza	Brit.	Brig	do			4495	25020	557	
	23	Jasmine	Brit.	Luggar	do			3022	16202	230	
	5	Era	Brit.	Yaks	do			3700	21074	301	

	6	William	Brit.	Barg	Liverpool	2715	13950	2000	71171	160	
	12	Landord?	Brit.	Sloop	do	4391	23014				2353
	16	Iron □□□	Brit.	Barg	do	1763	9313	2400	13659	195	
	18	□□□ □□□	Brit.	Yaks	do	740	3976				
	14	Florence	Brit.	Yaks	□□□			3190	17121	256	
	30	□□□	B□□□	Brig	New York			3000	16624	237	
	4	Olinda	Brit.	Barg	□□□			5233	28171	402	
	7	Sir □□□ □□□	Brit.	Barg	Liverpool	1843	9822	857	4720	67	
	15	Vulcan	Brit.	Barg	do	1602	8300	1311	7158	102	
	16	Saphin Wood	Belg.	Barg	do	1500	7879	1250	7097	101	
	18	□□□ Magall	Brit.	Sloop	do	4400	22922	2800	15395	220	
	22	Linda	Brit.	Barg	do	1805	9649	1267	6831	97	
	23	Isabelle Ridley	Brit.	Barg	Channel			4730	26650	381	
					Total	68780	350726	95771	532216	7602	5420

United States Consular Agency
Maceio 1st September 1865.

J. Borstelmann
Consular Agent

[Maceio Consular Agency U. S. A.]

Summary of Exports from Port of Maceio During year ending 30th June 1865.

To United Kingdom and Channel for □□□	Cotton		Sugar			Hides	
	Bags	awbs.	Tons	Bags	awbs	Tons	Nos
To New York To Hawaii	67896	349361	1991	92771	515592	7365	5420
				3000	16624	237	
bgs	834	4365	62				
bgs							
Coastwise: Ao Rio de Janeiro □□□ — Cotton bags 225; Sugar bags 15872, as 85520; Hides 375	225	1155	16	15872	85521	1221	275
	68955	354881	5069	111643	617737	8823	5795
against year ending 30th June 1864.	43006	226050	3229	96421	533198	7616	9040
against year ending 30th June 1863.	49430	265908	3799	165958	897686	12815	8491
against year ending 30th June 1862.	43200	237675	3395	175500	965315	13790	9690
against year ending 30th June 1861.	26456	145368	2080	108227	595290	8504	8887

United States Consular Agency
Maceió September 1st 1865.
J. Borstelmann
Consular Agent

[2-030]

[No 14.

Rec Dec. 14
Ack Dec. 15]

U. S. Consulate, Macao.
Sept. 30, 1865.

Sir:

Permit me to hand you herewith my Returns of "Arrivals & Departures" (with statements of Fees, Froms 44 & 45), "Navigation & Commerce", and "Names of Deceased Citizens" – in all 4 enclosures.

[to Auditor Nos 1–4. Quarterly Return]

Quarterly Returns to the Sect. of the Treasury and to the Fifth–Auditor also my "Annual Commercial Report" will go forward, in the same mail – but in past under cover to the Gov't Despatch Agent London.

I remain,
Your Obedient Servant
W. P. Jones
U. S. Consul.

[The Hon. W. H. Seward
Secretary of State for the United States
Washington D. C.]

[Macao. Sept. 30. 1865
W. P. Jones. Consul.
No. 14.
4 Enclosures
Received
Quarterly Returns.

Enclosure,
With Despatch No 14,
Names of Deceased
Am. Citizens
No. 4,
Macao. Sept 30, 1865.]

Names of all deceased American citizens, including □□□ or mariners, together with the value of personal affects belonging to them, and taken possession of by as deposited with the Authorities U. S. Consul at, Macao. during the Quarter ending Sept. 30. 1865.

Date of decease	Names of persons	Of what place a native or resident	If a seaman to what vessel belong's	Where deceased	Value of affect	Disposition made thereof	
1865 July	9	Jacob W. Haves	Hyannis, Mass		Chilian Board'g House		Taken by Authorities
			Address[d] Mrs Sylvia Haves, Hyannis, Mass, his mother				

U. S. Consulate
Macao, Sept, 30. 1865

W. P. Jones
U. S. Consul

[□□□□□□□□□□□□□□□□□□□□□□□□□
□□□□□□□□□□□□□□□□□□□□□□□□□]

[2-031]

[Recd Jan 22
Ack Jan 28

No. 15

Statiscal]

U. S. Consulate Macao.
Sept. 30. 1865.

Sir:

Referring to my annual report of 1864, Despatch No. 12, for a brief sketch of the History, Geography, Climate, Geology, Population, Agriculture, Manufactures and past Commerce of Macao I now have the pleasure to hand you Table Nos. 1–10 inclusive exhibiting the principal trade statistics of the year ending June 30. 1865. – From

[Annual Report.]

Table N[os] 1 to 3.

It appears that the Imports into this Colony for the year named amounted to–

In Foreign rigged vessels–		5,010,829
In Chinese junks–		840,915
	Total	$5,851,744

And that the Exports for the same period amounted to–

In Foreign rigged vessels		3,201,917
In Chinese junks		500,965
	Total	$3,702,882

[Imports & Exports of 1864–5]

[The Honorable William H. Seward.

Secretary of State for the United States.

Washington. D. C.]

I am sorry to have to remark that these tables are extremely unsatisfactory, as is easily accounted for when it is understood that the values are merely the estimates of masters of vessels or shippers, who have generally no willingness to exhibit their business to the public but rather wish to conceal the value and nature of their shipments – Of course in the absence of any official inspection, （since the abolition of Customs） it is easy for all to furnish such statements as best suit them. A comparison of the Opium imported viz: $2,535,974 and the amount of the same exported viz: $357,090, indicate the unreliability of this exhibit – the greater part of this difference being naturally bought by the Chinese and Parsee Merchants and sent up the coast and into the interior in Chinese junks, which manage to smuggle it past the Customs Houses.

[Defects of the tables Value of the tables.]

The principal value of the tables therefore is to exhibit the variety of Imports and Exports, and by careful collating show what are the chief of these, e.g: Opium, Rice, Tea, Silk, Cinnamon, Paper, Salt, Aniseed & Oil, Fire Crackers. &c.

[Valueof Tables]

Table N° 4.

Illustrates the coolie Traffic from this Port, which under increasing restrictions is still but little diminished in the members of emigrant, while the health & comfort of these poor creatures are very nearly as well guaranteed before leaving here as it is possible for any police regulations to serve them. The melancholy part of the lives of these victims is not during the voyage but after their arrival beyond the seas. Few probably leave this harbor without their own full consent, but they little apprehend the fate to which they hasten.

[Coolie Traffic]

Table N° 5.

Is my Navigation & Commercial Report for the year ending with date.

[Nav. & Com. Report.]

Tables N°s 6 & 7

Show the Nationality of the sailing vessels entered or cleared from this Port during the year: None of these bore our flag – which has however been represented during this period by Five American Merchant Steamers, one of them running regularly between this & Canton and another of late plying daily to & from Hong Kong.

[Nationality of Vessels Entered and Cleared. Direct & Indirect trade]

Table N° 8.

Represents the number of vessels and tonnage employed in Direct or Indirect trade.

Table N° 9.

Furnishes a comparison of vessels entered & cleared for the several years from July 1st 1860 to June 30, 1865.

[Comparative Statement]

Tables No. 10.

Is a statement of the average market prices throughout the year of the principal Imports & Exports –

For the usual commissions, Port Charges &c. at Macao I beg to refer to enclosure N° 10. with my annual report for 1864.

[Average market Prices.]

Light House.

It take much pleasure in communicating the intelligence that his Colony under the energetic lead of its present enterprising Executive, has set a most important example to all China & Japan by the creation of a light house with a superior American revolving light, upon the loftiest hight of the Macao promontory. Were such light established on all the prominent ports of the China Coast and upon the Prata & Paracelle Shoals many lives and millions of property would be saved annually.

[Light House.]

As soon as the bearings &c. of this light （now in preparation） are published I will forward the same to the several interested Departments at Washington, and to the collectors of our principal ports.

American Capital.

Is still employed at Macao only in Merchandizing, and that principally in purchases which are either shipped directly to Great Britain or hence to Whampoa, or HongKong, （where they are invoiced） and thence to the United States.

Hoping that the indications of a revival of commerce under our flag （now beginning to be noted in neighboring ports） may be soon followed by something like our prosperity before the war, and that it may so appear in my next annual report.

[Am. Capital]

I have the honor to remain,
your Obedient Servant.
W. P. Jones,
U. S. Consul at Macao

[Table No. 1 With an Repost of 1865.]

Tabular statement showing the Imports into the port of Macao, distinguishing.
the countries whence imported quantities, and values for the year ending June 2[3]0. 1865.

Names of Articles	From Spain □□□□		From Straits		From □□□ □□□		From China		Quantity	Total Value
	Quantity	Value	Quantity	Value	Quantity	Value	Quantity	Value		Dollars
□□□ picul			2680	4633					2680	4633
□□□ Box					30	248			30	240
□□□ picul	16	220	1742	21505	643	19290			1659	41115
□□□ nut picul	2	620	16	890			27	2020	45	3530
□□□ nut picul			4000	9000					4000	9000
□□□ picul			139	278					139	278
□□□ No	20575	1130							20575	1130
□□□ picul					2193	48402	78	2496	2271	50898
□□□ Boxes	12	1324							12	1324
□□□ picul			691	2455					491	2455
□□□ No.			2	200					2	200
□□□ No.					100	10000			110	10000
Lamp Oil picul	1400	11200							1400	11200
□□□ Tree picul	764	3130							764	3130
□□□ ad picul			584	7600	230	1900			814	9500
□□□ ney □□□						594566		141619		734185
Opium Chest			1001	508235	5489	2027739			6440	2535774
□□□ piculs			170	510					170	510
□□□ty. piculs	2040	4864							3040	4864
□□□der Bbls			300	2800					300	2800
Pepper piculs			2444	15692					2444	15692
□□□ piculs	39688	123000	485120	1102246	9385	28155			534193	1253401
□□□ piculs					196	3800	150	4500	18982	49946
□□□ piculs	3425	4643	3997	28432					7422	33075
□□□ piculs			1864	7456			50	250	1914	7706
□□□ Box			10	5000	90	34350	468	110638	568	149888
□□□ pieces			2724	13393					2724	13393
□□□ Box			10	80	2195	23358			6933	44422
□□□ Box			392	1462			4728		960	1880
□□□ bbls					75	500	568	20984	75	500
□□□ picul			3	150					3	150
□□□ picul					12195	23358			12195	23358
□□□ picul							1568	448	1568	448
□□□ Skin picul			4500	5100					4500	5100
□□□ box			968	24180					968	24180
Turtle Shell picul					40	400		418	40	400
		$150231		1761297		2815958		283343		$5010829

No. 130.

NAVIGATION AND COMMERCE of the United States at the Port of Macao, during the quarter ending Sept. 30. 1865.

VESSELS				CARGOES–							
ENTERED		CLEARED.		INWARD.				OUTWARD			
No. of vessels.	WHERE FROM	No. of vessels.	WHERE FOR	No of vessels	DESCRIPTION.	VALUE Dollars.	VALUE Cents.	No. of vessels.	DESCRIPTION.	VALUE Dollars.	VALUE Cents.
1	In port	1	In port	1	U. S. stores			1	vessel in port		
2	HongKong daily	1	Sold HongKong daily	1	BallaSt	$		1	Sold		
		1		1	Passengers & Gen'l Cargo	116064		1	Passengers & Gen'l cargos	38899	--
1	Canton–Triweekly	1	Canton Triweekly	1	Passengers & Gen'l Cargo	133360		1	Passengers & Gen'l cargos	46292	--
4		4		4		$249424		4		$85191	--

W. P. Jones

U. S. Consul.

Classes of vessels entered: 3 steamers, and 1 ship in port

Classes of vessels cleared: 2 steamers and 1 steamer sold, and in port（ship）

Aggregate tonnage entered: steamer sold 163 $\frac{10}{55}$ Tons; 1 steamer running daily for 20 day 520 $\frac{37}{55}$ Tons; 1 steamer Triweekly of 600 Tons.

Aggregate （2）=

[Enclosure
With dispatch No.14
"Navigation & Commerce"
No.3
Macao. Sept. 30. 1865.
Statistical
Portugal]

[□□□, Sept. 30. 1865.
W. P. Jones. Consul.
No. 15.
10 Enclosures
Received
Annual Report for 1865.]

Number of Vessel arrived in 1865 to Day

Portuguese	89
English	188
French	20
American	5
Prussian	6
Russian	3
Italian	3

Peruvian 2
Egyptian 1
Swedish 1
Macklim Burguese 1
Norwegian 2
Danish 1
Spanish 2
Bremen 1
France 1
Oldin Burguese 1
Hanoverian 1
Dutch 3
Vessels arrive up to Dec 31 1865 331
of these 63 are men of war
Dec 31 1865
U. S. Consulate
Funchal Dec 31st 1865

[Enclosure
Funchal Consulate
With Dist. N° 33

Statement of the number
of vessels and their
Nationality, that arrived
in Funchal harbor
for the year 1865

Dec 31/65
Feby 26]
[Table No. 4]

Map of Ships, cleared from the Port of Macao, during
The year of 1864, with Chinese Emigrants, contracted in compass
With the regulations of this Colony.

Dates	Ships	Tonnage	Captains	Destination	Passengers
□□□□ 3.	Port□ Clipper "Don Fernando"	984	José de Senna	Havana	492
□□□□ 6.	Peruvian Clipper "General Prim"	294	A de Alans	Callas of Liona	182
□□□□ 17.	Peruvian Bark "Clatilde."	357	S. Bollo	Callas of Liona	220
□□□□ 18.	Peruvian Bark "Sol de Lima"	222	B. Abarva	Callas of Liona	110
□□□□ 30.	Peruvian Clipper "Theresa"	796	M. Sieard	Callas of Liona	500

□□□□	31.	Port□ Bark "S. V□□□ de Pau[lo]"	423	E. P. da Silva	Callas of Liona	262
□□□□	31.	Spanish Bark Raze Camen	368	J. Maristoni	Callas of Liona	328
□□□□	14.	Chilian Brig "Emma"	307	H. Wich	Callas of Liona	168
□□□□:	5	French Brig Gaston	317	Le Balle	Callas of Liona	200
□□□□	20.	Peruvian Clipper "Cezar"	499	I. Nissan	Callas of Liona	519
□□□□	23	Dutch Bark "Ourust"	836	B. J. Jonquer	Callas of Liona	510
□□□□	24	Peruvian Clipper "Julias"	834	C. dee □□□	Callas of Liona	500
April	7	Peruvian Bark "Lima"	328	B. J. Castaniola	Callas of Liona	184
April	22	Peruvian Bark "Vitalia"	403	I. P. Susal	Callas of Liona	260
May	13	Peruvian Bark "Mandarina"	258	"F. S. Rossi"	Callas of Liona	152
June	8	Peruvian Clipper N. Canavars	1215	"R. Dunaro"	Callas of Liona	300
June	8	French Bark "Baleman"	500	"Menard"	Callas of Liona	308
□□□□	11.	Perv' Clipper "Camilo Pavow"	1326	"I. de Landabaso"	Callas of Liona	600
□□□□	21.	French Bark "Claire"	498	"L. Robert."	Callas of Liona	312
□□□□	1.	French Bark "Medoe"	648	Dutiel	Callas of Liona	324
□□□□	29.	Belgian Clipper "L Cateaux"	832	A. Nicaise	Havana	416
□□□□	31.	Spanish Clipper "Emigrante"	720	M. S. de Hereta	Havana	360
Nov[r]	2.	French Bark "St. Joseph"	784	J. Rousseau	Havana	366
Nov[r]	3.	Port□ Clipper "D[a] M Pia"	774	J. T. das Lautos	Callas of Liona	425
Nov[r]	12	Peruvian "Aurora"	668	Jorge Mrill	Callas of Liona	377
Nov[r]	23	Span. Clipper "Encamation"	567	R. Vara	Havana	283
Nov[r]	29	Port□ "□□□ da Almeira"	1142	V. A. dos □□□	Havana	571
Dec	8	French Bark Isabel	542	□□□	Havana	271
Dec	8	French Bark "Charlotte"	541	F. Moroass	Havana	270
Dec	18	Spanish Clipper "Guadalope"	913	R. Munaz.	Havana	456
Dec	18	French Clipper "David"	842	Robert.	Havana	421
Dec	20	Portuguese Clipper "Emma"	478	C. J. Siqueira	Havana	239
Dec	24	Peru□ Brig "Thereza"	240	J. Seafino	Callas of Liona	143
		Total Ton.				20450

Total □□□

[□□□□ No. 4
With Annual Report
Dispatch No.15,
Macao, Sept, 30, 1865]

[Table No. 6.]

Tabular statement of the shipping, tonnage and crew, entered at the port of Macao during the year ending June 30, 1865 together with tonnage and crews.

Nationality.	Entered								
	With Cargoes			In Ballast			Total		
	Vessels	Tons	Crews	Vessels	Tons	Crews	Vessels	Tons	Crews
Belgian				1	832	21	1	832	21
Bremen	7	2290	86	5	1814	61	12	4104	147
Chilian				3	1395	44	3	1395	44
Danish	10	2245	93	15	3445	150	25	5690	165(243)
Dutch	9	2892	157	11	4180	61	20	7072	218
English	36	16057	651	19	11172	495	55	27229	1146
French	6	1930	78	18	8154	319	24	10084	197
Hanoverian	4	922	52	2	995	27	6	1917	79
Hamburg	21	5449	273	14	4435	186	34	9884	459
Italian	1	329	13	8	7265	177	9	7594	190
Norweden				2	489	24	2	487	24
Oldenburg	2	926	44	1	518	15	3	1444	59
Peruvian				8	5907	151	8	5907	151
Portuguese	8	3510	174	4	2366	67	12	5876	241
Prussian	1	580	17	3	1203	50	4	1783	69
Total entered	104	37.130	1688	114	54.168	1848	218	91298	3482

[Table No. 6
With Annual Report
Dispatch No.15.
Macao Sept. 30, 1865]

[Table No.7.]

Tabular statement of the shipping, tonnage and crew, cleared from the port of Macao during the year ending June 30, 1865 together with tonnage and crews.

Nationality.	Cleared								
	With Cargoes			In ballast			Total		
	Vessels	Tons	Crews	Vessels	Tons	Crews	Vessels	Tons	Crews
Belgian	1	832	24				1	832	24
Bremen	9	3118	110				9	3118	110
Chilian	2	599	27				2	599	27
Danish	17	3946	175	7	1603	76	24	5549	251

Dutch	15	5327	242				15	5327	242
English	35	17183	799	13	4419	196	48	21602	795
French	20	8977	368	3	871	38	23	9848	406
Hamburg	20	5700	255	15	4168	191	35	9868	446
Hanoverian	4	1577	63	1	343	15	5	1920	78
Italian	8	7514	271				8	7514	271
Norwegian	2	505	24				2	505	24
Oldenburg	2	121	34	1	340	25	3	1471	59
Peruvian	4	3470	120				4	3470	120
Portuguese	16	8540	382	2	960	27	16	8540	382
Prussian	1	450	11				3	1410	38
Siamese	1	250	15				1	250	15
Sweden				2	895	28	2	895	28
Spanish	14	4400	316	6	1544	107	20	5944	423
Total cleared	171	73519	3236	50	15143	703	221	88662	3939

[Table No.7.
With Annual Report
Dispatch No. 15,
Macao, Sept. 30, 1865]

[Table No.8.]

Tabular statement of the shipping, tonnage engaged in direct and indirect tradeat the port of Macao, during the year ending June 30, 1865.

Nationality.	Entered						Cleared					
	Direct trade		Indirect trade		Total		Direct trade		Indirect trade		Total.	
	Vessels	Tons	Vessels	Tons	Vessels	Tons	Vessels	Tons	Vessels	Tons	Vessels	Tons
Belgian			1	832	1	832			1	832	1	832
Bremen	5	1814	7	2290	12	4104			9	3118	9	3118
Chilean			3	1395	3	1395			2	599	2	599
Danish			25	5690	25	5690			24	5549	24	5549
Dutch			20	7072	20	7072			15	5327	15	5327
English	20	10.419	35	16.810	55	27229	39	18260	9	3342	48	21602
French	4	1.475	20	8.609	24	10.084	5	1.312	18	8536	23	9848

Hamburg			34	9.884	34	9.884	2	435	33	9433	35	9868
Hanoverian			6	1.917	6	1.917			5	1920	5	1920
Italian			9	7.594	9	7.594			8	7514	8	7514
Noweigian			2	487	2	487			2	505	2	505
Oldenburg			3	1444	3	1444			3	1471	3	1471
Peruvian	1	240	7	5667	8	5907	4	3470			4	3470
Portuguese			12	5876	12	5876	1	236	15	8304	16	8540
Prulican			4	1783	4	1783			3	1410	3	1410
Siamese									1	250	1	250
Sweden									2	895	2	895
Spanish							14	3383	6	2561	20	5944
Total	30	13.948	188	77.350	218	91.298	65	27.096	154	61.566	221	88.662

[Table No.8
With Annual Report.
Dispatch No. 15.
Macaò, Sept. 30, 1865]

[Table No.9]

Comparative statement of the aggregate navigation returns of the port of Macao, for the past five years, showing number of arrivals and clearances, tonnage and crews.

Years	Arrived			Cleared		
	Number of Vessels	Tonnage	Number of Crews	Number of Vessels	Tonnage	Number of Crews
1860	287	104.613	5513	288	120.398	5898
1861	231	84.992	4245	220	94.145	4469
1862	195	75.819	3333	198	75.422	3619
1863	172	63.280	2809	171	62.075	2854
1864	218	91.298	3482	221	88.662	3939
Total	1103	420.002	19382	1098	440.702	20.779
Average of five years	220	84.000	3876	219	88.140	4155

[Table No.9.
With annual report
Dispatch No.15,
Macao. Sept. 30. 1845.]

[From No. 6.]

[From No.6—Continued]

Return of the Arrival and Departure of American Vessels, &c., and Statement of Fees received at the United states Consulate at Macao during the quarter ending Sept. 30 165.

DATE 1865		VESSELS.										CARGO. INWARD.					CARGO. OUTWARD.				
Month.	Day.	Class.	Name.	Tonnage.	Where from.	When built.	Where built.	Where belonging.	Where bound	Owners.	Masters.	Where produced.	Where manufactured.	Description.	Quantity.	Value.	Where produced.	Where manufactured.	Description	Quantity.	Value.
July	15	str.	Fee Pang	163 $\frac{10}{95}$	Hong Kong	1841	Eaden's Land'g.	Hong Kong	Sold	Geo. V. Sands	M'Coslin			In Ballast					Sold		
July	1	ship	U. S. S Relief		In Port				In Port					U. S. Stores							
July	1–20	str.	White Cloud	520 $\frac{52}{95}$	Hong Kong				Hong Kong	Russell & Co.	G. V. Sands	With–Passengers & Gen'l Cargo–Daily				$116.064	With Passengers & Gen'l Cargo–Daily				38.899
July–Sept	1–30		Spark	100	Canton				Canton	J. B. Endicott	G. H. Brady	With–Passengers & Gen'l Cargo=Triweekly				183.360	With–Passengers & Gen'l Cargo–Triweekly				46.292
				783												$249.424					$85.191

CREWS. INWARD.		CREWS. OUTWARD.		DISCHARGED.		SHIPPED.		TONNAGE FEE.		FEES FOR. Noting protest.	Certified copy of same.	Extending protest.	Certified copy of same.	Orders of survey and recording.	Amounts paid of Surveyors.	Certified copy of surveys.	Arrest and release.	Certificates to crew list and articles.		Other certificants and services		DECEDENTS' ESTATES FEES.		TOTAL FEES.		DATE OF CLEARANCE.		Note.–United States consuls are specially interested to state in additional columns, to be prepared by them, the amount of any and every fee received by them for receivers other than those above specified. This form is to be followed by U. S. consuls residing at ports, and to be transmitted quarterly to the Departments of State. REMARKS.
American.	Foreign.	American.	Foreign.	No.	Amount Fees.	Dollars.	Cents.	Dollars.	Cents.									No.	Amount.	No.	Amount.	Dollars.	Cents.	Dollars.	Cents.			
	4			at Hongkong				1	63															15	79			
																					$\$14.^{16}$							
								5	20															5	20	Daily		
								1	00															1	00	Triweekly		
								7	83												$14.^{16}$			$21	99			

[2-032]

[Enclosure
With Dispatch No. 14.
"Arrivals & Departures"
& Fees. {No.1
Macao Sept. 30. 1865]

[Table No.9
With annual report
Dispatch No.15
Macao, Sept. 30. 1865]

U. S. Consulate, at Macao.
Sept. 30. 1865–

W. P. Jones
U. S. Consul.

[Recd. Dec. 14
Ack Dec. 15
N°.13.]

U. S. Consulate Macao
Sept. 30, 1865.

Sir:

I have the pleasure to hand you, contained herein, my Account for Miscellaneous Expenses for the quarter now terminating: See enclosure No.1 together with copies of the Letter Registers (Enclosure Nos. 2 & 3), and Vouchers 1 to 4 inclusive.

[No. 1 Mis. Ex. a/c. Nos 2 & 3, Letter Registers & 4 Vouchers]

If appears therefore that after deducting the Fees of the quarter (amounting to $28^{\underline{49}}$) there remains a balance to my credit of $9^{\underline{51}}$, which I carry to the debit of the miscellaneous Ac't of the next Quarter; and remain.

[Balance carried to next quarter.]

Your Obediently
W. P. Jones
U. S. Consul

[Hon. W. H. Seward
Secretary of State for the United States

Washington, D. C.]

[Macao, Sept. 30. 1865.
W. P. Jones– Consul.
No.13.
7. Enclosures
Received
Explaining Accompanying
miscel. Ex a/c.]

[2–033]

[Recd Dec, 14
Ack Dec, 15
No.12.]

U. S. Consulate Macao
Sept. 30, 1865.

Sir:

Enclosed please find my account for Office Rent of the Quarter now ending, am'tg to $37^{50}, as per enclosure No.1.

[No. 1 Ac'ct for Rent.]

Enclosures Nos. 2 &3 are the required vouchers the latter being for logs per exchange in the sale of my dft for the amount above claimed–made to James American, Esq. of Hong Kong at 25% discount on its face:

[Nos 2 & 3. Vouchers.]

Please see Miscellaneous Expense a/c of this date, whereon all fees of the quarter will be found credited.

Your Obedient Servant
W. P. Jones
U. S. Consul

[The Hon. W. H. Seward
Secretary of State for the United States.
Washington, D. C]

[Macao, Sept. 30. 1865.
W. P. Jones Consul.
No.12.
3 Enclosures
Received
Acct for Office Rent.]

[2-034]

[No.16.

Mr. Jones
Recd. Jan. 22.
Ack Jan. 23]

U. S. Consulate, Macao
October 28, 1865.

Sir:

I have the honor to inform the Department that consequent upon the death of Mr. Irwin, our lamented Consul at Amoy, Consul General, Geo. F. Seward, Esq, has deemed it expedient to commission me to take charge provisionally of that Consulate, （please see Enclosure No.1. copy）, and that I have therefore, with his approval, appointed J. Q. Barton, Esq, vice Consul for the United States in this Colony from this date until my return, or pending the receipt of instructions from Washington.

[□□□ and □□□ J. Q. Barton vice Consul Macao.]

His Excellency Governor Amaral has been pleased to signify his willingness to recognize Mr. Barton in the capacity named.

[Barton, □□□ & Governor.]

It is my duty as well as pleasure to state that Mr. Barton is a native of Portland, Maine, a graduate–of Bowdoin College, and a member of the Maine bar. He has

[□□□ charge □□□ of Mr. Barton]

[The Honorable
W. H. Seward,
Secretary of State for the United States
Washington, D. C.]

acted as an Assistant Paymaster in the U. S. Navy during a considerable portion of the war, is a temperate, intelligent, patriotic gentleman, and every way worthy to represent our country in the position to which he has been temporarily called.

Hoping that the Honorable Secretary will in all things approve of my action in this matter.

I have the honor to □□□ myself
Your Obedient Servant
W. P. Jones
U. S. Consul at Macao.

[U. S. Consulate.
Macao, Oct. 25,1865.

W. P. Jones–Consul.
No.16.
Enclosure 1
Received.–

Departure to take charge
of the Consulate at Amoy
&
Appointment of
J. Q. Barton
Vice Consul at Macao.]

[Copy]

Hong Kong, October 21, 1865.

To W. P. Jones, Esquire,
United States Consul, Macao,
Sir:

Pending the receipt of instructions from Peking, I hereby authorize you to take charge of the property pertaining to the United States Consulate at Amoy and to discharge the business of that office.

Should you consent to remain in the office permanently I will recommend Dr. Williams Charge[①] d'Affaires at Peking, to join with me in nominating you to the Secretary of State for appointment.

I have …………&………..
(Signed) Geo. F. Seward
U. S. Consul General in China

[With Dispatch, No.16.
Copy of the Consul General
Seward's authority for me
to take charge of the
Amoy Consulate
No.1.
Macao, Oct. 28, 1865.]

[2–035]

[Recd. Jan. 22
No.17]

United States Consulate,
Macao, October 28. 1865.

① Sic.

Sir:

Referring you to my No16 for explanation of my rendering accounts at this time in the quarter, I now have the honor to hand you my account for Consular Office Rent, from Oct, 1st to Oct 31st 1865. Please see enclosure No. 1, being the said account for 12^{50} and logs per exchange in the sale of my draft 4^{17}, together with vouchers Nos.1 & 2 in support of the same.

[No 1. Rent a/c for October 1865 Vouchers Nos 1–2]

An examination of the voucher accompanying my September accounts will show my landlords acknowledgement for receipt of rent to Oct 31st agreeing with my own voucher above. The vouchers for the past two years have all shown this anticipation of the one month's rent now claimed and this doubly vouched for by myself and the landlord.

I have the honor to be
Your Obedient Servant.
W. P. Jones.
U. S. Consul.

[The Hon.
W. H. Seward.
Secretary of State for the United States
Washington, D. C.]

[Macao, Oct. 28, 1865
W. P. Jones Consul
No.17.
1 Enclosure
Received
Dispatch with Rent
a/c.]

[2-036]

[Recd. Jan. 22,
No.18]

United States Consulate,
Macao, Oct. 28, 1865.

Sir:

Respectfully referring to my No.16, announcing the appointment of Mr. Barton as U. S. Vice Consul at this Port, for an explanation of my rendering accounts for a fractional quarter, I now beg to hand you my Miscel. Ex. a/c for the period from Oct. 1st to 28th inclusive in settlement of my claims under this head to the date of my departures to take charge of the Consulate at Amoy: See Enclosure No.1. showing a balance due me of 43^{21}, together with enclosure Nos 2 & 3 (letter lists) and voucher No. 1 to 3 inclusive.

The Sworn statement of Fees received during the month, (Amtg to 2^{50}), I have sent to the Secretary of the

Treasury, with my account for salary.

[No 1. Miscel. Ex a/c. Nos 2 &3. Letter lists Vouchers 1–3.]

I am Sir ,
Yours Obediently
W. P. Jones
U. S. Consul.

[The Honorable
W. H. Seward
Secretary of State for the United States
Washington, D. C.]

[Macao, Oct. 28, 1865.
W. P. Jones– Consul
No.18.
6 Enclosures
Received
Missel. Ex a/c to date]

[2–037]

[Received March 19
Ack March 19
No.3.]

United States Consulate
Macao, Dec. 31th, 1865.

Sir:

Herewith permit me to hand you my quarterly returns of this date, Enclosures Nos 1 to 3 inclusive, being respectively my Return of "Arrival and Departure" / with statement of Fees forms Nos. 44 & 45 attached, "Navigation and Commerce" ; and annual "Aggregate Return of Fees" Form no. 138.––

Quarterly Return to the Secretary of the Treasury and to the Fifth Auditor will go forward by the same opportunity.

[Sr auditor Sr]

I have the honor to be
Your Obdt. Servant
J. Q. Barton.
U. S. Vice Consul.

[To
Hon. Wm H. Seward
Secretary of State for the United States
Washington, D. C.]

[U. S. Consulate, Macao
December 31. 1865.

J. Q. Barton U. S. Vice Consul
No.3.
3 Enclosure
2 accompany
Quarterly Return]

[2-038]

[No.1

Received–March 19
Ack March 19

File]

United States Consulate
Macao, Dec 31st, 1865.

Sir

Enclosured please find my account for office Rent for the two months ending with date as above showing a balance due me （after deducting all official fees received during the same time） of $4.01 which I have carried to the Debit of the office rent account for next quarter, and have the honor to be.

[No. 1 Acc't for Office Rent. & Voucher.]

Your Obt. Servant
J. Q. Barton
U. S. Vice Consul

[To
Hon Wm H. Seward
Secretary of State for the United States
Washington, D. C.]

[U. S. Consulate, Macao
Dec, 31st, 1865.
No.1.
J. Q. Barton Vice Consul
□□□ Enclosures
Dispatch with
Acc't for Office Rent]

[2-039]

[No.2
Received March,19
Ak March 19]

United States Consulate
Macao, Decbr, 31st 1865.

Sir

Herewith I have the pleasure to hand you my account for miscellaneous expense for the quarter ending with date as above; the enclosure no.1. together with copies of the Letter Registers （Enclosure nos. 2 & 3, ） and vouchers 1 & 2.

[Nos 1. 2. & 3. Miscellaneous Ex. account.]

The entire official Fees received during this fractional quarter having been applied to the payment of office rent as par my dispatch no.1, the amount of the above account will be carried to the Debit of my miscellaneous account for next Quarter.

I am Sir
Your Obdt. Servant,
J. Q. Barton
U. S. Vice Consul,

[To the
Hon Wm H. Seward
Secretary of State for the United States
Washington D. C.]

[Recd Decr 26. 1867]

[Macao, Dec.31st, 1865.
J. Q. Barton. Vice Consul.
No.2.
3 Enclosures
Despatch with Miscell Ex. a/c.]

AGGREGATE RETURN of all Fees received at the Consulate of the United State at Macao and the Consular Agencies connected with it from January 1st to December 31st,1865, inclusive.

NAME OF CONSULAR OFFICER.	OFFICE.	WHERE LOCATED.	Fees for the quarter ending March 31.	Fees for the quarter ending June 30.	Fees for the quarter ending Sept.30.	Fees for the quarter ending Dec.31.	TOTAL.	REMARKS.
J. Q. Barton	Macao	China	$6.35	$16.55	$28.49	$23.49	$74.88	
						TOTAL.	$74.88	

U. S. CONSULATE at Macao
December 31, 1865.

J. Q. Barton
United States, Vice Consul.

NOTE.–This Form is to be transmitted to the Department of State, with the blanks properly filled, at the close of every year, in order that the information may be communicated to Congress, as required by law. The amounts are to be given in American currency, and the total amount to be stated.

[Enclose
With Dispatch No.3.
Arrival aggregate of
Fees
No 3.
Macao Dec[r] 31st, 1865.]

[2-040]

[Red 13 April
Ack Ultim 14]

Clements

United States Consulate at Macao
Jany. 26th, 1866.

Sir:

I have the honor to acknowledge the receipt this day of your despatch dated 21st November last, addressed to W. P. Jones, U. S. Consul at Macao, notifying him that the salary of this consulate would cease upon receiving your communication, and that hereafter only the fees which away be collected, will be allowed as compensation for consular services.

Very Respectfully
Your Ob[t] Servant.
J. Q. Barton.
U. S. Vice Consul.

[To
Hon W[m] H. Seward
Secretary of States for
The United States,
Washington.]

[2-041]

[Recd, June 29,
Ack July 5
No.6.]

United States Consulate,
Macao, April 20, 1866,

Sir:

As will be more fully stated in my No. 8 of this same date, it now devolves upon me, upon the eve of my final departure for my new post of duty at Amoy, to close the accounts of this consulate to this time.

[Final Statements of Acc't at Macao.]

Under this cover therefore I now beg to hand you the Miscellaneous Expense account of the Macao Consulate from Jan. 1. 1866, to April 20th including balance brought over from the account of Dec. 31. 1863: Enclosure No 1 with voucher 1 to 4 inclusive.

[No. 4 Macao □□□ & 4 Vouchers.]

Of voucher No. 4. for exchange, I must remark that it is impossible to sell these small drafts at a more favorable rate than is here truthfully vouched for. Larger drafts could now be sold on better terms, as the promptings with which the Government meets consular drafts and the general faith in our public finances begin to affect the money market whereas formerly I had to solicit merchants to

[to]

[Exchange]

[The Honorable
W. H. Seward, Esq.
Secretary of State for the United States,
Washington, D.C.]

beg, my drafts as a personal favor, of date such drafts are inquired for; not however in such small sums and on such □□□ accounts as these I now make.

Enclosure Nos 2 & 3 are copies of the Letter Registers and Enclosure 4, shows that when vice Consul Barton withdrew I settled with him for the accounts advanced by him on these accounts.

[2 & 3 Letter Registers.]

Let me finally request that the drafts made upon this and other accounts at this closing of matters at Macao, may be as promptly paid as hitherto, and all errors in accounts be carried to my accounts at Amoy.

[4 Mr. Barton's receipt for monies now claimed by me Errors to be charged to my account at Amoy if any errors appear]

I have the honor to be
Your Obedient Servant
W. P. Jones.
U. S. Consul.

[2-042]

[Recd, June 29.
No.7.
Ack, June 5]

United States Consulate,
Macao April 20. 1866.

Sir:

Before the late Vice Consul had received notice of the President's order of Sept. 28, 1865, informing him that the salary of this consulate must cease from receipt of such notice, he had, （as the inclosed voucher No.1 shows）, paid Office Rent to March. 31; in compliance with the custom of this country and the term of the Office Lease.

Notice of the President's order was received Jan 26th, I have paid Mr. Barton the sum so advanced by him, as in honor bound to do, and have full faith that the Honorable Secretary of State will now approve reimbursement of the same to me, as claimed in the Account, Enclosure No1, and vouched for in voucher No.1.

[Agent]

Since March 31, I have paid the office rent as before, but regret that I have no confident hope state claim for the account

[would]

[To Honorable
W. H. Seward,
Secretary of State &c
Washington, D. C.]

would be allowed, so do not now draw for it my enclosure, the new vice consul, will remove. the offices to his own premises before the termination of the present month.

I have the honor to be
Your Obedient Servant
W. P. Jones.
U. S. Consul.

[Macao, April 20, 1866.
W. P. Jones–Consul.
No.7.
1 Enclosure
2 vouchers
Received
Dispatch with Office
Rent a/c.]

[2–043]

[Recd. June 29,
Ack. July 5
Mr. □□□

Copy to Comm. as appropriation
Jany 15th

No.8.]

United States Consulate,
Macao, April 21, 1866

Sir:

I have the honor to acknowledge receipt of your No. 24, from the Acting Secretary, respecting my appointment to the Consulate at Amoy, and having prepared the incidental accounts of this Office down to date will forward herein the same mail with this, and, immediately, removing my family to Amoy, esteeming connection with this office virtually at concluded.

[Receipt of No. 24, approving my transfer to Amoy Preparations for my removal]

Your approval of my nomination of J. Q. Barton to be Vice Consul, I regret to say, arrived after that gentleman had been compelled to retire from the office which he is creditably filled. I have therefore, in the absence of any suitable permanent American resident, solicited and empowered Henirich Ebell, Esq, Prussian Vice Consul for Macao to be Acting Vice Consul

[for]

[Retirement of the late Vice Consul Nomination of Mr. Ebell. to be Acting Vice Consul.]

[The Honorable
W. H. Seward
Secretary of States for the United States,
Washington, D. C.]

for the United States, until the pleasure of the President is made known. The official title, "Acting Vice Consul" is so worded, at the request of the gentleman himself, who is governed in this choice by the rules of his own service.

Mr. Ebell, a native of Prussia, and as before intimated Prussian Vice Consul for Macao, is a polite, liberally educated gentleman, already familiarized with the discharge of Consular duties. In the relation to our government now proposed His Excellency Governor Amaral has been pleased to express himself most happy to recognize him.

[Governor Amaral recognize Mr. Ebell Begin the President's confirmation requested and a salary of $1000 with permission to □□□business □□□]

I cannot but hope that the President will both confirm the appointment of Mr. Ebell and at the same time recommend the appropriation of $1000 salary in addition to the trivial fees now allowed him, since the labors of this office are principally of those descriptions for which there are no fees chargeable and which nevertheless consume so much of the officer's time that it seems not at all respectable for a first class Government to expect that he should long perform them gratuitously.

If such an appropriation of salary is made and with the understanding that he may continue to transact mercantile business, Mr. Ebell will consent to serve the Government for several years.

I beg to enclose for you a copy in English, of His Excellency's final official favor, evincing his customary politeness, and uniform good will, and approving of the nomination of Mr. Ebell. I may add that he has tendered me his barge for my embarkation and ordered a consular salute.

[□□□ Enclosure No 1. Governor Amaral recognition of Mr. Ebell and parting courtesies Nos 2 & 3. Invoicing.]

Finally I enclose, (No. 2), Mr. Ebell's receipt for the Consular Archives surrendered to him & joint Certificate form.

I have the honor to remain
Your Obedient Servant.
W. P. Jones
U. S. Consul.

[Macao, April, 20, 1866.

W. P. Jones–Consul.

No. 8.

---

3 enclosures

Received

Despatch upon retirement
from the Consulate at
Macao & removal to Amoy
Appointment by Vice Consul
&c.]

Consulate of the United States
at Macao, April 20th, 1866.

We certify that on this the 20th day of April 1866, the services of W. P. Jones ceased, and he is entitled to his salary, or fees, including said day, and that the services of Henrich Ebell as a Acting Vice Consul commenced the day following, he having received the archives as specified in the 79th Section of the General Instructions.

W. P. Jones
H. Ebell.

[With Dispatch No.8.

Joint Certificate
on change of office

No. 3.

Macao, April 20, 1866.]

Inventory of Consular Archives Delivered to Heinrich Ebell Esq. Acting U. S. Vice Consulate Macao, April 20, 1866.

□□ Book Case & Desk
□□ Leather Bound Consular Record books
□□ Paper or Muslin Bound Record books
□□ A number of Consular Blanks
□□ A number of Consular Files
□□ Seal Press
□□ Brass and 1 Ivory seal
□□ Consul's Manuals
□□ Reams （more or less） of Despatch Paper
□5 Reams （more or less） of note Paper
□1/2 Reams （more or less） of Letter Paper
□□ Packages of large Despatch envelopes
□3 Packages of Small envelopes
2 Boxes steel pens
2 1/2 Dozen skeins of red tape
Lime wafers & quills
1 Bible
□ Volumes Diplomatic correspondence
4 Patent Office Reports
1 Wheaton's Instructional Law
1 Vol Navigation and Commerce
6 Vols. Commerce Relations
1 Leather bound vol. 7 Japan bound statistics at Large
1 Coat of Arms
1 Ensign - with Flag staff & Halliards - （very ordinary）
Last Few office Sundries.

Fee book
Arrivals and Departures
2 Protests Books.
Record Book
2 Despatch Books
3 Letter Books.
1 Ship Journal
1 Passport Book
2 Miscel Return & Record
2 Bound Volumes of Despatches received

W. P. Jones.
H. Ebell.

[□□□□
With Dispatch No. 8.

Inventory of Archives
delivered to Mr. Ebell

No.2.

Macao, April 21, 1866.]

Translation

Foreign Affairs
N[o] 14.
Sir:

I have the honor to acknowledge your Official letter of this date, in which you inform me of your having been transferred from the post of Consul of the United States at Macao, to the exercise of the Consular office at Amoy, and requesting me to recognise, in the capacity of Vice Consul of the United States for Macao, Mr. Heinrich Ebell, until your government either confirms the nomination of Mr. Ebell, or makes other appointment.

Granting your request, I also avail of this opportunity, to express, any regret at your departure from this city; since your department here has ever been grave, dignified, and every way appropriate to the representation of a country so intimately leagued with Portugal in the most cordial relations. On the other hand I beg you to accept the sincere wish I entertain for your more complete happiness in the new port to which you are now called. God preserve you.

Macao, 21st April 1866.

(Signed) José Rodrigues Cóelho de Amaral
Governor of Macao

[Wm P. Jones Esq
U. S. Consul.
at Macao]

[□□□8.
Translation of □□□
□□□ □□□□□□□
Mr. Ebell Acting
Vice Consul
□□□
Macao, April□□□1866.]

[2-044]

[Recd, June, 29
Ack July 20

No.9]

United States Consulate
Macao April 20, 1866.

Sir:

I beg to hand you herewith my Transcript of Fee Book for period therein Stated ending at this date.

[Enclosed N°1 transcript of Fees]

I regret that I am not permitted to report any Arrivals or Departures from this Consulate during the past quarter and this fractional quarter, which concludes my term of service at Macao; except the triweekly arrivals and departures of the little Steamer "Spark", plying between this and Canton with Imports (in general Cargo), Amounting to $142,000 – and Exports (of same description) estimated at $58,500. The U. S. Flag Ship "Hartford", U. S. S "Wyoming", U. S. S "Wachusett" and supply ship "Relief", have made this their rendezvous for the most of this period. These accept this dispatch in view of form 14, 44, 45 & 128, the matter of which is here stated.

I am, Sir,
Yours Obediently
W. P. Jones
U. S. Consul

[The Honorable
W. H. Seward.
Secretary of State
Washington D. C.]

[Macao, April 20, 1866.

W. P. Jones Consul

No.9.
1 Enclosure

Received
Despatch in Cons of
Forms No. 44, 45, & 128]

Date of Certificate 1866		Name of the vessel or party for whom service is rendered	Where bound or whither sent	Kind and character of the good or Merchandise	Where Produced	Value including cost & exchange	
May No.1	26	Raynals Co. & Brit. Barque Ann Lucy	New York to Orden	Tea	China	$9,461	31

May	28	Raynals Co. & Brit Barque Ann Lucy	New York to orden	1 Box Tea, 1 Box fans	China	$8	25
May	31	Johannes & Co. & Brit. Barque Ann Lucy	New York Brown Shipley of London	Fans	China	$2,899	59
Macao 31st December 1866.– H. Ebell, Actg U. S. Vice Consular							

[Macao
State
for Port Commerce
Report Book
□□□ A□□□□□□□]

[2–045]

[Dept of State
ack. May 25.]

United States Consulate
Macao 27th, Feby 1867.

Sir.

Herewith I have the pleasure to hand you (enclosure N°. 1–9) Record of Treasury fees, Copy of Invoice Book, Registers of official letter received and sent, Return of arrivals and departures of American vessels, Return of fees received on account of vessels, return of fees not contained in form N° 44, Aggregate of fees received and my account of miscellaneous Expenses, for the Period from 1st May to ult° December, 1866.–

[Com[l] to state a/c for postage in request]

Against the trifling amount of my miscellaneous expenses I do not draw, but carry the same over to the credit of my miscellaneous expense for the next quarter.–

[To
The Hon W[m]. H. Seward
Secretary of State for the United States
Washington D. C.]

I intended to have added to the above Documents statistics with regard to the trade of this Colony during the year 1866, but as no publication to this effect has as yet appeared in the Government Gazette, I am under the necessity to pospone it till a later period.

I have the honor to be
Your Obd[t]. Servant
H. Ebell
Act[g]. U. S. Vice Consul

[No.44.]

Statement of Fees, received at the United States Consulate at Macao from 1st May 1866 to ultimo December 1866.–

Date of arrival		Name of the Vessel	□□□	Crews								Tonnage fees		Noting marine Protest	Certificates				Recording documents in Consular records.–		Letters to authorities; □□□ and Signature of consul To clearence and papers, note, bill of health.		Acknowlegements of masters or merchants to □□□ bonds, bills of Sale and other informants of writing.		Declaration of □□□ of master to ship bill □□.		Total of fees received on account of this vessel		Date of Clearance		Remarks
				Inward		Outward		Disch arged		Shipped					To crew list & shipping articles of destinations, deaths and of probable American Seaman		De□□□, invoice currency, ownership; and □□□ on □□□ □□□, &c &c &c.														
Month	Day		Tons	No tons	No fees	No tons	No fees	No	Tons	No	Dols	Dols	Cts	Dollar	N°.	tons.	N°.	tons	N°.	tons	N°.	tons	N°.	tons	N°.	tons	Dollars	Cts	Mon.	Day.	
□□□	9	Pangnin	583	6	8	6	8					$5	83								1	$2					$7.	83.			
□□□	10	Kamrya	(Siamese Schooner)											$2.–													$2.	--			
□□□	25	S° Jozé	204	1.	8	1.	8			8	$4.	$2.	04		4	$3.	1	$2	3	$3.					1	50¢	$19.	54.			
□□□	30	Str. Sports										$1.															$1.	--.			
□□□	30	Str Spark										$1.															$1.				
□□□	31	Str Sports										$1.															$1.	--.			
																											$32.	37.			

Macao 31st. Decbr 1866.

H. Ebell.

Actg Vice Consul of the U.S. of America

[No.1]

Record of Treasury Fees

Fees received at the United States Consulate at Macao from 1st May to ult° December 1866

Date	N°	Name of Vessel	Name of the party paying the fee	Nature of Service rendered	Amount of fees paid		Remarks
May 9	1	Penguin	Capt Moore	Tonnage fees etc	$7.	83	
May 10	2		Capt Botsford	Noting Marine Protest	$2.	--	
May 26	3		Raynals Co.	Invoice Verific and 1 Copy	$3.	50	
May 28	4		Raynals Co.	Invoice Verific and 1 Copy	$2.	50	
May 31	5		T P. Johannes	Invoice Verific and 1 Copy	$2.	50	
June 22	6		E. Lehmann	4 Acklg^mt^ of Signatures	$8.	--	
June 25	7	St Jozé	C. Lee Moses	Certificate of Ownership	$2.	--	
				Certificate to Shippg Articles	$2.	--	
				Certificate to Appoint^mt^ of Master	$2.	--	
				Certificate to Copy of Ships Register	$2.	--	
				Preparing Sea letter	$3.	--	
				Recording Bill of Sale	$1.	50	
				Recording Sea letter	$1.	--	
				Recording appoint^mt^ of Master	--.	50	
				Declar. & oath of master to not being able to procure 2/3 of a crew of Amer Steamer	--.	50	
				Tonnage fees	$2.	04	
				Carried forward	$42.	87	
				Brought over	$42.	87	
June 25	7	St Joz é	C. Lee Moses	Shipping 8 Mariners & Seaman	4.	--	
				Noting protest	2.	--	
				Certificate of Crew list	2.	--	
				□□□To deposition	--.	50	
				Filing deposition	--.	25	
June 25	8		E. Lehmann	Acklg^mt^ of Signature	2.	--	
June 30	9	St^r^ Spark	L. d'Almeida	Tonnage Fees	1.	--	
(Oct)Sept. 30	10	St^r^ Spark	L. d'Almeida	Tonnage Fees	1.	--	
Oct. 12	11		Emil Lehmann	2 Certific. of Copies	4.	--	
Oct. 29	12		Emil Lehmann	1. Certific of Signature	2	--	
Dec. 14	13		Luis Ant. Franco.	2. Certific of Signature	4	--	
Dec. 31	14	St^r^ Spark	L. d'Almeida	Tonnage Fees	1.	--	
					$66.	62	
Six sixty six Dollars and sixty two Cents							

H. Ebell

Macao 31st Decb[r] 1866

Actg U. S. Vice Consul

On the Thirty first day of December 1866, before me the undersigned, personally appeared H. Ebell, acterig U. S. Vice Consul at Macao and made oath that the above and foregoing account or report of fees is a full and perfect transcript of the register, which he is by law required to keep; that the same is true and correct and contains a full and accurate statement of all fees, received by him as such Consular officer, or for his use, for his official services, to the Seal of his knowledge during the period of time Herin mentioned.–

Sworn before me.

H. Ebel

[CONSULATE OF The UNITED STATES MACAO]

Actg U.S. Vice Consul

Netherlands Consul for Canton

in china

□N°12

Register of Official Letters receid at the U.S. Consulate at Macao from 1st, May to ulto Decbr. 1866

Name of writer	N°	Place and Date of letter	When rec[d]	On what Subject	N. of Enclosures	Postage paid	
T. Ribeiro	1	Government Secret. Macao	May 11	Report at an Am Subject, arrested by Police			
□ Secretary	2	Washington	June 6	Enc[l]. 1 Despatch for Payments of Han□□□□	1	_	32
□Moses	3	Macao June 5	June 5	Soliciting a Sailing Letter for Brig. S[t] Jozé			
□Kurman	4	Chiukiary May 28	June 22	Entrances upon duty			
□Secretary	5	Washington March 19	June 27	Circular N°58			16
□Auditor	6	Washington April 23	July 4	Adjustment of acct.			16
□□□ller	7	Washington April 24	July 4	Adjustment of acct.			16
Secretary of State	8	Washington May 14	July 21	Acknow[lg], receipt of Desp of J. H. Barton	1		32
	9	Washington Apr 20	July 21	Circular N.59			16
□J	10	Washington June 18	Aug. 18	Circular announce death of Louis Case			16
□Mācao	11	Macao Aug 28	Aug. 23	Acknow[lg] recp[t] of Desp. announcing Death of Louis Cass.			
□□ Agent	12	London July 26	Sept. 21	Entrances upon duty			16
□□ Depart[mt]	13	Washington	Sept. 23	6 Desp. to the Payments of U. S. Squadron	6		32
□□ Depart[mt]	14	Washington	Sept. 23	3 Desp. to the Payments of U. S. Squadron	3		16
	15	Washington Aug 3	Oct. 4.	Adjustmt of account			16
□□ Depart[mt]	16	Washington	Nov. 23.	1 Desp. for Payments of Wyoming			16

□□uny Dep.	17	Washington	Nov. 24	List of Value of foreign Sp□□□ D□□			16
□□Justice	18	Macao Dec. 10	Dec. 10	Request to remove William Murray, on Am ..Subject, from this Colony			
R Britton	19	New York Oct. 2	Dec. 15th	Request information about his Son H. B. Brinton			8.
						$2	64

Macao 31st Decbr 1866
H. Ebell
Actg. U. S. Vice Consular

[No. 3
Letter Received]

Register of Official Letters post from the U.S. Consulate at Macao from 1st May to ulto Decbr 1866.

Date		No	To whom sent and what place	On what Subject	No of Enclose.	Postage paid	
May 1866	11	1	Govern. Secretary, Macao	Concerng an American Sailor (arrested)			
June	8	2	Harbor Master, Macao	Inform that Port. Brig St Jozé has been sold to C. Lee Moses, an Am Citizen.			
June	24	3	U. S. Consul, Chuckiary	Acknowlg receipt of his Desp.			16c
Aug.	21	4	President of Govern. Counsel Macao	Announcing Death of Lewis Cass.			

Macao 31st Decb. 1866
H. Ebell
Actg. U. S. Vice Consul

Return of fees, prescribed in Form N. 44, received at the Consulate of the United States at Macao from 1st May to ulto Decbr. 1866.

No.	Date		Name of vessel	Name of party paying the fee	Nature of the service rendered	Amount	
3	May	26		Raynalz Co.	Invoice verific and 1 Copy	$3.	50
4	May	28		Raynalz Co.	Invoice Verifications	$2.	50
5	May	31		J. P. Johannes	Invoice Verifications	$2.	50
6	June	23		E. Lehmans	4 Acknowlgmt of Signature	$8.	--.
7	June	25	St Jozé	C. Lee Moses	preparing Sea Letter	$3.	--.
					Noting protest	$2.	--.
					Administering oath to depositions	--.	50
					filing deposition	--.	25

8	June	25		E Lehmans	Acknowlg^{mt} of signature	$2.	--.
11	Oct.	12		E Lehmans	2 Certific of Copies	$4.	--.
12	Oct.	29		E Lehmans	Acknowlg^{mt} of signature	$2.	--.
13	Dec.	14		Luis Ant. Franco.	2 Acknowlg^{mt} of signature	$4.	--.
						$34.	25

Macao 31st Decb^{r} 1866.
H. Ebell
Act^{g} U. S. Vice Consul.

□□□□□□□□□□□ to ult^{o} Decb^{r} 1866.

Name of the Consular Officer	Office	Where located	Fees for the quarter ending March 31.	Fees for the quarter ending June 30.	Fees for the quarter ending Sept 30.	Fees for the quarter ending Decr 31.	Total	Remarks.
H. Ebell	Consulate	Macao	~	$54.62	$1.–	$11.	$66.62	Fees for the Quarter ending March 31. $3.– have been reported by Consul W. P. Jones April 20th 1866.

Macao 31st December 1866.
H. Ebell
Act^{g} U. S. Consul.

[2-046]

[ack. May 28]

United States Consulate.
Macao, 27 February, 1867.

Sir:

The purpose of the present is principally to draw your attention to Despatch N° 8 of 20th April 1866, addressed to you by Consul W. P. Jones at the time he charge me temporally with his Official Duties at this Colony.

Although highly gratified with this personal appointment, still I must convey to you the intimation that the duty attracted to this function are more onerous than I anticipated and under the circumstances, the approval of the yearly Salary of $1000, offered to me as an inducement, having been withheld till the present

[moment]

[To

Hon: Wm H. Seward

Secretary of State for the United States
Washington D. C.]

moment. I beg respectfully to submit to you the urgent request to reconsider. M[r] Jones's proposal, as in the absence of any salary additional to the trifling fees, which I received would though unwillingly be obliged to solicit my dismission.

I have the honor to be
Your Obd[t] Servant
H. Ebell
Act[g] U. S. Vice Consul

[2-047]

[Received
ack Mar 7
No.1]

United States Consulate
Macao, December 4, 1867

Sir:

I have the honor to inform you that having delivered the consular achieves and seal of the Canton Consulate to E. M. Ruis, Esq, as per Instructions of the Department, I have returned to my post of duty at this Port as per requirement of the Consular Instructions.

I have the honor to be
Sir,
Your Obedient Servant
W. P. Jones
U. S. Consul.

[The Honorable William H. Seward
Secretary of State for the United States
Washington, D. C.]

[Macao
W. P. Jones Consul
No.1
Return to Office
at Macao.]

[2-048]

[Macao
Mr J. Smith
Received
No.1
□□□□□□□□□□□□
□□□□□□□□□□□□]

Washington, D. C.
May 29, 1868.

Sir:

I have the honor to inform you that on the 1st day of February last, I left Amoy, recently my post of duty as Consul by transfer from Macao, enroute for the United States, and arrived in this city, now my temporary residence, on yesterday the 28th.

The whole of the above mentioned period from Feb, 1st to May 28th was actually and necessarily consumed in making my transit except 19 days in February, spent in visiting the cities of Canton and Macao.

[Return to the U. S.]

I have the honor to be,
Sir,
Your Most Obedient Servant
W. P. Jones
Late U. S. Consul,
Amoy.

[To the Honorable
William H. Seward,
Secretary of State for the United States, Washington, D. C .]

[2-049]

[Macao Mr. P Suite
Amoy
□□□□□□□□□□□□
□□□□□□□□□□□□
□□□□□□□□□□□□]

Washington June 7, 1868

Hon. F. W. Seward

Assistant Secretary of State

Washington, D. C.

Sir:

My attention has been called to my despatch from Macao, indicate of December 4, 1867, announcing that I had returned to my post of duty at that port, which I beg to withdraw, for the following reasons:

I wrote it under the impression that it was my duty to return to Macao and then resign before returning house. The letter was written immediately upon my arrival and mailed, but upon conversation with the Vice Consul. I discovered that it would be disagreeable to him to have me resume the office, and then go through the formula of reappointing him, notifying the Local Government of these changes &c &c –, and that he would not consent to accept the office again after he was once relieved. Indeed I discovered that he was scarcily willing to retain it without these excuses for abandoning it, and in case of his refusal I knew there was no one so situated has to accept the position.

Moreover upon for this considerations I felt persuaded that my resumption of the office would be of poor expediency every way. Mr. Ebell was recognized by the Department as Vice Consul. I had had no responsibilities connected with the office for two years. I had been recognized at other official posts and been regularly retired. In the time of my absence the salary at Macao had ceased and not being a mercantile man, but sent out under bonds not to trade, I found myself on the other side of the globe without any means of supporting my family and with a child too sick to remain any longer in the country. I concluded that my relation to the Macao consulate was of such an ambiguous nature that if entitle to demand the archives the position was so wholly untenable （without any means of support） and it would be so utterly impossible for me to leave the office is any betters position than it then was that I ought not to demand possession of the archives. Accordingly I did not resume possession of the office, and on the following day departed for Amoy.

[□□□ doubtless]

The fact then is that I have not performed any official functions at Macao since the appointment of Mr. Ebell to be Vice Consul at that Port and that the letter of the 4th December last is to be correctly □□□ only with this explanation intended to operate as a withdrawal there of that the records of the Department may correspond with the facts of the case.

I have the honor to be

Sir,

Your Obedient Servant

W. P. Jones.

[2-050]

[Macao

Received

Jun 9 1868]

Washington, June. 8, 1868.

Honorable F. H. Seward

Consulate Secretary of State

Washington, D. C.

Sir:

In relation to my claim fee salary while making my transit from Amoy to this city I beg to submit the following statement of facts and arguments:

Wm Irvin, Consul at Amoy died of cholera Sept. 10, 1865. The country in the immediate vicinity of that port was then in a very troubled condition, owing to the presence of rebel hordes, which had destroyed the great city of Changchow, but 25 miles distant and had attracted a large number of unprincipled adventurers of all nationalities to Amoy for the purposes of illicit trade &c. But a short time before my arrival General Burgevime, an American, had been arrested, charged with endeavoring to make his way through the imperial lines and had been forcibly carried though the city into the interior, in contempt of the demand of the Consul that the he had surrendered to him for trial.

[Other]

Other reckless Americans were still in the city and threating trouble – For want of someone to take charge of the Consulate the archives, seals &c had be come scattered into no less than four parts of the settlements, and judicial cases were entirely neglected.

[Narrative of my appointment to Amoy.]

In this condition of affairs the Consul General at Shanghai felt constrained to visit the port and immediately afterwards called on me at Macao and desired me to leave the less important duties of that office to a Vice Consul and go to Amoy. I represented the inconvinence & expense of the transfer, and he assured me that he had communicated with the acting minister, and they would both take such action as they doubted not would lead to my permanent appointment.

I went to the port immediately and after waiting eight months to be certain that my position was understood at the Department. I sold my furniture at Macao, at a □□□ and removed my family to Amoy. In less than three months afterwards I was advised that Gen. C. W. Legendic was appointed my successor.

I was regarded in China as a Consul transferred to Amoy and was as addressed & treated by our own civil and naval officers, by the native officials and the consuls of other powers, and upon no other understanding would I have gone there.

In not claim salary at the rate of the Amoy office during my transit home, on the ground that I was a Consul of the regular services; under bonds; of that close entitled by law to transit home, that I filled vacancy at Amoy, in which I was subordinate and responsible to no principal but the government; and that both as such Consul, and as filling the vacancy I was entitled to all the vacated privileges left by the death of Consul Irwin. （grounds of my claim for transit）

I make the point that the opinion of the Attorney General referred in the Section 424 of the Consuls Manual (1849) – declaring that "an acting Consul in charge of a Consulate" during actual vacancy of the Consulate is "entitled to receive the statute compensation of the office" – covers the claim for transit home as a part of that compensation.

[For]

For I understand that a vice Consul placing in charge by a principal officer during his absence looks to his agreement with his principal for his compensation – and a the principal officer collects the transit home there is good reason why the Government □□□ not also pay the vice Consul's transit – □□□ in the case of a vacancy by death the person who is summoned by the proper authority to fill the vacancy takes all the rights vacated by his predecessor.

I argue from the equity of the case – ; 1st That I had good reason to presume that the government would respect the arrangements made by its highest representatives in China, and yield to their recommendations that my appointment should be made permanent – without such an understanding I should not have in carried the trouble & Expense of removing to Amoy.

2d The Expenses resulting from the sale of my furniture at Macao (not ordered until the expiry of my lease there and offer eight months waiting for the action of the government.), my removal to Amoy, my purchasing of new furniture there, my removal thence, & the transit–house have accounted to about 2800 silver dollar

[the cost]

(the cost from Hong Kong to Washington, alone having amounted to upwards of $1400), against which my whole claims for transit to Amoy ($86.08) and transit home ($781.93) accounts to only $868.01.

I enclose a letter from His Excellency Mr. Burlingame, endorsing my claim.

Trusting that the above statements may prove satisfactory grounds for allowing my claims for transit.–

I have the honor to be
Sir,
Your Obedient Servant
W. P. Jones.
Late Consul
& c. Amoy.

to use this
letter

Your Obt Servt
Anson Burlingame.

Peking
M □ 15th 1867

My dear Mr Jones

In reply to your letter of Oct. 12th 1867, I have to say that it seems to me that you have at least, an equitable claim

[W. P. Jones Eqr late
U. S. Consul Canton]

for transit as stated by you.

I know that you were of the greatest service to the Government and that you performed your Consular duties, with □□□□□□□□□□ ability.

I wish to urge upon the Govt a settlement in accordance with your statement and to that end.

Yours

[2-051]

[Macao
Mr. J. Smith]

Washington D. C.
June 10, 1868.

Hon, F. W. Seward
Assistant Secretary of State
Washington. D. C.

Sir:

I find that the exact language of the Attorney General's opinion referred to in my official of the 8th instant vouching my claim for transit from Amoy is as follows: "The Acting Consul, who under the old system retained the fees as if he were commissioned Consul may in my opinion now receive the salary attached to the office as if he were commissioned Consul, if such be the Will of the Department" Vol VII P. 716,

May I not hope that the Department will exercise its discretions, so that a Consul has served his Government faithfully in an unhealthy foreign clime, at the farthest verge of the globe, shall not have to bear the entire burden of the heavy expenses of his voyage half way around the world back to his residence.

The Attorney General after showing that a Vice Consul is only, entitled to what his principal agrees to pay him, says (page 215) "When the Consulate was actually vacant by the death of the Consul or otherwise, and the duties were discharged by an Acting Consul under approval of the Department, the latter received the fact to his own benefit precisely the same as if he had been duly commissioned as Consul"; Thus plainly intimating that a man who fills a vacancy stands in other rights than an ordinary Vice Consul, with a principal between him and the government to whom he looks for his ruts of compensation and becomes possessed of the □□□ Consul's rights in full – one of which right is – in such salaried Consulates as Amoy the allowance of salary while returning home.

There is a fact which I hope the Secretary will kindly bear in mind – viz: that the Salary at Macao ceased during the period when I was at Amoy. So that if I am not adjudged entitled to the compensation from Amoy □□□ home – it will result that I have lost in transit home while obeying the wishes of the minister and the Consul General – by filling a vacancy which the highest interests and honor of the public service required me to □□□.

I understand that my temporary stay at Canton which was under agreement with Mr. Perry, the Consul – and plainly an ordinary Vice Consular arrangement not entitling me to transit （that being given to the Consul himself, by our agreement as well as by the law which provides against paying two transits by disallowing the transit of a person who does not fill a vacancy） – my stay at Canton, did not affect my claim for transit from Amoy – which place I embarked from on the 1st of Feburary last.

I am told in the Treasury Department that if I was entitled to transit from Amoy when I was relieved in Dec. 1866 I am still entitled to it, as much as if insread of serving Mr. Perry at Canton I had merely delayed in HongKong in other employment.

It ought also to be bare in mind that at my despatch of 8th instant shows I never resumed the functions of Consul at Macao. I believe that my recognition & commission at Amoy operated as a resignation of the Macao Office – （See Consuls Manual P425 – page 214）

[this]

This belief together with the reasons in the interest of the government set forth in my despatch of the 8th inst. on this point, will also explain why I have sent in no resignation of the Macao Consulate.

Had there been no such reasons, you will nevertheless grant that the necessities of my position would excuse me from returning to a port from which support had been suddenly cut off in my absence.

Perhaps it may be of some consequence （technically） that my accounts have been over the signature of Acting Consul – for the time I was at Amoy – and are so entered on the books of the Register of the Treasury.

I need the money claimed in this account. The facts in my case are most of them □□□ of record – and show that my expense □□□ necessarily have for exceeded my claim □□□ were made in obedience to the wishes of the government & under such reasonable expectation of confirmation as permanent Consul at Amoy that since this failed – I may rationally anticipate that the Department will exercise all □□□ powers of discretion to promote the allowance of ninety of my expenses now sought for.

I have the honor to be, Sir
Your Obedient Servant
W. P. Jones.

Postscript to Despatch of June 10, 1868.

I beg to add the following extracts from the opinions of the Attorney General – Vol IX p 80.

"It is settled that a consul retained in office under the Act of 1855 – is a consul appointed under that Act so far as regard compensation. That compensation was a salary to he counted from the time when he reached his port of duty down to the time when he left it. To give him more was expressly forbidden."

"But in 1856 the system was again reworded. By that 8th Section of the Act then passed a consul was to receive salary not only for the time spent at the place of his official duty – but in addition to that, for the time spent in awaiting his instructions, in traveling to his port of duty – and in returning home at the close of his service."

"The result of all this legislative – which does not seem at the first blush to be very plain – is that a consul who served only under the old law received fees and nothing else. If he was retained after July 1855, he got a salary for the time he

[remained]

remained at his post. If he held office after the Act of 1856 went into operation he got paid in addition for the time he spent in coming home."

"I submit that the above opinion sustain my inference in despatches of June 8th & June 10th 1868 that as the Att'ny General （Vol XII p. 716） says that the acting consul filling an actual vacancy caused by the death of a consul, is entitled to the statute compensation of the office precisely as if he were commissioned consul – this compensation is to be taken to include transit home as much as it does salary when in charge of the office."

Respectfully
W. P. Jones

[2-052]

[Mr. J. Smith
Department Rceeived
Nov 30]

United State Consulate at Macao.
October 9th 1869.–

Sir,

The call of others duties rendered it necessary for me to resign the post of Actg U. S. Vice Consul, which I have held at this place since the 21st April, 1866.

In the absence of any permanent American resident adapted to fill this office and not having succeeded in finding among the Portuguese and foreign Community some suitable personage, who was inclined to take charge of the same, I am obliged to transmit the Archives and furniture of the Consulate into the hands of U. S. Consul at Hongkong, leaving it to the decision of the President to appoint another Consular officer for this Colony.

I have the honor to be,
Sir,
Your Obedient Servants.
H. Ebell.
Actg. U. S. Vice consul.

[To
the Honorable Hamilton Fish,
Secretary of State
Washington D. C.]

[2-053]

Macao, China
Report

Mr Ebell, the Vice Consul in charge since April 1866 having resigned, the Consulate is left vacant. There is no salary attached to it and I know of no American who will take the Consulate without salary. I think the Consulate had better be left vacant than to appoint a foreigner to the position. There is very little trade with this country from that port, and it is so near Hong Kong that I think no great inconvenience will be felt if the Consulate is suppressed.

I advise that no appointment be made them unless Congress shall provide for a salary to a Consul.

Respectfully Submitted
Jasber Smith
Dec 6th 69

[END
THE NATIONAL ARCHIVES OF THE UNITED STATES 1934]

後　記

衆所周知，澳門是西方國家來華活動的橋頭堡。明清以來，隨着多國人士陸續抵達澳門，舉世聞名的中外文化經貿交流活動隨之展開，其多樣性的成果成爲澳門學研究的主要内容。近代澳門與美國的關係作爲中西文化交流的重要組成部分，已引起學者們的重視。

近年來，我們對有關澳門與美國關係的史料進行了蒐集、整理與研究，先後發表了若干著述。其中，《美國駐澳門領事館領事報告（1849—1869）》是研究近代澳門與美國關係的重要史料，也是構建近代澳門乃至近代中國與美國關係的基本材料之一，在中美關係史研究領域有其重要的價值。爲此，我們組織力量將其進行轉寫，以期爲研究者使用該檔案提供一些便利。

經過四年的努力，轉寫工作得以完成。感謝澳門大學爲此次研究及轉寫工作所提供的支持；感謝參與轉寫和校對的同學和朋友：澳門大學碩士研究生楊珊泓、陳逸鋒同學完成前期錄入及初校，美國司徒晨陽（Kenneth Edward Stewart）先生負責校閲；感謝廣東人民出版社社長曾瑩女士、副社長肖風華先生、編輯梁茵女士等爲此書的編校及出版所付出的辛勤努力。

整理者

2016年4月28日

即將出版

海上絲綢之路史料叢刊・中外關係卷

海上絲綢之路史料叢刊・洋商卷

海上絲綢之路史料叢刊・华商卷

海上絲綢之路叢刊・研究卷

海上絲綢之路叢刊・譯叢卷

海上絲綢之路叢刊・港澳卷